HANDBOOK OF RURAL AGING

The *Handbook of Rural Aging* goes beyond the perspective of a narrow range of health professions, disciplines, and community services that serve older adults in rural America to encompass the full range of perspectives and issues impacting the communities in which rural older adults live. Touching on such topics as work and voluntarism, technology, transportation, housing, the environment, social participation, and the delivery of health and community services, this reference work addresses the full breadth and scope of factors impacting the lives of rural elders with contributions from recognized scholars, administrators, and researchers. This *Handbook* buttresses a widespread movement to garner more attention for rural America in policy matters and decisions, while also elevating awareness of the critical circumstances facing rural elders and those who serve them.

Merging demographic, economic, social, cultural, health, environmental, and political perspectives, it will be an essential reference source for library professionals, researchers, educators, students, program and community administrators, and practitioners with a combined interest in rural issues and aging.

Dr. Lenard W. Kaye is Professor of Social Work at the University of Maine School of Social Work and Director of the University of Maine Center on Aging. A prolific writer in the field of health care and aging, he has published more than 175 journal articles and book chapters, and 15 books on specialized topics in aging, including social isolation, home health care, men's health, productive aging, rural practice, family caregiving, support groups for older women, and congregate housing. His recent books include *A Man's Guide to Healthy Aging: Stay Smart, Strong, and Active* (with Edward Thompson, Jr., 2013) and *Social Isolation of Older Adults: Strategies to Bolster Health and Well-Being* (with Clifford M. Singer, 2019).

Dr. Kaye is lead evaluator for AgingME, Maine's Geriatrics Workforce Enhancement Program and co-director of evaluation of an ACL/DHHS-funded, technology-driven, nutrition enhanced self-management program for older adults with multiple chronic diseases. He is also a co-principal investigator of The Mayer-Rothschild Foundation-supported Designation of Excellence in Person-Centered Long-Term Care initiative. He was the lead organizer of the International Symposium on Safe Medicine and a founding board member of the International Institute for Pharmaceutical Safety; and has managed a series of John Hartford Foundation-funded gerontological social work education programs at the University of Maine.

Dr. Kaye was the 2010 recipient of the Career Achievement Award of the Association for Gerontology Education in Social Work (AGESW) and has served on the National Advisory Committee for Rural Health and Human Services of the U.S. Department of Health and Human Services. He is a research scientist at Northern Light Eastern Maine Medical Center and past president of both the Maine and New York State Gerontological Societies. He is the past chair of the National Association of Social Worker's Section on Aging, sits on the editorial boards of the *Journal of Gerontological Social Work* and *Journal of Aging Life Care*, and is a fellow of the Gerontological Society of America.

HANDBOOK OF RURAL AGING

Edited by Lenard W. Kaye

Routledge
Taylor & Francis Group
NEW YORK AND LONDON

First published 2021
by Routledge
52 Vanderbilt Avenue, New York, NY 10017

and by Routledge
2 Park Square, Milton Park, Abingdon, Oxon, OX14 4RN

Routledge is an imprint of the Taylor & Francis Group, an informa business

Library of Congress Cataloging-in-Publication Data
A catalog record for this book has been requested

ISBN: 978-0-367-65189-3 (hbk)
ISBN: 978-0-367-72282-1 (pbk)
ISBN: 978-1-003-12826-7 (ebk)

Typeset in Bembo
by Apex CoVantage, LLC

To Dyan Walsh, for her unwavering support, extraordinary understanding, and wise counsel on all matters of aging and common sense thinking during the course of preparing this volume.

CONTENTS

PREFACE

A comprehensive resource guide in the form of a *Handbook of Rural Aging*, that is dedicated to understanding the aging experience in rural communities broadly defined, has, until now, remained unavailable. This has been the case even though small-town America has consistently registered higher proportions of older adults residing there than in urban and suburban communities. Handbooks have existed addressing the aging process generally and rural living generally, but not rural aging specifically. Other books, considerable in number, that focus on the aging process more generally, have traditionally focused on the experience of urban aging and the challenges facing older adults in more populated regions of the country and have not made needed distinctions between the circumstances and needs of urban, suburban, and rural-dwelling elders.

The books that do exist on rural aging have explicit, well-defined frames of reference such as the delivery of human services or health care, or else they focus on the roles of particular health care professionals such as social workers or nurses and physicians in sparsely populated communities. They are intentionally more narrow or circumscribed in breadth and scope, focusing on one or more of a limited number of themes—either health, service delivery, program and policy, culture, professional practice, etc. The *Handbook of Rural Aging* addresses all of these topics and much more, making it the first such comprehensive reference source for library professionals, researchers, educators, students, and community administrators and practitioners.

The *Handbook of Rural Aging* proceeds beyond the perspective of a narrow range of health professions and disciplines and community services that serve older adults in rural America to the full range of professional perspectives and issues impacting the infrastructure of the communities in which rural older adults reside, including, but not limited to, work and voluntarism, technology, transportation, the environment, housing, information, social participation, as well as health and community services. In this way, it endorses many of the dimensions of the built and social environment that AARP (2020) has specified are the multiple domains of a livable community (one that is safe and secure, has housing and transportation options that are affordable and appropriate, and offers supportive community features and services) and the impact those domains have on the quality of life of rural-dwelling older adults. *Simply put, the aim of this single volume has been to address the full breadth and scope of factors impacting the lives of rural elders. As a result, the* Handbook of Rural Aging *aims to fill a significant knowledge gap and serve as a one-stop reference source on the rural aging phenomenon, providing demographic, economic, social, cultural, health, environmental, and political perspectives.*

The *Handbook of Rural Aging* is intended to both support a widespread movement to place rural America on the policy radar screen while elevating the attention given to the critical circumstances facing rural elders and those who serve them, including stakeholders in the fields of aging, government, academia, technology, business, health care, and the nonprofit, faith-based, and community service sectors. Best practices and techniques that encourage effective and efficient rural community and cross sector collaboration, partnerships, information dissemination and sharing, and improved access and utilization of services and resources will be emphasized. These strategies are, in many cases, not the same as those that have been enacted in metropolitan regions of the country given the dramatically different nature of urban and rural community geography, infrastructure, resource availability, and culture.

The target audiences for the *Handbook* include:

- Practitioners and program administrators who work at agencies and organizations serving older adults in small towns and rural communities
- Government and community policymakers and program planners in rural communities
- Students in gerontology and geriatrics degree and certificate programs with a focus on rurality and/or aging
- Reference librarians and acquisition decision-makers in public and academic-based libraries
- Students in interdisciplinary and interprofessional degree and certificate programs focusing on rural issues
- Educators teaching about and researchers studying the rural aging experience

The approximately 80 entries by more than 120 contributing authorities in the *Handbook* are purposefully brief (most being 1,500 to 2,500 words in length), interdisciplinary and interprofessional in orientation, and written in easy-to-digest language with limited but highly relevant and current references including, in some cases, recommendations for further reading.

Unless otherwise stated in an individual entry, the term "rural" as used in this *Handbook* will refer to populations, regions, territories, communities, towns, and housing not included within a designated "urban area" as defined by the U.S. Census Bureau. Applying principles of residential population density and several different land use characteristics, the Census Bureau has defined two categories of "urban area": 1. "urbanized areas" composed of 50,000 or more people; and 2. "urban clusters" composed of at least 2,500 but fewer than 50,000 people. Thus, rural areas are any and all locations having fewer than 2,500 inhabitants. Suffice it to say, residents of rural areas can be characterized as living in towns and communities reflecting "low density, sparse population, not built up, and at a distance from urban areas" (Smith & Trevelyan, 2019, 6). For a more detailed definition of urban and rural, see Ratcliffe, Burd, Holder, and Fields (2016).

Lenard W. Kaye

References

AARP. (2020, November 16). *AARP network of age-friendly states and communities*. Retrieved from https://www.aarp.org/livable-communities/network-age-friendly-communities/

Ratcliffe, M., Burd, C., Holder, K., & Fields, A. (December 2016). *Defining rural at the U.S. Census Bureau, ACSGEO-1*. Washington, DC: U.S. Census Bureau.

Smith, A. S., & Trevelyan, E. (2019). *The older population in rural America: 2012–2016, ACS-41, American Community Survey Reports*. Washington, DC: U.S. Census Bureau.

FOREWORD
The Federal Scene

As Americans increasingly express a preference for aging at home, rural America can offer tremendous benefits. Rural areas often bring a wealth of strengths that can support healthy aging, including tight-knit communities, pristine outdoors, a lower cost-of-living, and a less hectic lifestyle. They also present unique challenges, such as limited infrastructure, dispersed populations, and economic barriers. Such embedded hurdles can make connecting rural older adults to needed services that support healthy aging more difficult.

The inaugural publication of the *Handbook of Rural Aging* brings much-needed information to practitioners and program administrators, government and community policymakers, students, educators, and others who strive to serve older adults in rural communities across the country. The federal government provides critical services to meet key needs, including nutrition through home-delivered and congregate meals, transportation through state-based driving networks, and caregiver support through respite networks and caregiver resources and training materials. The federal government also helps older adults in rural areas age at home through programs that provide personal care services, homemaker services, and home repairs. These services cut across agencies, including the Department of Health and Human Services (DHHS), the Department of Housing and Urban Development, the Department of Transportation, the Department of Agriculture, and the Department of Veterans Affairs.

For researchers and policy practitioners seeking insight about "who does what" at the intersection of federally funded programs focused on issues of a rural *and* an aging population, we recommend a review of DHHS's Moyer table, a useful cross-tabbed document that delineates funding by subject area. Highlighted here are those federal programs aiming to address the unique challenges rural older Americans face, focusing on the following agencies and areas:

- Administration for Community Living (ACL): Community-Based Agencies and Senior Support Services
- Health Resources and Services Administration (HRSA): Rural Hospital Support, Telehealth, and Geriatric Programs and Education
- National Institute on Aging (NIA): Geographic Health Disparities
- U.S. Department of Veterans Affairs (VA): Rural Health Program Expansion
- U.S. Department of Agriculture (USDA): Affordable Housing and Repairs.

Challenge 1: Limited Infrastructure

Fewer transportation options, homes in need of age-appropriate modifications, limited access to caregiver support, and fewer resources specialized in health care for older adults create obstacles for rural older adults wishing to age-in-place. ACL and HRSA—both agencies housed within DHHS—are particularly focused on helping local agencies overcome these rural resource challenges.

Administration for Community Living (ACL)

Drawing on funds from the Older Americans Act (OAA), the ACL was created "around the fundamental principle that older adults and people of all ages with disabilities should be able to live where they choose, with the people they choose, and with the ability to participate fully in their communities" (ACL, 2019). While the ACL provides funding and support for a broad network of community-based agencies, the Area Agencies on Aging (AAAs) are designated as public or nonprofit organizations primarily responsible for a geographic area—sometimes referred to as Planning and Service Areas (PSAs). AAAs may be categorized as county, city, regional planning council or council of governments, private, or nonprofit.

Title III of the OAA requires states to target services to older adults living in rural areas. Program areas focused on limited infrastructure challenges include:

- *Supportive Services and Senior Centers*: provides funding to states and AAAs to provide a wide range of services to help older Americans remain in their homes and communities. Funding can be used for activities at the local level, including transportation, homemaker support, case management, adult day programming, tax counseling and assistance, and home modifications.
- *Nutrition*: nutrition services are intended to reduce hunger and food insecurity, promote socialization, and delay the onset of adverse health conditions.
- *Disease Prevention and Health Promotion Services*: states and territories receive grants that fund evidence-based disease prevention and health promotion programs (such as falls prevention, chronic disease self-management, and brain health) to help older Americans better manage their chronic conditions, thereby reducing the need for more costly medical interventions.
- *Lifespan Respite Care Programs*: these grants to states help lift the immense burden placed on our nation's 46 million family caregivers, who provide an estimated $470 billion in uncompensated care each year, by providing opportunities for them to take a break from their duties. An astounding 85% of caregivers do not receive any respite services at all.

Health Resources and Services Administration (HRSA)

HRSA administers rural-focused programs through the Federal Office of Rural Health Policy (FORHP). These programs support health services in rural areas that include support for services for older adults, but all programs are not necessarily specifically targeted toward older adults.

- *Rural Health Information Hub (RHIhub)*: Established in 2002 as a rural health and human services information portal, RHIhub "offers information, resources, and technical assistance for rural community health organizations, providers, and government health officials at both state and local levels." RHIhub is a collaboration of the University of North Dakota Center for Rural Health (UND-CRH), the Rural Policy Research Institute (RUPRI), and the NORC Walsh Center for Rural Health Analysis.

- *Rural Hospitals*: FORHP provides technical assistance and support to address the unique needs of rural hospitals, which represent more than half of all hospitals in the U.S. FORHP aims to build essential access to inpatient, outpatient, and emergency medical services in rural communities.
- *Rural Community Programs*: the Community-Based Division (CBD) grant programs provide funding to increase access to care in rural communities and to address their unique health-care challenges. Most of CBD's programs require community organizations to share resources and expertise using evidence-based models of care in networks of two or more health-care services providers.
- *Telehealth Programs*: the Office for the Advancement of Telehealth (OAT) promotes the use of telehealth technologies for health-care delivery, education, and health information services. Telehealth is especially critical in rural and other remote areas that lack sufficient health-care services, including specialty care.
- *Geriatrics Workforce Enhancement Program (GWEP)*: The Geriatrics Workforce Enhancement Program provides grants to health profession schools, health-care facilities, and programs leading to nursing assistant certification. Programs aim to improve health care for older adults (with a special emphasis on opioids and Alzheimer's disease and related dementias). GWEP programs maximize patient and family engagement by transforming clinical environments into integrated geriatric-focused primary care systems that are characterized by increased community coordination.
- *Geriatrics Academic Career Award Program (GACA)*: The Geriatrics Academic Career Award Program provides grants to support the career development of individual geriatrics faculty at accredited schools of allopathic medicine, osteopathic medicine, nursing, social work, psychology, dentistry, pharmacy, and allied health. GACA recipients focus on developing the necessary skills to lead health-care transformation in a variety of settings (including rural and/or medically underserved communities) and to provide training in clinical geriatrics (including the training of interprofessional teams).

Challenge 2: Dispersed Populations

Reaching older adults in remote, sparsely populated areas can add to the cost and effort of providing services. The NIA and VA offer broad sets of programs that seek to address the challenges that rural environments can often present for older adults seeking specialized care.

The National Institute on Aging (NIA)

The NIA—a division of the National Institutes of Health—"leads a broad scientific effort to understand the nature of aging and to extend the healthy, active years of life" (NIH, 2017). As one of its strategic initiatives, the NIA has created the Health Disparities Research Framework, a "resource for scientists interested in investigating health disparities related to aging" (NIA, n.d.). Focusing specifically on environmental factors (i.e., geography) among its four key levels of analysis in disparity research, the NIA uniquely serves as a clearinghouse for research on rural and aging issues.

U.S. Department of Veterans Affairs (VA)

The Office of Rural Health (ORH) works "to see that American veterans thrive in rural communities by establishing and expanding national programs, as well as cultivating partnerships at the federal, state, and local level" (VA.gov: Veterans Affairs, 2020).

- *Enterprise-Wide Initiatives*: numerous enterprise-wide initiatives provide funding to support the expansion of national VA program offices' health-care efforts to sites that serve rural veterans. Programs focus on increasing rural veterans' access to home-based primary and long-term care, as well as services in telehealth and lifestyle change (i.e., healthy behaviors). Through these programs, older veterans receive expanded access to mental health, transportation, and care coordination services as well. Initiatives supported through this program also focus on connecting rural VA facilities with specialized practitioners (e.g., clinical pharmacists) and resources (e.g., genomic counseling).
- *Rural Promising Practices*: rural promising practices supply seed funding to innovative local projects aimed at addressing rural veterans' health-care and access challenges. ORH also offers either "mentored" (i.e., ORH-led) or "direct" (i.e., published guidelines) implementation support for projects that demonstrate "significant impact based on select criteria" (VA.gov: Veterans Affairs, 2019). Models implemented nationwide address needs such as increasing access to care and services in rural communities and sharing clinical and operational knowledge among health-care delivery professionals who serve rural veterans. Several innovative and promising models directly impact rural older adults. The VA Geriatric Scholars Program was established to address the shortage of care workers with geriatric-specific skills by training VA general clinicians in the treatment of older, rural veterans. The GRECC Connect Project, meanwhile, improves access to geriatric care while reducing the distance veterans are required to travel by training VA providers to "manage medically complex cases through case-based conferences, electronic consultations, virtual meetings, and clinical video telehealth" (VA.gov: Veterans Affairs, 2019). Older veterans can also gain access to telehealth services through the Interdisciplinary Tele-Geriatrics Program, which provides remote video consultation focused on medication, education, and caregiver support in geographic areas where geriatric expertise may be limited.
- *Geriatrics and Extended Care*: aside from the VA's rural health-focused initiatives, the agency also offers an extended geriatrics care suite aimed at veterans, caregivers, and health professionals. The Extended Care suite provides information and programs that cover a variety of age-related topics, many of which offer benefits for rural older veterans, especially. Older adults can find veteran-specific programs focusing on dementia/Alzheimer's care and homemaker/home health support. Guides help older adults navigate the aging landscape, providing overviews on topics such as advanced care planning. Health-care professionals, additionally, can access geriatric resources, like data reports and links to further educational opportunities. Particularly applicable to older rural veterans is the VA's remote monitoring care program, which allows VA physicians or nurses to monitor medical conditions remotely using home monitoring equipment.

Challenge 3: Economic Barriers

Median household income is substantially lower in rural areas compared to urban areas. U.S. Department of Agriculture programs help rural residents buy or rent safe, affordable housing and make health and safety repairs to their homes.

The U.S. Department of Agriculture (USDA) Rural Development

The USDA is "committed to helping improve the economy and quality of life in rural America" (USDA, 2019). Aging-specific USDA rural programs include:

- *Section 504 Home Repair Program/Rural Repair and Rehabilitation Grants*: these programs provide grants to very low-income older homeowners (62 and older) in rural areas to remove health and safety hazards in their homes.
- *Multi-Family Housing Programs and Rental Assistance*: this program provides housing support for low-income, older, or disabled individuals and families in eligible rural areas. Tenants must be very low-income to moderate-income families or individuals, persons aged 62 or older, or have a disability. Rental assistance is also available for qualifying very low-income rural tenants at Rural Development funded properties.
- *Community Facilities, Direct Loan and Grant Program*: this program provides funding to develop "essential community facilities" in rural areas. Defined as a facility that provides an essential service for the orderly development of the community in a primarily rural area, these facilities do not include private, commercial, or business undertakings. Eligible community organizations that serve older adults could apply.

Aging can bring numerous obstacles, with some being inevitably more challenging for those residing in rural regions. Fortunately, for many years now, policymakers, community leaders, patients and families, and health-care professionals have worked diligently to recognize and address the challenges that impact aging Americans living in sparsely populated communities. There is still much work to be done, but it is hoped that this guide provides helpful documentation of the context driving these challenges and, importantly, the resources available to address them.

Senator Susan M. Collins, Chairman of the Senate Aging Committee,
and Senator Angus S. King, Jr.

References

ACL. (2019). *Advancing independence, integration, and inclusion throughout life*. Retrieved from https://acl.gov/

National Institute on Aging (NIA). (n.d.). *Health disparities framework*. Retrieved from www.nia.nih.gov/research/osp/framework

National Institutes of Health (NIH). (2017, March 1). Retrieved from www.nih.gov/about-nih/what-we-do/nih-almanac/national-institute-aging-nia

USDA. (2019, December 18). *About RD*. Retrieved from www.rd.usda.gov/about-rd

VA.gov: Veterans Affairs. (2019, December 12). Retrieved from www.ruralhealth.va.gov/providers/promising_practices.asp

VA.gov: Veterans Affairs. (2020, July 13). Retrieved from www.ruralhealth.va.gov/aboutus/programs.asp

A SPECIAL NOTE ON COVID-19, PANDEMICS, AND RURAL AGING

During the final stages of preparing the *Handbook of Rural Aging*, the novel coronavirus pandemic (COVID-19) was having significant national and global impacts. The threat to individual and community health and well-being was, in many respects, having unprecedented effects as this disease was sickening and killing individuals young and old alike at the same time that it was negatively impacting the economic well-being of individuals, families, organizations, and nations. Severe shortages of medical supplies and equipment, intensive care beds, and a wide range of basic food and household staples were commonplace, at least in the early stages, as was limited access to many, normally readily accessible, health and human services supports and other basic community infrastructure resources.

While it could be argued that in terms of sheer numbers, the hardest hit COVID-19 geographic regions were more likely to be higher population density metropolitan areas as compared to small towns and rural communities, it became clear, early on, that the highest risk individuals were adults 60 years of age and older and those with preexisting chronic conditions and compromised immune systems. Staying healthy, informed, and connected for these individuals during the COVID-19 pandemic became a major challenge. At the same time, official directives and public health emergency declarations emphasized the importance of social distancing and sheltering-in-place.

What also became apparent during the pandemic is that particular subgroups of individuals generally, including older adults in both rural and urban communities, were at higher risk of experiencing the potentially deadly consequences of contracting COVID-19. This has certainly included older people in nursing homes who have significantly lowered immunity and an increased number of chronic medical conditions (i.e., diabetes, cancer, cardiovascular and pulmonary disease, and other conditions) where high infection and death rates have been repeatedly documented.

Notably, increased risk levels have also been documented among individuals of color (i.e., people who are black, Latino, and Native American) in regions across the nation. These individuals have experienced the consequences of inequalities in access to health care, including heightened adverse COVID-19 health outcomes (higher infection and death rates) at the same time that they are more likely to be living at or near poverty levels, suffering from food insecurity, grappling with transportation barriers, and because of concerns for the out-of-pocket costs of health care, hesitating to access treatment in a timely fashion (Henning-Smith, 2020; Kijakazi, 2020; Gerontological Society of America, 2020).

If measured by the absolute numbers of those infected and the number of deaths resulting from COVID-19, rural areas represented a fraction of the rate recorded in major cities (3% as of March 23, 2020). In fact, in March of 2020, the nation's largest metropolitan areas reported an infection rate of more than seven times that of the nonmetropolitan rate. Approximately nine out of every ten cases reported by March of 2020 were situated in major metropolitan counties (metropolitan areas with one million or more residents) even though those counties had only about 56% of the U.S. population (USA Facts, 2020). It is likely that transmission rates of COVID-19 will ultimately prove to be lower in rural areas, but the percentage of cases resulting in death and other serious complications is expected to be measurably higher in rural compared to urban areas (Monnat, 2020). It is true that low population density in rural areas reduced the opportunities for such a virus to spread. Yet, other features of rural populations and communities were predicted to increase their risk of coronavirus-related mortality and other negative long-term health impacts including the fact that rural populations are older, have higher rates of chronic health conditions, lack adequate and affordable health insurance, have more fragile local economies and health-care infrastructures (characterized by widespread hospital and medical practice closures), and are exposed to more severe health disparities (Henning-Smith, 2020; Keating & Karklis, 2020). Additionally, large proportions of rural workers are employed in lower paid jobs that do not lend themselves to working remotely as was encouraged during this public health emergency. The National Council on Aging (2020) has predicted that pandemic-caused financial hardships will push between 1.4 million and 2.1 million older Americans alone into poverty. All of these factors pose significant implications for negative longer-term rural population health outcomes for public health emergencies like COVID-19 (Ajilore & Willingham, 2020; Kaye, 2020b; Monnat, 2020, Sun, 2020, Weber, 2020). (For a comprehensive listing of COVID-19 news stories especially relevant to rural communities, see Rural Health Information Hub at www.ruralhealthinfo.org/topics/covid-19/news (2020).

The COVID-19 outbreak, even in its earlier stages, has taught us many lessons. For older adults residing in rural communities and those who serve them, lessons learned center around being more aware in the future of the consequences that can be expected of pandemics and other public health emergencies for rural-residing older adults, their families, and community service and health-care providers. Also learned is the imperative that policymakers, providers, and older adults themselves plan ahead more systematically and implement both common sense and creative strategies for ensuring that older rural Americans stay connected to others in their communities at the same time that the risk of increased isolation, loneliness, and anxiety during challenging times is minimized (Kaye, 2020a; U.S. Senate Special Committee on Aging, 2020). Similarly, it is clear that we need to engage, perhaps with renewed energy and commitment, in efforts to develop policies and programs that reflect the enactment of new service delivery models, standards, and program criteria that ensure older adults and their families residing in rural communities stay safe and supported during public health crises. The dramatic and rapid transition to the remote transmission of information, resources, and clinical supports during the COVID-19 crisis, while impressive, also served to underscore how critical expanded availability of broadband and affordable communication technologies as well as digital literacy among rural residents is in the most rural and frontier regions of the U.S. not only for older adults but individuals of all ages. The COVID-19 pandemic also highlighted the importance of collaboration among governments, community organizations, and businesses. These alliances and the many selfless examples of civic engagement of individuals and groups helped ensure the availability of services and products (home-delivered meals, household supplies, mental and physical health-care services, etc.) to older adults who live independently and in congregate residences who found themselves suddenly isolated, anxious, and scared. During public health emergencies, vulnerable older adults and the rural communities in which they reside are particularly dependent on resources being made available that will better ensure their safety, health, and well-being.

Lenard W. Kaye

References

Ajilore, O., & Willingham, Z. (2020, March 5). *Rural Americans are vulnerable to the Coronavirus*. Center for American Progress. Retrieved from www.americanprogress.org/issues/economy/news/2020/03/05/481340/rural-communities-vulnerable-coronavirus/

Gerontological Society of America. (2020, May). *Understand ageism and COVID-19*. Retrieved from www.geron.org/images/gsa/reframing/AgeismInfographic_final.pdf

Henning-Smith, C. (2020, June 1). The unique impact of COVID-19 on older adults in rural areas. *Journal of Aging & Social Policy*, *32*(4–5), 396–402. doi:10.1080/08959420.2020.1770036

Kaye, L.W. (2020a, April 23). Older adults are facing dual public health emergencies. *Bangor Daily News*. Retrieved from https://bangordailynews.com/2020/04/21/opinion/contributors/older-adults-are-facing-dual-public-health-emergencies/?_ga=2.208326610.130714167.1587331829-918642114.1581903447

Kaye, L.W. (2020b, September 8), Retrieved from https://www.centralmaine.com/2020/09/08/scholars-strategy-network-the-pandemic-has-hit-older-adults-particularly-hard/.

Keating, D., & Karklis, L. (2020, March 19). Rural areas may be the most vulnerable during the coronavirus outbreak. *The Washington Post*. Retrieved from www.washingtonpost.com/nation/2020/03/19/rural-areas-may-be-most-vulnerable-during-coronavirus-outbreak/?arc404=true

Kijakazi, K. (2020). *COVID-19 racial health disparities highlight why we need to address structural racism*. Urban Institute. Retrieved from www.urban.org/urban-wire/covid-19-racial-health-disparities-highlight-why-we-need-address-structural-racism

Monnat, S. (2020, March 24). *Research update: Why Coronovirus could hit rural areas harder*. Syracuse: Population Health Research Brief Series. Lerner Center for Public Health Promotion, Syracuse University.

National Council on Aging. (April 16, 2020). Retrieved from https://www.ncoa.org/uncategorized/covid-19-pandemic-will-impoverish-millions-of-aging-americans/.

Rural Health Information Hub. (2020, June 24). *Rural response to coronavirus disease 2019 (COVID-19)—news*. Retrieved from www.ruralhealthinfo.org/topics/covid-19/news

Sun, Y. (2020, March 25). *COVID-19 cases are clustered in large urban hubs, but rural areas surrounding those hubs are also increasingly affected*. Population Health Research Brief Series. Syracuse: Lerner Center for Public Health Promotion, Syracuse University.

USA Facts. (2020, June 23). *Coronavirus in the United States: Mapping the COVID-19 outbreak*. Retrieved from https://usafacts.org/visualizations/coronavirus-covid-19-spread-map/

U.S. Senate Special Committee on Aging. (2020, June 11). *Combating social isolation and loneliness during the COVID-19 pandemic*. Retrieved from www.aging.senate.gov/hearings/combating-social-isolation-and-loneliness-during-the-covid-19-pandemic

Weber, L. (2020, March 21). Coronavirus threatens the lives of rural hospitals already stretched to breaking point. *Kaiser Health News*. Kaiser Family Foundation.

INTRODUCTION

Lenard W. Kaye

Rural aging issues are gaining increased attention by a variety of notable organizations. Grantmakers in Aging, a membership organization composed of all types of philanthropies with a common dedication to improving the experience of aging, initiated a three-year initiative to create ways to connect and support key stakeholders concerned with rural aging, including sharing knowledge and expanding the available resources and services available to older adults in rural areas of the country. A report by Grantmakers in Aging (Krout, 2019), using the definition of rural as outside of a metropolitan area, found that two-thirds of the nation's 3,142 counties are rural and include well over 50 million people who reside there. The rural population represents approximately 10 million people ages 65 and older. Additionally, rural communities have a higher overall median age than urban communities (51 years vs. 45 years) (Rural Health Research Gateway, 2018). Approximately 25% of Americans older than age 65 live in a small town or other rural area. In some states, the percentage of rural dwelling older adults is extremely high; for example, in Maine, 58% of adults older than age 65 live in rural areas and it is important to note that approximately 95% of U.S. territory is still officially designated as rural.

Change-makers in the field of aging are increasingly dedicating themselves to advancing the well-being of rural dwelling older adults. The 2017, 2018, and 2019 Connectivity Summits convened in Portsmouth, New Hampshire; Portland, Maine; and Nashville, Tennessee, respectively, are but three examples of increased interest and priority aimed at spreading the word about the importance of rural aging in America. At the inaugural Connectivity Summit in 2017, Donato Tramuto, then-chief executive officer of Tivity Health, conveyed the overarching goal of the summit—namely, to foster a nationwide *movement* by means of:

- Partnering to identify the unique challenges of rural aging,
- Using the participants' collaborative IQ to create targeted solutions, and
- Sharing the outcomes to inform policy debates and educate industry leaders and consumers.

A website growing out of the Connectivity Summits with resources and special points of focus on social isolation, infrastructure, nutrition, health care, and community is now available (www.ruralage.com). Developments like these bode well for elevating the importance and attention being given to rural aging issues.

In similar fashion, the number of academic centers focusing on aging-related research and education have increased over the years, such as those at rural-based institutions that include rurality as a central focal point (e.g., Center on Aging at the University of Maine; Center for Aging Research and Education (CARE) at UW-Madison School of Nursing; Interdisciplinary Network on Rural Population Health and Aging at Penn State University; Syracuse University; University of Colorado Boulder; and University of Mississippi).

Other leading organizations have recognized the significance of the rural aging phenomenon, including the Robert Wood Johnson Foundation and Campbell University, which have partnered to conduct an 18-month national study on philanthropy to improve health in rural communities. The project (The Rural Philanthropic Analysis) is designed to identify new ideas and insights to improve charitable organizations' support for healthy, equitable rural communities given that only 7% of private philanthropic investments are currently directed toward these locations (Campbell University, 2019). Still other foundations have announced special grant initiatives that encourage community-based health and human service organizations to think creatively and collaboratively on special issues that affect rural older adults in significant ways, such as the risks inherent in being lonely and living socially isolated from others (i.e., Bader Philanthropies Inc. in Wisconsin and Moses Taylor Foundation in northeastern Pennsylvania).

Even as growing interest in rural aging is evidenced, authoritative sources that define the challenges rural communities face and provide guidelines for better coordination of the efforts of government, policymakers, health-care systems, nonprofits, the business community, and philanthropic organizations continue to be badly needed. For example, in the government sector, even when multiple agencies in a rural area have relevant programs, they may not be well coordinated. Furthermore, local governments, nonprofits, and community members may not have much awareness of what is available; conversely, data and feedback about local needs and strengths may not be shared.

The Graying of Rural America

Rural Population Trends and the Aging Phenomenon

While population aging is a global phenomenon, the growth in the number and proportion of older citizens residing in small towns and rural communities is advancing at a particularly rapid rate. Rural America covers approximately 75% of land area in the U.S. and accounts for some 15% of the population. One in four Americans over the age of 65 lives in rural regions of the country (based on the 2013 Office of Management and Budget definition of nonmetropolitan counties—containing fewer than 50,000 people). By 2040, 25% of households in rural communities will be 65 years of age or older compared to 20% of households in urban communities (Pendall, Goodman, Zhu & Gold, 2016).

There are, no doubt, several reasons why the pace of aging in rural communities is accelerating. Since 2010, rural America has experienced a notable loss in overall population. Some 1,350 nonmetropolitan counties lost population from 2010 through 2016 because of a combination of younger residents moving away from rural counties and death rates outpacing birth rates, the latter which have remained at historic lows. Deaths exceed births in numerous regions of rural America including the South, the Northeast, and especially in and around Appalachia. Those rural counties that have been spared population loss are likely to have been beneficiaries of a boom in oil or natural gas production, represent border metropolitan areas, or are home to scenic coastal and mountain attractions.

It should be noted that there is evidence that the decline in rural population generally, which began in 2010, has begun to reverse itself. In 2016–2017, rural counties, overall, added population for the first time in eight years. Even so, an Urban Institute (Pendall, Goodman, Zhu, and Gold, 2016) analysis projects that between 2020 and 2030, rural populations will increase by just 1% while urban areas will grow by 8%.

Rural counties continue to rapidly age and represent the vast majority (85%) of those counties in the U.S. with 20% or greater of their population 65 years and older. Nineteen percent of the rural U.S. population are 65 years of age and older compared to 15% of metropolitan or urban areas (Economic Research Service, U.S. Department of Agriculture, 2018).

Not only are many rural communities composed of rapidly growing numbers and proportions of aging long-term residents, such locales are also proving to be attractive in-migration retirement destinations for older Americans because nonmetropolitan areas tend to have a relative lower cost of living, a greater sense of safety, and, of course, pristine natural surroundings and a variety of attractive lifestyle amenities. Those counties that represent retirement destinations and offer recreation or scenic attractions are especially likely to have seen higher net immigration in recent years that has led, in turn, to rapidly aging resident populations. On the other hand, other rural counties have registered dramatic increases in their aging populations because of long-term outmigration (primarily of young adults). Of course, a number of rural counties have simultaneously experienced both phenomena. Rural aging experiences in terms of both well-being and economic prospects can be expected to vary considerably depending on whether a region is considered a recreation/retirement county (characterized by having a larger population, located closer to large cities, and having more needed services) or an older age, chronic population loss county (characterized by having a smaller population, at greater distance from large cities, and having fewer needed services) (Economic Research Service, U.S. Department of Agriculture, 2018).

Notable, also, is that since 2000, rural rates of mortality have increased for middle-aged adults (partly because of the opioid epidemic) but are decreasing for older individuals, representing yet another factor that could result in an acceleration of rural aging (Economic Research Service, U.S. Department of Agriculture, 2018).

Rural Aging Well-Being and Quality of Life

Attracting both those who have aged in place and transplanted older adults, many small towns and rural communities can lay claim to a variety of enviable qualities:

- Pristine surroundings, including (depending on the rural state in which you reside) beautiful forests, mountains, lakes, and seashores. These outdoor venues are characterized by open spaces, a lack of crowding, and clean air and water and lend themselves to kayaking, canoeing, hiking, snowshoeing, cross-country skiing, and more.
- A greater sense of safety and security.
- A relatively lower cost of living.
- A tight-knit social fabric reflected in the presence of families, friends, and neighbors, who, while respecting your privacy, are almost always ready to step up and come to the aid of citizens during times of need.
- A more personalized relationship with the business and social and health-care networks that one interacts with.

- A less abrupt and potentially traumatic transition to retirement because individuals tend to have subscribed to a more balanced lifestyle in terms of the importance placed on work versus family and community.
- A generally more serene and less stressful lifestyle and reasonably high levels of life satisfaction (Kaye, 2015).

Of course, all is not well in rural America. Consider the challenges that are continuously confronted that lead to the distinction of rural populations being described as "older, sicker and poorer" than urban populations (Rural Health Research Gateway, 2018). A report by NPR, Robert Wood Johnson Foundation, and Harvard T.H. Chan School of Public Health (2019) reaffirms that at the same time that rural Americans see their communities as more safe than those nationally, sizable proportions experience difficulties affording medical bills, housing, or food as well as having ready access to adequate health care. Generally, older adults living in rural communities are less educated, have fewer employment opportunities, are living on lower incomes, are more food insecure, and are less healthy as they grapple with higher rates of chronic health conditions compared to their urban and suburban counterparts. Rates of high cholesterol, hypertension, arthritis, diabetes, heart disease, and COPD are also higher among rural residents than urban residents (Rural Health Research Gateway, 2018). Rural individuals are more limited in physical activity and live in older and less adequate housing stock. Rural elders have also been shown to have lower levels of social functioning, social networks, social support, and participation in the community compared to urban elders (Baernholdt, Yan, Hinton, & Rose, 2012). Additionally, they have less access to readily available formal transportation services and a variety of community health and social services, including specialized medical, mental health, and long-term care programs (Bipartisan Policy Center, 2018; Kaye, 2015; Krout, 2019). Service shortage in rural communities is accompanied by severe scarcity in terms of the availability of a wide range of professional health-care providers, including physicians, nurses, social workers, and other allied health professionals with specialized education and training in the care of older adults. Older adults in rural settings in spite of poorer general health are less likely to visit health-care professionals when needed (Baernholdt, Yan, Hinton, Rose, & Mattos, 2012).

Rural communities are more limited as well in resources, activities, connectivity, and infrastructure, including accommodations that are specifically designed for older adults, such as assisted living facilities, skilled nursing homes, and retirement communities (Rural Health Information Hub, 2019). Rural elders also appear to be at greater risk of what has been described as one of the great contemporary threats to societal well-being—social isolation and relatedly, loneliness (Bipartisan Policy Center, 2018; Kaye, 2017; Kaye & Singer, 2019; Walker & Warner, 2020). Taken together, these challenges lead to significant disparities in rural communities in terms of well-being, quality of life, economics, and health. In response, there are increasing calls to focus on quality of care, workforce development, and increased research especially focusing on health-care issues and the need to expand the implementation of evidence-based rural health programming. The Milbank Memorial Fund and the Reforming States Group (Parento, 2019) have explicitly identified as issues of critical importance to policymakers at the state level the incentivizing of investments in community health and developing programs for training and retaining health-care providers, including leveraging technology and telehealth services.

Diversity and the Rural Aging Experience

The inclination has been to characterize rural America in relatively homogeneous terms. While there is less racial and ethnic diversity in rural communities, compared to urban ones, differences exist, and those differences are increasingly visible. Rural communities can be predominately white, black, Hispanic, or Native American. However, diversity is especially notable in rural America in terms of differences in geographic, economic, cultural, social, and national origin traditions. Communities that are more agricultural compared to those that have more diversified economies present differently in terms of population characteristics and lifestyles (Krout, 2019). Taken together, the rural population is approximately 80% white compared to 58% in urban communities. The remainder of the rural population is made up of Hispanics (9%), blacks (8%), American Indians (2%), Asians (1%), Pacific Islanders (.01%), and multiple races (1.8%). Rural population losses have recently occurred among whites and blacks and gains made by Hispanics and Native Americans. It should be noted that rural poverty rates have dropped annually from a peak in 2013 for all racial and ethnic groups but remain highest among racial and ethnic minority populations (Economic Research Service, U.S. Department of Agriculture, 2018).

The Challenge of Getting Aging Rural America on the Radar Screen

The challenges faced by metropolitan areas have traditionally dominated policy discussions in our nation in large part because 85% of the nation's population reside there along with the lion's share of development, innovation, artistic expression, and wealth creation (Pendall, Goodman, Zhu, and Gold, 2016). Krout (2019) has summarized additional reasons behind why rural aging, specifically, has tended to draw less attention from researchers and funding sources: 1. The term "rural" is variously defined by state and federal agencies, making consistent and meaningful analysis difficult. In fact, it has been noted that there are some 11 different ways in which an area might be designated as rural (Hash, Morrow, & Weirich, 2019). 2. Rural community issues draw less interest compared to problems that can be studied more readily at the individual level such as Alzheimer's disease or falls prevention. 3. Advocacy for rural aging issues is less commonplace unless they affect rural individuals of all ages such as smoking and obesity.

There is a trend toward increased attention by elected officials and federal departments aiming to address the challenges of aging in rural America (Harvey, 2019). At the state level, policy and program innovation is evidenced as well. Much of it focuses on strategies for increasing services that enable older adults to remain in their homes and immediate communities, growing and training the caregiver workforce, expanding transportation access and services, and implementing Medicaid delivery system reforms (Kaye & Long, 2019). Given the call to recognize, once and for all, that rural older adults will continue to resist moving away from their homes and communities when their health fails and their needs increase (Stone, 2020), such a trend is encouraging. Yet, the need for continued attention and investment through enacted policies and strategic and innovative programming is undeniable.

Putting the Uniqueness of the Rural Experience in Context

No matter how long the list of challenges confronting older adults in small towns and rural communities across America becomes, let there be no confusion as to why large proportions of older individuals choose to remain. Perhaps, like Dennis Dudley, a long-time advocate for rural elders, they remain firm in their belief in the promise and the future of a rural America given the attitude and the tenacity of its residents. Dudley is driven by the fact that rural Americans have traditionally been underserved and overlooked and have not benefited from the same array of services and programming as urban dwellers. This is at the root of his mission of social justice and equity to access for older rural Americans (Dudley, 2019). Ultimately, Kathy Greenlee's personal reflections of her rural roots as a fifth-generation Kansan speak volumes:

> I know where I am from. I have a physical sense of my roots. I was raised rural because my people were rural. My hometown is also my family history. . . . I live in Kansas City, but will eventually return to be buried with many generations of my family. For now, you can hear the rural girl inside of me each time I complain because I cannot see the stars. It breaks my heart.
>
> (Greenlee, 2019, 8)

References

Baernholdt, M., Yan, G., Hinton, I., Rose, K., & Mattos, M. (Fall 2012). Quality of life in rural and urban adults 65 years and older: Findings from the National Health and Nutrition Examination Survey. *J Rural Health*, 28(4), 339–347.

Bipartisan Policy Center. (July 2018). *Rural aging: Health and community policy implications for reversing social isolation*. Washington, DC: Bipartisan Policy Center.

Campbell University (2019). *About rural philanthropy*. Retrieved from https://www.campbell.edu/about/research/rural-philanthropic-analysis/about-rural-philanthropy/.

Dudley, D. (2019). Keeping the faith in rural America: A longtime denizen speaks about equity and advocacy. *Generations: Journal of the American Society on Aging*. 43(2), 4–5.

Economic Research Service, U.S. Department of Agriculture. (November 2018). Rural America at a glance: 2018 Edition, Economic Information Bulletin 200. Washington, DC: United States Department of Agriculture.

Greenlee, K. (2019). Why people choose the rural life. *Generations: Journal of the American Society on Aging*. 43(2), 6–8.

Harvey, D. (Summer 2019). Perceptions of and policy making around aging in rural America. *Generations: Journal of the American Society on Aging*. 43(2), 66–70.

Hash, K.M., Morrow, F., & Weirich, M.R. (2019). The social implications of growing old in small towns and rural communities. In Kaye, L.W. & Singer, C.M. (Eds.), *Social isolation of older adults: Strategies to bolster health and well-being*. New York, NY: Springer Publishing Company, pp. 253–270.

Kaye, L.W. (Summer/Fall 2015). The demographic transition in Maine (and beyond) is in full swing. *Maine Policy Review*, 24(2), pp. 10–12.

Kaye, L.W. (2017). Older adults, rural living, and the escalating risk of social isolation. *Public Policy & Aging Report*, 27(4), 139–144. doi:10.1093/ppar/prx029

Kaye, L.W., & Singer, C.M. (Eds.). (2019). *Social isolation of older adults: Strategies to bolster health and well-being*. New York, NY: Springer Publishing Company.

Kaye, N., & Long, K. (September 12, 2019). Toolkit: State strategies to support older adults aging in place in rural areas. National Academy for State Health Policy. https://nashp.org/wp-content/uploads/2019/09/State-Strategies-to-Support-Older-Adults-Aging-in-Place-in-Rural-Areas_9_13_2019–1.pdf

Krout, J.A. *Rural aging*. (2019). Retrieved from www.giaging.org/issues/rural-aging/.

NPR, Robert Wood Johnson Foundation, & Harvard T.H. Chan School of Public Health. (May 2019). *Life in rural America: Part II. www.rwjf.org/en/library/research/2019/05/life-in-rural-america--part-ii.html*

Oh, H., Noh, H., Sims, O.T., Guo, Y., & Sawyer, P. (2018). A comparison of urban and non-urban African American older adults on health-related characteristics. *Social Work in Health Care*, 57(9), 762–773.

Parento, E.W. (May 2019). *Supporting rural health: Practical solutions for state policymakers. Issue brief.* Milbank Memorial Fund and The Reforming States Group. www.milbank.org/wp-content/uploads/2019/05/IssueBrief_RSG_RuralHealth_final_v2.pdf

Pendall, R., Goodman, L., Zhu, J., & Gold, A. (October 20, 2016). *The future of rural aging. Research report.* Washington, DC: Urban Institute.

Ratcliffe, M., Burd, C., Holder, K., & Fields, A. (December 2016). Defining rural at the U.S. Census Bureau, ACSGEO-1, U.S. Census Bureau, Washington, DC.

Rural Health Information Hub. (2019). *Demographic changes and aging population*. Retrieved from www.ruralhealthinfo.org/toolkits/aging/1/demographics.

Rural Health Research Gateway. (November 2018). *Rural communities: Age, income, and health status, Rural Health Research RECAP.* Grand Forks, ND: University of North Dakota Center for Rural Health.

Smith, A.S., & Trevelyan, E. (2018). The older population in rural America: 2012–2016, ACS-41, *American Community Survey Reports,* U.S. Census Bureau, Washington, DC.

Stone, R. (November 9, 2020). *Promoting quality of life among rural older adults.* Retrieved from https://www.ltsscenter.org/promoting-quality-of-life-among-rural-older-adults/.

Walker, E., & Warner, C. (2020). *Leveraging the power of connection: Demystifying "social determinants of health" to promote healthier aging in the 21st century.* Highlights of the 2019 Connectivity Summit on Rural Aging, August 14–15, 2019, Nashville, TN.

1
ADULT DAY SERVICES

William A. Zagorski

Introduction

Home and community-based services (HCBS) continue to be the fastest-growing sector of long-term supports and services in the U.S. (Harris-Kojetin, Sengupta, Lendon, et al., 2019) and adult day services (ADS) are a vital and cost-effective subset of HCBS. "ADS are professional care settings in which older adults, adults living with dementia, or adults living with disabilities receive individualized, therapeutic, social, and health services, for some, or all of the day" (National Adult Day Services Association, 2018). This definition is inclusive of several different models of noninstitutional care provided across the United States mostly to older adults with cognitive or physical limitations, and younger individuals with intellectual or developmental disabilities. ADS centers provide services to participants in the programs, as well as a much-needed break (respite) to caregivers, allowing them to fully engage in the community.

ADS Models and Participants

ADS are not regulated at the federal level, and therefore the regulations, licensing, and service delivery models vary widely from state to state (O'Keefe, O'Keefe, & Shrestha, 2014). In fact, some states do not regulate or license ADS at all, while others license ADS as a general social service, like childcare. In other states, ADS is licensed into differential levels of care dependent on the services provided. In general, ADS can be categorized as a social model, including respite, medical model, or a combination of both. Social model programs generally focus on socialization and some preventive services for the participants, and respite for caregivers. Medical model programs, more commonly known as adult day health care (ADHC), or Medical Adult Day Care (MADC) provide health assessment, treatment, stabilization, and therapeutic services in a social setting while still providing respite to caregivers. No matter the model of the program, the services provided generally address many facets of daily living, including but not limited to nutrition, transportation, socialization, therapeutic recreation, health or health-related care, and caregiver respite.

At the center of ADS and ADHC is the provision of health and related services by means of assisting with activities of daily living (ADLs) and instrumental activities of daily living (IADLs). Of the more than 4,800 ADS providers across the U.S., currently serving more than 280,000 individuals, more than 90% of ADS centers provide assistance with ambulation and transfers, toileting and personal care, and feeding assistance. Some 65–85% of ADS centers provide meals and nutrition to the participants, most at no charge. Many centers provide transportation services to and from the facilities. Nearly half of centers provide on-site therapeutic services (recreation therapy, art therapy, music therapy, speech therapy, physical therapy, etc.) while the vast majority provide ongoing active and social supportive services. Furthermore, more than 80% of centers offer some health-related services such as blood pressure and weight monitoring, diabetic management, and medication assistance. Nearly 65% of ADS providers offer significant nursing supports and services including medication administration, injections, wound care, and other health and mental health-related services (Harris-Kojetin L, Sengupta, Lendon, et al., 2019; MetLife, 2010). The services are provided by on-site, direct care staff and professionals of multiple disciplines, including nursing, social work, activity therapists, nutritionist, and more. In addition to the services provided to the participants in the programs, ADS provide respite to the caregivers, thus allowing them to fully participate in the community through ongoing employment, volunteerism, exercise, and socialization and have meaningful engagement in the community.

ADS are the most diverse sector of long-term care with participants more representative of the population. Roughly 16% of participants are African American and more than 22% are Hispanic. While 42% of participants are Caucasian, nearly 20% are non-Hispanic and non-African American, more than double the number served in residential settings. ADS participants range in age from 18 to well over 100, with roughly 64% of participants over the age of 65 and 58% of participants are women, according to the 2016 National Study of Long-Term Care Providers. One of the most striking trends in the last decade has been the inclusion of service provisions to individuals of varying physical, cognitive, and intellectual diagnoses. Only 30% of ADS participants suffer from Alzheimer's and other dementias, while the remaining majority suffer from a myriad of other chronic conditions such as heart disease, arthritis, asthma, kidney disease, diabetes, hypertension, and osteoporosis; physical disabilities such as cerebral palsy, post CVA, morbid obesity, Huntington's Disease, and ALS; and intellectual and developmental disabilities such as Down Syndrome, Grave's disease, autism, and more (Harris-Kojetin, Sengupta, Lendon, et al., 2019). Together, ADS provides comprehensive services and support to individuals who would otherwise rely on institutionalization, and thus allow them to age-in-place for the remainder of their lives.

Funding for ADS varies similar to regulations and licensing and is highly complex. To date, traditional Medicare does not pay for ADS; however, Medicaid programs remain one of the main direct payors of ADS services, paying for over 65% of participants' receipt of services at some level. In addition to Medicaid programs, the Veterans Administration is the second largest public assistance funding source, followed by Medicare Programs for the All Inclusive Care for the Elderly (PACE) programs, National Family Caregiver Support Program, and as of 2019, some Medicare Advantage (MA) plans have begun paying for ADS as a supplemental benefit. MA plans will soon cover more ADS (among other services) and these benefits are expected to significantly expand in the coming decade. Additionally, most long-term care insurance plans provide reimbursement for ADS, although less than 5% of participants possess such plans. Not-for-profit providers can assist participants and caregivers through grant funding and donations; however, private funding remains the second most common payment source, covering nearly 25% of participants (Harris-Kojetin L, Sengupta M, Lendon J, et al., 2019). ADS remain the most cost-effective long-term care (LTC) service, averaging less than $72 per day across the U.S. (Genworth, 2018).

Challenges and Trends in Rural Areas

The greatest challenge in rural, micropolitan, and even many urban and suburban areas is access to care. There are two main issues that prevent access: availability of services and transportation to those locations. While there were more than 4,600 ADS locations in 2012 (likely 8,000–10,000 as of 2019), over 85% are in urban or suburban areas (Harris-Kojetin, Sengupta, Lendon, et al., 2019). Of the remaining 15%, two-thirds are in micropolitan areas (populations centers between 10,000 and 50,000) and one-third are in rural areas, meaning there are less than 500 ADS centers in rural areas of the U.S. There are countless reasons behind this, but the more prominent is the viability and sustainability of an endeavor in a rural setting. No matter the regulatory environment where the ADS center is located, appropriate and cost-effective space must be available for a facility. Freestanding buildings of the appropriate size are often more costly than attached, or semi-detached suites in marketable locations, either of which may not be available in rural settings. The cost of renovations is often an excluding factor, as appropriate Americans with Disabilities Act (ADA)-compliant bathroom space, cooking and food service space, and activity and office space must all be available and approved by local and state authorities, making new openings capital intensive. Once a decision is made to open a location and the approved renovations are complete, some of the ongoing challenges for operators is the nationwide caregiver shortage. Direct care staffing in LTC, as well as professional staff (business operations, nonprofit management, nursing, social work, therapeutic recreation, etc.) can be a challenge in any arena but is often extremely difficult in a rural setting, because of the limited availability of trained and willing personnel in close proximity. The weather patterns are another issue in many areas of the U.S. Many rural locations in the Northeast and Northern U.S. are not able to remain open during colder months because of impassable roads and conditions that are not conducive for older adults, frail adults, or younger individuals with disabilities or mobility restrictions to safely leave their homes. This causes ADS centers to operate in a seasonal manner, which is challenging to long-term viability. Compounding the lack of locations, many older adults and individuals with disabilities do not have reliable or cost-effective access to transportation services, preventing participation in ADS centers altogether. Finally, there are significant social pressures and stigmas in the ADS arena. Not only do many participants not want to "go to day care" or feel that they "don't need help," there is also the stigma associated with the caregiver's accepting the need for and accepting the time for a break in the caregiving responsibilities. Taken together, the challenges of ADS use, especially in rural areas, are many, but many creative solutions can already be found.

Over the past decade, the LTC industry has expanded and continues to change based on the needs of the baby boomer generation. ADS has continued to innovate with this expansion as well. What began as general social support services has expanded into a multilevel continuum inclusive of services for individuals of all acuity levels. Along with the expansion of the care continuum, the marketing and terminology have changed and continue to change. The primary area of expansion has been the medical model ADHC services discussed earlier. Two additional models that have shown value in rural areas in addition to helping to expand the continuum of ADS are respite and early memory care (EMC) programs. Some states have identified programs, generally associated with religious organizations, that offer services for individuals in a central location for a limited number of hours and days, thus allowing regular respite for caregivers, and licensure exemptions (e.g., Tennessee). The Brookdale Foundation Group provides modest grants as startup funding for group respite programs. Not only have respite programs been shown to be beneficial to caregivers (Zarit, Kim, Femiaa, Almeida, & Klein, 2014), many have also seen modest success in rural areas. The rural success can be partially attributed to the low overhead when partnering with religious institutions, as well as reduced staffing needs due to the dearth of volunteerism in local communities. The issue of stigma remains, and many programs have started framing respite as a positive day out with friends for participants, instead of merely respite for a caregiver. Long-term sustainability in these programs remains in question but has also led to the advent of EMC and similar other programs as a next step. EMC programs funded by the Brookdale Foundation Group have shown success recently and can generally be viewed as a next step in the ADS care continuum. These programs serve individuals with mild cognitive impairments and early stages of dementia and utilize evidence-based programs to stimulate memory and cognitive exercises, while still providing respite for caregivers. These programs have the potential to supplement group respite and ADS in rural communities.

Further expanding on the continuum of ADS services, as well as reducing the stigma of terminology, many organizations that began in urban areas have expanded their programs into multilocation, multilevel programs to include ADS and ADHC. Some companies have expanded through franchise opportunities into urban, suburban, micropolitan, and rural areas, thereby meeting the needs of the individual communities. Many organizations in the south (specifically Tennessee and Kentucky) have found success in expanding services by opening satellite locations in suburban and micropolitan areas surrounding an urban core. The concept of satellites, or hub and spoke models of ADS is not new and has been successful in several states and opens the door to further expansion in the coming years. Another innovative concept in rural access to ADS is mobile adult day care. Although the terminology suggests a mobile facility, it refers to multiple centers to be operated in rural communities and the staff and operation of which are mobile. These programs have been shown to be successful in Georgia and may be a model for expansion in other states across the U.S. but would require legislative action in most areas.

Assuming many of the previously mentioned solutions were implemented across rural America, the limiting factor of available, accessible, and affordable transportation still exists. Most urban cores have accessible paratransit systems, some even free for older or disabled individuals (Pittsburgh); however, micropolitan and rural areas have severely limited publicly funded transit programs. There are many federal resources available for rural areas and local municipalities to create or expand on existing transit infrastructure through the National Aging and Disability Transportation Center and the National Rural Transit Assistance Program. There are additional resources and funding available for rural transportation initiatives through Grantmakers in Aging. Some organizations have found success in creating, maintaining, and managing temporary group respite "meeting locations" where multiple individuals from rural areas can meet at a safe access point and an ADS provider can transport all participants at a predetermined time to the center and return them at a drop-off time. This concept only works in some areas because of licensure and regulations and is only viable with paid support or regular volunteerism and safe weather conditions. Other communities have found moderate success in recent volunteer transportation initiatives. In Tennessee, the Senior Volunteer Transportation Network is a recent program consisting of older adults providing volunteer hours to transport other older adults within a given area. The program started in multiple sites in 2018 and currently serves more than 20, mostly rural counties, with plans to open 10 more each year for the next two years. Public funds and grants help to sustain and expand such programs, which rely heavily on volunteer hours as well. Ride-sharing organizations have begun to feel the market pressures to offer discounted rates to older adults, and industry analysts believe these organizations will soon expand their ability to offer quality and reduced cost transportation services to older and disabled adults throughout the networks.

Conclusions and the Future of ADS

The ADS industry has seen a prolific expansion over the last two decades. Participants, caregivers, professionals, and many others readily agree that this expansion will continue well into the next two decades. Many challenges remain across the ADS continuum, most notably, access to care and network adequacy, and others, such as the digital divide in rural settings, social networks in smaller communities, lack of health-care access, and increased chronic ailments in rural America. Many of the trends and benefits of ADS focus on the cost and social determinants of health of participants and caregivers. Additional research is ongoing and shows the benefits of ADS to include significant reduction of high cost health-care utilization and the value of standardized measurement of outcomes in ADS (Anderson K.A., Geboy L., Jarrott S, et al., 2018), which will allow for a standard language to be used when discussing these benefits. This will allow larger health systems to engage providers in all settings and help promote the expansion of ADS across all communities, especially in rural settings where network adequacy is not yet near attainment. Additionally, recent changes in MA plans will allow health maintenance organizations (HMOs) to cover ADS (and transportation) in the coming years as a supplemental health benefit, further expanding funding and access to ADS in rural areas. In the face of numerous challenges, innovations in ADS and alignment with like-minded organizations and strategic partners continue to allow the growth and use of ADS in urban, suburban, and especially rural areas.

Resources for Further Reading

The Brookdale Foundation Group. Retrieved from www.brookdalefoundation.net/Respite/respiteprogram.html

California Association for Adult Day Services. Retrieved from http://caads.org

Dementia Friendly Communities. Retrieved from www.dfamerica.org/

Easter Seals and the National Alliance for Caregiving—Caregiving in Rural America. Retrieved from http://es.easterseals.com/site/PageServer?pagename=ntl_rural_caregiving

The Gathering. Retrieved from www.lyngblomsten.org/community-services/gathering/

Grantmakers in Aging. Retrieved from www.giaging.org/initiatives/rural-aging/

Indiana Association of Adult Day Service. Retrieved from www.iaads.net

Kentucky Association of Adult Day Centers. Retrieved from http://kaadonline.org

Mobile Adult Day Care. Retrieved from https://aging.georgia.gov/caregiver-programs and, http://dhs.georgia.gov/sites/aging.georgia.gov/files/imported/DHR-DAS/DHR-DAS_Publications/Mobile%20Day%20Care%20Fact%20Sheet%202010.pdf

National Aging and Disability Transportation Center. Retrieved from www.nadtc.org

National Association of Adult Day Services. Retrieved from http://nadsa.org

National Rural Transit Assistance Program. Retrieved from www.nationalrtap.org

Pew Research—Digital Divide. Retrieved from www.pewresearch.org/topics/digital-divide/

Pittsburgh PA, Older Persons Transportation Plan. Retrieved from www.alleghenycounty.us/Human-Services/Programs-Services/Basic-Needs/Transportation/Older-Persons-Transportation-Program.aspx

Senior Volunteer Transportation Network. Retrieved from www.tn.gov/aging/our-programs/transportation-assistance.html

Tennessee Association of Adult Day Services. Retrieved from www.taads.net

References

Anderson, K. A., Geboy, L., Jarrott, S., Missaelides, L., Ogletree, A. M., . . . Zarit, S. H. (2018). Developing a set of uniform outcome measures for adult day services. *Journal of Applied Gerontology*. Published ahead of Print. doi:10.1177/0733464818782130

Genworth Financial (Genworth). (2018). *Cost of care survey*. Retrieved April 20, 2019, from www.genworth.com/aging-and-you/finances/cost-of-care.html

Harris-Kojetin, L., Sengupta, M., Park-Lee, E., Valverde, R., Caffrey, C., Rome, V., & Lendon, J. (2019). *Long-term care providers and services users in the United States: 2015–2016.* Retrieved from www.cdc.gov/nchs/data/series/sr_03/sr03_43-508.pdf

MetLife Mature Market Institute (MetLife). (2010). *The MetLife national study of adult day services.* Retrieved from www.metlife.com/assets/cao/mmi/publications/studies/2010/mmi-adult-day-services.pdf

National Adult Day Services Association (NADSA). (2018). *About adult day services.* Retrieved from www.nadsa.org/learn-more/about-adult-day-services/

O'Keefe, J., O'Keefe, C., & Shrestha, M. (2014). *Regulatory review of adult day services: Final report, 2014 edition.* Retrieved from https://aspe.hhs.gov/basic-report/regulatory-review-adult-day-services-final-report-2014-edition#CA

Zarit, S. H., Kim, K., Femiaa, E. E., Almeida, D. M., & Klein, L. C. (2014). The effects of adult day services on family caregivers' daily stress, affect, and health: Outcomes from the Daily Stress and Health (DaSH) study. *Gerontologist, 54*(4), 570–579. doi:10.1093/geront/gnt045

2
ADVOCACY AND ACTIVISM

Jessica L. Maurer

We're all called upon at different times in our lives to be advocates and activists, but we don't often think of ourselves in this way, nor do we always know how to be effective in these roles in different settings. The truth is, however, that we all have the skills needed to be effective advocates, and our advocacy is critical if we're going to ensure we can all live healthy, engaged, and secure lives as we age in our homes in rural communities.

As we age, the systems that have always worked for us in the past may not work for us as our bodies, abilities, and finances change. For instance, in rural communities, we all rely on single passenger vehicles to get to all the services and activities we need. Since there are few and too often no public transportation options, when we can no longer drive, we either become reliant on others to get around or we have to leave our homes. The same is true if our homes no longer work for us or if we cannot get the in-home care we need where we live.

To ensure we can age in our homes in the rural communities we love, becoming an advocate for change may well be necessary. This may include learning how to ask municipal, state, and federal decision-makers to change laws and ordinances and make new investments in the infrastructure that supports healthy aging. To be effective in this, one needs to know how decisions are made and how to best influence those decisions. Recommendations for engaging in effective advocacy in rural towns and communities follow.

Be Informed

Whether you're asking the town council to change a zoning ordinance or advocating for the passage of a bill before the legislature, fully understanding the scope of the problem and the potential solutions is critical for effectively advocating for change. Therefore, the first rule of effective advocacy is to be inquisitive. What's the history of the current law or ordinance? What is the proof that it needs to be changed? How have other communities or states addressed the issue in a different way? Is it working? Every situation will be different, but it helps to go into any conversation or hearing with the facts that support your cause.

Find the credible sources of information on your issue from organizations that publish information in your state. Can't find the data you're looking for? Reach out to the organization in your state most likely to have the information you need and ask someone to help. In Maine, for example, there are several credible sources for information on a multitude of issues impacting the health and well-being of older Mainers. These include the Maine Council on Aging, AARP Maine, the Maine Center for Economic Policy, Maine Affordable Housing Coalition, and Maine Equal Justice Partners, just to name a few. These each have excellent resources on their websites that can help you become better informed about various issues. You might also look for regional sources of information. For instance, the Tri-State Learning Collaborative on Aging (serving Vermont, Maine, and New Hampshire) is an important place to go to learn about issues impacting the region. These kinds of organizations can help you identify information about rural-specific problems in your state or community and potential solutions.

Know the Process

Our legislative processes are far from intuitive, and understanding them will help you know when and how best to communicate your message. There are a few ways to do this. You can talk to your town manager or a selectperson about the process for changing an ordinance or appropriating funding for an initiative. You can go online and read about the state and federal legislative processes. You can also ask your representative or senator how the state process works, or ask a congressional staffer how to engage the federal process. In the course of conversations with elected officials, you can ask them to help you. Most state legislators, but not all, will put in a bill for a constituent, even if they don't support the bill, just to make sure the idea gets consideration. Don't just ask about the formal process, but also ask when and how you can participate in it.

Communicate Effectively

It turns out, words really do matter. What we say and how we say it does have an impact on the people who hear our words. Thankfully, some national organizations have worked with the FrameWorks Institute to help us all understand how to effectively communicate about issues related to aging, older people, and our changing demographics. Their recommendations help people hear what you have to say without imposing their own bias or misunderstandings about aging and older people. Their recommendations are based on empirical research they conducted with thousands of Americans across the country, and they've been able to demonstrate that reframing reduces age-related bias (Busso, Volmert, & Kendall-Taylor, 2019). Here's what they recommend:

- *Use neutral words and avoid stereotypes* (Sweetland, Volmert, & O'Neil, 2017). Generally, people associate the terms "elder," "elderly," and "senior" with the oldest, least competent people among us. Conversely, they associate the terms "older people" and "older adults" with younger, more competent people. Using the neutral term "older people" helps people see themselves in the solution you're proposing. Also, too many people think aging is about living large in retirement, or decline, disability, and death, when the truth is somewhere in the middle and includes both extremes. To avoid stereotypes, avoid terms like "vulnerable" and "frail."
- *Be inclusive* (Sweetland et al., 2017). We are all aging. Messaging should emphasize that *we* need to pass this law to ensure *we can all* age well at home, something we all want to do. This encourages people to appreciate that they're a part of what's happening and that this law is for everyone; it helps avoid triggering the "us v. them" kind of thinking that too often happens.

- *Avoid crisis metaphors and terms that invoke impending catastrophe* (Sweetland et al., 2017). The favorite crisis metaphor is "the silver tsunami," which invokes a wave that cannot be stopped and will end in disaster. This kind of language makes people feel overwhelmed, as if there is nothing they can do to avoid the inevitable. Instead, even when dealing with a problem that has reached crisis proportions, the recommendation is to start by reminding the audience that human ingenuity has solved serious problems in the past and it helps to use an example. Then, describe the problem in real terms, avoiding all but the most important statistics. Finally, offer a credible solution.
- *Solutions matter* (Sweetland et al., 2017). Offer concrete, credible, and conceivable solutions that are collective. It's never enough to say, "We have to do something." Rather, we need to say, "The Town of Cumberland is offering property tax assistance that helps older people remain in their community. Our community should adopt the same solution because too many of our older residents cannot afford to meet their basic needs, repair their homes, and pay their property taxes."

Beyond the words we choose and the way we frame them, how we communicate these words also matters. There are a few basic ways we can advocate for change with decision-makers. We can testify at a town meeting or legislative hearing. We can write letters, send emails, and make calls. We can meet in person with our elected officials and ask them to act in a certain way. We can write letters to the editor and talk to our friends. These are all effective ways to communicate and there are a few basic strategies to consider with each:

- When communicating with an elected official in writing, show respect by using their title, "Honorable Jane Doe" or "Senator Jane Doe." When sending a letter, send it to the legislative office, not their home. When sending an email, never forward a mass-produced email to everyone in the legislature or on a legislative committee. While it's easier to copy and paste, mass emails are often ignored by legislators. Sending one personalized email at a time with a different subject line than others might be sending will get the email read. Always include your address, phone, and email address in written correspondence.
- When making phone calls, connect with legislators during the day at the statehouse through their legislative office or cell phone, or at home in the evening or on a weekend. When calling at home, avoid dinner time, early morning, or late night, and ask upfront if this is a convenient time for them to talk.
- When meeting in person, schedule the meeting. Usually, the best place to meet is in their local district, but you can also ask for a meeting at the statehouse or in a congressional office, particularly if you're traveling to the state capital or Washington, D.C. Elected officials often have tight schedules and planning to catch them in the halls as they rush from one meeting to the next is not an effective way to have a conversation.
- Regardless of how you have the discussion, keep in mind the following guidelines. Keep the message short and persuasive. In some legislative hearings, you'll only have a few minutes for public testimony; you only get 300 words in a letter to the editor. You have to be able to tell your story in a soundbite. Give a bill number or other specific information when it's known. Include local arguments and facts when possible. Use data, but only in connection with stories that help to make the data real. Tell the official exactly what you want them to do and ask for a commitment and a formal response. If you are one of their constituents, make sure they know it.
- Finally, always follow through if they ask for additional information.

Don't Go It Alone

Coalition building is critical to effective advocacy and activism. Whether you're starting a new volunteer initiative in your community to address an unmet need of older residents, or trying to get a bill passed at the legislature, you'll be more effective if you build a diverse group of people who believe in what you're trying to do. To build an effective coalition, the first question is, what is the problem I'm trying to solve? The next question is, who else cares about this problem? We might start with the "usual suspects," but in brainstorming with our allies, we may realize there are more unusual partners who may want to join us in our work. Issue-based coalitions need not reach consensus on all issues, just on the issue at hand. For instance, in thinking about a home modification tax credit, you might start thinking about older people who need to modify their homes and their caregivers. But you can easily expand your reach and include people with MS, veterans, and people with disabilities. Next, you might well want to consider reaching out to builders, realtors, and even health-care providers. Expanding the coalition increases your chances for success.

Grassroots support is just as important as the support of organizational stakeholders, and the way to garner grassroots support for an initiative or proposal is through conversation. Conversation is particularly powerful when addressing issues that impact older people. Many older people want to talk about the challenges we're experiencing. Even if we are uncomfortable talking about ourselves, we are often more readily willing to talk about how aging is impacting our friends, relatives, and neighbors. More importantly, involving older people in thinking about and designing solutions to community challenges make those proposed solutions all the more credible and potentially easier to enact at the local level.

For instance, small towns in rural communities often have an affinity for single-family zoning and are often loath to allow development of multifamily homes. But allowing more flexibility in modifying single-family homes to include a second unit is a very real solution for some older people who need a live-in caregiver, who need the extra income they could get from a rental unit, or who could build a second, universally designed home on their property to meet their changing physical needs. Building support for changes to local accessory dwelling unit ordinances can happen simply through community conversation about the housing needs of older adults. This can occur at a town meeting, through a series of discussion groups, through focus groups, or even one-on-one conversations. This can happen formally, through a comprehensive planning process, or informally by a group of people who want to host a conversation. Including elected officials is key because they need to hear what people are saying they need. No matter how it happens, once you've started conversations in your community about an issue, you'll find grassroots support growing for solutions that work, even controversial ones such as accessory dwelling units.

Be the Change You Want to See

Change is hard for all of us and our inclination is to keep doing things the way we've always done them. Unfortunately, far too many older adults in rural communities find out the hard way that the supports and services they need to keep them living well at home aren't available. We can keep doing the same thing while expecting different results, or we can take action to make sure what we need is available in our communities as we age. You don't have to start big; you just have to start somewhere. No act of advocacy or activism is too small. Here are a few suggestions for getting started:

- *Start with friends, family, and neighbors.* Find out what resources are available to help older people in your rural community and become a resource for others who need help.
- *Become active in your community.* Is there an "aging-in-place" or "age friendly community" initiative in your town? If there is, join them. If not, find out what towns around you are

doing to support healthy aging and talk to your town manager and friends about starting a local initiative. There are simple tools on the Tri-State Learning Collaborative on Aging's website that can help you get started. Is your town engaged in comprehensive planning? Make sure they include the needs of older rural residents, like transportation solutions and access to broadband in the planning process. Find out how your town shares information about resources available to older people and identify ways they can increase access to information and resources.

- *Stay informed and connected.* Knowing more and sharing with others, even just through informal conversations, will help build support for the kinds of reforms and investments needed, particularly in rural communities. Join a mailing list hosted by a statewide body advocating for older adults in your state or the state chapter of AARP to learn about advocacy opportunities in the statehouse. Correspond directly with your elected officials about issues that matter to you and your community. Whether it's one email or a call to a legislator or a well-timed conversation with a local selectperson, your advocacy matters.

We don't need a million person march on Washington, D.C., to change the systems that support healthy aging in rural communities. We need to start locally, with our friends and community leaders. We need to be inquisitive and have conversations. Understanding what resources and services are and are not available is essential. Strengthening the services and supports available to your rural community by learning from and replicating what other rural communities are doing is a best practice. Where there are systemic problems or investments needed by the government, investigating what state and national advocacy groups recommend and supporting their efforts is strategic. In short, everyone needs to take action to ensure we can age in our homes in our rural communities long into the future.

References

Busso, D., Volmert, A., & Kendall-Taylor, N. (2019). Reframing aging: Effect of a short-term framing intervention on implicit measures of age bias. *The Journals of Gerontology: Series B*, *74*(4), 559–564.

Sweetland, J., Volmert, A., & O'Neil, M. (2017). *Finding the frame: A frameworks research report.* Retrieved from http://frameworksinstitute.org/assets/files/aging_elder_abuse/aging_research_report_final_2017.pdf

3
AGE-FRIENDLY COMMUNITIES

Patricia A. Huffman-Oh

Introduction

One of the greatest public health success stories of our century is the growing number of people living into their 90s and beyond. With longer lives comes a desire for something more than just added years. People want to age in their own homes and remain engaged in their communities during those bonus years, even when the social and physical environment of the community is not ideal (Black, Dobbs, & Young, 2015).

Rural areas are aging more rapidly than cities. The median age of rural residents is 43, compared with 36 for urban dwellers (Day, Hays, & Smith, 2016). The challenges of rural aging include limited housing and transportation options, the lack of specialty healthcare, little or no high-speed internet, and social isolation (Winterton et al., 2016; Bond, Brown, & Wood, 2017). However, there are strengths. It can, for example, be easier to identify partners and form coalitions for change (Menec & Brown, 2018). The aging of the population is an opportunity for rural communities to think differently about community and economic development, to plan so that children, young families, and people in their 90s and beyond have the opportunity to live safe, healthy, and rewarding lives (Beard et al., 2016).

Age-Friendly Communities

Age-friendly initiatives target changes in policies, infrastructure, and services in the economic, physical, social and service environments that make it easier for older people of all backgrounds, abilities, and lifestyles to enjoy active, healthy, engaged aging (WHO, 2018). Communities with age-friendly features—such as safe, walkable streets; friendly and supportive neighborhoods; free recreational activities; and accessible businesses and public spaces—make it easier for older people to enjoy the best possible health and well-being. The benefits aren't only for older people; young families also enjoy walking, shopping at local businesses, and time with friends at an accessible park with benches and playground equipment for all ages. Age-friendly communities are places where people of all ages, abilities, race, ethnicities, and economic levels have what they need to thrive.

AARP Network of Age-Friendly States and Communities (AARP NAFSC)

In 2006, the World Health Organization (WHO) asked people in 23 countries what older residents needed to thrive in their communities (WHO, 2018). The answers were:

1. Safe, affordable, and appropriate transportation;
2. Housing for all stages of life;
3. Community support and health services;
4. Accessible public spaces and buildings;
5. Easy-to-find information about programs, services, and activities and reliable technology to communicate with friends and relatives;
6. Social participation;
7. Civic engagement and paid employment; and
8. Respect and social inclusion.

To promote municipal planning in these eight domains of livability, WHO launched the Global Network for Age-Friendly Cities and Communities (WHO-GNAFCC) in 2010 (WHO, 2018). Two years later, in 2012, AARP became an organizational affiliate of the WHO-GNAFCC to promote age-friendly municipal planning in the U.S. and provide technical support for communities that join. Although the network was not created specifically for rural communities, AARP has developed rural-specific resources and facilitates peer learning among rural communities nationwide (AARP, 2019a). For example, in June 2019, AARP hosted a national workshop about rural livability and, based on the proceedings, published a report that highlights innovative solutions to the challenges of rural aging (Stanton & Oh, 2020).

Characteristics of Rural Communities Enrolled in the AARP NAFSC

On December 31, 2019, 429 municipalities, six states, and one territory were members of the AARP NAFSC (AARP, 2019b). Although most municipalities were urban, 155 (43%) of the 364 member cities and towns had a population of less than 20,000 people and 8 (12%) of the 65 member counties were 50% or more rural in the 2010 census. Rural members were found in 28 states from California to Florida. The first rural community, Newport, Vermont, joined in 2013. Since then, the number of rural communities has steadily increased (see Figure 3.1)

Demographic characteristics of communities have been associated with municipal decision-making about age-friendly planning (Menec et al., 2015; Spina & Menec, 2015). On December 31, 2019, the median population size of rural cities and towns in the AARP NAFSC was 5,327, with a range of 41 in Hart's Location, New Hampshire, to 19,843 in Hudson, Massachusetts (see Figure 3.2). Rural municipalities with a higher median income than the state median were more likely to join the network; 53% of rural communities had a median income higher than the state median (see Figure 3.3). Although a majority of rural AARP NAFSC members had a higher percentage of residents 65+ than their state, 28% had a lower percentage of older residents (see Figure 3.4). Although demographics may play a role, municipalities are also influenced by community capacity (Menec & Brown, 2018).

Age-friendly initiatives are more likely to develop when older volunteers are seen as productive, active, and engaged members of the community; the municipality is highly committed, and regional partners are able to provide technical support, encouragement, and funding for

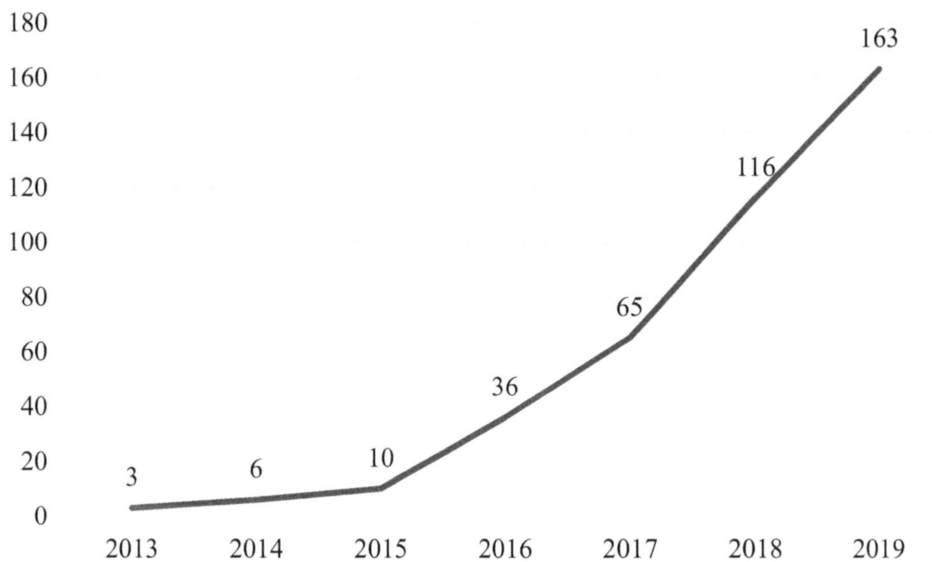

Figure 3.1 Growth in the Number of Rural Municipalities (Cities, Towns, and Counties) That Have Joined the AARP NAFSC, 2013–December 31, 2019 (n=155 cities/towns and 8 counties)

Source: AARP Livable Communities. 2019, July 2. *AARP Network of Age-Friendly States and Communities: The member list.* Retrieved from www.aarp.org/livable-communities/network-age-friendly-communities/info-2014/member-list.html

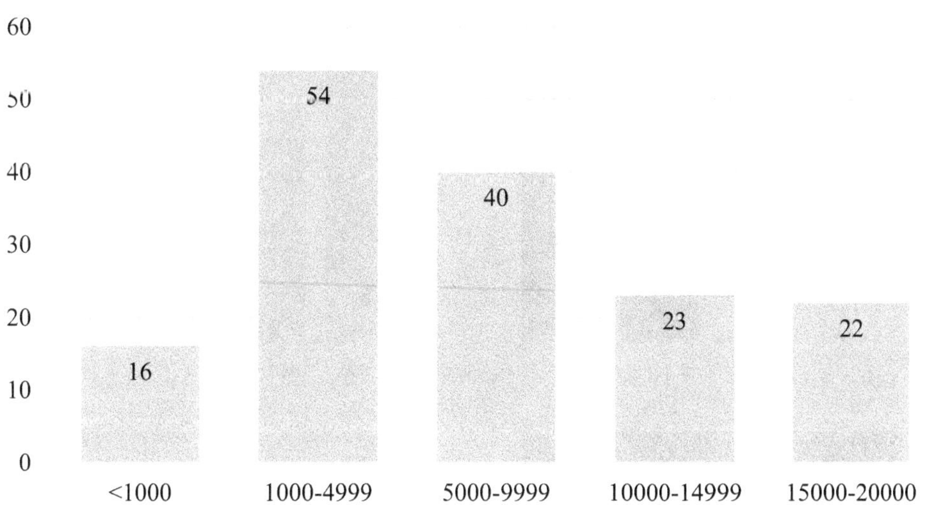

Figure 3.2 Population Size of Rural Towns and Cities Enrolled in the AARP Network of Age-Friendly States and Communities (n=155 rural cities/towns)

Note: Population size taken from ACS, 2013–2017, 5-year estimates, Table S0101

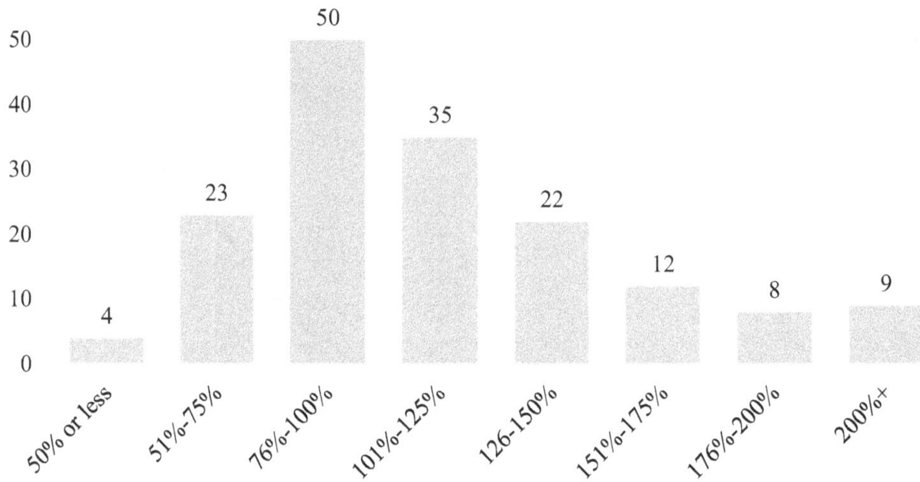

Figure 3.3 Median Income of AARP NAFSC Member Rural Town, Cities, and Counties as Percentage of State Median Income (n=155 cities/towns and 8 counties)

Note: Median household income taken from 2013–2017 American Community Survey, 5-year estimates. Table DP-03, Household Income in the Past 12 Months

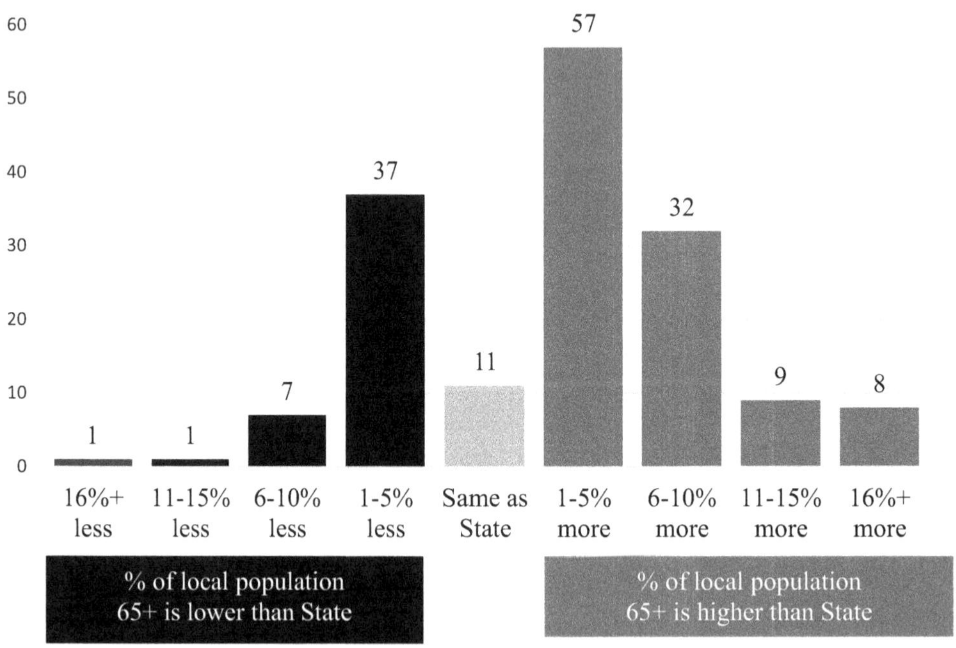

Figure 3.4 Difference Between Percentage of the Population 65+ in AARP NAFSC Member Rural Municipalities and for the Overall State (n=155 cities/towns and 8 counties)

Note: Percentage of the population 65+ taken from 2013–2017 American Community Survey, 5-year estimates. Table S0101, Age and Sex

start-up and implementation (Neville, Napier, Adams, Wham, & Jackson, 2016). Inclusion of older residents who are well respected in the community is important to build trust and for the work to be seen as responsive to community needs and preferences for change (Wiersma & Koster, 2013). Municipal involvement is critical for implementation of changes and for long-term sustainability of the initiative (Winterton, Warburton, Clune, & Martin, 2014). Regional and local partners play a critical role, taking the lead on projects that fit with their organizational mission and using resources at their disposal to move the age-friendly work forward (Russell, Skinner, & Fowler, 2019). Rural communities are most likely to embrace age-friendly community and economic development when all older residents, the municipality, and partner organizations have a history of successfully working together.

Although the majority of communities that join the AARP NAFSC join as individual members, small towns and villages may join forces with nearby municipalities that have, historically, shared resources. For example, the Mount Washington Valley Regional Age-Friendly Initiative includes 11 communities. At the end of 2019, 31% (n=51) of rural AARP NAFSC members were part of a regional approach. Working together allows small towns to develop community-specific initiatives (for example, advocating for an accessory dwelling unit policy or establishing a weekly social opportunity) while collaborating with other communities on regional issues such as transportation or housing.

Motivation to Join the AARP NAFSC

Municipalities that join the AARP NAFSC submit an action plan within two–three years of joining the network that is publicly available on the AARP NAFSC member list web pages (AARP, 2019b). A review of 39 action plans covering 57 rural communities as of December 31, 2019, showed that 86% joined to make their community an easier place to live for older residents, 73% include a reference to increasing accessibility, 64% have a goal of increasing economic security, and 48% want to increase social engagement. By making age-friendly changes, municipalities provide what longtime residents need to thrive in their community and are able to entice recent retirees and tourists looking for a community where they are welcome (Serow, 2003; Wiersma & Koster, 2013).

While providing what older residents need is an obvious motivation for communities, it is not the only reason municipalities join the AARP NAFSC. Nearly all of the age-friendly action plans (95%) stated that the age-friendly initiative wanted to make the community a better place to live for all ages. Age-friendly communities promote engagement. Some rural age-friendly initiatives, such as the ones in Emeryville, California; Newport, Vermont; and Old Orchard Beach, Maine, developed specifically to increase community engagement by younger people.

Age-Friendly Initiatives in Rural Communities

Joining the AARP NAFSC does not make a community age-friendly; the age-friendly team must cultivate community engagement, develop collaborations with diverse stakeholders, mobilize resources, and document achievements. Community is at the center of the action plans reviewed; all of the plans stressed the importance of developing strong multi-sector collaborations of stakeholders. For example, the mission of the Mount Washington Age-Friendly initiative is to "combine the talents and resources from all of our 11 towns to further develop the Mount Washington Valley as a place for people of all ages and abilities to thrive." In rural communities, where resources may be scarce, it is particularly important for the age-friendly team to partner with municipal governments and existing organizations to mobilize resources and expand capacity (Spina & Menec, 2013). The AARP NAFSC program model emphasizes the importance of tracking progress and celebrating achievements for accountability and to build trust in the community, with funders, and with other partners. All but one of the action plans (n=38) listed output metrics the team planned to collect to show progress on action steps and explained how the team would know that a goal was achieved.

Municipalities use a holistic approach to plan in the eight domains of livability. Increasing opportunities for social participation, for example, may include addressing needs in transportation and making outdoor spaces and buildings accessible. Given the breadth of these initiatives, tight fiscal budgets, and limited municipal staff in many rural areas, success often depends on volunteers who donate their knowledge, skills, and life experience. What follows are a few examples of age-friendly rural work in each of the eight domains of livability.

Housing

Many rural communities lack accessible housing options and affordable home maintenance services (Pendall, Goodman, Zhu, & Gold, 2016). To increase housing options, the Mount Washington Valley, New Hampshire age-friendly team developed a brochure about accessory dwelling units and created a home sharing program that matches older people who are interested in sharing their home with others. Shorewood Connects Neighbors, the age-friendly team in Shorewood, Wisconsin, partnered with a local vocational high school to develop small home kits that are affordable and well-insulated and have age-friendly features. Age-Friendly Readfield, Maine, partnered with local service organizations to create a volunteer program that helps older people with home maintenance and seasonal chores.

Transportation

The lack of transportation options in rural areas is well documented (Dize, 2019; Dobbs & Strain, 2008). In Bucksport, Maine, the age- and ability-friendly team increased access to public transportation by providing $1 vouchers for taxi rides to the bus. In Sausalito, California, a volunteer driver program provides up to four one-way rides/day within the community. In Sullivan, Maine, the age-friendly team partnered with a regional volunteer program to train local volunteers to give rides to residents for medical appointments, socialization, and errands. Although the needs are similar, solutions reflect community capacity and available resources.

Walkability is a concern in rural communities, much as it is in urban areas (Meyer et al., 2016). Westwood, New Jersey, installed pedestrian flags at dangerous crossings and promoted their use. Goshen, Massachusetts, added wayfaring signs and developed a walking map. In nearby Williamsburg, the age-friendly team conducted a pedestrian safety training for older residents. The West Chester, Pennsylvania, team conducted a walk audit and successfully advocated for sidewalk improvements and traffic calming measures.

Community Support and Health Services

Access to health care, especially specialty medicine, is challenging in rural areas (Rechel et al., 2016). Age-friendly initiatives have reduced the transportation barrier and created activities that encourage residents to participate in wellness opportunities and access health care. A volunteer transportation program in Surry, Maine, provides rides to medical appointments. In Grayson County, Virginia, the team advocated to expand Recreation Department offerings to include adult programs and outdoor recreation. Age-Friendly Bowdoinham, Maine, partnered with a dental school in a neighboring county to provide care for residents who hadn't seen a dentist in decades.

Age-friendly rural initiatives are using innovative ideas to enhance access to community support services. The age-friendly initiative in Hyattsville, Maryland, sponsors an annual self-care workshop for care partners. In Raymond and Saco, Maine, the age-friendly initiatives developed elevated-bed intergenerational gardens to promote social engagement and enhance food security. In Skowhegan, Maine, the team uses interactive improvisational theater to create community conversations about topics of concern to residents. The emphasis in Charles City, Iowa, and Clinton County, Ohio, was on economic development. Both developed age-friendly business programs to promote tourism and to ensure that residents of all abilities can remain engaged in the local economy.

Outdoor Spaces and Buildings

The accessibility of outdoor spaces and buildings typically open to the public affects the independence and quality of life of residents who have a temporary or long-term mobility limitation (Peace, 2013). Some rural age-friendly communities, such as Jackson Hole, Wyoming, have increased the number of benches in downtown areas. Others have increased the number of handicapped parking spaces, worked with local businesses to make them more accessible, advocated for accessibility improvements to municipal buildings, and partnered with funders to develop parks and trails that include ADA features.

Communication and Information

Age-friendly rural communities have developed resource guides, created Facebook pages to highlight local events, and developed social event phone trees to help residents stay connected. One key to increasing access to information about resources and activities is learning how older residents prefer to communicate (Yuan, Hussain, Hales, & Cotten, 2016). By using several different communication methods, age-friendly communities ensure that all residents can stay connected.

A challenge in many rural communities is access to broadband and communication technology. The Macon County, Georgia, age-friendly team is working to increase the number of older adults with internet access. A number of rural communities have partnered with their local libraries or lifelong learning programs to offer training in using technology. The increase in connectivity and comfort with internet technology makes it easier for older people to use the internet to stay connected and to access telehealth and other resources.

Civic Participation and Employment

Older people do not stop contributing to their communities when they turn 65 or 85 or 105. An age-friendly community provides opportunities for residents who want to or need to work past traditional retirement age and encourages people of all ages to volunteer and participate in the political process. The age-friendly team in Kennebunk, Maine, partnered with the Chamber of Commerce to develop a job fair for people 50 and over. In Fairfax, California, and Newport, Vermont, they launched educational campaigns to show employers the value of hiring and retaining older workers. In North Yarmouth, Maine, the goal was to increase civic engagement by younger people so the age-friendly team provided child care during the annual town meeting.

Social Participation

Rural dwellers have a higher risk for social isolation than their urban peers (Kaye, 2017). Age-friendly initiatives frequently focus their work on encouraging social participation (Oh, 2019). Communities ensure that events are accessible, provide transportation, and/or explore new ways to communicate about events and activities to increase access. In places where a lack of social opportunities is identified in the age-friendly needs assessment, the team works to create the types of opportunities people want. In Norcross, Georgia, the age-friendly initiative sponsored a social event for people 50+ that included dancing, food, and music. Some age-friendly initiatives try to build community connections through social opportunities for residents of all ages. In Shorewood, Wisconsin, the age-friendly team developed neighborhood events to promote neighbor-to-neighbor connections. The Community Friendly Connection committee in Old Orchard Beach, Maine, worked with partners to revitalize a basketball court and create a pop-up bakery with welcoming outdoor seating to allow residents to see that the block could be a safe, welcoming place to gather.

Respect and Social Inclusion

Communities that join the AARP NAFSC have committed to include an age-friendly lens in community and economic development, which implies that municipal officials want older residents to remain active and engaged in all aspects of community life. In North Yarmouth, Maine, a member of the age-friendly team greets each new resident with a welcome package that includes information about how to get involved in the community. In Carbondale, Colorado, the *Our Town, One Table* community picnic celebrates the diversity in the community. The age-friendly team developed a table at the event to celebrate the inclusion of older people in community life. When older residents are viewed as contributors to our communities, they have the opportunity to be as active and engaged as they want to be and everyone in the community wins through their contributions to community life.

Conclusion

Rural age-friendly initiatives are as different as each community but all of these examples make life easier and more enjoyable for residents of all ages and promote community and economic development. Given the breadth of the initiatives, tight fiscal budgets, and lack of municipal staffing, age-friendly rural communities rely on older volunteers who participate in the planning efforts and are actively engaged in implementation. Far from being a drain on their communities, older residents are building on community strengths to develop vital, inclusive communities that are good places to grow up and to grow old.

Suggestions for Further Reading

While many of the cited articles provide valuable background to understanding rural age-friendly community development, a few provide an excellent overview and critique:

Menec, V., & Brown, C. (2018). Facilitators and barriers to becoming age-friendly: A review. *Journal of Aging & Social Policy*, 1–23. doi:10.1080/08959420.2018.1528116

Neville, S., Napier, S., Adams, J., Wham, C., & Jackson, D. (2016). An integrative review of the factors related to building age-friendly rural communities. *Journal of Clinical Nursing*, *25*(17–18), 2402–2412. doi:10.1111/jocn.13299

For those interested in the history of the WHO-GNAFCC, the best overview is:

WHO, 2018. *The Global Network for Age-friendly Cities and Communities: Looking back over the last decade, looking forward to the next.* Retrieved from https://apps.who.int/iris/bitstream/handle/10665/278979/WHO-FWC-ALC-18.4-eng.pdf;jsessionid=6A638C81565882AD611262B00F6E4B32?sequence=1

Two edited volumes also provide a good introduction to rural age-friendly development:

Hennessy, C. H., Means, R., & Burholt, V. (2014). *Countryside connections: Older people, community, and place in rural Britain.* Bristol: Policy Press.

Stafford, P. B. (2019). *The global age-friendly community movement: A critical appraisal* (Part IV, Rural Aging). New York: Berghahn Press.

References

AARP. (2019a). *AARP livable communities: Rural livability.* Retrieved from www.aarp.org/livable-communities/archives/info-2014/rural-livability.html

AARP. (2019b). *AARP Network of Age-Friendly States and Communities: The member list.* Retrieved from www.aarp.org/livable-communities/network-age-friendly-communities/info-2014/member-list.html

Beard, J. R., Officer, A., De Carvalho, I. A., Sadana, R., Pot, A. M., Michel, J. P., . . . Thiyagarajan, J. A. (2016). The world report on ageing and health: A policy framework for healthy ageing. *The Lancet, 387*(10033), 2145–2154. doi:10.1016/S0140-6736(15)00516-4

Black, K., Dobbs, D., & Young, T. L. (2015). Aging in community: Mobilizing a new paradigm of older adults as a core social resource. *Journal of Applied Gerontology, 34*(2), 219–243. doi:10.1177/0733464812463984

Bond, M., Brown, J. R., & Wood, J. (2017). Adapting to challenge: Examining older adult transportation in rural communities. *Case Studies on Transport Policy, 5*(4), 707–715.

Day, J. C., Hays, D., & Smith, A. (2016). *A glance at the age structure and labor force participation of rural America.* Retrieved from www.census.gov/newsroom/blogs/random-samplings/2016/12/a_glance_at_the_age.html

Dize, V. (2019). Getting around in rural America. *Generations, 43*(2), 33039.

Dobbs, B., & Strain, L. (2008). Staying connected: Issues of mobility of older rural adults. In N. Keating (Ed.), *Rural aging: A good place to grow old?* (pp. 87–95). Bristol: Policy Press.

Kaye, L. W. (2017). Older adults, rural living, and the escalating risk of social isolation. *Public Policy & Aging Report, 27*(4), 139–144. doi:10.1093/ppar/prx029

Menec, V. H., & Brown, C. (2018). Facilitators and barriers to becoming age-friendly: A review. *Journal of Aging & Social Policy*, 1–23. doi:10.1080/08959420.2018.1528116

Menec, V. H., Hutton, L., Newell, N., Nowicki, S., Spina, J., & Veselyuk, D. (2015). How "age-friendly" are rural communities and what community characteristics are related to age-friendliness? The case of rural Manitoba, Canada. *Ageing & Society, 35*(1), 203–223.

Meyer, M. R. U., Moore, J. B., Abildso, C., Edwards, M. B., Gamble, A., & Baskin, M. L. (2016). Rural active living: A call to action. *Journal of Public Health Management and Practice: Journal of Public Health Management and Practice, 22*(5), E11. doi:10.1097/PHH.0000000000000333

Neville, S., Napier, S., Adams, J., Wham, C., & Jackson, D. (2016). An integrative review of the factors related to building age-friendly rural communities. *Journal of Clinical Nursing, 25*(17–18), 2402–2412. doi:10.1111/jocn.13299

Oh, P. H. (2019). Designing age friendly communities as a strategy for enhancing social connectedness. In L. Kaye & C. Singer (Eds.), *Social isolation of older adults: Strategies to bolster health and well-being* (pp. 89–102). New York: Springer.

Peace, S. (2013). Social interactions in public spaces and places: A conceptual overview. In G. Rowles & M. Bernard (Eds.), *Environmental gerontology: Making meaningful places in old age* (pp. 25–49). New York: Springer.

Pendall, R., Goodman, L., Zhu, J., & Gold, A. (2016). *The future of rural housing.* Washington, DC: Urban Institute. Retrieved from www.urban.org/sites/default/files/publication/85101/2000972-the-future-of-rural-housing_6.pdf

Rechel, B., Džakula, A., Duran, A., Fattore, G., Edwards, N., Grignon, M., . . . Ricciardi, W. (2016). Hospitals in rural or remote areas: An exploratory review of policies in 8 high-income countries. *Health Policy, 120*(7), 758–769. doi:10.1016/j.healthpol.2016.05.011

Russell, E., Skinner, M. W., & Fowler, K. (2019). Emergent challenges and opportunities to sustaining age-friendly initiatives: Qualitative findings from a Canadian age-friendly funding program. *Journal of Aging and Social Policy*. doi:10.1080/08959420.2019.1636595

Serow, W. J. (2003). Economic consequences of retiree concentrations: A review of North American studies. *The Gerontologist, 43*(6), 897–903. doi:10.1093/geront/43.6.897

Spina, J., & Menec, V. H. (2013). What community characteristics help or hinder rural communities in becoming age friendly? Perspectives from a Canadian prairie province. *Journal of Applied Gerontology, 34* (4), 444–464. doi:10.1177/0733464813496164

Stanton, M., & Oh, P. (2020). *AARP rural livability workshop report: How and why small towns and remote communities are working to become more livable for older adults and people of all ages* (eBook ed.). Retrieved from www.aarp.org/livable-communities/tool-kits-resources/info-2020/rural-livability-workshop-report.html

WHO. (2018). *The Global Network for Age-friendly Cities and Communities: Looking back over the last decade, looking forward to the next.* Retrieved from https://apps.who.int/iris/bitstream/handle/10665/278979/WHO-FWC-ALC-18.4-eng.pdf;jsessionid=6A638C81565882AD611262B00F6E4B32?sequence=1

Wiersma, E. C., & Koster, R. (2013). Vulnerability, volunteerism, and age-friendly communities: Placing rural northern communities into context. *Journal of Rural and Community Development, 8*(1), 62–76. Retrieved from https://journals.brandonu.ca/jrcd/article/view/683/152

Winterton, R., Warburton, J., Clune, S., & Martin, J. (2014). Building community and organizational capacity to enable social participation for ageing Australian rural populations: A resource-based perspective. *Ageing International, 39*(2), 163–179. doi:10.1007/s12126-013-9187-2

Winterton, R., Warburton, J., Keating, N., Petersen, M., Berg, T., & Wilson, J. (2016). Understanding the influence of community characteristics on wellness for rural older adults: A meta-synthesis. *Journal of Rural Studies, 45*, 320–327. doi:10.106/j.jrurstud.2015.12.010

Yuan, S., Hussain, S. A., Hales, K. D., & Cotten, S. R. (2016). What do they like? Communication preferences and patterns of older adults in the United States: The role of technology. *Educational Gerontology, 42*(3), 163–174. doi:10.1080/03601277.2015.1083392

4
AGING-IN-PLACE

Mindy O. Renfro

The vast majority of older adults prefer to continue living in their homes for as long as possible. According to the AARP, nearly 90% of adults over 65 want to remain in their current homes as they grow older (University of Southern California, 2019). This preference is referred to as "aging-in-place." Living at home allows older adults to maintain a sense of independence and control over their lives in a familiar and nurturing environment of their own design. For many of us, staying both physically and emotionally connected to the years of gathering memories, possessions, and furnishings is important to our quality of life and satisfaction.

An older adult's ability to successfully age-in-place is determined by "three legs of the stool" working together:

1. Personal capacities/physical abilities or *intrinsic factors*;
2. Home and community characteristics or *extrinsic factors*; and
3. Support of family, friends, and community or *societal factors*.

What Are the Differences in Rural Communities?

Currently, 10,000 "Baby Boomers" celebrate their sixty-fifth birthday each day and become eligible for Medicare. Approximately 20% of them live in rural areas (U.S. Census Bureau, 2019). All older adults face certain universal challenges associated with aging; however, the consequences of low population density combined with the heightened risk of physical and social isolation in a rural setting can make common problems of daily living especially daunting. Health-care and social service providers are limited, public transportation may not exist, and neighbors may reside at great distance. Farmers and ranchers may have depended upon children who have now grown and moved away. Successful aging-in-place requires planning, money, and time. In a rural area, planning may take on particular significance because of limitations in service providers, home modification contractors, and markedly greater distances from much-needed resources.

Personal Capacities/Physical Abilities: Intrinsic Factors

Changes in the body as one ages will increase the challenge of successfully aging-in-place. However, one has the capacity, in many cases, to forestall the negative impact of physical and/

or cognitive decline on functional independence with timely adoption of and adherence to healthy behaviors. Indeed, some health outcomes are within our control. Most chronic diseases and disabilities can be managed at home with quality health care and careful self-management. Even so, as we age, personal capacity and physical ability inevitably decline. It is important to understand that these changes are part of the aging process and can potentially impact our capacity to remain in our homes.

1. *Risk for falls and injury from falls increases with age.* About 28% of people age 65 and older will fall each year (CDC, 2019). This is a fact. However, it is also a fact that most falls are preventable with knowledge of the risks, balance improvement, leg strength exercises, home modifications, and medication review. Taking preventive steps is critical (CDC, 2019). The following resources offer sound advice and strategies for preventing the occurrence of falls:
    a. National Institutes of Health (NIH) www.nia.nih.gov/health/prevent-falls-and-fractures
    b. National Council on Aging (NCOA) www.ncoa.org/healthy-aging/falls-prevention/
    c. CDC's Take a Stand on Falls www.cdc.gov/features/older-adult-falls/index.html
2. *Aging muscles will lose fibers and may lose power.* After age 30, you begin to lose as much as 3% to 5% of your muscle mass every ten years. Most men will lose about 30% of their muscle mass during their lifetimes (Harvard Medical School, 2019). Loss of muscle mass can impede our ability to care for our yard, our home, and even ourselves. Well-designed exercises and diets high in lean protein can slow the process. Resources on how to preserve muscle mass can be found at the following sites:
    a. Harvard Medical School www.health.harvard.edu/staying-healthy/preserve-your-muscle-mass
    b. Stay Strong: four ways to beat the frailty risk (John Hopkins) https://www.hopkinsmedicine.org/health/wellness-and-prevention/stay-strong-four-ways-to-beat-the-frailty-risk
    c. International Council on Active Aging's "build back my muscles" https://www.icaa.cc/blog/2017-06/New-nutrition-resources-to-help-build-back-my-muscles-1.htm
3. *Brain function or cognition will change as you age.* As a person grows older, changes occur in all parts of the body, including the brain. Certain parts of the brain shrink, especially those important to learning and other complex mental activities. In certain brain regions, communication between neurons (nerve cells) can be reduced. Blood flow in the brain may also decrease. These changes in the brain can affect mental function, even in healthy older people. For example, some older adults find that they don't do as well as younger people on complex memory or learning tests. Given enough time, though, they often will perform equally well. There is growing evidence that the brain remains "plastic"—able to adapt to new challenges and tasks—as people age. You can learn more about keeping the brain sharp here:
    a. The older, healthy brain (NIH) https://www.nia.nih.gov/health/how-aging-brain-affects-thinking#:~:text=Some%20changes%20in%20thinking%20are,have%20more%20problems%20with%20multitasking
    b. How memory and thinking ability change with age (Harvard) https://www.health.harvard.edu/mind-and-mood/how-memory-and-thinking-ability-change-with-age#:~:text=Medications%2C%20poor%20vision%20and%20hearing,in%20middle%20age%20and%20beyond
    c. Don't Forget About You (AARP) https://stayingsharp.aarp.org/about/brain-health/brain-health-awareness/?cmp=KNC-DSO-Adobe-Google-SSS-NonBrand-

BrainHealth&ef_id=EAIaIQobChMI183Q9Nq85AIVB9tkCh3teQKoEAAYASAAEgLOHPD_BwE:G:s&s_kwcid=AL!4520!3!354973754839!e!!g!!keeping%20the%20brain%20healthy

Home and Community Characteristics: Extrinsic Factors

Making home modifications in midlife (i.e., your 50s) is advisable. Such alterations should be undertaken before a crisis arises and you are forced to vacate your home prematurely. Rather than installing a Jacuzzi and/or lap pool when the kids move out, it may be wiser to make sure that your home is "aging or disability friendly." Aging-in-place is reinforced when an older adult's home is:

1. *Located in an age-friendly community close to critical services.* Is your town age-friendly? You can learn more at AARP's Network of Age-Friendly States & Communities: www.aarp.org/livable-communities/network-age-friendly-communities/info-2014/an-introduction.html. Your community reflects age-friendly principles, which support aging-in-place, if it provides:

    a. Quality health-care services within a reasonable distance from your home;
    b. Social services including meals-on-wheels, a community or senior center, home health-care services, and a responsive 911 system;
    c. Transportation that is public, affordable, safe, accessible, and reliable should you be unable to drive (Transportation for America, 2019);
    d. Social, educational, and wellness classes for older adults that support a physically active, cognitively stimulated, and socially engaged lifestyle; and
    e. Sidewalks, cross walks, and walking paths that are lit and well maintained.

2. *Updated with key aspects of universal design (UD).* Simply defined, UD is human-centered design that seeks to create environments and products that offer safety and comfort for all people with no need for adaptation or functional change. The evolution toward UD began in the 1950s with new attention to design for people with disabilities. Barrier-free design was developed to remove obstacles in the built environment for people with physical disabilities (Place.org, 2019). These structural changes enhance independence when physical challenges arise. A brief video providing an overview of UD is found here: www.youtube.com/watch?v=yINSxTduC6A (AARP, 2019a). Key features of UD include:

    a. An accessible entrance without steps and/or thresholds and doorways that are wide enough for walker and/or wheelchair access and door hardware that can be managed by aging hands such as a keyless entrance with lever handles not knobs.
    b. The ground floor has an open floor plan and includes:

        i. Safe and easy entrance and egress out of the house
        ii. Master bedroom with roomy bed access on both sides and wide doorway
        iii. Full bathroom large enough for wheelchair access
        iv. Well-lit and user-friendly kitchen
        v. Living room area that does not include steps, ramps, or thresholds
        vi. Door handles and sink faucets with levers, not knobs.

    c. Fall prevention measures are in place or can be easily added including:

        i. Low slip flooring, new and well-installed carpet, smooth transitions
        ii. Grab bars by all toilets and bathing areas

iii. Shower chair built-in or room to use a shower chair/bench
iv. Any stairways and walkways are well-lit with firm railings on both sides and are wide enough for stair-glide installation
v. Front door has automatic lighting, door locks, and a table under a protective roof to set things down while opening doorways.

3. *Wired to support home technology*. With the growing popularity of being able to age-in-place, gerotechnology can help older adults live in their homes with greater ease and safety. As this population ages in homes that haven't been designed to accommodate individuals surviving into extended old age, considerable risks to older people's health and safety arise. Many older adults aging-in-place, especially in rural communities, may not have access to caretakers or health-care professionals on a day-to-day basis. Accidents and falls are a major concern for people living alone. Available technologies having considerable application value in rural settings include the following (Savoy, 2019):

   a. Wearable technology that monitors your movements: devices that monitor and track your health are becoming more popular among all age groups. However, for older adults aging-in-place, especially those without a caretaker in the home, these technologies can be lifesaving. They represent a major advance from the "I've fallen and can't get up" generation of pendants worn around the neck.
   b. Health technologies bring the doctor to you: mobility limitations may make trips to the doctor's office exceedingly difficult. Many doctor's offices now offer video consultation for those who cannot come in for an appointment. This technology is ideal for those aging-in-place and suffering from ailments that do not require an in-person visit to the primary care practitioner. Moreover, medication regimens can be difficult to adhere to, leading to misuse of a prescription and potentially serious health outcomes. One technology on the rise, especially for older adults without personal assistance in the home, is smart pill counters or medication dispensers designed to alert and properly dispense medications that need to be taken.
   c. Activity sensors through the house are becoming more and more popular to monitor loved ones who are living unassisted at home. These sensors can be placed in many discreet locations around the house: doors, cabinets, windows, beds, etc. These sensors can track movement around the house and report back to a caretaker and/or a central monitoring service (Savoy, 2019).
   d. Traditional smart home technology: most devices can now be operated through applications on your smartphone. While there may be a slight learning curve, this technology should be embraced to enhance aging-in-place. Other common technologies that can benefit older adults include smart lights for hassle-free professional lighting; smart security cameras that can be placed in the home for monitoring by caregivers; and personal assistance devices like Amazon Alexa and Google Home that have features that can set reminders for individuals to take medications (Savoy, 2019).

Tech Enhanced Life.com (www.techenhancedlife.com/) represents a resource that offers older adult perspectives of selected technology including fall alarms and personal emergency response systems (PERS).

Support of Family, Friends, and Community: Societal Factors

Federal funds through the Older Americans Act are distributed on a per capita basis. For those who reside in a community with many aging individuals, there will be greater federal support allocated for services and programs for older adults. Rural communities, by definition, reflect lower absolute numbers of older adults, which in turn reduces the allocation of federal funds in support of community services, which may jeopardize one's ability to successfully age-in-place in the home of your choice.

Towns that have organized themselves to qualify as members of the roster of AARP's Aging-Friendly Communities are more likely to endorse a local infrastructure that reinforces the efforts of individuals to age-in-place (AARP, 2019b).

Having family and friends locally available and/or easily accessible is an important consideration that can counteract, at least in part, limitations in publicly funded programming. Planning for retirement and where you would like to live should factor in access to family and friends, faith-based communities, universities, etc. Loneliness and social isolation threaten the ability of older adults to successfully age-in-place in rural communities. Isolated and lonely older adults are more likely to suffer from depression, physical inactivity, and poor health. Interventions and activities aimed at reducing social isolation and loneliness, in turn, promote successful efforts at remaining at home and in one's community (Gardiner, 2016). If able, older adults are encouraged to reside in a new home location for a one-year trial rental period prior to making a home purchase (Kiplinger, 2019).

If the cost of making your home safer and more responsive to your changing capabilities as an aging adult is prohibitive, consideration should be given to downsizing into a smaller residence. At the same time, it is essential that one is mindful that a community that supports aging-in-place is also going to reflect the presence of informal supports (family, friends, and/or neighbors), accessible health and social services, transportation options, and ample opportunities for social interaction.

References

AARP. (2019a, September 5). *Universal design AARP award winning residence by Mannigan design*. YouTube. Retrieved from www.youtube.com/watch?v=yINSxTduC6A

AARP. (2019b, September 5). *AARP Network of Age-Friendly States and Communities*. An Introduction About the Program. Retrieved from www.aarp.org/livable-communities/network-age-friendly-communities/info-2014/an-introduction.html

Aging in Place.org. (2019, September 6). How universal design creates a seamless aging-in-place experience. *AgingInPlace.org*. Retrieved from www.aginginplace.org/how-universal-design-creates-a-seamless-aging-in-place-experience/

Centers for Disease Control and Prevention. (2019, September). *Important facts about falls*. Centers for Disease Control and Prevention. Retrieved from www.cdc.gov/homeandrecreationalsafety/falls/adultfalls.html

Gardiner, C. (2016, July 13). Interventions to reduce social isolation and loneliness among older people: An integrative review. *Health & Social Care in the Community*, *26*(2), 147–157. Epub. doi:10.1111/hsc.12367

Harvard Medical School. (2019, September). Preserve your muscle mass. In *Declining muscle mass is part of aging, but that does not mean you are helpless to stop it*. Retrieved from www.health.harvard.edu/staying-healthy/preserve-your-muscle-mass

Kiplinger. (2019, September 5). *Should you move or stay put in retirement?* Retrieved from www.kiplinger.com/article/retirement/T010-C022-S002-should-you-move-or-stay-put.html

Padilla, C. (2019). Aging today. *American Society on Aging*. Retrieved from www.asaging.org/blog/aging-healthcare-rural-america-overlooked-needs-quiet-strength

Savoy, T. (2019, September 5). Technology that can foster aging in place. *Washington Post*. Retrieved from www.washingtonpost.com/news/where-we-live/wp/2018/02/26/technology-that-can-foster-aging-in-place/?noredirect=on

Transportation for America. (2019, September 5). *HUD: Aging in place, stuck without options: Fixing the mobility crisis threatening the baby boom generation*. Retrieved from https://t4america.org/docs/SeniorsMobilityCrisis.pdf

University of Southern California. (2019). USC Leonard Davis school of gerontology. In *Resources: The value of aging in place*. Retrieved from https://gerontology.usc.edu/resources/articles/the-value-of-aging-in-place/

U.S. Census Bureau. (2019, August 30). Rural America. In *How does the Census Bureau define rural?* Retrieved from https://gis-portal.data.census.gov/arcgis/apps/MapSeries/index.html?appid=7a41374f6b03456e9d138cb014711e01

5
AMERICAN INDIANS AND ALASKA NATIVES

R. Turner Goins and Collette Adamsen

Who Are American Indians and Alaska Natives (AI/ANs)?

AI/ANs are generally understood as individuals who are enrolled members or eligible to be enrolled in a federally recognized AI/AN community. Individual tribes or tribal entities determine for themselves who is eligible for membership. A minimum blood quantum or degree of tribal ancestry is usually required by tribes and these membership criteria differ by tribe. Thus, there is not a single universally accepted definition of who is an AI or AN as various cultural, social, political, and administrative definitions exist. There are currently 574 federally recognized nations (Bureau of Indian Affairs, 2020). However, not all AI/ANs are enrolled in a federally recognized tribe—some individuals belong to a state-recognized tribe, and others self-identify as AI/ANs but are not enrolled in a tribe. Tribal membership has important implications for access to benefits. Members and descendants of members of federally recognized tribes have more broad access to certain federal benefits and services than AI/ANs who are not members of these tribes. The diversity across AI/AN communities cannot be overstated, including the number of enrolled members, cultural practices, language, geography, landmass, economics, public health priorities, and aging-related services and programs.

Demographics

Numbers, Age, and Gender

U.S. Census data distinguishes between AI/ANs who self-identify as AI/AN alone and AI/ANs who self-identify as such in combination with another race and/or ethnicity. As of 2017, there were 2,726,278 AI/ANs alone of any age (U.S. Census Bureau, 2019a). From the 2012–2016 American Community Survey, there were 235,124 AI/ANs alone aged ≥65 years and of these, 101,792 resided in rural areas (Smith & Trevelyan, 2019). The number of AI/ANs alone aged ≥65 years will increase to 657,000 by 2030 and to 996,000 by 2050 (Ortman et al., 2014). The AI/AN alone population is younger than the general U.S. population with a median age of 29 years compared to 37.2 years, respectively. Among AI/ANs alone aged ≥65 years, 44% are males and 56% are females (U.S. Census Bureau, 2019a), which is identical for the same-age total U.S. population (Roberts, Ogunwole, Blakeslee, & Rabe, 2018).

Economics

As an aggregate, AI/ANs report higher rates of poverty and lower educational attainment than the general U.S. population. AI/ANs of all ages have a larger proportion of their population who live below the poverty threshold compared to the general U.S. population (11% vs. 22%, respectively (Kaiser Family Foundation, 2019). Mean annual income of AI/ANs alone or in combination with another race and/or ethnicity aged ≥50 years is $29,391 compared to $39,584 for the U.S. general population (Goins et al., 2015). Nineteen percent of AI/ANs alone aged ≥65 years live in poverty compared to 9% of the same-age general U.S. population (Administration for Community Living, n.d.).

The American Communities Project (2019) examined income inequality, which is defined as the ratio of household income at the 80th percentile to income at the 20th percentile. "Native American Lands," which included 43 counties across the U.S., scored the highest on income inequality across the 11 rural community types, with the inequality primarily from income differences between racial/ethnic groups. Also, "Native American Lands" and "African American South" tied for having the highest unemployment rate (6%) across the 11 rural community types examined.

Marital Status and Living Arrangements

Forty-eight percent of AI/ANs alone aged ≥65 years are married, 27% are widowed, 16% are divorced or separated, and 9% have never been married (Administration for Community Living, n.d.). Among AI/ANs alone and in combination with another race and/or ethnicity aged ≥50 years, half are married compared to 61% of the same-aged U.S. general population. Also, in this same age group, a greater percentage are divorced or separated and approximately the same percentage are widowed compared to the same-aged U.S. general population (Goins et al., 2015).

AI/AN alone households tend to be larger than non-AI/AN households (Pindus et al., 2017). Among AI/ANs alone or in combination with another race and/or ethnicity aged ≥50 years, a larger percentage reside in households with ≥ three generations compared to the same-aged U.S. general population (10% vs. 7%). Their average household size is similar to the same-aged U.S. general population (2.3 vs. 2.2 persons), and 32% live alone compared to 28% of the same-aged U.S. general population (Goins et al., 2015).

Where They Live

Geography

Tribes hold more than 56 million acres of land across the U.S. There are approximately 326 Indian land areas in the U.S. administered as federal Indian reservations. The Navajo Nation has the largest reservation that is approximately, 27,000 square miles, while there are some reservations that are a few acres and some tribes with no land (National Congress of American Indians, 2019).

Not all AI/ANs live on tribal lands. The number and proportion of AI/ANs residing in urban areas has increased (National Urban Indian Family Coalition, 2008) where most are not classified as rural residents. Among AI/ANs aged ≥50 years, 36% of AI/ANs alone and 28.7% of AI/ANs alone or in combination with another race or ethnicity lived in a nonmetropolitan location. While it is not the majority, it is greater than the same-aged general U.S. population

(18%). Forty-four percent of the AI/AN population who are aged ≥50 years live on tribal lands. The percentage of AI/ANs aged ≥50 years who live on tribal lands increases for those who are AI/AN alone (57.9%) and for those who are aged ≥65 years regardless of whether they are AI/AN alone (60.8%) or alone and in combination with other races/ethnicity (46.1%) (Goins et al., 2015).

Older AI/ANs reside in all 50 states. States with the greatest numbers of AI/ANs alone aged ≥65 years include Oklahoma (31,876), Arizona (25,539), California (23,058), New Mexico (17,983), and North Carolina (14,233) (Administration for Community Living, n.d.). States with the highest proportion of AI/ANs alone or in combination with another race and/or ethnicity aged ≥50 years include Alaska (14%), Oklahoma (9.1%), New Mexico (7.3%), South Dakota (5%), and Montana (4.7%) (Goins et al., 2015).

Housing

Overall, housing in tribal areas reflects more problems compared to housing for the general U.S. population. A greater percentage of AI/AN households in tribal areas compared to the general U.S. population households have problems with the following: general condition (8.1% vs 0.8%), plumbing (5.6% vs. 1.3%), kitchen (6.6% vs. 1.7%), heating (12% vs. 0.1%), and overcrowding (15.9% vs. 2.2%). The average home value for AI/AN homeowners is lower than the general U.S. population or about 66% (Pindus et al., 2017).

Health

Life Expectancy

Period life tables were estimated for AI/ANs and found that life expectancy at birth was 71.1 years compared to 73.9 years for the non-Hispanic black population, 78.4 years for the non-Hispanic white population, and 80.8 years for the Hispanic population (Arias, Xu, & Jim, 2014). According to U.S. population projections, life expectancy at birth will continue to be low for AI/ANs. However, AI/ANs are projected to experience one of the largest increases in life expectancy between 2017–2060. Specifically, life expectancy at birth for AI/ANs is anticipated to increase by about ten years for males and eight years for females (U.S. Census, 2019b).

Chronic Health Conditions

Useful descriptive information on chronic health conditions was recently published from survey data collected between 2011 and 2014 from 14,632 Older Americans Act Title VI service users who were aged ≥55 years (Adamsen, Schroeder, LeMire, & Carter, 2018). Survey respondents reside on or near tribal lands. Results indicated that the highest-ranking prevalent conditions were hypertension (59%), diabetes (54%), and arthritis (47%). Ninety percent of respondents reported being diagnosed with at least one of ten diseases surveyed. Seventy percent reported being diagnosed with ≥ two conditions, and 45% reported being diagnosed with ≥ three conditions.

Physical Functioning

Available data suggest that AI/ANs experience a higher prevalence of physical impairments than their white counterparts. In particular, AI/ANs alone aged ≥55 years compared to same-aged whites had a higher prevalence of functional limitations (36% vs. 25%), mobility disability (21% vs. 17%), and self-care disability (12% vs. 9%) (Goins, Moss, Buchwald, & Guralnik, 2007). Fifty-eight percent of AI/ANs alone aged ≥65 years had a disability compared to 42% of all other race/ethnic groups the same age (Moss, Schell, & Goins, 2006). More recent studies have examined performance-based physical functioning measures among American Indians (Goins et al., 2018; Goins, Innes, & Dong, 2012). Using the short physical performance battery (SPPB) (Gurlanik et al., 1994), "good" lower body functioning was determined by a SPPB score of ≥10. One of the studies found that 48% of the sample (n=328) had "good" lower body functioning (Goins et al., 2012), while the other study found that 25% of the sample (n=818) had "good" lower body functioning (Goins et al., 2018).

Cognitive Functioning

Only a few studies have examined cognitive impairment in this population and what we do know is not specific to rural-dwelling older AI/ANs. Among the 2014 Medicare fee-for-service beneficiaries aged ≥65 years, 10.5% of AI/ANs met criteria for all-cause dementia compared to 11.3% of whites (Mathews et al., 2018); but these rates were not age-adjusted to account for the shorter life expectancy of AI/ANs. Meanwhile, other research suggests that AI/ANs suffer from substantial dementia disparities. Indeed, AI/ANs exhibited the second-highest dementia incidence (Mayeda, Glymour, Quesenberry, & Whitmer, 2016) and the second-shortest median survival among all race and ethnic groups aged ≥60 years (Mayeda et al., 2017).

Programs and Services

Availability of and access to programs and services vary across tribal communities as they do across any type of community. Tribal communities can finance elder-related programs and services through multiple sources, such as Medicaid, Medicare, the Older Americans Act, Department of Justice, and tribal revenue. The extent to which tribal revenue sources are accessible and available to be invested in such a way varies by community. Some tribes, including the Eastern Band of Cherokee Indians and the Choctaw Nation of Oklahoma, can offer a wide variety of tribally delivered services for their aging members (Goins, Scarton, & Winchester, 2019), while there are other tribes that cannot.

A survey of four key informants at 305 tribal entities queried perceptions of service availability for elders and adults with disabilities with respect to health and human services (Goins, Bogart, & Roubideaux, 2010). Among health services, the most available services were wellness/disease management, case management/care coordination, and personal care services; the least available services were nursing home, speech therapy, and adult day care. Among human services, the most available services were nutrition/congregate meal site, transportation, and home-delivered meal program; the least available services were translation services, older adult legal services, and financial planning.

The National Resource Center on Native American Aging (NRCNAA) routinely gathers information on program and services that older AI/ANs use. The most commonly used programs and services were congregate meals (18.1%), home-delivered meals (15.8%), and senior center programs (15.4%). The least commonly used programs and services were employment services (1%), retirement communities (0.9%), and nursing facilities (0.8%).

Conclusion

While we present aggregated information to describe rural older AI/ANs, the diversity across AI/AN communities cannot be overstated, including number of enrolled members, cultural practices, language, geography, landmass, economics, public health priorities, and aging-related services and programs. Misunderstandings and stereotypes are, unfortunately, rampant regarding AI/ANs. Each federally recognized tribe is a sovereign nation and deserves to be understood individually, which is beyond the scope of this entry. Those seeking to know AI/ANs and AI/AN communities need to appreciate that if you know one tribal community, you only know one tribal community and to use caution when generalizing. Appreciating the experiences and needs of older AI/ANs will be critical as between 2020 and 2050, the number aged ≥55 years is estimated to experience a 1.8-fold increase, aged ≥65 years is estimated to experience a 2.2-fold increase, and aged ≥85 years is estimated to experience a 5-fold increase (U.S. Census, 2017).

References

Adamsen, C., Schroeder, S., LeMire, S., & Carter, P. (2018). Education, income, and employment and prevalence of chronic disease among American Indian/Alaska native elders. *Preventing Chronic Disease, 15*, E37.

Administration for Community Living. (n.d.). *2017 profile of American Indians and Alaska natives age 65 and over.* Retrieved from https://acl.gov/sites/default/files/Aging%20and%20Disability%20in%20America/2017OAProfileAIAN508.pdf

American Communities Project. (2019). *A new portrait of rural America.* Retrieved from www.americancommunities.org/chapter/overview-2/#Major%20Findings

Arias, E., Xu, J., & Jim, M. A. (2014). Period life tables for the non-Hispanic American Indian and Alaska Native population, 2007–2009. *American Journal of Public Health, 104*(S3), S312–S319.

Bureau of Indian Affairs. (2020). Indian tribes recognized by and eligible to receive services from the United States Bureau of Indian Affairs. *Federal Register, 85*(20), 5462–5467.

Goins, R. T., Bogart, A., & Roubideaux, Y. R. (2010). Service provider perceptions of long-term care access in American Indian and Alaska Native communities. *Journal of Health Care for the Poor and Underserved, 21*(4), 1340–1353.

Goins, R. T., Innes, K., & Dong, L. (2012). Lower body functioning prevalence and correlates among older American Indians in a southeastern tribe: The Native Elder Care Study. *Journal of the American Geriatrics Society, 60*(3), 577–582.

Goins, R. T., Moss, M., Buchwald, D., & Guralnik, J. M. (2007). Disability among older American Indians and Alaska Natives: An analysis of the 2000 Census public use microdata sample. *The Gerontologist, 47*(5), 690–696.

Goins, R. T., Scarton, L., & Winchester, B. (2019). The first rural community: Indian Country. *Generations, 43*(2), 76–83.

Goins, R. T., Schure, M. B., Crowder, J., Baldridge, D., Benson, W., & Aldrich, N. (2015). *Lifelong disparities among older American Indians and Alaska Natives.* Research Report No. 2015–8. Washington, DC: AARP.

Goins, R. T., Schure, M. B., Jensen, P. N., Suchy-Dicey, A., Nelson, L., Verney, S. P., Buchwald, D. (2018). Lower body functioning and correlates among older American Indians: The Cerebrovascular Disease and Its Consequences in American Indians Study. *BMC Geriatrics, 18*(6), 1–9.

Gurlanik, J. M., Simonsick, E. M., Ferrucci, L., Glynn, R. J., Berkman, L. F., Blazer, D. G., . . . Wallace, R. B. (1994). A short physical performance battery assessing lower extremity function: Association with self-reported disability and prediction of mortality and nursing home admission. *Journal of Gerontology, 49*, M85–M94.

Kaiser Family Foundation. (2019). *State health facts: Poverty rate by race/ethnicity. Timeframe 2017.* Retrieved from www.kff.org/other/state-indicator/poverty-rate-by-raceethnicity

Mathews, K. A., Xu, W., Gaglioti, A. H., Holt, J. B., Croft, J. B., Mack, D., & McGuire, L. C. (2018). Racial and ethnic estimates of Alzheimer's disease and related dementias in the United States (2015–2060) in adults aged ≥65 years. *Alzheimer's & Dementia, 15*(1), 17–24.

Mayeda, E. R., Glymour, M. M., Quesenberry, C. P., Johnson, J. K., Perez-Stable, E. J., & Whitmer, R. A. (2017). Survival after dementia diagnosis in five racial/ethnic groups. *Alzheimer's & Dementia, 13*, 761–769.

Mayeda, E. R., Glymour, M. M., Quesenberry, C. P., & Whitmer, R. A. (2016). Inequalities in dementia incidence between six racial and ethnic groups over 14 years. *Alzheimer's & Dementia, 12*, 216–224.

Moss, M. P., Schell, M. C., & Goins, R. T. (2006). Using GIS in a first national mapping of functional disability among older American Indians and Alaska natives from the 2000 census. *International Journal of Health Geographics, 5*(37).

National Congress of American Indians. (2019, May). *Tribal nations and the United States: An introduction*. Retrieved from www.ncai.org/tribalnations/introduction/Tribal_Nations_and_the_United_States_An_Introduction-web-.pdf

National Urban Indian Family Coalition. (2008). *Urban Indian America: The status of American Indian and Alaska Native children and families today*. A report to the Annie E. Casey Foundation. Retrieved from https://www.aecf.org/resources/urban-indian-america/

Ortman, J. M., Velkoff, V. A., & Hogan, H. (2014). *An aging nation: The older population in the United States*. Current Population Reports No. P25–P1140. Washington, DC: U.S. Bureau of the Census.

Pindus, N., Kingsley, G. T., Biess, J., Levy, D., Simington, J., & Hayes, C. (2017). *Housing needs of American Indians and Alaska Natives in tribal areas: A report from the assessment of American Indian, Alaska Native, and Native Hawaiian housing needs*. U.S. Department of Housing and Urban Development, Office of Policy Development and Research. Retrieved from https://www.huduser.gov/portal/publications/HNAIHousingNeeds.html

Roberts, A. W., Ogunwole, S. U., Blakeslee, L., & Rabe, M. A. (2018, October). *The population 65 years and older in the United States: 2016*. American Community Survey Reports ACS-38. Retrieved from www.census.gov/content/dam/Census/library/publications/2018/acs/ACS-38.pdf

Smith, A. S., & Trevelyan, E. (2019). *The older population in rural America: 2012–2016*. American Community Survey Reports, ACS-41. Washington, DC: U.S. Bureau of the Census.

U.S. Census Bureau. (2017). *2017 national population projections datasets, table 1. Projected population by single year of age, sex, race, and Hispanic origin for the United States: 2016 to 2060*. www.census.gov/data/datasets/2017/demo/popproj/2017-popproj.html

U.S. Census Bureau. (2019a). *Selected population profile in the United States: 2017 American Community Survey 1-year*. Retrieved from https://factfinder.census.gov/faces/tableservices/jsf/pages/productview.xhtml?src=bkmk#

U.S. Census Bureau. (2019b). *2017 national population projections datasets, table 1: Projected population by single year of age, sex, race, and Hispanic origin for the United States: 2016 to 2060*. Retrieved from www.census.gov/data/datasets/2017/demo/popproj/2017-popproj.html

6
AREA AGENCIES ON AGING

Sandy Markwood

Introduction

For nearly five decades, the nation's Area Agencies on Aging (AAAs) have been addressing the needs of older adults in rural America. Whether providing congregate meals in senior centers or a home-delivered meal, arranging a needed ride to the doctor, offering fall prevention and chronic disease self-management classes, providing in-home personal care support or chore services, or adding grab bars or a wheelchair ramp to an older adult's home, AAAs and the critical support they provide often serve as a lifeline for older adults living in rural and frontier areas.

The mission of AAAs is to ensure that every older American has the opportunity to age with dignity and independence in his or her home and community. Over 11 million older adults are served every year across the United States, through the work of AAAs (Department of Health and Human Services, 2016). AAAs were authorized by the 1973 reauthorization of the Older Americans Act (OAA) and are charged with responding to the needs of Americans 60 and over in every community across the country. The 622 AAAs serve virtually every community in the U.S. and are a part of the Aging Network, which includes the federal Administration on Aging, State Units on Aging, and other community-based providers that AAAs partner with to provide services.

AAAs assess community needs and develop area plans to address these needs, coordinating services and supports to ensure that older Americans have the opportunity to age-in-place. The OAA requires that AAAs provide certain core services, including supportive services such as transportation and legal services, nutrition, health and wellness, caregiver supports, and elder rights. Since AAAs are charged with responding to the needs of older adults in their communities, many provide additional services, such as care management, options counseling, and home repair and modifications. Through their information and referral programs, AAAs also connect older adults to additional resources in their communities.

Rural AAA Settings and Structures

Every three years, the National Association of Area Agencies on Aging (n4a) conducts a survey of all AAAs in the country for the U.S. Administration for Community Living to track services

Table 6.1 AAA Service Areas

Describe the area served by your organization:	*Frequency*	*Percent*
Predominantly rural	209	43%
A mix of urban, suburban, and rural	123	25%
A mix of suburban and rural	53	11%
A mix of urban and suburban	51	11%
Predominantly urban	21	4%
Predominantly suburban	17	4%
Predominantly remote or frontier	13	3%

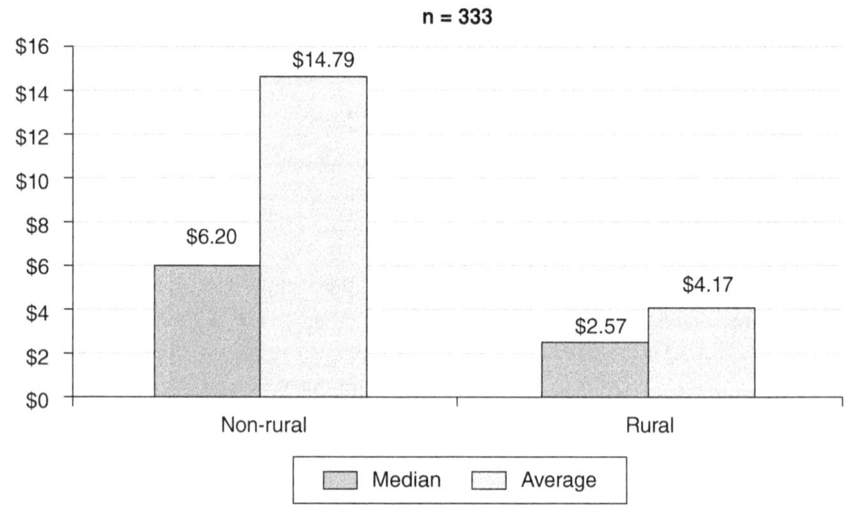

Figure 6.1 Rural and non-rural AAA budget (in millions)

and emerging trends. This entry draws data from a 2019 AAA National Survey and a 2018 data issue brief, "Rural AAAs Structure and Services."

Addressing the unique needs of older adults in rural America is particularly relevant for AAAs. According to the results of the 2019 National Survey of Area Agencies on Aging, 43% of AAAs serve a predominantly rural area (n4a, 2020). An additional 36% of AAAs serve a mix of rural and suburban and/or urban areas. Three percent of AAAs serve predominantly remote or frontier areas (n4a, 2020). For the purposes of the remainder of this article, n4a defined rural AAAs as those that self-identified as "predominantly rural" or "predominantly remote or frontier" and defined non-rural as all other categories.

Regarding their organizational structure, most rural AAAs operate private nonprofit organizations (41%) or operate as part of regional councils of governments or planning and development districts (32%). The remainder of rural AAAs are incorporated within a city or county government (20%) (n4a, 2020).

Rural AAA Budgets

Rural AAAs have smaller budgets than their non-rural counterparts. The average budget for a rural AAA is approximately $4.17 million annually as compared to a budget of $14.79 million annually for their counterparts, as depicted in Figure 6.1 (n4a, 2018). Rural AAAs reported that most of their funding comes from the Older Americans Act (35% of their budgets), Medicaid waiver (24%), state general revenue (21%), and local government funding (8%), as shown in Figure 6.2 (n4a, 2018). These numbers are calculated based upon those AAAs that report any funding from the funding source.

Rural AAA Staffing

Given their more limited budgets, rural AAAs, not surprisingly, operate their agencies with fewer staff. Rural AAAs operate with almost half of the full-time staff support of non-rural AAAs. Whereas rural AAAs have a median of 15 staff members, their non-rural counterparts have a median of 29 full-time staff. Both rural and non-rural AAAs have five part-time staff, as depicted in Figure 6.3 (n4a, 2018).

Rural AAA Services

Even with their comparatively smaller budgets and staffing levels, rural AAAs provide a broad range of services and supports for older adults in their communities. As previously noted, all

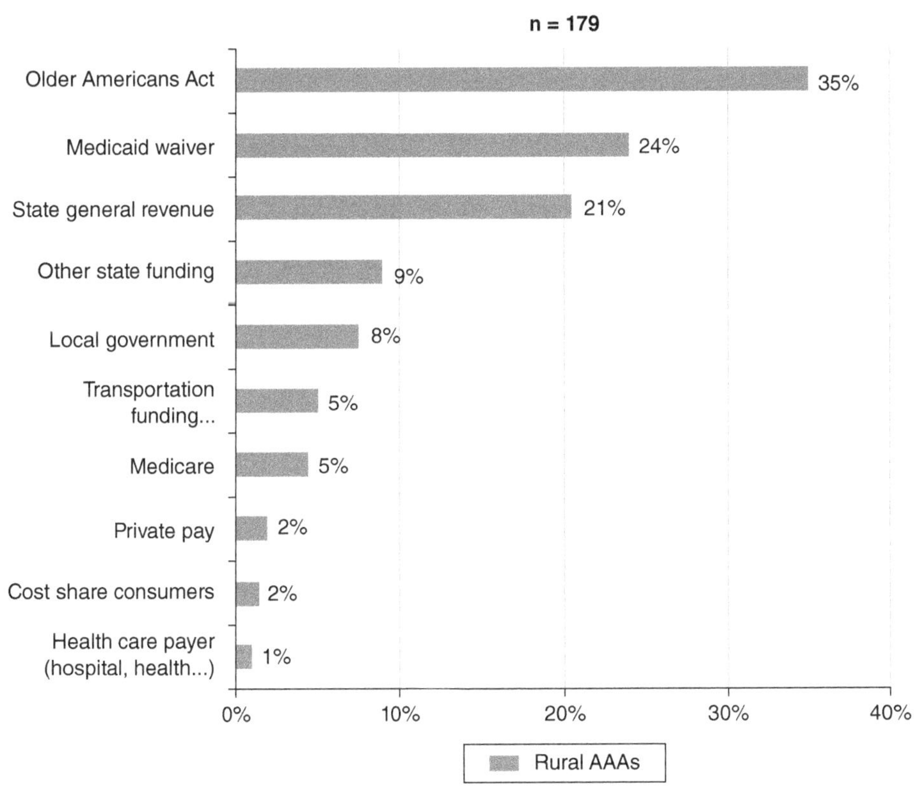

Figure 6.2 Proportion of rural AAA budget by source (median) (calculated based upon those AAAs that report any funding from the source)

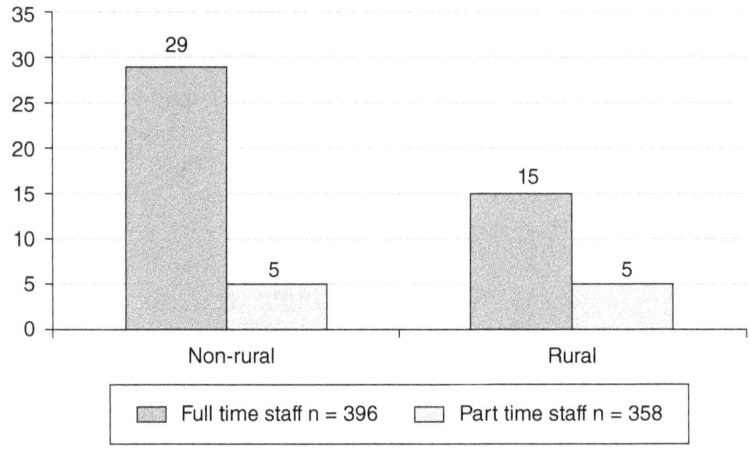

Figure 6.3 Number of full and part-time staff (median)

Table 6.2 AAA Service n=179

Common Services Offered by AAAs (Beyond OAA Core Services)	*Percent of Rural AAAs Offering This Service*
Adult day services	41%
Case management	79%
Chore services	54%
Enrollment assistance	62%
Evidence-based caregiver program	46%
Homemaker services	72%
Personal assistance/personal care services	69%
Home repair or modification	63%
Senior center programming	64%
Medical transportation	65%
Nonmedical transportation	87%

AAAs are required, through the OAA, to provide certain core services: supportive services such as transportation and legal services, nutrition, health and wellness, caregiver supports, and elder rights. However, many rural AAAs offer additional services to meet the unique needs of older adults in their communities. Common services rural AAAs offer, beyond the core required services, are depicted in Table 6.2.

Rural AAAs' Involvement in Integrated Care

A growing number of AAAs across the country are involved in integrated care initiatives.

Integrated care is a broad approach to care that connects multiple systems—such as primary care, behavioral health, long-term services and supports, and acute care—to achieve a more coordinated and person-centered approach and to improve health outcomes. Integrated care is

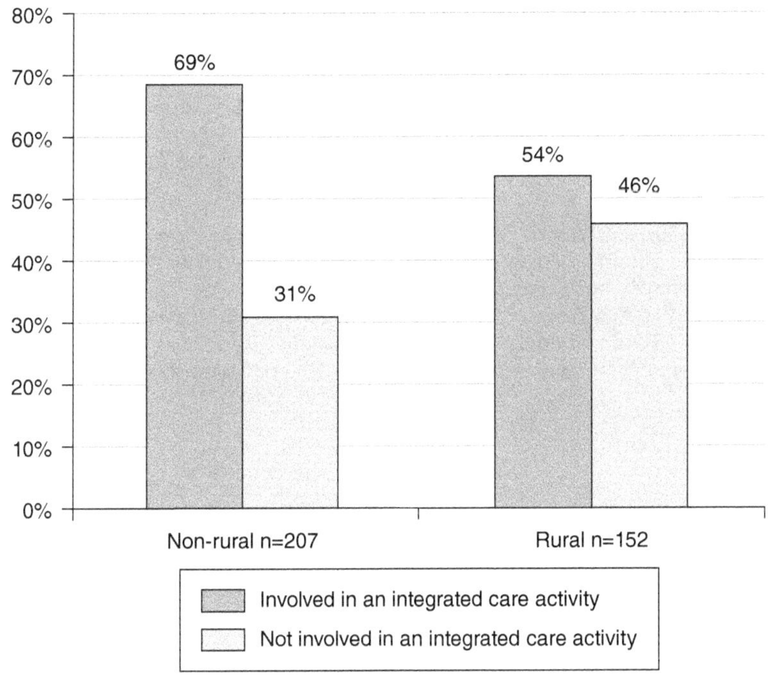

Figure 6.4 Rural and non-rural involvement in integrated care

particularly important for rural residents who have higher rates of chronic conditions than those in non-rural areas; however, to date, rural AAAs are less likely than non-rural AAAs to report being involved in an integrated care activity, as depicted in Figure 6.4.

Nationally, the integrated care initiatives that AAA survey respondents are most likely to provide are Medicaid 1915(c) waivers (34%), Veteran-Directed Home and Community-Based Services (25%), and Medicaid Managed Care 1915(b) Waiver programs (14%). Although the numbers of rural AAAs involved in integrated care initiatives is lower than non-rural AAAs, there are only modest differences between the types of integrated care initiatives that rural and non-rural AAAs are involved in. For example, rural AAA survey respondents are less likely to participate in Medicaid Managed Care waiver programs and in the HRSA-funded Geriatrics Workforce Enhancement Program. In addition, AAAs serving rural areas are significantly more likely to report no involvement in integrated care initiatives.

Summary

Whereas older adults living in rural America often face unique challenges, such as shortages of health-care professionals and lack of transportation options, AAAs serving rural communities often face significant challenges of their own, having smaller budgets and fewer staff than non-rural AAAs to address rural older adults needs. Despite these barriers, rural AAAs deliver a wide array of services and programs every day to meet the needs of older adults living in rural communities. Additionally, rural AAAs are continuing to innovate, to find new ways to expand the scope of their services that draw upon the assets of rural older adults and rural communities as well as explore new integrated care initiatives to improve the health and well-being of the older adults they serve. Through their efforts, the AAAs in rural America will continue to serve as a lifeline for the millions of rural older Americans who want to age with dignity and independence in the rural communities they call home.

References

Department of Health and Human Services. (2016). *FY 2016 report to congress: Older Americans Act.* Retrieved from https://acl.gov/sites/default/files/about-acl/2019-02/FY2016_OAApercent20 Reportpercent20topercent20Congress.pdf

National Association of Area Agencies on Aging (2018). *Rural AAAs structure and services: Information & planning issue brief.* Retrieved from www.n4a.org/buildingcapacity

National Association of Area Agencies on Aging (n4a) (2020). *2020 national survey of area agencies on aging report.*

7
ASIAN AMERICANS AND PACIFIC ISLANDERS

Fengyan Tang and Ke Li

General Information and Statistics

Asian Americans and Pacific Islanders (AAPIs) are one of the fastest-growing older populations in the U.S. (National Asian Pacific Center on Aging, 2013). Particularly, the Asian older adult population (aged 65 and older) increased by 73%, and the Native Hawaiian/Pacific Islander (NHPI) older population increased by 50% between 2000 and 2010 (National Asian Pacific Center on Aging, 2013). In 2012, there were about 1.6 million AAPI older adults, constituting 9% of the total AAPI population (National Asian Pacific Center on Aging, 2013). It is projected that the number of AAPI older adults will continuingly grow 352% to 7.3 million, making up about 21% of the total AAPI population by 2060 (National Asian Pacific Center on Aging, 2013). Among the general older population in the U.S., it is projected that 7.1% will be Asians and 0.3% will be NHPI by 2050 (Ritenour, Rodriguez, & Wilson-Frederick, 2017).

California, New York, and Hawaii have the largest AAPI older adult populations (National Asian Pacific Center on Aging, 2013). The five largest ethnic groups among Asian older adults are Chinese, Filipino, Japanese, Indian, and Korean (National Asian Pacific Center on Aging, 2013). According to the U.S. Census Bureau (2010), Chinese older adults, with a population of 366,761, are the largest Asian American ethnic group, making up 26% of the AAPI older population, followed by Filipino (20%) and Japanese (13%) (National Asian Pacific Center on Aging, 2013). Approximately 85% of AAPI older adults are foreign-born, and 65% are naturalized citizens (National Asian Pacific Center on Aging, 2013).

Ambiguity and Misuse of the Term AAPIs

The U.S. Census Bureau groups Pacific Islanders together with Asian Americans, which has resulted in a designation of AAPIs. As of the 2000 Census, Pacific Islanders, who are immigrants or descendants of immigrants from one of the Pacific Islands to the United States, including Hawaii, Samoa, Fiji, Guam, and the islands of Micronesia, were officially separated from Asian Americans (Kalibatseva & Leong, 2011). Asian Americans refer to persons having origins in any of the original people of the Far East, Southeast Asia, or the Indian subcontinent including, for example, Cambodia, China, India, Japan, Korea, Malaysia, Pakistan, the Philippines, Thailand, and Vietnam (Kalibatseva & Leong, 2011).

Asian Americans and Pacific Islanders are still grouped or termed together, probably because both groups had shared experiences with colonialism and had historically been linked through trade and cultures (Spickard, 2007). However, there is significant heterogeneity in this group. AAPIs have roots in at least 29 Asian countries and 20 Pacific Islander cultures, and members of this group speak over 100 languages and belong to numerous religions (Ghosh, 2003). Thus, it is important to understand the complexity of cultural identity, country of birth, and linguistic diversity when working with AAPI populations.

AAPIs and Racial Diversity in Rural Communities

In general, rural areas are less racially and ethnically diverse than urban areas in the U.S. The total rural population remained close to 46.1 million since 2013, with quite small change until 2016–2017 (U.S. Department of Agriculture, 2018). Relatively few AAPIs live in rural areas, accounting for about 1.1% of the rural population (U.S. Department of Agriculture, 2018). That is to say, there are approximately 50,000 AAPI rural residents, and possibly less than 9% of them are aged 65 and older. By contrast, whites make up nearly 80% of the rural population, compared with 58% of the urban population (U.S. Department of Agriculture, 2018). Hispanics are the fastest-growing rural population group but only constitute 9% of the rural population, compared with 20% in urban areas (U.S. Department of Agriculture, 2018). Blacks make up 8% of the rural population (U.S. Department of Agriculture, 2018). American Indians are the only minority group with a higher rural than urban population share (2% versus 0.5%) (U.S. Department of Agriculture, 2018).

Settlement in Rural Areas

Asian Americans have long been known to settle in metropolitan cities, such as New York and San Francisco, where they have built ethnic enclaves such as Chinatowns and Koreatowns (Weng, 2016). Particularly, recent older immigrants often join family or kin in such places for social and material support (Treas & Mazumdar, 2002). Compared with U.S.-born Asian Americans, foreign-born Asian Americans are more likely to reside in urban areas. For example, 90% of foreign-born Asian Americans lived in urban communities, as shown in a study about Asian and white Medicare beneficiaries (Ngo-Metzger et al., 2003). Recent immigrants, and Asians in particular, tend to settle down in the suburban areas that have been dominated by native-born white Americans (Chiang & Leung, 2011). A qualitative study among Chinese immigrants indicated that they have made a home in rural communities because they feel that their careers or business are secure or promising and they are certain they have come to the right places for their work and family (Chiang & Leung, 2011).

Challenges Facing APPI Older Adults

Immigration in later life appears to increase risk for adverse health outcomes, with increasing barriers and challenges to accessing social resources and adjusting to life in the U.S. (Diwan, 2008). Older Asian immigrants, in particular, experience many challenges because of cultural and language differences, limited social networks, and different family roles (Kim, Dattilo, & Heo, 2011). Compared with other racial groups, they are disproportionately affected by mental health issues and psychological distress, facing such psychological stressors as social isolation, stressful life events, recency of immigration, poor perceived health, and dissatisfaction with family (Dong, Chang, Wong, & Simon, 2012). Living in a rural community may increase the risk of social isolation and dependence on family and kin.

Older Asian immigrants' health and health care are still largely unknown, especially among those who live in rural areas (Winton, 2015). It is very likely that health disparities occur more often in rural medically underserved areas than in urban areas (Winton, 2015), probably because rural areas have a documented undersupply of health-care professionals and facilities (Bolin et al., 2015). Health service use is determined by place and race, and the health status of rural minorities is worse than rural whites, with very limited access to quality health services (Bolin et al., 2015). In addition to systems and linguistic barriers, cultural values of filial piety and interdependence on family and friend networks may prevent AAPIs from seeking health services, especially nursing home and hospice care (Fuller-Thomson & Chi, 2012; Ngo-Metzger et al., 2003).

AAPIs are underrepresented in social science research and usually excluded in racial or cultural comparative studies. Lesser is known about AAPI older adults living in rural areas, and most studies do not include rural residents or compare rural and urban differences. The dearth of research on this population is problematic for several reasons. First, the AAPI older population is large and growing, with a large proportion foreign-born and recently arrived (Flippen & Kim, 2015). Second, the population is geographically dispersed, with a very small number of rural residents. Because of the geographical distribution of Asian Americans, it is quite challenging for researchers to find representative and adequate sample sizes when conducting research with Asian Americans outside of the major states of California and New York (Kalibatseva & Leong, 2011). Third, AAPIs are among the fastest-growing racial groups with great heterogeneity, representing very diverse populations in terms of ethnicity, language, culture, education, income level, English proficiency, and sociopolitical experience (Office of the Surgeon General, 2001). Although cultural ties exist among different AAPI communities, it is important to recognize and understand the differences among them (Office of the Surgeon General, 2001). Future work needs to apply community-based participatory research methodologies to engage AAPI older adults in rural settings, rely on infrastructure support to conduct research that has theoretical and policy significance for the population, and investigate the impacts of ethnic, linguistic, and cultural factors on health and health-care disparities.

References

Bolin, J. N., Bellamy, G. R., Ferdinand, A. O., Vuong, A. M., Kash, B. A., . . . Helduser, J. W. (2015). Rural healthy people 2020: New decade, same challenges. *The Journal of Rural Health*, *31*(3), 326–333. doi:10.1111/jrh.12116

Chiang, S. Y., & Leung, H. H. (2011). Making a home in U.S. rural towns: The significations of home for Chinese immigrants' work, family, and settlement in local communities. *Community, Work & Family*, *14*(4), 469–486. doi:10.1080/13668803.2011.574871

Diwan, S. (2008). Limited English proficiency, social network characteristics, and depressive symptoms among older immigrants. *The Journals of Gerontology Series B: Psychological Sciences and Social Sciences*, *63*(3), S184–S191. doi:10.1093/geronb/63.3.S184

Dong, X., Chang, E. S., Wong, E., & Simon, M. (2012). Perception and negative effect of loneliness in a Chicago Chinese population of older adults. *Archives of Gerontology and Geriatrics*, *54*(1), 151–159. doi:10.1016/j.archger.2011.04.022

Flippen, C., & Kim, E. (2015). Immigrant context and opportunity: New destinations and socioeconomic attainment among Asians in the United States. *The Annals of the American Academy of Political and Social Science*, *660*(1), 175–198. doi:10.1177/0002716215577611

Fuller-Thomson, E., & Chi, M. (2012). Older Asian Americans and Pacific Islanders with activities of daily living (ADL) limitations: Immigration and other factors associated with institutionalization. *International Journal of Environmental Research and Public Health*, *9*(9), 3264–3279. doi:10.3390/ijerph9093264

Ghosh, C. (2003). Healthy people 2010 and Asian Americans/Pacific Islanders: Defining a baseline of information. *American Journal of Public Health, 93*(12), 2093–2098. doi:10.2105/AJPH.93.12.2093
Kalibatseva, Z., & Leong, F. T. (2011). Depression among Asian Americans: Review and recommendations. *Depression Research and Treatment*, 1–9. doi:10.1155/2011/320902
Kim, J., Dattilo, J., & Heo, J. (2011). Education and recreation activities of older Asian immigrants. *Educational Gerontology, 37*(4), 336–350. doi:10.1080/03601271003609058
National Asian Pacific Center on Aging. (2013). Retrieved July 25, 2019, from www.napca.org/
Ngo-Metzger, Q., McCarthy, E. P., Burns, R. B., Davis, R. B., Li, F. P., & Phillips, R. S. (2003). Older Asian Americans and Pacific Islanders dying of cancer use hospice less frequently than older white patients. *The American Journal of Medicine, 115*(1), 47–53. doi:10.1016/S0002-9343(03)00258-4
Office of the Surgeon General (U.S.), Center for Mental Health Services (U.S.), National Institute of Mental Health (U.S.). (2001). *Mental health: Culture, race, and ethnicity. Supplement to mental health: A report of the surgeon general.* Rockville, MD: Substance Abuse and Mental Health Services Administration (U.S.).
Ritenour, D., Rodriguez, J., & Wilson-Frederick, S. (2017). *Understanding the health needs of diverse groups of Asian and Native Hawaiian or other Pacific Islander Medicare beneficiaries.* Retrieved July 25, 2019, from www.hosonline.org/globalassets/hos-online/publications/cms-omh-data-highlight-vol10-aug-2017.pdf
Spickard, P. (2007). Whither the Asian American coalition? *Pacific Historical Review, 76*(4), 585–604. doi:10.1525/phr.2007.76.4.585
Treas, J., & Mazumdar, S. (2002). Older people in America's immigrant families: Dilemmas of dependence, integration, and isolation. *Journal of Aging Studies, 16*(3), 243–258. doi:10.1016/S0890-4065(02)00048-8
U.S. Census Bureau (2010). *2010 Census.* Retrieved from https://www.census.gov/programs-surveys/decennial-census/decade.2010.html
U.S. Department of Agriculture. (2018). *Rural America at a glance.* Retrieved July 25, 2019, from www.ers.usda.gov/webdocs/publications/90556/eib-200.pdf?v=5899.2
Weng, S. S. (2016). Asset mapping for an Asian American community: Informal and formal resources for community building. *Psychosocial Intervention, 25*(1), 55–62.
Winton, M. B. (2015). Korean immigrants health and healthcare practices in rural America: A systematic review. *Online Journal of Rural Nursing and Health Care, 16*(1), 23–58. doi:10.14574/ojrnhc.v16i1.368

8
BIOETHICS

Angeline Bushy

Historically, health-care bioethics evolved from several focal areas. The *Encyclopedia of Bioethics* indicates five areas of inquiry that contribute to the discipline of bioethics—theoretical, clinical, regulatory, policy, and culture. *Theoretical health-care ethics* addresses principles of moral reasoning as applied to health-care-related issues. *Clinical ethics* refers to challenges encountered in patient care. *Regulatory and policy health-care ethics* refers to organizational and legal attributes of health-care-related ethical questions and situations. *Cultural health-care ethics* refers to the systematic examination of health-care ethics issues in relation to the social and cultural context in which the event occurs. An important cultural subgroup of bioethical inquiry is the rural context. More specifically, inquiry can address the manner in which rural contextual factors can influence ethical situations that a health-care provider may encounter in serving patients generally, and older patients in particular, such as (geographic) remoteness, low population density, cultural preferences, informal social networks, economic structures, and available resources. These factors can interact and influence care-seeking behaviors that could contribute to bioethical situations. Examined here are those rural contextual features that can impact bioethical events (Bushy, 2006; Nelson, 2006, 2010).

Table 1: Select Rural Contextual Characteristics

- Low population density in large geographical areas
- Informal social structures; shared network connections/experiences
    - Individualism; strong sense of self-reliance/independent thinking
    - Shared historical and cultural values among residents
    - Incongruent community/patient versus professional values
- Diffuse, overlapping personal-professional relationships
- Limited access to health-care services, providers, specialists, ethics resources
    - Small (critical access) hospitals with 25 or fewer beds
- Limited economic infrastructures; fewer employment opportunities; prevalence of hazardous occupations (fishing, agriculture, timber, mining, etc.)
    - Higher proportion of residents of low socioeconomic status
    - Higher rates of underinsured/uninsured

Table 2: Select Rural Contextual Features Influencing Health-Care Ethical Situations

- Community and/or older adult values/beliefs that differ from professional standards
- Overlapping personal-professional boundaries/roles in the community
- Threats to anonymity, confidentiality, privacy
- Real or perceived geographic and/or professional isolation
- Limited access to specialist health-care services/providers
- Socioeconomic factors (e.g., low income, lack of adequate insurance, limited health literacy, low education level)
- Clinician stress associated with community expectations, professional isolation, personal/family versus professional community expectations
- Patients preferred reliance on informal (nonprofessional) health-care support networks
- Limited rural ethics resources (i.e., rural ethics literature, ethicists, continuing education, rural-sensitive ethics committees)

Low Population Density in Large Geographical Areas

There are several widely accepted definitions for "rural" that can be used to differentiate such regions from urban areas. These definitions, taken together, tend to be somewhat imprecise and oftentimes conflicting. Essentially, all of the rural definitions include the concept of *low population density*, alluding to fewer people residing in a designated geographical area. In the U.S., approximately 20% of the total population resides within about 75% of the nation's land mass. Population dispersion has implications for the manner in which residents live, work, and interact, as well as the available needed services and resources. These intersecting contextual features should always be considered when examining a bioethical situation that presents in a rural practice (Bushy, 2020).

Informal Social Structures: Overlapping Professional-Personal Boundaries

In a small community, many residents are acquainted if not related. In turn, most residents know their local physicians, nurses, and other health professionals and frequently interact with them outside of health-care settings. Thus, a common feature of the rural context is described as diffuse professional-personal and overlapping boundaries among clinicians and their older patients and family members. Informal social dynamics characterize a small tight-knit community. Realistically, a health-care provider very likely will interact with community members (i.e., who also may be patients) in various settings. For instance, a nurse or physician may serve on the local school board or as a county commissioner, of which, other board members may also be patients or relatives of a patient. Or, a physician's children may attend schools and participate in youth activities (i.e., sports, band) with patients' children or grandchildren. Or, a social worker may attend the same church as one or more of his or her clients. Such informal professional-patient exchanges are not as likely to take place in a highly populated community. On the one hand, informal relationships could enhance health-care outcomes. On the other hand, these informal exchanges and social interactions can complicate the clinician-patient relationship that could lead to an ethical situation. Anecdotally, some rural clinicians report informal interpersonal exchanges enable them to better understand a patient's lifestyle and belief systems, which, in turn, allows for personalizing the care plan. However, diffuse professional-personal boundaries can pose threats to objectivity in the provision of patient care. Essentially, rural ethical situations often are influenced and shaped by overlapping clinicians' professional-personal boundaries, roles, and responsibilities (Nelson, 2010).

Threats to Confidentiality, Privacy, and Anonymity

Diffuse, overlapping boundaries with professional-patient relationships can lead to advertent and inadvertent threats to a patient's anonymity, confidentiality, and privacy. For example, associated with informal kinship networks, a rural health-care provider often hears patients report that they do not trust anyone in the community. In other words, there is no one they feel comfortable with whom to discuss a personal problem. Partly this cautious perspective is attributable to small-town residents' genuine interest in the lives of neighbors, friends, and relatives. Be it rural or urban, it can be devastating for everyone involved when a personal problem becomes public knowledge. For these reasons, implementing HIPAA regulations (Health Insurance Portability and Accountability Act) or addressing HCAHPS scores (Hospital Consumer Assessment of Healthcare Providers and Systems) can be challenging and next to impossible for a small-town health-care facility or clinician (Nelson, 2006, 2010).

For example, in the waiting room of a physician's office, local residents often interact with each other and, in this setting, often discuss community news as well as personal and family matters. Likewise, in a small hospital, when one person visits a patient, it is not unusual to run into other locals who are visiting another patient (i.e., family member, friend, relative). Again, this is an opportunity for visitors to exchange information about patients, their conditions, and treatment. Subsequently, that information may be shared with family members, friends, and relatives and further disseminated via the "informal grapevine." Furthermore, residents in a small town often are recognized by the car they drive. Thus, even seeing someone's vehicle in a parking lot can jeopardize patient confidentiality and anonymity. Consequently, when bioethical situations occur in a rural setting, threats of privacy, confidentiality, and anonymity must always be considered.

Community's Values Versus Professional's Values

A comprehensive discussion on rural cultural preferences is beyond the scope of this entry. However, it is important to emphasize that each community is unique demographically and in its cultural preferences. With that in mind, a community's cultural, religious, and political beliefs about illness and health care could conflict with those of the health-care provider (Karimi-Dehkordi, Spiers, & Clark, 2019).

For instance, an ethical situation could occur when a patient's understanding about the cause of an illness and the appropriate treatment differ from a clinician's practice patterns or the recommended evidence-based protocols. Ethical situations often stem from miscommunication, misunderstanding, and low health literacy by a patient or family members. Miscommunication can also occur when a provider does not display respect for the cultural beliefs of patients and their families. Insensitivity on the part of the clinician exacerbates mistrust by patients. For example, a patient or family's etiological explanation for an illness and the appropriate manner of treating it (e.g., indigenous healer, traditional medicine) may be in direct conflict with the professional's treatment approach. Or, the belief that at the end-of-life, an individual should remain in the home surrounded by family, while extended family, friends, and neighbors care for the dying person. First and foremost, the clinician in rural practice should make every effort to understand prevailing community values and then, as much as possible, integrate treatment approaches that are congruent with a community's beliefs and preferences and those of their older patients (Nelson, 2010). Rural-focused academic and clinical experiences could facilitate awareness and promote mutual sensitivity and trust among clinicians and patients. Rural exposure will inform clinicians considering rural practice. Awareness, in turn, can go a long way in preventing an ethical situation from occurring and when and how to intervene early on to prevent the situation from escalating to a bioethical conflict.

Limited Access to Services and Providers

Inherent with low population density in a geographical area is the lack of a critical mass to viably support public and private resources, which can be a factor contributing to an ethical situation. For instance, in the rural context, the lack of a geriatrics service(s) or specialist(s) may demand that a general practitioner or primary care provider perform specialized interventions that are beyond one's expertise and skill level. Or, when a physician is not readily available, a nurse, social worker, or pharmacist becomes the de facto primary care provider. Such occurrences are not uncommon in a community designated as a health professional shortage area (HPSA). Medically underserved communities place significant demands on clinicians who may be forced to provide care outside of their expertise. This reality heightens risk for errors and threatens quality care, all of which can lead to a bioethical event (Bushy, 2020).

Socioeconomic Factors

Socioeconomic factors influence an individual's and family's choice and use of health-care services. An older adult's willingness to accept recommended care may be restricted by economics especially among patients who are uninsured or underinsured. In rural areas, health-care professionals regularly encounter situations in which they must decide whether to provide needed care to a patient with little or no reimbursement; or, when a health professional is aware of the patient's economic situation deciding not to explain all options that might be available to treat this condition. Such actions could jeopardize both the patient's health and the provider's practice reputation in the community. Lack of access to desired services by a patient can be a difficult decision for a clinician and conflict with a patient's expectations of the clinician (Nelson, 2010).

Consider also a patient requesting (demanding) a specific medication or medical intervention he or she recently became aware of through a media advertisement but which the provider does not believe is appropriate for the diagnosis. Since most residents know local health-care providers, such practice decisions can quickly become public knowledge based on word-of-mouth reports by a disgruntled patient or family. Subsequently, should the patient's condition worsen, this could be perceived as neglect or malpractice by the individual or family. In other words, access and allocation of health-care services are contextual factors that should be considered when discussing rural ethical situations.

Clinician Stress and Burnout

Clinicians tend to be held in high esteem by residents in small towns, perhaps especially older adults, but this reality makes it difficult for these professionals to have a life outside of work. A major factor contributing to provider stress and burnout is real or perceived professional isolation. In a small health-care facility, there may not be other health professionals with whom one can readily consult. In medically underserved communities, there may only be one physician or a nurse practitioner in the community. Residents may expect the provider to be on-call 24/7. The provider may not actually be "on duty" at all times; nevertheless, locals expect that the health-care provider will be readily accessible when needed. Consequently, fatigue, burnout, and disrupted personal relationships contribute to stress and professional burnout that can result in miscommunication and unsound decision-making (Bushy, 2020).

Another challenge in underserved areas is clinicians maintaining expertise in certain specialties, for example obstetrics, pediatric care, or psychiatric and behavioral health. While telecommunication can address certain aspects of professional isolation, in some more remote rural settings or in emergency situations, telecommunication technology may not be reliable or available. Accessing continuing education also could be problematic for a rural-based clinician when professional relief is unavailable or technology capability is limited (i.e., limited cellular connections, lack of broadband services). These realities are examples of factors that should be considered in actual or potential rural bioethical situations.

Limited Ethics Resources

It is not unusual for a rural health-care facility to not have access to ethics resources such as an ethics committee much less an in-house ethicist. When a rural hospital is part of a large urban-based health-care system, an ethics committee generally is available in the sponsoring institution. Unfortunately, these urban-based system ethics committees tend to be unaware of the rural context and cultural dynamics. Little information is available on rural bioethics. Thus, it is important that urban-based ethics committees be educated about rural contextual features, including the special issues that may arise when working with older adults, and consider such factors in ethics discussions and decision-making (Nelson, 2010).

Administrators of rural health-care facilities have a responsibility to identify local ethics resources and how to access them; then, disseminate the information to local clinicians. Continuing education programs should be offered to rural providers to inform them about the prevention and early identification of potential ethical situations along with systematic ethical decision-making processes. Consideration can be given to inviting experts from within a health-care system to speak on various ethics topics to local clinicians. Managers should also make printed and electronic reading materials readily available on clinical units that can be readily accessed by staff.

Table 3: Select Rural Bioethics Resources

- Local, regional ethics committees
- Multi-facility/system-wide ethics committee
- Academic medical center's ethics educational programs
- University/college ethics department
- Web-based resources provided by health professional organizations
- Proprietary and commercial continuing education programs

Unfortunately, published materials and evidence focusing on rural bioethics is limited and, in many cases, dated. Table 4 highlights an agenda with major topic areas needed to expand the rural bioethics knowledge base. In turn, this information should be disseminated to inform rural-based as well as urban-based clinicians (Vermont Ethics Network, 2019).

Table 4: Rural Health-Care Ethics Agenda

- Develop a clearer understanding of what constitutes "rural health-care ethics"
- Increase awareness of rural health-care ethics issues and how these differ from ethics events that occur in urban settings
- Understand rural health-care ethics decision-making processes and how these interface with the rural context
- Develop guidelines that address common rural ethical situations
- Develop models for ethics decision-making in small rural health-care facilities
- Provide evidence-based rural ethics perspectives to health-care administrators and policymakers

Finally, living and working as a clinician in a rural community is unique. Most describe the experience as rewarding both personally and professionally. Compared to more populated settings, older rural residents may live further from health-care resources and hold cultural beliefs regarding health, illness, and care-seeking. Health care in a medically underserved community more than likely is provided by a clinician with whom patients are personally acquainted or, perhaps, even related. Rural contextual features such as these often enhance health-care outcomes; however, they can also contribute to bioethical situations encountered by clinicians.

References

Bushy, A. (2006). Nursing in rural and frontier areas: Issues, challenges, and opportunities. *Harvard Health Policy Review*, 7(1), 17–27.

Bushy, A. (2020). Population-centered nursing in rural and urban environments. In M. Stanhope & J. Lancaster (Eds.), *Public health nursing population-centered health care in the community*. St. Louis, MO: Elsevier.

Karimi-Dehkordi, M., Spiers, J., & Clark, A. (2019). An evolutionary concept of analysis of patients' values. *Nursing Outlook*, *67*(5), 523–529.

Nelson, W. (Ed.). (2006). *Handbook for rural healthcare ethics: A practical guide for professionals*. Retrieved October 20, 2019, from https://geiselmed.dartmouth.edu/cfm/resources/ethics/full-book.pdf

Nelson, W. (2010). Health care ethics and rural life. *Health Progress*. Retrieved October 20, 2019, from www.chausa.org/publications/health-progress/article/september-october-2010/health-care-ethics-and-rural-life

Vermont Ethics Network. (2019). *Advancing health care ethics: Rural health care ethics (website)*. Retrieved October 20, 2019, from https://vtethicsnetwork.org/; https://vtethicsnetwork.org/medical-ethics/rural-health-care-ethics

9
BROADBAND SERVICE

Sharon Strover

Geography, Broadband Quality, and Cost

A long-standing gap in broadband service reach and quality exists between metropolitan and rural areas. The national Federal Communications Commission (FCC) standard for what constitutes broadband service as of 2020 is 25 Mbps download and three Mbps upload speed, and approximately 93.5% of Americans have access to fixed broadband at those speeds. However, the deployment is skewed toward urban areas, where 98.3% of the population has access to this quality level of broadband compared to 73.6% of the rural population (FCC, 2019a). Many observers, including FCC commissioners, believe even these statistics inflate actual levels of rural access to broadband and that rural and tribal areas have even lower availability rates (FCC, 2018; Meinrath et al., 2019). Conventionally "fixed broadband" is delivered by some type of wire-based (e.g., cable, fiber, phone lines) connection, in contrast to mobile or "wireless" access, such as what one might have using a mobile phone.

Many consider the FCC's standards modest or even inadequately low for the range of applications now available such as streaming video, but those standards frame what is called "broadband." As a private service generally offered by cable or telecommunications companies, broadband services' historical development across the country illustrates that the more populous and lucrative markets garnered the earliest and most attention from providers; rural areas were generally secondary, and over several years consistently lagged behind metro regions in broadband service availability by at least 10% (Whitacre, Gallardo, & Strover, 2014). Better service quality and more competitive alternative providers are present in more heavily populated regions (FCC, 2019a; Levin & Mattey, 2017). Competition is an important factor in keeping costs lower, and rural regions have less competition (Molnar & Savage, 2017; Mahoney & Rafert, 2016). While some policymakers argue that mobile access (such as through one's smartphone) is an adequate substitute for fixed service even though its bandwidth is more limited, many disagree (FCC, 2019a).

What do deployment, service quality, and cost statistics mean for a rural aging population? In rural areas, 17.5% of the population is over 65 years of age compared to 13.8% in urban areas (Smith & Trevelyan, 2019), and rural regions lead urban regions in the proportion of individuals 85 years and over who call it their home. Together with broadband deployment statistics, this means that older rural populations have less access to broadband. For those rural dwellers who do use the internet, the service quality is likely to be less reliable and slower. With fewer competing providers in rural areas, costs are likely to be somewhat higher than in metro areas.

Census statistics confirm that individuals 65 and older use broadband services less frequently: 63.1% of that group used the internet at any location in 2018 compared to a national average of 77.7% (NTIA, 2018). Indeed, age has been a powerful factor in predicting "digital divides" since the introduction of computers. Older Americans indicate they "don't need" or are "not interested" in going online at home more frequently than any other age group (71.5% of unconnected older Americans say this).

Mobile technology use such as smartphones, laptops, and tablets grew generally in the 2010–2020 decade among all age groups, and by 2017 more households had mobile data plans than had wired broadband services (Redl, 2018). Older and rural populations use mobile technologies less often, underscoring their reduced use of the internet more generally. Pew Research (2019) reports that among people 65 and older, 49% used an internet-enabled mobile device as of 2017 compared to a national average of 64%. Another 2019 Pew survey confirms those rural and age-related figures that underscore lower mobile internet use: rurally based individuals have lower smartphone use rates compared to urban individuals, 71% compared to 83%, and 53% of people 65 and older had a smartphone (Pew Research, 2019).

Digital Literacy and the Older Rural Population

Another important factor associated with rural aging and broadband access and use is digital literacy. The older population reports consistently lower levels of digital literacy, often defined as capability or comfort with computer technology, compared to other age groups. Older adults, particularly those who have spent their lives in rural regions and who did not grow up with computers, typically have not had a great deal of exposure to digital technologies, contributing to a "second order" digital divide characterized by limited self-efficacy and technical skills (Martin, 2019). Some even report feeling they are "too old to learn" (Pew Research, 2017). Lower levels of digital skills also are related to education and income, and again, age may interact with both of these factors.

In 2017, one-third of adults 65 and older reported they never use the internet. Among older adults, those closer to 65 are far more likely to go online compared to people 80 and older (Pew Research, 2017). That said, older adults who do use the internet tend to use it frequently (Pew Research, 2017). The mean age of people who say they do not use the internet because they have "neither need nor interest" is 62.8 years (NTIA, 2019), while the mean age of people saying they do not use the internet because it is "too expensive" is 48.7 years. Older adults face barriers to technology that include costs and poor design (such as small buttons or complicated interfaces), and they often possess negative attitudes about the utility of broadband and low assessments of their competence (Delello & and McWhorter, 2015; Horrigan, 2010).

Being older appears to be compounded by rural location when it comes to lower levels of internet usage as well as having devices such as smartphones capable of accessing the internet. Affordability may also be a factor. The Census reports that rural householders age 65 and over have lower incomes compared to their counterparts in urban areas (Bishaw & Posey, 2016). Hence, the cost of internet services could explain why older rural dwellers choose not to have broadband access through smartphones or home connections. However, when older individuals do use the internet, they frequently find their experiences rewarding and useful, suggesting that more attention to cultivating digital literacy among older adults is one strategy for enabling rural older citizens to make greater use of online resources.

Broadband and Services for Aging Populations

Broadband internet may provide strategies for remediating loneliness, social isolation, medical problems, unemployment, and educational needs in rural areas. Highlighting rural-specific, age-related issues, the U.S. Department of Agriculture observes that

> travel time by car is 28% longer (74 minutes) for older-age persistent population-loss [rural] counties. These population and spatial differences affect socioeconomic conditions and come with policy implications for programs serving the needs of older populations. Transportation, healthcare, retail, and other needed services are generally harder to access and maintain in more sparsely settled, remote regions where persistent population-loss counties are concentrated.
>
> (USDA, 2018, 6)

Each of these services can be made more readily available by broadband internet if connectivity is available and affordable, and if the older population in these regions is willing to use the relevant technology. Even in rural areas that are not losing population, these same broadband-based amenities can positively affect the lives of older residents.

Health Services and Broadband

Health needs for older residents in rural areas are growing alongside the presence of increasingly older populations. Rurally based health services already are challenged by cost issues. For example, many rural hospitals have either shrunk or closed—over 100 have closed between 2010 and 2019 (Ramesh & Gee, 2019). Compounding limited medical services, simply getting to a rural physical location for medical services may be challenging during times of poor weather or when gasoline prices spike. Simultaneously, rural populations in general reflect higher rates of obesity, mental health issues, diabetes, cancer, and opioid addiction, and most of these conditions are exacerbated among older populations (Fernandez, 2019). Finally, many older people want to "age-in-place," and they require the social and medical support to do so. Broadband connectivity can increase an individual's ability to remain in their home.

Telehealth or "connected care" facilities can address health conditions including heart conditions, opioid dependency, stroke, mental health needs, and diabetes, among others (FCC, 2019b). The FCC has piloted several Connected Care programs specifically to bring broadband-mediated care, often to rural populations out of easy reach of medical facilities. Services can include remote diagnoses, medical checks, and monitoring conditions such as diabetes or even mental health. A handful of states similarly are improving local rural broadband to connect rural locations to medical service providers (Clyburn, 2019), aiding populations of all ages.

Broadband services can be effective not only in improving doctor-patient care but also in launching campaigns and programs to improve health or disseminate health information. While older and rurally based populations might be less digitally connected overall, targeted broadband-based campaigns and medical services can bring much-needed information, support, and actual clinical care to regions where the conventional medical infrastructure is limited. Seeking health-related information is one of the most popular uses of the internet among older adults, and online users report that going online allows them to remain independent later in life (Seifert & Schelling, 2018).

Continuing Education and Work

While some believe that being 65 and older means an end to work and to education, this is not the case. Approximately 11% of the workforce is over 65 years of age (SHRM, 2018), and many older workers live in rural regions. One-fourth of the 2026 workforce will be over 55 years of age (U.S. Congress, 2017), which will necessitate a response to retirement needs, increased longevity, and burdensome housing and medical costs. While rural areas are not generally technology hubs, employment trends in America predict an aging workforce. Many of those jobs and workers will be in rural regions (Humphries, 2019), underscoring the significance of both digital literacy and broadband deployment. Older adults who work in rural communities likely will have to rely on broadband and digital technologies for re-skilling, underscoring their need for sound digital literacy.

Social Support and Connections in an Internet Age

Rural regions have a smaller share of social services compared to suburban and urban communities and need robust social support systems, given their aging populations. That said, rural regions reflect communities in which people historically have displayed significant measures of social capital based on face-to-face interpersonal contacts. Internet connectivity can help regions that are losing population and build interpersonal connections across generations and distances by facilitating the maintenance of existing social ties and creating opportunities to forge new ones.

Internet connectivity has been shown to provide various sources of support for older, rural-based adults by enabling people to more easily and cheaply stay in touch with family and friends, access relevant information, and more easily obtain the goods and services they desire. For example, Chopik (2016) and Gilbert, Karahalios, and Sandvig (2010) demonstrated that broadband-based services can facilitate interpersonal relationships for older adults and improve psychological health.

Suggestion for Further Reading

Humphries, B. (2019). *Demand for broadband in rural areas: Implications for universal access*. Congressional Research Service, R46108. Washington, DC: CRS Report. Retrieved from https://crsreports.congress.gov/product/pdf/R/R46108

References

Bishaw, A., & Posey, K. (2016, December 8). *A comparison of rural and urban America: Household income and poverty*. Washington, DC: U.S. Census Bureau. Retrieved from www.census.gov/newsroom/blogs/random-samplings/2016/12/a_comparison_of_rura.html

Chopik, W. (2016). The benefits of social technology use among older adults are mediated by reduced loneliness. *Cyberpsychology, Behavior and Social Networking*, *19*(9), 551–556. doi:10.1089/cyber.2016.0151. Retrieved from www.ncbi.nlm.nih.gov/pmc/articles/PMC5312603

Clyburn, M. (2019, October 16). *Engagement on equity: Connectivity and the future of healthcare*. Benton Institute for Broadband and Society, Digital Beat. Retrieved from www.benton.org/blog/engagement-equity-connectivity-and-future-healthcare

Delello, J., & McWhorter, R. (2015). Reducing the digital divide: Connecting older adults to iPad technology. *Journal of Applied Gerontology*, *36*(1), 3–28. doi:10.1177/0733464815589985

FCC. (2018). *Dissenting statement of Commissioner Mignon Clyburn*. 2018 Broadband Deployment Report. Washington, DC: Federal Communications Commission, 82–83. Retrieved from https://www.fcc.gov/reports-research/reports/broadband-progress-reports/2018-broadband-deployment-report

FCC. (2019a). *2019 Broadband deployment report.* Washington, DC: Federal Communications Commission. Retrieved from www.fcc.gov/reports-research/reports/broadband-progress-reports/2019-broadband-deployment-report

FCC. (2019b). *Notice of proposed rulemaking in the matter of promoting telehealth for low-income consumers.* WC Docket No. 18–213. Washington, DC: Federal Communications Commission. Retrieved from https://docs.fcc.gov/public/attachments/FCC-19-64A1.pdf

Fernandez, M. (2019, December 4). The urban-rural health divide is costing lives. *Axios.* Retrieved from www.axios.com/rural-america-leading-causes-death-ec78d7bb-5d7f-4530-80fa-a761de5e2969.html

Gilbert, E., Karahalios, K., & Sandvig, C. (2010). The network in the garden: Designing social media for rural life. *American Behavioral Scientist, 53*(9), 1367–1388. doi:10.1177/0002764210361690

Horrigan, J. (2010). *Broadband adoption and use in America.* OBI Working Paper Series No. 1. Washington, DC: Federal Communications Commission. Retrieved from https://transition.fcc.gov/national-broadband-plan/broadband-adoption-in-america-paper.pdf

Humphries, B. (2019). *Demand for broadband in rural areas: Implications for universal access.* Congressional Research Service, R46108. Washington, DC: CRS Report. Retrieved from https://crsreports.congress.gov/product/pdf/R/R46108

Levin, B., & Mattey, C. (2017). *In infrastructure plan, a big opening for rural broadband.* Washington, DC: Brookings Institution. Retrieved from www.brookings.edu/blog/the-avenue/2017/02/13/in-infrastructure-plan-a-big-opening-for-rural-broadband/

Mahoney, D., & Rafert, G. (2016, November). Broadband competition helps to drive lower prices and faster download speeds for U.S. residential consumers. *Analysis Group Whitepaper,* 21–22, 24. Retrieved from www.analysisgroup.com/globalassets/content/insights/publishing/broadband_competition_report_november_2016.pdf

Martin, M. (2019). *Deconstructing the digital divide: Identifying the supply and demand factors that drive internet subscription rates.* SEHSD Working Paper Number 2019–15. Washington, DC: US Census Bureau. Retrieved from www.census.gov/content/dam/Census/library/working-papers/2019/demo/sehsd-wp2019-15.pdf.

Meinrath, S., Bonestroo, H., Bullen, G., Jansen, A., Mansour, S., Mitchell, C., Ritzo, C., & Thieme, N. (2019). *Broadband availability and access in rural Pennsylvania.* College Park, PA: The Center for Rural Pennsylvania. Retrieved from www.rural.palegislature.us/broadband/Broadband_Availability_and_Access_in_Rural_Pennsylvania_2019_Report.pdf

Molnar, G., & Savage, S. (2017). Market structure and broadband internet quality. *The Journal of Industrial Economics, 65*(1), 101. doi:10.1111/joie.12106

National Telecommunications and Information Administration. (2018). *Digital nation data explorer.* Washington, DC: NTIA. Retrieved from www.ntia.doc.gov/data/digital-nation-data-explorer#sel=internetUser&demo=age&pc=prop&disp=chart

National Telecommunications and Information Administration. (2019). *Unplugged: NTIA survey finds some Americans still avoid home internet use.* Washington, DC: NTIA. Retrieved from www.ntia.doc.gov/blog/2019/unplugged-ntia-survey-finds-some-americans-still-avoid-home-internet-use

Pew Research. (2017, May 17). *Tech adoption climbs among older adults.* Pew Research Center Internet & Technology. Retrieved from www.pewresearch.org/internet/2017/05/17/tech-adoption-climbs-among-older-adults/

Pew Research. (2019, June 12). *Mobile fact sheet.* Pew Research Center. Retrieved from www.pewresearch.org/internet/fact-sheet/mobile/

Ramesh, T., & Gee, E. (2019, September 9). *Rural hospital closures reduce access to emergency care.* Center for American Progress. Retrieved from www.americanprogress.org/issues/healthcare/reports/2019/09/09/474001/rural-hospital-closures-reduce-access-emergency-care/

Redl, D. (2018). *New data show substantial gains and evolution in internet use.* NTIA. Retrieved from www.ntia.gov/blog/2018/new-data-show-substantial-gains-and-evolution-internet-use

Seifert, A., & Schelling, H. (2018). Seniors online: Attitudes toward the internet and coping with everyday life. *Journal of Applied Gerontology, 37*(1), 99–109. doi:10.1177/0733464816669805. Retrieved from https://journals.sagepub.com/doi/full/10.1177/0733464816669805

SHRM. (2018). *Number of older Americans at work has grown 35 percent.* Retrieved from www.shrm.org/resourcesandtools/hr-topics/employee-relations/pages/older-workers-.aspx

Smith, A., & Trevelyan, C. (2019, September). *The older population in rural America: 2012–2016.* American Community Survey Reports, U.S. Census Bureau. Retrieved from www.census.gov/content/dam/Census/library/publications/2019/acs/acs-41.pdf

U.S. Congress. (2017). *America's aging workforce: Opportunities and challenges: A report of the Senate Special Committee on Aging*. Washington, DC: U.S. Government Publishing Office. Retrieved from www.congress.gov/115/crpt/srpt191/CRPT-115srpt191.pdf

USDA. (2018). *Rural America at a glance, 2018 edition*. USDA. Retrieved from www.ers.usda.gov/webdocs/publications/90556/eib-200.pdf

Whitacre, B., Gallardo, R., & Strover, S. (2014). Broadband's contribution to economic growth in rural areas: Moving towards a causal relationship. *Telecommunications Policy*, *38*(11), 1011–1023. doi:10.1016/j.telpol.2014.05.005

10
CAREGIVERS

Lenard W. Kaye

The Prevalence of Informal, Family Caregiving

The majority of long-term care of older adults in the U.S., whether in small towns or in the largest of cities, has been, and probably always will be, provided by family, friends, and neighbors. Often considered the backbone of long-term care services and supports, informal or family caregivers represent some 65% of the exclusive care provided to older adults in need of assistance. Another 30% of older adults in need of assistance receive some combination of family care and care delivered by paid providers.

Family caregivers are individuals usually unpaid for the services they provide. Those services can include an exceedingly wide range of supports provided including, most commonly, assistance with various instrumental activities of daily living (IADLs) and, to a lesser degree, activities of daily living (ADLs). Caregiver assistance with IADLs can include meals preparation, housekeeping, giving medicines, arranging outside services, managing money, shopping, and transportation. The provision of support with ADLs includes help with walking, getting in and out of bed or a chair, dressing, bathing, toileting, feeding, and dealing with incontinence.

Approximately every five years, a nationally representative, probability-based, trended research series focused on family caregivers in the U.S. is conducted. The *Caregiving in the U.S.* studies represent one of the most comprehensive resources profiling the American caregiver. A comparison of informal caregiver prevalence rates in 2015 and 2020 confirms that adults continue to step up and provide care to family and friends 50 years of age and older when it is needed. In fact, those rates increased from 14.3% (34.2 million caregivers) to 16.8% (41.8 million caregivers) over that five-year period. In 2017, family caregivers across the U.S. provided some 34 billion hours of care with an estimated economic value of $470 billion (based on an average of 16 hours of care provided per week, at an average value of $13.81 per hour) (Reinhard, Feinberg, Houser, Choula, & Evans, 2019). If caregivers of family and friends of all ages are considered, more than one in five Americans (21.3% or 53 million adults) are providing care for someone with health and functional needs, having increased from 43.5 million caregivers in 2015 (AARP & National Alliance for Caregiving, 2020).

Five-year comparisons from 2015 to 2020 serve to further confirm greater proportions of caregivers of adults are helping more than one person (18% in 2015 and 24% in 2020) and are experiencing greater difficulty coordinating the care they provide (19% in 2015 and 26% in

2020). In terms of their demographic profile, caregivers span generations, racial/ethnic groups, income and educational levels, gender identities, and sexual orientations. However, the majority are caregivers caring for a relative (89%) (usually a parent or parent-in-law followed by a spouse or partner, a friend or neighbor, a grandparent or grandparent-in-law, or an adult child), and are white (61%, compared to 17% Hispanic or Latino, 14% African American, and 5% Asian American and Pacific Islander). Eight percent identify as LGBTQ. Sixty-one percent are women and 39% are men. Data also indicate that caregivers are increasingly helping adults with more complex, comorbid, health, and functional needs, including (most commonly) long-term physical conditions; mental health issues; and memory issues, such as Alzheimer's disease and dementia. Caregivers providing help for someone with Alzheimer's disease or dementia increased from 22% to 26% over the five-year period. And caregivers indicating their own health to be only fair to poor also increased during this period from 17% to 21%. An average of 24 hours of care is provided weekly by American caregivers, and 61% hold down jobs in addition to their caregiving responsibilities (AARP & National Alliance for Caregiving, 2020).

The Impact of Caregiving on Caregivers

Repeatedly, population-based studies indicate that many family caregivers evidence little strain associated with providing caregiving assistance (American Psychological Association, 2015). In fact, many caregivers report that the experience is rewarding and that they derive considerable satisfaction and experience personal growth from performing the tasks associated with helping someone else. It is seen as a positive experience and an opportunity to give back or reciprocate for the caring and support that they have previously received from a parent, spouse, or significant other. Even so, there is substantial evidence that confirms caregivers have higher levels of depression, anxiety, and other health problems compared to non-caregivers. Especially at risk of feeling burdened and stressed are individuals providing care at a distance, living more than an hour away from the care recipient (called long-distance caregivers) (National Alliance for Caregiving & AARP, 2020); those providing more hours of care (Family Caregiving Alliance, 2019); female caregivers (Office of Women's Health, U.S. DHHS, 2020; National Partnership for Women & Families, 2018); Hispanic and African American caregivers (Family Caregiving Alliance, 2019); those caring for individuals with Alzheimer's or other dementias (Alzheimer's Association, n.d.); and employed caregivers (Family Caregiver Alliance, 2016). And, research by the Rosalynn Carter Institute for Caregiving (2020) on the impact of the COVID-19 pandemic has documented that 83% of caregivers surveyed reported increased stress related to caregiving since the start of the COVID-19 pandemic, with 42% reporting that the number of other caregivers available to help them has declined during the pandemic. This research also confirmed that isolation, increased burden resulting from additional caregiving and household responsibilities, and worry about getting infected or a family member becoming infected with COVID-19 were major sources of stress. Financial concerns, instability, and resource insecurity were also highlighted as notable factors contributing to caregiver stress.

Caregiving Is Challenging, Especially in Rural America

Family caregiving is challenging no matter where it is carried out. However, research suggests that it can be particularly difficult in rural communities. One of the earlier surveys of caregiving in rural communities (Easter Seals Disability Services & National Alliance for Caregiving, 2004) identified no fewer than seven factors that create challenges for families and friends who assume caregiving responsibilities in rural areas of the U.S.: 1. the scarcity of services and limited use of services that do exist; 2. the impact caregiving has on rural workplaces; 3. the financial burden that rural caregiving places on low-income individuals; 4. the stress, burden, and difficulties coping that rural caregiving creates; 5. limitations in the availability and use of broadband and the internet; 6. the greater prevalence of work-related disability and chronic illness in the rural U.S.; and 7. the increasing numbers of veterans residing in rural areas in need of care. The out-migration of younger and middle-aged adults from rural communities also has likely placed greater strain on meeting the needs of older adults without available caregivers as have the lower marriage and birth rates generally, both of which are expected to lead to a smaller pool of available caregivers over time.

Profiling the Rural Caregiver

The average rural caregiver is a non-Hispanic, white, 48.8-year-old woman. She is likely caring for a 66.9-year-old parent or parent-in-law, providing 26.3 hours of care weekly and has been doing it for 4.2 years on average (AARP & National Alliance for Caregiving, 2020).

Current research strongly suggests that the special challenges faced by rural caregivers remain present and may even be increasing. Caregivers in rural communities are reporting sharper increases in relatives and friends with comorbid conditions over the last five years (an increase from 38% to 51%) compared to urban caregivers (an increase from 37% to 43%). Unlike caregivers in cities, caregivers in rural communities are more likely performing a wider range of helping tasks and are increasingly finding themselves to be the primary caregivers (the sole caregiver or the one providing the majority of assistance). For example, rural caregivers report providing help more frequently with medical and nursing tasks than their urban counterparts. Rural caregivers, unlike those in urban settings, are also increasingly assuming the role of advocate (60%) (especially women and those caring for the very old and lower income) and performing monitoring functions (70%) in terms of their relative or friend's condition to adjust care as needed. Furthermore, caregivers who live in rural areas more often care for multiple people (34% vs. 23% of caregivers who live in a suburban or urban area). And caregivers in rural areas are more often reporting that they had no choice in taking on care and also find the help they provide more difficult. Rural caregivers are more likely to report difficulty finding affordable services such as meal delivery, in-home health care, and transportation than urban caregivers (32% compared to 25%). Furthermore, while they are typically working in an hourly job in addition to performing their caregiving duties, they are more likely than urban caregivers to report financial strain resulting in delaying plans for saving, assuming more debt, not paying bills or doing so after they are due, and borrowing money from family and friends. They are less likely to have health insurance and more likely to have trouble managing their own health than urban caregivers (AARP & National Alliance for Caregiving, 2020).

It is also concerning that rural caregivers, more recently, are reporting having decreasing numbers of conversations with care providers about their own needs, including especially those who are primary, lower-income, and less educated caregivers. Rural caregivers, as well, go less often online to organize care activities and rarely use ride-share services (2% compared to 11% urban) (AARP & National Alliance for Caregiving, 2020; National Alliance for Caregiving & AARP, 2020). Equally worrisome is that only one in two rural caregivers (51%) have been found to use any community-based services (Buckwalter & Davis, 2011).

Rural Caregiving, COVID-19, and the Risk of Social Isolation

Even before the novel coronavirus outbreak in 2020, older adults were found to be living more isolated lives than ever before with as many as 43% of adults 60 years of age and older in the

U.S. reporting feeling lonely. The negative consequences of isolation and loneliness, especially for older adults, are not to be taken lightly. Isolated and lonely older adults exhibit significantly higher illness and death rates than the general population. There is a well-documented risk of caregivers of older adults becoming socially disconnected as well. COVID-19 has served to increase the threat of social isolation and loneliness for older adults sheltering-in-place and their caregivers, perhaps especially in rural communities. Rural caregivers can feel discouraged, stressed, and isolated by the time demands and intensity of their caregiving tasks, which, in turn, can lead to physical health problems and depression. These problems tend to increase in remote areas where transportation services and services support are more scarce, which exacerbate feelings of social and geographic isolation (McMaster University, 2020). Caregivers of the chronically ill and physically isolated older adults may be at particular risk of becoming socially isolated (Sun, Finkelstein, & Ouchida, 2019).

Future Needs and Recommendations

The National Advisory Committee on Rural Health and Human Services (NACRHHS) has issued the following recommendations in support of rural caregiving: 1. creating a comprehensive resource on aging and long-term services available to rural-residing older adults; 2. expanding flexibility in Medicare telehealth billing and providing a comprehensive resource of rural telehealth services; 3. promoting the establishment of rural age-friendly health systems; and 4. exploring the entry of Medicare Advantage Dual-Eligible Special Needs Plans into rural areas (NACRHHS, 2019).

The most successful rural caregiver assistance programs appear to be those that are developed with the strong support of community stakeholders, are planned in close partnership with caregivers themselves, employ individuals from or very familiar with the cultural and social traditions of the communities that are served, and reflect a balance of personal face-to-face services and supports in combination with available technology that ensures effective information sharing and communication (Buckwalter & Davis, 2011).

Key informant research conducted by Henning-Smith and Lahr (2018a) suggests several policy strategies for supporting rural caregivers including 1. increasing the funding of Medicaid services for families, paying caregivers for the help they provide, and making health care and housing more affordable in rural communities; 2. developing a national strategy for responding to their needs; and 3. expanding access to resources including in-home care and assistance, providing caregiver training to increase their confidence, preparation and comfort in performing needed tasks, and expanding access to broadband internet and remote technologies in the home. Henning-Smith and Lahr (2018b) also offer helpful resources for caregiving in rural communities. It is notable that in the National Alliance for Caregiving and AARP (2020) survey of caregiving in America, rural caregivers more frequently indicated that they would prefer programs that pay them directly for some of their time and effort as compared to urban-based caregivers. Also recommended is increased attention directed to the importance of social connectedness for both caregivers and their care recipients as a public health priority in all communities, but in rural areas especially.

References

AARP & National Alliance for Caregiving. (2020, May). *Caregiving in the United States 2020.* Washington, DC: AARP. doi:10.26419/ppi.00103.001

Alzheimer's Association. (n.d.) *Caregiver stress.* Retrieved from www.alz.org/help-support/caregiving/caregiver-health/caregiver-stress

American Psychological Association. (2015, February). *Mental and physical health effects of family caregiving.* Retrieved from www.apa.org/pi/about/publications/caregivers/faq/health-effects

Buckwalter, K. C., & Davis, L. L. (2011). Elder caregiving in rural communities. In R. C. Talley, K. Chwalisz, & K. C. Buckwalter (Eds.), *Rural caregiving in the United States: Research, practice, policy* (pp. 33–46). Cham, Switzerland: Springer Nature. doi:10.1007/978-1-4614-0302-9_3

Easter Seals Disability Services & National Alliance for Caregiving. (2004). *Caregiving in rural America.* Retrieved from www.caregiving.org/wp-content/uploads/2020/05/Easter-Seals_NAC_Caregiving_in_Rural.pdf#page=4

Family Caregiver Alliance. (2016). *Caregiver statistics: Work and caregiving.* Retrieved from www.caregiver.org/caregiver-statistics-work-and-caregiving

Family Caregiver Alliance. (2019, April 17). *Caregiver statistics: Demographics.* San Francisco, CA: Family Caregiver Alliance.

Henning-Smith, C., & Lahr, M. (2018a, August). *Perspectives on rural caregiving: Challenges and interventions.* Policy brief. Retrieved from https://3pea7g1qp8f3t9ooe3z3npx1-wpengine.netdna-ssl.com/wp-content/uploads/2019/01/1535633283UMNpolicybriefcaregivingchallenges.pdf

Henning-Smith, C., & Lahr, M. (2018b, August). *Resources for caregiving in rural communities: Policy brief.* Retrieved from https://3pea7g1qp8f3t9ooe3z3npx1-wpengine.netdna-ssl.com/wp-content/uploads/2019/01/1535129489UMNpolicybriefcaregivingresources.pdf

McMaster University. (2020, January 15). *Isolation and remoteness: Supporting family caregivers in hard-to-reach communities.* Hamilton, ON: McMaster Optimal Aging Portal.

National Advisory Committee on Rural Health and Human Services. (2019, August). *Supportive services and caregiving for older rural adults: Policy brief and recommendations to the secretary.* Retrieved from www.hrsa.gov/sites/default/files/hrsa/advisory-committees/rural/publications/2019-Older-Adults.pdf

National Alliance for Caregiving & AARP. (2020, May). *The "typical" caregiver of a care recipient living in a rural area: Fact sheet.* Unpublished document. doi:10.26419/ppi.00103.015

National Partnership for Women & Families. (2018, November). *The female face of family caregiving: Fact sheet.* Washington, DC: National Partnership for Women & Families.

Office of Women's Health, U.S. DHHS. (2020, June 3). *Caregiver stress.* Retrieved from www.womenshealth.gov/a-z-topics/caregiver-stress

Reinhard, S. R., Feinberg, L. F., Houser, A., Choula, R., & Evans, M. (2019, November). *Valuing the invaluable: Charting a path forward: Insight on the issues.* Washington, DC: AARP Public Policy Institute.

Rosalynn Carter Institute for Caregiving. (2020, October). *Caregivers in crisis: Caregiving in the time of COVID-19.* Americus, GA: Rosalynn Carter Ibstitute for Caregiving.

Sun, A. Y., Finkelstein, E., & Ouchida, K. (2019). Social isolation, loneliness and caregiver burden among paid and unpaid caregivers of homebound older adults. *Innovation in Aging, 3*(Suppl. 1), S967. doi:10.1093/geroni/igz038.3505

11
CHRONIC DISEASE

Shinduk Lee and Matthew Lee Smith

Chronic Disease in Aging Society

Approximately three-in-four deaths in the U.S. occur among older adults ages 65 years and older (Meit et al., 2014), and the top five causes of death among older Americans are chronic diseases (NCHS, 2018; Heron, 2019). Heart disease accounts for over 25% of all deaths among older adults, followed by cancer (20.7%), chronic lower respiratory disease (6.6%), stroke (6.1%), and Alzheimer's disease (5.8%) (Heron, 2019). These mortality statistics highlight only one aspect of the chronic disease burden among the aging population. Chronic disease imposes a burden on individuals, their interpersonal networks, and society by increasing risk for poor quality of life, disability, and health complications, all of which are associated with increased financial costs. The prevalence, mortality, determinants, prevention, and management of chronic conditions in rural communities are explored here.

Prevalence of Chronic Diseases in Rural Aging Communities

The 2018 Behavioral Risk Factor Surveillance System (BRFSS) data were used to estimate the age-specific prevalence of common chronic conditions (e.g., arthritis, cancer, cardiovascular disease, kidney disease, chronic obstructive pulmonary disease (COPD), and diabetes) in rural and non-rural areas (CDC, 2018a). In both rural and non-rural areas, the chronic disease prevalence increased with chronological age (Figure 11.1).

The most prevalent chronic condition among older adults in both rural and non-rural areas was arthritis (55.5% in rural and 53.3% in non-rural areas), followed by cancer (30.9% and 31.8%), diabetes (24.9% and 23.8%), cardiovascular disease (27% and 22.2%), COPD (15.6% and 13.3%), and kidney disease (7% and 7%). Older adults in rural areas were more likely to have arthritis, cardiovascular disease, and COPD than those in non-rural areas. This corroborates previous studies that have also reported a higher prevalence of arthritis (Boring et al., 2017), cardiovascular disease (Towne et al., 2019), and COPD (Croft et al., 2018) in rural areas compared to non-rural areas. These studies focused on the overall adult population and did not specifically examine rural-urban differences by age groups or focus on older adults.

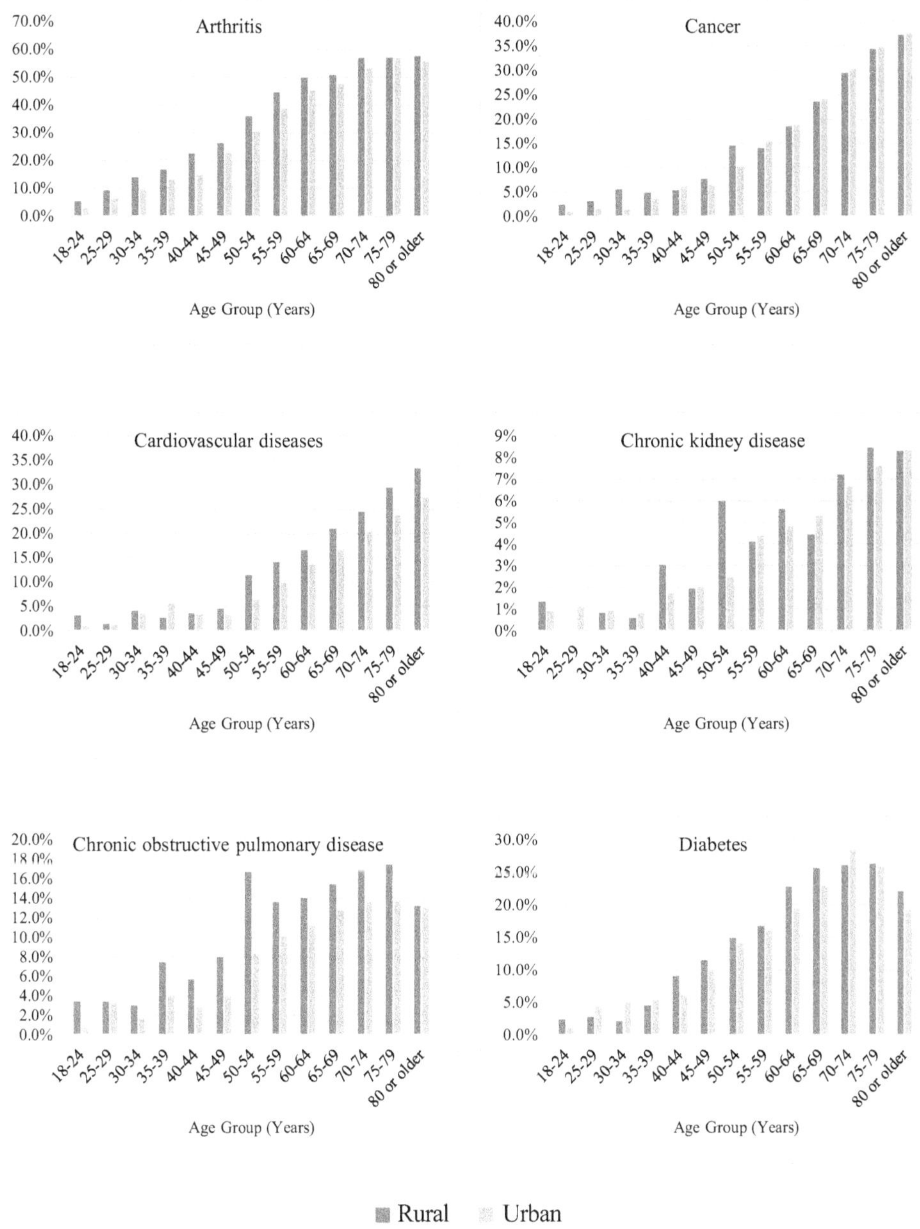

Figure 11.1 Prevalence of Chronic Diseases by Age and Rurality

Data source: 2018 Behavioral Risk Factor Surveillance System (BRFSS)

Chronic Disease Burden in Rural Communities

The Healthy People 2020 Initiative's objectives include the reduction of deaths from chronic conditions. Since the baseline year of 2007, the reduction in overall age-adjusted death rates was observed for all these chronic diseases (U.S. Department of Health and Human Services (HHS) & Office of Disease Prevention and Health Promotion (ODPHP), 2019). While the changes are in the desirable direction, chronic disease death rates are still disproportionately higher among older adults when compared to younger persons. For example, the overall age-adjusted cancer death rate among older adults was 1,030.3 per 100,000 persons in 2007 (i.e., baseline year) and decreased by over 18% to 841.3 per 100,000 persons in 2017 (HHS & ODPHP, 2019). Yet, the overall age-adjusted cancer death rate among older adults remained higher compared to their younger counterparts. Age-adjusted cancer death rates among adults ages 45–64 years decreased by almost 8% from 199 per 100,000 persons in 2007 to 183.5 per 100,000 persons in 2017. Age-adjusted cancer death rates among adults ages 18–45 years also decreased by almost 18% from 2007 to 13.3 per 100,000 persons in 2017 (HHS & ODPHP, 2019).

The 2014 Rural-Urban Chartbook, published by the Center for Rural Health, shows that the death rates for older adults tend to increase with rurality (Meit et al., 2014). A review of 1999–2014 mortality data found higher age-adjusted death rates and greater percentages of excess deaths from chronic diseases in rural areas compared to non-rural areas (Moy et al., 2017). In another study using cancer incidence and mortality data from 2004–2015, average annual age-adjusted cancer-related death rates were higher in rural counties than non-rural counties despite lower average annual age-adjusted cancer incidence rates in rural areas (Henley et al., 2017).

Figure 11.2 shows crude death rates from cancer, cardiovascular disease, chronic lower respiratory disease (CLRD), and diabetes between 2013 and 2017 by age groups and rurality. Overall, chronic disease-related crude death rates among older adults were higher in rural areas compared to non-rural areas. For example, the average crude CLRD death rates for older adults at ages 65–74 years were 131.0 per 100,000 persons in non-rural areas and 192.1 per 100,000 persons in rural areas (CDC, 2018b). The absolute differences in crude CLRD death rates between rural and non-rural areas were 104.4 deaths per 100,000 older adults at ages 75–84 years and 105.8 deaths per 100,000 older adults at ages 85 years and older.

Other than those associated with mortality, chronic disease burdens also include higher rates of chronic disease complications and worse quality of life. For example, of the over one million cases of diabetic foot ulcers that presented in emergency departments between 2006 and 2010, rural patients had a higher likelihood of having major or minor amputations or inpatient deaths relative to their urban counterparts (Skrepnek, Mills, & Armstrong, 2015). In another study using the 2015 BRFSS, Boring and his colleagues (2017) reported higher rates of arthritis-attributable activity limitation in rural areas than in non-rural areas.

Risk Factors and Prevention of Chronic Diseases in Rural Communities

There often are multiple underlying causes leading to the onset and progress of chronic diseases. Common predictors of chronic disease include low socioeconomic status and risky behaviors (e.g., tobacco use, unhealthy diet, insufficient physical activity levels, and excessive alcohol consumption) (CDC, 2019; WHO, 2019). Rural residents have higher rates of alcohol consumption, obesity, and insufficient physical activity levels than their non-rural counterparts (Matthews et al., 2017). Moreover, about 13% of rural residents reported being food

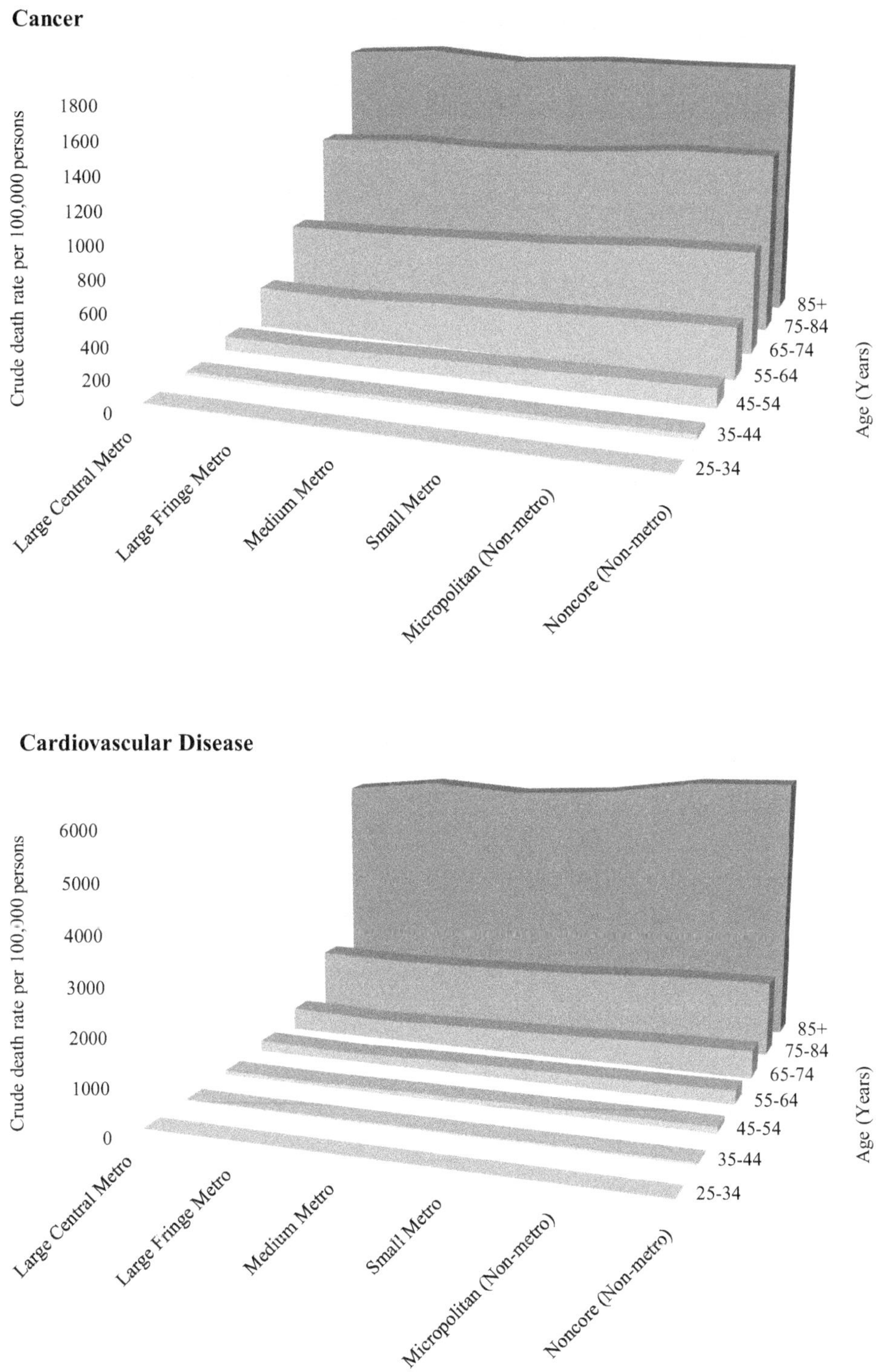

Figure 11.2 Chronic Disease-Related Death Rates

Data source: Centers for Disease Control and Prevention WONDER

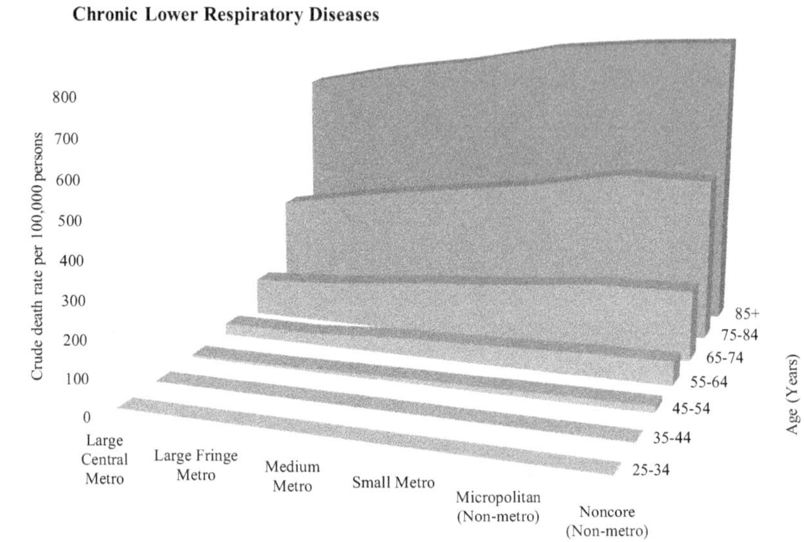

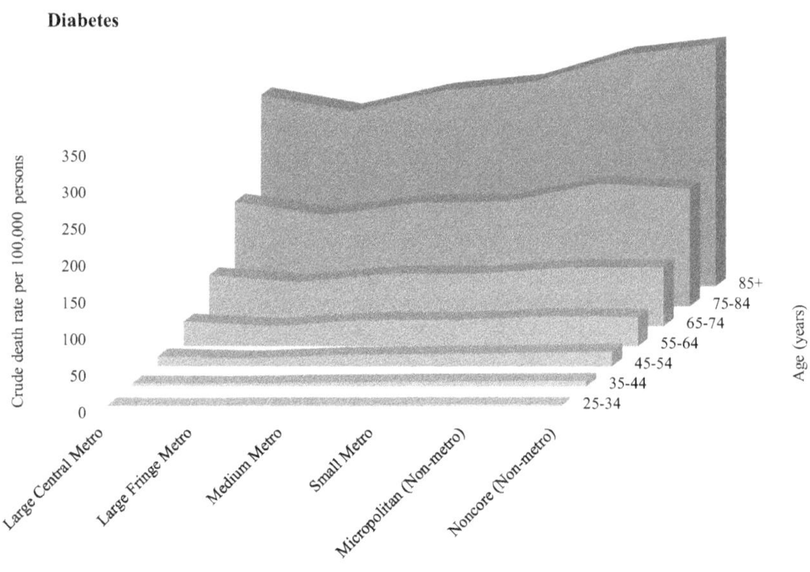

Figure 11.2 (Continued)

insecure (Coleman-Jensen, Rabbitt, Gregory, & Singh, 2018), which is associated with poorer diet quality and higher rates of chronic conditions (Ziliak & Gundersen, 2017). Analyses of cancer registry data indicated that while overall cancer incidence rates were higher among non-rural populations compared to rural populations, incidence rates of tobacco- and human papillomavirus-associated, and lung and bronchus, cervical, and colon cancer were often higher among rural populations than among non-rural populations (Zahnd et al., 2018). This study highlights that cancer incidence rates in rural areas can be largely influenced by healthier lifestyles and preventive care (e.g., cancer screening).

Limited access to health care in rural areas is an important risk factor in the chronic disease prevention and management in rural communities because it adversely influences rural residents' chronic disease screening and clinical care for their chronic conditions. Weisgrau (1995) described the challenges faced by rural health-care facilities as low population volume, low profitability, and shortages of health professionals. Unfortunately, many rural health-care facilities still face similar issues. Almost two-in-three primary care health professional shortage areas (HPSA) are located in rural areas (HRSA, 2019), and rural hospital closures remain a persistent public health concern (Kaufman et al., 2016). While Critical Access Hospitals (CAHs) were introduced in 1997 to enhance rural health services (Rural Health Information Hub, 2019), almost 120 rural hospitals, including CAHs, have closed since 2010 (NC Rural Health Research Program, 2019). Alternatively, telehealth can be a potential solution to rural health care, yet further efforts are needed for telehealth utilization, implementation, and sustainment.

Management of Chronic Diseases in Rural Communities

While all chronic diseases are different, they are typically characterized by their slow onset and progress. Unlike acute conditions, many chronic conditions are not treatable and require ongoing disease management to prevent worsening of the disease and preventing or delaying the onset of further complications and loss of physical or mental functioning.

A Healthy People 2020 objective is to increase the proportion of older adults receiving Diabetes Self-Management Benefits to 12% in 2020 from 2% in the baseline year of 2008 (HHS & ODPHP, 2019). Unfortunately, the percentage has actually been decreasing slowly since 2008 (Figure 11.3) (HHS & ODPHP, 2019). Moreover, the percentage of Medicare beneficiaries receiving Diabetes Self-Management Benefits among 85-year-olds or older (0.6–0.8%) was almost one-third or one-fourth of the percentage among 65–74 years old (2.3–2.6%) (HHS & ODPHP, 2019). This may imply that older adults may not feel the need for repeatedly receiving diabetes self-management training and that health, aging, and community service providers

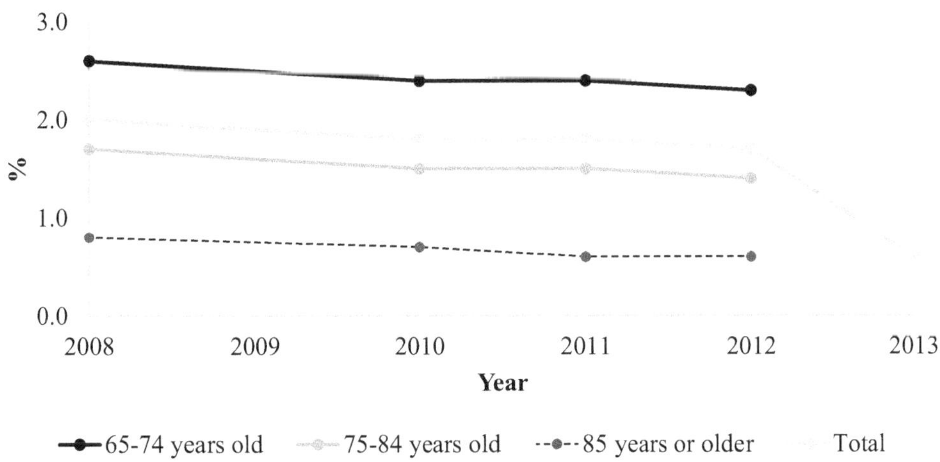

Figure 11.3 Percentage of Older Adults Receiving Diabetes Self-Management Benefits

Data source: As described by the HHS & ODPHP, 2019

should provide older adults with more educational opportunities and increase awareness of the availability of (and their eligibility for) such disease-related benefits among older adults. Further efforts should be invested in understanding the disparity in the receipt of self-management training among older adults.

As disparity exists among older adults, not all rural communities are equal in their opportunities and challenges. Rutledge, Masalovich, Blacher, and Saunders (2017) showed that over 1,000 diabetes self-management education (DSME) programs were delivered in 38% of rural counties in 2016. In other words, DSME programs were not available in almost two-thirds of rural counties. The likelihood of having at least one DSME program increased with the proportion of insured, higher socioeconomic status, and number of persons with diabetes. It should be noted that although the average number of persons with diabetes was greater in those rural counties with at least one DSME program than the counties without any DSME program, the counties without any DSME program had higher diabetes prevalence and incidence rates. In another study using national repository data from 47 states, Smith and colleagues (2017) showed that only about 8% of chronic disease self-management education (CDSME) programs were delivered in rural counties between 2009 and 2016. Aligned with Rutledge's study, Smith's study reports inequity in the availability of CDSME programs in rural communities. Furthermore, Smith's study also shows that various resources and settings (e.g., educational institutions, workplaces, and tribal centers) can be used for CDSME program delivery in rural areas.

Conclusion

The chronic disease prevalence and impacts have been outlined and described, as well as interventions targeting chronic disease among older adults in rural areas. Older adults in rural areas have higher rates of chronic disease than their counterparts in non-rural areas. Chronic disease prevention and management in rural areas can be enhanced by reducing risky behaviors and reinforcing healthy lifestyles and preventive care utilization. Limited access to health care in rural areas has been a persistent public health issue that poses a unique challenge for preventing and managing chronic disease in rural settings. Telehealth has long been a suggested solution for the problem of rural access to health care, but combined efforts from policymakers, health professionals, industry, and community will be needed to embed this technology into common practice. Other innovative solutions beyond telehealth should also be encouraged and evaluated. Additionally, a large and growing body of literature exists about chronic disease prevention and management, but limited studies distinguish between chronic disease prevention and management in rural and non-rural aging communities. This indicates the knowledge gap in the field, and further efforts are needed to understand both challenges and opportunities in chronic disease prevention and management in rural aging context.

References

Boring, M. A., Hootman, J. M., Liu, Y., Theis, K. A., Murphy, L. B., Barbour, K. E., . . . Croft, J. B. (2017). Prevalence of arthritis and arthritis-attributable activity limitation by urban-rural county classification—United States, 2015. *MMWR: Morbidity and Mortality Weekly Report, 66*(20), 527–532. doi:10.15585/mmwr.mm6620a2

Centers for Disease Control and Prevention (CDC). (2018a). *Behavioral risk factor surveillance system survey data.* Atlanta, GA: U.S. Department of Health and Human Services, Centers for Disease Control and Prevention.

Centers for Disease Control and Prevention (CDC). (2018b). *Underlying cause of death, 1999–2017 on CDC WONDER online database.* Retrieved from https://www.ncbi.nlm.nih.gov/pmc/articles/PMC6800725/

Centers for Disease Control and Prevention (CDC). (2019). *About chronic diseases.* Retrieved from www.cdc.gov/chronicdisease/about/index.htm

Coleman-Jensen, A., Rabbitt, M. P., Gregory, C. A., & Singh, A. (2018). *Household food security in the United States in 2017.* Economic Research Report Number 256, US Department of Agriculture, Economic Research Service. Retrieved from https://www.ers.usda.gov/webdocs/publications/90023/err-256.pdf

Croft, J. B., Wheaton, A. G., Liu, Y., Xu, F., Lu, H., Matthews, K. A., . . . Holt, J. B. (2018). Urban-rural county and state differences in chronic obstructive pulmonary disease—United States, 2015. *MMWR: Morbidity and Mortality Weekly Report, 67*(7), 205–211. doi:10.15585/mmwr.mm6707a1

Health Resources & Services Administration (HRSA). (2019). *Shortage areas.* Retrieved from https://data.hrsa.gov/topics/health-workforce/shortage-areas

Henley, S. J., Anderson, R. N., Thomas, C. C., Massetti, G. M., Peaker, B., & Richardson, L. C. (2017). Invasive cancer incidence, 2004–2013, and deaths, 2006–2015, in nonmetropolitan and metropolitan counties—United States. *MMWR: Morbidity and Mortality Weekly Report, 66*(14), 1–13. doi:10.15585/mmwr.ss6614a1

Heron, M. (2019). Deaths: Leading causes for 2017. *National Vital Statistics Reports, 68*(6).

Kaufman, B. G., Thomas, S. R., Randolph, R. K., Perry, J. R., Thompson, K. W., Holmes, G. M., & Pink, G. H. (2016). The rising rate of rural hospital closures. *The Journal of Rural Health, 32*, 25–43. doi:10.1111/jrh.12128

Matthews, K. A., Croft, J. B., Liu, Y., Lu, H., Kanny, D., Wheaton, A. G., . . . Eke, P. I. (2017). Health-related behaviors by urban-rural county classification—United States, 2013. *MMWR: Morbidity and Mortality Weekly Report, 66*(5), 1–8. doi:10.15585/mmwr.ss6605a1

Meit, M., Knudson, A., Gilbert, T., Yu, A. T., Tanenbaum, E., Ormson, E., . . . NORC Walsh Center for Rural Health Analysis. Mortality. (2014). *The 2014 update of the rural-urban chartbook.* Bethesda, MD: Rural Health Reform Policy Research Center.

Moy, E., Garcia, M. C., Bastian, B., Rossen, L. M., Ingram, D. D., Faul, M., . . . Iademarco, M. F. (2017). Leading causes of death in nonmetropolitan and metropolitan areas—United States, 1999–2014. *MMWR: Morbidity and Mortality Weekly Report, 66*(1), 1–8. doi:10.15585/mmwr.ss6601a1

National Center for Health Statistics (NCHS). (2018). *Table 20. Leading causes of death and numbers of deaths, by age: United States, 1980 and 2016. Health, United States, 2017: With special feature on mortality.* Hyattsville, MD: NCHS.

NC Rural Health Research Program. (2019). *161 rural hospital closures: January 2005-present (119 since 2010).* Retrieved from www.shepscenter.unc.edu/programs-projects/rural-health/rural-hospital-closures/

Rural Health Information Hub. (2019). *Critical access hospitals (CAHs).* Retrieved from www.ruralhealthinfo.org/topics/critical-access-hospitals

Rutledge, S. A., Masalovich, S., Blacher, R. J., & Saunders, M. M. (2017). Diabetes self-management education programs in nonmetropolitan counties—United States, 2016. *MMWR: Morbidity and Mortality Weekly Report, 66*(10), 1–6. doi:10.15585/mmwr.ss6610a1

Skrepnek, G. H., Mills, J. L., Sr., & Armstrong, D. G. (2015). A diabetic emergency one million feet long: Disparities and burdens of illness among diabetic foot ulcer cases within emergency departments in the United States, 2006–2010. *PloS One, 10*(8), e0134914. doi:10.1371/journal.pone.0134914

Smith, M. L., Towne, S. D., Herrera-Venson, A., Cameron, K., Kulinski, K. P., Lorig, K., . . . Ory, M. G. (2017). Dissemination of chronic disease self-management education (CDSME) programs in the United States: Intervention delivery by rurality. *International Journal of Environmental Research and Public Health, 14*(6), 638–651. doi:10.3390/ijerph14060638

Towne, S. D., Jr., Callaghan, T. H., Ferdinand, A. O., Akinlotan, M., Primm, K., & Bolin, J. (2019). *Prevalence and mortality of heart disease and related conditions: Disparities affecting the south, rural areas, and American Indian and Alaska Natives.* Policy Brief. Southwest Rural Health Research Center. Retrieved from https://srhrc.tamhsc.edu/docs/srhrc-pb5-towne-heartdisease.pdf

U.S. Department of Health and Human Services (HHS), & Office of Disease Prevention and Health Promotion (ODPHP). (2019). *Healthy people 2020.* Retrieved from www.healthypeople.gov/

Weisgrau, S. (1995). Issues in rural health: Access, hospitals, and reform. *Health Care Financing Review, 17*(1), 1–14.

World Health Organization (WHO). (2019). *Noncommunicable diseases and their risk factors*. Retrieved from www.who.int/ncds/en/

Zahnd, W. E., James, A. S., Jenkins, W. D., Izadi, S. R., Fogleman, A. J., Steward, D. E., . . . Brard, L. (2018). Rural-urban differences in cancer incidence and trends in the United States. *Cancer Epidemiology, Biomarkers & Prevention*, *27*(11), 1265–1274. doi:10.1158/1055-9965.EPI-17-0430

Ziliak, J. P., & Gundersen, C. (2017). *The health consequences of senior hunger in the United States: Evidence from the 1999–2014 NHANES*. Retrieved from www.feedingamerica.org/sites/default/files/research/senior-hunger-research/senior-health-consequences-2014.pdf

12
COMMUNITY DEVELOPMENT

Cornelia Butler Flora

Rural communities are aging. And many rural communities are seeing the services available decline, and with it their quality of life (Thiede, Brown, Sanders, Glasgow, & Kulcsar, 2017). Yet the assets provided by older adults in the community can contribute to community ecosystem health, economic security, and social inclusion. By examining the assets of each older individual in the community, the opportunities for community development can be enhanced and the community strengthened from the inside (Russell, 2011).

The many assets that contribute to community development can be classified as "capitals"—assets invested over a long time horizon (Flora, Flora, & Gasteyer, 2015). Increasing an asset only for short-term goals, such as quarterly profits, is speculation. Community developers around the world have found the following capitals useful in rural areas: natural, cultural, human, social, political, financial, and built. Addressing them in that order is helpful in appreciating the uniqueness of each rural community.

It is also important to recognize the special assets that older adults bring to a community, as their long lives provide much to be shared. Some elders have aged-in-place. They are living near where they have grown up and seen much change over time. Other elders have chosen to either return to their home community because of friends and relatives there or an attraction to one or another of the assets a community has available.

Natural Capital

Natural capital provides the possibilities and limits to human action. It influences and is influenced by human actions. It includes air quality, wind, and sun, water (both quantity and quality), soils and minerals, biodiversity, landscape, temperature, and extreme events. Memory of how nature once was by those with long ties to the community can help a community aspire to again have clean water and breathable air. And newcomers can protect that natural capital that attracted them to settle there. Both may have the time to walk in the woods or the countryside or sit on their porch and listen to birds, see the local animals, hear the insects calling, and share that knowledge with others. As a result, the community can better plan and act in concert with natural systems, rather than overcoming or destroying them.

Cultural Capital

Cultural capital determines how we see the world, what we take for granted, what we value, and what things we think possible to change. It includes how we connect the seen to the unseen, food and language, and being, and definitions of what can be changed. The diverse cultural capitals of older adults in the community can increase the options considered to continuously improve the community. Elders can express and value cultural differences in the meanings given to and the use of all categories of capitals. They can help maintain ancestral knowledge and language, including the cultivation and preparation of local food. They can also can take the time to help others in the community understand and build on different ways of knowing.

Human Capital

Human capital refers to the characteristics of individuals that are determined by the intersection of nature (genetics) and nurture (interactions with other people and the environment). It includes education over a lifetime, skills that are learned informally, through experience, health, self-esteem, and self-efficacy—the belief that one can make a difference in the community. Older adults are often delighted to share skills with "grandchildren" within the community, such as the African American grandmother helping the Hmong boy grow greens in the community garden. As local skills and abilities are recognized across all ages, they can be recombined to increase the health and well-being of a community.

Social Capital

Social capital is made up of interactions among individuals that occur with a degree of frequency and comfort. Bonding social capital consists of interactions within a specific group, such as at a senior center or a church, while bridging social capital consists of interactions across social groups. When the knowledge and skills of older adults are shared in a community meeting, bridging capital within the community is strengthened. Older adults often have connections with institutions and people in other places they have lived that can enhance community development as local groups learn about the networks that can bring resources from the outside to fulfill community visions. The social capital of older adults makes it easier to build first on internal resources before needing to look elsewhere for alternative ways to respond to constant change.

Political Capital

Political capital is the ability of a group to influence standards, regulation, and enforcement of those policies that determine the distribution of resources and the manner in which they are used. Local political capital requires organization, connections, voice, and power. Older adults help form basic community organizations that can articulate local issues and often have the experience to link them to specific policies. Health care is an important issue for older adults—and all community residents. The frequent closing of rural hospitals means that new ways of providing health services must be developed. Connections to local and regional elected and appointed officials can often be made by older citizens in the community, articulating local issues and possible actions to resolve them.

Inclusion of older adults with other community members contributes to civic action for deeper democracy and a just society. Older adults can demand accountability (and have an impact doing so) from elected and appointed officials, particularly since they are likely to vote at a higher rate than other cohorts (Russell, 2011). At a community level, they can mobilize around their direct self-interest and around the collective interests of the community for the common good.

Financial Capital

Financial capital consists of forms of currency used to increase capacity. It is often privileged because it is easy to measure. There is a tendency to think of other capitals in financial capital terms. Older adults often bring with them savings, pensions, and Social Security benefits they have accumulated over years of hard work. But they can also be a source of income generation, as local people provide services for them, or they establish businesses based on their human, cultural, and social capital that contribute to economic security in rural areas. Older adults pay local taxes and user fees that keep the community able to provide public goods. The skills of aging individuals can be used to support appropriately diverse local economies as services evolve to serve them and they develop small businesses. These local economies seek to reduce poverty, increase firm efficiency, increase firm diversity, and increase the assets of local people.

Built Capital

Built capital is human-constructed infrastructure that contributes to other community capitals. It includes recreation centers for older adults where children can also come, accessible trails, sidewalks where individuals of all ages can stroll in comfort, greeting neighbors and making new friends. It includes alternative energy sources controlled and managed by the rural community. That physical infrastructure enhances the other capitals because it serves multiple users; can be locally maintained and improved; links local people together equitably; and connects local people, institutions, and businesses to the outside.

In many rural communities, the centralization of the economy, coupled with declining population through the outmigration of young people, has resulted in declining numbers of businesses, with fewer of them locally owned (Carr & Kefalas, 2009).

When aging individuals are viewed as community assets, the community can spiral up. Drawing on the cultural capital of older adults, "old timers" and newcomers, social capital can increase, resulting in coordinated political capital. That political capital can be used to invest in human capital, from health care, to schools, to childcare. The increased human capital, including healthy, active elders, can contribute to better use of natural capital, improve built capital, and finally increase financial capital, not just for the few but for all. The result of involving older adults as partners and leaders can increase financial security for all, a healthier ecosystem, and promote inclusion of all community members working for a healthier community for all its citizens. It creates a community that others will find attractive as a residence and the basis for a business or opportunity to provide services.

The impact of an aging population is most positive when a community is organized enough to identify who their aging citizens are and engage them in the life of that community, often through community asset-mapping strategies. Unless there is a conscious effort to look for the assets *all* residents bring to a community, many will be left out and alienated. Building social capital by linking all age groups, but especially older adults, to natural, cultural, and human capital can create an aging population committed to the future of *their* community. While Russell (2011) stresses utilizing elder assets to co-produce healthy lifestyles, those assets, combined with healthy lifestyles, co-create dynamic rural communities for young and old alike.

References

Carr, P., & Kefalas, M. J. (2009). *Hollowing out the middle: The rural brain drain and what it means for America*. Boston, MA: Beacon.

Flora, C. B., Flora, J. L., & Gasteyer, S. P. (2015). *Rural communities: Legacy and change* (5th ed.). Boulder, CO: Westview Press.

Russell, C. (2011). Pulling back from the edge: An asset-based approach to ageing well. *Working with Older People*, *15*(3), 96–106.

Thiede, B. B., Brown, D. L., Sanders, S. R., Glasgow, N., & Kulcsar, L. J. (2017). A demographic deficit? Local population aging and access to services in rural America, 1990–2010. *Rural Sociology*, *82*(1), 44–74.

13
CULTURE

E. Helen Berry

Authors who describe rural culture often comment that all rural places are thought of as being alike and that rural places are generally thought of as being "other" or different from urban places. Rural places are described as having a singular culture and set of traditions and behaviors. The culture of rural places is believed to be different from urban places, resulting in real differences in lifestyles and attitudes, with concomitant implications for the older population.

Whether there is a rural culture is an interesting question. Claude Fischer (1978) argued that rural is different from urban because the heterogeneity, density, and size of cities results in innovations occurring first in cities, then diffusing, somewhat more slowly, to rural places. As a result, there is a real rural-urban difference in cultures because of the differential diffusion of ideas and innovations. Berry and Okulicz-Kozaryn (2011) describe a gradient of subjective well-being or happiness that rises from its lowest levels in large central cities to its highest levels on the small-town/rural periphery. The gradient is not necessarily consistent across countries: for example, Shucksmith, Cameron, Merridew, and Pichler (2009) find that when urban–rural differences in income and deprivation are controlled, the richer countries of Europe show little evidence of significant urban–rural difference but rural areas in the poorer countries have much lower levels of perceived welfare and quality of life.

Still, Cloke (2016) and Jackson (1985) describe rural culture as the ideal and posit that living in rural areas is perceived to be living in an ideal landscape, a place where everyone would like to live. Indeed, the U.S. suburbs with their moats of green grass landscaping around each house (Jackson, 1985) are miniature reproductions of the open spaces of agriculture and rural America. Other authors, particularly in examining how rural places view themselves, illustrate that rural peoples do not always feel as comfortable about rural life, or at least about their own lives. Both Hochschild (2016) and Cramer (2016) describe being rural as a social identity, a way to think about themselves relative to urban society. Correlated with this identity is a belief that rural places are left behind and that they are not getting the respect they deserve. Both find that this "rural resentment" (Cramer, 2016) comes partly from changes to rural life and partly from massive changes in the economy that leave rural people feeling overlooked and disrespected and seeing the American Dream passing them by.

In response, Kelly and Lobao (2019) illustrate that rural values, beliefs, and political choices are highly correlated with socioeconomic status. As a result, differences from urban and suburban places in values and choices can be largely explained by social status, employment, and other sociocultural attributes like race, ethnicity, and education. When social status, employment, and other sociocultural attributes are controlled, there is no difference in values and beliefs across the geographic urban-rural continuum. Still, such a result does not negate the feeling that some, or even many, rural places are left behind.

What are the consequences for rural older adults? First, one should keep in mind that the places where rural elders reside are not all alike. Specifically, as Cromartie (2019) points out, some rural places have larger proportions of older people because elders choose to move there: these are counties whose economies are based in recreation and retirement, and older adults are attracted by the benefits of living in amenity-rich areas. Other counties that have been losing population for many years, called persistent population-loss counties, are places where higher proportions of older adults are left behind because younger persons, particularly youth, move away because of the lack of economic opportunities in those places. One can safely say that residents of the persistent population-loss counties are those who feel left behind, whereas residents of counties that are migration destinations, like the retirement/recreation counties, are experiencing more gains.

Clearly, there is an interplay between the types of counties in which older adults live and their experience of aging. One of the key factors that make rural living different from urban life is the greater distances between home and services. First, the greater distances that are, by definition, part of rural life, mean that there are fewer care facilities and those are farther apart. Second, as people age, there is increased likelihood that they will experience greater health-care needs and greater age-related disability. Third, rural places have, overall, fewer economic advantages, less community development, and, as a result, fewer and less specialized services available for the older adult population. Distance to services plus the overall paucity of services has been made particularly evident by the particularly harsh impact of the Covid-19 pandemic on rural populations.

Persistent population-loss counties feel all of these factors much more so than do retirement and recreation destination counties. Regarding the distance issue, the distance to and from places is not so much greater in such places. Rather, the consistent loss of population in those places results in the related loss of facilities in those areas. Thus, distance becomes more important. Further, no matter how distance is measured, whether as in the long distances and remoteness of the rural West or Alaska, or if measured as the still isolated, but "closer-in" suburbs of large cities like St. Louis or New York, there are long commutes from homes to jobs, to health-care professionals and to grocery stores or even convenience stores. The effect is that it takes time to get anywhere plus the costs of gas, vehicle depreciation, and the challenge of finding drivers if one is past driving oneself. A related outcome is that the possibility of community engagement becomes substantially more limited, thereby depriving the community as a whole of the benefits and skills of those who cannot or do not easily transcend the distances and also depriving older adults of the benefits of community.

The distance issue also has a knock-on effect related to elders' health. Although the "young old" (ages 65–74) almost always drive themselves, once past 75, individuals often rely on other driving options (Glasgow & Blakely, 2000). Rural roads are also notably riskier, partly because of riskier behaviors by rural drivers (no seatbelts, DUI) but also because of challenges of road design (e.g., Rakauskus et al., 2009). The effect is a loss of independence and self-efficacy.

Regarding rural health-care disparities, recreation/retirement counties have the kind of infrastructure more often found where incomes are higher and thus, are more like suburban or even metro counties in terms of available services. Unfortunately, the persistent population-loss counties are where hospitals and clinics are closing and, increasingly, there are fewer services. Relatedly, rural communities have a higher prevalence of age-related disability and lower life expectancy relative to the nation as a whole. Rural areas face the obstacles of low tax-bases, dwindling numbers of small businesses and economic opportunities, plus the associated out-migration of youth, older housing, and, of course, the opioid crisis. These obstacles tend to result in inadequate resources to serve elders (Skoufalos, Clarke, Ellis, Shepard, & Rula, 2017).

When it comes to accepting services, if they are available, rural residents are often uncomfortable about getting help, especially when considering mental health care, but also medical or other types of assistance. There is the added discomfort of longtime residents in accepting services. Slama (2004) documents that rural peoples, because of their socioeconomic and socio-ethnic differences from urban residents, tend to accept health support less than elsewhere. Mental health care is even less accepted. "Independence & self-reliance are survival values when you live at distances from services and other people" (Slama, 2004, p. 10). Slama adds that knowing everyone around you makes it even harder to accept support since the lack of privacy in rural areas means people are less likely to accept help.

Thus, the circumstances for older adults in rural and urban places differ. Rural attitudes and physical circumstances, as discussed by authors cited earlier, result in more challenging circumstances for elders. At the same time, not all rural places are the same and thus the effect on rural older residents is not uniform from place to place. Elders who choose to move to retirement/recreation destinations, or who, by good fortune, find themselves in such places, generally have access to infrastructure and services. For rural elders in population-loss counties, the culture tends to be less optimistic, for the very real reasons related to the economic and political circumstances of life in relatively deprived places. In both types of places, the sense of community and the likelihood of knowing and helping one's neighbors is similar because the density of acquaintanceship is high—or, if one prefers, because everyone knows everyone else.

Further Readings on Rural Culture

Cramer, K. J. (2016). *The politics of resentment: Rural consciousness in Wisconsin and the rise of Scott Walker.* Chicago, IL: University of Chicago Press.

Hochschild, A. R. (2016). *Strangers in their own land: Anger and mourning on the American right.* New York: New Press.

Kelly, P., & Lobao, L. (2019). The social bases of rural-urban political divides: Social status, work, and sociocultural beliefs. *Rural Sociology, 84*(4), 669–705.

References

Berry, B. J. L., & Okulicz-Kozaryn, A. (2011). An urban-rural happiness gradient. *Urban Geography, 32*(6), 871–883. doi:10.2747/0272-3638.32.6.871

Cloke, P. (2016). Rural life-styles: Material opportunity, cultural experience, and how theory can undermine policy. *Economic Geography,* 72(4), 433–449.

Cramer, K. J. (2016). *The politics of resentment: Rural consciousness in Wisconsin and the rise of Scott Walker.* Chicago, IL: University of Chicago Press.

Cromartie, J. B. (2018, December). *Rural aging occurs in different places for very different reasons.* Research and Science, U.S. Department of Agriculture. Retrieved December 16, 2019, from www.usda.gov/media/blog/2018/12/20/rural-aging-occurs-different-places-very-different-reasons

Fischer, C. S. (1978). Urban-to-rural diffusion of opinions in contemporary America. *American Journal of Sociology, 84*(1), 151–159. doi:10.1086/226744

Glasgow, N., & Blakely, R. M. (2000). Older nonmetropolitan residents' evaluations of their transportation arrangements. *Journal of Applied Gerontology, 19*(1), 95–116. doi:10.1177/073346480001900106

Hochschild, A. R. (2016). *Strangers in their own land: Anger and mourning on the American right.* New York: New Press.

Jackson, K. T. (1985). *Crabgrass frontier: The suburbanization of the United States*. New York: Oxford University Press.

Kelly, P., & Lobao, L. (2019). The social bases of rural-urban political divides: Social status, work, and sociocultural beliefs. *Rural Sociology*, *84*(4), 669–705. doi:10.1111/ruso.12256

Rakauskas, M. D., Ward, N. J., & Gerberich, S. G. (2009). Identification of differences between rural and urban safety cultures. *Accident Analysis & Prevention*, *41*(5), 931–937. doi:10.1016/j.aap.2009.05.008

Shucksmith, M., Cameron, S., Merridew, T., & Pichler, F. (2009). Urban–rural differences in quality of life across the European Union. *Regional Studies*, *43*(10), 1275–1289. doi:10.1080/00343400802378750

Skoufalos, A., Clarke, J. L., Ellis, D. R., Shepard, V. L., & Rula, E. Y. (2017). Rural aging in America: Proceedings of the 2017 connectivity summit. *Population Health Management*, *20*(Suppl. 2), S1–S10. doi:10.1089/pop.2017.0177

Slama, K. (2004). Rural culture is a diversity issue. *Minnesota Psychologist*, *53*(1), 9–12.

14
DEMENTIA

Clifford M. Singer

Epidemiology of Dementia

As a community's average age increases, its population at greatest risk of Alzheimer's disease and related disorders (ADRD) grows. Because of its aging population, the number of people in the U.S. with Alzheimer's disease is expected to reach 8.4 million by 2030, a staggering increase in just a few years from the current estimate of 5.8 million people with the disease in the U.S. (Alzheimer's Association, 2020). The population of rural areas in the U.S. are significantly older than suburban and urban populations and prevalence of dementia is higher, although relative risk of dementia may actually be lower in rural areas (Weden, Shih, Kabeto, & Langa, 2018). Disease prevalence estimates that rely on Medicare beneficiary data may underestimate the prevalence of dementia in rural areas because of low rates of screening or documentation of cognitive diagnoses in primary care (Abner, Jicha, Christian, & Schreurs, 2016). Residents in rural and remote areas have less access to specialty clinics for the assessment of cognitive disorders and may be less likely to have confirmation and documentation of a dementia diagnosis.

Access to Outpatient and Home Health-Care Services

Primary care providers (PCPs) in rural areas take on much of the burden of planning dementia care, although they are keen to utilize specialists' help when available. They often lack confidence in making specific diagnoses of ADRD in distinguishing these disorders from normal cognitive aging, depression, and other conditions. PCPs welcome multidisciplinary assistance in care (Kosterniuk, Morgan, Innes, & Keady, 2012). People with dementia in rural areas may need more support services than in urban areas because of leaner family support. They are also more likely to report unmet health-care needs beyond dementia care (Forbes, Morgan, & Janzen, 2006). Dementia specialists, such as geriatricians, geriatric psychiatrists, behavioral neurologists, and neuropsychologists tend to work at academic medical centers or tertiary care hospitals located in larger towns and cities. Long travel distances to medical services may be especially challenging for persons with dementia and their families. Winter weather adds an additional obstacle for people in some regions. Technological innovations, such as telehealth and in-home monitoring, are promising options for people who have access to these resources. Cognitive assessment via telehealth has been shown to be acceptable and reliable (DeYoung & Shenal, 2019). Unfortunately, Medicare doesn't yet reimburse for telehealth at home, so persons needing cognitive assessment still have to travel to clinics with telehealth connections. The US Center for Medicare and Medicaid loosened their regulations during the 2020–2021 COVID-19 pandemic, allowing telehealth visits from people's homes. These changes have allowed safe, effective outpatient care during the pandemic and to be very popular with patients. At the time of this writing, we do not know whether these regulations will endure post-pandemic. Overall, there have been mixed results from studies assessing quality and cost from telehealth. However, the effects of mental health treatment by telehealth have been well studied, including in nursing home patients. The benefits of telemental health are positive and make up a significant part of telehealth services reimbursed by Medicare (MedPac, 2018).

Project ECHO is another way to provide specialist consultation to rural health-care providers (Project ECHO, 2020). Project ECHO was started by Dr. Sanjeev Arora at the University of New Mexico and is both an acronym (Extension for Community Health Outcomes) and a metaphor for the reverberation and spread of knowledge that occurs in ECHO programs. There are several Project ECHOs around the world that focus on dementia care in outpatient and community settings. In this model, PCPs gather online with specialists in a "hub and spoke" format over a video conferencing platform and present cases that are then discussed. Treatment recommendations are provided by the group. This format provides new learning for the participants and reduces the sense of isolation that often accompanies practice in remote areas. Most importantly, it provides clinically meaningful recommendations to help patients and families.

Other models exist that rely on mixtures of face-to-face care and remote telehealth. Many rely on initial visits to a specialized care clinic. In Canada, the Rural Dementia Action Research Team was organized in 2003 to serve people with dementia living in rural Saskatchewan. Their work is focused on improving accessibility and acceptability of services in their rural and remote communities. The original projects were the development of a "one-stop telehealth assisted interdisciplinary Rural and Remote Memory Clinic" (RRMC), a study of health-care utilization by persons with dementia and their caregivers in rural settings and an evaluation of a special program ("Enhancing Care Program") in two rural long-term care facilities. A study of 30 rural family caregivers of patients seen at the RRMC in Saskatchewan found that help-seeking by the family was usually initiated by a "need to know what was happening" to their loved one and whether it was normal or not for aging. They also wanted to know prognosis or "what to expect" and to receive advice on available services. At a second interview six months later, they reported that receiving a diagnosis helped "with acceptance and moving forward," "relief," "validation," and "improved access to services" (Morgan et al., 2014).

Even when assessment for cognitive symptoms is available, many people decline the evaluations. Almost 22% of older adults will refuse memory screening when offered. Furthermore, rural older adults may score differently on memory screening tests. In a study done of rural, suburban, and urban older adults in Indiana, rural residents showed a lower rate of positive screens (impairment) despite a higher average age. Higher levels of education and lower levels of chronic illness in this particular cohort likely offset the effects of higher age. These trends may not hold for all rural residents but indicate the hazards of trying to generalize assumptions about the rural older populations (Fowler et al., 2018).

If residents in remote locations can access specialty care for dementia, they are likely to realize benefits that very busy primary care providers in their small towns don't have the time, staff, or expertise to provide. Beyond expertise in diagnosis, specialized memory clinics will create treatment plans and make referrals for services if available in the patient's rural location. They may also offer unique, grant-funded services. In 2019, the RRMC in Saskatchewan, Canada, began incorporating specific interventions and research protocols covering the comprehensive multidisciplinary support services of the program (Rural & Remote Memory Clinic, 2020).

These services, including cognitive rehabilitation, driving safety assessment, and social support are among many recommended for high-quality dementia care in the outpatient setting by several published clinical practice guidelines. US Medicare also encourages this type of comprehensive assessment and treatment planning for cognitive impairment and dementia through the use of a special billing code (CPT 99483). This provides enhanced reimbursement for time spent doing cognitive assessment, treatment planning, counseling and coordination of care.

Access to programs promoting wellness is also challenging for people in rural areas. Programs aimed at maximizing physical and brain health can also be offered remotely through videoconference technologies. Encouraging physical activity is one of the best evidence-based strategies for healthy aging and is associated with delayed onset of dementia. Remotely directed group exercise classes via telehealth have been shown to be acceptable and enjoyable to both the person with dementia and family. Not surprisingly, willingness to participate in a group class was the most significant predictor of participation in one published outcome study. The exercise classes in one study were attended at a rural local health facility with telehealth capability and both patient and caregiver participated (Fowler et al., 2018).

Rural areas also have less access to Medicare-reimbursed skilled home care that is "hands on" and requires long travel distances for nurses and rehab therapists (Probst, Towne, Mitchell, Bennett, & Chen, 2014). On the other hand, palliative and hospice care may be augmented by telehealth. Alzheimer's and most of the other diseases that cause dementia are progressive over time and ultimately fatal. As dementia progresses to terminal stages, there may not be access to palliative and hospice care in remote communities to oversee comfort measures at the end of life. A study of telehealth-delivered hospice home care showed that this may be a good way to augment but not replace in-person care (Read, Salmon, Sinnarajah, & Spice, 2019).

Hospital Care

Hospital care can be especially hazardous for people with dementia given their high risk for delirium (acute mental status changes from surgery, illness, or medications) and poor outcomes from surgery and medical treatment. In the U.S., there is a national movement to certify hospitals and systems "age friendly" and hospitals meeting this certification are often critical access hospitals in rural areas that are part of larger systems (American Hospital Association, 2020). Hospitals with "Age Friendly Healthcare System" designation use the "4M framework" (mentation, mobility, medications, matters) approach, focusing on reducing risk of delirium, maintaining mobility, minimizing medication side effects and focusing on the outcomes that matter most to patients and families. A few hospitals in rural areas even have emergency services that are specially designed to reduce risk to older patients and those with dementia (PR Newswire, 2020).

Apart from dementia-friendly hospital and non-hospital settings for acute care, finding health-care workers with dementia-capable skills is not easy in remote regions. In the U.S., the federal government's Health Resources and Services Administration (HRSA) sponsors grants to increase geriatrics training opportunities for health-care workers (HRSA, 2020). The Geriatrics Workforce Enhancement Program (GWEP) is funded through HRSA's Bureau of Health Workforce and supports programs in 37 states and territories (some states have more than one program). Many of the programs focus on improving clinical geriatrics skills of health-care professionals in rural areas. For example, the GWEP in Maine (AgingME) reaches providers in many rural communities and includes case-based dementia education through both Project ECHO and on-site mini-fellowships in the hospital setting. HRSA also has professional school loan-repayment programs that improve recruitment of health-care workers to rural regions.

Caregivers and Community Support Services

Caring for a person with dementia is difficult in any setting, but in rural areas where support services may not be easily accessible, it is particularly challenging. Access to dementia-specialists who can give persons with dementia the treatment they need and the family caregivers the information they can benefit from may require distant travel. Canadian investigators mailed questionnaires and conducted telephone interviews to determine what health-care professionals and families of people with dementia perceived as needs that should be addressed by planned dementia care services in "rural and remote" Saskatchewan. Both physicians and non-physician health-care providers identified more long-term care facilities and community support programs as needs. Non-physician providers specifically noted "increased community services, better coordination between services, travel burden to get care and staff education in dementia care" as needs or problem areas. One-third of family caregivers were unsatisfied with services available to them, pointing to lack of diagnosis and long wait time for services (Dal Bello-Haas, Cammer, Morgan, Stewart, & Kostenuik, 2014). The author of this entry is medical director of a memory disorders clinic that serves the most rural parts of Maine. People often drive three hours and wait months for appointments. Caregiver support groups are also less likely to be found in rural areas and these can be very helpful in reducing social isolation and lack of information that are significant problems for family caregivers. Online support groups held via remote video conferencing is one way to address this problem.

Long travel distances are not the only reason for lack of assessment and treatment in rural regions of the country. A survey identified eight barriers to obtaining community services in rural areas: stigma, lack of privacy, a culture of self-reliance producing guilt when asking for help, lack of awareness that help was available, acceptability and accessibility of services, service delivery challenges (client doesn't let person in, caregivers not available, etc.), and lastly, the client was "not ready to receive help" (Morgan, Semchuk, Stewart, & D'Arcy, 2016).

Older adults in rural settings need access to a variety of affordable care options to keep them in their communities without financial impoverishment. Programs to support aging-in-place require integration of health and social programs and are generally less available in rural areas. Care managers who provide coordination, navigation, and transportation to and from care resulting in the reduction in loneliness and social isolation would be of tremendous help (American Research Institute, 2016). Nearly 44 million people in the U.S. provide unpaid care to a vulnerable older adult, many with dementia. Those in rural areas are more likely than urban areas to face the challenges of social isolation, lack of transportation, and lack of flexible employment options and caregiver support services (Henning-Smith & Lahr, 2018). Tax policies to help offset direct care costs, increased access to technology (such as internet-based caregiver education and support), and paid family leave could address the needs of unpaid caregivers for older adults with dementia.

Summary

Major areas of concern for people with cognitive decline and dementia and their families residing in rural areas have been considered and promising solutions to overcome challenges highlighted. A helpful policy summary of recommendations for future directions can be found in an August 2019 report to the U.S. Secretary of the Department of Health and Human Services (DHHS) entitled "Supportive Services and Caregiving for Older Rural Adults by the National Advisory Committee on Rural Health and Human Services" (NACRHHS) (NACRHHS, 2019).

References

Abner, E. L., Jicha, G. A., Christian, W. J., & Schreurs, B. G. (2016). Rural-urban differences in Alzheimer's disease and related disorders diagnostic prevalence in Kentucky and West Virginia. *Journal of Rural Health*, *32*(3), 314–320.

Alzheimer's Association website. Retrieved January 30, 2020 from www.alz.org/alzheimers-dementia/facts-figures

American Hospital Association website. Retrieved January 30, 2020, from www.aha.org/center/new-payment-and-delivery-models/age-friendly-health-systems

American Research Institute Issue Brief #1. (2016, December). *All together now: Integrating health and community supports for older adults*. Retrieved from www.air.org/system/files/downloads/report/Integrating-Health-and-Community-Supports-for-Older-Americans-Nov-2016.pdf

Dal Bello-Haas, V. P., Cammer, A., Morgan, D., Stewart, N., & Kostenuik, J. (2014). Rural and remote dementia care challenges and need: Perspectives of formal and informal care providers residing in Saskatchewan, Canada. *Rural Remote Health*, *14*(3), 2747.

Dal Bello-Haas, V. P., O'Connell, M. E., Morgan, D. G., & Crossley, M. (2014). Lessons learned: Feasibility and acceptability of telehealth-delivered exercise intervention for rural dwelling individuals with dementia and their caregivers. *Rural and Remote Health, 14*, 2715. Retrieved from www.rrh.org.au

DeYoung, N., & Shenal, B. V. (2019). The reliability of the Montreal Cognitive Assess using telehealth in a rural setting with veterans. *Journal of Telemedicine and Telecare*, *25*(4), 197–203.

Forbes, D. A., Morgan, D., & Janzen, B. L. (2006). Rural and urban Canadians with dementia: Use of health care services. *Canadian Journal on Aging*, *25*(3), 321–330.

Fowler, N. R., Perkins, A. J., Gao, S., Sachs, G. A., Uebelhor, A. K., & Boustani, M. A. (2018). Patient characteristics associated with screening positive for Alzheimer's disease and related dementia. *Clinical Interventions in Aging*, *13*, 1779–1785.

Henning-Smith, C., & Lahr, M. (2018, August). *Perspectives on rural caregiving challenges and interventions: University of Minnesota Rural Health Research Center Policy Brief*. Retrieved from https://3pea7g1qp8f3t9ooe3z3npx1-wpengine.netdna-ssl.com/wp-content/uploads/2019/01/1535633283UMNpolicybriefcaregivingchallenges.pdf

HRSA website. Retrieved January 30, 2020, from www.hrsa.gov/sites/default/files/hrsa/advisory-committees/rural/publications/2019-Older-Adults.pdf

Kosterniuk, J., Morgan, D., Innes, A., & Keady, J. (2012). Who steers the ship? Rural family physicians' views on collaborative care models for patients with dementia. *Primary Health Care Research & Development*, *15*(1), 104–110.

MedPac. (2018, March). *Mandated report to Congress: Medicare payment policy telehealth services and Medicare program*. Retrieved from www.medpac.gov/docs/defaultsource/reports/mar18_medpac_ch16_sec.pdf?sfvrsn=0)

Morgan, D. G., Semchuk, K., Stewart, N., & D'Arcy, C. (2016). Rural families caring for a relative with dementia: Barriers to use of formal services. *Social Science & Medicine*, *55*(7), 51–64.

Morgan, D. G., Walls-Ingram, S., Cammer, A., O'Connell, M. E., Crossley, M., Bello-Haas, V. D., . . . Stewart, N. (2014). Informal caregivers' hopes and expectations of a referral to a memory clinic. *Social Science & Medicine*, *102*, 111–118.

NACRHHS. (2019, August). *Supportive services and caregiving for older rural adults: Policy brief and recommendations to the secretary*. Washington, DC: NACRHHS.

PR Newswire website. Retrieved January 30, 2020, from www.prnewswire.com/news-releases/dartmouth-hitchcock-health-west-health-partner-to-create-nations-first-rural-geriatric-emergency-department-300943899.html

Probst, J. C., Towne, S., Mitchell, J., Bennett, K. J., & Chen, R. (2014, June). *Home health care agency availability in rural counties*. South Carolina Rural Health Research Center. Retrieved from https://sc.edu/study/colleges_schools/public_health/research/research_centers/sc_rural_health_research_center/documents/112hhcagencyavailability2014.pdf

Project ECHO website. Retrieved January 30, 2020, from https://echo.unm.edu/

Read, P. L., Salmon, C., Sinnarajah, A., & Spice, R. (2019). Web-based videoconferencing for rural palliative care consultation with elderly patients at home. *Supportive Care Cancer*, *27*(9), 3321–3330.

Rural & Remote Memory Clinic website. Retrieved January 30, 2020, from https://cchsa-ccssma.usask.ca/ruraldementiacare/Rural%20Remote%20Memory%20Clinic.php

U.S. Health Resources & Services Administration website. Retrieved January 30, 2020, from www.hrsa.gov

Weden, M. M., Shih, R. A., Kabeto, M. U., & Langa, K. M. (2018). Secular trends in dementia and cognitive impairment of U.S. rural and urban older adults. *American Journal of Preventive Medicine*, *54*(2), 164–172.

15 DEMENTIA FRIENDLY COMMUNITIES

Meredith Hanley

Overview

Researchers estimate that nearly six million Americans are living with Alzheimer's disease, which is the most common form of dementia (Alzheimer's Association, 2019). With age being the greatest risk factor for the development of Alzheimer's disease, this number could climb to 14 million by the year 2050 (Alzheimer's Association, 2019). This equates to one in ten people over the age of 65. Other common types of dementia include vascular dementia, frontotemporal dementia, and Lewy Body dementia. It is estimated that 14% of adults over the age of 71 have some form of dementia (Alzheimer's Association, 2019).

Research also has shown that 80% of people with dementia live in their homes or with family and nearly a quarter of people with dementia are living alone (Lepore, Ferrell, & Wiener, 2017). The role of the 16 million caregivers in the U.S. who provide vital support to individuals living with dementia is critical to helping people with dementia remain at home. While rewarding, caregiving can also come with a physical and emotional toll. Caregivers for people with dementia are more likely to have depression and report emotional difficulty than other caregivers (Family Caregiver Alliance, National Center on Caregiving, n.d.).

Given these statistics and that, proportionally, the number of people 65 and older is higher in rural areas compared to urban areas (Baernholdt, Guofen, Hinton, Rose, & Mattos, 2012), it is important that rural communities consider how to best prepare to support the growing number of residents who have or may develop Alzheimer's disease or a related dementia, as well as their caregivers.

About Dementia Friendly Communities

A dementia friendly community is informed, safe, and respectful of individuals with dementia and their families and provides supportive options that foster quality of life (Dementia Friendly America, n.d.b). In the U.S., dementia friendly community efforts are spearheaded at the national level by the Dementia Friendly America (DFA) initiative. There have also been a number of international organizations supporting dementia friendly communities in their respective countries such as the Alzheimer's Society in the United Kingdom and Alzheimer's Association Japan (Alzheimer's Disease International, 2017). While research continues to search for a cure, treatment, or prevention of Alzheimer's disease and other forms of dementia, dementia friendly communities work to support people who are affected by dementia as well as their families and caregivers.

DFA is administered by the National Association of Area Agencies on Aging in partnership with over 35 national and leading organizations that serve on its National Council, including the Alzheimer's Association, AARP, LeadingAge, the LEAD Coalition, USAgainstAlzheimer's, BrightFocus Foundation, HomeInstead Senior Care, and Connected Living (Dementia Friendly America, n.d.a) Also serving on the National Council are people living with dementia and caregivers. DFA is based on Minnesota's successful statewide initiative, ACT on Alzheimer's, which since 2011 has worked to support the development of dementia friendly communities in Minnesota (ACT on Alzheimer's, n.d.). DFA launched in 2015 with eight pilot communities, and currently the initiative directly or in partnership with statewide dementia friendly community leads, supports, and engages approximately 300 dementia friendly communities across the country.

Joining the Dementia Friendly Movement

When communities join the DFA network, it means that the community is engaged in a process of becoming more dementia friendly. Communities pledge that their efforts include the following points of focus:

- Connecting Across Sectors. They convene a cross-sector team across three or more community sectors to advance dementia friendliness. Key sectors promoted in dementia friendly communities include business and banking; law enforcement and first response; health-care systems; faith communities; local government; community members; and residential care and community services. A cross-sector team includes at a minimum, government, clinical, and community-based organizations.
- Inclusion and Leadership of People Living With Dementia. People living with dementia and their caregivers are key to leading and shaping dementia friendly communities.
- Adoption and Communication of Dementia Friendly Practices and Change Goals. Communities foster sector-specific dementia friendly practices across their communities. DFA offers a publicly available toolkit to guide communities through a process that fosters adoption of dementia friendly practices.
- Champion Organization and Coordination Capacity. DFA communities identify an organization that is willing to champion, coordinate, and, if needed, serve as a fiscal sponsor. The champion organization may help recruit and partner with a senior leader of local government in the effort (e.g., mayor, city council member, other elected officials).

Many communities are integrating age-friendly and dementia friendly community initiatives. AARP and DFA partnered to develop "Better Together: A Comparative Analysis of Age-Friendly and Dementia Friendly Communities" to illustrate how age-friendly and dementia friendly efforts relate by providing case studies and an overlay that reflect the World Health Organization's eight domains of age-friendliness alongside key characteristics of dementia friendly communities (Dementia Friendly America, n.d.b).

Each dementia friendly community establishes its own unique goals and aims to better support people in their communities. Common goals of dementia friendly communities include increasing coordination across community sectors; increasing community awareness and sensitivity toward those living with dementia; increasing access to and inclusion in community life;

increasing respite and support services; increasing dementia friendly business and financial practices; improving the effectiveness of public services (such as law enforcement, first response, and transportation) in responding to people with dementia; increasing rates of detection/diagnosis; and increasing rates of advance planning.

Unique Challenges and Opportunities in Rural Areas

Dementia friendly communities work to ensure that people living with dementia and their caregivers have the best quality of life possible and can engage and thrive in day-to-day living. While many people with dementia face challenges with early and accurate diagnosis, transportation, and social isolation, these challenges are often exacerbated in rural areas. Highly trained physicians are typically less available, which can result in difficulty receiving an early and accurate diagnosis. This can affect treatment and care decisions. There are fewer social and health-care services, particularly those aimed at people with dementia, to help individuals remain living at home safely and independently. There are fewer transportation options and greater travel distances. While people in the early stages of dementia may continue to drive, typically at some point in the disease process, driving is no longer possible. Lack of transportation options in rural communities can then lead to social isolation as well as negatively impact access to nutrition and health-care services.

However, rural communities also offer assets that help to support people with dementia that many larger communities may not benefit from, such as a strong sense of community and the willingness of neighbors to help neighbors (Alzheimer's Society, n.d.). The spirit of collective action—leaders and community members from various backgrounds and perspectives coming together to offer their unique contributions—is often the most critical aspect of a successful dementia friendly community effort.

Examples of Rural Dementia Friendly Communities in Action

Dementia Friendly Shenandoah Valley, Virginia, which launched in 2018, is a partnership between Central Shenandoah Health District and Valley Program for Aging Services. Both of these organizations serve the counties of Augusta, Bath, Highland, Rockbridge, and Rockingham and the cities of Buena Vista, Harrisonburg, Lexington, Staunton, and Waynesboro. This region of Virginia is predominantly rural (Rural Health Information Hub, n.d.), and in four counties (Augusta, Bath, Highland, and Rockbridge) the population 60 and older exceeds 30% (Weldon Cooper Center for Public Service, University of Virginia, n.d.). The initiative initially started in Lexington, Virginia, but later expanded to include the broader Shenandoah Valley. Participants on the Steering Committee include representatives from banks, faith communities, aging/social services, business, health care, housing, libraries, and law enforcement/first response as well as community members and people with dementia. The library established a monthly memory café at its Lexington location with plans to expand to all five branches. A library also established a collection of books, puzzles, CDs, DVDs, and other materials geared specifically for people with dementia and caregivers. Dementia Friends awareness-raising sessions are held at local organizations and have included a hospital and senior center. Dementia Friendly @ Work education sessions have been held for a hospice, ministerial association, museum, library, nursing home, hospital department heads, churches, home care company, and the fire and rescue team. The initiative is evaluating the impact of these sessions using a toolkit from the U.S. Administration for Community Living. Dementia Friendly Shenandoah established a partnership with a local weekly newspaper to feature a monthly article on dementia and caregiving. They disseminate business card-size cards for caregivers that inform others that their companion has dementia along with simple tips. Dementia Friendly Shenandoah has found that information about the initiative has been widely spread by word-of-mouth throughout their region serving to reinforce the initiative's momentum.

According to the U.S. Census Bureau, West Virginia is the most rural state in the South with over half of its residents living in rural areas (U.S. Census Bureau, n.d.). The state of West Virginia was one of DFA's original pilot sites and launched its West Virginia CARES—Coordinated Action, Response, Education and Support—program in 2015 with the goal of helping organizations and individuals across multiple sectors (nonprofit, law enforcement, faith, and business) learn about dementia so they can help to enhance the quality of life of individuals living with dementia. West Virginia University Health Science Center leads the effort in collaboration with key partners throughout the state including the Claude W. Benedum Foundation, AARP-West Virginia, Alzheimer's Association-West Virginia Chapter, the Joan C. Edwards School of Medicine at Marshall University, the West Virginia Bureau of Senior Services, the West Virginia Parkinson's Network, the West Virginia Sheriff's Association, and West Virginia University's Rockefeller Neuroscience Institute. Activities of the West Virginia CARES initiative include partnering with the West Virginia Council of Churches to engage the faith community in dementia education, hosting virtual town halls in partnership with AARP that included Alzheimer's 101 presentations and Q&A with a neurologist, conducting law enforcement training, hosting professionally facilitated regional listening sessions of caregivers of people with dementia to learn about their needs and concerns, and holding evidence-based "Dealing with Dementia" training sessions for caregivers through the state.

Summary

Dementia friendly communities in rural areas play a critical role in supporting people with dementia and their caregivers. They help to address the unique challenges faced by people with dementia in rural areas, such as lack of transportation, health-care access, a need for greater services and supports, and the risk of loneliness and social isolation. In a dementia friendly community, each sector of the community—whether it is business, banking, legal services, transportation, law enforcement/first response, faith communities, social services, or residential care—is willing to step forward and ensure their organization, business, or sector is dementia friendly. As the Shenandoah Valley, Virginia, and the statewide West Virginia examples have shown, community members and leaders coming together can make a remarkable difference.

References

ACT on Alzheimer's. (n.d.). *Minnesotans work together on the impacts of Alzheimer's*. Retrieved February 24, 2020, from https://actonalz.org/about

Alzheimer's Association. (2019). *2019 Alzheimer's disease facts and figures*. Retrieved from www.alz.org/media/Documents/alzheimers-facts-and-figures-2019-r.pdf

Alzheimer's Disease International. (2017, September). *Dementia friendly communities: Global developments* (2nd. ed.). Retrieved February 24, 2020, from www.alz.co.uk/adi/pdf/dfc-developments.pdf

Alzheimer's Society. (n.d.). *Dementia-friendly rural communities guide*. Retrieved February 24, 2020, from www.alzheimers.org.uk/get-involved/dementia-friendly-communities/rural-communities

Baernholdt, M., Guofen, Y., Hinton, I., Rose, K., & Mattos, M. (2012). Quality of life in rural and urban adults 65 years and older: Findings from the National Health and Nutrition Examination survey. *Journal of Rural Health*, *28*(4), 339–347.

Dementia Friendly America. (n.d.a). *Leadership*. Retrieved February 24, 2020, from www.dfamerica.org/leadership

Dementia Friendly America. (n.d.b). *What is Dementia Friendly America (DFA)?* Retrieved February 24, 2020, from www.dfamerica.org/what-is-dfa

Family Caregiver Alliance, National Center on Caregiving. (n.d.). *Depression and caregiving*. Retrieved February 24, 2020, from www.caregiver.org/depression-and-caregiving

Lepore, M., Ferrell, A., & Wiener, J. (2017). *Living arrangements of people with Alzheimer's disease and related dementias: Implications for services and supports*. Retrieved February 24, 2020, from https://aspe.hhs.gov/advisory-council-july-2017-meeting-presentation-living-alone-dementia

Rural Health Information Hub. (n.d.). *Am I rural?* Retrieved February 24, 2020, from www.ruralhealthinfo.org/am-i-rural

U.S. Census Bureau. (n.d.). *Rural America*. Retrieved February 24, 2020, from https://gis-portal.data.census.gov/arcgis/apps/MapSeries/index.html?appid=7a41374f6b03456e9d138cb014711e01

Weldon Cooper Center for Public Service, University of Virginia. (n.d.). *Population estimates for age & sex, race & Hispanic, and towns*. Retrieved February 24, 2020, from https://demographics.coopercenter.org/population-estimates-age-sex-race-hispanic-towns

16
DENTAL AND ORAL HEALTH

R. Constance Wiener, Patricia A. Findley, and Chan Shen

Introduction

There are a number of disparities associated with rural life that limit access to medical and oral health care. Among these disparities are difficulties with scheduling, transportation, availability of specific services, time away from work, traveling greater distances for services (Hamano, Takeda, Tominaga, Sundquist, & Nabika, 2017), and financial burden. Overall, in 2014, more people reported financial barriers to dental care compared to any other type of health-care (Vujicic, Buchmueller, & Klein, 2016).

Disparities are important to consider as research in oral epidemiology shows the cumulative effects of disparities over the life course. Health-care utilization in general, and oral health-care utilization in particular, is influenced by social determinants, including individual behaviors, local culture, and customs; health literacy; general education; economics; availability of services (Newton, 2005); and metropolitan/urban/rural residence. For example, Wiener, Shen, Sambamoorthi, and Findley (2017) found that veterans from a national sample with 57% of participants ages 65 years and above, and living in rural areas, were less likely than their urban counterparts to have a dental visit in the past year. Residence matters, particularly for oral health care.

Oral Health Status in Older Adults in Rural America

The older adult population is not a homogenous group in terms of oral health. Many young-old adults (born in/after 1957) had access to community water fluoridation or fluoride supplements; whereas, older-old adults (born before 1957) did not. Additionally, Procter and Gamble introduced Crest® with Fluoristan in 1955 (Crest, 2019), which was followed by many other fluoridated toothpastes available to the young-old. The young-old, unlike the older-old adults saw many television public service announcements to "brush after every meal" in their youth. They also had dental care that was more efficient and less uncomfortable than the older-old adults had, as there were advancements in instrumentation (high-speed handpieces, etc.) and materials (white composite dental restorations, etc.).

Older-old adults had fewer treatment options and fewer preventive aids (for example, tooth powders, baking soda, salt, and other alternative products were commonly used to clean teeth).

Older-old adults are more likely to have tooth loss than the young-old. Additionally, many do not consider oral health care as important to their overall health and well-being as the young-old do (Kiyak & Reichmuth, 2005; Dolan, Atchison, & Huynh, 2005). Therefore, attitudes vary widely within the demographic of older adults.

Rural residence of older adults has not been shown to have an effect on many clinical oral health indicators, except tooth loss. One study documents 18.5% of rural older adults and 18.2% of urban older adults with at least one untreated carious tooth; and 21.9% of teeth of rural older adults and 21.8% of teeth of urban older adults had caries (Vargas, Yellowitz, & Hayes, 2003). The disparity noted between rural and urban residence in oral health was in edentulism (having no teeth) and regular dental care (Vargas, Yellowitz et al., 2003).

In a study of rural older adults (over age 65 years) in Colorado, tooth loss was associated with older age (odds ratio = 1.09; p = 0.02) (Tiwari, Scarbro, Bryant, & Puma, 2016). In another study, rural blacks, ages 50 years and above, had a higher rate of tooth loss (28%) and a lower rate of dental visits (34.3%) than their urban counterparts (18.7% and 49.3%, respectively) (Caldwell, Lee, & Cagney, 2017). Similarly, older rural whites had a higher rate of tooth loss (17.5%) and a lower rate of dental visits (62.4%) than their urban counterparts (11.1% and 73.5%, respectively) (Caldwell et al., 2017). Having access to primary health care had improved oral health outcomes; however, it did not close the difference between older rural whites and blacks (Caldwell et al., 2017). Additionally, living in a rural area had more health-care-related disadvantages that are independent of poverty and the availability of health-care providers (Caldwell, Ford, Wallace, Wang, & Takahashi, 2016). For example, there are higher rates of smoking and smokeless tobacco use by rural residents (Skillman, Doescher, Mouradian, & Brunson, 2010). Tobacco use is a factor in tooth loss. Unfortunately, rural regions are poorly understood, have less research conducted, and are difficult to include in public health discourse because of the lack of data (Caldwell et al., 2016).

It is important to recognize that rural America is highly diversified in social and economic conditions across geographical contexts (Caldwell et al., 2016). Despite this, oral health *perceptions* are often similar in rural areas. Overall, 50.7% of rural dentate older adults perceive their dental status to be poor (Vargas, Yellowitz et al., 2003). Socioeconomically, 62.9% of the rural poor and near-poor older adults perceive their dental status to be poor, and 40.7% of the non-poor perceive their dental status to be poor (Vargas, Yellowitz et al., 2003).

Oral Health-Care Seeking Behavior

Rural Beliefs and Self-Care Practices

As stated earlier, rural older adults are not monolithic; however, certain attitudes and cultural nuances persist. For example, many older rural adults consider health to be the absence of illness. That is, if someone is able to work, or do activities of daily living, he or she would be considered "healthy." With this definition of health, wellness visits are not deemed necessary. Researchers using National Health and Nutrition Examination Survey (NHANES) reported rural older adults were less likely to be regular users of dental care than urban older adults (33.9% and 45.9%, respectively) (Vargas, Yellowitz et al., 2003; Vargas, Dye et al., 2003).

Pain also motivates people to seek needed medical and dental attention. However, older adults may avoid professional preventive dental care for many of the previously mentioned reasons until motivated by pain. Additionally, some rural older adults have *limited or inaccurate oral health knowledge* concerning dental care. For example, in Appalachia, rural older adults are known to relate a child's stomach or intestinal pain with a problem associated with a mandibular canine. Hence, the mandibular canine is referred to as the "stomach tooth." Other misconceptions in some rural areas include the belief that tooth loss is inevitable; that each pregnancy takes calcium out of the woman's teeth; that one tooth is lost with each pregnancy; and that it is appropriate to put a baby to bed with a bottle. Many rural older adults have *unique personal oral health self-care behaviors*. Researchers have noted that self-care behaviors have included over-the-counter medicines (12.1%), over-the-counter dental products (84.3%), salt (51.0%), prayer (6.1%), and complementary therapies (18.2%) to treat bleeding gingiva, dry mouth, and other oral conditions (Arcury et al., 2009) with varying levels of success. Furthermore, anecdotal reports of older adults in rural areas include those of families using household pliers to extract family member's carious teeth, and itinerant dentists going home-to-home to provide dental care, extractions, and fabricate dentures while staying with local families.

Other reasons rural older adults do not have the same level of professional dental care as their urban counterparts include *high dental anxiety* (Bell et al., 2011); *limited access* (Vargas, Yellowitz et al., 2003); *lack of dental insurance—low incomes* (Arcury et al., 2009); *lack of transportation and declining infrastructure* (Caldwell et al., 2016); and *beliefs or perceptions about not needing professional preventive dental care.* A question posed by Dolan et al. (2005) is: would the disparities be alleviated by increasing the availability of dental professionals or financial resources in rural areas; or would unfavorable attitudes toward oral health care that preclude professional dental service use be a more significant barrier even if the services were more readily available?

The availability of services is an important consideration requiring further research. Poor oral health may have systemic health consequences in older adults. Researchers have found associations of periodontal disease with systemic diseases from diabetes (Schallhorn, 2016; Jin, Liao, He, Meng, & Li, 2019); to cardiovascular disease (Simone & Hennekens, 2018; Vedin et al., 2015); to kidney disease (Kapellas, Singh, Bertotti, Nascimento, & Jamieson, 2019; Ricardo et al., 2015); to Alzheimer's disease (Singhrao, Kesavalu, & Crean, 2017); and to cognitive decline (Ide et al., 2016). Also, individuals with severe mental illness are at higher risk of developing periodontal disease, due in large part to the side effects of their psychotropic medications such as antipsychotics, antidepressants, and mood stabilizers (Kisely, 2016). It is therefore important for all older adults to have appropriate preventive oral care, including those who are edentulous. However, because of the financial burdens occurring with the Great Recession (December 2007 to June 2009), general dentist visits declined to a low of 38.4% in 2010 and have not significantly recovered (Guay & Blatz, 2019). Overall, in 2012, the supply of dentists was greater than the demand for oral health care (Guay & Blatz, 2019). In a 2015 report, urban areas had 36.7 practicing dentists per 100,000 people; whereas, rural areas had 24.3 practicing dentists per 100,000 people (Rural Health Information Hub, 2019).

Initiatives to Improve the Oral Health of Older Rural Adults

There are ways in which the dental health of older rural adults may be improved. Community water fluoridation has been very successful in reducing dental caries. Education is important. There is a need for in-office patient education about brushing, flossing, diet, and tobacco cessation; public health education to reach rural older adults in public forums about the same topics; and train-the-trainer interprofessional education initiatives to encourage other professionals to help with oral health education, diet, treatment options, and dental referrals of their patients. Although the demand for oral health care is lower than prior to 2010, there is a need to recruit students into the dental profession as many rural general dentists are nearing retirement age. Recruiting from rural areas, providing rural experiences while in dental school, and providing loan repayments to practice in rural shortage areas are potential ways to increase the dental professional pool in rural areas. Mobile clinics and telehealth are also potential resources that could be used in rural areas. There is a need to evaluate such programs and scale them to a sustainable level if they are successful. Whatever program(s) is/are deemed worthy of governmental support should be sustainable. Dental health is important and rural older adults deserve the care that all Americans are afforded.

References

Arcury, T. A., Bell, R. A., Anderson, A. M., Chen, H., Savoca, M. R., Kohrman, T., & Quandt, S. A. (2009). Oral health self-care behaviors of rural oral adults. *Journal of Public Health Dentistry, 69*(3), 182–189.

Bell, R. A., Arcury, T. A., Anderson, A. M., Chen, H., Savoca, M. R., Gilbert, G. H., & Quandt, S. A. (2011). Dental anxiety and oral health outcomes among rural older adults. *Journal of Public Health Dentistry, 72*(1), 53–59.

Caldwell, J. T., Ford, C. L., Wallace, S. P., Wang, M. C., & Takahashi, L. M. (2016). Intersection of living in a rural versus urban area and race/ethnicity in explaining access to health care in the United States. *American Journal of Public Health, 106*(8), 1463–1469.

Caldwell, J. T., Lee, H., & Cagney, K. A. (2017). The role of primary care for the oral health of rural and urban older adults. *The Journal of Rural Health, 33*(4), 409–418.

Crest. History of Toothpaste. (2019). Retrieved from https://crest.com/en-us/oral-health/why-crest/faq/history-toothpaste

Dolan, T. A., Atchison, K., & Huynh, T. N. (2005). Access to dental care among older adults in the United States. *Journal of Dental Education, 69*(9), 961–974.

Guay, A. H., & Blatz, A. (2019). The effect of the Great Recession on the demand for general oral health care and orthodontic care. *Journal of the American Dental Association, 150*(4), 287–293.

Hamano, T., Takeda, M., Tominaga, K., Sundquist, K., & Nabika, T. (2017). Is accessibility to dental care facilities in rural areas associated with number of teeth in elderly residents? *International Journal of Environmental Research and Public Health, 14*(3), E327.

Ide, M., Harris, M., Stevens, A., Sussams, R., Hopkins, V., Culliford, D., . . . Puenter, U. (2016). Periodontitis and cognitive decline in Alzheimer's disease. *PLoS One, 11*(3), e0151081.

Jin, D. S., Liao, Y. T., He, L., Meng, H. X., & Li, P. (2019). Study on periodontal status of patients with pre-diabetes. *Chinese Journal of Stomatology, 54*(3), 157–163.

Kapellas, K., Singh, A., Bertotti, M., Nascimento, G. G., & Jamieson, L. M. (2019). Perio-CKD collaboration. Periodontal and chronic kidney disease association: A systematic review and meta-analysis. *Nephrology, 24*(2), 202–212.

Kisely, S. (2016). No mental health without oral health. *The Canadian Journal of Psychiatry, 61*(5), 277–282.

Kiyak, H. A., & Reichmuth, M. (2005). Barriers to and enablers of older adults' use of dental services. *Journal of Dental Education, 69*(9), 975–986.

Newton, J. T., & Bower, E. J. (2005). The social determinants of oral health: New approaches to conceptualizing and researching complex causal networks. *Community Dentistry and Oral Epidemiology, 33*(1), 25–34.

Ricardo, A. C., Athavale, A., Chen, J., Hampole, H., Garside, D., Marucha, P., & Lash, J. P. (2015). Periodontal disease, chronic kidney disease and mortality: Results from the third National Health and Nutrition Examination survey. *BMC Nephrology, 16*(1), 97.

Rural Health Information Hub. (2018). *Rural aging*. Retrieved March 20, 2019, from https://www.ruralhealthinfo.org/topics/aging

Rural Health Information Hub: Oral Health in Rural Communities. (2019). *Do rural areas have sufficient dental health workforce?* Retrieved from www.ruralhealthinfo.org/topics/oral-health

Schallhorn, R. A. (2016). Understanding the inter-relationship between periodontitis and diabetes: Current evidence and clinical implications. *Compendium of Continuing Education in Dentistry, 37*(6), 368–370.

Simone, T. S., & Hennekens, C. H. (2018). Interrelationships of periodontal disease, systemic inflammation, and cardiovascular disease. *Annals of Dentistry and Oral Health, 2*, 108.

Singhrao, S. K., Kesavalu, L., & Crean, S. (2017). Putative association of periodontitis with Alzheimer's disease. *Advances in Alzheimer's Disease, 5*, 183–196.

Skillman, S. M., Doescher, M. P., Mouradian, W. E., & Brunson, D. K. (2010). The challenge to delivering oral health services in rural America. *Journal of Public Health Dentistry, 70*(2020), S49–S57.

Tiwari, T., Scarbro, S., Bryant, L. L., & Puma, J. (2016). Factors associated with tooth loss in older adults in rural Colorado. *Journal of Community Health, 41*(3), 476–481.

Vargas, C., Dye, B. A., & Hayes, K. (2003, Summer). Oral health care utilization by US rural residents, National Health Interview Survey 1999. *Journal of Public Health Dentistry, 63*(3), 150–157.

Vargas, C., Yellowitz, J. A., & Hayes, K. L. (2003). Oral health status of older rural adults in the United States. *Journal of the American Dental Association, 134*, 479–486.

Vedin, O., Hagström, E., Gallup, D., Neely, M. L., Stewart, R., Koenig, W. . . . Held, C. (2015). Periodontal disease in patients with chronic coronary heart disease: Prevalence and association with cardiovascular risk factors. *European Journal of Preventive Cardiology. 22*(6), 771–778.

Vujicic, M., Buchmueller, T., & Klein, R. (2016). Dental care presents the highest level of financial barriers, compared to other types of health care. *Health Affairs, 35*(12), 2176–2182.

Wiener, R. C., Shen, C., Sambamoorthi, U., & Findley, P. A. (2017). Rural veterans' dental utilization, Behavioral Risk Factor Surveillance Survey, 2014. *Journal of Public Health Dentistry*, 77(4), 383–392.

17 DIRECT CARE WORKERS

Robert Espinoza

Introduction

With proper long-term services and supports, older people in rural America can maintain independence in their homes and communities as long as possible, as well as receive support in residential or skilled nursing homes if needed. Unfortunately, the poor quality of direct care jobs—coupled with a range of unique barriers to care experienced by rural residents—makes it difficult to achieve this ideal. To create a strong long-term care system for rural older people, policymakers and industry leaders must strengthen the direct care workforce through multiple public policy and workforce interventions that are rooted in research and endorsed by an educated and engaged public.

Provided here is a detailed national snapshot of the direct care workforce, including key demographics, job characteristics, and employment projections. Four major challenges facing this workforce are described—low compensation, inadequate training, limited career advancement, and a strained system worsened by high turnover—as well as a review of the unique workforce considerations in rural areas. Finally, a structural approach is proposed for improving direct care jobs in rural areas through policy reforms, workforce interventions, research, and public education.

A Detailed Snapshot of the Direct Care Workforce

Direct care workers provide daily support to older adults and people with disabilities across a variety of environments, including private homes, residential care settings, and nursing homes (PHI, 2019b). This workforce is composed of three primary occupations. Personal care aides assist their clients with activities such as dressing, bathing, and eating, as well as housekeeping, errands, appointments, and community engagement. Home health aides and nursing assistants perform many of the same activities as personal care aides, as well as clinical tasks, such as blood pressure readings, assistance with range-of-motion exercises, and more.

Nationwide, there are 4.5 million direct care workers—half of these workers are in the home care industry while the other half are employed in nursing homes, residential care, and other industries (PHI, 2019e, 2019f). The vast majority (86%) of these workers are women; 59% are people of color; and 26% are immigrants. The median age for direct care workers is 41 years, and almost one in four workers is aged 55 and older. As the number of older people in the U.S. continues to surge, and as the average American lives longer, the need for these workers will rise—across urban, suburban, and rural areas. Between 2016 and 2026, the long-term care industry will need to fill 7.8 million job openings in direct care (Campbell, 2019).

Key Challenges Facing Direct Care Workers

To meet growing demand for direct care and strengthen recruitment and retention among direct care workers, several job-related challenges must be addressed.

Low Compensation

Despite their clear value, direct care workers struggle financially in jobs that are poor in quality, exemplified in large part by individuals receiving persistently low wages and reflecting high poverty rates. The median hourly wage for direct care workers is $12.27, a figure that has increased only slightly in the last decade (adjusted for inflation) (PHI, 2019g). Additionally, 30% of direct workers work part-time, and their median annual earnings are $20,200. In turn, one in five direct care workers lives in poverty, and 44% live in low-income households.

Inadequate Training

The training policy landscape and delivery infrastructure for direct care workers remain underdeveloped and inconsistent across settings and occupations. While home health aides and nursing assistants are federally required to complete at least 75 hours of training, personal care aides have no federal requirement and are governed by state laws and policies that vary widely; only 15 states and the District of Columbia require 40 or more hours of training for personal care aides (PHI, 2019a, 2019c, 2019d). Furthermore, the dearth in public funding for training in direct care means that states often struggle to implement high-quality, adult learner-centered training curricula and programs that reliably train all direct care workers across occupations, settings, and learning styles (PHI, 2019h).

Limited Career Advancement

The direct care workforce is also limited in terms of advancement opportunities that are designed to improve care for consumers and provide a gratifying career path for workers. Advanced roles—which position workers to play a more expansive role in the delivery of care—are generally lacking at the state and provider level, despite the growing body of evidence that these roles improve care quality for consumers and job satisfaction among workers (Drake, 2019).

A Strained System, High Turnover

Long-term care costs continue to rise, which prevents individuals and families from accessing much-needed care (PHI, 2019h). Moreover, as state lawmakers grapple with the growing public cost of this system, in a time of strained state-level budgets, providers are faced with inadequate reimbursement rates that complicate their abilities to deliver proper care and enact job improvements for direct care workers. In states and localities across the country, a recruitment and retention crisis in direct care has emerged, with turnover among direct care workers hovering around 60% or higher and job vacancies being common across the sector (PHI, 2019b).

Unique Rural Barriers

Preparing the direct care workforce to efficiently deliver care in rural areas requires an understanding of the unique barriers facing older people in these communities.

- Widening "Care Gap." In rural areas (more so than in urban areas), the growth in the number of working-age women (the typical demographic for direct care jobs) is not keeping pace with the growth in the number of people aged 65 and older (PHI, 2017).
- Fewer Younger People. As younger people in rural areas reach adulthood, they are likely to migrate to metropolitan areas (PHI, 2017). This trend leaves their older loved ones without family support and the field with a smaller candidate pool of workers.
- High Unmet Need. Older people in rural areas (and urban areas) are challenged with finding support from personal care aides (Henning-Smith, Wu, & Lahr, 2019). As a result, they are likely to remain isolated in their homes, experience mistakes with their medications, and go without buying groceries, eating regular meals, and managing other necessary household chores, among other necessities.
- Limited Health and Social Services. Compared to people in cities and suburban communities, rural residents live in areas with fewer health and social services, including hospitals, health-care clinics, and long-term care supports (Brown, Lash, Wright, & Tomisek, 2011).
- Reliance on Institutional Services. Rural residents are less likely than their non-rural counterparts to have access to home and community-based supports, forcing them to rely more on institutional services, such as nursing homes (Coburn & Lundblad, 2017).
- High Rates of Chronic Conditions. Older people in rural areas report higher rates of chronic conditions, which often result in the need for paid support (Hirsch, 2019), yet training related to these specific conditions is generally lacking.
- Limited Public Transportation. Public transportation is less developed in rural areas than in urban areas, which makes it difficult and often expensive for older people to travel to their appointments (PHI, 2017). In rural areas, home care workers must also travel long distances by car to reach clients, an added expense not covered by many employers.
- Vast Geographic Distances. For many home care workers, traveling from one client to another in large, geographically dispersed rural areas can take hours, permitting them to reach only a few clients each day (PHI, 2017). Additionally, long-distance commuting results in additional wear and tear and damage to automobiles, yielding various travel-related expenses for workers and their employers.
- Broadband Deserts. In many parts of rural America, access to broadband is thin or non-existent. Access to high-speed internet, which is what is needed for many technology products and software programs in health care, is especially limited (Turner-Lee, 2019).

A Structural Solution: Key Areas for Action

To address the challenges facing the direct care workforce in rural communities, four key areas must be addressed: policy reforms, workforce interventions, research, and public education.

Policy Reforms

State lawmakers can enact a range of policies that strengthen direct care supports in rural areas (PHI, 2019h). Policies that improve the quality of direct jobs—by increasing compensation, boosting training standards and programs, and creating advanced roles, as three leading examples—would improve recruitment and retention in this sector, among other outcomes (Espinoza, 2017). These job improvements would require an increase in both general funding and reimbursement rate levels for long-term services and supports—with attention to the needs of rural residents; these improvements would in turn expand access for rural consumers and ensure that long-term care providers have the capacity to provide sufficient services and offer high-quality jobs. Additionally, government leaders could improve data collection on this workforce, fund matching service registries that pair consumers with workgroups, and create statewide workgroups to craft action plans in support of this workforce.

Workforce Interventions

Upskilling and advanced role approaches—which provide direct care workers with condition-specific competencies, enhanced communication skills, and more—have shown success in improving workers' capacity to support clients and participate in care teams (Drake, 2019). Advanced roles can also improve job satisfaction, increase compensation, and reduce turnover—all necessary in an unstable sector. The direct care training infrastructure—requirements, personnel, training materials, and testing and certification systems—could be strengthened at the state level, with attention to both improving training in core competencies for workers in rural areas and developing enhanced training related to chronic conditions that are prevalent in rural communities (PHI, 2019h). Finally, despite the broadband challenges described earlier in this chapter, technology could be leveraged to improve direct care supports in rural areas, without replacing workers. Areas for technological intervention include training and skills development (through e-learning approaches); facilitating interdisciplinary communication (such as through mobile devices to improve reporting on client conditions); and recruiting and managing the workforce (through social media recruitment and worker scheduling, as two examples) (Scales, 2019). To be effective, technology innovations would need proper screening, testing, and funding to support consumers across the board and not replace workers.

Research

More research is needed to fully understand the direct care workforce needs in rural areas. Better data on direct care workforce volume, stability, and compensation would help the field target resources to rural areas, among other benefits (National Direct Service Workforce Resource Center, 2009). The industry could also build evidence on successful workforce interventions in the areas of upskilling, advanced roles, training, and technology. Research on the needs, experiences, and aspirations of direct care workers would help the public-private sector support these workers on the job and in their daily lives, as well as create relevant interventions, products, and services.

Public Education

Public education campaigns can help raise awareness about the direct care workforce and the needs of rural residents (Espinoza, 2018). These types of campaigns can also target online users by zip code, effectively reaching people who live in rural counties, and they can foster online dialogue and digital advocacy. Finally, the stories of both workers and consumers can build empathy and inform policy and practice interventions from the grassroots level. These campaigns should account for accessibility issues, digital literacy implications, broadband limitations, and cultural and linguistic differences.

Conclusion

Direct care workers are key to helping rural older adults and people with disabilities thrive in their communities—but only if public policy and industry practice transform these jobs through the range of interventions described here.

Moreover, the primary demographics of this workforce (women, people of color, and immigrants) have long been culturally devalued—and their clients (older persons and people with disabilities) have also been pushed to the margins across institutions. Confronting the structurally biased systems that perpetuate these inequalities will be central to creating a strong direct care workforce and long-term care sector.

Direct care workers are also part of a broader caregiving system that includes a variety of health and social professionals, as well as family caregivers. A comprehensive approach to strengthening rural caregiving will ensure that the full spectrum of practitioners and family caregivers have the funding and institutional support to make a difference in the lives of rural older people.

Finally, as the demand for care in rural America intensifies, innovations in long-term care will become more urgent. However, any innovation, as with the rest of long-term care, will rely on a robust financial investment from government. To support older adults regardless of where they live, we must imagine a well-funded long-term care system that everyone can afford and access—one that will create strong direct care jobs for the years ahead.

References

Brown, D., Lash, S., Wright, B., & Tomisek, A. 2011. *Strengthening the direct service workforce in rural areas.* The Centers for Medicare & Medicaid website. Retrieved from www.medicaid.gov/medicaid/ltss/downloads/workforce/rural-area-issue-brief.pdf

Campbell, S. (2019, January 4). *New research: 7.8 million direct care jobs will need to be filled by 2026.* Blog post. Retrieved from https://phinational.org/news/new-research-7-8-million-direct-care-jobs-will-need-to-be-filled-by-2026/

Coburn, A., & Lundblad, J. (2017). *Rural long-term services and supports: A primer.* Rural Policy Research Institute website. Retrieved from the www.rupri.org/wp-content/uploads/LTSS-RUPRI-Health-Panel-2017.pdf

Drake, A. (2019, March 4). *How "upskilling" can maximize home care workers' contributions and improve serious illness care.* Blog post. Retrieved from www.healthaffairs.org/do/10.1377/hblog20190227.420595/full/

Espinoza, R. (2017). The changing policy landscape of the direct care workforce. *Public Policy & Aging Report, 27*(3), 101–105. doi:10.1093/ppar/prx014

Espinoza, R. (2018, December 7). *Savvy social media: 6 lessons from Minnesota and Wisconsin.* Blog post. Retrieved from https://phinational.org/savvy-social-media-6-lessons-from-minnesota-and-wisconsin/

Henning-Smith, C., Wu, Z., & Lahr, M. (2019). *Unmet need for personal care assistance among rural and urban older adults.* The University of Minnesota Rural Health Research Center website. Retrieved from https://rhrc.umn.edu/publication/unmet-need-for-personal-care-assistance-among-rural-and-urban-older-adults/

Hirsch, S. (2019). Rural America by the numbers. *Generations: Journal of the American Society on Aging, 43*(2), 9–16.

National Direct Service Workforce Resource Center. (2009). *The need for monitoring the long-term care direct service workforce and recommendations for data collection.* Retrieved from www.medicaid.gov/medicaid/ltss/downloads/workforce/monitoring-dsw.pdf

PHI. (2017). *State of care: Minnesota's home care landscape.* Retrieved from https://phinational.org/resource/state-of-care-minnesotas-home-care-landscape/

PHI. (2019a). *Home health aide training requirements by state.* Retrieved September 19, 2019, from https://phinational.org/advocacy/home-health-aide-training-requirements-state-2016/

PHI. (2019b). *Key facts and FAQ.* Retrieved September 19, 2019, from https://phinational.org/policy-research/key-facts-faq/

PHI. (2019c). *Nursing assistant training requirements by state.* Retrieved September 19, 2019, from https://phinational.org/advocacy/nurse-aide-training-requirements-state-2016/

PHI. (2019d). *Personal care aide training requirements by state.* Retrieved September 19, 2019, from https://phinational.org/advocacy/personal-care-aide-training-requirements/

PHI. (2019e). *U.S. home care workers: Key facts (2019).* Retrieved from https://phinational.org/resource/u-s-home-care-workers-key-facts-2019/

PHI. (2019f). *U.S. nursing assistants employed in nursing homes: Key facts (2019).* Retrieved from https://phinational.org/resource/u-s-nursing-assistants-employed-in-nursing-homes-key-facts-2019/

PHI. (2019g). *Workforce data center.* Retrieved September 19, 2019, from https://phinational.org/policy-research/workforce-data-center/

PHI. (2019h) *Workforce matters: The direct care workforce and state-based LTSS social insurance programs.* Retrieved from https://phinational.org/resource/workforce-matters/

Scales, K. (2019, August 7). *Leveraging technology to support—not supplant—the home care workforce.* Blog post. Retrieved from www.healthaffairs.org/do/10.1377/hblog20190805.54553/full/

Turner-Lee, N. (2019). Can emerging technologies buffer the cost of in-home care in rural America? *Generations: Journal of the American Society on Aging, 43*(2), 88–93.

18
DISABILITIES

Stephen Gilson and Elizabeth DePoy

Rural populations aging with disability are examined here and three models that differently conceptualize and shape responses to disability and aging in the context of rurality are presented. The application of theory-based principles through which to redesign aging and disability as part of the valued fabric of rural life are then proposed and illustrated.

Definitions

Defining disability in later life is a herculean task, as is distinguishing the aging body from the aging disabled body. (Note the term body refers to the body as the vessel for the totality of life experience (Malacrida & Lowe, 2016)). As pejoratively stated by Tidy (2016), "Disability in old age is frequent and lowers the quality of life." Words such as those penned by this author reflect aging itself as disproportionately debilitating (e.g., disabling) and further suggests that any change in functional status related to advancing years means that a person is damaged. However, given the increase in both aging and disabled bodies, recent scholarship has aimed to wrest both aging and disability away from a decline model, repositioning it within the expanse of human diversity. As discussed next, how aging and disability are conceptualized, in large part, guides responses to this conflated population, promising multiple scaffolds for engaging in innovative analysis and advancing the possibility of a rich life in rural settings for those in advanced years, their families, and communities.

Exploring Disability

Disability is a relatively new word applied to select human traits and states. Before the twentieth century, atypical human phenomena that are now identified as disabling conditions were explained as divine, moral, or karma (Williamson, 2019). Because of many factors, these ideas have been supplanted with the three primary theoretical models now inhabiting the disability literature: the medical, the social, and the disjuncture models. Each brings diverse understandings of and responses to the phenomenon of disability.

Although it meets with significant opposition, the medical model of disability remains predominant in the twenty-first century. This schema posits disability as an embodied phenomenon in which its inhabitant has an internal condition limiting age-referenced function

(DePoy & Gilson, 2011). Through the medical lens, disability is seen as abnormality of the physical or psychological corpus resulting in impairment and inviting tinkering or fixing. For example, unlike infancy when children cannot yet walk, in adulthood, the need for wheeled mobility to support movement that should be accomplished by ambulation is considered a disability. Moreover, developmental theory sets the stage for marrying advanced years to medical debility.

Prevalence and incidence statistics fit within this model, as the impaired body can be counted by type, age, location, income, function, and so forth. According to the most recent census, 15.2% of rural residents report one or more disabling conditions (U.S. Census, 2017). This percentage rises disproportionately by age (Myers, Greiman, von Reichert, & Seekins, 2016). Because of the nascency of rural disability research, percentage data on disability type in rural areas are unavailable. However, given the relatively stable percentage distribution in the U.S., extrapolating from national data provides a reasonable estimate of rural impairment type. Over 14% of the over 65 population cannot live at home independently. Comorbid health conditions such as obesity are disproportionately high in the disabled older adult population (U.S. Census, 2017).

Peering down the medical tunnel to disability responses, professional intervention is most often the leitmotif. With specialized knowledge, professionals guide disabled persons, families, and caregivers to move the atypical body toward the norm through compensatory or accommodative strategies. The medical framework is useful in illuminating the atypical medicalized body and guiding professional intervention. What it does not disclose, however, is the nature of well-being and how to craft communities to achieve this aim gracefully. We turn to the social and disjuncture models of disability for this discussion.

In the social model, the impaired body starring on the medical model stage is supplanted by a leading villain, the environment. The hostility and inaccessibility of environmental attributes, not the body itself, is the locus of disability. For example, staired entrances, not the bodies unable to navigate them, are the seat of disability through this approach. Emerging from this perspective are legislative initiatives such as the Americans with Disabilities Act (ADA). Following in the footsteps of civil rights movements, the social model spurs activism for target populations such as wheelchair users and individuals with hearing and visual impairment. While this view invites environmental surveillance and change, it does so for only some impaired bodies, leaving others outside the rural ramparts.

Because each of the previously mentioned disability models has value but is incomplete, recent theorists have activated disability. Early interactive models still acknowledge disability as impairment but look to the resolution from thoughtful changes in context. The disjuncture approach (DePoy & Gilson, 2011) foregrounds individual inability to reach a goal as the seat of disability. As such, disability may be attributed to "any body" regardless of the presence of impairment. For example, in a recent study of aging farmers (DePoy, Brzozwski, & Gilson, 2018), economics trumped embodied changes as the most disabling factor in agricultural career continuation. Viewing disability as belonging to anyone engorges the population and creates a multidimensional canvas for painting responses but does not lend itself to epidemiological surveillance. However, disjuncture presents many paths for a textured response approach.

Words on the Meaning of Aging

Implicit in the term "aging" is the chronometric categorization of humans (Baars, 2012), in which the accumulation of years over time brings with it loss of youth, function, and social value. Although beyond the scope of this discussion, attention to the multiple theories of decline and senescence illustrates the host of factors that are identified as causal of damage as lived time accrues (Cavanaugh & Blanchard-Fields, 2019).

Now, recall the brief introduction to the role of age norms outside of which disability resides. While such developmental theory proposes prototypes for older adults on the basis of chronometric age, it is curious that impairment is ascribed to these norms thereby swelling the ranks of disability in later years (e.g., hearing and vision changes, differences in strength and endurance, and so forth). So, in this sense, the medical model of disability, while alive and well in aging, is no longer seen as atypical or abnormal but rather is essentialized as the norm for older adults. Thus, the medical model applied to later life (Lawrence-Lightfoot, 2009), diagnoses advancing years as inevitable embodied decline spiraling to dysfunction.

Picturing Rural Geographies

While bucolic, rural areas often are infamous for sparse health and social services (RHIB, 2002–2019). Thus, medical model and developmental theory proponents of disability and aging deservedly decry the dearth of limited professional services as the primary reason that aging with disability in rural communities is difficult. Scarce or absent public transportation systems, long distances to specialized health and social services, and caregiver shortages are of particular note. Further, because people with disabilities have encountered employment discrimination during younger years, conflated with chronically limited rural job opportunities, poverty is disproportionately high among rural residents with diagnosed atypical bodies. However, meager services met with limited income and unrequited need create a fallow field awaiting to be seeded with innovative redesign.

Redesign

Redesign, a creative process, requires both forensic and asset analysis; in other words, querying what has failed and what has been productive in meeting needs respectively. Because rural geographies are not homogenous, the implementation of universal strategies and those imported from urban communities is contraindicated. Instead, well-developed, theory-based redesign principles relevant to rurality, aging, and disability can flexibly guide action specifically tailored to each rural area. Three redesign principles, skepticism, proximity, and seamless integration are particularly germane to recrafting rural communities as welcoming to those who are aging with disability.

1. *Skepticism* refers to productive questioning of "what is," "why it is," and what needs to change.
2. Ensuring that each community is seen as unique in which solutions are aligned with inherent assets and needs embodies *proximity*.
3. *Seamlessness* refers to continuity. This principle is a guide for reenvisioning disability (regardless of age cohort) as simply a part of humanness rather than an essential category. Dissolution of the categorical perimeters of disability in chronometric aging leaves a cultivatable space for redesigning disability, aging, and disability in aging in rural areas as part of human diversity that capitalizes on often overlooked proximal ingenuity and human capital in non-urban geographies.

Principle 1: Skepticism begins with the knowledge that scarcity of resources is likely to continue, particularly in geographies with low population densities. Thus, the skeptic questions how to best rework the medical model service structures relying on on-site, resource-rich systems unlikely to relocate and relinquish profitability of real estate in populated areas. The social model demands environmental redesign, but when borrowed from urban spaces (ramps, automated doors, sophisticated navigation systems, and so forth), it may not be feasible or relevant to all rural communities. Through redesign, how existing services can be revised, repurposed, and augmented such that they are respectful, relevant, and have a wide rural girth is in order. Enter the consultative model, integrating everyday technology as one example of how professional services delivered in traditional office spaces can be reconfigured, as illustrated in the following example.

Principle 2: Proximity involves closeness and responsiveness to the actual rural community in question and those within, who are objects of well-meaning but overloaded service systems begging for redesign. Mining and fitting community assets into revised models of community support for those aging with disability is indicated.

Principle 3: Guided by seamlessness, specialized person-to-person, office-based service models can be reinvented into consultative approaches in which professionals share expertise with community members to capitalize on existing lay assets.

Example: A Study of Farm Ingenuity

Farming is central to many, but not all rural communities. Nevertheless, the principles extracted from a recent study (DePoy et al., 2018) can be extrapolated for diverse non-urban areas characterized by low population density and service scarcity.

Services to assist aging and disabled farmers to adjust to embodied challenges are offered through many rural university-community partnerships. And while well-intended, they are often underutilized because they are perceived as irrelevant, not needed, not trusted, or not resonating with the fundamental needs of eligible recipients (Reed, 2015).

The study, visited only briefly here, exposed important knowledge to inform service revision. First, respondents recognized their bodies as aging and changing, but were *skeptical* that the provider-client model would be an approach through which they would learn to adapt. To the contrary, farmers exhibited their own ingenuity most often through *seamless strategies* and products available to anyone. Some examples include pruning apple trees so that tree heights were easily accessible to those unable to climb, adding off-the-shelf equipment such as simple winches to tractors to raise and lower objects without having to dismount, using commercially available motorized carts, hydraulic lifts, and hand trucks to manage livestock feeding, using colorful feed and plant pails for visual cues, harvesting crops over more days than needed to avoid fatigue, making prototypes from bailing twine before fabricating permanent devices, using an all-terrain vehicle already equipped with hand controls as a tractor when unable to use one or both legs to accelerate and brake, creating driving collaboratives for those unable to drive after dark or at all, forming farmer-to-farmer cooperatives to job-share and exchange innovations, using readily available smart watches as fall detection devices, and using YouTube videos as instructive, among many others.

Thus, these seamless strategies, using available products and personal inventiveness to adapt the body to context and vice versa, were not informed through professional instruction but rather through "passive YouTube consultation," an underutilized professional service medium.

Illustrating proximity, a major articulated unmet need was an equipment sharing collaborative. For those unable to afford their own equipment, distributing the economic burden among many would have significantly reduced costs. For this strategy, resources and differing purchasing and maintenance models are awaiting professional-farmer cooperative harvesting.

Conclusion

Aging and impairment can be reinvented as primary stimuli for rural innovation. This realization forms a powerful direction for rural redesign in which all citizens are valued and have a role. Kluge, Zagheni, Loichinger, and Vogt (2014) "argue that there may be positive unintended side effects of population aging that can be leveraged to address pressing environmental problems" such as those identified in rural communities. Population trends are not limited to crisis. They create need and foster profound cultural, technological, educational, intellectual, and economic change.

We recognize that farming adaptation is not the only dilemma faced by rural communities as aging and disability increase. While all unmet needs cannot be addressed here, we would be remiss not to acknowledge caregiver scarcity and isolation. Existing faith communities (Gleckman, 2019) and communication technology have been proposed as seamless vehicles for meeting surveillance and caregiving needs.

And finally, a major lesson speaks loudly to higher education. If rural citizens aging with disability or becoming disabled are to continue as valued members of their communities, a major shift in professional education is warranted. Teaching professional knowledge and skill to students through direct service models can and should be augmented by consultation and community organizing approaches to implementing the three design principles presented earlier. One rural university system in Northern New England has recognized the role of advanced education in contributing to a flourishing rural life, as exemplified by a "Grand Challenge" call for educational innovation in rural health and wellness. Reimaging how a rural environment can be reinvented to meet increasing human diversity represents an excellent rural redesign opportunity.

References

Baars, J. (2012). *Aging and the art of living*. Baltimore, MD: Johns Hopkins University Press.

Cavanaugh, J., & Blanchard-Fields, F. (2019). *Adult development and aging*. Boston, MA: Cenage.

DePoy, E., Brzozwski, R., & Gilson, S. (2018). *Aging farmers with disabilities: From omission to belonging*. Washington, DC: AUCD.

DePoy, E., & Gilson, S. (2011). *Studying disability*. Los Angeles, CA: Sage Publications.

Gleckman, H. (2019, October 28). The special challenges of nearly 11 million seniors who live in rural communities. *Forbes*.

Kluge, F., Zagheni, E., Loichinger, E., & Vogt, T. (2014). The advantages of demographic change after the wave: Fewer and older, but healthier, greener, and more productive? *PLoS One*, *9*(9).

Lawrence-Lightfoot, S. (2009). *The third chapter: Passion, risk, and adventure in the 25 years after 50*. New York: Sarah Crichton Books.

Malacrida, C., & Lowe, J. (2016). *Sociology of the body: A reader*. New York: Oxford University Press.

Myers, A., Greiman, L., von Reichert, C., & Seekins, T. (2016). *Rural matters: The geography of disability in rural America*. Missoula, MT: The University of Montana Rural Institute for Inclusive Communities.

Reed, D. (2015). Protecting ourselves from harm: Voices of aging farmers. *Journal of Agricultural Safety and Health*, 269–279.

RHIB. (2002–2019). *Aging in place in rural communities*. Rural Health Information Hub. Retrieved from www.ruralhealthinfo.org/toolkits/aging/1/rural-issues

Tidy, C. (2016, January 28). *Disability in older people*. Retrieved from https://patient.info/doctor/disability-in-older-people

U.S. Census. (2017). *American factfinder*. Retrieved from https://factfinder.census.gov/faces/tableservices/jsf/pages/productview.xhtml?pid=ACS_17_5YR_S1810&prodType=table

Williamson, B. (2019). *Accessible America*. New York: New York University Press.

19
DISASTERS

Kim Mosby, Traci Birch, Aimee Moles, and Katie E. Cherry

When natural or technological hazards strike unpopulated or underpopulated areas, they are generally not considered disasters. More often, society tackles the issues of disaster impacts and recovery only when natural hazards or technological accidents disrupt people's lives, destroy infrastructure, and damage resources (Quarantelli, 1985; Kroll-Smith & Couch, 1991). While different types of disasters occur across the world, social scientists recognize that disasters do not impact all people equally. Some populations are more vulnerable to the adverse effects of disasters because of social stratification systems that limit resources based on social characteristics (Wisner, Blaikie, Cannon, & Davis, 2004; Phillips, Thomas, Fothergill, & Blinn-Pike, 2010). Groups with greater political influence and power may retain the resources to remove themselves and their property from harm and repair any damages they may sustain (Wisner et al., 2004; Phillips et al., 2010). People on the margins of society, such as women, minorities, the impoverished, and/or disabled, often have fewer resources to respond to threats, and they may recover from disasters more slowly (Wisner et al., 2004; Phillips et al., 2010). In addition, they may be forced to live in more risky environmental situations in which housing is often less expensive (Wisner et al., 2004; Bullard & Wright, 2012).

Older adults, especially frail individuals, are one group that has traditionally been viewed as vulnerable to disasters, having higher morbidity and mortality rates than their younger counterparts (Cutter, Boruff, & Shirley, 2003, World Health Organization, 2008; Tuohy & Stephens, 2012). Population-based health statistics show that older adults are more likely to die during disasters than younger people (Johnson & Galea, 2009). This outcome can happen for a number of reasons. Older adults are more likely to have chronic health conditions that require routine medication and medical care. The CDC estimates that among older adults 80% have a chronic health condition and 50% have two or more, which increases their vulnerability to disasters (Aldrich & Benson, 2008). Severe disasters can often disrupt support services and access to medications or necessary care. Older adults are also more susceptible to extreme temperatures that may happen if a disaster interferes with electrical systems that control heating or air conditioning systems. Additionally, if disasters result in displacement, those older adults with Alzheimer's disease and related disorders may experience a more rapid deterioration in their mental and physical health as a result of being displaced from their familiar environment. How disasters impact older adults is important because the World

Health Organization (2008) estimates that the number of people 65 and older increases by 10,000 people every day in the U.S. By 2030, this age group will comprise 20% of the nation's population (Morken & Warner, 2012).

A critical, though often overlooked, variable in disaster planning and management concerns where people live, especially frail elders. Location, as well as limited financial and social resources, likely increases older adults' vulnerability to disasters. Population studies show that rural areas have higher proportions of older residents than urban areas but have fewer resources available to support the needs of older adults (Kinsella, 2001; Morken & Warner, 2012). In general, those in rural areas tend to be more isolated, have lower incomes, and have higher rates of chronic illness and disability than do their urban counterparts (Morken & Warner, 2012; Skoufalos, Clarke, Ellis, Shepard, & Rula, 2017). Isolation can increase vulnerability because rural dwellers may have less access to outside assistance when a disaster strikes. This assistance could be in the form of help preparing a home before a storm, evacuating to a safer location, or rebuilding after a disaster. Having lower incomes can increase their vulnerability because older persons may struggle to buy adequate supplies to shelter-in-place; to afford travel, hotel, and food costs if evacuation is necessary; and to pay for clean-up and repairs they may be physically unable to perform themselves.

Although older adults may be vulnerable to disasters as a demographic group, other evidence suggests that some older adults may be more resilient than their younger counterparts (Cherry, Allen, & Galea, 2010). Older adults often experience less disaster-related stress than do middle-aged adults because they may have fewer responsibilities, consistent with the burden hypothesis (Cherry et al., 2011). Middle-aged adults may be responsible for caring for their children and their parents after a disaster as well as meeting work responsibilities. Previous life experiences with disaster and trauma can bolster older adults' ability to cope with the negative impacts of disasters (Cherry, Silva Brown, & Galea, 2009; Tuohy & Stephens, 2012; Brockie & Miller, 2017). Prior life experience may increase their capacity for resilience in comparison with younger age groups because older adults can evaluate negative situations in light of prior hardships.

To illustrate how geographic location can affect the vulnerability and resilience of older adults and the communities they reside in (Kaye, 2017), consider the flooding that occurred in Baton Rouge, Louisiana, in 2016. A resiliency index was created to assess environmental factors that may affect recovery at both individual and community levels. Specifically, an index was developed to better measure the impact of a natural disaster (flooding) on community well-being by spatially differentiating locations with flooding and those without. The index was used to understand how adults over age 65 may impact the vulnerability and resilience of rural and urban communities. Recommendations on improving resilience for older adults and the communities where they live are considered.

Case Illustration: Rural and Urban Older Adults After a Flood

The Great Flood of 2016 covered a wide geographic area, affecting a sizable proportion of south Louisiana residents in both rural and urban communities. Monday, August 8, 2016, began as a typical rainy day. A storm system hovered over south Louisiana bringing a torrential downpour that lasted for several consecutive days. By Friday, August 12, local schools were closed because of the perilous threat of flash flooding. Local rivers rose to unimaginable heights. Creeks overtopped their banks, and drainage ditches spilled over, flooding neighborhoods and homes. A relentless environmental event, this flood brought a swath of destruction that impacted personal properties, homes, schools, businesses, and places of worship alike. Thirteen people lost their lives and billions of dollars in damages resulted (Sergent, Padilla, Loerkhe, Petras, & Thorson, 2016).

When disasters happen suddenly like the Great Flood of 2016, first responders and local citizens are catapulted into action to save lives and rescue people who have been stranded. For instance, The Cajun Navy, an impromptu rescue group of concerned citizens, used their own boats, time, and resources to bring stranded residents to safety. Scores of individuals, young and old, were boated out of their flooded homes and neighborhoods to staging areas, where they were eventually airlifted to higher ground. Faith-based communities, among other volunteer organizations, played a pivotal role in caring for disaster survivors in the immediate aftermath of the 2016 flood (Cherry, Calamia, & Elliott, 2021).

An important question is whether older adults influence the overall wellness and resilience of a community during or after an event such as a severe flood. Using an index developed by Moles et al. (2021), it is possible to examine the global effect of the percentage of adults older than 65 on indicators including: community stress, economic health, environmental health (natural and built environments), and public health and safety. A higher percentage of older adults had positive impacts on overall well-being and two of the components of the index, community stress and economic health. Older adults were more likely to live in communities with high occupancy rates, telephone access, nonprofit organizations, and religious organizations. Home ownership and per capita income were also higher in communities with higher percentages of older adults. However, rural communities in the study area saw lower benefits from an aging population while urban communities improved their well-being when older adults were present in higher concentrations. An important takeaway is that significant spatial variations may exist in local impacts of an aging population on well-being.

Community resilience and well-being are nuanced and composed of many factors. The literature shows older adults as a physically vulnerable population in need of special care in disasters because of health risks and physical limitations. Yet studies also show that older adults are mentally more resilient because of previous life experiences with trauma and disasters. The index shows the inclusion of older persons can bring important economic and social resources to a community. These resources may improve a community's overall well-being and the likelihood it can bounce back quickly after a disaster. According to the index, the benefits of having older adults in a community are more pronounced in urban areas than rural areas. This trend is expected because the older adults in urban areas tend to have more financial resources and opportunities for social interactions than those in rural communities.

Recommendations and Future Directions

As climate change increases the frequency and intensity of storms, and as the U.S. population continues to age, planning for vulnerable populations and community resilience will continue to rise in importance, especially in rural areas. Social ideas concerning older adults reflect the reality that aging residents may require special attention and care. Prior research and the index referred to earlier show that persons 65 years and over have valuable knowledge and resources that can help their communities recover from disasters (Cherry et al., 2009; Tuohy & Stephens, 2012). Rural communities could strengthen their resilience by developing programs to encourage intergenerational social cohesion and interaction (Tuohy, Stephens, & Johnston, 2014; Brockie & Miller, 2017). Because many rural older adults do not have family close by, helping elders establish bonds within the community can reduce their dependence on local government. Support structures that naturally emerge in the face of disasters, such as faith-based organizations, together with intergenerational social programming can allow older adults to form meaningful social bonds that may help them prepare and recover in times of disaster. Recognizing older adults' life experiences may also help younger generations make sense of disasters and cope successfully with potential negative psychological effects of disaster-related trauma (Cherry, 2020).

References

Aldrich, N., & Benson, W. F. (2008). CDC's disaster planning goal: Protect vulnerable older adults. *Centers of Disease Control and Prevention*, 1–17.

Brockie, L., & Miller, E. (2017). Understanding older adults' resilience during the Brisbane floods: Social capital, life experience, and optimism. *Disaster Medicine and Public Health Preparedness*, *11*(1), 72–79.

Bullard, R. D., & Wright, B. (2012). *The wrong complexion for protection: How the government response to disaster endangers African American communities*. New York: New York University Press.

Cherry, K. E. (2020). *The other side of suffering: Finding a path to peace after tragedy*. New York: Oxford University Press.

Cherry, K. E., Allen, P. D., & Galea, S. (2010). Older adults and natural disasters: Lessons learned from hurricanes Katrina and Rita. In P. Dass-Brailsford (Ed.), *Crisis and disaster counseling: Lessons learned from hurricane Katrina and other disasters* (pp. 115–130). Thousand Oaks, CA: Sage Publications.

Cherry, K. E., Calamia, M. R., & Elliott, E. M. (2021). When disasters strike: Navigating the challenges of "sudden science." In K. E. Cherry & A. Gibson (Eds.), *The intersection of trauma and disaster behavioral health* (pp. 127–143). New York: Springer.

Cherry, K. E., Silva Brown, J. L., & Galea, S. (2009). Natural disasters and the oldest-old: A psychological perspective on coping and health in late life. In K. E. Cherry (Ed.), *Lifespan perspectives on natural disasters: Coping with Katrina, Rita and other storms* (pp. 171–193). New York: Springer.

Cherry, K. E., Silva Brown, J. L., Marks, L. D., Galea, S., Volaufova, J., Lefante, C., . . . Jazwinski, S. M. (2011). Longitudinal assessment of cognitive and psychosocial functioning after hurricanes Katrina and Rita: Exploring disaster impact on middle-aged, older, and oldest-old adults. *Journal of Applied Biobehavioral Research*, *16*, 187–211.

Cutter, S., Boruff, B. J., & Shirley, W. L. (2003). Social vulnerability to environmental hazards. *Social Science Quarterly*, *84*, 242–261.

Johnson, J., & Galea, S. (2009). Disasters and population health. In K. E. Cherry (Ed.), *Lifespan perspectives on natural disasters: Coping with Katrina, Rita and other storms* (pp. 281–326). New York: Springer.

Kaye, L. W. (2017). Older adults, rural living, and the escalating risk of social isolation. *Public Policy & Aging Report*, *27*(4), 139–144. doi:10.1093/ppar/prx029

Kinsella, K. (2001). Urban and rural dimensions of global population aging: An overview. *The Journal of Rural Health*, *17*(4), 314–322.

Kroll-Smith, S., & Couch, S. R. (1991). What is a disaster? An ecological-symbolic approach to resolving the definitional debate. *International Journal of Mass Emergencies and Disasters*, *9*(3), 355–366.

Moles, A., Birch, T., Chan, Y. L., Yang, D., Zhu, H., & Cherry, K. E. (2021). Community vulnerabilities and wellbeing after disaster. In K. E. Cherry & A. Gibson (Eds.), *The intersection of trauma and disaster behavioral health* (pp. 247–269). New York: Springer.

Morken, L., & Warner, M. (2012). *Planning for the aging population: Rural responses to the challenge*. Issue brief. Washington, DC and Ithaca: National Association of Area Agencies on Aging and Cornell University. Retrieved from cms.mildredwarner.org/p/146

Phillips, B. D., Thomas, D. S. K., Fothergill, A., & Blinn-Pike, L. (Eds.). (2010). *Social vulnerability to disasters*. Boca Raton, FL: CRC Press.

Quarantelli, E. L. (1985). What is disaster? The need for clarification in definition and conceptualization in research. In B. J. Sowder (Ed.), *Disasters and mental health* (pp. 41–73). Washington, DC: U.S. Department of Health and Human Services and National Institute of Mental Health.

Sergent, J., Padilla, R., Loerkhe, J., Petras, G., & Thorson, M. (2016, August 23). *Louisiana's historic floods*. Retrieved from www.usatoday.com/pages/interactives/la-floods-august-2016/

Skoufalos, A., Clarke, J. L., Ellis, D. R., Shepard, V. L., & Rula, E. Y. (2017). Rural aging in America: Proceedings of the 2017 Connectivity Summit. *Population Health Management*, *20*(Suppl 2), S3–S10.

Tuohy, R., & Stephens, C. (2012). Older adults' narratives about a flood disaster: Resilience, coherence, and personal identity. *Journal of Aging Studies*, *26*(1), 26–34.

Tuohy, R., Stephens, C., & Johnston, D. (2014). Older adults' disaster preparedness in the context of the September 2010–December 2012 Canterbury earthquake sequence. *International Journal of Disaster Risk Reduction*, *9*, 194–203.

Wisner, B., Blaikie, P. M., Cannon, T., & Davis, I. (2004). *At risk: Natural hazards, people's vulnerability, and disasters* (2nd ed.). London and New York: Routledge.

World Health Organization. (2008). *Older persons in emergencies: An active ageing perspective*. Retrieved February 21, 2019, from www.who.int/ageing/en

20
DRUG AND ALCOHOL ADDICTION

Sarabeth Biermann and Carl Leukefeld

Addiction is an excess, a reinforcing compulsion, an inability to control dependency behavior and attitudes that can be harmful or beneficial. For alcohol and drug misuse, addiction is clearly harmful. The addiction life span approach suggests that our genetic makeup (tolerance to drug and alcohol use) is linked to our thinking as well as our environment (psychological and social factors), which influences the amount and number of times we use and/or misuse drugs and alcohol (Daugherty & Leukefeld, 1998). Clearly, these parameters change as we age biologically; however, there is limited information about aging and addiction.

When we think about rural settings and substance use, images can pop into our heads. These images frequently range from alcohol stills, revenuers enforcing tax laws, and most recently doctor shopping for prescription opioids. We could add older rural adults selling their prescription medications to supplement their income. These images can include rural older adults who have recently been spotlighted by the popular press as the opioid epidemic devastates Appalachian and other rural regions. This devastation includes drug overdoses and associated criminal activities.

Nora Volkow, Director of the National Institute on Drug Abuse, set the stage about older adults in 2011 when she indicated that the percentage of American 50 to 59 years old who reported abusing an illicit or prescription drugs during the past year more than doubled, from 2.7% to 6.2%, between 2002 and 2009. Baby boomers born between 1946 and 1964 have experience with and histories of illicit drug use and comprise nearly 30% of the U.S. population. In addition, the social and physical changes that accompany the aging experience may increase vulnerability to drug-related problems. The loss of loved ones, juggling of multiple roles, and retirement or loss of employment and income may cause some older adults to self-medicate especially those with a history of taking drugs to cope. Furthermore, the effects of drugs of abuse in older adults may be influenced by age-related health conditions and medications—contingencies that are more problematic when patients hide their drug abuse (National Institute on Drug Abuse, NIDA NOTES, 2011).

This entry, like others in this volume, uses the U.S. Census Bureau definition of rural as any population, housing, or territory that is not in an urban area—"Urban Clusters," with a population of 2,500 to 50,000 or "Urbanized Areas," with a population of 50,000 or more. However, the definition of older adults varies as noted next.

So, who are the rural older adult drug and alcohol misusers? What drug and alcohol services are available? And what are possible implications for rural older adults?

Rural Older Adult Drug and Alcohol Misuse

According to data from the combined 2007 to 2014 National Survey on Drug Use and Health, nearly 16.2 million adults aged 65 or older drank alcohol in the previous month, with 3.4 million reporting binge alcohol use and 772,000 reporting heavy alcohol use. These data also indicate that on an average day, six million older adults used alcohol. Older adults who used alcohol drank an average of approximately two (1.8) drinks per day when they drank with an average of 11.1 days per month of alcohol consumption. In addition, 132,000 older adults used marijuana and 4,300 older adults used cocaine (Mattson et al., 2017).

The National Drug Abuse Warning Network data collected in U.S. emergency rooms indicate that on an average day in 2011, there were 2,056 drug-related emergency department visits by older adults. Of these, 290 involved illegal drug use, nonmedical use of pharmaceuticals, or use of alcohol combined with other drugs (Mattson et al., 2017). In addition, for adults 65 and older, opioid-related overdose deaths increased 17.2% from 2016 to 2017, which was the only age group with an increase in overdose deaths from prescription opioids during that time (Scholl, Seth, Kariisa, Wilson, & Baldwin, 2019).

Overall, tobacco, alcohol, and illicit drug abuse costs the US more than $740 billion annually in terms of crime, lost work productivity, and health care needs. Recently, the nationwide rise in opioid abuse and the associated risks of dependence, overdose, and the spread of infectious diseases such as HIV and hepatitis C has was recognized by Congress and the general public which resulted in targeted funding to support expanded opioid treatment and other services for older rural adults (National Institute on Drug Abuse, 2019).

Rural Older Adult Drug and Alcohol Services

Overall substance abuse treatment and interventions do not typically focus on older adults. Consequently, like urban older adults, rural older adults do not receive specialized services, particularly in rural areas because services are limited when compared to urban areas and frequently require greater travel distances and time for those wishing to access them. Rural treatment addiction services are usually outpatient with expanding medication-assisted treatment for opioid misuse and dependency. This treatment uses medications such as methadone, suboxone, or naltrexone. In addition, rural, residential treatment is becoming more available but tends not to tailor services for older adults seeking addictions treatment. Rural hospitals and public health clinics can also provide addiction services including prevention and education but are limited. Like urban areas, health insurance is important to better ensure receiving rural addictions treatment, which includes older rural adults. Even with insurance, it is important to note that there are fewer providers in rural areas and fewer who specialize in the care of treating older adult addiction.

When we try to understand who is receiving treatment services, data from the national Treatment Episode Data Set (TEDs) can be used. These data indicate that there were 14,230 substance misuse admissions to treatment by older adults 65 and over to U.S. treatment programs and on an average day in 2012, there were 29 admissions by older adults for alcohol use and six admissions to treatment for heroin or other opiates (Mattson et al., 2017). Substance abuse treatment referrals for 65 or older adults were made by: self-referral or by other individuals (17), by the criminal justice system (10), by other health-care providers (5), by community organizations (4), and by alcohol or drug abuse care providers or others (3).

The National Survey on Drug Use and Health in 2017 estimated that nearly 21 million people, aged 12 and older, needed substance use treatment in 2017 but only four million received treatment in the previous year. If we apply the 30% figure (the estimated proportion of baby boomers comprising the U.S. population) cited previously by Volkow for 2011 and the 21 million people in need of treatment, it can be estimated that about 6.7 million older adults need addictions treatment but only 14,230 received treatment in 2012. This estimate is similar to that of Colliver et al. (2006), who estimated that the number of adults aged 50 or older with a substance use disorder was projected to double from 2.8 million in 2002–2006 to 5.7 million in 2020 given the high substance use rate of baby boomers. Consequently, addiction treatment is limited for older adults, particularly rural older adults, since there are fewer addiction treatment programs in rural areas.

Implications for Rural Older Adults Addictions

Rural areas like all parts of the U.S. are youth-oriented. For example, most advertisements favor our youth-oriented culture. However, there are exceptions including both print and media drug company ads, which develop and reinforce the need for older adults to use medications that are prescribed by a physician or purchased over the counter to ease a variety of disorders including pain. Consequently, older adults, as they age, may be more prone to mixing medications, swapping medications, and not disposing of expired medications properly or at all, which can put them in harm's way.

It is not clear how older rural adults respond to addiction treatment since treatment is usually not age and culturally sensitive. In addition, estimates of the number of rural older adults who need addiction treatment are not geographically precise. When the limited data and the number of specialized rural addiction practitioners are considered along with the small number of addiction treatment services for older adults, rural older adults will continue to find themselves in difficult situations for recovering and may continue to have to rely on self-help groups like Alcoholics Anonymous and Narcotics Anonymous if available in rural areas.

Given the current surge in opioid misuse in rural areas and the number of overdoses, rural older adults, as parents and grandparents, can find themselves serving as the "fabric" of many rural families and communities. Their roles can include caregivers for their grandchildren whose parents have overdosed and died, are in jail or prison, or are active users. These important caregiving roles receive limited recognition and even less support in many rural areas. On the other hand, for those addicted to alcohol and/or drugs who are older Americans, these addictions can be associated with a constellation of other addictions including eating and related disorders such as cancer, coronary heart disease, and diabetes, particularly in rural areas.

We conclude with the idea that rural support systems are stretched and limited particularly for older adults. Planning for rural addictions services should embrace older adult services as well as education to ensure knowledgeable and caring practitioners. This area is ripe for creativity as well as research to better understand rural older adults who are addicted, particularly to alcohol as well as tobacco. This includes smoked, vaped, and spit nicotine. Although differences have been noted among rural adults including rural narcotic addiction (O'Donnell, 1996), rural "meth" use (Booth, Leukefeld, Falck, Wang, & Carlson, 2006), and the rural medical misuse of prescription Oxycontin (Leukefeld, Walker, Havens, Leedham, & Tolbert, 2007), rural older adults are largely not included in these kinds of studies. This is a major limitation that needs to be rectified. Clearly, there is a need for not only developing and evaluating novel prevention interventions but also specialized, targeted education and training for treating addictions among rural older adults. Future initiatives must incorporate refining evidence-based addiction practices for older adults including cognitive and behavioral efforts such as motivational interviewing and skill-based approaches.

References

Booth, B. M., Leukefeld, C., Falck, R., Wang, J., & Carlson, R. (2006). Correlates of rural methamphetamine and cocaine users: Results from a multistate community study. *Journal of Studies on Alcohol, 67*(4), 493–501.

Colliver, J. D., Compton, W. M., Gfroerer, J. C., & Condon, T. (2006). Projecting drug use among aging baby boomers in 2020. *Annals of Epidemiology, 16*(4), 257–265.

Daugherty, R., & Leukefeld, C. (1998). *Preventing alcohol and drug problems across the life span.* New York: Plenum.

Leukefeld, C., Walker, R., Havens, J., Leedham, C. A., & Tolbert, V. (2007, Summer). What does the community say: Key informant perception of rural prescription drug use. *Journal of Drug Issues*, 503–524.

Mattson, M., Lipari, R. N., Hays, C., & Van Horn, S. L. (2017, May). *A day in the life of older adults: Substance use facts.* Rockville, MD: Center for Behavioral Health Statistics and Quality, Substance Abuse and Mental Health Services Administration.

National Institute on Drug Abuse (2019). *Costs of substance abuse.* Retrieved from https://www.drugabuse.gov/drug-topics/trends-statistics/costs-substance-abuse

National Institute on Drug Abuse, NIDA NOTES (2011, December 19). *Substance aAbuse among older adults.* Retrieved from https://archives.drugabuse.gov/news-events/nida-notes/2011/12/substance-abuse-among-older-adults on 2020, November 19.

O'Donnell, J. A. (1996). *Narcotic addicts in Kentucky.* PHS Publ. 1881. Washington, DC: U.S. Government Printing Office.

Scholl, L., Seth, P., Kariisa, M., Wilson, N., & Baldwin, G. (2019, January 4). Drug and opioid-involved overdose deaths—United States, 2013–2017. *Morbidity and Mortality Weekly Report, 67*(5152), 1419–1427.

21
DYING, DEATH, AND BEREAVEMENT

George E. Dickinson

Most definitely, dying and death are situations occurring with a high degree of frequency among older adults, as almost two-thirds of individuals who die in the United States each year are 65 and older. The human body obviously is not structured to last forever. As the Biblical quotation in Ecclesiastes notes, "there is time to be born and a time to die." We will all die, and most likely beyond the age of 65 years. Indeed, dying seems to go with growing old.

Older adults bring a unique set of needs and demands to the health-care system, the complexity of which is increased through rurality (Tedder, Elliott, & Lewis, 2017). Rural counties in the U.S. continue to age and represent the majority (85%) of counties with 20% or greater of their population being 65 years and older (Economic Research Service, 2018). Though numerous variables contribute to death, the simple fact of where one lives can have a huge impact on health (Frostenson, 2017). Geography and the difference that rural versus urban living can have on an individual's longevity is notable.

Death Anxiety and Religion

The idea of growing old is fearful to some, as the term gerontophobia suggests. Aging anxiety is perpetuated by ageist stereotypes that lead one to fear her/his own aging. Such attitudes can become a self-fulfilling prophecy as older persons repeatedly confront stereotypical assumptions of being useless, thus beginning to perceive themselves as others see them. Yet, while older individuals tend to think of death more often than younger adults, overall, they appear to have less fear concerning death. Older persons, therefore, discuss death more openly and accept it more peacefully. Such death-related experiences and attitudes toward death are more likely to influence their adjustment toward their own aging process (Missler et al., 2012).

French sociologist Emile Durkheim (1915) argues that it is the ceremonial acts that are mainly responsible for the life-enriching effects of religion; thus shared meanings and values through group participation certainly give support to an individual regarding the fear of death. Religiosity tends to play a role regarding death fear, and because older individuals are more likely to be religious, a sense of comfort should be provided as they approach death. The sheer ceremonial act of regular attendance at religious services contributes to lower death anxiety.

Overall, religious individuals are known to report lower levels of death anxiety (Jonas & Fischer, 2006). Bereavement could be enhanced by such sharing and interaction. Certainly, it has been suggested that grief shared is grief relieved.

Issues With Dying and Death in Rural Areas

The American system of health-care delivery is not evenly distributed geographically, with primary care physicians being underrepresented, particularly in rural areas. Physicians generally prefer to practice in urbanized settings. The unequal distribution of physicians is evident with one out of every 20 counties in the U.S. not having a single physician (Cockerham, 2017). In some rural areas, nurse practitioners fill in for medical doctors. Though many small communities try to recruit physicians, the uneven distribution remains. Geriatricians are especially in demand, both in rural and urban areas. Geriatrics ranks at the bottom of medical specialties that internal medicine residents choose to pursue (Hafner, 2016).

Nurses' aides provide the greater part of hands-on care in institutions that serve persons with terminal illnesses (Denham, Meyer, & Rathbun, 2006). For those dying in rural areas in facilities, however, the staff may have insufficient training in the important area of palliative care with its focus on comfort and the psychological, social, and spiritual well-being of dying individuals. On the positive side, however, living in a rural area with much of the care often provided by nurses' aides, the aides tend to remain in their positions longer than those in urban areas and are more likely to know the families with whom they work, thus feeling a strong connection to the people they serve, note Sharon Denham and colleagues (2006). Such closeness could be a positive factor in bereavement in rural areas because of cultural homogeneity, as opposed to cultural heterogeneity more likely found in urban areas.

Rural areas have higher incidences of poverty and less access to community resources such as activity centers, pharmacies, grocery stores, emergency care centers, and hospitals (Snedeker, 2017). A study of rural-urban differences in Minnesota revealed rural enrollees more likely to report no past year preventive care compared to urban enrollees in health care (Loftus, Allen, Call, & Everson-Rose, 2018). Isolation and being away from emergency services is more of an issue in rural areas, thus having an impact on health. Older adults in the U.S., for example, die from falls at a very high rate, about 74 per day, thus timing in getting the individual to an emergency care unit would be more of an issue in rural areas because of distance (CDC, 2016).

Lack of public transportation for older adults in rural areas can limit their ability to connect with family and friends, thus contributing to social isolation and depriving them of social interaction, a key ingredient to overall health for older adults. In fact, Kirk Johnson (2009) noted that public transportation is almost unheard of in rural areas.

The probability of living alone increases with age, as nearly one-third of older adults in America live alone, outside of a nursing home or hospital (Institute on Aging, 2010). Though living alone does not mean that one is lonely, the possibility of such is increased. For some individuals, isolation and being alone can contribute to depression, and depression correlates with ill health.

Drug use in rural areas tends to be heavier than in urban areas among older adults. For example, rural participants over 85 years of age in Oregon use significantly more prescription medications than their urban cohorts, perhaps appropriate given that rural individuals have a higher disease burden (Goeres et al., 2016). The opioid epidemic is overwhelmingly concentrated in rural pockets of the U.S. as are related overdose deaths; thus, limited access to trauma centers that can quickly treat emergency situations is again a major issue (Frostenson, 2017).

Death Etiology in Rural Areas

Residents of rural areas in the U.S. tend to be older and sicker than their urban counterparts, with higher rates of cigarette smoking, high blood pressure, and obesity. Obesity causes its own kind of liver disease and can be lethal in combination with other conditions such as diabetes, heart attacks, and strokes. The average American woman today weighs as much as an American man did in the early 1960s (Bernstein, Hull, & Kindy, 2016). Those in rural areas report less leisure-time physical activity and lower seat belt use than urban dwellers (CDC, 2017).

Rates of drug overdose deaths are rising in rural areas, surpassing rates in urban areas, with the effects of use being higher (CDC, 2017). Most overdose deaths occur in homes in rural areas where rescue efforts may fall to relatives with limited knowledge of, or access to, overdose follow-up care. Additionally, suicide rates are higher in rural areas than in urban America, and the gap between the two geographical areas grew steadily between 1999 and 2015.

Rural Americans are more likely to die from heart disease, cancer, unintentional injury, chronic lower respiratory disease, and stroke than their urban counterparts. Unintentional injury deaths are some 50% higher in rural areas, partly because of greater risk of death from motor vehicle crashes and opioid overdoses (CDC, 2017).

Addressing the Issue of Dying, Death, and Bereavement in Rural Areas

For social workers and policymakers, understanding differences in illicit drug use and drug overdose deaths in urban and rural areas can help public health professionals to better monitor, identify, and prioritize responses, suggests the CDC (2017). Health-care providers should follow CDC guidelines when prescribing opioids for chronic pain and educate patients on the risks and benefits of opioids. Additionally, better screening for high blood pressure, comprehensive cancer control programs focusing on prevention, screening, education, and access to care would be helpful. Encouraging physical activity and healthy eating to address obesity and promoting smoking cessation would both contribute to healthier living. Providing motor vehicle safety programs for older adults could assist in preventing unintentional deaths.

Telehealth programs for health-care delivery, education, and health information services is especially critical in rural and other remote areas (HRSA, 2019). Traditional models of telehealth involve care delivered to a patient at an originating site from a specialist working at a distant site. Technologies include video conferencing, the internet, store-and-forward imaging, streaming media, and terrestrial and wireless communications. The Office for the Advancement of Telehealth provides funds to promote and improve telehealth services in rural areas. With suicide rates higher in rural areas, internet counseling can be of benefit in isolated areas. Likewise, bereavement counseling via chat lines can be comforting to one suffering from the death of a significant other.

A nurse-led navigation program model to provide early palliative care in rural areas in Canada for older adults living with advanced chronic illness is a promising innovation for these adults (Pesut et al., 2017). This person-centered approach, with complex issues being addressed on an individual basis, provides continuity for patients and families who are seeing multiple health-care providers and has resulted in a high degree of satisfaction from participants.

The shortage of physicians in rural areas is being addressed, though perhaps not intentionally, because some urban areas have an oversupply of doctors (Cockerham, 2017). Towns in rural areas occasionally advertise and try to attract doctors with special incentives to move to their locale. A few states have programs for such attraction by giving medical students scholarships or paying their tuition, with the promise that the student, after graduation, would "pay back" by setting up practice in a rural community.

Conclusion

A look at the differences that rural versus urban living can make in the longevity of older adults is a wakeup call to address these discrepancies. Applying Everett Rogers's stages of the adoption process (1962) (awareness, interest, evaluation, trial adoption, and adoption), the first stages of "awareness" and "interest" of health discrepancies in rural areas are rapidly coming to fruition. Therefore, it is now time to move on to the other stages to eventually reach "adoption" of various policies and caregiving strategies. With rural counties in the U.S. continuing to age and with rural residents tending to be older and sicker than their urban counterparts, government policies and access to health care need to be stepped up. Hopefully, the future will hold promise for closing the gap between rural and urban differences in health care.

Suggestions for Further Reading

Cann, C. K. (2018). *The Routledge handbook of death and the afterlife*. New York: Routledge.

Dickinson, G. E., & Sanders, B. S. (2019). *Aging in the family*. London: Routledge.

Kaye, L. W., & Singer, C. M. (Eds.). (2019). *Social isolation of older adults: Strategies to bolster* health *and well-being*. New York: Springer.

Leming, M. R., & Dickinson, G. E. (2020). *Understanding dying, death and bereavement 9e*. Stamford, CT: Cengage Publishers.

Loe, M. *Aging our way: Lessons for living from 85 and beyond*. London: Oxford University Press.

Silverman, I. I., & Siegel, E. B. (Eds.). (2018). *Aging wisely: Wisdom of our elders*. Burlington, MA: Jones & Bartlett Learning.

Staudt, C., & Ellens, J. H. (2014). *Our changing journey to the end: Reshaping death, dying, and grief in America*. Santa Barbara, CA: Praeger.

References

Bernstein, L., Hull, A., & Kindy, K. (2016). *A new divide in American death*. Retrieved March 26, 2019, from www.washingtonpost.com/sf/national/2016/04/10/a-new-divide-in-american-death/

CDC (Centers for Disease Control and Prevention). (2016). *Older adults fall prevention*. Retrieved March 4, 2019, from www.cdc.gov/media/dpk/healthy-living/injury-falls-older-adults/older-adult-falls.html

CDC (Centers for Disease Control and Prevention). (2017). *Rural health*. Retrieved April 22, 2019, from www.cdc.gov/ruralhealth.html

Cockerham, W. C. (2017*). Medical sociology*. London: Taylor & Francis.

Denham, S. A., Meyer, M. G., & Rathbun, A. (2006). Knowledge of rural nurses' aides about end-of-life care. *Family Community Health, 29*(3), 229–241.

Durkheim, E. (1915). *The elementary forms of religious life*. New York: George Allen and Unwin.

Economic Research Service, U.S. Department of Agriculture. (2018, November). *Rural America at a glance: 2018 Edition*. Economic Information Bulletin 200. Washington, DC: U.S. Department of Agriculture.

Frostenson, S. (2017). The death rate gap between urban and rural America is getting wider. *Vox*. Retrieved from www.vox.com/science-and-health/2017/1/13/14246260/death-gap-urban-rural.amer . . .

Goeres, L. M., Gille, A., Furuno, J. P., Erten-Lyons, D., Hartung, D. M., Calvert, J. F., . . . Lee, D. S. H. (2016). Rural-urban differences in chronic disease and drug utilization in older Oregonians. *The Journal of Rural Health, 32*, 269–279.

Hafner, K. (2016, January 25). As the population ages, where are the geriatricians? *The New York Times*.

HRSA (Health Resources & Service Administration). (2019, January). *Telehealth programs*. Retrieved from www.hrsa.gov/rural-health/telehealth/index.html

Institute on Aging. (2010). *Information on senior citizens living in America*. Retrieved from www.ioaging.org/aging-in-america

Johnson, K. (2009, December 9). For elderly in rural areas, times are distinctly harder. *New York Times*. Retrieved from www.nytimes.com/2009/12/10/us/10rural.html

Jonas, E., & Fischer, P. (2006). Terror management and religion: Evidence that intrinsic religiousness mitigates worldview defense following mortality salience. *Journal of Personality and Social Psychology*, *91*, 553–567.

Loftus, J., Allen, E. M., Call, K. T., & Everson-Rose, S. A. (2018). Rural-urban differences in access to preventive health care among publicly insured Minnesotans. *The Journal of Rural Health*, *34*, 48–55.

Missler, M., Stroebe, M., Geurtsen, L., Mastenbroek, M., Chmoun, S., & van der Houwen, K. (2012). Exploring death anxiety among elderly people: A literature review and empirical investigation. *Omega*, *64*(4), 357–379.

Pesut, B., Hooper, B., Jacobsen, M., Nielsen, B., Falk, M., & O'Connor, B. P. (2017). Nurse-led navigation to provide early palliative care in rural areas: A pilot study. *Biomed Central Palliative Care*, *16*, 37–46.

Rogers, E. M. (1962). *Diffusion of innovations*. New York: The Free Press.

Snedeker, L. (2017). Aging and isolation—causes and impacts. *Social Work Today*, *17*(1), 24–29.

Tedder, T., Elliott, L., & Lewis, K. (2017). Analysis of common barriers to rural patients utilizing hospice and palliative care services: An integrated literature review. *Journal of the American Association of Nurse Practitioners*, *29*, 356–362.

22
ELDER ABUSE

Laura Mosqueda and Julie Schoen

Background and Types of Elder Abuse

Older adults should be treasured and revered members of our communities. Too often, however, older adults are targeted by unscrupulous criminals for fraud or are subjected to other forms of physical, emotional mistreatment, and neglect. Elder abuse is complex and far-reaching; you will probably encounter an incident involving you or a loved one sometime in your lifetime. Among the 46 million older adults who live in the United States (15% of the population), more than 10% are victims of abuse each year (Breckman et al. 2018). Elder abuse has been identified as an urgent problem for individuals, their families, communities, and societies, leading to increased rates of hospitalization, nursing home placement, financial ruin, severe emotional distress, and even increased rates of mortality. Given the number of people affected and the devastating outcomes that result, the Centers for Disease Control and Prevention (CDC) has identified elder abuse as a public health crisis (Centers for Disease Control and Prevention, 2019).

Definitions of Elder Abuse

As defined by the CDC, "Elder abuse is an intentional act, or failure to act, by a caregiver or another person in a relationship involving an expectation of trust that causes or creates a risk of harm to an older adult (An older adult is defined as someone age 60 or older.)". Forms of elder abuse include:

- *Physical Abuse*: the intentional use of physical force that results in acute or chronic illness, bodily injury, physical pain, functional impairment, distress, or death. Physical abuse may include, but is not limited to, violent acts such as striking (with or without an object or weapon), hitting, beating, scratching, biting, choking, suffocation, pushing, shoving, shaking, slapping, kicking, stomping, pinching, and burning.
- *Sexual Abuse or Abusive Sexual Contact*: forced or unwanted sexual interaction (touching and non-touching acts) of any kind with an older adult. This may include forced or unwanted:
    - Completed or attempted contact between the penis and the vulva or the penis and the anus involving penetration
    - Contact between the mouth and the penis, vulva, or anus

- Penetration of the anal or genital opening of another person by a hand, finger, or other object
- Intentional touching, either directly or through the clothing, of the genitalia, anus, groin, breast, inner thigh, or buttocks

These acts also qualify as sexual abuse if they are committed against a person who is not competent to give informed approval.

- *Emotional or Psychological Abuse*: verbal or nonverbal behavior that results in the infliction of anguish, mental pain, fear, or distress. Examples include behaviors intended to humiliate (e.g., calling names or insults), threaten (e.g., expressing an intent to initiate nursing home placement), isolate (e.g., seclusion from family or friends), or control (e.g., prohibiting or limiting access to transportation, telephone, money, or other resources).
- *Neglect*: failure by a caregiver or other responsible person to protect an elder from harm, or the failure to meet needs for essential medical care, nutrition, hydration, hygiene, clothing, basic activities of daily living, or shelter, which results in a serious risk of compromised health and safety. Examples include not providing adequate nutrition, hygiene, clothing, shelter, or access to necessary health care; or failure to prevent exposure to unsafe activities and environments.
- *Financial Abuse or Exploitation*: the illegal, unauthorized, or improper use of an older individual's resources by a caregiver or other person in a trusting relationship, for the benefit of someone other than the older individual. This includes depriving an older person of rightful access to, information about, or use of, personal benefits, resources, belongings, or assets. Examples include forgery, misuse, or theft of money or possessions; use of coercion or deception to surrender finances or property; or improper use of guardianship or power of attorney (Centers for Disease Control, 2019).

The National Center on Elder Abuse as a Primary Resource

To provide a clearinghouse for all types of information pertaining to elder abuse, the National Center on Elder Abuse (NCEA) was formed by the federal Administration for Community Living (ACL). The hosting agency for the NCEA is currently the Keck School of Medicine at USC. The mission of the NCEA is "To improve the national response to elder abuse, neglect, and exploitation by gathering, housing, disseminating, and stimulating innovative, validated methods of practice, education, research, and policy" (NCEA, 2018). It serves as a national resource center dedicated to engaging and empowering older people so that they may be an advocate for themselves and their communities. The NCEA recognizes that it is up to all of us as a community to ensure the right social structures are in place so people can remain connected to their communities and to society as a whole, reducing the likelihood of abuse. Through evidence-based policies, initiatives, education, and civic engagement, we can create a sturdy social structure that can support us as we grow older. The NCEA is committed to working with other like-minded organizations to promote elder justice in all communities. This concept of elder justice refers to a society's response to elder abuse, which includes physical abuse, neglect, financial exploitation, psychological abuse, and sexual abuse.

Elder Abuse in Rural and Tribal Communities

Crimes against older adults in rural communities pose a special challenge. Part of the NCEA's goal is to inform and educate communities that are most susceptible to these forms of mistreatment. In many rural areas, law enforcement agencies can be spread thin and there often are fewer support services available. Approximately 25% of older adults reside in rural communities across America (Economic Research Service, U.S. Department of Agriculture, 2018). Many rural communities are grounded in the institutions of faith and family bound by tradition and strong commitments to the community. They turn to family and friends for comfort and support. Older rural adults can be fiercely independent and interdependent, with community members concerned for the welfare of one another. This close-knit model of society should be very beneficial in preventing elder abuse. At the same time, rural and tribal communities face challenges that put them at greater risk of elder abuse. The lack of proximity to elder justice professionals alone is a huge impediment to accessing support and services.

Risk Factors

Risk factors that may increase the potential for abuse of an older person can be identified at community, individual, relationship, and sociocultural levels (World Health Organization, 2019).

Community

Social isolation is one of the largest risk factors predicting elder abuse. As older adults sometimes become less interactive in community affairs, they may become more socially isolated. Many older adults are isolated because of loss of physical or mental capacity, or through the loss of friends and family members. Large geographic distance compounded by staffing shortages impose significant demands on rural service providers who often have to wear many hats and handle a wide array of matters. Statistically, rural older adults are more likely to own their own homes, making them targets for financial exploitation.

Individual

Risks at the individual level include poor physical and mental health of the older adult as well as mental disorders and alcohol and substance abuse. Other individual-level factors, which may increase the risk of abuse, include the gender of the victim and a shared living situation. While older men have the same risk of abuse as women, in some cultures where women have inferior social status, older women are at higher risk of neglect and financial abuse (such as seizing their property) when they are widowed. Women may also be at higher risk of more persistent and severe forms of abuse and injury. In rural communities, access to programs that support the individual and provide services may be few and far between.

Relationship

A shared living situation is a risk factor for elder abuse. It is not yet clear whether spouses or adult children of older people are more likely to perpetrate abuse. An abuser's dependency on the older person (often financial) also increases the risk of abuse. In some cases, a long history of poor family relationships may worsen as a result of stress when the older person becomes more care dependent. Finally, as more women enter the workforce and have less spare time, caring for older relatives becomes a greater burden, increasing the risk of abuse. In rural areas, younger family members moving away to seek employment and career opportunities leaving older family members alone can exacerbate this (*Rural and Tribal Elder Justice Resource Guide*, https://www.justice.gov/elderjustice/rural-and-tribal-resources2018).

Sociocultural

Sociocultural factors that may affect the risk of elder abuse include:

- Ageist stereotypes that depict older adults as frail, weak, and dependent
- Erosion of the bonds between generations of a family
- Systems of inheritance and land rights, affecting the distribution of power and material goods within families often common in rural communities
- Lack of funds to pay for care.

In rural areas, even locating care assistance and residential care facilities can be very limited and too costly.

Prevention of Elder Abuse in Rural Communities

The lack of or limited infrastructure may contribute to the incidence of elder abuse and impede accessing or receiving elder abuse services. However, many resources are available and many more are in development. Next is a listing of current programs and resources to end social isolation and prevent elder abuse.

Broadband/Telehealth

It is widely recognized that access to broadband is not simply a luxury, but important to many aspects of living in today's society. By being connected, there is a pathway to current events and resources to prevent social isolation. The Federal Communications Commission (FCC) has programs and tools to assist with expanding services and identifying available broadband in address specific locations. The USDA Rural Utilities Services (www.rd.usda.gov/about-rd/agencies/rural-utilities-service) has programs to encourage more high-speed broadband to be installed in high-need areas by awarding grants to rural and tribal areas. Access to broadband will help to connect communities and provide timely access to telehealth programs and adult protective services.

Transportation

A well-integrated system of transportation is critical for enabling older adults to maintain independence. In contrast, the absence of or limited public transportation fosters reliance on others and increased dependency, factors associated with elder abuse. The National Rural Transit Assistance Program (RTAP) (www.nationalrtap.org/Home) is a technical assistance center to connect older adults with available transportation systems.

Health and Nutrition Resources

Health and nutrition are foundational to successful aging by maintaining independence. Studies have shown that rural older adults often suffer higher rates of poor health. In addition, there are generally fewer health-care services available. However, the National Association of Rural Health Clinics (NARHC) (https://narhc.org/) is dedicated exclusively to improving the delivery of quality, cost-effective health care in rural underserved areas through the Rural Health

Clinics Program. Access to these health resources is key to preventing physical and emotional elder abuse.

Summary

Elder abuse is a problem with a variety of solutions. The most significant ways we can prevent and address elder abuse are by reducing risk factors to abuse. Everyone can do their part and ensure that our communities have the strong set of social support beams that are needed to protect our society from elder abuse. Keep in mind some of these tips on how to prevent and address elder abuse in rural communities.

- Consider better public transportation and use of assistive transportation services;
- Understand and access current available supportive resources, including broadband and telehealth services;
- Strengthen elder abuse training and awareness resources for care providers, law enforcement, and others who interact with older people so they can identify the signs of abuse and learn how to prevent and address it; and
- Support research funding on elder abuse.

No one deserves to be mistreated, whether they are young or old, rural or urban. By reducing the conditional factors that can contribute to elder abuse, we can minimize the emotional, financial, and social costs and allow everyone the opportunity to thrive.

References

Breckman, R., Burnes, D., Ross, S., Marshall, P. C., Suitor, J. J., Lachs, M. S., & Pillemer, K. (2018). When helping hurts: Nonabusing family, friends, and neighbors in the lives of elder mistreatment victims. *The Gerontologist, 58*(4), 719–723. doi:10.1093/geront/gnw257

Burnes, D., Acierno, R., & Hernandez-Tejada, M. (2018). Help-seeking among victims of elder abuse: Findings from the National Elder Mistreatment Study. *The Journals of Gerontology: Series B, 74*(5), 891–896. doi:10.1093/geronb/gby122

Burnett, J., Dyer, C. B., Clark, L. E., & Halphen, J. M. (2018). A statewide elder mistreatment virtual assessment program: Preliminary data. *Journal of the American Geriatrics Society, 67*(1), 151–155. doi:10.1111/jgs.15565

Cannell, B., Gonzalez, J. M. R., Livingston, M., Jetelina, K. K., Burnett, J., & Weitlauf, J. C. (2019). Pilot testing the detection of elder abuse through emergency care technicians (DETECT) screening tool: Results from the DETECT pilot project. *Journal of Elder Abuse & Neglect, 31*(2), 129–145. doi:10.1080/08946566.2018.1564104

Centers for Disease Control and Prevention. (2019). *Elder abuse definitions*. Retrieved September 9, 2019, from www.cdc.gov/violenceprevention/elderabuse/definitions.html

Cornes, M., Manthorpe, J., & Haselden, N. (2010). Rural dimensions of elder abuse: Contributions to the No Secrets review from rural older people. *Journal of Adult Protection, 12*(3), 20–29. doi:10.5042/jap.2010.0411

Dimah, K. P., & Dimah, A. (2003). Elder abuse and neglect among rural and urban women. *Journal of Elder Abuse & Neglect, 15*(1), 75–93. doi:10.1300/J084v15n01_06

Economic Research Service, U.S. Department of Agriculture (2018). Retrieved from https://www.justice.gov/opa/pr/justice-department-department-agriculture-host-inaugural-rural-and-tribal-elder-justice.

Galdamez, G., Avent, E., Rowan, J., Wilber, K. H., Mosqueda, L., Olsen, B., & Gassoumis, Z. D. (2018). Elder abuse multidisciplinary teams and networks: Understanding national intervention approaches. *Innovation in Aging, 2*(Suppl 1), 763. doi:10.1093/geroni/igy023.2823

Lichtenberg, P. A., Hall, L., Gross, E., & Campbell, R. (2019). Providing assistance for older adult financial exploitation victims: Implications for clinical gerontologists. *Clinical Gerontologist, 42*(4), 435–443. doi :10.1080/07317115.2019.1569190

Marshall, K. A., & Hale, D. (2018). Elder abuse. *Home Healthcare Now, 36*(1), 51–52. doi:10.1097/ nhh.0000000000000648

NCEA. *Mission statement.* (2018). Retrieved from ncea.acl.gov2018.

Rosen, T., Elman, A., Dion, S., Delgado, D., Demetres, M., Breckman, R., . . . Burnett, J. (2019). Review of programs to combat elder mistreatment: Focus on hospitals and level of resources needed. *Journal of the American Geriatrics Society, 67*(6), 1286–1294. doi:10.1111/jgs.15773

Rowan, J., Gassoumis, Z., Homeier, D., Rath, L., & Wilber, K. (2018). Person-centric care of elder mistreatment: Lessons learned from a service advocate. *Innovation in Aging*, 2(Suppl 1), 526–527. doi:10.1093/geroni/igy023.1946

Rural and Tribal Elder Justice Resource Guide. (2018). Department of Justice Elder Justice Initiative; graphics utilized by express permission of Dept. of Justice, Elder Justice Initiative 2018. Retrieved September 9, 2019, from www.justice.gov/elderjustice/book/file/1110846/download

Vandsburger, E., Curtis, V. S., & Imbody, B. A. (2012). Professional preparedness to address abuse and neglect among elders living in the rural south: Identifying resiliency where stress prevails. *Ageing International, 37*(3), 356–372. doi:10.1007/s12126-010-9081-0

Vincenti, V. (2015). *Researchers study elder financial exploitation. Reflections: College of Agriculture and Natural Resources research report* (pp. 15–17). Laramie: University of Wyoming.

Weissberger, G. H., Goodman, M. C., Mosqueda, L., Schoen, J., Nguyen, A. L., Wilber, K. H., . . . Han, S. D. (2019). Elder abuse characteristics based on calls to the National Center on Elder Abuse resource line. *Journal of Applied Gerontology*. doi:10.1177/0733464819865685

World Health Organization. (2019). *Elder abuse: Risk factors.* Retrieved September 13, 2019, from www. who.int/news-room/fact-sheets/detail/elder-abuse

23
LEGAL SERVICES

Kathy Greenlee and Rebecca C. Morgan

Introduction

Access to an attorney is critical to all older adults for many reasons, not the least of which are representation in legal matters, access to justice, education on legal issues, and help in developing a plan for the final phase of the individual's life. Elder law is a unique area of legal practice that focuses on the needs of the older person or that person's family who is involved in caring and supporting the older person. Although elder law might be viewed as a single specialty legal practice area, because it has the potential to encompass a wide range of legal issues, we view it as a broader area of legal practice with elder law attorneys frequently specializing in some but not necessarily all of those many subject areas (Sabatino, 2012).

Types of Legal Issues Confronting Older People

Older people living in rural areas may need access to legal assistance for a wide variety of reasons. Some of the more common legal matters include:

- Assistance with drafting estate planning documents, such as wills, trusts (testamentary trusts, revocable living trusts, special needs trusts, and pet trusts, for example), health-care directives, and durable powers of attorney for financial decisions;
- Designating an agent for surrogate decision-making and the intricacies of family dynamics;
- Access to income and health benefits, such as Social Security (disability, retirement, and dependent and survivors' benefits), Supplemental Security Income (SSI), Medicare (including original, Medicare Advantage, and Part D), Medicaid, Veterans benefits, pensions (private and public) and insurance;
- Protection from or response to elder abuse, including physical abuse, psychological abuse, sexual assault, neglect, and financial exploitation;
- Planning for and options for diminished capacity, including supported decision-making, maximizing capacity, and the use of durable powers of attorney;
- Assistance in obtaining a guardianship or conservatorship if the older person is unable to care for herself or her property. An older person may also need guidance on lesser restrictive alternatives to a guardianship or conservatorship;

- Managing housing and home ownership, including active adult housing, reverse mortgages, federally subsidized housing, legal ownership of a home, and homestead protection;
- Planning long-term care, including selecting nursing home care, assisted living facilities, or continuing care retirement communities; and
- Protection from or recourse for discrimination, including options available through the Age Discrimination in Employment Act, the Americans with Disabilities Act, and other state and federal protections.

Legal issues facing older people living in rural areas are, for the most part, the same as those facing older people in urban areas. The difference in these locales is more readily apparent when older people confront health and long-term care challenges. With fewer resources available, rural areas may not have programs and services that support older people as they age in such a community (Pruitt & Williams, 2018). One of the greatest dilemmas older people and their families confront is the lack of locally available in-home care or congregate long-term care services. These health-care challenges make it especially important for rural older adults to plan in advance for their future care needs.

Land ownership may be the area of law most unique to rural older people. While every rural older person is differently situated with regard to their real and personal property, there are older adults who own tracts of land that may include water rights, mineral rights, etc. For these individuals, passing the land to the next generation requires the guidance of an attorney who is expert in property and tax law to guarantee successful transfer of title while navigating the tax implications of such transfer. To qualify for public assistance for long-term care through the state Medicaid program, there are also strict rules that govern transfer of assets and whether those assets should remain available to the older person to offset the cost of care.

Native Americans who own tribal land held in trust by the U.S. Government need specialized assistance for estate planning. The Bureau of Indian Affairs, U.S. Department of the Interior, has basic trust estate planning information available on their website. This information is designed to provide a general introduction to the complexities of this topic (see U.S. Department of the Interior, Indian Affairs, n.d., www.bia.gov/bia/ots/dres/estate-planning).

Attorney Generalists and Specialists

As in other professions, lawyers frequently specialize in a particular area of law. Elder law attorneys, for example, understand a broad range of issues facing older clients. However, attorneys in general private practice may also represent older clients. An attorney who is familiar with preparing wills and trusts—called a probate attorney—is likely also familiar with powers of attorney and the requirements for guardianships and alternatives to guardianship. An attorney who does estate planning may also be familiar with the rules about applying for Medicaid. A general real estate lawyer may or may not know the unique housing options available to older adults. An older person seeking legal assistance needs to find an attorney who knows the subject matter at issue *and* how that issue impacts older people.

The variety of topics and the intricacies of many of the subjects involved in the practice of elder law illustrate the benefit of rural older people seeking the representation of an elder law attorney.

An elder law attorney needs to know more than the law. Elder law attorneys can recognize nonlegal issues as well as legal issues, as the nonlegal issues are often intertwined with, or in some way, exacerbating the legal issue. Elder law attorneys recognize that a client may have health issues, diminished capacity, need assistance with activities of daily living, or lack adequate income, all of which can compound the client's legal problem. As well, elder law attorneys are familiar with programs and services available to the older person that may provide solutions to the legal problem or may be one component to the solution crafted by the elder law attorney. Elder law attorneys know other professionals in fields of aging who may be helpful to clients who need supportive services. Using a holistic approach, elder law and special needs planning attorneys often work with other professionals in various fields to provide quality service and ensure clients' needs are met. (NAELA Consumer Resources, n.d.c).

Elder law attorneys know how to communicate with clients with diminished capacity, can recognize whether the client has capacity to make the decisions needed in the course of legal representation, can recognize the red flags indicating potential elder abuse, and can suggest supportive programs and services available to help a client age with dignity.

Elder Law Is Unique

What distinguishes elder law from other practice areas, other than the fact that the client is likely "older"? One expert offers this view:

> [f]irst, elder law places emphasis on issues arising from a long life, rather than death. . . . Second, elder law integrates legal planning and problem solving into a larger picture of personal planning needs. . . . Thus, elder law has always embraced a "big-picture," holistic approach. . . [and] strives for an interdisciplinary planning perspective. Social workers, geriatricians, other health practitioners, geriatric case managers, financial planners, and others all serve as allies in the legal planning work of elder law attorneys.
>
> (Sabatino, 2012, pp. 77–78)

Elder law is also different from other areas of law in that the practice is defined by the client rather than the subject[1] (Radford, 2019). This means that an older client could have one of many types of legal problems, rather than a problem in one legal area. A client could have a family law matter, may need to appeal a denial of public benefits, update her estate planning documents, be a victim of elder abuse, have diminished capacity, or be unable to make decisions about her property or her self-care. Thus, "[r]ather than being defined by technical and legal distinctions, elder law and special needs planning is defined by the clients to be served" (NAELA Why Hire A NAELA Member, n.d.).

The National Academy of Elder Law Attorneys or NAELA, the preeminent organization of attorneys who practice primarily in the field of elder law, describes the practice area as:

> helping such persons and their families with planning for incapacity and long-term care, Medicaid and Medicare coverage (including coverage of nursing home and home care), health and long-term care insurance, and health care decision-making. It also includes drafting of special needs and other trusts, the selection of long-term care providers, home care and nursing home problem solving, retiree health and income benefits, retirement housing, and fiduciary services or representation.
>
> (NAELA About NAELA, n.d.b)

Unique Ethical Issues

In addition to the substantive knowledge needed to practice elder law, elder law attorneys also need to be prepared to deal with unique ethical issues that may arise in an elder law practice.

> When assisting clients with planning or the implementation of plans, elder law . . . attorneys often will represent clients who have diminished capacity. Family members and other persons with fiduciary responsibilities also may be involved. The client-attorney relationship in elder law and special needs planning is not always as clear-cut and unambiguous as in other areas of law.
>
> (NAELA Aspirational Standards, n.d.)

For example, if the client has diminished capacity, the attorney will need to determine whether the client has the requisite capacity first to hire the attorney and, if so, whether the client has the requisite capacity to undertake the legal matter for which the client seeks representation. The attorney needs to know the capacity threshold needed for the act in question and determine whether the client demonstrates that requisite capacity. The attorney needs to understand and be able to implement various communication techniques to maximize the client's capacity.

Another example of a potential ethical pitfall is when the family of the client oversteps their roles. One of the critical principles of the client-attorney relationship is confidentiality of information (see ABA Model Rule 1.6, 2018). Family members may insist on being present for the attorney's conversations with the client or actively seek to learn what the attorney has told the client. Elder law attorneys are prepared for this potentiality (see ABA, *Why Am I Left in the Waiting Room*, n.d.). In addition, elder law attorneys are attuned to the potential of someone exerting undue influence[2] over the client and how to recognize when that may be happening.

When the older person and an adult child come into the attorney's office, the question of who the attorney represents is in play. Client identification is critical for all areas of practice, but the potential for the issue of "who is the client" is greater in an elder law practice because others may be involved in the client's life.

Finding an Elder Law Attorney in a Rural Setting: Access to Justice

Rural areas are likely not to have an abundance of attorneys in the community,[3] and it is even less likely that an elder law attorney would locate a practice in a small town, unless the demographics show a significant percentage of older persons in the community. There are various organizations that have directories of elder law attorneys that might be useful, such as NAELA, AARP's Legal Counsel for the Elderly, state bar associations, and local legal aid offices.

Even if there is no elder law attorney in the community, the older person may still be able to meet with an elder law attorney. The older person can travel to the community where the elder law attorney is practicing, but if the older person is unable to drive or there is a lack of transportation options for the older person in her community, an in-person meeting may not be possible. The attorney may be able to make a "house call," but that may also increase the cost of representation. Technology can remove the transportation barrier, and it is possible to communicate with the elder law attorney by phone. For those clients who have internet access, the client may be able to have a videoconference meeting with the attorney, but there still exists a "digital divide" between urban and rural areas given more limited broadband, less infrastructure, and less use of elder law attorneys in rural communities (Perrin, 2019).

Conclusion

The ability of an older person to be represented by an elder law attorney may have hurdles stemming from the rural location of the client. Further, living in a rural area may limit the older person's legal solutions or access to supportive programs and services. This is all to say that in rural America, legal issues may be quite intertwined with limits on availability of transportation, social services and supports, and more.

Notes

1. *But see* Sabatino suggesting that "it is increasingly common for elder law attorneys to serve younger generations of clients who seek to do their own planning and, especially, younger clients with special needs. 'Elder and special needs law' more accurately describes a large segment of the practice today. In addition, the paradigm allows for a great deal of flexibility in the evolution of elder and special needs law. While the core goals and general challenges remain the same over time, the particular benefits, financial planning options, housing options, and health-care options and issues are likely to change significantly in the years to come." Sabatino, C. (2012, July–August). The longevity of Elder law. *BiFocal*, 33(6), 77–78. Retrieved from www.americanbar.org/groups/law_aging/publications/bifocal/vol_33/issue_6_aug2012/longevity_of_elder_law/.
2. "The improper use of power or trust in a way that deprives a person of free will and substitutes another's objective; the exercise of enough control over another person that a questioned act by this person would not have otherwise been performed, the person's free agency having been overmastered" in Garner, B.A. (Ed.), *Black's Law Dictionary* (11th ed. 2019).
3. American Bar Association, Legal Profession Statistics (2019a, May 31). Retrieved from www.americanbar.org/about_the_aba/profession_statistics/ (Current statistical data have been gathered to assist with research on lawyers and the legal profession.) Lawyer population by state (ABA, 2019b) is available here: www.americanbar.org/content/dam/aba/administrative/market_research/national-lawyer-population-by-state-2019.pdf. *See also* Runge, R. Addressing the access to justice crisis in rural America. *Human Rights Magazine*, *40*(3). Retrieved from www.americanbar.org/groups/crsj/publications/human_rights_magazine_home/2014_vol_40/vol_40_no_3_poverty/access_justice_rural_america/.

References

American Bar Association (ABA). (2019a, May 31). *Legal profession statistics*. Retrieved from www.americanbar.org/about_the_aba/profession_statistics/

American Bar Association (ABA). (2019b). *Lawyers by state*. Retrieved from www.americanbar.org/content/dam/aba/administrative/market_research/national-lawyer-population-by-state-2019.pdf

American Bar Association (ABA). (2018). *Model rules of professional conduct, rule 1.6 confidentiality*. Retrieved from https://www.americanbar.org/groups/professional_responsibility/policy/ethics_2000_commission/e2k_rule16rem/

American Bar Association (ABA). (n.d.). *Why am I left in the waiting room?: Understanding the Four C's of Elder law ethics (4 Cs brochure)*. Retrieved from www.americanbar.org/products/inv/brochure/211008886/

Garner, B. A. (Ed.). (2019). *Black's law dictionary* (11th ed.). Eagan, MN: Thomson Reuters.

NAELA. (n.d.a). *Aspirational standards*. Retrieved from www.naela.org/Web/About_Tab/History_and_Standards/History_and_Standards_Sub_landing/Aspirational_Standards.aspx

NAELA. (n.d.b). *About NAELA*. Retrieved from www.naela.org/Web/About/ImportTemp/About_NAELA_New.aspx?hkey=feb0efd3-bd62-4508-9ca4-20de373d478

NAELA. (n.d.c). *Consumer resources*. Retrieved from www.naela.org/Web/ConsumerResources/ImportTemp/Consumer_Resources_Landing_New.aspx?hkey=1e07503a-588d-4e61-98c0-a975d05fb4a6

NAELA. (n.d.d). *Why hire a NAELA member*. Retrieved from www.naela.org/Web/Consumers_Tab/Consumer_Resources/Why_Hire_a_NAELA_Member.aspx

Perrin, A. (2019). *Digital gap between rural and nonrural America persists*. Pew Research Center FactTank. Retrieved from www.pewresearch.org/fact-tank/2019/05/31/digital-gap-between-rural-and-nonrural-america-persists/

Pruitt, L. R., & Williams, R. H. (2018, March). Rural justice. *L.A. Law*, *41*, 26.

Radford, M. F. (2019, February). *A comparison of the 2016 American College of Trust and Estate Counsel commentaries with the 2017 NAELA Aspirational Standards (special ed.) 71*. Online version. Retrieved from www.naela.org/NewsJournalOnline/NewsJournalOnline/Journal_Articles/2019/Aspirational_Standards/AComparison.aspx

Sabatino, C. (2012, July–August). The longevity of elder law. *Bifocal*, *33*(6), 77–78. Retrieved from www.americanbar.org/groups/law_aging/publications/bifocal/vol_33/issue_6_aug2012/longevity_of_elder_law/

U.S. Department of the Interior, Indian Affairs. (n.d.). *Estate planning*. Retrieved from www.bia.gov/bia/ots/dres/estate-planning

24
ENTITLEMENTS AND BENEFITS

Brandy Bauer, Leslie Fried, Ann Kayrish, and Genevieve Waterman

Introduction

In 2017, approximately ten million (one out of four) older adults resided in small towns or rural areas in the U.S. (Skoufalos, Clarke, Ellis, Shepard, & Rula, 2017). Older adults who reside in rural areas are more likely to be at a disadvantage compared to older adults who reside in urban areas. This population is more likely to experience geographic isolation, lower socioeconomic status, and lower Social Security benefits (Skoufalos et al., 2017). Coupled with longer life spans and higher rates of chronic conditions, rural residents are more likely to outlive their retirement savings, leaving them vulnerable to significant financial burden.

Physical and financial health are intertwined. Economic factors affect not only access to health care and nutritious food, but also shape healthy behaviors, which are a primary determinant of premature death. This is especially challenging for older adults, who often have no means of boosting their income in retirement, especially in rural areas that may face job scarcity.

Numerous public benefit programs are available to assist struggling older adults with freeing up financial resources and enabling them to meet critical health needs. These benefits also are proven to reduce the burden and costs on the health-care system. The Medicare Savings Programs (MSPs), administered and paid through state Medicaid agencies[1], pay the monthly Part B premium, and other cost-sharing for those with very low income. The Part D Low-Income Subsidy, or Extra Help, helps older adults afford medications and increase prescription adherence, which in turn helps them better manage chronic conditions and reduce falls.

Access to the Supplemental Nutrition Assistance Program (SNAP, formerly Food Stamps) reduces hospital admission rates and the need for emergency room visits among older adults, and on average can save $2,100 a year in medical costs (Samuel, Szanton, Cahill, Wolff, Ong, Zielinskie, & Betley, 2018). SNAP assistance facilitates healthier eating, which also can lessen the adverse side effects of chronic conditions. Rural households spend a higher percentage of their incomes on home energy bills than the average American household (Ross, Drehobl, & Stickles, 2018). Utility benefits such as the Low-Income Home Energy Assistance Program (LIHEAP) provide vital assistance to help rural older adults offset the costs of heating and cooling their homes, thereby reducing respiratory disease symptoms and emergency room visits.

Barriers to Benefits Enrollment for Rural Older Adults

Public benefits can offer rural older adults the critical help needed to remain independent and in their own homes and communities. Yet millions of older adults who are eligible to receive assistance from these programs are not enrolled. It is estimated that three in five older adults who qualify for SNAP are not receiving the benefit; roughly half of those who are eligible for the MSPs are not enrolled (Caswell & Waidmann, 2017).

There are myriad reasons why older adults are reluctant to apply for these programs. A comprehensive telephone survey with over 1,000 low-income older adults sponsored by the National Council on Aging (NCOA) in 2016 revealed that the four greatest barriers to participation were:

1. *Lack of awareness of programs.* Only 24% of respondents had heard of the MSPs; roughly half had knowledge of LIHEAP. For SNAP, while awareness was high, many older adults had misconceptions that the program was only for families with children (National Council on Aging, 2017).
2. *Not knowing where to begin to apply.* Awareness of certain resources in their communities that can help with benefits applications, such as the State Health Insurance Assistance Programs (SHIPs), which work to enroll Medicare beneficiaries into the MSPs and Extra Help, was low among survey respondents.
3. *Assuming the application process is tedious.* Some benefits program applications can be upwards of 25 or more pages. This, combined with the need to gather and submit documentation and possibly attend an interview, can be a major deterrent to applying. In rural areas, this is compounded by the lack of transportation to administering agency offices and lack of broadband internet access to facilitate online applications.
4. *Believing other people need more help.* While several of the core benefits programs noted earlier, including SNAP and the MSPs, expand to meet the need, there is often the belief that accepting assistance takes away from someone else in need. Better education about the nature and availability of benefits, as well as positive affirmations about older adults having earned the right to claim benefits as a result of taxes paid into these programs, can mitigate this concern.

In addition, many older adults are reluctant to apply for benefits programs because of stigma and negative associations with the concept of "welfare" (National Council on Aging, 2016). For rural residents, who may especially value an ethic of self-reliance, there is often a fear that neighbors will become aware that they are receiving assistance. NCOA's stigma research also revealed that exposure to others who enroll in benefits programs makes older adults less likely to feel isolated and embarrassed as a result of participation, which can be difficult in rural areas that lack a high penetration of social services.

Community-Based Approaches to Addressing Health and Wealth Disparities

One mechanism being used to assist economically insecure rural older adults is a network of Benefit Enrollment Centers (BECs). Supported by NCOA, BECs are community or state agencies that assist low-income individuals with Medicare to access programs that pay for health care, food, and more. Using web-based tools and person-centered approaches, the BECs help low-income older adults and individuals with disabilities find and enroll in all the benefits programs for which they are eligible and create coordinated, community-wide systems of benefits access. The BECs focus on connecting Medicare beneficiaries with limited incomes to five core benefits: Medicare Part D Extra Help, MSPs, Medicaid, SNAP, and LIHEAP. BECs also assist older adults and individuals with disabilities to apply for other programs, such as Supplemental Security Income (SSI), state pharmaceutical assistance program (SPAPs), local transportation assistance, tax relief, and other local programs.

BECs are supported with funding from the Medicare Improvements for Patients and Providers Act (MIPPA) and administered through the U.S. Administration for Community Living (ACL). As the MIPPA Resource Center, NCOA's Center for Benefits Access has supported the creation of BECs since 2009. Currently, there are 85 BECs located in 43 states. Since 2009, the BECs have assisted over 535,000 older adults and individuals with disabilities with over 800,000 applications for benefits estimated to be worth over $1.3 billion. Of the 85 BECs, approximately half are currently located in rural locations or provide assistance to clients who are socially isolated in rural areas across the country.

BEC Promising Practices for Serving Rural Clients

Trust, costs, and messaging underline much of the work of NCOA's Center for Benefits Access and its grantees in connecting lower-income individuals to the programs and services to which they are entitled. The following are several examples from the BEC network of how they have mitigated these concerns and positioned themselves to be able to boost enrollment in programs like Medicare Savings Programs, SNAP, and Medicaid.

Promising Practice 1: Meet Communities Where They Are

The Northern New Mexico Benefit Enrollment Center (NNM BEC) provides benefits outreach and enrollment assistance to residents living in its 8,000 square mile service area, which consists of many Native American communities. The NNM BEC collaborated with the Rio Arriba Community Senior Advisory Committee for guidance on how to introduce the BEC and the outreach and enrollment activities within the community. The NNM BEC received advice of community elders who volunteer their time to ensure that their local senior centers meet the unique needs of the older adults in their rural/frontier communities. During the initial engagement process, the Senior Advisory Committee provided feedback on the BEC's strategic plan and facilitated listening sessions at 11 area senior centers to allow for the NNM BEC to receive direct feedback from community members. The BEC's community integrated planning approach has proven successful by assisting 2,054 low-income Medicare beneficiaries to enroll in benefits since 2016. The NNM BEC and the Advisory Committee continue to collaborate to connect residents to benefits, and the Advisory Committee continues to refer clients to NNM BEC daily.

Promising Practice 2: Avoid Stigma by Protecting Anonymity

One of the issues commonly raised in smaller communities is that familiarity among community members makes residents reluctant to seek assistance. A BEC in North Carolina that serves rural areas and homebound individuals resolved this issue by putting locked boxes at local venues that are frequented by potential clients, such as pharmacies and libraries. The potential client has an opportunity to fill out a form to request more information and schedule an initial session with a BEC counselor. By making the initial contact private, the BEC mitigates the stigma that is associated with inquiring about benefits eligibility at a public office where an individual may be seen by peers.

Promising Practice 3: Utilize Health Providers to Assist With Outreach

Older adults regularly see their health-care provider as a trusted source of information for medical and nonmedical advice. It is essential to the health and well-being of older adults to educate physicians, nurses, pharmacists, and other aging professionals on the value of benefits especially for those who are struggling. A BEC in Kentucky cultivated a relationship with Kentucky One Health and external medical providers through an awareness campaign that included outreach to financial aid departments and medical clinics. The BEC designed a mock prescription pad that includes the BEC's contact information with instructions to schedule an initial meeting with a BEC counselor. "Prescribing" a benefits screening takes the patient out of the role of asking for assistance and reaffirms the notion that improved financial stability is essential to their overall health and well-being.

Conclusion

The Benefit Enrollment Center network has made great strides in the establishment of coordinated care networks that provide enrollment assistance services to many rural communities across the country. As the number of older adults who are struggling continues to increase, it is essential to develop strategies aimed at providing streamlined care that is customized to the unique needs of each rural community.

Note

1. Medicare Savings Programs include the Qualified Medicare Beneficiary (QMB) program, the Specified Low Income Medicare Beneficiary (SLMB) program, and the Qualified Individual (QI) program. QMB and SLMB are funded entirely through state Medicaid, while the QI is a federally funded program.

Recommendation for Further Readings

Cunnyngham, K. (2018). *Trends in Supplemental Nutrition Assistance Program participation rates: Fiscal year 2010 to fiscal year 2016*. United States Department of Agriculture. Retrieved from https://fns-prod.azureedge.net/sites/default/files/snap/Trends2010-2016.pdf

National Council on Aging. (2016). *An end to stigma*. Challenging the stigmatization of public assistance among older adults and people with disabilities. Retrieved from www.ncoa.org/wp-content/uploads/An-End-to-Stigma-Issue-Brief-NCOA.pdf

References

Caswell, K. J., & Waidmann, T. A. (2017). *Medicare Savings Program enrollees and eligible non-enrollees*. Report for Medicaid and CHIP Payment and Access Commission (MACPAC). Retrieved from www.macpac.gov/wp-content/uploads/2017/08/MSP-Enrollees-and-Eligible-Non-Enrollees.pdf

National Council on Aging. (2016). *An end to stigma: Challenging the stigmatization of public assistance among older adults and people with disabilities*. Retrieved from https://d2mkcg26uvg1cz.cloudfront.net/wp-content/uploads/An-End-to-Stigma-Issue-Brief-NCOA.pdf

National Council on Aging. (2017). *What the research says*. Retrieved from www.ncoa.org/centerforbenefits/outreach-toolkit/what-the-research-says/

Ross, L., Drehobl, A., & Stickles, B. (2018). The high cost of energy in rural America. Household energy burdens and opportunities for energy efficiency. *American Council for an Energy-Efficient Economy*. Retrieved from https://assets.ctfassets.net/ntcn17ss1ow9/NYfb0e4UpPPpmWa3At1VC/60f46af9f8b43ab99542e4f458f6d5c3/EEFA_AEEE_Rural_Energy_burden_report_.pdf

Samuel, L. J., Szanton, S. L., Cahill, R., Wolff, J. L., Ong, P., Zielinskie, G., & Betley, C. (2018). Does the Supplemental Nutrition Assistance Program affect hospital utilization among older adults? The case of Maryland. *Population Health Management, 21*(2), 88–95. doi:10.1089/pop.2017.0055

Skoufalos, A., Clarke, J. L., Ellis, D. R., Shepard, V. L., & Rula, E. Y. (2017). Rural aging in America: Proceedings of the 2017 connectivity summit. *Population Health Management, 20*(2), S3–S9. doi:10.1089/pop.2017.0177

25
EVIDENCE-BASED PROGRAMS

Matthew Lee Smith, Shinduk Lee, Samuel D. Towne, Jr., Andrew C. Pickett, Scott A. Horel, and Kristie P. Kulinski

Overview

The burdens of disease complications and preventable hospitalizations from falls may be ameliorated by leveraging medical and nonmedical solutions. To complement traditional medical care, a diverse array of evidence-based programs (EBPs) have been developed and employed across the U.S. to meet older adults' health needs (Ory & Smith, 2015). These programs can be delivered in multiple settings and were developed to empower older adults by giving them practical and usable skills to manage their health and avoid negative health-related consequences. EBP topics include, but are not limited to, chronic disease self-management, fall prevention, physical activity, caregiving, behavioral health/mental health, and general wellness. Despite national efforts to promote the dissemination of these programs, unique challenges persist regarding the reach, adoption, and implementation of EBPs in rural communities and organizations (Smith et al., 2017, 2018). This chapter highlights the concurrent national dissemination of evidence-based chronic disease self-management education (CDSME) and fall prevention programs in rural communities from January 2009 to January 2019.

Criteria

Many credible organizations have developed their own criteria for defining EBPs for older adults. One such organization is the Administration for Community Living (ACL), a division of the U.S. Department of Health and Human Services (https://acl.gov). States can independently apply ACL's criteria to programs to identify interventions that are appropriate for Older Americans Act Title III-D funding, or they can select interventions that have been vetted by an independent Review Council.

The Review Council, composed of select experts in the academic, health-care, government, and community sectors, performs a thorough, two-stage review of submitted programs on an annual basis. Stage One assesses the available evidence about program effectiveness for older adults. Only after meeting the criteria outlined in Stage One can programs undergo Stage Two review. Stage Two assesses program information regarding the implementation, training, dissemination materials, available supports, and other essential elements for grand-scale program dissemination. Across the two stages, programs are evaluated on the five criteria that comprise ACL's definition of evidence-based programming: 1. demonstrated through evaluation to be effective for improving the health and well-being or reducing disease, disability, and/or injury among older adults; 2. documented effectiveness with older adult population, using an experimental or quasi-experimental research design; 3. published results in a peer-reviewed journal; 4. translated in one or more community sites; and 5. developed dissemination products that are available to the public (ACL, 2020). To date, approximately 60 programs are listed as having met these ACL criteria (National Council on Aging (NCOA), 2020).

ACL Funding Initiatives

National data were examined from two ongoing and concurrent ACL-funded EBP dissemination efforts (Boutaugh et al., 2014; Boutaugh & Lawrence, 2015). All data were collected from ACL grantees from 2009 to 2019, each required to report reach and adoption information into a national data repository (Kulinski et al., 2015). The primary purpose of these ACL funding initiatives is to develop capacity for, bring to scale, and/or sustain evidence-based CDSME and fall prevention programs. Through these funding mechanisms, special attention is given to vulnerable and at-risk populations, which are defined primarily as older adults and adults with disabilities. In addition, a 2020 funding opportunity specifically targeted behavioral health and chronic pain among these populations.

Rural Reach and Adoption

Each county was assigned a Rural-Urban Continuum Code (RUCC), which were developed by the U.S. Department of Agriculture (U.S. Department of Agriculture, 2017; Hall, Kaufman, & Ricketts, 2006). Counties with RUCC of four or higher on the nine-point scale were classified as nonmetropolitan, which we refer to throughout as "rural." Of the 3,221 U.S. counties, 1,911 counties (59.3%) delivered at least one EBP. Of the 1,911 counties that delivered one or more EBPs, 53% (1,012) were rural counties.

For the chronic disease self-management education (CDSME) program dissemination, data from January 2009 to January 2019 were analyzed, which included 19 unique program types. A total of 32,355 workshops were delivered to 385,770 participants across 48 states and two territories. Approximately 20% of these workshops (6,292) were offered in rural counties, which served 17.5% (67,326) of reached participants. The most commonly delivered CDSME program workshops in rural counties were the Chronic Disease Self-Management Program (CDSMP, 76.1%), Diabetes Self-Management Program (DSMP, 16.4%), Chronic Pain Self-Management Program (CDSMP, 3.7%), and *Tomando Control de su Salud* (Spanish CDSMP, 2.1%). The most common implementation site types for CDSME program workshops in rural counties were health-care organizations (23.8%), senior centers (21.6%), residential facilities (11.5%), and faith-based organizations (7.1%).

For the fall prevention program dissemination, data from January 2014 to January 2019 were analyzed, which included nine unique program types. A total of 7,040 workshops were delivered to 88,016 participants across 30 states. Approximately 22% of these workshops (1,534) were offered in rural counties, which served 20.8% (18,270) of reached participants. The most commonly delivered fall prevention workshops in rural counties were the A Matter of Balance (AMOB, 50.0%), Stepping On (18.8%), Tai Ji Quan (13.6%), and Tai Chi for Arthritis (12.9%). The most common delivery implementation types for fall prevention workshops in

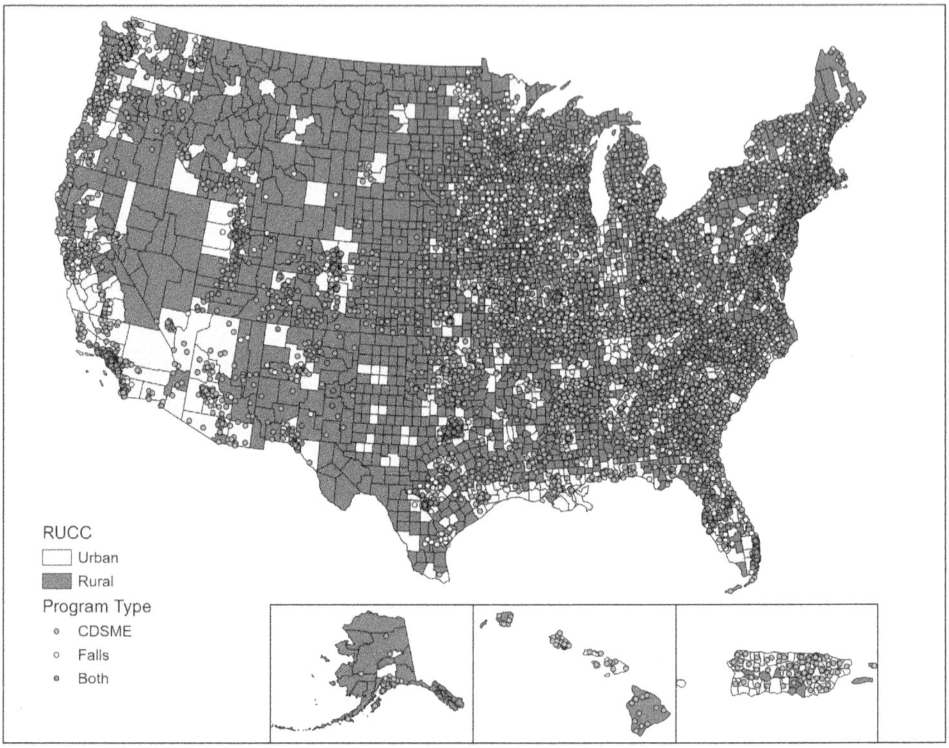

Figure 25.1 National Dissemination of CDSME and Falls Programming—2009 to 2019

rural counties were senior centers (29.8%), residential facilities (15.8%), health-care organizations (14.7%), faith-based organizations (8.9%), and community centers (8.6%).

While a larger proportion of CDSME participants from urban areas participated in residential facilities (23%) than in health-care organizations (19%), a larger proportion of CDSME participants from rural areas participated in health-care organizations (22%) than in residential facility (16%). Furthermore, a larger proportion of fall prevention program participants from remote areas participated in a health-care organization (20%) than the participants from urban areas (16%).

Figure 25.1 illustrates the combined national dissemination of these EBPs, which is complemented by the data in Table 1. Despite rural counties representing 53% of all counties that delivered one or more EBPs, only 18.1% of participants reached and 21.7% of implementation sites were in rural counties. Compared to urban counties, larger proportions of rural counties offered CDSME Programs Only (27.1% versus 36.6%) and Falls Programs Only (1.5% versus 3.1%); however, a larger proportion of urban counties offered both CDSME and Falls Programs (18.5% vs. 13.3%). In regard to counties that offered Falls Programs Only, rural counties served more participants and had more implementation sites than urban counties.

Table 25.1 CDSME and Falls Program Delivery by Rurality

	Participants			*Implementation Sites*			*Unique Counties Reached*		
	Urban	*Rural*	*Total*	*Total*	*Urban*	*Rural*	*Urban*	*Rural*	*Total*
CDSME Only	123,160 (26%)	46,686 (9.9%)	169,846 (35.9%)	5,248 (25.6%)	2,313 (11.3%)	7,561 (36.8%)	517 (27.1%)	699 (36.6%)	1,216 (63.6%)
Falls Only	1,124 (0.2%)	1,646 (03%)	2,770 (0.6%)	67 (0.3%)	112 (0.5%)	179 (0.9%)	28 (1.5%)	59 (3.1%)	87 (4.6%)
CDSME and Falls	263,878 (55.7%)	37,264 (7.9%)	301,142 (63.6%)	10,763 (52.4%)	2,023 (9.9%)	12,786 (62.3%)	354 (18.5%)	254 (13.3%)	608 (31.8%)
TOTAL	**388,162 (81.9%)**	**85,596 (18.1%)**	**473,758 (100%)**	**16,078 (78.3%)**	**4,448 (21,7%)**	**20,526 (100%)**	**899 (47.0%)**	**1,012 (53.0%)**	**1,911 (100%)**

Implications and Opportunities

The dissemination of these CDSME and fall prevention programs reinforces that EBPs can be introduced and embedded into rural communities through a diverse infrastructure of implementation sites (Smith et al., 2017, 2018; Towne, Smith, Ahn, & Ory, 2015). Collectively, about 18% of the participants served by these EBPs were in rural counties. Given that 19% of Americans reside in rural counties, this is promising (U.S. Census Bureau, 2020a). While it is encouraging that 53% of workshops were implemented in rural counties, these 1,012 counties only represent 51% of the 1,985 rural counties in the U.S. Further, programs were limited and almost nonexistent in predominantly rural states with larger proportions of older adults (e.g., Montana, North Dakota, South Dakota, Nebraska, Kansas, and Oklahoma) (U.S. Census Bureau, 2020b). This suggests the need for continued support to expand the reach of EBPs in rural America. It is important to note that EBP dissemination efforts reported here do not fully represent the complete delivery of evidence-based programming nationwide in rural or urban settings, as only ACL grantees were required to enter data into the national repository.

Innovations are needed to expand the reach of EBPs in rural communities. Rather than "recreating the wheel," best practices recommend using existing EBPs and tailoring them for embedment and sustainability in local communities. However, this process must be performed rigorously and thoughtfully to avoid program drift or loss of essential intervention elements (Chen, Reid, Parker, & Pillemer, 2013; Rakowski, 1999; Tomioka & Braun, 2015). CDSMP is an exemplar of such tailoring, where translated versions have increased the reach to rural populations. The language- and culture-based CDSMP translations of *Tomando Control de su Salud* (Spanish CDSMP) and *Ke Ola Pono* (meaning "health in balance" and translated in Pidgin (Hawaiian English)) (Tomioka, Braun, Compton, & Tanoue, 2012) in Hawaii are examples of tailored EBPs successfully implemented in rural areas. Tailoring and cultural translations of EBPs enhance the intervention appropriateness for wider audiences, especially those harder-to-reach populations (Smith et al., 2018).

Common barriers of implementing EBP workshops in rural and remote areas include 1. recruitment and retention of trained program facilitators; 2. enrolling and retaining a sufficient number of program participants to host workshops with fidelity; and 3. travel distance to workshop locations (for the facilitators and participants). Compared to urban areas, rural and remote areas have a smaller pool of potential leaders, which introduces larger delivery burden and attrition. Careful workshop delivery site selection can assist facilitators and participants to overcome transportation barriers and attend more workshop sessions. For example, offering workshops in locations that are visited routinely (e.g., faith-based organizations are often visited weekly) can improve attendance and retention. Innovative transportation solutions (e.g., carpools, ride-share vouchers) may also reduce distance-related barriers for remote populations.

Technology offers another innovative opportunity for expanding EBP reach in rural communities (Smith et al., 2017, 2018). If implemented successfully, online delivery of EBPs can overcome distance-related barriers by enabling workshop facilitators from one location to teach participants from one or more rural and remote communities. Internet-based, virtual delivery of programming may make content available to new audiences (e.g., homebound persons, those in more remote areas). However, older adults and rural populations may have reduced access to high-speed internet compared to their metropolitan counterparts (Federal Communications Commission, 2020), which may serve as a barrier to full online implementation of EBPs in these communities (Smith et al., 2017, 2018). To date, many existing EBPs have been translated to online delivery formats (e.g., CDSMP, Otago Exercise Program), and more information can be learned on their respective websites.

Strategic Planning for Implementation in Rural Communities

Understanding the program delivery infrastructure in rural communities can provide an opportunity for expanding the program reach in these communities. Compared to urban communities, rural communities are more likely to lack the resources required to sustain multiple programs, which may explain the larger proportion of urban counties offering both CDSME and falls programs than rural counties. To maximize the chances of successful program implementation in rural areas, organizations should leverage limited resources available in their community. In rural areas, senior centers and aging service organizations were the predominant delivery sites. With limited community resources, senior centers, aging service organizations, and health-care organizations may be a common place for congregating and seeking health-related resources in rural areas. Involving these organizations in the implementation planning process and program delivery can increase program reach in these areas. However, diversifying organizational recruitment (e.g., faith-based organizations) in rural areas may strengthen participant reach (Smith et al., 2015).

Furthermore, program delivery sites also differed based on program types. Health care was the most predominant in rural counties for CDSME, but not for falls (senior centers). Despite some differences, the same implementation site types served the most participants in CDSME and falls programs, which confirms that location matters in attracting the intended audience (e.g., falls programming typically attracts older and less ambulatory individuals compared to CDSME, hence larger proportions of falls programs being offered in senior centers and residential facilities).

Notably, compared to falls programming, CDSME has had a larger footprint, based on its longer and more substantive funding history (Boutaugh et al., 2014). However, there is a large overlap of counties adopting both CDSME and falls programming. The delivery of *multiple* EBP types helps potentially vulnerable populations meet their numerous and distinct needs and results in increased available options, which a *single* EBP is not capable of providing alone. Exposure to multiple EBPs that taken together can complement or even build off the knowledge gained in multiple distant EBPs may be critical, thereby leaving a participant better equipped to age more successfully (Lee, Smith, Towne, & Ory, 2018; Towne, Smith, Ahn, Altpeter et al., 2015). Given the potential benefit from delivering multiple distinct EBPs in a given area, it is encouraging that nearly one-third of U.S. counties were reached by organizations delivering both CDSME and falls programming. Additional support and ongoing efforts are needed so EBP adoption and delivery can be increased and sustained nationwide.

References

Administration for Community Living. (2020). *Health promotion*. Retrived April 1, 2020, from https://acl.gov/programs/health-wellness/disease-prevention

Boutaugh, M. L., Jenkins, S. M., Kulinski, K. P., Lorig, K. L., Ory, M. G., & Smith, M. L. (2014). Closing the disparity: The work of the Administration on Aging. *Generations*, *38*(4), 107–118.

Boutaugh, M. L., & Lawrence, L. J. (2015). Fostering healthy aging through evidence-based prevention programs: Perspectives from the Administration for Community Living/Administration on Aging. *Frontiers in Public Health*, *2*, 236. doi:10.3389/fpubh.2014.00236

Chen, E. K., Reid, M. C., Parker, S. J., & Pillemer, K. (2013). Tailoring evidence-based interventions for new populations: A method for program adaptation through community engagement. *Evaluation & the Health Professions*, *36*(1), 73–92.

Federal Communications Commission. (2018). *2018 broadband deployment report*. Retrieved April 1, 2020, from www.fcc.gov/reports-research/reports/broadband-progress-reports/2018-broadband-deployment-report

Hall, S. A., Kaufman, J. S., & Ricketts, T. C. (2006). Defining urban and rural areas in U.S. epidemiologic studies. *Journal of Urban Health*, *83*, 162–175.

Kulinski, K. P., Boutaugh, M. L., Smith, M. L., Ory, M. G., & Lorig, K. (2015). Setting the stage: Measure selection, coordination, and data collection for a national self-management initiative. *Frontiers in Public Health, 2*, 206. doi:10.3389/fpubh.2014.00206

Lee, S., Smith, M. L., Towne, S. D., Jr., & Ory, M. G. (2018). Effects of sequential participation in evidence-based health and wellness programs among older adults. *Innovations in Aging, 2*(2), 1–12. doi:10.1093/geroni/igy016. Retrieved from www.ncoa.org/news/resources-for-reporters/get-the-facts/falls-prevention-facts

National Council on Aging. (2020). *Highest tier evidence-based health promotion/disease prevention programs*. Retrieved April 1, 2020, from www.ncoa.org/wp-content/uploads/Title-IIID-Highest-Tier-EBPs-January-2019.pdf

Ory, M. G., & Smith, M. L. (2015). Research, practice, and policy perspectives on evidence-based programming for older adults. *Frontiers in Public Health, 3*, 136. doi:10.3389/fpubh.2015.00136

Rakowski, W. (1999). The potential variances of tailoring in health behavior interventions. *Annals of Behavioral Medicine, 21*(4), 284.

Smith, M. L., Ory, M. G., Ahn, S., Belza, B., Mingo, C. A., Towne, S. D., Jr., & Altpeter, M. (2015). Reaching diverse participants utilizing a diverse delivery infrastructure: A replication study. *Frontiers in Public Health, 3*, 77. doi:10.3389/fpubh.2015.00077

Smith, M. L., Towne, S. D., Jr., Herrera-Venson, A., Cameron, K. A., Horel, S. A., Ory, M. G., . . . Skowronski, S. (2018). Delivery of fall prevention interventions for at-risk older adults in rural areas: Findings from a national dissemination. *International Journal of Environmental Research and Public Health, 15*(12), 2798. doi:10.3390/ijerph15122798

Smith, M. L., Towne, S. D., Jr., Herrera-Venson, A., Cameron, K. A., Kulinski, K. P., Lorig, K., . . . Ory, M. G. (2017). Dissemination of chronic disease self-management education (CDSME) programs in the United States: Intervention delivery by rurality. *International Journal of Environmental Research and Public Health, 16*(6), E638. doi:10.3390/ijerph14060638

Tomioka, M., & Braun, K. L. (2015). Implementing evidence-based programs: A four-step protocol for assuring replication with fidelity. *Health Promotion Practice, 14*(6), 850–858. doi:10.1177/152483991 2469205

Tomioka, M., Braun, K. L., Compton, M., & Tanoue, L. (2012). Adapting Stanford's chronic disease self-management program to Hawaii's multicultural population. *The Gerontologist, 52*(1), 121–132. doi:10.1093/geront/gnr054

Towne, S. D., Jr., Smith, M. L., Ahn, S., Altpeter, M., Belza, B., Kulinski, K. P., & Ory, M. G. (2015). National dissemination of multiple evidence-based disease prevention programs: Reach to vulnerable older adults. *Frontiers in Public Health, 2*, 156. doi:10.3389/fpubh.2014.00156

Towne, S. D., Jr., Smith, M. L., Ahn, S., & Ory, M. G. (2015). The reach of chronic disease self-man agement education programs to rural populations. *Frontiers in Public Health, 2*, 172. doi:10.3389/fpubh.2014.00172

U.S. Census Bureau. (2020a). *Rural America*. Retrieved April 1, 2020, from https://gis-portal.data.census.gov/arcgis/apps/MapSeries/index.html?appid=7a41374f6b03456e9d138cb014711e01

U.S. Census Bureau. (2020b). *Older population in rural America*. Retrieved April 1, 2020, from www.census.gov/library/stories/2019/10/older-population-in-rural-america.html

U.S. Department of Agriculture. (2017). *Rural-urban continuum codes*. Retrieved April 1, 2020, from www.ers.usda.gov/data-products/rural-urban-continuum-codes.aspx

26

FALLS AND INJURIES

Mindy Renfro

Each year, millions of older adults—those 65 and older—fall. In fact, more than one out of four older adults falls each year, but less than half inform their doctors. Falling once doubles your chances of falling again (CDC, 2019). The basic facts about falls in older adults are frightening:

- One out of five falls causes a serious injury such as broken bones or a head injury;
- Each year, three million older adults are treated in emergency departments for fall injuries;
- Over 800,000 patients a year are hospitalized because of serious falls, most often because of a resulting head injury or hip fracture;
- Each year, at least 300,000 older adults are hospitalized for hip fractures;
- More than 95% of hip fractures are caused by falling, usually by falling sideways;
- Falls are the most common cause of traumatic brain injury (TBI); and
- In 2015, the total medical costs for falls exceeded $50 billion. Medicare and Medicaid shouldered 75% of these costs. This does not include the out-of-pocket costs to the patient and/or their family (CDC, n.d.).

According to CDC's Burns and Kakara, among persons aged ≥65 years, the rate of falls increased by almost a third (31%) from 2007 to 2016, with increases reported in 30 states and the District of Columbia for both men and women (Burns & Kakara, 2018). Falls can result in fractures and other injuries, disability, and fear and can trigger a decline in physical function and loss of autonomy (Lord & Close, 2018).

Falls are classified into three groups:

1. *Near falls*: a stumble event or loss of balance that would result in a fall if sufficient recovery mechanisms were not activated. Near falls predict subsequent falls (Nagai et al., 2017).
2. *Falls*: loss of balance resulting in striking a lower supporting surface such as the floor, furniture, or a wall. Falls without injury do predict subsequent falls with injuries.
3. *Falls with injury*: a fall that results in an injury requiring medical care. Injury falls can be life altering for the older adult and their entire family.

Most falls are preventable! There are four critical steps to prevention:

1. *Physical activity*: strength and balance exercise geared to an individual's ability level.
2. *Home safety*: removing clutter and providing well-designed spaces with reduced hazards.
3. *Medication management*: annual review of medications.
4. *Vision care*: annual update of eyeglasses and comprehensive vision care.

Fall Risk Factors

There is not a single approach to the reduction of fall risks that is effective for all individuals. An array of fall risk factors needs to be considered and a determination made as to which needs to be addressed for a particular individual. There are two main types of fall risk factors:

1. *Intrinsic Fall Risk Factors*: these are specific to you and your body and include factors such as previous falls, previous injury or current illnesses, cognition, balance, vision issues, dizziness, taking four or more medications, lack of physical activity, and/or limited social engagement.
2. *Extrinsic Fall Risk Factors*: these are the characteristics of your environment—especially your home—that can create fall hazards such as the presence of stairs, poor lighting, household clutter, engaging in risky behavior such as climbing up on chairs or ladders, the absence of grab bars in bathrooms, loose scatter rugs, etc.

Smith et al. (2018) studied falls specific to rural areas. They reported that there is no single solution to combat falls among older adults. The known risk factors are multifactorial and they can be associated with biological, psychosocial, and environmental causes. One extrinsic risk factor for falls is residing in rural areas. Rural-dwelling older adults are at an increased risk for falls relative to their urban-dwelling counterparts because of differences in the physical environment and lifestyle activities.

There is a three-step process to evaluating your own fall risk:

1. *Your Community*: determine if you are living in a livable community by assessing the AARP Livability Index for your small town or rural community (https://livindexhub.aarp.org/). If your community is not highly rated, learn what is needed to improve that score. If you are considering a move, read about the most livable communities before making a choice.
2. *Your Home*: determine if it is time to install grab bars and additional lighting instead of moving out. Whenever possible, make these modifications before retirement. Making your home safe will increase your ability to age-in-place successfully.
3. *Your Body*: determine your basic fall risk by using the brief home self-evaluation of your basic fall risk, using the CDC's Stay Independent home self-evaluation questionnaire (www.cdc.gov/steadi/pdf/STEADI-Brochure-StayIndependent-508.pdf). If you score above a four, it is recommended that you discuss your fall risk profile with your primary care practitioner. Patient-health provider discussion should include attention to the following:
    a. *Falls*: any near falls and actual falls with or without resulting injury you have had in the past one to two years.
    b. *Medications*: whether current dosages should be reduced as you age. The body's ability to metabolize medications diminishes as you age and it is therefore important to consider whether a decrease in dosing is advised. Taking four or more prescription

medications is associated with an elevated fall risk. Drugs that affect your mood, sleep, and/or pain are the most critical to review. Medications that may result in a sudden decrease in blood pressure when standing up should be discussed.

c. *Vision*: your last eye doctor appointment, eyeglass repair, and/or replacement, and use of multifocal or bifocal lenses. Looking down through reading lenses while walking is particularly dangerous. The use of filters, sunglasses, and/or eye protection while in the sun, driving, and/or using computer/phone screens is also important to protect and preserve vision. Seeing your eye doctor every year once you turn 60 is strongly advised.

d. *Physical Activity*: what level and types of activity are safe for you? Where are the best programs in your community for older adults? Should you begin with a physical therapy (PT) consult? Would it be best to begin with an evidence-based fall prevention course such as Stepping On, Matter of Balance, or Tai Ji Quan: Moving for Better Balance? (see www.ncoa.org/healthy-aging/falls-prevention/falls-prevention-programs-for-older-adults-2/). Is it time for a bone scan (www.mayoclinic.org/tests-procedures/bone-density-test/about/pac-20385273)? Is it time for a blood test for vitamin D levels (www.health.harvard.edu/blog/vitamin-d-whats-right-level-2016121910893)?

e. *Home Safety*: bring your home safety evaluation, too. Your doctor may refer you to a PT or an occupational therapist (OT) for a home evaluation and/or to recommend home modifications. Be sure to have a signed referral form with you when you leave the office. Learn about and locate certified home modification experts in your area here https://homemods.org/

Once you have identified your individual fall risks, each should be addressed with effective evidence-based interventions and management.

Physical Activity and Evidence-Based Programs

Physical activity includes exercise, physical work, play, gardening, and/or simply being outdoors. What matters most is remaining physically active in ways that are safe as our bodies and needs change. Activities to engage in should be selected with caution and changes to activity plans carried out that are appropriate for the body's capabilities and limitations. Plans should not be undertaken without first consulting with one's primary care provider (PCP)—doctor, nurse practitioner, or physician's assistant.

There is robust evidence that exercise can reduce falls in older adults. Systematic review of evidence from 88 trials (with 19,478 participants) indicates exercise can reduce the rate of falls in community-dwelling older people by 21% with greater effects seen from exercise programs that challenge balance and are delivered in higher doses. Higher doses of an intervention intended to promote fall prevention are defined as at least 50 hours of progressively difficult exercise within each six-month period (Sherrington et al., 2008). A continuous exercise schedule is essential as the benefits realized will quickly vanish otherwise.

Not all exercise is effective for fall prevention or fall risk reduction. Most geriatrics fall prevention experts agree that fall prevention exercises should aim to challenge balance in three ways:

1. Reducing the base of support (e.g., standing with both legs close together, standing with one foot directly in front of the other, i.e., a tandem stance position and, if possible, standing on one leg).

2. Movement of the center of gravity—control of the body's position while standing (e.g., reaching safely, transferring the body weight from one leg to the other, stepping up onto a block).
3. Reducing the need for upper limb support with exercises in standing that do not use the arms for support. If this is not possible, the aim should be to decrease reliance on the arms (e.g., hold onto a bar with one hand instead of both hands, rest one finger on a table rather than the whole hand). (Sherrington, Tiedemann, Fairhall, Close, & Lord, 2011).

These three aims are all met with evidence-based fall prevention programs, such as

1. Tai Ji Quan: Moving for Better Balance (TJQMBB)—a higher-level balance exercise (https://tjqmbb.org/) that has some similarities to Tai Chi programs;
2. Alternatively, Stepping On may be a preferred starting point (https://wihealthyaging.org/stepping-on-consumer); and
3. If an individual has difficulty leaving home or working with a group, beginning with a physical therapist at home using the Otago Exercise Program is a safe point of entry (visit www.med.unc.edu/aging/cgec/exercise-program/).

Home Safety and Use of Technology

Ideally, whether residing in rural or urban communities, we would all live in homes created with universal design (UD) (http://universaldesign.ie/What-is-Universal-Design/) allowing older adults, children, and/or people with disabilities to safely visit and for older adults to easily adapt the home as we age-in-place. Since UD is not a building code requirement, it is not uncommon for the home environment (especially in rural communities with older housing stock) to severely limit its safe use. While adapting the home to age-in-place can be expensive and difficult to accomplish for rural-residing older adults with limited assets, it should nevertheless be considered.

There are five main steps to successful aging-in-place with many resources available to inform the process (www.nia.nih.gov/health/aging-place-growing-older-home):

1. First, decide if you want to age where you are currently living. Consider the community, the year it was built, the expense of needed upgrades, and its location with respect to your family, friends, health-care providers, and access to recreation and social engagement. What are the alternatives for transportation when you decide not to drive? Do you have the support that you may need?
2. If you are going to stay, get the best help to evaluate the match between your physical abilities and your home's structural needs. Begin by speaking with your PCP and gaining a referral to a PT or an OT with experience in home modifications and assistive technology. Always check the Home Modifications Resource list here https://homemods.org/national-directory/. With a referral from your doctor, the initial home visit and recommendations should be covered by your health insurance.

   You can also check with your senior center or Area Agency on Aging to see if the CAPABLE program is offered in your area. Community Aging in Place—Advancing Better Living for Elders is a five-month home visit program that helps low-income older adults age-in-place. This program was developed by the Johns Hopkins School of Nursing. There are currently 28 CAPABLE sites across the country, three of which are in rural communities (www.ruralhealthinfo.org/project-examples/1064).

3. Find funding for the needed modifications, materials, and service.

   a. The CAPABLE program has limited funding for simple projects such as grab bars, toilet replacements, and ramps up to about $1,200/home. Other programs include Rebuilding Together and state-funded projects through your aging services providers.
   b. The Veterans Administration does provide home modifications for veterans when it will stop or delay admission to a nursing home. Visit your VA center and/or www.veteransaidbenefit.org/home_renovation_grants.htm.
   c. If you are a homeowner with good credit, consider a second mortgage, a reverse mortgage, a refinance, or other bank loan to cover the costs.
   d. In some cases, the cost of home modifications can be used as a tax deduction for local city and state tax returns and sometimes, they can also be used as a deduction on federal taxes (https://legaleaglecontractors.com/tax-deductions-for-accessible-home-modifications/).

4. Get the work done by reputable builders and/or handymen. Check for handymen that are CAPS certified as a Certified Aging in Place Specialist (https://www.nahb.org/education-and-events/education/Designations/Certified-Aging-in-Place-Specialist-CAPS). Call the local senior center, Area Agency on Aging, local church, Rebuilding Together organization (https://rebuildingtogether.org/find-your-local-affiliate), and/or the Better Business Bureau for recommendations. Be sure that agreements are in writing and are only partially paid up front with the balance due at completion.
5. For any older adults living alone or alone for extended periods of time, use of a fall alarm or Personal Emergency Response System (PERS) is critically important. This technology changes frequently and you should carefully select the correct equipment. https://www.techenhancedlife.com/).

Medication Management

Older adults who take more than four prescription medications daily are considered to be at higher fall risk (Zia, Kamaruzzaman, & Tan, 2015). In particular, drugs that impact mood, sleep, or brain function markedly increase fall risk. In addition, drugs that are beta-blockers (some blood pressure and/or cardiac medications) can result in dizziness when standing up from a bed or chair. Whenever changing prescriptions (start, stop, and/or modify the dosing), there may be an increased fall risk, especially during the first two to three weeks.

Preventive steps to decrease your fall risk from medications include the following:

1. Fill all prescriptions with one pharmacy so the pharmacist is aware of all drugs taken and possible interactions. Schedule annual medication reviews with pharmacists. If fall risk issues are evidenced, pharmacists are encouraged to speak to the PCP. Medicare will cover pharmacist annual drug reviews if it is scheduled and preapproved.
2. Ask doctors if there are any drugs that could be decreased or stopped. As we age, the liver and kidneys are less effective in clearing drug metabolites from the system. This can result in an increase in side effects.

3. Avoid sleeping aids—prescribed and/or OTC. Instead, use meditation for relaxation, exercise to improve sleep, and herbal teas during your bedtime rituals to avoid the need for drugs to aid sleep. Learn more at www.mayoclinic.org/healthy-lifestyle/adult-health/in-depth/sleep-aids/art-20047860
4. Organize and manage medications. Use of pill sorters and medication dispensers can be very helpful to avoid missing or doubling medications, both of which could be very dangerous. Automated systems are currently under objective review at www.techenhancedlife.com
5. Never change your drugs without speaking to your PCP and/or pharmacist—this includes OTC medications.

Vision Care

Establishing balance is achieved using many parts of our nervous system including our vision. As we age and some systems decline (i.e., loss of sensation in the legs or feet, inner ear, leg strength), we depend more on vision. To minimize fall risk, it is important to maintain our vision through annual eye exams and vision correction. Using progressive or multifocal lenses while we are walking increases fall risk (Lord, Smith, & Menant, 2010). As we age, using separate eyeglasses for reading and for distance is advisable.

In addition to eye care, lighting is also a factor to be considered. The older eye adjusts slower to changes in light intensity. Walking from the sunshine to the indoors or vice versa can be temporarily blinding resulting in a fall. As lighting changes, stopping to give the eyes a minute to adjust before proceeding is advisable. Using bright lights when working in the kitchen or office and/or to walk safely through the house is important. Use of automatic motion-detector night lights in the home and at the front door should be considered.

References

Burns, E., & Kakara, J. (2018, May). *Deaths from falls among persons aged ≥65 years—United States, 2007–2016*. CDC Morbidity and Mortality Report. Retrieved from www.cdc.gov/mmwr/volumes/67/wr/mm6718a1.htm#suggestedcitation

CDC. (2019). *Cost of older adult falls*. Retrieved from https://www.cdc.gov/homeandrecreationalsafety/falls/data/fallcost.html

CDC. (n.d.). *Important facts about falls*. Home & Recreational Safety. Retrieved from www.cdc.gov/homeandrecreationalsafety/falls/adultfalls.html

Lord, S. R., & Close, J. C. T. (2018, July). New horizons in falls prevention. *Age and Ageing*, *47*(4), 492–498. doi:10.1093/ageing/afy059

Lord, S. R., Smith, S. T., & Menant, J. C. (2010, November). Vision and falls in older people: Risk factors and intervention strategies. *Clinics in Geriatric Medicine*, *26*(4), 569–581. doi:10.1016/j.cger.2010.06.002

Nagai, K., Yamada, M., Komatsu, M., Tamaki, A., Kanai, M., Miyamoto, T., . . . Tsuboyama, T. (2017, October). Near falls predict substantial falls in older adults: A prospective cohort study. *Geriatrics & Gerontology International*, *17*(10), 1477–1480. doi:10.1111/ggi.12898

Sherrington, C., Tiedemann, A., Fairhall, N., Close, J. C. T., & Lord, S. R. (2011). Exercise to prevent falls in older adults: An updated meta-analysis and best practice recommendations. *NSW Public Health Bulletin*, *22*, 78–83. doi:10.1071/NB10056

Sherrington, C., Whitney, J. C., Lord, S. R., Herbert, R. D., Cumming, R. G., & Close, J. C. (2008). Effective exercise for the prevention of falls: A systematic review and meta-analysis. *Journal of the American Geriatrics Society*, *56*(12), 2234–2243. doi:10.1111/j.1532-5415.2008.02014.x

Smith, M. L., Towne, S. D., Herrera-Venson, A., Cameron, K., Horel, S. A., Ory, M. G., . . . Skowronski, S. (2018). Delivery of fall prevention interventions for at-risk older adults in rural areas: Findings from a national dissemination. *International Journal of Environmental Research and Public Health, 10–15*(12), 2798. doi:10.3390/ijerph15122798

Zia, A., Kamaruzzaman, S. B., & Tan, M. P. (2015, April). Polypharmacy and falls in older people: Balancing evidence-based medicine against falls risk. *Postgraduate Medicine, 127*(3), 330–337. doi:10.1080/00325481.2014.996112

27
FAMILY LIFE

Erik Blanco and Roseann Giarrusso

Introduction

Sociological theory on the differences between rural and urban areas leads us to propose that social interaction among families differ in rural and urban communities. As the population in the U.S. continues to age and the baby boomer generation continues to transition into retirement, the differences between family life in rural and urban regions will become a pinnacle area in the study of aging. In particular, traditions, structural, and demographic changes show an impact of rural environments in the daily life of older adults. Many older adults who live in rural communities prefer to age-in-place; however, that decision comes with unique challenges (Morken & Warner, 2012) potentially affecting their ability to live closer to nature and a place where a slower rhythm to daily life is preferred.

Family Demographics

There are several factors that play a role in shaping the demographics of rural communities with one of the most substantial being that a higher proportion of older adults reside there. The most noticeable dynamic between urban and rural communities is the migration of individuals (Morken & Warner, 2012). Young adults moving to urban areas and older adults relocating to rural communities have resulted in rural areas in the U.S. becoming disproportionately old (Glasgow & Brown, 2012). Additionally, lower individual and family income levels result in increased levels of poverty in rural communities. This is partly because of fewer employment opportunities available for individuals generally, and older adults in particular, in rural communities (Krout, 2014).

There are two types of households in rural communities. On the one hand, there are households occupied by multiple generations, co-residence of older adults and their children, or other types of large households. On the other hand, there are households where older adults live with a spouse only or by themselves (Kendall & Angelwicz, 2018). There has been an increase in numbers of the latter. Because rural older adults are more likely to live alone, there has been an accompanying increase in the number and proportion of aging individuals living in physical and emotional isolation (Morken & Warner, 2012).

Increased job opportunities outside of rural communities is an important factor affecting family life. Significant numbers of rural families have members of the household commuting considerable distances for employment, living away for extended periods of time, or sometimes relocating to urban areas to secure employment. In addition, more women have entered the workforce to supplement the household income in rural communities.

Regardless of these trends in household structure and composition, cultural expectations appear to remain high. Even when younger generations have chosen to relocate to urban spaces, leaving older members of the family behind, individuals from rural communities still expect that interactions among relatives will remain strong, more so than their urban family counterparts (Mair & Thivierge-Rikard, 2010). That expectation provides rural-residing older adults with a measure of assurance that the family will remain intact and functional regardless of the physical separation of its members.

More recently, however, the unrelenting migration of younger generations out of rural places has resulted in alterations in the social structure of those communities. Specifically, the sense of filial piety, the important virtue and primary duty of children to respect, obey, and care for one's parents and other aging family members, is beginning to weaken (Sheng & Zhuo, 2018). This appears to be stressing and even altering the traditional culture and helping traditions of many rural families. Support that had long been available is now lost. Tight-knit, loyal, and supportive families, long a source of pride in rural communities are being put to the test as sons, daughters, and grandchildren are convinced that the new economy is not working for them, resulting in them having to leave their neighborhoods of origin (Ulrich-Schad & Duncan, 2018).

Family Caregivers

People living in rural spaces tend to have more traditional values and cultural traditions (Gruijters, 2017; Krout, 2014). It is commonplace in these settings for families and close friends to provide the majority of services and support needed by older adults during times of need such as bathing, cleaning, cooking, and shopping. Recent studies confirm that families and close friends serving as caregivers have taken on increasingly more complex responsibilities such as medication management and operating medical equipment (Ewing, 2014). This is especially the case in those rural communities where access to health-care providers and services is limited, resulting in older adults who prefer to age-in-place having to rely on family and friends to act as caregivers. Studies confirm that private in-home service providers are accessed less often in rural compared to urban settings, and only as a last resort, when informal support was unavailable (Bacsu, Jeffery, Johnson, Martz, Novik, & Abonyi, 2012). Furthermore, family members who are expected to provide assistance often have to make the difficult decision of coming to the aid of an older relative or friend and remaining employed (Ewing, 2014). Thus, even when a sense of filial piety remains strong for a given rural family, the decision to care for an older relative can be a difficult one.

Challenges of Rural Spaces

It is important to note that not all older adults living in rural communities have strong family networks and those individuals may be forced to face many challenges largely on their own (Bacsu et al., 2012). These challenges include lack of transportation, the risk of becoming socially isolated, financial worries, and mobility issues. More importantly, older adults who choose to age-in-place in their rural communities frequently face multiple challenges to their health and well-being, potentially creating even greater demands on their informal support networks (Galvin, 2019).

Even when community services exist, there are frequent gaps in terms of when assistance is available. For instance, public transportation services may not be available on the weekends or in the evening, and older adults may find it difficult to participate in programs, get to appointments, and visit friends, all of which help to preserve a sense of social connectedness (Rural Health Information Hub, 2019). Service scarcity in rural communities can mean that older adults living in rural communities rely more on themselves and their social networks for transportation, but staying connected can be difficult if older adults are living alone or without a nearby family member. In addition, the shortage of supportive services can worsen already existing health issues, which further highlights the importance of having and maintaining a strong support system in rural spaces.

Health and Well-Being

The integrity of an older adult's social network can have a significant impact on his or her health and well-being. In particular, regular contact with friends and neighbors positively correlated with subjective well-being (Mair & Thivierge-Rikard, 2010). Even though there is increased spatial dispersion and lower population density in rural areas, the lasting bonds older adults create with friends and neighbors appear to be very important (Morken & Warner, 2012). This is because older adults in rural communities tend to have less phone contact with others, meaning that face-to-face contact can take on particular significance in terms of their sense of well-being.

Rural culture defines health in terms of function. In this sense, a healthy person is seen as a person who has the ability to work. Older adults tend to want to do things independently and are well served by their beliefs. This self-resilience places independence at a high value (Gessert, Elliott, & Peden-McAlpine, 2006) and in turn positively affects health because it gives older adults motivation and purpose (Hassani, Izadi-Avanji, Rakhshan, & Alavi, 2017).

Conclusion

As the number and proportion of Americans age 65 and older continues to increase, the needs of older adults living in rural communities will necessarily increase in significance. Many of the challenges that older adults face every day are magnified by the remoteness and lack of infrastructure characteristic of rural communities. The family plays a major role in such settings in supporting individuals who aim to remain independent and age-in-place. The changing economy is creating a gap between families, ever changing the culture and traditions of filial piety.

Future studies in the field of family life in rural communities can be informed by experiences in rural settings internationally. Indeed, many rural communities around the world are thriving and in some cases are doing better than urban communities (Elo, Hendi, Ho, Vierboom, & Preston, 2019). In other industrialized countries, life expectancy is higher, rural residents face fewer barriers to healthy aging, and there is less of a difference when comparing the economic well-being of families residing in rural versus urban communities.

References

Bacsu, J., Jeffery, B., Johnson, S., Martz, D., Novik, N., & Abonyi, S. (2012). Healthy aging in place: Supporting rural seniors' health needs. *Online Journal of Rural Nursing and Health Care, 12*(2), 77–87.

Elo, I. T., Hendi, A. S., Ho, J. Y., Vierboom, Y. C., & Preston, S. H. (2019). Trends in non-Hispanic white mortality in the United States by metropolitan-nonmetropolitan status and region, 1990–2016. *Population and Development Review, 45*(3), 549–583.
Ewing, J. (2014). Helping rural seniors age in place. *National Conference of State Legislatures*, 1–5.
Galvin, G. (2019). An age-friendly rural America. *Healthiest Communities*. Retrieved from https://www.phac-aspc.gc.ca/seniors-aines/alt-formats/pdf/publications/public/healthy-sante/age_friendly_rural/AFRRC_en.pdf
Gessert, C., Elliott, B., & Peden-McAlpine, C. (2006). Family decision-making for nursing home residents with dementia: Rural-urban differences. *The Journal of Rural Health, 22*(1), 1–8.
Glasgow, N., & Brown, D. (2012). Rural aging in the United States: Trends and contexts. *Journal of Rural Studies, 28*(4), 422–431.
Gruijters, R. (2017). Family care-giving and living arrangement of functionally impaired elders in rural China. *Aging and Society, 37*, 633–655.
Hassani, P., Izadi-Avanji, F., Rakhshan, M., & Alavi, H. (2017). A phenomenological study on resilience of the elderly suffering from chronic disease: A qualitative study. *Psychology Research and Behavior Management, 10*, 59–67.
Kendall, J., & Angelwicz, P. (2018). Living arrangements and health at older ages in rural Malawi. *Aging and Society, 38*(5), 1018–1040.
Krout, J. (2014). Rural aging. In *Grantmakers in aging: Issue briefs*. Retrieved from https://www.giaging.org/issues/rural-aging/
Mair, C., & Thivierge-Rikard, R. (2010). The strength of strong ties for older rural adults: Regional distinctions in the relationship between social interaction and subjective well-being. *International Journal of Aging and Human Development, 70*(2), 119–143.
Morken, L., & Warner, M. (2012). Planning for the aging population: Rural responses to the challenge. *National Association of Area Agencies on Aging, n4a*, 1–8.
Rural Health Information Hub. (2019). *Aging in place in rural communities*. Retrieved October 3, 2019, from www.ruralhealthinfo.org/toolkits/aging/1/rural-issues
Sheng, L., & Zhou, F. (2018). The anomie of the filial piety culture and dilemma of family support for the elderly in the context of rural social structure. *Social Construction, 5*, 62–73.
Ulrich-Schad, J., & Duncan, C. (2018). People and places left behind: Work, culture, and politics in the rural United States. *The Journal of Peasant Studies, 45*(1), 59–79.

28
FARMERS*

Carl Zulauf

A topic of ongoing public interest in the U.S. is the older age of farmers and the need to replace them (for example, see Kurtzleben, 2014; Stone, 2014). Examined here will be the average age of U.S. farmers over time, their role, and the accompanying policy implications. Although farmers have been older as a group than the U.S. population and labor force since at least 1960, their age as a group has increased by less. They account for about one-quarter of farm production and are as involved as younger farmers in farm decisions. Most importantly, it is suggested that a policy of enhancing the ability of older U.S. farmers to remain active and perform at a high level in their chosen profession offers benefits for them and all Americans.

Average Age of U.S. Farmers

The average age of U.S. farmers was first reported in the 1945 *Census of Agriculture*. It was 47.8 years (see Figure 28.1). The average age in the 2017 *Census of Agriculture* was 57.5, or 9.7 years higher. The 2017 average is, however, 0.8 years younger than the 2012 census average. The only other census in which average age of farmers declined more than 0.1 year from the immediately preceding census was the 1978 census. Both of these declines overlap to some extent with an extended period of farm prosperity: 1973–1980 for the 1974 and 1978 censuses and 2007–2013 for the 2012 and 2017 censuses. A decline in average age during periods of prosperity is consistent with a pattern of prosperous times attracting new entrants. A change in survey methodology may also be a factor in the lower average age in the 2017 census. The 2017 census collected characteristics for up to four operators per farm compared with three operators per farm in the 2012 census. In the 2017 census, the average age was 58.6 for the principal farm operator vs. 52.8 for non-principal farm operators (second, third, and fourth operators).

The average age of U.S. farmers is younger on the larger farms that produce most U.S. farm products. For example, the 2017 census reported 76,865 farms had $1 million or more in sales of farm products U.S. Department of Agriculture, National Agricultural Statistics Service, 2019). They were 3.8% of all U.S. farms but accounted for 68% of all sales of U.S. farm products. The average age of farmers on these largest U.S. farms was 53.8 years, or 3.7 years younger than the average age of all U.S. farmers.

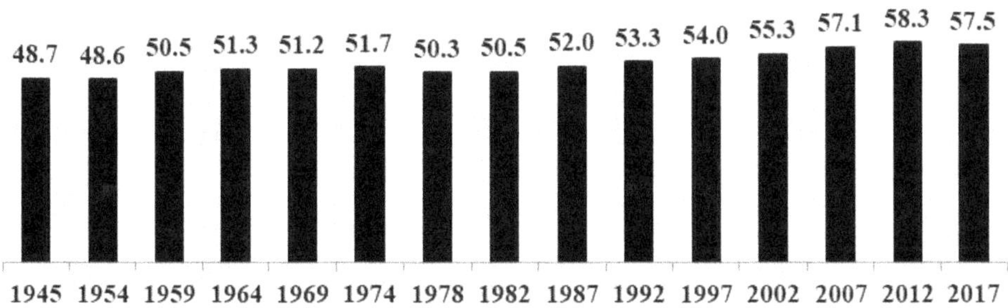

Figure 28.1 Average Age of Farmers, U.S., 1945–2017

Source: Census of Agriculture (various years)

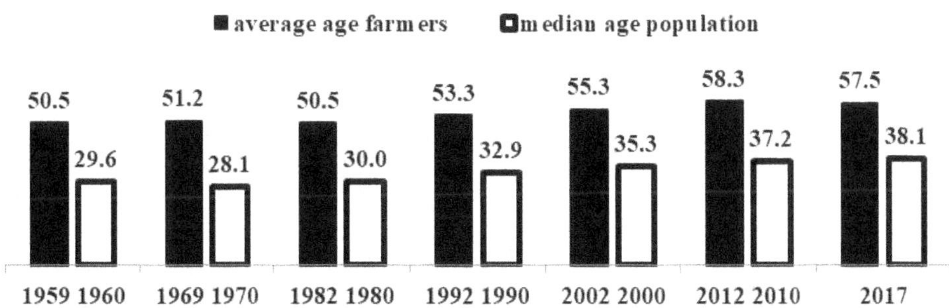

Figure 28.2 Average Age of Farmers and Median Age of Resident Population, U.S., 1959–2017

Sources: Census of Agriculture (various years) and Wikipedia (July 2019)

Comparison With U.S. Population

The average age of U.S. farmers is compared with the median age of the U.S. resident population for decennial population census years starting in 1960, with 2017 added as the latest observation. The average age of farmers is for the agricultural census year nearest to the decennial population census year. The source for the median age of the U.S. resident population is Wikipedia (July 2019).

In 2017, the median age of the U.S. resident population was 38.1, or 19.4 years younger than the average age of U.S. farmers (see Figure 28.2). This difference was the smallest since 1960. The largest difference was 23.1 years for the 1970 decennial census (see Figure 28.3). Thus, while U.S. farmers have been notably older than the U.S. resident population since 1960, the average age of U.S. farmers have increased less than has the median age of the U.S. resident population.

Comparison With U.S. Workforce

U.S. farmers are older than the U.S. population in part because farming is a business occupation, but U.S. farmers are also older than the U.S. labor force. The latter represents workers 16 and

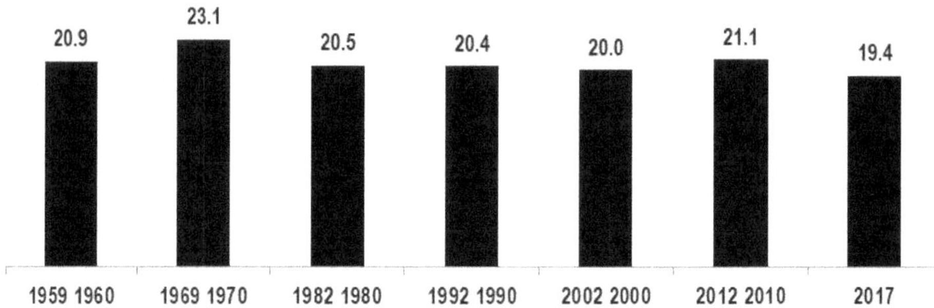

Figure 28.3 Difference: Average Age of Farmers Minus Median Age of Resident Population, U.S., 1959–2017

Source: Calculated from values in Figure 28.2

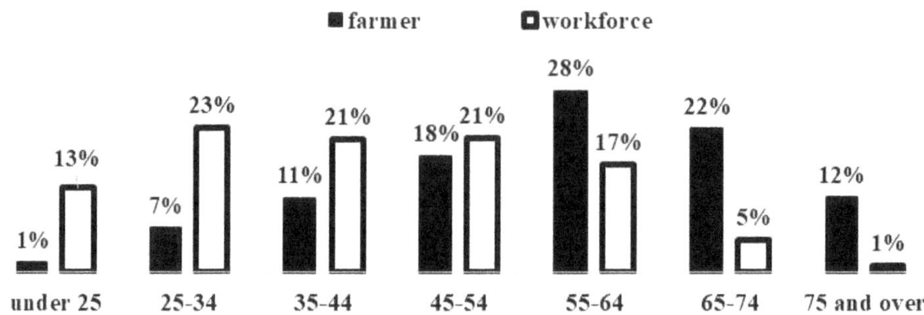

Figure 28.4 Age Distribution, Farmers vs. Workforce, U.S., 2017

Source: *2017 Census of Agriculture* and U.S. Department of Labor, Bureau of Labor Statistics (July 2019)

above. In 2017, one-third of U.S. farmers were older than the commonly discussed retirement age of 65 (see Figure 4). Only 6% of the U.S. workforce were 65 and older (see Figure 28.4). Moreover, only 14% of self-employed U.S. workers in nonagricultural business were 65 and older (U.S. Department of Agriculture, Economic Research Service, 2017).

Involvement of Farmers 65 and Older in Production and Management

Farmers age 65 and older account for 23%, or nearly a quarter, of U.S. farm sales (USDA, 2017). A new question in the 2017 census asked about involvement in selected business decisions. At least 74% of farmers 65 and older reported involvement in each of these decision categories: day-to-day, crop-related, and financial (see Figure 28.5). Their shares in decisions were similar to that of farmers younger than 65. Compared with younger farmers, farmers 65 and older were slightly less involved in livestock-related decisions but slightly more involved in estate or succession planning. Farmers of all ages were least involved in these two decision categories. Less involvement with livestock likely reflects both the on-going specialization in livestock

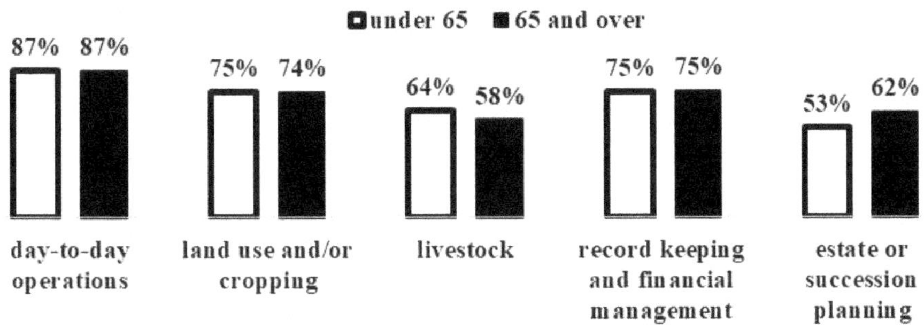

Figure 28.5 Involvement in Decision-Making by Age, U.S. Farmers, 2017

Source: 2017 Census of Agriculture

production and the daily attention they require. People of all ages, but especially younger individuals, often postpone or avoid estate and succession decisions.

Policy

A number of programs exist to help new entrants into farming, including mentorship programs that pair younger with older farmers. The focus of these programs is on helping new entrants, but they can also provide older farmers with labor and management supports, as well as estate transfer and financial benefits. Interested individuals can contact their local Extension office or state Department of Agriculture for information on new entrant assistance programs.

Tauer (1995) found that productivity declined for older U.S. farmers. At the same time, U.S. farmers as a group will likely remain notably older than other American workers for the foreseeable future. These observations raise the question, "Should the U.S. private and public sectors be more involved in raising the productivity of older farmers and helping them remain active members of the workforce?"

An underappreciated impact of technology is its role in allowing older farmers to remain active in their desired profession. A recent example is Global Positioning Systems (GPSs) for tractors and combines, which has greatly reduced the stress of planting and harvesting. A national policy aimed at enhancing and capitalizing on technology's role in allowing older farmers to remain active members of the labor force has the potential for economic, social, and quality-of-life benefits. Robotics, in particular, appears to offer considerable promise.

Summary Observations

For as long as data have been available, U.S. farmers have been older as a group than the average American (U.S. Department of Agriculture, 2019). It takes time for someone to accumulate the capital needed to compete in U.S.-style farming, either via inheritance, or savings, or both. However, the average age of U.S. farmers has not increased as much as the median age of the U.S. resident population. Moreover, the decline in average age associated with the farm prosperity of the 1970s and 2007–2013 suggests a willing supply of new farmers exist and will enter when farming provides their desired returns. In short, it is not evident the U.S. now has or will in the future have a problem replacing its farmers.

With U.S. farmers likely to remain older than the average American worker for the foreseeable future, a reasonable argument can be made that U.S. public policy and private efforts need to go beyond the current focus on transitioning farms to a new generation. A national effort aimed at enhancing the ability of older U.S. farmers to remain active in a farming profession they love can benefit all Americans by improving the economic efficiency and noneconomic efficacy of this important sector of the American economy and cultural identity.

Note

* The author thanks Allan Lines, Gary Schnitkey, Ani Katchova, and David Orden for their review, comments, and suggestions on an earlier draft.

References

Kurtzleben, D. (2014, February 24). The rapidly aging U.S. farmer. *U.S. News and World Report*. Retrieved from www.usnews.com/news/blogs/data-mine/2014/02/24/us-farmers-are-old-and-getting-much-older

Stone, A. (2014, September 19). American farmers are growing old, with spiraling costs keeping out young. *National Geographic*. Retrieved from https://news.nationalgeographic.com/news/2014/09/140919-aging-american-farmers-agriculture-photos-ngfood/

Tauer, L. (1995). Age and farmer productivity. *Review of Agricultural Economics, 17*(1), 63–69.

U.S. Department of Agriculture. (2019, July). *Census of agriculture: 1945–2002*. Cornell University Mann Library. Retrieved from http://agcensus.mannlib.cornell.edu/AgCensus/homepage.do;jsessionid=5FC0D4A36B0C8979034F0A0DEA1B1AC2

U.S. Department of Agriculture, Economic Research Service. (2017). *America's diverse family farms*. Economic Information Bulletin No. 185. Retrieved from www.ers.usda.gov/publications/pub-details/?pubid=86197

U.S. Department of Agriculture, National Agricultural Statistics Service. (2019, July). *Census of agriculture: 2007, 2012, and 2017*. Retrieved from www.nass.usda.gov/AgCensus/index.php

U.S. Department of Labor, Bureau of Labor Statistics. (2019, July). *Labor force statistics from current population survey*. Retrieved from https://data.bls.gov/PDQWeb/ln

Wikipedia. (2019, July). *Demography of the United States*. Retrieved from https://en.wikipedia.org/wiki/Demographics_of_the_United_States

29
FEDERAL POLICY

Robert Blancato and Meredith Whitmire

Introduction

Federal policy regarding rural aging remains a work in progress. More work has been done and progress has been made, but we are nowhere near having a clear, defined, and coordinated federal policy on rural aging.

Challenges Facing Rural Older Adults

Many older adults in rural areas face challenges that could be alleviated by sound federal policy. For example, 24% of rural older adult homeowners face housing costs (mortgage, utilities, etc.) of more than 30% of their income and more than half of rural older adult renters pay more than 30% of their income on rent (Anarde, 2019).

Transportation is another ongoing challenge. A poll by the National Aging and Disability Transportation Center found that less than half of rural elders felt they had access to good transportation alternatives to driving (Dize, 2019).

Similar research shows that people living in rural areas have a higher prevalence of chronic disease, a higher disability rate, and a lower percentage of healthy behavior (Dize, 2019). Another recent and concerning development is that while Medicare Advantage membership is growing in many states across the country, in major rural states the penetration rates hover under 20%—in Wyoming, for example, it is 3% (Kaiser Family Foundation, 2019).

Further, there is a real concern about social isolation among older adults in rural America. This situation is becoming more acute and is intensified because of the ongoing digital divide in rural America. According to the Federal Communications Commission (FCC), whereas 97% of Americans overall have access to high-speed fixed internet (broadband), in rural areas that drops to 65% and on tribal lands it goes even lower, to 60% (FCC, 2020).

What Is the Federal Government Currently Doing?

We are seeing some promising action on rural aging issues from both Congress and the administration.

Most prominently, the House of Representatives has passed its version of the 2019 Older Americans Act reauthorization, H.R.4334, which has three distinct features of note for rural areas. First, services authorized under the act (including home and community-based services, congregate and home-delivered meals, and other programs) would, for the first time, have to provide social isolation screening. The reauthorization would also maintain rural older adults as one of the groups to whom the act's funds must be targeted. Finally, the reauthorization would also recommend ways to improve caregiver assessments in rural areas.

The Senate version of the Older Americans Act reauthorization, S.3057, also has a few provisions regarding rural areas, including the House caregiver assessments provision and the maintenance of targeting rural older adults. It also contains provisions calling for a study on social isolation in rural areas and a study on nutrition program waiting lists, including those in rural and underserved areas.

Further, Senate bill S.2677, the Older Americans Social Isolation and Loneliness Prevention Act, would incorporate the House provisions on social isolation into the Senate version of the Older Americans Act reauthorization.

The House Ways and Means Committee has started a bipartisan Rural and Underserved Communities Health Task Force, which "will convene members and experts to discuss the challenges of delivering health care in rural and underserved areas, and explore holistic bipartisan policy options that could improve outcomes and care in these communities" (House Ways and Means Committee, 2019). This task force issued a Request for Information (RFI) in November 2019, which elicited close to 100 comments and suggestions for policy changes.

In addition, many other bills have been introduced in the 116th Congress to address rural concerns that impact older adults, most of which are bipartisan, including:

- S.454—Office of Rural Broadband Act, which would establish an Office of Rural Broadband within the Federal Communications Commission (FCC);
- H.R.2601—Office of Rural Telecommunications Act, which would establish an Office of Rural Telecommunications within the FCC;
- H.R.3999—Rural Broadband Connectivity Act of 2019, which would provide tax credits for companies providing broadband service in rural areas;
- S.2411/H.R.4898—Rural Health Innovation Act of 2019, which would establish a rural health center innovation awards program and a rural health department enhancement program;
- S.1190/H.R.2594—Rural Access to Hospice Act of 2019, which would allow federally qualified health centers (FQHCs) and rural health centers (RHCs) to receive payment under Medicare for hospice services, since currently FQHCs and RHCs may not receive payment under Medicare for such services; and
- S.2518—Rural Economic Infrastructure Equity Act of 2019, which would create an Assistant Secretary for Rural Economic Investment and an Office of Rural Economic Investment within the Department of Transportation.

Congressional appropriators have also allocated additional funding to support rural communities, incorporating the concerns of rural older adults, in the final spending bills for federal fiscal year 2020 (H.R.1865), including programs such as:

- $1 million "to support a model program . . . to increase and strengthen the eldercare workforce in rural counties where there are health care disparities related to access and delivery of care";

- $2 million "to encourage investment in research by universities and other eligible entities that seek to develop technologies that allow for independent living, address the disabled aging populations, and target rural, frontier, and tribal communities";
- $4 million to specifically "combat opioid abuse in rural communities";
- $555 million for the "Re-Connect program to increase access to broadband connectivity in unserved and underserved rural communities";
- $300 million for the Veterans Administration (VA) Office of Rural Health and its Rural Health Initiative;
- $30 million to "increase [VA] telehealth capacity in rural and highly rural areas"; and
- $40 million for rural transit infrastructure grants.

Some branches of the federal Department of Health and Human Services (DHHS) have rural health-care plans that include older adult health concerns. For example, the Center for Medicare and Medicaid Services (CMS) has a "CMS Rural Health Strategy," and there is an advisory committee on rural health, the National Advisory Committee on Rural Health and Human Services (CMS, 2018). The Health Resources and Services Administration also has a Federal Office of Rural Health Policy.

The FCC is actively working to solve the "digital divide" issue; in January 2020, they issued a schedule for implementation of the newly adopted reforms in the Rural Health Care Promoting Telehealth Report and Order, which seeks to efficiently allocate funding for rural telehealth services (Federal Register, 2020).

What Else Could Be Done?

Distinct problems for older adults include a growing lack of health-care facilities as well as a lack of medical specialists. In fact, according to an article in the American Society on Aging's journal *Generations*, 64 rural hospitals, including critical access hospitals, closed between 2013 and 2017—more than twice as many as had closed in the previous five years (MacKinney, 2019).

Some solutions to rural older adult health challenges are developing but must be expanded. One prime example is an expansion of telehealth services (and Medicare coverage for these services) with the important caveat that this expansion must be accompanied by an absolute commitment to close the "digital divide."

The federal government must ensure that adequate resources reach rural America from the federal funds being committed to combat the opioid crisis, since rural America has been disproportionately affected by this epidemic. The government should consider rural hospital closures to be a public health emergency, which could allow time to hopefully avert the closure and its corresponding devastating impact to entire communities.

As health experts focus more attention and eventually more federal resources into the social determinants of health, special attention must be given to the unique issues facing rural America. The federal government should more specifically address rural health-care workforce issues. Further, rural PACE (Program of All-Inclusive Care for the Elderly) programs need more funding.

Community-based programs need more assistance as well. The Government Accountability Office (GAO) found in a May 2019 report that HHS could help rural service providers by centralizing information on promising practices (GAO, 2019). More specifically, the GAO found that the Administration for Community Living (ACL) within HHS, which has jurisdiction over Older Americans Act programming and other federally funded community-based programs for older adults, should provide a hub for resources for rural programs. The GAO also stated that

ACL should make the information that is currently available through various national resource centers more prominent.

Conclusions

Seventeen years ago, the West Virginia University Center on Aging published a handbook entitled *Best Practices in Service Delivery to the Rural Elderly*, which has lessons applicable to today's work.

First, the handbook addressed the need to create a standardized definition of "rural," which has still not been entirely established across various fields.

Second, the handbook stated that HHS should work to coordinate what were then more than 225 federal programs in HHS alone listed as serving rural communities, "each with unique application and evaluation requirements." The handbook recommended "a formal structure within HHS . . . to coordinate rural policy initiatives among these programs," which "could be a catalyst for similar coordination efforts which must be undertaken in other federal agencies that also have hundreds of individual programs for rural America with little or no coordination." Much has been done in this area, but the work must continue.

Further recommendations that still seem relevant include the reform of Medicare programs to ensure parity for rural beneficiaries by "providing inducements to attract provider plans to rural areas," which could address the Medicare Advantage disparity, and the promotion of "awareness-raising activities around key issues affecting older people in rural and remote areas, including those issues related to homeland security."

As the West Virginia University report recommended in 2003, we need to approach present and future rural policies with an eye on several cross-cutting issues, leading with economic development policy specifically for rural America. This must include infrastructure, employment, and the closing of the digital divide. We must have a standardized definition of rural for everything from how the 2020 Census is conducted to how the term is used for program designation. Finally, we need to bring coordination where fragmentation exists today. Having hundreds of different federal programs that have rural aspects of one kind or another really serves no purpose if they are in individual silos. Using existing resources more effectively to serve rural America needs to be a priority of the future.

Hopefully, in recognition of the fact that every senator represents a rural area, as do many House members, and that the rural vote is important in presidential elections, we will see the development and implementation of new federal policies to aid rural older adults as a nonpartisan issue and one that has a strong and enduring political imperative.

References

Anarde, S. (2019). Home sweet home: Aging in place in rural America. *Generations*, *43*(2), 17–23.

Centers for Medicare and Medicaid Services (CMS). (2018). *CMS rural health strategy*. Retrieved from www.cms.gov/About-CMS/Agency-Information/OMH/Downloads/Rural-Strategy-2018.pdf

Dize, V. (2019). Getting around in rural America. *Generations*, *43*(2), 33–39.

Federal Communications Commission (FCC). (2020). *Bridging the digital divide for all Americans*. Retrieved from www.fcc.gov/about-fcc/fcc-initiatives/bridging-digital-divide-all-americans

Federal Register. (2020). *Wireline competition bureau provides guidance on the implementation schedule for reforms adopted by the rural health care program promoting telehealth report and order*. Retrieved from www.federalregister.gov/documents/2020/01/17/2020-00759/wireline-competition-bureau-provides-guidance-on-the-implementation-schedule-for-reforms-adopted-by

Government Accountability Office. (2019, May). *Older Americans Act: HHS could help rural service providers by centralizing information on promising practices*. Retrieved from www.gao.gov/assets/700/699298.pdf

House Ways and Means Committee. (2019, July 16). *Ways and Means Committee launches Rural and Underserved Communities Task Force.* Retrieved from https://waysandmeans.house.gov/media-center/press-releases/ways-and-means-committee-launches-rural-and-underserved-communities

Kaiser Family Foundation. (2019, June 6). *Medicare Advantage.* Retrieved from www.kff.org/medicare/fact-sheet/medicare-advantage/

MacKinney, C. (2019). Aging well in rural America—the role and status of healthcare. *Generations*, *43*(2), 46–54.

30
FOOD INSECURITY

Mary Ellen Camire

What Is Food Insecurity?

Food insecurity is the inability to get enough nutritious food; thus, both the quantity and nutritional quality of available food must be considered. The U.S. Department of Agriculture (USDA) Economic Research Service (ERS) has defined four levels of food security: high, marginal, low, and very low (Figure 30.1). Hunger may accompany food insecurity, but people sometimes opt for less-nutritious and inexpensive foods to avoid hunger. Nutrient-dense foods may be more expensive in rural stores than in their urban counterparts (Hardin-Fanning & Rayens, 2015). Food insecurity may persist steadily throughout a year or occur seasonally (Coleman-Jensen, Rabbitt, Gregory, & Singh, 2019).

Inadequate financial resources are often responsible for food insecurity, but other factors may be involved. For example, the lack of private or public transportation to food stores can be a barrier to acquiring healthful foods in rural areas. Local neighborhood stores may only offer energy-dense foods, making it impossible for consumers to buy fresh fruits and vegetables and other healthful foods. The term "food desert" was coined to describe areas where access to nutritious foods is limited. Rural areas are quite diverse across the U.S., so their food environments cannot be easily characterized (Lenardson, Hansen, & Hartley, 2015).

Measurement of Food Security

The USDA ERS conducts an annual survey with a Food Security Supplement to estimate the extent and severity of food insecurity; this information guides federal aid program allocations. The ten-question survey tool requires yes/no answers or selection of a frequency of occurrence (often, sometimes, never) (Coleman-Jensen et al., 2019). An additional eight questions are asked when households include one or more children under the age of 18. A key bias in the ERS's reporting is the lack of data for homeless individuals. The Food Abundance Index evaluates food access, diversity, quality, density, and affordability (Murrell & Jones, 2020) but has not been tested in rural locations.

No single surveillance tool assesses the nutritional status and food security of older adults living in the community and long-term care and other facilities. The National Health and Examination Survey (NHANES) measures a cross-section of Americans but does not include

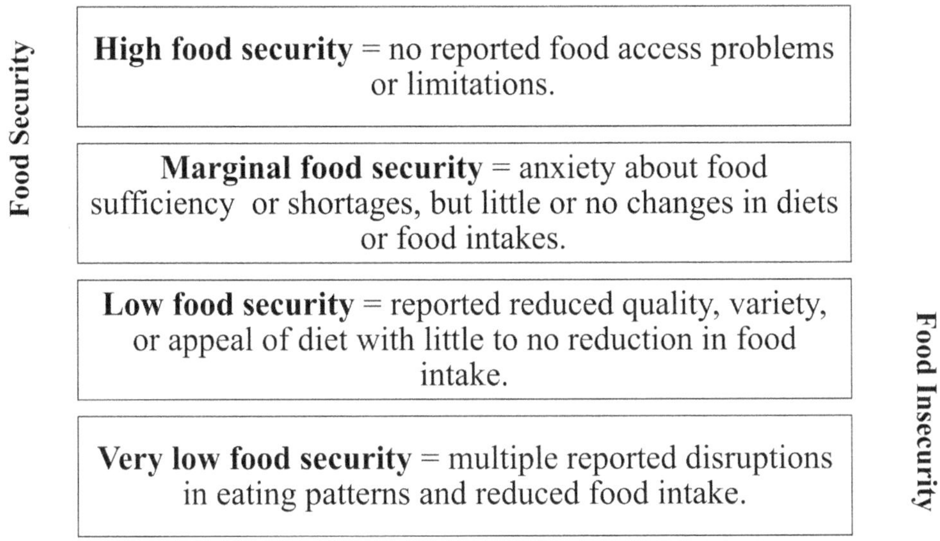

Figure 30.1 USDA Definitions of Food Security

persons over the age of 85 years. As the proportion of the oldest older adults grows, more comprehensive monitoring is needed.

Incidence of Food Insecurity Among Older Adults

The 2018 Food Security Supplement reported that 7.5% of households containing older adult members and 8.9% older adults who lived alone were classified as food insecure, while 2.6% of households with older adults and 3.4% of older adults living alone experienced very low food security (Coleman-Jensen et al., 2019). In 2018, approximately 5.3 million Americans aged 60 or older were food insecure, and that number may increase in 2020 because of economic and food supply problems associated with the novel coronavirus COVID-19 (Ziliak & Gundersen, 2020). West Virginia, District of Columbia, Mississippi, Alabama, Louisiana, Texas, Kansas, New Mexico, and Nevada had food insecurity rates exceeding 10% among older adults. Americans living in rural parts of the country tend to be older, more likely to be disabled, and have less education than their urban counterparts. The 2018 poverty rate for persons over the age of 65 living in nonmetropolitan areas of the U.S. was 10.2% and was over 16.5% in completely rural regions in 2017 (Pender, Hertz, Cromartie, & Farrigan, 2019).

Risk Factors

Food insecurity involves many social and demographic factors. Park, Saint Ville, Schwinghamer, and Melgar-Quiñonez (2019) assessed food insecurity among older adults in 48 developed nations and found several factors that predicted food insecurity including being in their 60s; single, or widowed and living alone; residing in a rural home; unemployed; having an income in the four lowest quintiles; high school education; and low community basic, daily experience, and social life indices. Being nonwhite, mentally ill, and a smoker was significantly associated with food insecurity in a U.S. study (Brostow, Gunzburger, Abbate, Brenner, & Thomas, 2019).

The added financial burden of winter heating bills or summer air conditioning expenses in warm climates can limit food purchasing and thus impact food security. Nord and Kantor (2006) reported that the odds for very low food security were 43% lower in the summer for residents of states with high winter heating needs, and 27% higher in the summer for persons living in areas requiring high cooling. Health-care costs can also deplete finances. Food insecure older adults may choose to take less medication to save money (Afulani, Herman, Coleman-Jensen, & Harrison, 2015). Dys, Hake, Morgan, and O'Leary (2015) found that 63% of older adult Feeding America clients said that they had to choose between buying food and medical care.

Special Considerations for Older Adults

As a person ages, subtle changes in body systems over time culminate in problems that lead to poor health and malnutrition. A systematic review has identified numerous risk factors for malnutrition in older adults (Fávaro-Moreira et al., 2016). Tooth loss may require the use of dentures that may be uncomfortable to use and that make eating painful. Some people may be edentulous (toothless) and must rely on foods that can be swallowed without the grinding and tearing action of teeth (Azzolino et al., 2019). Dysphagia is a common issue in older adults that occurs when the mouth and throat muscles can no longer move food normally. Specially thickened liquids and pureed foods for dysphagia may be too expensive or difficult to prepare for food-insecure people, especially those who live alone. Food may be aspirated into the lungs, leading to hospitalization for pneumonia (Sura, Madhavan, Camaby, & Crary, 2012).

A work-limiting disability, functional limitations, and problems managing money increased the probability of being food insecure among both adults aged 19–59 years and persons aged 60 or older who participated in the NHANES between 1999 and 2014 (Heflin, Altman, & Rodriguez, 2019). The preservation of one's mental faculties is essential for independent living but takes on greater importance for older adults living in rural areas. Food-insecure people aged 60–85 years had lower cognitive function compared with food-secure cohorts (Frith & Loprinzi, 2018). Forgetting to take medications correctly, not following dietary recommendations, and unsafe food preparation may accompany cognitive deficits. Well-intentioned health-care providers may recommend specific diets to aid clients with dementia or other cognitive problems. Still, short-term dietary interventions may lead to unwanted weight loss and burden on caregivers (Yerstein & Mendez, 2020), as well as additional food expenses.

The possibility of hospitalization can severely affect the health outcomes and lifestyles of older adults. Hypertension, arthritis, and diabetes were the most common chronic illnesses among food-insecure adults over the age of 50 (Garcia, Haddix, & Barnett, 2018). Frailty, a generalized loss of functional ability, and sarcopenia, a loss of muscle mass and function that often accompanies frailty, are frequently found in hospitalized older patients (Keevil & Romero-Ortuno, 2015). The reduction in mobility during hospitalization may induce acute sarcopenia or exacerbate existing conditions, leading to extended stays in rehabilitation centers and reduced capacity to care for oneself (Welch, Hassan-Smith, Greig, Lord, & Jackson, 2018). Food insecurity was associated with past and concurrent hospitalization among adults over the age of 50 but was not a predictor for future hospital stays (Bergmans, Mezuk, & Zevin, 2019).

Interventions to Increase Food Security

Persons who are food insecure use a variety of actions or coping strategies to acquire food and pay bills. Rural residents may use large freezers to store food for long periods or rely on food supplied by hunting, fishing, foraging, or mobile food vendors (Lenardson et al., 2015). The Coping Strategies Index (CSI) was developed by Maxwell and Caldwell (2008) to measure how households deal with insufficient food. Home and community gardens can offer seasonal fruits and vegetables. A pilot group garden project in rural Alabama reduced food insecurity among older African American women (Everhardt, Bradley, & Cellon, 2019).

Food pantries distribute donated food to persons in need, but like supermarkets and other food stores in rural areas, may not be accessible or convenient for older adults to use. Mobile food pantries deliver food to isolated older adults in rural Alabama (Povich, 2018), and similar programs have begun in other regions. The Rural Health Information Hub (2020) has developed an online Rural Food Access Toolkit to assist organizations that want to increase food access in rural areas.

The U.S. federally funded Supplemental Nutrition Assistance Program (SNAP), which was formerly known as Food Stamps, supplies food to low-income Americans. Analysis of longitudinal data from the Health and Retirement study indicated that although SNAP participation may have offset physical health problems in food-insecure adults over the age of 60, the aid was significantly associated with depression and negative self-attitudes among this group (Pak & Kim, 2020). It is not clear how much the social stigma of receiving food aid inhibits older adults from taking advantage of this program. The effect of rural versus urban living was not analyzed and should be assessed in future work.

The Title III-C Nutrition Services Program (NSP) includes congregate meals at community centers and home-delivered meals for older adults via state and regional agencies. Approximately 25% of participants in each program live in rural areas, and about 60% live alone (Mabli et al., 2017). The "Meals on Wheels" programs may also supply meals for persons with dysphagia, diabetes, and other medical conditions.

Conclusions

Reducing food security and hunger to 6% of American households is one recommendation of Healthy People 2020 (U.S. Department of Health and Human Services, 2020). The Academy of Nutrition and Dietetics advocates for "systematic and sustained action" to achieve food security in the U.S. (Holben & Marshall, 2017). Future research should focus on how food security can be improved for rural residents, with emphasis on communities of Native Americans, African Americans, and people of Hispanic or Latino backgrounds.

References

Afulani, P., Herman, D., Coleman-Jensen, A., & Harrison, G. G. (2015). Food insecurity and health outcomes among older adults: The role of cost-related medication underuse. *Journal of Nutrition in Gerontology and Geriatrics*, *34*(3), 319–342. doi:10.1080/21551197.2015.1054575

Azzolino, D., Passarelli, P. C., De Angelis, P., Piccirillo, G. B., D'Addona, A., & Cesari, M. (2019). Poor oral health as a determinant of malnutrition and sarcopenia. *Nutrients*, *11*(12), 2898. doi:10.3390/nu11122898

Bergmans, R. S., Mezuk, B., & Zivin, K. (2019). Food insecurity and geriatric hospitalization. *International Journal of Environmental Research and Public Health*, *16*(3), 2294. doi:10.3390/ijerph16132294

Brostow, D. P., Gunzburger, E., Abbate, L. M., Brenner, L. A., & Thomas, K. S. (2019). Mental illness, not obesity status, is associated with food insecurity among the elderly in the Health and Retirement Study. *Journal of Nutrition in Gerontology and Geriatrics*, *38*(2), 149–172. doi:10.1080/21551197.2019.1565901

Coleman-Jensen, A., Rabbitt, M. P., Gregory, C. A., & Singh, A. (2019). *Household food security in the United States in 2018*. ERR- 270. U. S. Department of Agriculture, Economic Research Service. Retrieved from www.ers.usda.gov/webdocs/publications/94849/err-270.pdf

Dys, T. D., Hake, M., Morgan, B., & O'Leary, M. (2015). Baby boomers and beyond: Facing hunger after fifty. *Feeding America.* Retrieved from www.feedingamerica.org/sites/default/files/research/senior-hunger-research/baby-boomers-executive-summary.pdf

Everhardt, S. L., Bradley, C., & Cellon, J. (2019). Food insecurity among older, female African-Americans: A pilot project. *Activities, Adaptation & Aging, 43*(1), 51–64. doi:10.1080/01924788.2018.1469941

Fávaro-Moreira, N. C., Krausch-Hofmann, S., Matthys, C., Vereecken, C., Vanhauwaert, E., Declerq, A., . . . Duyck, J. (2016). Risk factors for malnutrition in older adults: A systematic review of the literature based on longitudinal data. *Advances in Nutrition*, 7(3), 507–522. doi:10.3945/an.115.011254

Frith, E., & Loprinzi, P. D. (2018). Food insecurity and cognitive function in older adults: Brief report. *Clinical Nutrition, 37*(5), 1765–1768. doi:10.1016/j.clnu.2017.07.001

Garcia, S. P., Haddix, A., & Barnett, K. (2018). Incremental health care costs associated with food insecurity and chronic conditions among older adults. *Preventing Chronic Disease, 15*, E108. doi:10.5888/pcd15.180058

Hardin-Fanning, F., & Rayens, M. K. (2015). Food cost disparities in rural communities. *Health Promotion Practices, 16*(3), 383–391. doi:10.1177/1524839914554454

Heflin, C. M., Altman, C. E., & Rodriguez, L. L. (2019). Food insecurity and disability in the United States. *Disability and Health Journal, 12*(2), 220–226. doi:10.1016/j.dhjo.2018.09.006

Holben, D. H., & Marshall, M. B. (2017). Position of the Academy of Nutrition and Dietetics: Food insecurity in the United States. *Journal of the Academy of Nutrition and Dietetics, 117*(12), P1991–P2002. doi:10.1016/j.jand.2017.09.027

Keevil, V. L., & Romero-Ortuno, R. (2015). Ageing well: A review of sarcopenia and frailty. *Proceedings of the Nutrition Society*, 74(4), 337–347. doi:10.1017/S0029665115002037

Lenardson, J. D., Hansen, A. Y., & Hartley, D. (2015). Rural and remote food environments and obesity. *Current Obesity Reports, 4*(1), 46–53. doi:10.1007/s13679-014-0136-5

Mabli, J., Gearan, E., Cohen, R., Niland, K., Redel, N., Panzarella, E., & Carlson, B. (2017). *Evaluation of the effect of the Older Americans Act Title III-C nutrition services program on participants' food security, socialization, and diet quality.* Administration for Community Living, U.S. Department of Health & Human Services. Retrieved from https://acl.gov/sites/default/files/programs/2017-07/AoA_outcomesevaluation_final.pdf

Maxwell, D., & Caldwell, R. (2008). *The Coping Strategies Index: Field methods manual* (2nd ed.). Retrieved from www.spring-nutrition.org/publications/tool-summaries/coping-strategies-index-field-methods-manual-2nd-edition

Murrell, A., & Jones, R. (2020). Measuring food insecurity using the Food Abundance Index: Implications for economic, health and social well-being. *International Journal of Environmental Research and Public Health, 17*(7), 2434. doi:10.3390/ijerph17072434

Nord, M., & Kantor, L. S. (2006). Seasonal variation in food insecurity is associated with heating and cooling costs among low-income elderly Americans. *Journal of Nutrition, 136*(11), 2939–2944. doi:10.1093/jn/136.11.2939

Pak, T. Y., & Kim, G. (2020). Food stamps, food insecurity, and health outcomes among elderly Americans. *Preventative Medicine, 130.* doi:10.1016/j.ypmed.2019.105871

Park, J. Y., Saint Ville, A., Schwinghamer, T., & Melgar-Quiñonez, H. (2019). Heterogeneous factors predict food insecurity among the elderly in developed countries: Insights from a multi-national analysis of 48 countries. *Food Security, 11*, 541–552. doi:10.1007/s12571-019-00934-x

Pender, J., Hertz, T., Cromartie, J., & Farrigan, T. (2019). *Rural America at a glance, 2019 Edition.* EIB-212. U. S. Department of Agriculture, Economic Research Service. Retrieved from www.ers.usda.gov/publications/pub-details/?pubid=95340

Povich, E. S. (2018). *Mobile food banks roll to isolated, rural poor.* Retrieved from www.pewtrusts.org/en/research-and-analysis/blogs/stateline/2018/07/16/mobile-food-banks-roll-to-isolated-rural-poor

Rural Health Information Hub. (2020). *Rural food access kit.* Retrieved from www.ruralhealthinfo.org/toolkits/food-access

Sura, L., Madhavan, A., Camady, G., & Crary, M. A. (2012). Dysphagia in the elderly: Management and nutritional considerations. *Clinical Interventions in Aging*, 7, 287–298. doi:10.2147/CIA.S23404

U.S. Department of Health and Human Services, Office of Disease Prevention and Health Promotion. (2020). *Healthy people 2020.* Retrieved from www.healthypeople.gov/

Welch, C., Hassan-Smith, Z. K., Greig, C. A., Lord, J. M., & Jackson, T. A. (2018). Acute sarcopenia secondary to hospitalisation—an emerging condition affecting older adults. *Aging and Disease, 9*(1), 151–164. doi:10.14336/AD.2017.0315

Yerstein, O., & Mendez, M. F. (2020). Dietary recommendations for patients with dementia. *Alzheimer's & Dementia, 6*(1), e12011. doi:10.1002/trc2.12011

Ziliak, J. P., & Gundersen, C. (2020). The state of senior hunger in America 2018: An annual report. *Feeding America.* Retrieved from www.feedingamerica.org/sites/default/files/2020-05/2020-The%20State%20of%20Senior%20Hunger%20in%202018.pdf

31
GEOGRAPHIES AND ENVIRONMENTS

Jessica M. Finlay

Where Is Rural America and What Does It Look Like?

"Rural America" is a deceivingly simple term for a diverse assortment of spaces and places. Rather than a concrete definition, this abstract concept often invokes landscape images of rolling hills, farms, and ranches. However, rurality encompasses a much broader expanse of spaces beyond agriculture. It includes food processing plants, manufacturing parks, and warehouses strung along county highways; industrial regions and towns centered around the extraction, processing, and shipping of coal, oil, natural gas, and ore; timber and pulp mills nestled in forested regions; sprawling exurban residential areas outside major cities and their suburbs where residents seek idyllic lifestyles; and fast-growing recreational areas near lakes, oceans, and mountains for vacationers, wedding parties, cabin goers, and sports enthusiasts (Johnson, 2017). Rurality is broad and vague and not consistently defined by state and federal agencies (Krout, 2017). While the U.S. Census Bureau defines rural as any population, housing, or territory not in an urban area, the Office of Management and Budget uses a different county-based definition of areas outside of metropolitan or micropolitan statistical areas (Skoufalos, Clarke, Ellis, Shepard, & Rula, 2017). Rural America, according to these definitions, covers a wide range of territory representing approximately 75% of land area across the country.

Aging populations in rural areas are generally understood to live in a wide range of smaller, dispersed, less-densely populated, and under-serviced settlements (Skinner & Winterton, 2018). The majority of rural populations are clustered in the vicinity of metro areas given historical settlement on farms and in mill towns to produce goods for nearby urban centers (U.S. Census Bureau, 2019). However, communities, regions, and states vary widely in how rural they are, as do the natural climates, topographies, demographics, sociocultural fabrics, and local economies of these areas (Krout, 2017). Thus, the experiences and needs of older adults in rural communities also vary widely.

Geographic Implications for Rural Aging Populations

Given increased risk for multiple health conditions and reduced mobility (including losing the ability to drive), older adults may be particularly susceptible to and influenced by their rural surroundings. Commonly cited geographic challenges are that distances to destinations are greater and places more isolated. This makes it more difficult to access and secure resources necessary for health and quality of later life, including housing, healthy foods, transportation services, social opportunities, health care, caregiving, and community services (Skoufalos et al., 2017). Rural older adults' spaces of care are more likely to encompass voluntary sector or informal supports as a result, including delivery of goods, services, and care by family members and friends (Bascu et al., 2012). With out-migration of younger generations for education and employment, however, older adults are less likely to have proximal connections to assist with care and services (Skinner & Winterton, 2018). This socio-geographic isolation coupled with the dispersion and relative lack of infrastructure, services, and amenities often results in significant social isolation for rural older adults (Kaye, 2017). The result is a "double-jeopardy" scenario (Joseph & Cloutier-Fisher, 2005), in which rising numbers of older adults, many of whom have multiple health conditions, are aging in increasingly vulnerable communities with declining tax revenues struggling to provide necessary services and supports. The risk of residential home admission increases with level of rurality given fewer resources to address the in-home needs of older adults (Gilbert, Todd, May, Yardley, & Ben-Shlomo, 2010). As a result, it may not be feasible or safe for older residents to continue living independently in their rural homes and communities to age-in-place.

Regarding the natural environment and desires to age-in-place, weather and climate are often mentioned as factors impacting older adults' well-being and quality of life (Finlay, 2017). Given the frequent need to travel greater distances for services and amenities, rural older adults can be particularly affected by weather. Fears of falling and dangerous driving on icy, snowy, and wet roadways and sidewalks can contribute to limited mobility and social isolation, especially during winter months. Older residents may be "cooped up" at home for lengthy periods without regular social contact. Despite these pitfalls, winter can also provide opportunities for recreation and enjoyment, such as walking and skiing on trails and enjoying seasonal landscape views of nearby parks, lakes, and forests (Novek & Menec, 2014). Neighbors may socialize and support one another more during inclement weather conditions, such as providing assistance with snowplowing and bonding over a harsh climate (Finlay, 2017).

Some rural landscapes offer pristine natural surroundings, including forests, mountains, lakes, oceans, rolling hills, and open plains. These locales are appealing to retirement in-migration given scenic attractiveness, lifestyle amenities, and quality of life opportunities (Stockdale, 2017). Gentrifying rural areas across the U.S. tend to be recreation-dense and high-amenity destinations with in-migration of retiring and aging baby boomers. Housing used seasonally and/or for recreation purposes may become more regular or permanent as residents retire (Nelson, Oberg, & Nelson, 2010). These homes may need to be retrofitted if residents become less independent given physical and/or cognitive limitations. However, renovations, installations, and upgrades can be cost-prohibitive. For older adults with less resources, it is especially critical to ensure access to safe, accessible, and affordable housing. There is a need for a broader range of housing options in rural areas, including rental units, smaller one-floor apartments and condominiums, rehabilitation and repair programs, housing with services, and independent and assisted living (Oberdorfer & Wiley, 2014).

Future Directions for Research and Policy

Despite the unique geographies of rural aging, these contexts remain relatively under-examined in terms of research and policy development (Skinner & Winterton, 2018). Improving opportunities, accessibility, support, and viability of rural areas for people of all ages and abilities is critical—both to the 60 million people who live there (U.S. Census Bureau, 2019), as well as the much larger urban population who depend upon rural areas for goods, resources, socio-geographic diversity, and environmental well-being. A key area to address is the social determinants of health in rural areas exacerbated by spatial isolation. Aging rural residents have to travel greater distances to fulfill basic everyday needs, including obtaining healthy foods, quality health care, reliable transportation, and social sustenance. Unaddressed geographic conditions contribute to health disparities and the lower life expectancy of rural populations (Rural Health Research Gateway, 2018).

Technology can provide useful tools to help overcome geographic challenges of rural aging. Examples include telehealth (the use of telecommunication technologies to remotely deliver, manage, and enhance health-care services), online service access and delivery (e.g., groceries and household supplies), and virtual socialization (e.g., video calls with grandchildren, online chatrooms). This is not to suggest entirely substituting or replacing direct and in-person interactions, but rather enabling and supplementing such exchanges (Kaye, 2017). While the telecommunications capability gap between urban and rural areas has narrowed recently, over 26% of Americans in rural areas still lack high-speed broadband access in comparison to only 1.7% of Americans in urban areas (Federal Communications Commission, 2019). Rural areas more often lack in-home modern technology (Skoufalos et al., 2017), which is an important limitation to address moving forward.

Geographical and social gerontologists caution against an oversimplified and generalized concept of rurality (Skinner & Winterton, 2018). Local strengths and needs assessments must be ascertained through research and policy development to determine precise socio-geographic conditions in specific areas, instead of an abstract and vague concept of rurality that applies to no one person or region in particular. Engaging stakeholders and strategic partners at multiple levels are key steps to better understand and address the varied rural contexts in which people grow old. This includes moving our attention beyond overarching demographic, physical, and spatial characteristics to critically examine and consider the diverse sociocultural and political contexts of rurality, such as local norms, values, and attitudes that impact older adults. Geographical and environmental gerontologists are poised to critically investigate and articulate the various opportunities and constraints of rural aging in varied spaces and places that alternatively empower or disenfranchise older adults. Experiences of rural aging result from multi-scalar interconnections between places that range from the local community to region, nation, and globe.

References

Bascu, J. R., Jeffery, B., Johnson, S., Martz, D., Novik, N., & Abonyi, S. (2012). Healthy aging in place: Supporting rural seniors' health needs. *Online Journal of Rural Nursing and Health Care, 12*(2), 77–87.

Federal Communications Commission. (2019). *2019 broadband deployment report*. Washington, DC. Retrieved from www.fcc.gov/reports-research/reports/broadband-progress-reports/2019-broadband-deployment-report

Finlay, J. M. (2017). "Walk like a penguin": Older Minnesotans' experiences of (non)therapeutic white space. *Social Science & Medicine, 198*, 77–84. doi:10.1016/j.socscimed.2017.12.024

Gilbert, R., Todd, C., May, M., Yardley, L., & Ben-Shlomo, Y. (2010). Socio-demographic factors predict the likelihood of not returning home after hospital admission following a fall. *Journal of Public Health (Oxford), 32*(1), 117–124. doi:10.1093/pubmed/fdp077

Johnson, K. (2017). Where is "rural America," and what does it look like? *The Conversation*. Retrieved from https://theconversation.com/where-is-rural-america-and-what-does-it-look-like-72045

Joseph, A. E., & Cloutier-Fisher, D. (2005). Ageing in rural communities: Vulnerable people in vulnerable places. In G. J. Andrews & D. R. Phillips (Eds.), *Ageing and place: Perspectives, policy and practice* (pp. 133–146). London: Routledge.

Kaye, L. W. (2017). Older adults, rural living, and the escalating risk of social isolation. *Public Policy & Aging Report*, *27*(4), 139–144. doi:10.1093/ppar/prx029

Krout, J. A. (2017). Rural aging. *Grantmakers in Aging*. Retrieved from www.giaging.org/issues/rural-aging/

Nelson, P. B., Oberg, A., & Nelson, L. (2010). Rural gentrification and linked migration in the United States. *Journal of Rural Studies*, *26*(4), 343–352. doi:10.1016/j.jrurstud.2010.06.003

Novek, S., & Menec, V. H. (2014). Older adults' perceptions of age-friendly communities in Canada: A photovoice study. *Ageing and Society*, *34*(6), 1052–1072. doi:10.1017/s0144686x1200150x

Oberdorfer, E., & Wiley, K. (2014). *Housing an aging rural America: Rural seniors and their homes*. Washington, DC: Housing Assistance Council Report.

Rural Health Research Gateway. (2018). *Rural communities: Age, income, and health status*. Grand Forks, ND. Retrieved from www.ruralhealthresearch.org/assets/2200-8536/rural-communities-age-income-health-status-recap.pdf

Skinner, M. W., & Winterton, R. (2018). Rural ageing: Contested spaces, dynamic places. In M. W. Skinner, G. J. Andrews, & M. P. Cutchin (Eds.), *Geographical gerontology: Perspectives, concepts, approaches* (pp. 136–148). New York: Routledge.

Skoufalos, A., Clarke, J. L., Ellis, D. R., Shepard, V. L., & Rula, E. Y. (2017). Rural aging in America: Proceedings of the 2017 connectivity summit. *Population Health Management*, *20*(Suppl 2), S1–S10. doi:10.1089/pop.2017.0177

Stockdale, A. (2017). From "trailing wives" to the emergence of a "trailing husbands" phenomenon: Retirement migration to rural areas. *Population, Space and Place*, *23*(3). doi:10.1002/psp.2022

U.S. Census Bureau. (2019). *Rural America*. Retrieved from https://gis-portal.data.census.gov/arcgis/apps/MapSeries/index.html?appid=7a41374f6b03456e9d138cb014711e01

32
GERIATRIC CARE MANAGERS

Cathy J. Cress

What Is Geriatric Care Management?

Almost 20 years ago, Lenard Kaye argued that rural practice in geriatric care management might be the last interventive frontier in the field (Kaye & Sherman, 2002). It could also have been said at the time that it was perhaps the most challenging. Reviewed here are the major hurdles to practicing private geriatric care management in rural areas as well as the advantages that rural geriatric care managers (GCMs) will experience by having a rural practice. Also outlined is the type of geriatric care management practice that will function best in the rural U.S.

What is private geriatric care management? It is a profession that emerged in the 1970s to offer adult children and family members one-stop professional navigation to aging services, when there was no central point of entry for information about services to help with the then-ballooning aging population in the U.S.

Fifty years later, there is still really no effective, well-advertised central point of entry for national navigation to aging services for adult children and family members. Over this same period of time, the U.S. older adult population has swollen steadily and starkly, from 25.5 million in 1980 (11.3% of the total population) to a projected 64.3 million (21.1% of the total population) in 2030—more than doubling in size over the 50-year period (Gilford, 1988). Even more ominous, 60 million Americans live in rural America, or one in five people (U.S. Census Bureau, 2019).

GCMs have changed as well. Their umbrella professional association is now called Aging Life Care Association (ALCA) and includes practitioners from all over the U.S. This association was formerly known as the National Association of Geriatric Care Management. GCMs still charge privately, as Medicare does not yet cover their services. They offer certification through the National Academy of Certified Care Managers (NACCM) and accept other certifications from the American Nurses Association (ANA) and the National Association of Social Workers (NASW). The bulk of GCMs is highly skilled, with 64% holding a master's degree in the field of health care or geriatrics. Members are divided according to their skill and experience level, so that those older adults or family members trying to find such a professional can choose the most qualified GCM in their area.

What Are the Major Problems Confronting Rural GCMs?

The first challenge to GCMs practicing in rural areas is that of establishing a profitable business. Consequently, few members of the Aging Life Association practice in rural areas currently. The largest proportions of GCMs is found on both coasts of the U.S. and in the sunbelt, and the smallest membership is situated in the central part of the country, where the bulk of rural older adults reside (National Association of Professional Geriatric Care Managers, 2014).

GCMs are a for-profit service, not covered by Medicare. Profitability remains a major challenge for GCM businesses in rural America. GCMs function much like concierge physicians, who have existed as a profession for decades before doctors began to revert back to private pay status. Concierge physicians serve older adults like the pre-HMO, multiple-practice, pre-1950s physicians who presided over freestanding solo practices. As a private, for-profit business, GCMs are pressed to target their services to the top 10% of the population because that is the segment that can afford them long-term. They offer 24-hour service coverage, house calls, and personalized care. GCMs, like private-pay concierge physicians, serve the same higher income demographic and promise the same individualized concierge care.

GCMs who bill privately can only remain in business if they bill 85% of their time and are financially successful. It is difficult to be financially successful in the business of geriatric care management if you have a rural practice. GCMs operate small boutique businesses and have steep overhead, including 24/7 on-call services and costly technology that is required today to serve older adults effectively and efficiently. They employ care managers who are highly trained professionals with advanced degrees in the health-care field (RNs, gerontological social workers, and physical therapists) and have either a certificate, degree, or experience in geriatric care management.

The cost of private for-profit geriatric care management is too expensive for the average older adult who resides in rural America (Florida, 2019). On the other hand, the per hour charge for care management services is relatively affordable for the top 25% of the U.S. population. GCMs charges range from $125 to $150 an hour on both coasts, and $80–$90 an hour in the central U.S., where most rural residents reside (National Association of Professional Geriatric Care Managers, 2014). But even a $90 hourly rate is too costly for the average rural elder based on the median income in rural America.

As clients age and become increasingly vulnerable, they are in greater need of care management and related interventions. The number of hours for which a GCM is needed can be expected to increase as well as greater need for care is evidenced. This, too, makes affordability in rural communities more of a challenge. Affordability challenges extend to low-density remote areas in the nation's heartland, in Appalachia from eastern Kentucky to Maine, and in high-poverty areas in the Southeast and border areas in the Southwest. This includes parts of North Dakota, Montana, New Mexico, Texas, and Pennsylvania (Cromartie, 2018).

The second challenge to establishing a geriatric care management practice in the rural U.S. is the frequent lack of a continuum of care in these regions. Such a continuum is a linked infrastructure of care, including social services and health care for older adults at every stage of the aging process. Such a continuum extends from light nonmedical care to 24-hour care at home or in a skilled nursing facility. This service continuum or thread is used by a GCM to weave a care plan and map out solutions to an older adult's life challenges. In the absence of an existing community care continuum and accompanying health-care team, as is the case in too many rural communities, it is difficult for the GCM to construct an effective care plan. In addition, the scarcity of a wide range of well-trained health and human service professionals in rural areas needed to comprise the health-care team that delivers care complicates the task further for the GCM.

Indeed, the individual whom most care rests on, the paid caregiver, is at a premium in rural areas (Seegert, 2017). As Kaye said in 2002, the scarcity of a wide range of well-trained health and human service professionals, including care practitioners in non-urban regions of America, is becoming well-documented. In some cases, the problem is reaching crisis proportions (Kaye, 2002). That was in 2002. In 2020, the crisis is fully pronounced. Unfortunately, rural communities continue to lack the requisite resources required to develop a continuum of long-term care. In addition, it continues to be difficult to recruit health-care professionals to remote, lower-paying jobs in rural America (Redford & Krout, 1998).

Conditions are exacerbated by a lack of family caregivers. There has been and continues to be an outbound migration of younger family members from small towns and rural communities. The lack of employment in rural areas, made so apparent by the 2018 midtrm election, and driven by the offshoring of manufacturing jobs, has left younger rural Americans with declining job prospects. Thus, an outbound population of rural family members, who could otherwise function as caregivers, is lost, leaving older relatives without the centuries-old buttress of available family care. This accelerating out-migration trend by young people in rural communities has continued unabated for the last 20 years and resulted in a continuing depletion of the supply of relatives and other informal supports able and willing to care for older adults (Kaye & Sherman, 2002).

Distance is yet another barrier that limits GCMs from working successfully in rural areas. A geriatric care management practice should be limited to a 50-mile required travel radius between the office of the GCM and a client's home to be financially stable. Greater distances to travel in rural regions result in many GCMs spending significant time on the road; as a consequence, they spend less time with clients, and, in turn, gain fewer billable hours. Such conditions also result in greater expense in terms of fuel bills and automobile maintenance. Thus, GCMs are unable to benefit from the usual economies of scale that result from working in higher population density regions of the country with greater numbers of clients living in closer proximity to each other.

What Makes a Successful Rural Geriatric Care Management Practice?

The most financially successful GCM practice, based on a limited survey of 30 ALCA members, is a mixed rural and urban practice, or a practice in an urban area that is co-located within a rural area. An example of this is in Santa Cruz County, California, with coastal urban towns and a large redwood forest in the Santa Cruz Mountains hovering above the coast. The contrasting geography creates a rural/urban mix that provides the GCMs the income they need to be profitable. The majority of the rural care managers polled for the survey referred to earlier stated that this mixed urban-rural caseload made them profitable.

A second strategy for establishing a successful rural GCM practice is to locate an agency in a nonmetropolitan area that has proven particularly attractive to retirees. Some rural counties have a rapidly aging population profile because they represent a particularly attractive destination for retirees. One-third of older-age counties—concentrated in the Upper Great Lakes, the Appalachians and Ozarks, Texas Hill country, and throughout the Rocky Mountain West—are classified as either retirement destinations or as places with recreation-based economies. Most of these counties have seen an upturn in population growth caused by baby boomer retirees (Cromartie, 2018).

A GCM can also create a sustainable rural practice by employing telehealth technologies. Telehealth is the use of electronic information and telecommunications technologies to support long-distance clinical health care, patient and professional health-related education, public health, and health administration (Rural Health Information Hub, 2019).

Telehealth can assist GCMs who are daunted by the long distance they must travel to make home visits to rural clients. Telehealth allows the GCM to speak to the client via videoconference. Telehealth can be used to supplement in-person home visits, reduce the burden of travel, and serve as a tool for delivering client health education and one-on-one assessments, as well as convening family meetings and training for families and paid caregivers. The National Consortium of Telehealth Resource Centers, which has 14 telehealth resource centers that serve all rural areas of the U.S., provides technical assistance and education for health-care providers who provide services at a distance (see National Consortium of Telehealth Research Centers).

An additional strategy for enabling GCMs to more successfully practice in rural settings is through the utilization of lay trained outreach workers who are trained and supervised to perform selected outreach functions for the GCM supported by technology.

Paraprofessional, GCM-supervised care does not necessarily have to be provided by nurses or home health aides, which can be costly. Instead, a GCM could utilize health outreach workers who know about the needs of older adults, specialize in older adult concerns, and can actually perform a number of important functions including providing fall prevention education and exercises, health screenings, and information and referral; assisting clients in completing applications for health benefits; visiting homes to check on individuals with specific health conditions; driving clients to medical appointments; picking up and delivering medications, and generally increasing the quality of life and reducing social isolation risk of GCM clients. Many GCM practices already employ assistant GCMs who perform such tasks that are billed at a lower rate, and who, in turn, save GCMs' time so that GCMs can focus on providing major clients' assessments and interventions. Stephen Bartels, director of the Dartmouth Centers for Health and Aging, suggests the use of a health-care aide called a community health worker who lives in the areas where the GCMs' rural clients reside, and so are closer to the clients, understand the culture, and can perform assistant care manager tasks more cost-efficiently and with, perhaps, a greater degree of client trust, because the provider comes from the rural area where clients live (Seegert, 2017). This strategy could be supported with the professional supervision of the assistant GCM and by employing appropriate technology.

The Positives of Practicing in a Rural Setting

On the positive side, having a GCM practice in rural America features a lifestyle enriched by open space and less crowding. The rates of violent and property crime are much lower than those in large cities. The air is cleaner because there is less traffic and fewer factories and other facilities that emit pollution. Life in rural areas is thought to be slower-paced, resulting in lower levels of anxiety and a greater sense of relaxation. For these and other reasons, rural residents exhibit heightened mental health on average than do urban residents (Barkan, 2016). Working in rural America can mean living in a safer environment with a strong sense of community, where people have the time and inclination to be friendlier and more concerned for their neighbors.

An additional advantage of locating a GCM business in a rural area is that housing is less costly. This makes starting a business less financially burdensome. Most GCMs start in their homes. Internet access makes home-based geriatric care management start-ups easier to launch and operate. The location has a direct impact on your business costs, including the cost of labor, supplies, and inventory, and other expenses such as business insurance, all of which are likely less costly in rural areas. While urban GCM companies slightly edge out rural companies at the top end of revenue, the exact same percentage of rural and urban GCM businesses (21%) are in the under-$100,000 revenue range. When you account for urban household spending (which is substantially higher than rural households), rural businesses may actually be holding their own compared to urban businesses in terms of revenue. Profitability ultimately depends on whether you operate a "lean" business. The more expenses your business has, the lower your take-home profits will be. The five largest GCM business expenses are insurance, advertising, taxes (income taxes, property taxes, etc.), staff salaries, and the owner's compensation. Virtually all of these expenses can be expected to be lower when you operate in a rural area.

Finally, small business owners need access to affordable capital to accomplish their goals. Rural businesses can be expected to secure business loans more easily than urban companies. In rural areas, there are more small banks who will lend to you more readily than large banks, if you present good credit scores and take advantage of available personal connections. Rural banks may have more leeway, providing you with a better chance of getting business loans (Prakash, 2018).

References

Barkan, S. (2016). Problems of rural life. *GitHub Pages*. Retrieved from https://saylordotorg.github.io/text_social-problems-continuity-and-change/s17-04-problems-of-rural-life.html

Cromartie, J. (2018, November). Rural America at a glance: 2018 edition. *Economic Information Bulletin, 200*. Retrieved from www.ers.usda.gov/webdocs/publications/90556/eib-200.pdf

Florida, R. (2019, September 3). The future of the middle class depends on upgrading service jobs. *CityLab*. Retrieved from www.citylab.com/equity/2019/09/service-jobs-employment-data-inequality-politics/597118/

Gilford, D. M. (Ed.). (1988). *The aging population in the twenty-first century: Statistics for health policy*. National Academy Press. Retrieved from www.ncbi.nlm.nih.gov/books/NBK217737/pdf/Bookshelf_NBK217737.pdf

Home Care Pulse. (2014). *Care Management Benchmarking Study*. National Association of Professional Geriatric Care Managers. Retrieved from https://www.homecarepulse.com/latest-news/geriatric-care-manager-study/

Kaye, L. W. (2002). Guest editor's message: Care management and rural health care delivery. *Journal of Geriatric Care Management, 12*(1), 2–3. Retrieved from https://pdfs.semanticscholar.org/8527/c1941ff-bae5cbb01a4c489976bb3d0f4badb.pdf

Kaye, L. W., & Sherman, K. (2002, January). Geriatric practice in rural America: The last frontier. *Social Work Today*, 7, 13–15.

National Consortium of Telehealth Research Centers. Retrieved from www.telehealthresourcecenter.org/

Prakash, P. (2018, June). Rural small businesses earn better profits and more financing vs. city ones. *Fundera, 25*. Retrieved from www.fundera.com/blog/rural-vs-urban-business-financing

Redford, L., & Krout, J. A. (1998). Public policy and the rural elderly. In *Aging in rural settings: Life circumstances and distinctive features* (pp. 267–286). New York: Springer.

Rural Health Information Hub. (2019, March 26). *Telehealth use in rural healthcare*. Rural Health Information Hub. Retrieved from www.ruralhealthinfo.org/topics/telehealth#different-from-telemedicine

Seegert, L. (2017, January 6). Geriatric workforce training supports rural elderly. *AHCJ, Association of Health Care Journalists*. Retrieved from https://healthjournalism.org/blog/2017/01/geriatric-workforce-training-supports-rural-elderly/

U.S. Census Bureau. (2019, May 23). *What is rural America?* U.S. Census Bureau. Retrieved from www.census.gov/library/stories/2017/08/rural-america.html

33

GERIATRICS AND GERONTOLOGY EDUCATION AND TRAINING

Judith L. Howe

Introduction

A number of approaches have been used to increase the rural geriatrics and gerontological workforce in the last three decades (Howe & Kramer, 2019). In 2008, the latest year that data were made available, approximately 90% of geriatricians were located in urban areas. In addition, there is a lack of university, college, and continuing education programs to meet the needs of the aging services network. Reasons for this shortage include difficulties in recruitment to and retention of health-care providers and staff in rural areas (Rabinowitz, Diamond, Markham, & Santana, 2011; Cohen, Cook, Sando, & Sabik, 2018) and the well documented out-migration of younger generations from rural areas.

The Institute of Medicine (IOM) concluded in its landmark report, "Retooling for an Aging America: Building the Healthcare Workforce," that prior initiatives to promote specialization in geriatrics were generally inadequate and that "immediate and substantial action is necessary by both public and private organizations to close the gap between the status quo and the impending needs of future older Americans" (IOM, 2008, p. 30). The IOM report notes that to meet the need for flexibility, health-care professionals should have distance learning opportunities to increase skills and knowledge in geriatrics.

In rural America, family practitioners perform 42% of physician visits (McGrail, Wingrove, Petterson, & Bazemore, 2017). For rural older persons, the lack of geriatrics specialists has serious implications since they are more likely to have higher rates of chronic disease and disability, lower incomes and education, and greater dependence on government entitlement programs than their urban counterparts (Cohen et al., 2018; Wallace et al., 2010). The movement to "geriatricize" health-care professionals so that they are equipped to recognize and treat common geriatrics conditions has proven to be successful in a variety of health-care settings and is particularly relevant to rural elders (Callahan, Tumosa, & Leipzig, 2017; Lee, Burton, & Lundebjerg, 2017; Hwang et al., 2013; Chen & Steinman, 2016; Friedman et al., 2013).

Challenges in Recruitment and Retention of Rural Health-Care Professionals

Challenges to health-care practice in rural areas include scarce resources, high patient volume and needs, limited time off, fewer opportunities for professional development and continuing education, insufficient supervision, and lack of professional colleagues (Arora et al., 2011). On the positive side, rural practitioners appreciate opportunities for rapid development of professional and administrative skills, diverse caseloads, autonomy, and a rural lifestyle (Chipp et al., 2011). Multiple studies have found that the most important predictor to being a rural health-care practitioner is having lived in a rural area (MacQueen et al., 2018). In addition, medical schools that offer preclinical or clinical rotations in rural locations have been found to contribute to a decision for rural practice (Crump, Fricker, 2015; Myhre, Bajaj, & Jackson, 2015).

Strategies to Increase the Rural Health-Care Workforce

Given the urgent need to increase the number of individuals providing health care, services, and programs to rural elders, different strategies have been undertaken to fill the gap, some of which are described next.

Geriatrics Workforce Development

An exemplary example of a longitudinal professional development program is the Veterans Health Affairs (VHA) Geriatric Scholars Program, which integrates geriatrics into primary care practices. It uses a blended educational format, which includes required components of attendance at an intensive course in geriatrics and a quality improvement program aimed at improving care of older veterans. Available to clinicians in several disciplines, electives include clinical practica, rural interdisciplinary team training, webinars, and self-directed learning and mentoring opportunities (Kramer et al., 2016).

Distance Continuing Education (CE)

Distance learning can take on many forms and technologies, including the internet, intranet, videoconferencing, telephone, and CD-ROM. Since it is self-paced, and "anywhere, anytime" learning, it meets the needs of those working in rural areas because of increased flexibility in accessing information and self-directed instruction. For educators, it is ideal because of ease in updating information, the ability for widespread distribution, standardization of content, automated tracking of learners, and accountability (Ruiz, Mintzer, & Leipzig, 2006).

One exemplary program delivering geriatrics CE to rural health-care workers has been developed and disseminated by the University of Alabama (UAB). The web-based CE interprofessional geriatrics-specific curriculum provides CE to both urban and rural physicians in Alabama and Mississippi (Ford, Sawyer, & Brown, 2018). Another CE program was developed by the Penn State College of Nursing for nurses at eight critical access rural hospitals. A geriatrics nurse champion at each hospital designed a distance CE program meeting the specific needs of the local hospital. The program increased nurse-sensitive patient satisfaction scores (Buck, Kolanowski, Fick, & Baronner, 2016). Another example of a web-based CE program is the Geriatrics Scholars Program's virtual learning community. Health-care providers, staff, and trainees access www.gerischolars.org to learn more about conditions affecting older persons through clinical demonstrations, toolkits, and interactive case studies. The Specialty Care Access Network-Extension for Community Healthcare Outcomes (SCAN-ECHO) is used in the VHA national network of health-care facilities and rural clinics. It provides veterans greater access to specialty care and educates health-care staff about the treatment of specific diseases. Usually using videoconference, a case presentation is followed by a short didactic presentation (Guzman-Clark et al., 2016). One VHA application of the SCAN-ECHO model is a collaborative of 15 VHA Geriatric Research, Education and Clinical Centers (GRECCs), GRECC Connect, which links geriatrics expertise at GRECCs, located at urban tertiary medical centers, with rural clinic teams. Regularly scheduled case-based educational conferences focus on challenging clinical case discussions for primary care interdisciplinary teams using videoconference and telephone modalities (Hung et al., 2014).

In-Person Workshops and Conferences

Face-to-face learning is desirable because it provides opportunities for rural staff, who may feel professionally isolated, to have in-person interactions. However, substantial resources may be required, such as faculty travel to and from rural locations. One successful in-person education program is the Geriatric Scholars Rural Interdisciplinary Team Training (RITT) workshop for VHA rural providers and staff. RITT is a 4- or 6.5-hour team-based VHA accredited educational workshop to enhance the knowledge and skills of rural primary care clinicians and staff in caring for older veterans. It has trained 2,100 staff from 250 rural clinics. The program has positively affected teamwork and increased geriatrics knowledge (Howe, Penrod, Gottesman, Bean, & Kramer, 2019).

Rural Immersion Experiences

Students who were raised in rural areas or have rural immersion experiences while in training are more likely to practice in rural areas (Sterling et al., 2017; Mathew, Ryan, & Samarasena, 2017; Mitra, Gowans, Wright, Brenneis, & Scott, 2018). For instance, the federally funded Area Health Education Centers, which recruit and educate students to work in underserved communities, primary care, and rural settings, have been successful in recruiting medical students with rural clerkships into rural practice (Taylor & Goletz, 2016). Other factors contributing to consideration of rural practice include debt repayment and financial incentives, a spouse who was raised in a rural area, desire for professional autonomy, and a preference for small-town life (Myhre et al., 2015). For students from rural backgrounds or those with an interest in rural health care, consideration should be given to targeted mentoring during training (Mitra et al., 2018).

Developing and Reinforcing the Aging Services Network

Despite the increasing demand for workers in the aging services network, students, programs, and courses in aging are scarce. A helpful resource is the online directory of educational programs in gerontology, including those that have been "certified" through a Program of Merit, sponsored by the Academy of Gerontology in Education of the Gerontological Society of America (www.geron.org/programs-services/education-center). One study found that aging service organizations desired a workforce with a gerontology background but were unwilling to fund training (Maiden, Horowitz, & Howe, 2010). For instance, in New York State a study found that 137 colleges and universities of 241 surveyed did not offer gerontology courses; of the remaining schools, 4% had a major, 2% had a minor, 16% a certificate, and only one school offered a doctorate that is now defunct (Maiden et al., 2010). Nationally, there has been a downturn in the number of gerontology programs (Pelham, 2008). The Great Plains Interactive Distance Education Alliance (GPIDEA) was one of the first in the U.S. to offer exclusive online learning. The gerontology component consists of seven institutions from rural states in the central part of the U.S. A survey of GPIDEA students found that over 50% were interested in rural aging (Heinz, Martin, Doll, & Pearson-Scott, 2014). There are a handful of gerontology programs such as that offered at the University of Arkansas at Pine Bluff, which infuses all coursework with strong rural elements and offers a variety of electives and internships with a rural focus and setting (University of Arkansas at Pine Bluff, www.uapb.edu/academics/school_of_arts_sciences/social_behavioral_sciences/gerontology.aspx). There are initiatives in social work education to attract students to rural practice, with one study finding that almost one-fourth of students intend to practice in a rural setting (Barney, Barnett-Queen, Duran, & de la Rosa, 2010). The annual National Institute on Social Work and Human Services in Rural Areas conference sponsored by Murray State University at its regional campus in Paducah, Kentucky, has held a multiday conference on rural social work for 44 years (Murray State University, Social Work Conference, www.murraystate.edu/academics/CollegesDepartments/CollegeOfEducationandHumanServices/coehsacademicunits/CLHS/SocialWork/SocialWorkConference.aspx).

The Direct Service Workforce

Rural areas are faced with numerous direct service workforce challenges, with creative solutions being developed locally to meet local needs (Brown, Lash, Wright, & Tomisek, 2011). One example is the Alaska Native Tribal Health Consortium Behavioral Health Aides Project, which provides incentives for rural residents to remain in their communities through career ladders (https://anthc.org/behavioral-health-aide-program). There are also programs to support and educate rural family caregivers such as the "Powerful Tools for Caregivers" program, a six-week education course about self-care, communication, and decision-making, which has over 4,600 trained class leaders (Powerful Tools for Caregivers, www.powerfultoolsforcaregivers.org/caregivers).

Education and Lifelong Learning for Rural Elders

Adult lifelong learning programs are generally more scarce in rural areas than urban and suburban areas. For instance, public libraries often provide lifelong learning services such as computer instruction, arts and crafts instruction, and film and book discussions. A study by the National Center for Education Statistics (Lewis & Farris, 2002) found that libraries in rural areas were less likely than urban libraries to offer adult learning programs. However, there are notable exceptions such as the Osher Lifelong Learning Institutes, founded in 2010 by the Osher Foundation, with 123 lifelong learning programs on university and college campuses across the U.S., with at least one institute in each state as well as a national resource center. The institutes are geared for older adults who want to expand their horizons with no tests, papers, or graded assignments (The Bernard Osher Foundation, www.osherfoundation.org/index.php?olli). Maine, the most rural state in the nation in 2010, received the second grant from the foundation and now hosts the largest older adult lifelong learning program in the nation, with 17 colleges offering education on a variety of topics through the Maine Senior College Network (Kaye & Harvey, 2015). Another successful example is the Academy for Lifelong Learning of SUNY Empire State College located in Saratoga Springs, New York, which is located in the rural Adirondack region of the state. Founded in 1992, it is a nonprofit membership organization with 450 members offering a variety of educational programs for a modest annual fee, including classes, special interest groups, and local tours (SUNY Empire State College, www.esc.edu/all/the-academy-in-brief).

Conclusion

While there are barriers to meeting the health care and service needs of older adults living in rural areas, as well as obstacles to education for rural older adults, a number of innovative programs have proven to be successful in overcoming these challenges. Advances in technology, distance education, and telehealth have the promise to offer new solutions in the decades ahead.

References

Arora, S., Kalishman, S., Dion, D., Som, D., Thornton, K., Bankhurst, A., . . . Yutzy, S. (2011). Partnering urban academic medical centers and rural primary care clinicians to provide complex chronic disease care. *Health Affairs*, *30*(6), 1176–1184. doi:10.1377/hlthaff.2011.0278

Barney, D. D., Barnett-Queen, T., Duran, B., & de la Rosa, I. (2010). Social work student interests in rural practice. *Contemporary Social Work Journal*, *2*(1), 45–50. Retrieved from https://digitalcommons.murraystate.edu/crsw/vol2/iss1/6

The Bernard Osher Foundation. *Osher Lifelong Learning Institutes*. Retrieved August 21, 2019, from www.osherfoundation.org/index.php?olli

Brown, D. K., Lash, S., Wright, B., & Tomisek, A. (2011). *Strengthening the direct service workforce in rural areas*. Washington, DC: Center for Medicare and Medicaid Services, National Direct Service Workforce Resource Center, The Lewin Group.

Buck, H. G., Kolanowski, A., Fick, D., & Baronner, L. (2016). Improving rural geriatric care through education: A scalable, collaborative project. *Journal of Continuing Education in Nursing*, *47*(7), 306–313. doi:10.3928/00220124-20160616-06.

Callahan, K. E., Tumosa, N., & Leipzig, R. M. (2017, October). Big "G" and little "g" geriatrics education for physicians. *Journal of the American Geriatrics Society*, *65*(10), 2313–2317. doi:10.1111/jgs.14996

Chen, P., & Steinman, M. A. (2016). Perception of primary care physicians on the impact of comprehensive geriatric assessment: What is the next step? *Journal of Health Policy Research*, *5*, 46, eCollection.

Chipp, C., Dewane, S., Brems, C., Johnson, M. E., Warner, T. D., & Roberts, L. W. (2011). "If only someone had told me . . .": Lessons from rural providers. *Journal of Rural Health*, *27*(1), 122–130. doi:10.1111/j.1748-0361.2010.00314.x

Cohen, S. A., Cook, S. K., Sando, T. A., & Sabik, N. J. (2018, June). What aspects of rural life contribute to rural-urban health disparities in older adults? Evidence from a national survey. *Journal of Rural Health*, *34*(3), 293–303. doi:10.1111/jrh.12287

Crump, W. J., & Fricker, R. S. (2015). A medical school pre-matriculation program for rural students: Staying connected with place, cultivating a special connection with people. *Teaching and Learning in Medicine*, *27*(4), 422–430. doi:10.1080/10401334.2015.1077709

Ford, C. R., Sawyer, P., & Brown, C. J. (2018). Utilizing geriatrics-focused web-based continuing education to reach practitioners in rural practice. *TechTrends*, *62*, 286–295. doi:10.1007/s11528-018-0258-0

Friedman, S. M., Gillespie, S. M., Medina-Walpole, A. M., Caprio, T. V., Karuza, J., & McCann, R. M. (2013). "Geriatricizing" hospitalists: Identifying educational opportunities. *Gerontology and Geriatrics Education*, *34*(4), 409–420. doi:10.1080/02701960.2013.819802

Guzman-Clark, J., Harrell, K., Leff, A., Henriques, D., Ines, E., Rofail, M., . . . Castle, S. (2016). An ECHO-based program to provide geriatric specialty care consultation and education. *Federal Practitioner*, *33*(4), 40–45.

Heinz, M., Martin, P., Doll, G., & Pearson-Scott, J. (2015). The delivery of distance education—is it time for doctoral programs in gerontology? *Gerontology and Geriatrics Education*, *36*(4), 343–364. doi:10.1080/02701960.2014.925887

Howe, J. L., & Kramer, B. J. (2019). Workforce issues in geriatrics in rural America. *Current Geriatrics Reports*, *8*, 49–54. doi:10.1007/s13670-019-0271-7

Howe, J. L., Penrod, J. D., Gottesman, E., Bean, A., & Kramer, B. J. (2019). The rural interdisciplinary team training program: A workforce development workshop to increase geriatrics knowledge and skills for rural providers. *Gerontology and Geriatrics Education*, *40*(1), 3–15. doi:10.1080/02701960.2018.1454917

Hung, W. W., Rossi, M., Thielke, S., Caprio, T., Barczi, S., Kramer, B. J., . . . Howe, J. L. (2014). A multisite geriatric education program for rural providers in the Veteran Health Care System (GRECC-Connect). *Gerontology and Geriatrics Education*, *35*(1), 23–40. doi:10.1080/02701960.2013.870902

Hwang, U., Shah, M. N., Han, J. H., Carpenter, C. R., Siu, A. L., & Adams, J. G. (2013). Transforming emergency care for older adults. *Health Affairs*, *32*(12), 2116–2121. doi:10.1377/hlthaff.2013.0670

IOM (Institute of Medicine). (2008). *Retooling for an aging America: Building the health care workforce*. Washington, DC: The National Academies Press.

Kaye, L., & Harvey, S. A. (2015). Providing services to well older adults in rural areas. In K. M. Hash, E. T. Jurkowski, & J. A. Krout (Eds.), *Aging in rural places* (p. 148). New York: Springer.

Kramer, B. J., Creekmur, B., Howe, J. L., Trudeau, S., Douglas, J. R., Garner, K., . . . Barczi, S. (2016). Veterans Affairs Geriatric Scholars Program: Enhancing existing primary care clinician skills in caring for older veterans. *Journal of the American Geriatrics Society*, *64*(11), 2343–2348. doi:10.1111/jgs.14382

Lee, A. G., Burton, J. A., & Lundebjerg, N. E. (2017). Geriatrics-for-Specialists Initiative: An eleven-specialty collaboration to improve care of older adults. *Journal of the American Geriatrics Society*, *65*(10), 2140–2145. doi:10.1111/jgs.14963

Lewis, L., & Farris, E. (2002). *Programs for adults in public library outlets*. Washington, DC: U.S. Department of Education, National Center for Education Statistics, Westat.

MacQueen, I. T., Maggard-Gibbons, M., Capra, G., Raaen, L., Ulloa, J. G., Shekelle, P. G., . . . Hempel, S. (2018). Recruiting rural healthcare providers today: A systematic review of training program success and determinants of geographic choices. *Journal of General Internal Medicine*, *33*(2), 191–199. doi:10.1007/s11606-017-4210-z

Maiden, R. J., Horowitz, B. P., & Howe, J. L. (2010). Workforce training and education gaps in gerontology and geriatrics: What we found in New York State. *Gerontological and Geriatric Education*, *31*(4), 328–348. doi:10.1080/02701960.2010.532749

Mathew, M., Ryan, D., & Samarasena, A. (2017). Early-career work location of Memorial University medical graduates: Why the decline in rural practice? *Society of Rural Physicians of Canada*, *22*(2), 54–61.

Mitra, G., Gowans, M., Wright, B., Brenneis, F., & Scott, I. (2018). Predictors of rural family medicine practice in Canada. *Canadian Family Physician*, *64*(8), 588–596.

Murray State University, Social Work Conference. Retrieved August 21, 2019, from www.murraystate.edu/academics/CollegesDepartments/CollegeOfEducationandHumanServices/coehsacademicunits/CLHS/SocialWork/SocialWorkConference.aspx

Myhre, D., Bajaj, S., & Jackson, W. (2015). Determinants of an urban origin student choosing rural practice: A scoping review. *Rural and Remote Health*, *15*, 3483. Retrieved from www.rrh.org.au/journal/article/3483

Pelham, A. (2008, March–April). Can academic gerontology keep from becoming irrelevant? *Aging Today*, *28*(2), 3–4.

Powerful Tools for Caregivers. Retrieved August 21, 2019, from www.powerfultoolsforcaregivers.org/caregivers

Rabinowitz, H. K., Diamond, J. J., Markham, F. W., & Santana, A. J. (2011). Increasing the supply of rural family physicians: Recent outcomes from Jefferson Medical College's Physician Shortage Area Program (PSAP). *Academic Medicine*, *86*, 264–269. doi:10.1097/ACM.0b013e31820469d6

Ruiz, J. G., Mintzer, M. J., & Leipzig, R. M. (2006). The impact of e-learning in medical education. *Academic Medicine*, *81*(3), 207–212.

Sterling, S. A., Seals, Samantha R., Jones, A. E., King, Melissa H., Galli, R. L., Isom, K. C., Summers, R. L., & Henderson, K. A. (2017). The impact of the TelEmergency program on rural emergency care: An implementation study.. Research Article. *Journal of Telemedicine and Telecare* 23(6), 588-594. doi:10.1177/1357633X16657499

SUNY Empire State College. *Academy for lifelong learning*. Retrieved August 21, 2019, from www.esc.edu/all/

Taylor, J. D., & Goletz, S. E. (2016). Using area health education centers to promote interest in rural practice. *Rural and Remote Health*, *16*(3934).

University of Arkansas at Pine Bluff. *Overview of gerontology program*. Retrieved August 21, 2019, from www.uapb.edu/academics/school_of_arts_sciences/social_behavioral_sciences/gerontology.aspx

Wallace, A. E., Lee, R., Mackenzie, T. A., West, A. N., Wright, S. . . . Weeks, W. B. (2010). A longitudinal analysis of rural and urban veterans' health-related quality of life. *Journal of Rural Health*, *26*(2), 156–163. doi:10.1111/j.1748-0361.2010.00277.x

34
HEALTH DISPARITIES

Steven A. Cohen and Mary L. Greaney

Background

A health disparity is a specific difference, variation, or inequality in some measure of health status, health care, or population health in which socially, economically, or geographically disadvantaged people experience worse health than their counterparts (Braveman, 2014). A disparate population is one in which disease and/or death rates are significantly worse compared to the health or mortality status of the general or comparison population (Minority Health and Health Disparities Research and Education Act, 2000). Over the past decade, there has been increasing interest in expanding the definition of health disparities to include rural-urban health disparities, with rural populations considered to be disadvantaged compared to urban and suburban populations.

In the U.S., numerous examples of rural-urban health disparities exist. The well-documented gains in life expectancy in the U.S. over the past half century until 2015 are more attenuated in rural areas than urban areas (Singh & Siahpush, 2014b), while rural-urban disparities in all-cause mortality and mortality from major causes of death (e.g., heart disease, cancer, and diabetes) also have widened substantially over time (Singh & Siahpush, 2014a). Infant mortality is higher among rural Appalachian residents than in other U.S. populations (Singh, Kogan, & Slifkin, 2017). The prevalence of obesity (Hales et al., 2018) and incidence of stroke (Howard et al., 2017) were significantly higher among rural (4.8%) than urban (4.1%) populations. Smoking and related lung cancers were also significantly higher in rural areas than in other parts of the country (Jenkins et al., 2018). Furthermore, children in rural areas are more likely to be overweight or obese and are less likely to have routine medical and dental exams than urban and suburban children (Probst, Barker, Enders, & Gardiner, 2018).

Rural-urban health disparities have important implications for older adults, given that older adults are disproportionately concentrated in rural areas compared to younger adults and children (Glasgow & Brown, 2012). Furthermore, older adults use more health services than their younger counterparts, and the quality and availability of health services is generally lower in rural areas than non-rural areas (Lutfiyya et al., 2007; Caldwell, Ford, Wallace, Wang, & Takahashi, 2016). These disparities may reflect the continuum of rural versus urban or suburban living, and the potential influence place of residence and geographic location have on economics, health and well-being, and other aspects of life. Older adults living in rural areas may encounter higher economic hardship, geographic isolation, less access to and availability of quality health care, greater frequency of hospital closings, and other risk factors than those living in urban or suburban areas (Caldwell et al., 2016; Kaufman et al., 2016).

Examples of Rural-Urban Health Disparities Among Older Adults

Rural-urban health disparities may be present among older adults in a number of ways. One common subtype, differences by rural-urban status, can occur when rural older adults are at a relative health disadvantage compared to urban and suburban older adults. Another common subtype, moderation of other disparities by rural-urban status is when other types of disparities (e.g., racial or ethnic) are more pronounced among older adults living in rural areas than those living in urban and suburban areas. That is, where an older adult lives (i.e., rural vs. urban) moderates or amplifies existing demographic, social, or economic disparities.

Disparity Subtype 1: Differences by Rural-Urban Status

As discussed earlier, interest in understanding and addressing rural-urban health disparities in the U.S. has grown markedly over the past decade. Much of the research in this area, particularly among older adults, has focused on rural-urban differences in health status, behaviors, and outcomes. A study in the Appalachian region found that Medicare beneficiaries in rural counties were less likely to be diagnosed with Alzheimer's disease and related disorders than those beneficiaries in urban and suburban counties, despite presenting with similar clinical conditions (Abner, Jicha, Christian, & Schreurs, 2016). Similarly, Thorpe et al. found that rural older adults with dementia had higher levels of ambulatory care-sensitive hospitalizations than urban older adults, and that difference was not because of variations in patient behavior, caregiving status, or other community-based factors (Thorpe, Van Houtven, Sleath, & Thorpe, 2010). Rural older adults were less likely to participate in cancer screenings than older adults living in urban and suburban areas (Fan, Mohile, Zhang, Fiscella, & Noyes, 2012). Fan et al. also identified gradations in cancer screening rate by rurality, with older adults living in the most geographically isolated rural areas being less likely to get screened for colorectal cancer than those living in less isolated, but still rural areas. Similar findings in rural-urban gradients in the incidence of breast and cervical cancer also have been identified (Moss, Liu, & Feuer, 2017). However, McLafferty & Wang found the opposite trend, with a higher prevalence of lung, breast, colorectal, and prostate cancers in urban areas (McLafferty & Wang, 2009). The potential reasons for these paradoxical findings are unclear but may be because of lack of access to screening services in rural areas, rather than a true lower prevalence. Perhaps the cancer cases presenting in rural areas, though less, may be more severe than those presenting in more urban areas because of being diagnosed at later stages of disease progression (Campbell et al., 2001) or lower screening rates. Additionally, rural cancer survivors report significantly higher levels of comorbidity, psychological distress, and poor overall health than their urban counterparts (Weaver, Geiger, Lu, & Case, 2013).

After controlling for socioeconomic, demographic, and health-related factors, people living in rural areas are significantly more likely to have coronary heart disease than people living in urban or suburban areas (O'Connor & Wellenius, 2012). Rural-urban disparities in obesity are present among older adults, although the magnitude of the disparity depended upon the way in which rural-urban status was assessed (Cohen, Cook, Kelley, Foutz, & Sando, 2017). Rural-urban differences in health behaviors in older adults, namely consumption of fruits and vegetables, may, in part, explain these rural-urban disparities in obesity (Cohen, Greaney, & Sabik, 2018).

There are also important rural-urban disparities in health-care services utilization among older adults. Rural older adults were less likely than their urban counterparts to have bariatric surgery (Wallace, Young-Xu, Hartley, & Weeks, 2010) or receive care for chronic lower back pain (Goode, Freburger, & Carey, 2013). Terminally ill lung cancer patients in urban areas have more intensive care unit (ICU) days in the last 90 days of life and are more likely to have used hospice care services compared to rural patients (Nayar et al., 2014), although similar rural-urban disparities were not observed in terminally ill patients with ovarian cancers (Fairfield et al., 2012). O'Connor and Wellenius (2012) also found higher rates of type 2 diabetes among rural residents compared to urban residents.

Disparity Subtype 2: Rural-Urban Status Moderates Other Types of Disparities

Another mechanism through which place of residence (rural/urban) contributes to health disparities is by moderating other types of health disparities. In other words, rural-urban status may alter the magnitude and direction of other disparities (e.g., racial, ethnic, gender). Although studies suggest the existence of this type of disparity, this subtype is not as well studied as the simple differences by rural-urban status discussed in the previous section, particularly for older adults. For racial and ethnic disparities, rural-urban differences may be partially attributed to key demographic differences in the composition of racial and ethnic minority populations in rural areas compared to urban areas. Racial/ethnic minorities in rural areas tended to be younger, have less income, and have lower levels of educational attainment than rural whites and urban minorities (James et al., 2017).

Nonetheless, there are some examples of this subtype of rural-urban health disparity. Racial disparities in stroke mortality among older adults were more severe in rural areas of the

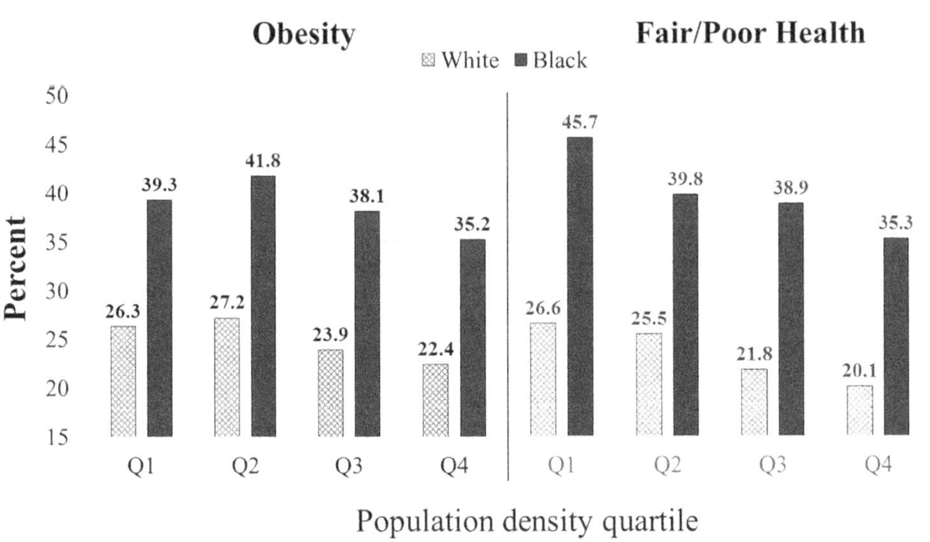

Figure 34.1 Percent of Whites and Blacks with obesity and fair or poor self-reported health by income and population density quartile

southeastern U.S. compared to other areas (Tassone, Waller, & Casper, 2009). Black/white disparities in all-cause mortality were significantly larger in rural areas of Tennessee than in more urban areas (Erwin, Fitzhugh, Brown, Looney, & Forde, 2010). Analysis of data from the 2012 Behavioral Risk Factor Surveillance System from adults aged 60 and older identified rural-urban gradients in the magnitude of black/white disparities in obesity and self-reported health (Figure 34.1). Although the relative differences between blacks and whites did not differ substantially by rural-urban status, the absolute differences decreased with increasing urbanicity. For self-reported health, the black/white difference in the most rural areas (Q1) was 19.1%, while in the most urban areas (Q4), the difference was "15.2%"—35.3–20.1=15.2, suggesting that racial/ethnic disparities may worsen with increasing rurality for older adults.

Conclusion

Rural-urban place of residence plays a significant role in the health and well-being of older adults. There are numerous pathways through which place of residence directly and indirectly influences population health and promotes health disparities that need to be explored. Despite the growing body of research documenting these rural-urban health disparities among older adults in the U.S., such disparities have been worsening over time. As the population ages, and older adults continue to be disproportionately concentrated in rural areas, there is a critical need to identify and understand the mechanisms promoting these disparities. Such research may lead to effective policies and programs designed to reduce rural-urban disparities and promote health for all older adults regardless of where they live.

References

Abner, E. L., Jicha, G. A., Christian, W. J., & Schreurs, B. G. (2016). Rural-urban differences in Alzheimer's disease and related disorders diagnostic prevalence in Kentucky and West Virginia. *The Journal of Rural Health*, *32*(3), 314–320.

Braveman, P. (2014). What are health disparities and health equity? We need to be clear. *Public Health Reports*, *129*(1_Suppl 2), 5–8.

Caldwell, J. T., Ford, C. L., Wallace, S. P., Wang, M. C., & Takahashi, L. M. (2016). Intersection of living in a rural versus urban area and race/ethnicity in explaining access to health care in the United States. *American Journal of Public Health*, *106*(8), 1463–1469.

Campbell, N. C., Elliott, A. M., Sharp, L., Ritchie, L. D., Cassidy, J., & Little, J. (2001). Rural and urban differences in stage at diagnosis of colorectal and lung cancers. *British Journal of Cancer*, *84*(7), 910.

Cohen, S. A., Cook, S. K., Kelley, L., Foutz, J. D., & Sando, T. A. (2017). A closer look at rural-urban health disparities: Associations between obesity and rurality vary by geospatial and sociodemographic factors. *The Journal of Rural Health*, *33*(2), 167–179.

Cohen, S. A., Greaney, M. L., & Sabik, N. J. (2018). Assessment of dietary patterns, physical activity and obesity from a national survey: Rural-urban health disparities in older adults. *PloS One*, *13*(12), e0208268.

Erwin, P. C., Fitzhugh, E. C., Brown, K. C., Looney, S., & Forde, T. (2010). Health disparities in rural areas: The interaction of race, socioeconomic status, and geography. *Journal of Health Care for the Poor and Underserved*, *21*(3), 931–945.

Fairfield, K. M., Murray, K. M., Wierman, H. R., Han, P. K., Hallen, S., Miesfeldt, S., . . . Earle, C. C. (2012). Disparities in hospice care among older women dying with ovarian cancer. *Gynecologic Oncology*, *125*(1), 14–18. doi:10.1016/j.ygyno.2011.11.041

Fan, L., Mohile, S., Zhang, N., Fiscella, K., & Noyes, K. (2012). Self-reported cancer screening among elderly Medicare beneficiaries: A rural-urban comparison. *The Journal of Rural Health*, *28*(3), 312–319.

Glasgow, N., & Brown, D. L. (2012). Rural ageing in the United States: Trends and contexts. *Journal of Rural Studies*, *28*(4), 422–431.

Goode, A. P., Freburger, J. K., & Carey, T. S. (2013). The influence of rural versus urban residence on utilization and receipt of care for chronic low back pain. *The Journal of Rural Health, 29*(2), 205–214. doi:10.1111/j.1748-0361.2012.00436.x

Hales, C. M., Fryar, C. D., Carroll, M. D., Freedman, D. S., Aoki, Y., & Ogden, C. L. (2018). Differences in obesity prevalence by demographic characteristics and urbanization level among adults in the United States, 2013–2016. *Journal of the American Medical Association, 319*(23), 2419–2429.

Howard, G., Kleindorfer, D. O., Cushman, M., Long, D. L., Jasne, A., Judd, S. E., . . . Howard, V. J. (2017). Contributors to the excess stroke mortality in rural areas in the United States. *Stroke, 48*(7), 1773–1778.

James, C. V., Moonesinghe, R., Wilson-Frederick, S. M., Hall, J. E., Penman-Aguilar, A., & Bouye, K. (2017). Racial/ethnic health disparities among rural adults—United States, 2012–2015. *MMWR: Surveillance Summaries, 66*(23), 1.

Jenkins, W. D., Matthews, A. K., Bailey, A., Zahnd, W. E., Watson, K. S., Mueller-Luckey, G., . . . Patera, J. (2018). Rural areas are disproportionately impacted by smoking and lung cancer. *Preventive Medicine Reports, 10*, 200–203.

Kaufman, B. G., Thomas, S. R., Randolph, R. K., Perry, J. R., Thompson, K. W., Holmes, G. M., & Pink, G. H. (2016). The rising rate of rural hospital closures. *The Journal of Rural Health, 32*(1), 35–43.

Lutfiyya, M. N., Bhat, D. K., Gandhi, S. R., Nguyen, C., Weidenbacher-Hoper, V. L., & Lipsky, M. S. (2007). A comparison of quality of care indicators in urban acute care hospitals and rural critical access hospitals in the United States. *International Journal for Quality in Health Care, 19*(3), 141–149.

McLafferty, S., & Wang, F. (2009). Rural reversal? Rural-urban disparities in late-stage cancer risk in Illinois. *Cancer, 115*(12), 2755–2764.

Moss, J. L., Liu, B., & Feuer, E. J. (2017). Urban/rural differences in breast and cervical cancer incidence: The mediating roles of socioeconomic status and provider density. *Women's Health Issues, 27*(6), 683–691.

Nayar, P., Qiu, F., Watanabe-Galloway, S., Boilesen, E., Wang, H., Lander, L., & Islam, M. (2014). Disparities in end of life care for elderly lung cancer patients. *Journal of Community Health, 39*(5), 1012–1019.

O'Connor, A., & Wellenius, G. (2012). Rural–urban disparities in the prevalence of diabetes and coronary heart disease. *Public Health, 126*(10), 813–820. doi:10.1016/j.puhe.2012.05.029

Probst, J. C., Barker, J. C., Enders, A., & Gardiner, P. (2018). Current state of child health in rural America: How context shapes children's health. *The Journal of Rural Health, 34*, S3–S12.

Singh, G. K., & Siahpush, M. (2014a). Widening rural–urban disparities in all-cause mortality and mortality from major causes of death in the USA, 1969–2009. *Journal of Urban Health, 91*(2), 272–292.

Singh, G. K., & Siahpush, M. (2014b). Widening rural–urban disparities in life expectancy, US, 1969–2009. *American Journal of Preventive Medicine, 46*(2), e19–e29.

Singh, G. K., Kogan, M. D., & Slifkin, R. T. (2017). Widening disparities in infant mortality and life expectancy between Appalachia and the rest of the United States, 1990–2013. *Health Affairs, 36*(8), 1423–1432.

Tassone, E. C., Waller, L. A., & Casper, M. L. (2009). Small-area racial disparity in stroke mortality: An application of Bayesian spatial hierarchical modeling. *Epidemiology (Cambridge, Mass.), 20*(2), 234.

Thorpe, J. M., Van Houtven, C. H., Sleath, B. L., & Thorpe, C. T. (2010). Rural-urban differences in preventable hospitalizations among community-dwelling veterans with dementia. *The Journal of Rural Health, 26*(2), 146–155.

U.S. Public Law. (2000). *Minority Health and Health Disparities Research and Education Act, 106–525*, 2498. Retrieved from https://www.ncbi.nlm.nih.gov/books/NBK57039/

Wallace, A. E., Young-Xu, Y., Hartley, D., & Weeks, W. B. (2010). Racial, socioeconomic, and rural–urban disparities in obesity-related bariatric surgery. *Obesity Surgery, 20*(10), 1354–1360. doi:10.1007/s11695-009-0054-x

Weaver, K. E., Geiger, A. M., Lu, L., & Case, L. D. (2013). Rural-urban disparities in health status among US cancer survivors. *Cancer, 119*(5), 1050–1057.

35
HEALTH INSURANCE

Erika Ziller and Yvonne Jonk

Introduction: The Medicare Program

Older adults—aged 65 and older—are one of the few populations in the U.S. that has near-universal access to health insurance coverage, through the Medicare program. Medicare was established by Congress in 1965 amid growing recognition of the challenges many older adults faced accessing coverage and care after retirement. In 1972, the Medicare program was expanded to include certain adults with long-term disabilities but, as of 2016, older adults represented 84% of all beneficiaries (MedPAC, 2019). Older adults make up a larger proportion of rural compared with urban communities; in 2017, about 19% of all rural residents were aged 65 and older compared with 15% of those living in urban locales (U.S. Census Bureau, 2017). Medicare has been credited with dramatically reducing the uninsured rate among older adults (from nearly half of all adults 65 and older to only 2%) and, by extension, extending the life expectancy of older adults by five years (Davis, Schoen, & Bandeali, 2015).

Medicare Parts and Benefits

Medicare has four different parts (A through D) representing different types of services that are covered and/or different modes of health insurance provision (Social Security Administration, 2018). *Medicare Part A* is required coverage for all beneficiaries and covers hospital stays, short-term stays in a skilled nursing facility, and in some cases home health or hospice care. *Medicare Part B* is optional, requires payment of monthly premiums by the beneficiary, and covers a portion of most ambulatory medical care provided by doctors and other health-care providers. It also covers durable medical equipment such as walking aids. In traditional Medicare, Parts A and B are provided and managed by the federal government, which collects premiums and pays claims on behalf of enrollees who use services. Beginning in 2006, Medicare introduced prescription drug coverage through *Medicare Part D*, which helps beneficiaries pay for their prescription medications. Except when covered through a Medicaid benefit (see later under supplemental coverage), Part D benefits are provided by private insurance companies that are authorized by Medicare to sell these plans.

Medicare Part C, more widely known as *Medicare Advantage*, is an option for elders to obtain Medicare coverage through a private health insurance company instead of the federal government's plan. Medicare Advantage plans cover the same services as traditional Medicare Parts

A and B and may also offer prescription drug coverage through a Medicare Part D option (Centers for Medicare & Medicaid Services, n.d.). Nearly one-third of all Medicare beneficiaries were enrolled in a Medicare Advantage plan in 2017 (Jacobson, Damico, & Neuman, 2017), although participation has been more limited among rural beneficiaries—25% compared with 31% of their urban counterparts (Centers for Medicare & Medicaid Services & RAND, 2018).

Most recently, Medicare Advantage has been authorized by Medicare to develop Special Needs Plans (SNPs). These plans are specifically tailored to the health-care needs of older adults with chronic health conditions such as diabetes, cancer, heart disease, or lung disorders. Medicare SNPs offer disease management services and more affordable cost-sharing for medications and other services related to the beneficiary's health condition.

Out-of-Pocket Costs and Affordability Issues for Rural Older Adults

High Total and Out-of-Pocket Spending Increases With Age and With Poorer Health

Total health-care spending increases with age, largely because of declining health status and a greater need for health-care services, including long-term care (Cubanski, Swoope, Damico, & Neuman, 2014). Among Medicare beneficiaries, total medical expenses for 90-year-olds were more than double that of 70-year-olds, largely because of nursing home expenses (De Nardi, French, Jones, & McCauley, 2016). Among older adults, rural residents tend to be older and sicker than urban residents and have more chronic conditions (Douthit, Kiv, Dwolatzky, & Biswas, 2015; James et al., 2017), which may affect their overall health-care use and spending.

At the same time that health-care spending is increasing, older adults generally experience lower incomes because of retirement, which can lead to high out-of-pocket costs relative to income. Approximately half of older Medicare beneficiaries live on less than $26,000 per year, yet in 2013, they paid an average of $5,680 out-of-pocket for health care including premiums, deductibles, and co-insurance (North Carolina Rural Health Research Program, 2017). The top 10% of patients with out-of-pocket expenses spend an average of $10,000 a year on such costs (Noel-Miller, 2017) and account for 52% of medical spending among Medicare beneficiaries (De Nardi et al., 2016). Premiums alone accounted for 50% to 66% of out-of-pocket expenditures for Medicare households, while health expenses equaled approximately 14% of Medicare household budgets in 2012 (Cubanski et al., 2014). About one-fourth of Medicare beneficiaries spent at least 10% of their household incomes on medical care, excluding premiums, and were thus considered underinsured (Schoen, Davis, & Willink, 2017).

Supplemental Health Insurance Coverage

Rural-residing older adults with Medicare are more likely to be enrolled in traditional fee-for-service (FFS) Medicare policies than they are in Medicare Advantage (Part C managed care) plans when compared with urban elders (Oyeka, Ullrich, & Mueller, 2019). In 2018, approximately 25% of rural Medicare beneficiaries were enrolled in Medicare Advantage (MA) plans compared to the national average of 34%. Although FFS plans typically have wider provider networks than managed care plans, they also tend to have less generous benefit packages. For example, beneficiaries in FFS Medicare face an almost $1,400 deductible for each hospitalization under Part A, pay premiums for Part B that cost $135 per month, and are responsible for the first $185 of outpatient care (e.g., physician visits) and then 20% of outpatient costs after that.

To address these potentially large out-of-pocket costs, many older adults enroll in private health insurance policies to supplement their Medicare coverage. Some obtain these policies from their former employers as a retirement benefit, although the proportion who have this type of coverage has been decreasing over time. Other beneficiaries may buy supplemental insurance directly from an insurance company and these plans tend to be higher cost than employer-based plans. Finally, some beneficiaries may be eligible for Medicaid, a shared state-federal program that covers low-income individuals and those with long-term disabilities. Medicaid is also the largest payer for long-term care services. Older adults with Medicare and Medicaid (dual eligible) generally face lower out-of-pocket expenses than those without Medicaid and tend to spend a lower share of their household income on health care than middle-income households not eligible for Medicaid (Cubanski et al., 2014).

Despite the risk of out-of-pocket spending under FFS, however, nearly one in five beneficiaries in this traditional Medicare option go without supplemental policies (Cubanski, Damico, Neuman, & Jacobson, 2018). Older adults living in rural communities are more likely than those in urban areas to lack any source of supplemental coverage, more likely to have a plan directly purchased from an insurer (Medigap), and less likely to have an employer-based plan (Ziller, Lenardson, & Coburn, 2015). They are about equally likely to be dually eligible for Medicare and Medicaid as are their urban counterparts (Ziller et al., 2015). All of this suggests that rural older adults living in their communities may face higher out-of-pocket health-care spending than their urban counterparts.

Health-Care Spending by Rural Older Adults

Studies have documented higher out-of-pocket expenses for prescriptions by rural beneficiaries compared to urban beneficiaries (Ziller et al., 2015), as well as for the following subpopulations: cancer patients compared to beneficiaries without cancer (Davidoff et al., 2013); those needing specialty type drugs (e.g., for treatment of cancer, hepatitis C, multiple sclerosis, arthritis) (Cubanski, Koma, & Neuman, 2019); and patients with dementia in the last five years of life (Kelley, McGarry, Gorges, & Skinner, 2015). Rural beneficiaries are also more likely to have chronic conditions than urban beneficiaries and are thus more likely to use more expensive, specialized services that usually require higher copayments than preventive or primary care visits, and lack the breadth of coverage that primary care services typically have (Machlin & Mitchell, 2018).

High out-of-pocket expenses may pose a substantial financial barrier to accessing needed health-care services. Financial barriers are a primary reason for beneficiaries receiving less than the recommended level of medical care (Kurichi et al., 2017). For example, among patients on statins, high copayments were a significant risk factor for patients reporting lower medication adherence (McRae, van Gool, Hall, & Yen, 2017). Studies assessing barriers to accessing care have found that rural beneficiaries were more likely to report that cost was an issue when deciding whether to seek medical services than urban beneficiaries (Fitzpatrick, Powe, Cooper, Ives, & Robbins, 2004; Goins, Williams, Carter, Spencer, & Solovieva, 2005; Schulte, Pink, Holmes, & Kirk, 2019). This suggests that rural older adults may be more likely to go without needed services and are more likely not to take or follow through with taking prescription medicines. Although problems accessing appropriate care have been associated with poorer health outcomes (North Carolina Rural Health Research Program, 2017), further research is needed to understand how these financial barriers may be affecting the health and well-being of rural elders.

Finally, in addition to incurring higher direct medical care expenses, rural older adults may face additional indirect costs associated with traveling long distances for care and updating and adjusting their home environment(s) to accommodate aging-in-place. For example, the prevalence of outdated housing stock in rural areas makes it challenging for older adults with functional limitations to stay in multilevel homes where the bedrooms and the only bathroom are on the second floor, the washer and dryer are in the basement, and flights of stairs pose significant barriers to using portions of the home. With limited home and community-based services available in rural communities, along with limited financial resources to tend to their housing needs, rural older adult Medicare beneficiaries are less likely to "age-in-place" and more likely to seek admission to nursing homes than their urban counterparts (Coburn, Ziller, Paluso, Thayer, & Talbot, 2019).

Conclusion

Although Medicare provides critically important health insurance coverage for older adults, the somewhat piecemeal history of the program and its benefit structure may leave some rural older adults with financial barriers to health-care services. For example, Medicare excludes many essential services such as long-term care, oral health, and vision services. And without supplemental insurance coverage, the cost-sharing requirements for health-care services can be high. This is compounded by the fact that adults past retirement typically have lower individual and family incomes than their working age counterparts. According to recent estimates, about one-quarter of all Medicare beneficiaries spend more than 20% of their income on a combination of premiums and cost-sharing for medical services (Schoen et al., 2017). Policymakers and rural advocates should monitor health-care access for rural older adults and make policy corrections as needed, to ensure that older adults in rural places have the services that they need for health and well-being in their post-retirement years.

References

Centers for Medicare & Medicaid Services. (n.d.). *Medicare Advantage Plans*. Retrieved from www.medicare.gov/sign-up-change-plans/types-of-medicare-health-plans/medicare-advantage-plans

Centers for Medicare & Medicaid Services, & RAND. (2018). *Rural-urban disparities in health care in Medicare*. Baltimore, MD: CMS.

Coburn, A. F., Ziller, E. C., Paluso, N., Thayer, D., & Talbot, J. A. (2019). Long-term services and supports use among older Medicare beneficiaries in rural and urban areas. *Research on Aging*, *41*(3), 241–264. doi:10.1177/0164027518824117

Cubanski, J., Damico, A., Neuman, T., & Jacobson, G. (2018). *Sources of supplemental coverage among Medicare beneficiaries in 2016*. San Francisco, CA: Kaiser Family Foundation.

Cubanski, J., Koma, W., & Neuman, T. (2019). *The out-of-pocket cost burden for specialty drugs in Medicare Part D in 2019*. Menlo Park, CA: Kaiser Family Foundation.

Cubanski, J., Swoope, C., Damico, A., & Neuman, T. (2014). *Health care on a budget: The financial burden of health spending by Medicare households*. Menlo Park, CA: Kaiser Family Foundation.

Davidoff, A. J., Erten, M., Shaffer, T., Shoemaker, J. S., Zuckerman, I. H., Pandya, N., . . . Stuart, B. (2013). Out-of-pocket health care expenditure burden for Medicare beneficiaries with cancer. *Cancer*, *119*(6), 1257–1265. doi:10.1002/cncr.27848

Davis, K., Schoen, C., & Bandeali, F. (2015). *Medicare: 50 years of ensuring coverage and care*. New York: Commonwealth Fund.

De Nardi, M., French, E., Jones, J. B., & McCauley, J. (2016). Medical spending of the US elderly. *Fiscal Studies*, *37*(3–4), 717–747. doi:10.1111/j.1475-5890.2016.12106

Douthit, N., Kiv, S., Dwolatzky, T., & Biswas, S. (2015). Exposing some important barriers to health care access in the rural USA. *Public Health*, *129*(6), 611–620. doi:10.1016/j.puhe.2015.04.001

Fitzpatrick, A. L., Powe, N. R., Cooper, L. S., Ives, D. G., & Robbins, J. A. (2004). Barriers to health care access among the elderly and who perceives them. *American Journal of Public Health, 94*(10), 1788–1794. doi:10.2105/ajph.94.10.1788

Goins, R. T., Williams, K. A., Carter, M. W., Spencer, M., & Solovieva, T. (2005). Perceived barriers to health care access among rural older adults: A qualitative study. *Journal of Rural Health, 21*(3), 206–213.

Jacobson, G., Damico, A., & Neuman, T. (2017). *Medicare Advantage 2018 data spotlight: First look*. Menlo Park, CA: Kaiser Family Foundation.

James, C. V., Moonesinghe, R., Wilson-Frederick, S. M., Hall, J. E., Penman-Aguilar, A., & Bouye, K. (2017). Racial/ethnic health disparities among rural adults—United States, 2012–2015. *MMWR: Surveillance Summaries, 66*(23), 1–9. doi:10.15585/mmwr.ss6623a1

Kelley, A. S., McGarry, K., Gorges, R., & Skinner, J. S. (2015). The burden of health care costs for patients with dementia in the last 5 years of life. *Annals of Internal Medicine, 163*(10), 729–736. doi:10.7326/m15-0381

Kurichi, J. E., Pezzin, L., Streim, J. E., Kwong, P. L., Na, L., Bogner, H. R., . . . Hennessy, S. (2017). Perceived barriers to healthcare and receipt of recommended medical care among elderly Medicare beneficiaries. *Archives of Gerontology and Geriatrics, 72*, 45–51. doi:10.1016/j.archger.2017.05.007

Machlin, S. R., & Mitchell, E. M. (2018). *Expenses for office-based physician visits by specialty and insurance type, 2016*. Statistical Brief #517. Rockville, MD: AHRQ.

McRae, I., van Gool, K., Hall, J., & Yen, L. (2017). Role of cost on failure to access prescribed pharmaceuticals: The case of statins. *Applied Health Economics and Health Policy, 15*(5), 625–634. doi:10.1007/s40258-017-0336-8

MedPAC. (2019). *Health care spending and the Medicare program: A data book*. Washington, DC: MedPAC.

Noel-Miller, C. (2017). *Medicare beneficiaries' out-of-pocket spending for health care*. AARP Public Policy Institute. Retrieved from https://www.aarp.org/ppi/info-2017/medicare-beneficiaries-out-of-pocket-spending-for-health-care.html

North Carolina Rural Health Research Program. (2017). *Rural health snapshot (2017)*. Chapel Hill, NC: NC RHRP.

Oyeka, O., Ullrich, F., & Mueller, K. (2019). *Medicare Advantage enrollment update 2018*. Iowa City, IA: RUPRI.

Schoen, C., Davis, K., & Willink, A. (2017). *Medicare beneficiaries' high out-of-pocket costs: Cost burdens by income and health status*. New York: Commonwealth Fund.

Schulte, A., Pink, G., Holmes, M., & Kirk, D. (2019). *Cost-sharing as a barrier to accessing care at FQHCs and RHCs for rural Medicare beneficiaries*. Chapel Hill, NC: North Carolina Rural Health Research and Policy Analysis Center.

Social Security Administration. (2018). *Medicare*. Pub. No. 5–10043. Woodlawn, MD: SSA.

U.S. Census Bureau. (2017, June 7). *American Community Survey 1-year estimates*. Retrieved from www.census.gov/programs-surveys/acs/technical-documentation/table-and-geography-changes/2017/1-year.html

Ziller, E. C., Lenardson, J. D., & Coburn, A. F. (2015). *Out-of-pocket spending among rural Medicare beneficiaries*. Portland, ME: Maine Rural Health Research Center.

36
HEALTH PROMOTION AND WELLNESS

Kelley A. Strout

Rural older adults who engage in wellness behaviors experience health benefits and may demonstrate a more positive attitude toward aging than those who do not engage in such behaviors. Wellness is a holistic representation of health that views older adults beyond their physical health to include the emotional, social, and intellectual domains (International Council on Aging, 2019). Older adults who engage in behaviors that promote multiple domains of wellness experience not only physical but mental health benefits as well (Strout, 2012; Strout et al., 2016; CDC, 2019). This is significant since older adults fear losing cognitive abilities more than any other bodily function as they grow older (Phelan, Anderson, LaCroix, & Larson, 2004). Research demonstrates that when older adults engage in wellness-related behaviors, they experience greater cognitive protection than those who do not (Strout et al., 2016). Wellness behaviors such as physical activity, positive thinking, displaying purpose in life, and engaging in rich social networks provide health-promoting benefits that can foster independence and physical and mental health protections (Strout, 2012; Strout et al., 2016).

Social Wellness

Positive social connections and rich social networks promote wellness among older adults. Older adults who are engaged socially demonstrate less risk for high blood pressure, obesity, depression, anxiety, Alzheimer's disease, and death (Centers for Disease Control and Prevention—CDC, 2017). Adults living in rural areas may experience challenges leaving their homes to engage in social activities because of transportation barriers or lack of social opportunities. Volunteer opportunities at local spiritual centers or churches, community food cupboards, and schools can provide positive experiences to help combat loneliness and promote social engagement. Higher education institutions often provide a venue for older adults to engage in the social process of learning something new. Some universities offer senior college and other lifelong learning opportunities that provide unique learning experiences for older adults that typically do not involve exams. For example, Maine has 17 senior colleges that provide intellectually engaging courses taught by volunteers and charge low tuition (www.maineseniorcollege.org/). Senior college is an ideal opportunity for older adults to meet other adults with similar interests and challenge their minds intellectually. For older adults who do not know where to begin, there are several national organizations that offer support connecting older adults to social opportunities.

Internet resources that support social engagement include:

- www.Encore.org connects older adults to both paid and unpaid activities that maximize their experience and knowledge
- AARP ExperienceCorps trains older adults to tutor elementary students who are not reading at their grade level
- Meetup.com allows users to find opportunities to engage in activities they enjoy, meet new friends, and try new activities
- VolunteerMatch connects individuals with volunteer opportunities at nonprofit organizations that align with the individual's values and priorities
- Create the Good links individuals with volunteer opportunities that align with their strengths and experiences.

Emotional Wellness

A positive outlook on life promotes health and wellness among older adults. Adults who demonstrate higher levels of anger, moodiness, anxiety, depressed mood, fear, or envy are at higher risk for cognitive decline than those who demonstrate more positive personality traits (Strout & Howard, 2012, 2015). Individuals can modify their personality types and circumvent the health outcomes associated with negative emotions through a process called the "undoing effect" (Fredrickson, Mancuso, Branigan, and Tugade, 2000). Intentional engagement in activities that promote positive emotions can build resilience and promote health (the preferred ratio of positive to negative emotions for reinforcing health promotion is three to one (Fredrickson, 2004)). Frederickson offers resources to promote positive emotions that include a positivity assessment (www.positivityratio.com) and free meditations support to increase positivity (www.positivityresonance.com/survey.php).

Physical Wellness

Physical health is the most common health promotion and wellness behavior indicator of older adult well-being. Those who engage in physical activity, healthy eating, and preventive exams demonstrate health benefits.

Physical Activity

Physical activity reduces the risk of onset of chronic disease and helps to better manage diseases that already exist. Physical activity also supports older adults' emotional health and ability to remain independent as they age. Older adults can begin a physical activity plan at any age. The Centers for Disease Control and Prevention (CDC, 2020) recommends that older adults focus on moving more and sitting less. For optimal health benefits, they recommend two hours and 30 minutes to five hours per week of moderate-intensity, or one hour and 15 minutes to two hours and 30 minutes of vigorous-intensity aerobic activity per week. Adults will experience additional benefits the more physical activity they engage in. Older adults should also engage in strength-training and balance exercises two days per week and include all muscle groups. They should always work with a primary care provider to identify health or safety concerns before starting a new exercise program (CDC, 2020).

Adults living in rural areas may find barriers to walking, which is the most common and basic form of physical activity. Rural environments often do no have sidewalks, and walking on streets may be dangerous, especially during winter months. Fortunately, some daily chores count as physical activity such as mowing the lawn, shoveling snow, and carrying groceries. Strength-training exercises such as pushups, planks, squats, and lifting hand-weights can also be performed indoors or outdoors without the need for expensive equipment or gym membership. Technology affords older adults an opportunity to engage in group fitness via phone applications, telephonic support, and online programs.

Evidence-based physical activity programs for older adults are available in many rural communities. Explore more options:

- Enhance Fitness: a low-cost adaptable physical activity program for all skill levels. https://projectenhance.org/locations/
- Fit and Strong: an 8-week physical activity program designed for older adults with osteoarthritis. www.fitandstrong.org/about/locations.aspx
- Healthy Moves: the program aims to improve strength, flexibility, and reduce falls and pain. These programs are available worldwide. www.eblcprograms.org/evidence-based/map-of-programs/
- Walk with Ease: a program designed to reduce pain associated with arthritis and improve overall quality of life. The program is offered online, via mobile app, videos, or at worksites. www.arthritis.org/living-with-arthritis/tools-resources/walk-with-ease/
- SilverSneakers: a physical activity and health program that is covered by most Medicare plans. (https://tools.silversneakers.com/).

Healthy Eating

Older adults who consume a healthy diet reduce risk and better manage chronic diseases. MyPlate (2015–2020) was developed to provide specific dietary recommendations for older adults. MyPlate (2015–2020) provides a simple visual to support optimal nutrition for older adults. It is recommended that older adults fill half of a standard size plate with fruits and vegetables, fill one fourth of a plate with whole grains, one fourth of a plate with lean proteins, one fourth of a plate with dairy, and a small portion in the center of a plate with healthy oils. MyPlate offers a website that provides shopping, salt alternatives, and recipes to assist older adults in achieving their health eating goals. For more information: https://hnrca.tufts.edu/myplate/ (Tufts University, 2020).

Older adults living in rural areas experience transportation barriers that limit access to shopping centers where fresh fruits and vegetables are available. Frozen fruits and vegetables provide the nutrients adults need for optimal health and often retain nutrient value more than store-bought fresh fruits and vegetables that have traveled great distances from their original source. Frozen fruits and vegetables also prevent frequent spoilage that single older adults often experience when purchasing fresh fruits and vegetables.

Gardening is another option for older adults who want to eat healthy and live in rural areas. Older adults who plant, harvest, cultivate, and consume fresh vegetables may experience numerous health benefits. Research suggests that gardening may promote purpose in life, physical activity, emotional well-being, sound nutrition, and cognitive health benefits among older adults (Wang & Glicksman, 2013). Gardens planted from seeds are inexpensive and provide immediate access to fresh food. Older adults who are interested in starting their own gardens should contact their local Cooperative Extension office for technical support and assistance locating supplies. Some Cooperative Extensions also offer Master Gardener training programs that provide in-depth training in the art and science of horticulture. To locate a Master Gardener program, visit: www.ahsgardening.org/gardening-resources/master-gardeners

Vision Statements and Goal Setting

Older adults want to maintain their independence and view wellness as an avenue that promotes realizing that goal. Health-care professionals often focus on specific physical health goals such as reducing weight or blood pressure, or prescribing specific diets based on a health diagnosis. While these measures of wellness are important, it is essential that older adults develop a vision statement that is centered around their personal desires and visions for the future. Vision statements provide an opportunity to reflect on what one's ideal self would look like. To create a vision statement, older adults should ask themselves the following questions (WellCoaches, 2009):

1. What do I value most in my life? Whom do I want to be?
2. What do I want to accomplish?
3. Why is this vision so important to me?
4. What behaviors do I want to do consistently?
5. Why do I want to accomplish this goal and engage in these behaviors now?
6. What strengths and past successes will support my accomplishment of this goal?
7. Who will help me and support me while I am trying to change my behaviors and achieve my goals?
8. What would I look and feel like if I achieved my ideal level of wellness?
9. What are the most important components of my vision?
10. Think about a time in my life when I felt my best, or I was close to or actually achieving the vision I desire today. Describe that time in detail. What was I doing? Who was supporting me?

After thoroughly answering these questions, older adults should reflect on all of the perceived barriers or challenges that they anticipate in accomplishing the target vision. It is best to write down every possible barrier. After all of the challenges and barriers are identified, older adults should brainstorm several possible solutions to each challenge. During a brainstorm, all options are on the table. Older adults should not overthink options to conquer challenges and emphasize creative solutions to common challenges.

Then, an older adult should draft a vision statement. A vision statement should be one sentence and reflect exactly how they see their future reality and connect their values. Examples of vision statements include:

- *I am socially engaged and happy.*
- *I exercise daily and live a full and independent life.*
- *I thrive on healthy eating, and I lose 10 pounds so that I look amazing in my dress at my granddaughter's wedding.*
- *I attend group fitness classes with my friends and remain fit so I can play with my grandchildren.*

After establishing a vision statement, it is important to put a plan into action. A SMART plan is an evidence-based goal setting framework that promotes the achievement of a goal (Doran, 1981). A SMART goal is specific, measurable, action-oriented, realistic, and time-oriented. To develop a SMART goal, ask the following questions:

1. Specific: what will you do, specifically? Be specific. Identify exactly what you will do, when you will do it, where you will do it, and whom you will do it with.

2. Measurable: how will you measure your progress? Will you write it in a journal? Will you document it on a calendar? Will you enter it in a smart phone?
3. Action-Oriented: use words to set your goal that indicate action. For example, "I will walk." Not, "I will try" or "I may."
4. Realistic: think about where you are now compared to where you want to be and develop a goal that is one step ahead of where you are now. For example, if your ultimate goal is to walk three miles per day every morning at 6 a.m., but currently you sit in a chair all day, a realistic goal would be to wake up at 6 a.m. by setting an alarm for a week. You do not want to start with a three-mile walk because long-term, you are less likely to be successful.
5. Time-Oriented: think about how long you need to work toward each segment of your goal. You can create new SMART goals in intervals. Your first goal could be accomplished in a week or a month. Once you achieve the first part of your goal, you can set another goal. Every goal should have an end point so that you can measure it and determine if it was realistic or not.

Once an older adult has set a SMART goal, it's important to assess his or her motivation and priorities about the goal to ensure that it is well conceived. Scales are an excellent method to assess motivation and priority (Prochaska, DiClemente, & Norcross, 1992). For example, on a scale of 1–10 (10 being the greatest), how motivated are you to accomplish this goal and how much of a priority is this goal in your life today? Why are you the number you identified? Why are you not a higher number? Why are you not a lower number? If the number for either scale is low (below 5), the older adult should reconsider the goal and determine if it is the best goal for him or her at this time and then set a goal that he or she is more motivated and a higher priority to achieve. Sometimes older adults feel pressured to set goals because other people or their providers think they should. Even after they proceed through the entire vision statement process, they still end up with a goal that doesn't align with their values and priorities. The motivation, priority, and confidence rulers are a final check to ensure that the goal is ideal for the older adult.

Conclusion

Wellness is a holistic framework to approach healthy aging. Rural older adults should explore a variety of wellness behaviors in the social, emotional, and physical domains and determine which domains are most important to them. Establishing an effective vision and goal will support their ability to work toward living life to their full potential.

References

Centers for Disease Control and Prevention. (2017). *Are you engaged?* Retrieved from www.cdc.gov/features/social-engagement-aging/index.html

Centers for Disease Control and Prevention. (2019). *Adults need more physical activity*. Retrieved from www.cdc.gov/physicalactivity/inactivity-among-adults-50plus/index.html

Centers for Disease Control and Prevention. (2020). *How much physical activity do older adults need?* Retrieved from www.cdc.gov/physicalactivity/basics/older_adults/index.htm

Doran, G. T. (1981). There's a S.M.A.R.T. way to write management goals and objectives. *Management Review*, *70*(11), 35–36.

Fredrickson, B. L. (2004). The broaden-and-build theory of positive emotions. *Philosophical Transaction of the Royal Society B: Biological Sciences*, *359*(1449), 1367–1378.

Fredrickson, B. L., Mancuso, R. A., Branigan, C., & Tugade, M. M. (2000). The undoing effect of positive emotions. *Motivation and Emotion*, *24*(4), 237–258. doi:10.1023/A:1010796329158

International Council on Aging. (2019). *Active aging and wellness*. Retrieved from www.icaa.cc/activeagingandwellness/wellness.htm

Phelan, E. A., Anderson, L. A., LaCroix, A. Z., & Larson, E. B. (2004). Older adults' views of "successful aging"—How do they compare to researchers definitions? *Journal of American Geriatrics Society*, *52*(2). doi: 10.1111/j.1532-5415.2004.52056.x

Prochaska, J. O., DiClemente, C. C., & Norcross, J. C. (1992). In search of how people change. *American Psychology*, *47*, 1102–1104.

Strout, K. A., David, D. J., Dyer, E. J., Gray, R. C., Robnett, R. C., & Howard, E. P. (2016). Behavioral interventions in six dimensions of wellness that protect the cognitive health of community-dwelling older adults: A systematic review. *Journal of the American Geriatrics Society*, *64*(5), 944–958. doi:10.1111/jgs.14129

Strout, K. A., & Howard, E. P. (2012). The six dimensions of wellness and cognition among older adults. Journal of Holistic Nursing, 30(3), 195–204.

Strout, K. A., & Howard, E. P. (2015). Five dimensions of wellness and predictors of cognitive health protection in community-dwelling older adults: A historical COLLAGE cohort study. *Journal of Holistic Nursing*, *33*(1), 6–18. doi:10.1177/0898010114540322

Tufts University. (2020). *MyPlate for older adults*. Retrieved from https://hnrca.tufts.edu/myplate/

Wang, D., & Glicksman, A. (2013). "Being grounded": Benefits of gardening for older adults in low-income housing. *Journal of Housing for the Elderly*, *27*. doi:10.1080/027638

WellCoaches. (2009). *Chapter 8: Vision, planning, and goals. Coaching psychology manual*. Retrieved from www.wellcoach.com/memberships/images/Chapter-8.pdf

37

HIGHER EDUCATION INSTITUTIONS

Melissa L. Cannon

Introduction

Institutions of higher education in the U.S. are key components of American culture and dominant features in hundreds of towns and cities across the country. The American college town, as Gumprecht (2003) describes, is a "city where a college or university and the cultures it creates exert a dominant influence over the character of the community" (p. 51). College towns have a number of common characteristics, such as relatively youthful, diverse populations, educated workforces, lack of heavy industry, and cultural opportunities, setting them apart as unique types of urban places (Gumprecht, 2003). Because early founders of higher education institutions believed that quiet, rural settings distant from city life were the only proper environments for learning, institutions of higher education are often located in small, rural towns. College and university campuses are largely American inventions (Gumprecht, 2003; Turner, 1984) and are considered high-quality places to live, serving as environments for learning and providing numerous activities for students and staff, as well as community members with no direct connection to the institution (Gumprecht, 2003; Mangan, 1994).

College towns have certain advantages that position them well as retirement destinations. As early as 1990, a book titled *The Future of Baby Boomers and Other Aging Americans* predicted that the baby boomers will work until they are 70 years old and then retire in college towns (Dunn, 1990). College towns typically have commercial districts with abundant business such as coffeehouses, bookstores, and ethnic restaurants that may appeal to retirees. In addition, they have a number of lifelong learning opportunities, athletic activities, and nearness to young people, which many older adults may find appealing. Land-grant universities, in particular, offer a number of opportunities such as impressive sports facilities, concert halls, and museums, and they often include medical schools and health-related colleges. This last point is particularly salient for residents in rural areas; lack of health-care facilities in rural areas has been identified as a problem by most retirees (Hass & Serow, 1993), and the availability of adequate hospitals and health-care facilities in the community or nearby area is one of the primary concerns of most retirees (Hu, Wei, Shlais, & Yeh, 2008).

The Age-Friendly University Movement

As the global population is aging, institutions of higher education are seeking opportunities to embrace age diversity among students, support older workers and retirees, and increase competency around the aging process among their communities. The Age-Friendly University (AFU) Global Network is a recent international effort, pioneered by an interdisciplinary team through Dublin City University and dedicated to embracing the role higher education can play in serving our aging populations. Institutions of higher education join the network by endorsing ten principles associated with becoming an age-friendly university. These principles fall under the domains of six major pillars: teaching and learning; lifelong learning; research and innovation; intergenerational learning; encore careers and enterprise; and civic engagement. The AFU network was launched in 2012 and continues to grow, currently listing over 50 institutional members (Gerontological Society of America, 2020). This movement presents unique opportunities for rural areas, where universities and colleges can engage older adults in the core activities of the institution and use the influence and resources of the institution to support older adults aging-in-place in these communities.

Engaging Rural Older Adults in Core Activities of Institutions of Higher Education

Colleges and universities should be anticipating increasing numbers of older adults enrolled in their programs as the U.S. population ages (Silverstein, Choi, & Bulot, 2001). As stated by Hu et al. (2008): "One of the great benefits of living in a land-grant university or college town is the opportunity to have a life-long learning experience" (p. 59). Lifelong learning has many demonstrated benefits for health and well-being as people age. Narushima, Liu, and Diestelkamp (2018) discussed several studies over the years that have documented positive impacts for older adults participating in lifelong learning, such as on their psychological and physical health, family and social relations, civic engagement, and healthy behaviors (Dolan, Fujiwara, & Metcalfe, 2012; Feinstein, Budge, Vorhaus, & Duckworth, 2008; Field, 2009, 2011; Manninen et al., 2014; Schuller, Preston, Hammond, Brassett-Grundy, & Bynner, 2004).

Many institutions, including those in largely rural states, have found ways to engage older adults in lifelong learning by extending access to college courses through waived or reduced tuition. For example, in South Dakota, older adults (65 years of age or older), who are residents, are eligible to receive a 45% reduction in the cost of tuition at six public universities and special schools (South Dakota Board of Regents, n.d.). The University of Wyoming allows adults 65 years of age and older to enroll in courses on a space-available basis at no cost (University of Wyoming, 2019). The state of Oregon also allows all residents 65 and over to audit courses tuition-free at all public universities (OregonLaws, 2014). Additionally, more than 100 colleges and universities across the U.S. offer continuing education programs for older adults with the support of the OSHER Lifelong Learning Institute (OLLI). These institutions affiliated with OLLI provide an array of non-credit courses and activities for adults aged 50 or older who seek opportunities to be involved in higher education and continue their learning (Bernard Osher Foundation, 2005).

Though many older adults are engaging in lifelong learning for the sake of learning, many are also re-tooling to remain in the labor force. According to the Bureau of Labor Statistics (2019), in 1990, 17.5% of people 65–74 were in the labor force, and by 2026, this is projected to increase to 30%; for people 75–84 of age, 10.8% are projected to be in the labor force by 2026. Many of those in the workforce at older ages are "re-careering" or seeking "encore careers" that focus on both making a living and making a difference in the second half of life (Snyder, 2014). Institutions of higher education can support this trend by providing training and education to those who wish to pursue their next careers. Several foundations and organizations have been established to assist with this. For example, the American Association of Community

Colleges has a "Plus 50 Initiative" to help change the ways that community colleges deliver their programs and services to learners aged 50 years and older; the Lumina Foundation has worked to support older students striving to complete credentials and degrees to help them get hired (Snyder, 2014); and the AARP Foundation's "Back to Work 50+ Initiative" has been connecting community colleges and employment services at over 20 locations throughout the U.S. to support workers 50 and older who are seeking employment (Gerontological Society of America, 2019).

A looming challenge for institutions of higher education will be serving older adults who have such a broad range of educational needs. In rural areas, in particular, over one-third (38.2%) of older people have a high school degree as their highest level of educational attainment. Of those with more than a high school degree, they were more likely to have attained some college or an associate's degree (23.9%) than to have achieved a bachelor's degree or higher (Smith & Trevelyan, 2018). These populations may be especially attracted to colleges and universities to continue their learning and perhaps complete degrees, whereas others may be participating in higher education for other reasons. Additionally, older adults will vary in their learning styles, and those living in rural and remote areas may be best served by online options that are specifically designed for their needs. Overall, institutions of higher education will need to be adaptive in order to respond effectively to the varied learning situations among older adults.

Supporting Rural Older Adults Aging-in-Place

Institutions of higher education extend benefits to older adults living in their communities in other ways as well. For example, by attracting relatively youthful, diverse populations to the community (Gumprecht, 2003), they may enhance the lives of older residents by fostering intergenerational connections. Benefits of intergenerational learning have been widely documented, such as bridging generational divides and cultural values, allowing older generations to pass along wisdom and life experience, and breaking down stereotypes around aging (Heffernan, Cesnales, & Dauenhauer, 2019; Leedahl et al., 2019).

Universities can also support research that focuses on evaluating age-friendly issues in communities, ultimately benefiting residents who are aging-in-place. For example, in the University of Manitoba Centre on Aging's "Age-Friendly Rural and Remote Communities and Places: A Summary Report," Hamilton, Menec, and Bell (2013) identified and analyzed the strengths, weaknesses, opportunities, and threats related to age-friendly rural and remote communities in Canada. The authors discussed the potential for enhanced research funding and student interest in age-friendly issues and engaged communities in active research to understand promising practices, necessary resources, and the value/impact of tools and resources. The University of Manitoba Centre on Aging also developed a guide based on their locally driven and bottom-up participatory approach involving ten focus groups from communities ranging in size from fewer than 600 to approximately 5,000 people. These focus groups were conducted with older adults (aged 60 and over) and informal caregivers of older adults who were not able to participate because of physical or mental impairment. An additional ten focus groups were conducted with service providers from the public, business, and voluntary sectors (University of Manitoba Centre on Aging, 2007). This kind of research can be highly impactful to help understand ways that older adults, caregivers, and service providers in rural communities can be best supported.

Institutions of higher education can also serve as important partners to organizations that support older adults in their communities. Faculty and staff can offer support in a number of ways, including serving on local boards (e.g., faculty serving on a senior center advisory board); advocating (e.g., for continued funding for city-supported positions); directing students to volunteer/internship positions within the organizations; helping with fundraising activities; partnering to extend access to higher education to employees of organizations (e.g., caregivers at long-term care communities); inviting guest speakers as experts in the field (e.g., an ombudsperson who can speak about their role); and bringing in experts from the field as participants at career fairs (e.g., Careers in Aging Week) or to serve as members of an advisory board for a gerontology program.

Conclusion

There are a number of ways that institutions of higher education can support individuals aging in rural communities. These institutions offer a number of benefits to their communities overall and may contribute to these communities establishing themselves as attractive retirement destinations. They often bring services and amenities to communities that would not otherwise exist, including opportunities for lifelong learning and intergenerational connections. As colleges and universities recognize the growing opportunities and challenges associated with an aging world, many are now seeking ways to be more age-friendly, and they are demonstrating exciting trends and opportunities for higher education to engage rural older adults on campus and to extend their influence and support older adults aging-in-place in their communities.

References

The Bernard Osher Foundation. (2005). *Osher Lifelong Learning Institutes*. Retrieved from www.osherfoundation.org/index.php?olli

Bureau of Labor Statistics. (2019). *Labor force participation rate for workers age 75 and older projected to be over 10 percent by 2026*. Retrieved from www.bls.gov/opub/ted/2019/labor-force-participation-rate-for-workers-age-75-and-older-projected-to-be-over-10-percent-by-2026.htm

Dolan, P., Fujiwara, D., & Metcalfe, R. 2012. *Review and update of research into the wider benefits of adult learning*. BIS Research Paper 20, London: Department for Business, Innovation & Skills. Retrieved from www.gov.uk/government/uploads/system/uploads/attachment_data/file/34671/12-1243-review-wider-benefits-of-adult-learning.pdf

Dunn, W. (1990, February 27). Boomers to work for fun, retire with class. *USA Today*, p. A1.

Feinstein, L., Budge, D., Vorhaus, J., & Duckworth, K. (Eds.). (2008). *The social and personal benefits of learning: A summary of key research findings*. London: Centre for Research on the Wider Benefits of Learning, Institute of Education.

Field, J. (2009). *Well-being and happiness*. Inquiry into the future for lifelong learning. Leicester: Thematic Paper 4, National Institute of Adult Continuing Education. Retrieved from https://dspace.stir.ac.uk/bitstream/1893/16487/1/IFLL-wellbeing.pdf

Field, J. (2011). Adult learning, health and well-being—changing lives. *Adult Learner (0790–8084)*, 13–25. Retrieved from http://hdl.handle.net/1893/15658

The Gerontological Society of America. (2019). Higher education and aging: The age-friendly movement. *What's hot: A newsletter of the gerontological society of America*. Retrieved from www.geron.org/images/gsa/documents/WhatsHotAgeFriendly.pdf

The Gerontological Society of America. (2020). *Age-Friendly University (AFU) global network*. Retrieved from www.geron.org/programs-services/education-center/age-friendly-university-afu-global-network

Gumprecht, B. (2003). The American college town. *Geographical Review*, *93*(1), 51–80. doi:10.1111/j.1931-0846.2003.tb00020.x

Hamilton, J., Menec, V., & Bell, S. (2013). *Age-friendly rural and remote communities and places: Summary report*. International Invited Symposium. Winnipeg, MB: Centre on Aging, University of Manitoba. Retrieved from https://pdfs.semanticscholar.org/d287/b6b5b77e7b20b0abfb26e7a4cbd8bf5d0669.pdf

Hass, W. H., & Serow, W. J. (1993). Amenity retirement migration process: A model and preliminary evidence. *The Gerontologist*, *33*, 212–220. doi:10.1080/02763890802096963

Heffernan, K., Cesnales, N., & Dauenhauer, J. (2019). Creating intergenerational learning opportunities in multigenerational college classrooms: Faculty perceptions and experiences. *Gerontology & Geriatrics Education*. doi:10.1080/02701960.2019.1613235

Hu, S. M., Wei, C. I., Shlais, M. R., & Yeh, J. M. (2008). The potential of a college town as a retirement community. *Journal of Housing for the Elderly*, *22*(1–2), 45–65. doi:10.1080/02763890802096963

Leedahl, S. N., Brasher, M. S., Estus, E., Breck, B. M., Dennis, C. B., & Clark, S. C. (2019). Implementing an interdisciplinary intergenerational program using the Cyber Seniors® reverse mentoring model within higher education. *Gerontology & Geriatrics Education*, *40*(1), 71–89. doi:10.1080/02701960.2018.1428574

Mangan, K. S. (1994, January 19). Retiring to alma mater. *Chronicle of Higher Education*, §A, 31.

Manninen, J., Sgier, I., Fleige, M., Thone-Geyer, B., Kil, M., Mozina, E., . . . Operti, F. (2014). *Benefits of lifelong learning in Europe: Main results of the BeLL-Project research report*. Retrieved from www.alice.ch/fileadmin/user_upload/alicech/dokumente/sveb/projekte/BELL_RESEARCH_REPORT_310514_Final.pdf

Narushima, M., Liu, J., & Diestelkamp, N. (2018). Lifelong learning in active ageing discourse: Its conserving effect on wellbeing, health and vulnerability. *Ageing and Society*, *38*(4), 651–675. doi:10.1017/S0144686X16001136

OregonLaws. (2014). 2013 ORS 351.658: Waiver of tuition for Oregon residents at least 65. *OregonLaws.org*. Retrieved from www.oregonlaws.org/ors/2013/351.658

Schuller, T., Preston, J., Hammond, C., Brassett-Grundy, A., & Bynner, J. (Eds.). (2004). *The benefit of learning*. London: Routledge Falmer.

Silverstein, N. M., Choi, L. H., & Bulot, J. J. (2001). Older learners on campus. *Gerontology & Geriatrics Education*, *22*, 13–30.

Smith, A. S., & Trevelyan, E. (2018). *The older population in rural America: 2012–2016*. Washington, DC: ACS-41, American Community Survey Reports, U.S. Census Bureau. Retrieved from www.advancingstates.org/sites/nasuad/files/acs-41.pdf

Snyder, P. (2014). *Older workers*. Grantmakers in Aging. Retrieved from www.giaging.org/issues/older-workers/

South Dakota Board of Regents. (n.d.). *Reduced tuition—persons 65 years of age and older*. Retrieved from www.sdbor.edu/student-information/Pages/Reduced-Tuition-65-or-older.aspx

Turner, P. V. (1984). *Campus: An American planning tradition*. Cambridge, MA: MIT Press.

University of Manitoba Centre on Aging. (2007). *Age-friendly rural and remote communities: A guide*. Document prepared for the Healthy Aging and Wellness Working Group of the Federal/Provincial/Territorial (F/P/T) Committee of Officials (Seniors). Retrieved from www.gov.mb.ca/seniors/afmb/docs/AFRRC_en.pdf

University of Wyoming. (2019). *University catalog*. Retrieved from www.uwyo.edu/registrar/university_catalog/admiss_other.html

38
HOME HEALTH CARE

Sandy Nesin

Defining Home Health Care

There is a dizzying array of ways to define home health care in the U.S. today. For the purposes of this entry, home health care refers to those services provided through use of licensed health-care workers (registered nurses, certified nurse assistants, physical therapists, occupational therapists, speech therapists, medical social workers, etc.) designed to meet the needs of home-bound and community-based patients. Many home health-care agencies are dually licensed to provide hospice services to care for those with terminal illness. Dually licensed agencies often allow for greater continuity of care for those who may experience a decline in health status while home health-care services are being provided. In rural and aging areas of the country, where demand is high and resources are scarce, agencies providing both home health and hospice care often rely on cross-trained teams and clinicians to meet both the home health care and the end of life care needs of their communities.

Across the country, there has been a dramatic shift in demographics during the past decade. This is particularly true in rural areas (U.S. Census Bureau, 2019). In addition to a rapidly aging population, rural home health-care patients have been found to have higher acuity health-care needs and poorer overall health status. A 2014 study found rural home health-care patients more likely to be severely ill, have more risk factors for hospitalization, and more often need respiratory treatments and therapies than their urban counterparts. (Probst et al., 2014). This study serves to highlight one of the greatest challenges we face in health care today: Ensuring adequate and consistent access to care for aging adults in rural America, many of whom seek to manage their care as independently as possible, and from the comfort and safety of their homes. This can be accomplished through continued evolution and expansion of home health-care delivery to allow for the maximization of its full potential within the health-care delivery system.

Predictions for the Future of Home Health Care

Demand for Home Health-Care Services Will Continue to Climb

In 2015, the Medicare Payment Advisory Commission (MedPAC) projected that Medicare enrollment would increase by more than 50% over the next 15 years—from 54 million to nearly

80 million in 2030. (The Medicare Payment Advisory Commission, 2015). As of 2020, Medicare enrollment hovers around 68 million, which represents a significant outpacing of the initial predictions in growth. According to the U.S. Census, the proportion of the nation's residents older than 65 will have nearly doubled from 2010 to 2030, with 20% of the overall population expected to be older than 65 in 2030—a benchmark already surpassed by many of the more rural areas and states across the country. (U.S. Census Bureau, 2014).

As American life expectancy increases, so, too, do the number of older adults living with multiple chronic conditions. The National Council on Aging (NCOA) estimates that 80% of older adults (those 65 or older) have at least one chronic disease, while 77% have at least two (National Council on Aging, 2020). The aging of the U.S. population provides compelling motivation for necessary changes in health care to meet the forthcoming demand. In doing so, it may present an opportunity to transform the ways in which home health care is currently delivered.

Home Health Care Will Become Technology-Enabled

As technology continues to change the delivery of health care across the care continuum, it will be necessary for the home health-care industry to adapt accordingly. For patients residing in rural areas, telehealth can meaningfully expand access to care by bringing health care to patients in their homes, eliminating the distance between providers and their patients. Technology can provide important enhancements in care, allowing for routine connection with care delivery teams and telehealth visits with otherwise hard to access specialist care providers. However, in the many rural areas, internet connectivity serves as a limiting factor, often complicating if not entirely inhibiting the ability of the care delivery team to provide the patient with remote care and monitoring equipment. It will be critical that broadband internet or Wi-Fi be made available across rural areas to allow for expansion of necessary telehealth services.

The onset of COVID-19 has accelerated adoption of telehealth services and remote monitoring in health care, as providers and home health-care agencies work remotely to support patients in remaining stable in their homes while preventing unnecessary exposures to the highly contagious disease. In addition to allowing for more robust and consistent care delivery to those living in rural areas, telehealth may increasingly be used as a key tool to address the growing issue of demand outpacing human resources available to provide necessary care.

Labor Shortages Will Continue to Challenge the Industry

As demand continues to rise for home health-care services, recruiting and retention of qualified home health-care workers continues to challenge the industry. The average turnover rate for home health-care agencies ranges between 40% and 67%. (Home Care Pulse, 2018). A 2018 market research survey conducted by Home Care Pulse found that turnover of staffing in the industry was so severe that more than 50% of the responding home health-care agencies had to decline patients referred to them for care because they did not have sufficient staffing (Home Care Pulse, 2018). Home health-care workforce issues are especially acute in rural areas, where growing numbers of the workforce are nearing retirement. Job development opportunities also tend to be more limited in rural communities with less health-care infrastructure, which results in more generalized care delivery and further inhibits opportunities for advancement through specialization.

Wage pressure from companies competing for lower-wage workers may result in a further labor crunch for some of the lower paid home health-care team members such as home health aides (CNAs), as home health-care workers opt for retail and food service positions that offer comparable wages and a reprieve from the often more demanding and high stress work of providing care. It will be critical for home health-care agencies to focus on opportunities for recruitment and retention of necessary team members. This can be accomplished by introducing unique opportunities for meaningful growth in their work, allowing for opportunities for advancement and commensurate salary adjustments, and addressing the common misconception of home health care as a lower, less clinical setting of care.

Home Health Care Will Continue to Become More Specialized

As the industry works to combat labor shortages and address recruitment and retention challenges, many home health-care agencies have deployed a strategy of launching specialized care programs. In doing so, the agencies are working to meaningfully shift the perception of home health care from non-skilled, lower value care to specialized patient-centered care programs. Specialized care programs now marketed by home health-care agencies include heart failure, COPD, dementia, and orthopedic surgery recovery programs. Opportunities remain for home health agencies providing care in rural areas to introduce specialized care programs tailored to meet the unique needs of their communities. For example, specialized care programs aimed at addressing substance use disorder, a disease of high prevalence in many rural communities, may become more commonplace over the next few years. In addition to helping aid in attraction and retention of clinicians, these specialized care programs often serve to drive profitability through market capture. Furthermore, home health agencies able to highlight established specialized care programs with demonstrated results in improving patient outcomes may be rewarded with unique opportunities to collaborate with Medicare Advantage plans. As Medicare Advantage plans look to better control costs, there is a natural opportunity to partner with home health-care agencies to keep their members at home and out of higher cost settings of care, like the hospital.

While specialized care programs represent a step in the right direction, the home health-care industry will need to continue to evolve in development of capabilities to treat higher acuity community-based patients with ever-growing complexity in their care needs. To do so, funding will need to transition from a traditional fee-for-service model to a more robust value-based model, aimed at providing incentives and necessary reimbursement for such evolution in care delivery.

Home Health Care Will Become a Well-Recognized and Valued Component of Value-Based Care Arrangements

Traditionally, Medicare has provided fee-for-episode reimbursements to home health-care agencies; meaning, agencies receive payment for the care provided. This model does not adequately provide incentives for high-quality, well-coordinated, and lower cost care and largely does not provide reimbursement for services that are essential to providing patient-centered care such as telehealth and care coordination work. Home health-care agencies working diligently to coordinate care across the care continuum through the use of telehealth and remote monitoring services, or who otherwise provide a positive and patient-centered experience are generally reimbursed the same amount as those delivering care without such deliberate efforts and advancements in care delivery. As the financial viability of the American health-care delivery system hangs in the balance because of the rapidly growing and poorly controlled costs of care delivery, value-based payment arrangements grow in importance. Home health-care provides a unique care model able to substantially improve patient outcomes while reducing the overall cost of care of those served. It serves as an opportunity to meaningfully shift the site of care to the lowest cost delivery setting (the home), while eliminating expensive and often avoidable inpatient or skilled nursing facility stays.

Additionally, there are opportunities for home health-care agencies to partner with accountable care organizations and other health-care organizations focused on providing evidence-based population health management. The home health-care agency infrastructure and team could be leveraged to provide necessary population health management aimed at improving patient outcomes while reducing cost of care. For example, home health-care clinicians and team members could provide in-home support in the form of education and evaluation of important self-management skills for patients and caregivers, while serving as an in-home extension of the primary care delivery team, focused collectively on enabling patients and caregivers to successfully manage their care within the community.

Conclusion

The home health-care industry is designed and well-positioned to meet the health needs of our country's aging population in rural areas. However, further evolution of the industry will be necessary to meet the ever-growing demand for services. Home health-care agencies will need to work to ensure their care delivery teams are empowered and extended, both in terms of overall capacity and service area reach, through the use of technology. It is only with significant technological adoption and advancements aimed at extending the often-limited available workforce and service areas that the industry will be able to meet future volume demands for care in rural areas. Specialized care programs will need to be more intentionally developed to meet the unique needs of rural communities, while allowing for professional advancement opportunities for members of the home health-care workforce in rural areas. Finally, the home health-care industry will need to enhance their capabilities to treat higher acuity patients in collaboration with other interested parties (payers, providers, and hospitals). Such engagement and collaboration across the care continuum will allow for the progression from traditional fee-for-service models toward value-based models of care, better aimed at providing incentives and reimbursement for advancements in care necessary to meet future demands. Our success in meeting these challenges will help to ensure people living in rural America have access to necessary care and an opportunity to age with dignity in a manner that meets their expectations, preferences, and individual care needs.

References

Home Care Pulse. (2018). *The 2018 Home Care Benchmarking Study*. Retrieved from www.homecarepulse.com/articles/home-care-pulse-releases-2018-home-care-benchmarking-study/

The Medicare Payment Advisory Commission. (2015). *Report to the Congress: Medicare and the health care delivery system*. Retrieved from www.medpac.gov/docs/default-source/reports/chapter-2-the-next-generation-of-medicare-beneficiaries-june-2015-report-.pdf?sfvrsn=0

National Council on Aging. (2020). *Healthy aging facts*. Retrieved June 9, 2020, from www.ncoa.org/resources/fact-sheet-healthy-aging/

Probst, J. C., & Bhavsar, G. P. (2014). *Differences in case-mix between rural and urban recipients of home health care*. South Carolina Rural Health Research Center. Retrieved from https://www.ruralhealthresearch.org/publications/936

United States Census Bureau. (2014). *Fueled by aging baby boomers, nation's older population to nearly double in the next 20 years, Census Bureau reports*. Retrieved from www.census.gov/newsroom/press-releases/2014/cb14-84.html

United States Census Bureau. (2019). *In some states, more than half of older residents live in rural areas*. Retrieved from www.census.gov/library/stories/2019/10/older-population-in-rural-america.html#:~:text=More%20than%201%20in%205,to%2013.8%25%20in%20urban%20areas

39
HOMELESSNESS

Joy Moses

In different parts of the world, a variety of contexts, and the mouths of diverse actors, homelessness is often associated with the concept of invisibility. Individual characteristics, geography, and other elements may factor into invisibility.

There are reasons why people experiencing homelessness in rural areas may go unseen. First, this group is relatively small. They only account for 18% of people experiencing homelessness nationally. Second, fewer Americans see rural homelessness on a daily basis—such communities are less populated and less dense than major cities.

Older homeless adults fall into the blind spots of some. Aspects of public discourse and policymaking focus on other subgroups (families with children or young/middle-age adults able to work their way out of homelessness). Lost in such contexts are those growing too old to work and in need of higher-level services. Shining a light on the overlapping group of older homeless adults in rural America is key to ensuring that they are not invisible. It is also the first step toward better addressing their needs.

By the Numbers

Data and research on homeless subpopulations are limited. A significant source is the Annual Homeless Assessment Report (AHAR) published by the Department of Housing and Urban Development (HUD). The agency tracks people living in shelters by age and location.

Notable trends are tied to people 62 and over. Since 2007, group members living in rural and suburban homeless shelters have more than doubled, growing by 157%. By contrast, cities only experienced a 48% increase among this group.

Growth has been significant, but the number of people is relatively small. Throughout 2017, only 18,157 people aged 62 (and over) stayed in rural and suburban shelters. Almost all (99%) were living on their own. This should be a manageable number of people to serve.

Unfortunately, the group just behind them on the age scale tends to be much larger. In 2017, there were 62,308 people aged 51 to 61 who stayed in rural and suburban shelters. Failure to stabilize this group could lead them to be homeless in their 60s and older. Research points to another reason to focus on this group. People experiencing homelessness age faster. Those who are 50+ have medical conditions typically found in patients who are 65+ (Brown et al., 2016).

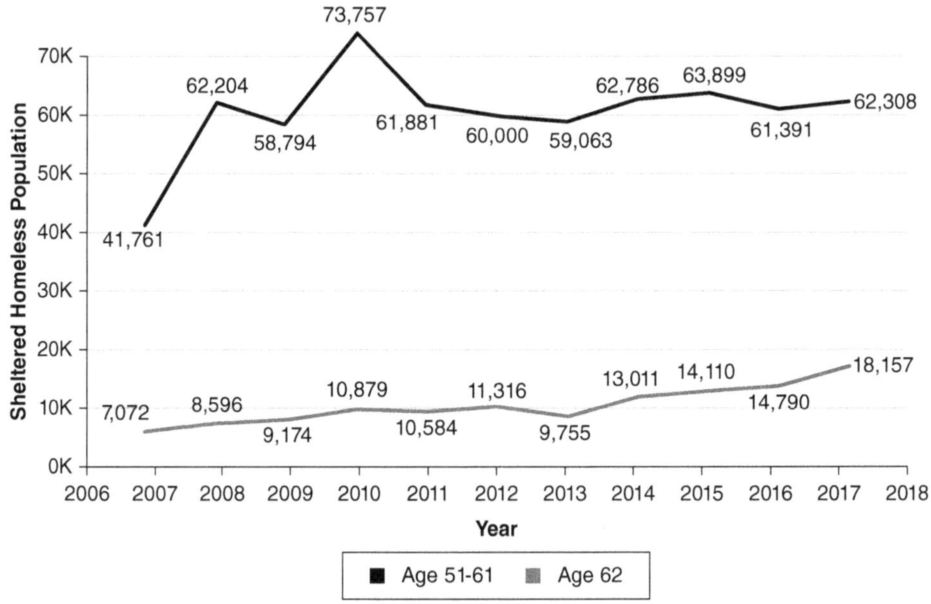

Figure 39.1 Rural/Suburban Sheltered Homelessness (by Age Group)

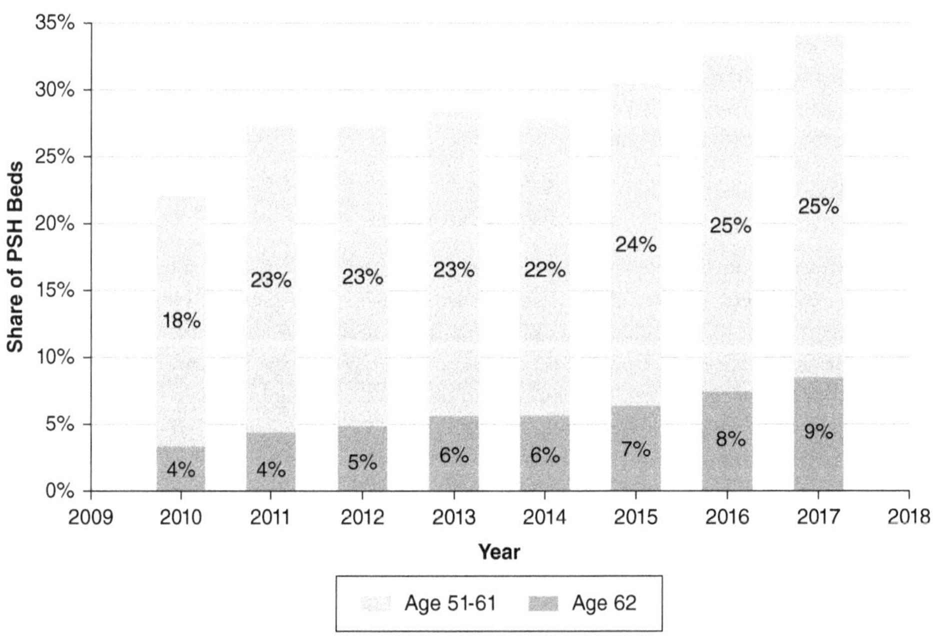

Figure 39.2 Age Group Shares of PSH Beds in Rural/Suburban Areas

Doctors have been urging earlier age screenings for challenges with walking, vision, hearing, falls, frailty, depression, and urinary incontinence.

None of these numbers account for people living unsheltered—in the woods, campgrounds, vehicles, abandoned structures, or other locations. The primary way the nation assesses the size of this group is through a Point-in-Time Count, which is a literal count of homeless people on a pre-scheduled day in January. This effort indicates that 41% of all people (all ages) experiencing homelessness in rural areas are unsheltered.

Additional Demographics

There is so much more to learn about homeless aging adults in rural areas. For instance, beyond their age, who are they and where do they live?

Many are veterans. Among those who are 51 and over and experiencing homelessness in rural/suburban areas, 25% are former military (HUD, 2007–2018). Veteran status is a significant identity in a society that values those who have served their country, but it is also relevant to exits from homelessness. These men and women are eligible for targeted supports from the U.S. Department of Veterans Affairs.

Additional clues shed light on the identities of those who are homeless and aging in rural America. HUD publishes general data on rural communities (which are not disaggregated by age). White people are a clear majority of the homeless population, with the full racial and ethnic breakdown being (Moses, 2019):

- White (71%)
- Black (17%)
- Hispanic (of any race) (14%)
- Multiracial (6%)
- Native American (5%)
- Pacific Islander (1%)
- Asian (0%).

Women are 34% of individual adults experiencing homelessness in rural areas. This figure is elevated compared to cities and the suburbs (Moses & Janosko, 2019). Women in those communities are only 27–28% of individual adults (Moses & Janosko, 2019).

Rural Landscapes: Physically Vast and Sparsely Populated

Across America, communities are wrestling with a lack of affordable housing, low wages, and an insufficient availability of services for those who need them. These factors contribute to homelessness. Rural areas face some additional and unique challenges that contribute to elder homelessness. Vast physical landscapes that are sparsely populated complicate efforts to locate, count, and serve older adults experiencing homelessness.

Annually, volunteers and workers go out into their communities to locate and count unsheltered people. In rural areas, there are typically far more square miles to search. Unlike in cities, there may not be any (or as many) centralized locations where people experiencing homelessness gather or receive services. For these reasons, rural areas are likely undercounting the population. Agencies that fall short in locating people may not fully understand the nature of homelessness in their communities. This makes it more challenging to craft solutions and to ensure those solutions reach those who need them.

Rural homeless services stand in stark contrast to those in cities. The differences are rooted in population size. With far more people to serve, cities often have multiple service providers covering a wide spectrum of needs—shelters targeting different subpopulations, permanent housing programs, street outreach, drop-in centers, meal programs, and school-based services. Urban areas also have more resources. Government funds often increase according to population size. And more citizens mean more people and/or businesses paying taxes and making donations. Rural homeless systems, with fewer consumers and resources, have far less infrastructure.

Other services are limited in rural communities for similar reasons (vast territories with sparse populations). One of them, transportation, significantly complicates access to services for people who are homeless or at-risk of homelessness (*see* HUD, 2017a). Consumers may have to travel great distances to reach centralized locations offering services. This could mean walking, trying to get a ride from someone with a car, catching multiple but infrequently running buses, and scraping together enough change to pay for such transportation. And, in rural areas, fewer nontraditional options like ride-share services may be available.

Alternatively, if consumers can't physically get to helpful services, the services must come to them. Providers must have the resources and staff time to travel across potentially vast territory to reach all those in need.

Transportation concerns become more complicated when the targeted group is older adults. Limitations in physical mobility and cognitive decline can impact a consumer's ability to get from point A to point B. Aging-related health challenges increase necessary doctor visits and trips to the hospital. Thus, aging adults may have more significant transportation needs. Those in rural areas may have fewer options for meeting those needs.

Homelessness and Housing Resources

There are resources available to tackle older adult homelessness in rural America. Homeless services systems offer various housing options throughout the country. In recent years, providers have been steadily increasing investments in permanent housing solutions. While emergency shelter was the most popular form of assistance a little over a decade ago, that title now belongs to permanent supportive housing (PSH) (National Alliance to End Homelessness, 2019).

PSH is affordable housing paired with support services. Ideally, residents spend no more than 30% of their income on rent (Corporation for Supportive Housing, 2013). Service offerings address challenges that hinder housing stability. Case management is typically available. Other common services include physical and mental health services, substance abuse treatment, and employment supports.

PSH is relevant to older adults. Institutionalization (nursing homes) should only be for those who absolutely need it. Many older adults can age-in-place within communities. They may simply require a little help—services offered through PSH can be that help.

Nationally, homeless services systems are actively serving older adults in PSH. It is revealing to focus on this population, the group of people not living in families. Among individuals in PSH, 57% are 51 and over (HUD, 2007–2018).

Rural and suburban communities contribute to this status quo. Since 2010, they have grown the number of older adults in PSH by 142% (HUD, 2007–2018). The share of beds going to 51- to 61-year-olds has been holding steady, but a greater and greater share of beds are going to people 62 and over.

Beyond homeless services, various housing programs are relevant to ending older adult homelessness in rural areas (see next table). They include the following:

Programs	*Target Population*	*Additional Information*
Rent Subsidies		
⋆Housing Choice Vouchers	Very low-income families, older adults, and the disabled.	This program is the largest source of federal housing help for older adults.
⋆Section 521	Rural residents with very low-, low-, and moderate incomes who are living in Section 515 or farmworker housing units.	34% of households are elderly.
Development—Land Purchase, Construction, and/or Rehabilitation		
⋆Section 515	Rural residents with very low-, low-, and moderate-incomes.	33% of units go to older adult households.
⋆Section 811	Very low- and extremely low-income adults with disabilities.	Provides supportive housing units.
Hybrid—Rent Subsidies plus Development		
⋆Section 202	Very low-income older adults.	20–25% of funds are set-aside for nonmetropolitan areas.
⋆Housing Trust Fund	Extremely low-income households.	Older adults are a target population in many states, with an estimated 16% of 2016-funded units going to this group.

Sources: Flores, 2017; USDA, 2019; Housing Assistance Council, 2014; Gramlich, 2018.

Future Considerations

A collection of powerful forces will shape the future of older adult rural homelessness. An issue that drives conversations across multiple policy circles is the aging of the baby boomer generation. They began turning 65 in 2011. Nationwide, the 65+ population is projected to nearly double between 2016 and 2060 (U.S. Census Bureau, 2017). This shift will be particularly relevant to rural communities. Their residents tend to be older. People 65 and over are more likely to be in rural communities than urban ones (Pendall, 2016). And this pattern is projected to continue into future years.

There are reasons to believe that some older adults will experience housing challenges. HUD tracks households with "worst case housing needs," which means they 1. have very low incomes, 2. do not receive housing assistance, and 3. have either severe rent burdens or severely inadequate housing (or both). The number of such households has been increasing in recent years. More than one in three very low-income renters in rural areas have worst case housing needs (HUD, 2017b). Of this group, 140,000 were older adults without children.

These housing needs coincide with housing stock challenges. Although rural areas are expected to have continued sluggish population growth, the Urban Institute projects an increased demand for housing. Reasons include people living longer and unusually old housing stock needing to be replaced or refurbished. In 2013, 63% of homes in nonmetropolitan areas were built before 1980 (Pendall, 2016). Some old homes fall into disrepair and become uninhabitable.

Certain demand concerns are explicitly tied to affordable housing. Development and rehabilitation programs (Section 515, Section 202, and Section 811) offer low-cost loans. Once the loans are paid off, owners are no longer obligated to rent their units at affordable prices. Over the years, advocates have sounded the alarm—these units have, and will, disappear from the low-cost housing market. Impacts felt now will continue into the future.

Additionally, multiple affordable housing programs have struggled in the federal appropriations process. For instance, Section 515 funds are less than half of what they were in the early 2000s (Strauss, 2019). And Section 202 lacked funds for new construction between 2010 and 2019—nearly a decade (National Low Income Housing Coalition, 2019).

To Do

When a challenge is invisible, a necessary first step is to shed light on it. Raising awareness about rural homelessness, older adult homelessness, and Americans at the intersection between both groups is critical. Various actors must play a role, including advocates, journalists, policymakers, and researchers.

The last group often focuses its efforts on urban communities. More research is needed to determine the extent to which such conclusions extend to people in rural areas. For instance, are people experiencing homelessness in rural communities aging at the same rate as their urban counterparts? How are personal challenges similar or different? Do interventions that have been proven in cities also work in rural areas?

An analysis of the amount of funding necessary to end homelessness and housing instability among rural older adults would also be helpful. This should be paired with an assessment of existing resources that includes all relevant government programs. Is America coming up short? By how much? Although such an effort seems simple, it relies on multiple variables and could be complicated. However, it would help in developing a plan to resolve this national challenge.

In the meantime, efforts must aim to shore up available resources. Programs like Housing Choice Vouchers and Sections 202, 811, 515, and 521 must not be allowed to languish. Constant vigilance over congressional appropriations is required.

Resources and fortitude are required to see through the creation and implementation of effective solutions for our nation's elders.

References

Brown, R. T., Hemati, K., Riley, E. D., Lee, C. T., Ponath, C., Tieu, L., Guzman, D., and Kushel, M. B. (2016). Geriatric conditions in a population-based sample of older homeless adults. *The Gerontologist, 57*(4), 757–766.

Corporation for Supportive Housing. (2013). *Dimensions of quality supportive housing*. Retrieved from https://d155kunxf1aozz.cloudfront.net/wp-content/uploads/2015/12/IL_Toolkit_Models_Combined.pdf

Flores, L. (2017). *Housing vouchers work: Helping seniors, people with disabilities afford homes that meet their needs.* Washington, DC: Center on Budget and Policy Priorities.

Gramlich, E. (2018). *Getting started: First homes being built with 2016 national Housing Trust Fund awards.* Washington, DC: National Low Income Housing Coalition.

Housing Assistance Council. (2014). *Housing an aging rural America: Rural seniors and their homes*. Washington, DC: Housing Assistance Council.

Moses, J. (2019). *Demographic data project: Race, ethnicity, and homelessness.* Washington, DC: National Alliance to End Homelessness.

Moses, J., & Janosko, J. (2019). *Demographic data project: Gender and individual homelessness.* Washington, DC: National Alliance to End Homelessness.

National Alliance to End Homelessness. (2019). *State of homelessness*. Retrieved from https://endhomelessness.org/homelessness-in-america/homelessness-statistics/state-of-homelessness-report/

National Low Income Housing Coalition. (2019). *HUD announces Section 202 Capital Advance NOFA*. Washington, DC: National Low Income Housing Coalition.

Pendall, R., Goodman, L., Zhu, J., & Gold, A. (2016). *The future of rural housing*. Washington, DC: Urban Institute.

Strauss, L. (2019). *USDA rural rental housing programs*. Washington, DC: National Low Income Housing Coalition.

U.S. Census Bureau. (2017). *2017 national population projections tables*. Retrieved from www.census.gov/data/tables/2017/demo/popproj/2017-summary-tables.html

U.S. Department of Agriculture. (2019). *Multi-family housing occupancy statistics*. Retrieved from http://ruralhome.org/storage/documents/rd_obligations/mfh-occupancy/occupancymfh2018.pdf

U.S. Department of Housing and Urban Development. (2007–2018). *Annual homeless assessment report*. Retrieved from www.hudexchange.info/homelessness-assistance/ahar/#2018-reports

U.S. Department of Housing and Urban Development. (2017a). *Housing challenges of rural seniors*. Retrieved from www.huduser.gov/portal/periodicals/em/summer17/highlight3.html

U.S. Department of Housing and Urban Development. (2017b). *Worst case housing needs 2017 report to Congress*. Washington, DC: U.S. Department of Housing and Urban Development.

40
HOUSING

Robyn I. Stone

The State of Housing for Older Adults Living in Rural Communities

Housing Tenure

A little less than one in five homeowners aged 65 and older and 14% of elderly renters lived in rural locations in 2017 (Joint Center for Housing Studies, 2019). Homeownership is more prevalent among rural older adults than their urban peers; over 83% of the housing units headed by individuals aged 65 and older in rural communities are owner-occupied compared to 79% of all elderly households across the country. Almost one-half of the increase in homeowner households headed by an older adult occurred in rural areas between 2000 and 2017 (Joint Center for Housing Studies, 2019). One-third of the increase in rental households headed by an older adult occurred in rural areas and the number of older renters in low-density areas outpaced the increase in high-density areas.

Housing Type

Single-family, detached homes make up most of the housing stock in rural communities with a little less than four out of five rural elderly homeowners living in this type of housing. The rural housing stock is older than that of the nation as a whole—as of 2013, 63% of rural homes were built before 1980 (Pendall, Goodman, Zhu, & Gold, 2016). These homes tend to be located on relatively large parcels of land; in 2009, the median size of a lot outside of a metropolitan area was 44,000 square feet compared with 14,000 square feet for all older adult homeowners nationwide.

Manufactured housing is an important low-cost residential option for many rural older adults. As of 2005, nearly two-thirds of all manufactured housing residences were built in rural areas of the country (Housing Assistance Council, 2016). The percentage of older adults living in this type of housing was higher in rural areas (11.1%) than among the older population across the country (8.5%).

Living Arrangements

Rural older adults are more likely than their urban counterparts to be living with others; 22.3% of people aged 65 and older in rural communities live alone compared with 27.6% of their peers in urban areas (Smith & Trevelyan, 2019). Older women who live alone account for almost 31% of all rural older adult households; the comparable estimate for men is 13%. Significantly fewer rural older adults (1.4%) live in nursing homes compared with their urban peers (3.1%). Factors explaining this geographic disparity in nursing home use include the emotional attachment that many rural older adults have to their homes and resistance to move to another setting when they need a higher level of care, limited availability of nursing homes in their communities, and the travel distance that is required for a family member to visit following a nursing home transfer.

Housing Challenges

Older adults in rural areas face many of the same challenges as those in urban and suburban areas, but in many cases those challenges are exacerbated by differences in demographics, economic conditions, infrastructure, and density.

Quality of the Housing Stock

Because of the age of the housing stock in rural America, older homeowners often face greater maintenance and repair requirements than their urban peers. Heating, ventilation, and air conditioning units typically last 15 to 25 years and shingle roofs last 20 years. Although the quality of manufactured housing has improved over the years (Joint Center for Housing Studies, 2019), older adults living in this type of housing are likely to reside in older units that result in many maintenance challenges for this subset of homeowners.

Older single-family homes are not likely to have features that are adaptable to the needs of an aging population. Many were built on multiple levels with steep stairways, narrow halls and doorways, dated electrical systems and hazardous bathrooms. Units owned by older adults are less likely than rental units, particularly those in publicly subsidized properties, to have universal design features including residential quarters on one floor, grab bars in bathrooms, and age-friendly door knobs and handles (Joint Center for Housing Studies, 2019). Simple measures, such as installing grab bars in bathrooms and railings on both sides of stairs, improving lighting in the home, and building ramps to improve access to the outside, could go a long way toward preventing falls and assisting older adults to remain in their homes. However, the price tag for these modifications is way beyond the budgets of many low-income older homeowners and all financially strapped older renters (Bipartisan Policy Center, 2016).

Inadequate housing poses major falls and other health-related risks to rural older adults. States with significant rural populations (e.g., Mississippi, West Virginia, Arkansas, and Kansas) tend to have the highest proportion of disabled older residents (Smith & Trevelyan, 2019). The combination of poor housing and increasing functional impairment is a recipe for negative health outcomes and costly health-care use including hospitalizations.

Housing Affordability

One in ten older residents of rural America lives below the poverty line, a large proportion are near-poor, and their income is lower than that of older adults nationally (HUD, 2017b). Although rural older adults have a high homeownership rate, nearly a quarter of them are still paying off their mortgages. Fifty-four percent of rural older adults who rent their homes are cost burdened (Housing Assistance Council, 2014). While the proportion of older adult renters is higher in urban than rural areas, the highest cost-burden rates among older renters in 2019 were in East Stroudsburg, Pennsylvania, and Lawrence, Kansas—two small towns in rural areas (Joint Center for Housing Studies, 2019).

Rural older adult homeowners face significant housing costs, including property taxes, utility costs, and property insurance. The costs of maintaining the home—particularly those built many years ago—and the large parcels of land surrounding the home add to the financial burden.

Lack of Residential Options to Support Successful Aging in Community

While many rural older adults prefer to "age in place," their communities often lack residential options. Housing-burdened individuals have little access to affordable rental properties, which are more limited in rural than urban areas. Housing, furthermore, is usually located away from shops, services, and other community resources; and given the lack of transportation alternatives, older adults with limited mobility may be largely homebound, making successful aging-in-place more difficult.

Alternative housing structures, such as accessory dwelling units (ADUs) can help older adults of all income levels realize their aspiration to age in their communities. An ADU located on an individual's property and then rented could provide a new stream of income to help finance the older person's retirement or serve as an offset to property taxes. ADUs also represent a potential source of housing for a caregiver to a disabled older adult. Given the fact that the homes of rural older adults are likely to be situated on large parcels of land, the ADU seems to be a viable option for lower-income older adults.

Unfortunately, because of concerns about the negative impact that ADUs and other alternate housing structures might have on housing values and demand for public services, communities impose zoning code overlays, ordinances that create extra requirements beyond simple land-use specifications, before an ADU can be approved. Complying with these overlays can be time-consuming and costly (HUD, 2018).

The Role of Federal Policy in Meeting the Housing Needs of Rural Older Adults

Federal Rental Assistance Programs

Federal rental-assistance programs are a critical source of help for low-income individuals and families, including older adults living in rural areas (Bipartisan Policy Center, 2016). Of the approximately 5.1 million households served by HUD programs, 36% were headed by someone aged 62 years or older (Stone, 2018). Older adults head 24% of the households served by the Housing Choice Voucher program, and they head even greater shares of households in public housing (32%) and the project-based Section 8 program (52%).

More than 60% of the renters assisted by the U.S. Department of Agriculture's (USDA) housing programs are older adults or people with disabilities (Housing Assistance Council, 2016). USDA's Section 515 program, which provides long-term, low-interest loans to support the construction and rehabilitation of multifamily housing, is a major source of funding for housing that serves low- and moderate-income older adults in rural communities. As of 2016, this program had funded almost 14,000 projects and 417,000 units. But Section 515's budget has dwindled over the past several decades, and no new units have been built since 2014.

HUD's Section 202 Supportive Housing for the Elderly program is the only federal rental-assistance program designed explicitly to serve older adults (HUD, 2017a). Since its creation in 1959, the Section 202 program, in partnership with the nation's leading nonprofit housing providers, has helped create nearly 400,000 affordable rental homes for older Americans in developments throughout the U.S.

Today, with federal resources stretched so thin, fewer than one in four households eligible for federal rental assistance receives any support (Joint Center on Housing Studies, 2019). The result is a system in which housing subsidies are allocated by lottery or through ever-growing waiting lists. The 2018 Congressional Appropriations bill provided a modest increase of $105 million for the HUD 202 program, resulting in about 760 new units for older adults. The 2018 bill also expanded eligibility to participate in the Rental Assistance Demonstration (RAD) program to 202 PRAC properties, which helped leverage additional capital for updating distressed properties.

While investments in federally subsidized rental housing has been limited, one policy area is receiving increased attention. Since 2010, HUD and the U.S. Department of Health and Human Services have jointly invested in demonstrations testing the efficacy and impact of housing-based teams (usually a service coordinator and wellness nurse) who engage in a range of prevention, health promotion, care management, and service coordination to help low-income older residents successfully "age-in-place" and reduce Medicare and Medicaid costs (Sanders, Stone, Cohen, Eldridge, & Grabowski, 2019). The Supports and Services at Home (SASH) program—implemented in over 140 housing properties in both urban and rural Vermont communities—was able to slow the growth of Medicare expenditures relative to two control groups over a four-year period and demonstrated reduction in Medicaid spending (Kandilov et al., 2018).

New Construction and Preservation of Affordable Housing

The Low-Income Housing Tax Credit (LIHTC) is the nation's key policy tool supporting new construction and preservation of affordable rental housing (Gudzinas, 2017). It is a capped federal incentive allocated to private developers through state housing finance agencies that receive an annual per capita allocation of credits indexed to inflation. Developers compete for credit awards and properties must be rented to tenants with incomes at or below 60% of the area median income at rents that are capped for a period of at least 30 years. In practice, the program typically serves households below this income threshold.

Since its creation, LIHTC has leveraged approximately $100 billion in private capital, helping to finance the construction and preservation of almost 2.8 million affordable rental homes for low-income families. Nearly one-third of LIHTC households include an older member (62+); 28.6% have a head of household who is an older adult. Some states provide set-asides and other preferences for older adult housing projects. In fact, the LIHTC program supports approximately 40,000 older adult-restricted affordable units annually.

HUD also administers the federally funded National Housing Trust Fund, a modest program that provides grants to states and aims to increase affordable housing. These trust funds serve housing needs of low-income families in nearly all states and more than 400 localities (Gudzinas, 2017).

Low Income Home Energy Assistance Program (LIHEAP)

Since 1981, LIHEAP has awarded grants to states and tribal organizations to provide financial assistance to households with low incomes that pay a high proportion of household income for home energy costs (Office of Community Services, 2018). Grantees can use funds for heating and/or cooling costs as well as up to 15% of their funding (or 25% with a waiver) for weatherization assistance. Average annual benefits range from $100 to $1,200. Emergency benefits are available for those who are at immediate risk of having their utilities turned off, are dangerously low on fuel, or have been impacted by a natural disaster. Requests are approved within 48 hours, with benefits ranging from $25 to $300 a year. According to a 2018 survey conducted by the National Energy Assistance Directors Association (2018), 46% of the 8.9 million households benefiting from this program had one or more older members. The average LIHEAP benefit was quite modest, covering about 50% of home heating costs.

Home Modification Programs

Several federal programs provide support to older adults who choose to modify their homes. Forty-eight out of the 50 states and the District of Columbia offer Medicaid waivers that allow low-income disabled older beneficiaries to purchase assistive devices or to modify their homes to accommodate their changing functional status and to help them avoid nursing home placement. One promising example is Michigan's Community Aging in Place, Advancing Better Living for Elders (CAPABLE) program, developed by researchers at Johns Hopkins University and incorporated into the state's Medicaid waiver. This person-centered, team-based intervention comprises an occupational therapist, a wellness nurse, and a handyman and provides up to ten home visits over a four-month period to qualified older homeowners and renters. A nurse assessment of the individual and physical environment is used to develop a care plan, which includes needed home modifications and assistive devices as well as education by the therapist to help beneficiaries better understand how to navigate and adapt to their home environment. Pilot study results indicate that 79% of the participants improved their self-care, the number of self-care tasks that participants had difficulty with were halved, and participants experienced a decrease in depressive symptoms similar to the decrease associated with antidepressant medication (Szanton, Leff, Wolff, Roberts, & Gitlin, 2016).

The federal government funds several other small programs that support home modifications for older adults, including the USDA's Section 504 home repair program. Grants are capped at $7,500 and loans are limited to $20,000.

Conclusion

With the older adult population poised to expand dramatically over the next 15 years, demand for affordable and accessible housing—both owner-occupied and rental properties—will intensify. The number of older households (aged 60 and above) eligible for federal rental assistance alone will likely increase by 1.3 million between 2011 and 2020, and another 1.3 million between 2020 and 2030 (Joint Center for Housing Studies, 2019). Despite the disproportionate growth of the older population in rural America, the housing challenges facing this subset of older adults have received relatively little attention and investment. Advocates for older adults and affordable housing need to challenge the status quo and encourage policymakers to address this crisis. The public and private sectors must collaborate on the development of new housing models, and researchers need to create an evidence base to support replication and sustainability.

References

Bipartisan Policy Center. (2016). *Healthy aging begins at home*. Report prepared by the Senior Health and Housing Taskforce. Washington, DC: Bipartisan Policy Center.

Gudzinas, B. (2017). *Low-income housing tax credits: Meeting the demand for affordable rental housing*. Fact Sheet #503. Washington, DC: AARP Public Policy Institute.

Housing Assistance Council. (2014). *Housing an aging rural America: Rural seniors and their homes*. Retrieved from www.ruralhome.org/storage/documents/publications/rrreports/ruralseniors2014.pdf

Housing Assistance Council. (2016). *USDA maturing multifamily mortgages*. Retrieved from rpn_maturing-mortgages-usda-2016.pdf

Joint Center for Housing Studies at Harvard University. (2019). *Housing America's Older Adults*. Retrieved from jchs.harvard.edu/sites/default/files/Harvard_JCHS_Americas_Older_Adults_2019.pdf

Kandilov, A., Keyes, V., van Hasselt, M., Sanders, A., Siegfried, N., & Stone, R. (2018). The impact of the Vermont Support and Services at Home program on healthcare expenditures. *CityScape: A Journal of Policy Development and Research*, *20*(2), 7–18.

The National Energy Directors' Association. (2018). *2018 national energy assistance survey final report: Report has been prepared by APPRISE for NEADA with support provided by the National Energy and Utility Affordability Coalition (NEUAC)*. Retrieved from http://neada.org/program-policy-reports/liheapsurvey/

Office of Community Services. (2018). *Low Income Home Energy Assistance Program fact sheet*. Retrieved from www.acf.hhs.gov/ocs/resource/liheap-fact-sheet-0

Pendall, R., Goodman, L., Zhu, S., & Gold, W. (2016). *The future of rural housing*. Research Report. Washington, DC: Urban Institute.

Sanders, A., Stone, R., Cohen, M., Eldridge, N., & Grabowski, D. (2019). *Exploring financing options for services in affordable senior housing communities*. Final Report prepared for the Gordon and Betty Moore Foundation, San Francisco, CA.

Smith, A. J., & Trevelyan, E. (2019). *The older population in rural America*. US. Census Bureau. Retrieved from census.gov/library/stories/2019/10/older-population-in-rural-America.html

Stone, R.I. (2018) The housing challenges of low-income older adults and the role of federal policy, Journal of Aging & Social Policy, 30:3-4, 227-243, DOI: 10.1080/08959420.2018.1462679

Szanton, S. L., Leff, B., Wolff, J. L., Roberts, L., & Gitlin, L. N. (2016). Home-based care program reduces disability and promotes aging in place. *Health Affairs*, *35*(9), 1558–1563.

U.S. Department of Housing and Urban Development (HUD). (2017a, Summer). *Housing for seniors: Challenges and solutions. Evidence Matters*. Office of Policy Development and Research. Retrieved from www.huduser.gov/portal/periodicals/em/summer17/highlight1.html

U.S. Department of Housing and Urban Development (HUD). (2017b, Summer). *Housing challenges of rural seniors*. Evidence Matters, Office of Policy Development and Research. Retrieved from www.huduser.gov/portal/periodicals/em/summer17/highlight3.html

U.S. Department of Housing and Urban Development (HUD). (2018). *Regulatory barriers clearinghouse*. Retrieved from www.huduser.gov/portal/rbc/home.html

41
IMMIGRANTS

Linda Silka

Demographic changes are reshaping America, with many more immigrants now living in the U.S. than in the recent past. Indeed, immigrants have become a major source of population growth and cultural change. From 2005 to 2050, for example, immigrants are projected to contribute 82% of the total increase of the U.S. population (Passel & Cohn, 2008). And, as the Migration Policy Institute notes, since the 1990s, many foreign-born people have been moving to small towns across rural America. Learning about recent immigrants' current residence is possible by way of the Migration Policy Institute's interactive data tools. The Rural Immigration Network (https://ruralimmigration.net/project/foundations-history-of-immigration-to-rural-america/) also points out that rural communities have not been home to new immigrant residents in large numbers since the 1920s when federal laws highly reduced opportunities for immigrants to come to the U.S.

To understand these shifts, rural states such as Iowa, Maine, and North Dakota have become the focus of many analyses and commentaries on the dramatic increase in immigrants and the impact of these changing demographics in rural states (Gimpbel & Lay, 2008; Gouveia, 1997; Lichter, 2012). Numerous books have been written that capture in detail the current changes and how dramatically they are impacting rural areas (Albarracin, 2016; Allegro & Wood, 2013; Cullen, 2018; Gordon, 2015; Lay, 2012; Yang, 2017; Yusuf, 2012).

Movement of immigrant families into rural areas partly reflects changing opportunities such as the availability of jobs and increasing numbers of compatriots from immigrants' home countries in some rural settings. Jobs—illustrated, for example, by shifts in the meatpacking industry to rural areas—have drawn immigrant families to rural towns (Broadway, 2007; Kandel & Parrado, 2005). Employers have encouraged immigrants to recruit family and friends to work at the plants, sometimes including family members. A large increase in culturally distinct immigrant families drawn by new economic opportunities in rural areas has been the result (Massey, 2008).

The result of multiple factors is that more immigrant elders live in rural areas than was the case in the recent past. Even so, it is important to keep in mind that in rural America, immigrant elders represent a new face yet not a new face. This seeming contradiction reflects the failure among many to remember and learn from the past in which much of rural America was settled by diverse immigrants (Adams, 2014; Barkan, 2013; Cantor, 2001). Past immigrants may have arrived from different countries than the older immigrants coming to today's rural settings, but it is important to remain aware that diversity among rural elders is far from new and there might well be much that could be learned from attending to past experiences of diverse older adults in rural communities.

The present demographic shifts are resulting in an increased focus on today's immigrant elders in rural communities and the special challenges they may encounter (Mui & Kang, 2006). A central theme in this growing literature is the importance of recognizing that immigrants are often living between two cultures (Das, 2007). As Silka (2007, 2015) notes, culture infuses every part of daily life. It is important to consider what cultural differences might be especially important to understand in trying to create practices that are effective across a range of cultures. Elder issues are deeply linked to family impact of structures and dynamics. As consideration is given to the impact of families, it will be important to understand what family means in different cultures. What is the role of the elder? What are the expectations for family life? What can be learned when intergenerational relationships are especially valued or take unfamiliar forms? Such questions are beginning to point to the need to envision new policies and approaches.

For policymakers struggling with the many dilemmas of aging-in-place, the perspectives and experiences of immigrants can provide alternative examples. Immigrants can assist us in thinking in expanded ways about nursing homes, assisted living, intergenerational living, support structures, and the role of faith organizations. What form might aging-in-place take in various immigrant communities? What customs, strategies, and ideas have people adopted and which of these could be adapted to U.S. rural settings?

Culture is important in other central ways that have significance in understanding older adult immigrants in rural areas. For example, seeking to understand the elder immigrant experience through the cultural lens of food has been found to be instructive. The food available through food pantries and food-support systems might not be familiar to immigrant families. Family traditions can be at odds with U.S. practices of when and what to eat and who decides all of this. In addition, many immigrants have been found to be unfamiliar with programs such as Meals on Wheels. The food is sometimes found to be inappropriate, for example, heavily emphasizing dairy products for populations with high rates of lactose intolerance. Food both divides and brings cultures together.

Health is also central to much thinking about aging, but here, too, the immigrant aging experience brings new issues to the forefront. With an eye to immigrant experiences, how do we understand aging and mental health issues? What would it mean to take into account health problems in which aging could be linked to the re-emergence of past trauma? Consider that today's immigrants who came here as young people not infrequently came from home countries that were battlegrounds. When they were young, many adapted well to the very different life in the U.S. Yet research is now showing the emergence of post-traumatic stress indicators during the course of growing older (Das, Dubus, & Silka, 2013; Lum & Vanderaa, 2010). Das et al. (2013) show that the experiences of refugees vary across the life course, creating new challenges as refugees grow older after resettlement. Past post-traumatic stress symptoms may emerge as different symptoms years later, with social role changes within the family and stressors triggered by the social environment surrounding the refugees. Refugees have disproportionately high rates of poor mental health related to conflict and resettlement stress as well as high rates of heart disease, hypertension, and type 2 diabetes. The increased risk of chronic disease is likely because of a combination of factors, including trauma from refugee circumstances and resettlement and from lifestyle changes on resettlement. Health care is often limited in rural areas for particular conditions, and these limits on resources add to the challenges immigrants living in rural areas may face.

The Increasingly Used Asset-Based Approaches

Rural areas have too often in the past been identified by what they lack rather than what they offer. A deficit analysis has too often prevailed. Increasingly, new analyses are aimed at understanding the assets and the many kinds of capital that can be found in rural areas and rural communities. A landmark example of this type of analysis is found in the book *Rural Communities* by Flora, Flora, and Gasteyer (2016). Here, the authors analyze in detail the community capital, natural capital, cultural capital, human capital, social capital, political capital, financial capital, and built capital that are available in rural communities. The book essentially provides a framework that could suggest ways that diverse older adults, including immigrant elders, may add capital to the rural regions in which they make their homes. Turcotte and Silka (2007) have suggested how a social capital analysis can be useful for understanding the opportunities that may emerge with older immigrants.

In short, recent analyses are moving more toward asset-based analyses that, while not ignoring the challenges to be found in rural settings, guide attention to the resources in rural areas that can be the basis for addressing some of the not infrequently found challenges. In the end, older immigrants may bring different forms of social capital that can help us all learn about strategies for exploring the aging experience in multiple productive ways.

References

Adams, B. (2014). *Old and new New Englanders: Immigration and regional identity in the gilded age*. Ann Arbor, MI: University of Michigan Press.

Albarracin, J. (2016). *At the core and in the margins: Incorporation of Mexican immigrants in two rural Midwestern communities*. East Lansing: Michigan State University Press.

Allegro, L., & Wood, A. G. (Eds.). (2013). *Latin American migrations to the U.S. heartland: Changing social landscapes in middle America*. Urbana, IL: University of Illinois Press.

Barkan, E. R. (Ed.). (2013). *Immigrants in American history: Arrival, adaptation, and integration*. Santa Barbara, CA: Abe-Clio Press.

Broadway, M. (2007). Meatpacking and the transformation of rural communities: A comparison of Brooks, Alberta and Garden City, Kansas. *Rural Sociology*, *72*(4), 560–582.

Cantor, J. L. (2001). *Jews in Michigan*. East Lansing: Michigan State University Press.

Cullen, A. (2018). *Storm Lake: A chronicle of change, resilience, and hope from a heartland newspaper*. New York: Viking Press.

Das, M. (2007). *Between two cultures: The case of Cambodian women in America*. New York: Peter Lang.

Das, M., Dubus, N., & Silka, L. (2013). Decades after resettlement: Later life experiences of aging Cambodian refugees. *Humanity and Society*, *37*, 327–345.

Flora, C. B., Flora, J. L., & Gasteyer, S. P. (2016). *Rural communities: Legacy and change* (5th ed.). Boulder, CO: Westview Press.

Gimpbel, J. G., & Lay, J. C. (2008). Political socialization and reactions to immigrant-related diversity in rural settings. *Rural Sociology*, 180–204.

Gordon, D. R. (2015). *Village of immigrants: Latinos in an emerging America*. New Brunswick: Rutgers University Press.

Gouveia, L. (1997). *Latino immigrants, meatpacking, and rural communities: A case study of Lexington, Nebraska*. Charleston: ERIC Clearinghouse.

Kandel, W., & Parrado, E. A. (2005). Restructuring of the U.S. meat processing industry and new Hispanic migrant destinations. *Population and Development Review*, *31*(3), 447–471.

Lay, J. C. (2012). *A midwestern mosaic: Immigration and political socialization in rural America*. Philadelphia: Temple University Press.

Lichter, D. T. (2012). Immigration and the new racial diversity in rural America. *Rural Sociology*, *77*(1).

Lum, T. Y., & Vanderaa, J. D. (2010). Health disparities among immigrant and nonimmigrant elders: The association of acculturation and education. *Journal of Immigrant and Minority Health*, *12*, 743–753.

Massey, D. S. (Ed.). (2008). *New faces in new places: The changing geography of American immigration*. New York: Russell Sage Foundation.

Migration Policy Institute. *Interactive data tools*. Retrieved from www.migrationpolicy.org/programs/data-hub/charts/us-immigrant-population-state-and-county

Mui, A. C., & Kang, S. Y. (2006). Acculturation stress and depression among Asian immigrant elders. *Social Work, 51*(3), 243–255.

Passel, J. S., & Cohn, D. (2008). *U.S. population projects: 2005–2050*. Pew Research Center. Retrieved from www.pewhispanic.org/2008/02/11//us-population-projections-2005-2050/

Silka, L. (2007). Immigrants in the community: New opportunities, new struggles. *Analyses of Social Issues and Public Policy*, 7, 75–91.

Silka, L. (2015). Immigrant elders: What can Maine learn from other states? *Maine Policy Review, 24*(2), 69–73.

Stuesse, A. (2016). *Scratching out a living: Latinos, race, and work in the Deep South*. Oakland, CA: University of California Press.

Turcotte, D., & Silka, L. (2007). Reflections on the concept of social capital: Complex partnerships in refugee and immigrant communities. In J. Jennings (Ed.), *Race, neighborhoods, and misuse of social capital* (pp. 109–132). New York: Palgrave Macmillan.

Yang, K. K. (2017). *The latehomecomer: A Hmong family memoir*. Minneapolis, MN: Coffee House Press.

Yusuf, A. I. (2012). *Somalis in Minnesota*. St. Paul, MN: Minnesota Historical Society Press.

42
INFORMATION SOURCES

Kathleen Spencer, Maren Niemeier, and Kristine Sande

Provided here is an annotated list of information sources relevant to understanding and responding to the rural aging experience. Several sources are focused solely on rural aging, and others are focused on aging, or rural with an aging component. Sources are organized by format: online portals and repositories, key reports, data sources, journals, research databases, and "gray" literature. Key organizations that produce information on rural aging are identified: federal agencies, research centers, foundations, and national organizations. Finally, sources of research assistance are identified.

Sources by Format

Online Portals and Repositories

Online portals and repositories provide opportunities to access a variety of resources including reports, government documents, policy briefs, webinars, and organizations related to a specific subject.

National Center on Elder Abuse Resources https://ncea.acl.gov/Resources.aspx
A collection of reports, webinars, podcasts, and databases related to elder mistreatment. Provides access to state resources and information on relevant state laws and regulations.

Rural Health Information Hub www.ruralhealthinfo.org
An online clearinghouse of information, data, and resources supporting health care and population health in rural communities. Includes the Rural Aging in Place Toolkit, www.ruralhealthinfo.org/toolkits/aging, and Rural Aging Topic Guide, www.ruralhealthinfo.org/topics/aging.

Rural Health Research Gateway www.ruralhealthresearch.org
Provides access to the research and findings of the Federal Office of Rural Health Policy's Rural Health Research and Policy Analysis Centers. See the Aging topic page, www.ruralhealthresearch.org/topics/aging, for relevant publications.

Key Reports Focused on Rural Aging

National Advisory Committee on Rural Health and Human Services. (2019). Supportive Services and Caregiving for Older Rural Adults. Retrieved from www.hrsa.gov/sites/default/files/hrsa/advisory-committees/rural/publications/2019-Older-Adults.pdf.

Policy brief and recommendations to the secretary of the U.S. Department of Health and Human Services on issues related to rural America with a focus on older rural Americans. Addresses long-term services and supports, telehealth, care coordination, transportation, social isolation, informal caregivers, and age-friendly communities and health systems.

National Association of Area Agencies on Aging. (2017). National Survey of Area Agencies on Aging 2017 Report and Toolkit. Retrieved from www.n4a.org/2017aaasurvey.

Identifies key issues affecting Area Agency on Aging (AAA) programs by tracking trends in services and funding. Includes information on rural AAAs and state-level reports.

U.S. Government Accountability Office. (2019). OLDER AMERICANS ACT: HHS Could Help Rural Service Providers by Centralizing Information on Promising Practices (Report GAO-19–330). Retrieved from www.gao.gov/products/GAO-19-330.

Focuses on services and resources authorized by the Older Americans Act to help older adults in rural communities age-in-place. Research included interviews with Administration for Community Living's (ACL) officials, several rural Area Agencies on Aging (AAAs), rural health experts, and stakeholder groups and a literature review.

Data Sources

The following sources provide access to data related to aging, often with a rural/urban breakdown, covering demographics, health status, health services, health disparities, housing, income and poverty, behavioral health, and the social determinants of health.

Administration for Community Living AGing Integrated Database (AGID) https://agid.acl.gov/Default.aspx

An online query system based on ACL-related data files and surveys allowing users to compare population characteristics by state and year. Data focuses on ACL's supportive services and care systems for older adults and people with disabilities. Data are not rural-specific.

AgingStats.gov: Federal Interagency Forum on Aging-Related Statistics http://agingstats.gov

Includes federal agencies that share a common interest in improving aging-related data. Data are not rural-specific.

American Community Survey (ACS) www.census.gov/programs-surveys/acs/

Includes data tables, ranking tables, population profiles, and geographic comparison profiles on demographic, social, economic, and housing information. Provides annual data that can be limited to rural.

America's Health Rankings: Senior Report www.americashealthrankings.org

A comprehensive report on the health of older adults on a national and state level. State rankings are based on 34 core measures of health, including healthy behaviors, health disparities by gender, social isolation, and the affordability of health-care services affecting unmet medical needs. Data are not rural-specific.

Explore Census Data https://data.census.gov/cedsci/

Provides access to U.S. Census Bureau data for the nation, and by county and state. Rural population data are available by age group, income, poverty, health insurance status, and disability, in table and map formats.

National Center for Health Statistics, Centers for Disease Control and Prevention www.cdc.gov/nchs/

Compiles statistical information on health topics from population and provider surveys, and vital records to guide actions and policies to improve health. The location of residence within or outside a Metropolitan Statistical Area (MSA) may be selected. Includes FastStats: Older Persons' Health, www.cdc.gov/nchs/fastats/older-american-health.htm.

National Rural Health Resource Center Population Health Portal—Put Data to Use www.ruralcenter.org/population-health-portal/data

Allows users to extract rural-specific data by state and county from a variety of federal and publicly available data sources supporting population health planning. Includes data for populations age 65 and older.

RHIhub Finding Statistics and Data Related to Rural Health Topic Guide www.ruralhealthinfo.org/topics/statistics-and-data
Offers resources and information to help locate and accurately use statistics and data on rural health needs and rural/urban disparities. Includes an annotated list of major rural-relevant data sources.

Journals

The journals selected are peer-reviewed and are known to publish articles relevant to rural aging.

Journal of Rural Health https://onlinelibrary.wiley.com/journal/17480361
A quarterly, peer-reviewed publication of the National Rural Health Association. Includes original research on rural health topics, case studies, and articles on rural policy issues including rural aging. Subscription required.

Journal of Aging Research www.hindawi.com/journals/jar/
A peer-reviewed, open access journal publishing research articles and clinical studies focused on gerontology and geriatrics.

Journal of Aging and Social Policy www.tandfonline.com/toc/wasp20/current
A peer-reviewed journal focused on policy issues affecting older adults, and the development of programs for elders in communities.

Rural and Remote Health www.rrh.org.au
An international, open access, online peer-reviewed journal supporting rural and remote health education, research, and practice.

Research Databases

Research databases offer access to citations, abstracts, and full-text for journal articles, reports, books, and other professional publications. The following list includes databases covering a variety of disciplines, including nursing, allied health, public health, and biomedical and life sciences. All databases listed include publications focused on rural aging and associated topics. Instructions on how to use their search mechanisms are available on their websites. Some of the databases listed are freely available from the internet; any subscription-based databases are identified as such and may be available through an academic library.

AgeLine www.ebsco.com/products/research-databases/ageline
A subscription database available from EBSCO of literature focused on social gerontology and aging-related issues of health, social work, sociology, psychology, economics, and public policy.

CINAHL Complete (Cumulative Index of Nursing and Allied Health Literature) www.ebscohost.com/nursing/products/cinahl-databases
A subscription database available from EBSCO Health of nursing and allied health journals and professional literature searchable by several fields.

PsycINFO www.apa.org/pubs/databases/psycinfo/
A subscription database produced by the American Psychological Association providing abstracts and citations of literature in the behavioral and social sciences.

PubMed www.ncbi.nlm.nih.gov/pubmed/
A free database from the National Library of Medicine providing citations and abstracts to life science journals and online books. See RHIhub's literature search, www.ruralhealthinfo.org/resources/3315, for a PubMed search on aging and rural health in the United States.

PubMed Central www.ncbi.nlm.nih.gov/pmc/
A free full-text database supported by the National Library of Medicine providing access to biomedical and life science journals.

Sociological Abstracts https://proquest.libguides.com/SocAbs
A subscription database available from ProQuest providing abstracting and indexing of international literature in sociology, social work, and related disciplines.

Gray Literature

Gray literature represents a variety of document types published by government, business, industry, and academic and research institutions outside of traditional commercial or academic publishing. They are of sufficient quality to be used by researchers and collected by libraries. Gray literature traditionally includes reports, white papers, policy briefs, and newsletter articles.

Gray literature can be found on the internet using search engines such as Google Scholar, https://scholar.google.com, and Microsoft Academic, https://academic.microsoft.com/home, by searching a variety of terms such as rural aging, rural seniors, and rural elders. Each search engine will have its own search syntax and requirements. Review the instructions or help information for guidance. Some common search options:

- A simple topic search such as *rural aging* may be sufficient. Using quotes around the query will typically find sources with the exact phrase included.
- Combination searches may be an option, using operators such as OR, AND, and NOT. For example: *rural aging* OR older adults.

Producers of Information on Rural Aging

Federal Agencies

The following list includes agencies providing relevant information on aging and rural aging.

Administration for Community Living (ACL) https://acl.gov
Supports the fundamental principle that older adults and people of all ages with disabilities should be able to live where they choose, with the people they choose, and with the ability to participate fully in their communities. Funds services and supports in local communities and invests in research, education, and innovation.

Centers for Medicaid and Medicare Services (CMS) www.cms.gov
An agency within the U.S. Department of Health and Human Services overseeing Medicare, which provides health insurance to people 65 and older, as well as Medicaid, in conjunction with state governments. Offers research, statistics, data, and general information by topic. Provides data on beneficiary demographics, health status, and health outcomes, as well as information on CMS programs and services.

Federal Office of Rural Health Policy (FORHP) www.hrsa.gov/rural-health/index.html
Coordinates activities related to rural health care and population health within the Health Resources and Services Administration (HRSA) under the U.S. Department of Health and Human Services.

National Institute on Aging (NIA) www.nia.nih.gov
A component of the National Institutes of Health (NIH) and the lead agency of the federal government in coordinating and supporting research on aging, and the health and well-being of older populations. Offers research and other publications with a focus on rural aging, or on providing a comparison of rural aging with urban aging.

Social Security Administration (SSA) www.ssa.gov
An agency of the federal government administering the Social Security program, an insurance program supporting retirement, disability, and survivor benefits. Provides publications about Social Security benefits, and other related retirement, disability, prescription drug, and nutrition programs.

Research Centers Focused on Aging in the U.S.

The following research centers have either a focus on rural aging, or on aging and related subfields such as health, economics, housing, and population growth regardless of geographic location. Most of the centers identified are affiliated with an academic institution and work with the federal government, state agencies, and/or health-care organizations to advocate on behalf of aging populations in rural communities, or at the national level.

Federal Office of Rural Health Policy—Rural Health Research Centers and Analysis Initiatives
www.ruralhealthresearch.org/centers
Among the research centers funded by FORHP, these conduct research related to rural older adults:

- Maine Rural Health Research Center
- Rural and Minority Health Research Center
- Southwest Rural Health Research Center
- University of Minnesota Rural Health Research Center

National Institute on Aging (NIA)—Centers on the Demography and Economics of Aging
www.nia.nih.gov/research/dbsr/centers-demography-and-economics-aging
The following NIA centers conduct research relevant to rural aging:

- Berkeley Center on the Economics and Demography of Aging (CEDA)
- Center for Demography of Health and Aging (CDHA) at UW-Madison
- Duke Center for Population Health and Aging
- Population Aging Research Center (PARC)
- RAND Center for the Study of Aging
- Stanford Center on the Demography and Economics of Health and Aging

Foundations

The foundations identified have either a rural aging focus, or more broadly cover the topic of aging.

Grantmakers in Aging (GIA) www.giaging.org
A national organization supporting a network of philanthropies, nonprofits, and government. Includes a variety of initiatives and resources focused on rural aging.

AARP Foundation www.aarp.org/aarp-foundation/
Works to reduce poverty among vulnerable people 50 years and older by developing and advocating for effective solutions that help support economic opportunity and reduce social isolation.

Robert Wood Johnson Foundation www.rwjf.org/en/our-focus-areas.html
Supports initiatives that identify the types of changes that would most improve health and bring together the many different stakeholders who need to be involved.

National Organizations

These national organizations address aging, health care, transportation, disability services, and other topics relevant to rural aging.

Administration for Community Living (ACL) Funded National Resource Centers https://acl.gov/node/2884
An annotated list of federally funded online resource centers providing information focused on a broad range of aging topics geared primarily for professional use.

American Society on Aging (ASA) www.asaging.org
Offers professional education, publications, and online training to increase the skills of individuals working to improve the quality of life for older adults and their families. Includes articles and reports focused on issues of concern for older adults in rural communities.

Meals on Wheels America www.mealsonwheelsamerica.org
The national organization supporting community-based programs providing home-delivered nutritious meals to older adults. Offers research publications demonstrating the importance of addressing hunger and social isolation.

National Aging and Disability Transportation Center (NADTC) www.nadtc.org
Advocates on behalf of older adults, people with disabilities, and caregivers for available and accessible transportation options. Publishes tools, guides, and website training focused on rural transportation.

National Association of Area Agencies on Aging (n4a) www.n4a.org
An organization for the nation's Area Agencies on Aging and Title VI Native American aging programs supporting the capacity of member agencies to provide options allowing older adults and people with disabilities to live in their homes and communities.

National Center for Equitable Care for Elders https://ece.hsdm.harvard.edu
Provides innovative and culturally competent models of care, interprofessional training and educational resources, and technical assistance to health-care professionals in community health centers who provide care to an increasingly vulnerable population: older adults.

National Council on Aging (NCOA) www.ncoa.org
Connects with nonprofit organizations, government entities, and businesses to support community programs and services for older adults. Offers a variety of resources focused on economic security, healthy living, and public policy, and includes resources focused on rural communities.

National Hispanic Council on Aging (NHCOA) www.nhcoa.org
An advocacy organization working to improve the lives of Hispanic elder populations by promoting and educating through research, policy, and practice.

National Indian Council on Aging (NICOA) https://nicoa.org
An advocacy organization supporting comprehensive health care, social services, and economic security for aging American Indian and Alaska Native Elders.

National Indigenous Elder Justice Initiative (NIEJI) www.nieji.org
Provides research, education, and training for the identification and prevention of elder abuse in Indigenous communities.

National PACE Association (NPA) www.npaonline.org
Advocates for the development and success of the Programs of All-Inclusive Care for the Elderly (PACE) model of care. Provides resources for the development of new PACE programs and includes a repository for the collection and analysis of data regarding enrollment, quality measures, demographic trends, and state policy.

National Resource Center on Native American Aging (NRCNAA) www.nrcnaa.org
Works to improve the quality of life and the availability of support services for Native American elders through the development of community-based solutions.

National Rural Health Association (NRHA) www.ruralhealthweb.org
Promotes leadership on rural health issues through advocacy, communications, education, and research. Consists of individual and organizational members who share a common interest in rural health.

Research Assistance

In conclusion, for help in accessing research and professional literature on the topic of rural aging, there are several options.

The Rural Health Information Hub (RHIhub) provides free customized assistance for those in need of research assistance. Information seekers can contact the RHIhub at 1-800-270-1898 or info@ruralhealthinfo.org.

Research assistance may also be available through an academic library. Academic librarians are trained in retrieving information and have the search tools to access professional literature. In addition, public libraries may also provide assistance and often have access to the same literature search tools as academic libraries.

43

INTERGENERATIONAL PROGRAMS

Lyn Holley

Intergenerational programming for rural older adults is emerging as an important resource. The challenges that may preclude consideration or implementation of this type of programming are discussed, and descriptions of this type of programming, examples of successful programs, and instructive resources likely to be accessible to those considering this type of programming as a service for rural older adults are offered.

Emergence of Intergenerational Programs for Rural Adults as a Resource

Despite the fact that each topic encompasses a significant feature of political and economic America that is of strategic importance for lifelong development of American citizens, neither rural aging nor intergenerational programming for rural older adults has been a high priority for research. Nonetheless, the research that has been done shows consistently that older adults who live in rural circumstances are substantially and consistently more likely to be on the adverse side of disparities in health, wealth, and wellness compared to their non-rural counterparts.

Major programs to benefit older Americans that include rural older adults do not take into account their rurality, or the potential impact of intergenerational relationships, and do not seek to create intergenerational opportunities; they mirror an economic structure that segregates the old even while programs for rural nutrition (Meals on Wheels) and some health services (e.g., rural Critical Access Hospitals) are well established, and Area Agencies on Aging continue to provide information and referral services to their extensive program and service areas. The adverse disparities have persisted, while programming and research intended to address them have focused almost exclusively on the physical health of rural older Americans.

That trend is changing and the U.S. Centers for Disease Control and Prevention (CDC), professional associations (Gerontological Society of America—GSA), powerful advocacy groups (e.g., AARP), and other organizations that fund research and programs have begun to focus on the social determinants of health (SDOH, also known as SDH). The CDC has identified determinants of health that include the social dimension of life, which can be addressed in part by positive intergenerational activity.

Results of research and reports of experience with intergenerational programming for rural older adults, although rare, typically suggest that intergenerational interventions can reduce loneliness, enhance meaning in life, and therefore positively influence mental and physical health at comparatively minimal cost. These results are consistent with results from research focused on grandparent/grandchild relationships in non-rural environments, and with reports from other countries (e.g., Poland, United Kingdom, China) and North American Indian populations (Baker, 2018; Norstrand & Xu, 2012).

Challenges to Intergenerational Programming and Research

Demographics

To be "intergenerational," an activity must include more than one generation. A generation is a group defined by age—when two generations meet, individuals in one will be older than individuals in the other. "Generations" are variously defined and there is little standardization. The common "demarcation" on the basis of chronological age is about a 20-year age difference between two population groups.

Traditionally, intergenerational programming has brought together "young" people who are "school age," i.e., preschool through college. One might ask—where are the young people rural older adults might share an activity with? A widely shared view of life in rural America is one in which young persons leave and go to urban areas to seek employment or other opportunities and that many young adults must leave home to attend high school.

Demographic data suggest that this may often be the case, i.e., although overall, one in four older adults lives in rural circumstances, overall, 79.2% live in "one generation" households in which no children are present (Hirsh, 2019; Huxhold & Fiori, 2019). The primary suggestion for connecting youth with older adults under these circumstances is to consider transportation options, internet-mediated communication, or simply the telephone or postal service. The classic "pen pal" programs of yore, or current telephone and home visiting program could be models (e.g., within Area Agency on Aging program service areas, or in connection with high school or college service or service learning programs).

Infrastructure

How about social media connections? Because of geographic isolation, rural older adults typically require transportation to travel in order to reach health care, or shop for medicine and food or to attend social activities. Rural areas typically lack the infrastructure required for public transportation services. Further, older adults who are among the 53% of rural area residents who lack high-speed broadband access are further separated (only 4% of those living in urban areas lack high-speed access) (Skoufalos, Clarke, Ellis, Shepard, & Rula, 2017).

Under these circumstances, geographic isolation can become social isolation, which research suggests is as damaging to health as smoking or other documented clinical factors (Pantell et al., 2013). Despite these challenges, creative application of the classic "pen pal" programs of yore, or current friendly visiting and telephone reassurance programs could incorporate elements of intergenerational activity until and unless infrastructure improvements are achieved (Warter & Grossman, 2001).

Funding

Funding is among the main foundational factors of "rural disadvantage" in access to services. There is an immediate need for low-cost programs that are accessible to the broad spectrum of older adults in rural areas (Hash, Jurkowski, & Krout, 2015). Intergenerational activities tend to be relatively inexpensive and accessible—the critical components of program design are readily available, namely youth and elders.

Recognition/Intentionality

Another challenge to considering or implementing intergenerational programs are the special problems this type of service intervention presents to evaluators and other researchers who compile the "evidence" concerning program effectiveness.

Evaluative challenges include the broad range of age groupings that can be studied, imprecision of definitions used, and the fact that much of this type of activity occurs informally, or is a latent (unintended) consequence of encounters that are happenstantial or a reaction to "news shared" (e.g., about the isolation, hardships, or triumphs of a youth or an older adult). Quantification of improvement (or not) in health or affect of youth and elders involved is often difficult to measure, and like much of program evaluation, the last priority for funding. Without "evidence" of effectiveness, however, funding is difficult to obtain. Collateral/latent outcomes of the programming also are difficult to assess, although successful programs may have effects reaching into many sectors: economic, wellness and health, and constructive civic engagement of older adults and youth.

Ageism

Ageism can be the factor underlying unwillingness of any stakeholder to even consider facing any of the challenges of intergenerational programming and research. Ageism, or age-based prejudice, is one of the most often "socially-condoned" prejudices, and it is embedded in our culture (Achenbaum, 2015; North & Fiske, 2012). Recent studies have found that in addition to the prejudice that American youth may hold against the old, older adults frequently evidence comparable prejudices against youth. The prejudice against older adults supports stereotypes of the old as somehow lesser, not part of the mainstream, takers who are not givers, unattractive and unhealthy (Achenbaum, 2015; North & Fiske, 2012). These prejudices can make positive connections, especially initial positive connections, between young and the old difficult. They can also preclude even consideration or awareness of the potential for intergenerational activity programming.

Ironically, actually participating in intergenerational activities can reduce ageism as these opportunities for feedback help include the "other" in the self, challenge negative unexamined assumptions with current observations, and enrich information about self and others. Another irony is that older adults are ageist themselves and as they age, they unconsciously conform to ageist expectations (e.g., to lack energy, economic significance, or to have at least one chronic illness), even while research about ways to combat ageism's negative effects suggests that holding positive self-perceptions of aging may increase functional health and longevity, and resistance to cardiovascular problems and hearing loss (Cadieux, Chasteen, & Packer, 2019; Levy, 2018).

Examples of Intergenerational Programming

In the rural U.S., organizations that may have a rich potential for engagement in intergenerational programming are as diverse as the heterogeneous older adults who could benefit from these programs. The LIFE Program described next is a "free standing" intentionally intergenerational project that evolved from Iowa State University's research. The Colorado Capital

Infrastructure—Intergenerational Physical Activity Program provides funding for capital infrastructure projects in rural or frontier communities; each community develops infrastructure that supports intergenerational physical activities and is accessible and open to all ages. The Onion River Time Bank established its original time bank program in 2008, and in 2010 it created an affiliated time bank initiative specific to the needs of older adults, called Rural Elder Assistance for Care and Health (REACH). This program has continued and it engages everyone, "no matter what age and ability" in meaningful community service. The Onion River program has been used as a model in surrounding communities in Vermont and in other states. The Time Bank exchanges supplement the established social service system, facilitate affordable access to care and services, and provides a place for individuals to participate as valued members of the community. It illustrates how the impacts of intergenerational activity programs can have effects in many sectors: economic, wellness and health, and constructive civic engagement of older adults and youth.

The LIFE (Living well through Intergenerational Fitness and Exercise) Program began as a research project by the Iowa State University Extension and Outreach. The project engaged college students as trainers and co-designers of a low-impact program of safe exercise that would be accepted by community-dwelling older adults. The "exergaming" exercise interactively combined exercise with video games. Since its launch in 2011, about 25 rural Iowa counties have offered the LIFE Program, over 340 older adults have enrolled, and over 100 younger adults have served as trainers. To read more about the project, and for contact information of knowledgeable persons, see: www.ruralhealthinfo.org/project-examples/774.

The Colorado Capital Infrastructure—Intergenerational Physical Activity Program provides funding for capital infrastructure projects to economically disadvantaged rural or frontier communities in Colorado that aim to promote creative and intergenerational physical activities accessible and open to the public for individuals of all ages and abilities. Funding may be used for:

- Activation: promotional materials and events;
- Community-based planning: to engage youth, parents, and community members of all ages and racial/ethnic backgrounds in the planning and designing process;
- Fitness stations and trails: to purchase and install fitness stations and trails in combination with active play equipment for kids that encourages intergenerational activity and supervision;
- Fixed infrastructure: tangible, immovable, age-appropriate, outdoor play space equipment for diverse age groups;
- Playground markings: painting the play area and public space with colorful, engaging, and stimulating game and activity patterns that encourage physical activity;
- Signage: purchase and install clear and identifiable signage and information in and around the public space to provide directions to the play spaces and to encourage use of the equipment; and
- Weather protection: purchase structures for sun, rain, and snow protection, including canopies and trees, to encourage intergenerational use year-round.

To read more about the project visit www.ruralhealthinfo.org/funding/4276,

or visit the program website at www.coloradohealth.org/funding-opportunities/capital-infrastructure-intergenerational-physical-activity.

The *Onion River Exchange Time Bank* is an example of how to provide services to older adults aging-in-place and also how to engage them in using their own talents to help their community. Since 2008, the program (and its "child," the REACH Program) have enabled more than 45,500 hours of service to be exchanged. This service exchange network is based upon the understanding that participants, no matter what age and ability, have valuable skills that they can share with each other. Based in the community, time bank participants give and receive services amongst each other. This, of course, includes older adults and individuals with disabilities, who share their skills and have access to services from other time bank members. These exchanges both supplement the established social service system and facilitate affordable access to care and services, as well as provide a place to participate as valued members of the community. Time spent or earned in services and activities is "banked" and can be redeemed for services offered by other program members. For more information about the Onion program, visit www.ruralhealthinfo.org/toolkits/aging/3/onion-river; and about REACH visit www.ciaip.org/grantees/montpelier/.

Resources for Intergenerational Programming

- Gerontological Society of America (GSA), Special Interest Group for Intergenerational Learning, Research and Community Engagement
- Generations United
- Rural Health Information Hub
- Retirement Research Foundation funding for 2020, which includes "intergenerational connectedness" on its list of priority areas
- Grantmakers in Aging: www.giaging.org/issues/intergenerational-strategies/
- U.S. Centers for Disease Control and Prevention www.cdc.gov/socialdeterminants/index.htm.

References

Achenbaum, W. A. (2015). A history of ageism since 1969. *Generations: Journal of the American Society on Aging, 39*(3), 10–16.

Baker, B. (2018, January 17). *Intergenerational programs thrive in rural Minnesota.* New York: Diverse Elders Coalition. Retrieved from www.diverseelders.org/2018/01/17/intergenerational-programs-thrive-in-rural-minnesota/

Cadieux, J., Chasteen, A. L., & Packer, D. J. (2019). Intergenerational contact predicts attitudes toward older adults through inclusion of the outgroup in the self. *Journals of Gerontology Psychological Sciences, Social Science, 74*(4), 575–584. doi:10.93/geronb/gbx176

Hash, K. M., Jurkowski, E. T., & Krout, J. A. (2015). *Aging in rural places: Policies, programs, and professional practice.* New York: Springer. ISBN:978-0-8261-9809-9

Hirsh, S. (2019). Rural America by the numbers: A demographic snapshot. *Generations: Journal of the American Society on Aging, 43*(2), 9–16.

Huxhold, O., & Fiori, K. L. (2019). Do demographic changes jeopardize social integration among aging adults living in rural regions? *Journals of Gerontology: Psychological Sciences Social Science, 74*(6), 954–963. doi:10.1093/geronb/gby008

Levy, S. R. (2018) Toward reducing ageismj: PEACE (positive education about aging and contact experiences) model. *Gerontologist, 58*(2), 226–232. doi:10.10/geront/gnw116

Norstrand, J. A., & Xu, Q. (2012) Social capital and health outcomes among older adults in China: The urban-rural dimension. *The Gerontologist, 52*(3), 325–334.

North, M. S., & Fiske, S. T. (2012). An inconvenienced youth? Ageism and its potential intergenerational roots. *Psychological Bulletin, 138*(5), 982–997. doi:10.1037/a0027843

Pantell, M., Rehkopf, D., Jutte, D., Syme, S. L., Balmes, J., & Adler, N. (2013). Social isolation: A predictor of mortality comparable to traditional clinical risk factors. *American Journal of Public Health, 103*(11), 2056–2062. doi:10.2105/AJPH.2013.301261

Skoufalos, A., Clarke, J. L., Ellis, D. R., Shepard, V. L., & Rula, E. Y. (2017). *Rural aging in America: Proceedings of the 2017 connectivity summit.* Retrieved from https://www.ncbi.nlm.nih.gov/pmc/articles/PMC5738994/

Warter, E. H., & Grossman, J. M. (2001). An application of developmental contextualism to service-learning (pp. 83–102). In A. Furco & S. H. Gillig (Eds.), *Service-learning: The essence of the pedagogy.* Greenwich, Connecticut: Information Age Publishing.

44

ISOLATION

James Lubben and Mercedes E. Bern-Klug

Isolation and Rural Aging

Social isolation is a serious health issue for people of all ages, but it appears to be especially devastating for older adults. The AARP Foundation has suggested that social isolation is a growing epidemic in America affecting over eight million older adults (AARP Foundation, 2016). Holt-Lunstad and colleagues advise that social isolation creates as much of a health risk as if one smoked 15 cigarettes a day (Holt-Lunstad, Smith, Baker, Haris, & Stephenson, 2015). Socially isolated individuals incur increased risk of an array of problems including abuse, cognitive impairment, depression, disability, extended hospital stays, falls, malnutrition and mortality (Lubben et al., 2018). Accordingly, Lubben (2017) argues that it is time for society to address social isolation as a potent killer!

Aspects of Social Isolation in Rural Communities

Rural older adults face a particularly high risk of social isolation (Kaye, 2017). Kaye also notes that "stoicism and fiercely independent spirit," which are much admired in rural communities, can be overrated and counterproductive qualities with respect to addressing social isolation (p. 140). In some cases, the methods of maintaining social connections used by rural older adults are at odds with family members and health providers. For example, Johnson (2002) describes the case of older adults who decided to continue driving against the advice of others, in part to remain socially connected.

Rural residents face significant barriers to accessing health care such as long distances between home and health facilitates as well as limited public transportation (Douthit, Kiv, Dwolatzky, & Biswas, 2015). Older minority rural adults may have even more difficulty accessing transportation than white older rural adults (Cromer, Wofford, & Wyant, 2019; Park et al., 2010). Social isolation compounds these transportation barriers to receiving timely and regular health care.

Rural older adults may have some advantages over their urban counterparts with respect to social connections. Using the National Social Life, Health, and Aging Project data, Henning-Smith and colleagues (2019) reported that rural older adults had more friends and close relatives than their urban counterparts. Rural older adults also reported having more living children and grandchildren than their urban counterparts. However, there were no significant differences in feeling isolated between the rural and urban older adults in this study.

Isolated Older Adults Challenge Rural Health-Care Systems

A major challenge in addressing social isolation is that social isolates are difficult to detect in the community. Social isolates are often first discovered when they encounter the health and mental care systems. The most extreme cases of social isolates are referred to as "unbefriended" older adults who show up in emergency rooms presenting tremendous challenges for health-care providers in their efforts to obtain consent for medical treatment. These individuals often have compromised cognitive functioning and are without any known relatives or friends who could sign consent forms. A related group of older adults are sometimes referred to as "adult orphans" in that they may have sufficient cognitive faculties to offer consent, but they also lack relatives or friends and thus are at high risk of becoming "unbefriended" older adults in the future. The American Geriatrics Society (Farrell et al., 2017) has developed a position paper addressing the health-care and legal issues presented by these two extreme groups of social isolates. Obviously, it would be preferred to identify these social isolates at an earlier stage when more options could be considered for addressing their isolation.

Expression of loneliness can be another example of social isolation. Some scholars have suggested loneliness can be viewed as perceived social isolation (Hawkley & Capitanio, 2015). Those older adults experiencing severe loneliness are also first detected when they come in contact with the mental health-care system. The previous examples of extreme social isolates as well as this example of those expressing severe loneliness suggest that health-care practice protocols are needed to screen for social isolation much as health professionals screen for other major behavioral health risks (Lubben et al., 2006; Lubben, 2017; Ciolfi, 2019; Perissinotto, Holt-Lunstad, Periyakoil, & Covinsky, 2019).

Community Responses to Social Isolation

Community organizations play a vital role in combating social isolation by providing opportunities for leisure, recreation, social connections, and the receipt of health, social, and financial services. National (e.g., AARP) and international organizations (e.g., WHO) promote the need for increased community awareness and action to mitigate social isolation among older adults, including those residing in rural areas. The AARP Foundation's *Connect2Affect* campaign is a good example of a public education approach to draw attention to social isolation (AARP Foundation, 2016).

The great heterogeneity among rural areas because of their varying economic and social histories, geography, density, climate, road conditions, proximity to larger urban areas, and the like, calls for tailored, context-specific interventions (Skinner & Winterton, 2018; Douthit et al., 2015; Durazo et al., 2011). Likewise, gender-specific interventions may need to be considered (Henning-Smith, Ecklund, Moscovice, & Kozhimannil, 2018). It is important to be mindful that each rural community will likely have its own combination of social resources and core organizational players including senior centers and Area Agencies on Aging. Brown and colleagues (2018) documented how rural communities can be resilient and effective in providing services to older adults when public and private organizations worked together to combat scarcity in terms of local service availability.

Colibaba and Skinner's (2019) case study of older adults as library volunteers speaks to the importance of the volunteer role in maintaining social connections for older adults and the value of the library and the volunteers to the community. They discuss the challenges of replenishing volunteers as older adults in rural communities find themselves no longer able to volunteer and, rather, become the recipients of needed community services, some of which also depend on the availability of volunteers. Another foundational resource in many rural communities is the religious institution, typically Christian churches, which increasingly provide not only spiritual support and opportunities for social interaction, but also social services, often without their staff and volunteers having received specialized training and support (Scott & Lovell, 2015).

The literature includes examples of how rural older adults, themselves, anticipate the possibility of becoming socially isolated and plan accordingly. Skemp, Maas, and Umbarger-Mackey (2013) describe how middle-income and affluent rural older adults decided to move to a small town motel to avoid the expenses and challenges of maintaining their own homes, and to enhance their social connections, including one couple who traveled daily from the motel to their farm to feed the animals. Rural community leaders need to be aware of these naturally occurring living arrangements and be ready to offer as needed support if the informal arrangements dissolve.

Rural older adults who have available the option of relocating to a neighboring college town will have resources and services not easily found in other settings. For example, Iowa City is the home of the University of Iowa and a popular retirement destination with access to cultural, social, and health-care resources. Diverse housing options are available in Iowa City ranging from federally subsidized apartments for older adults, affordable assisted living (a joint project between a local health-care provider and a housing company) with rent based on income, private assisted living, continuing care retirement communities, co-housing (Iowa City Cohousing, 2020), and recently, TRAIL (2020), a version of the Beacon Hill Boston Village movement, where people live in their own homes throughout the city and share information about resources (e.g., roofers and plumbers) and can participate in social activities with other TRAIL members.

Yet many rural older adults face serious obstacles (financial and social) when considering relocating, including the affordability of residing in more populated locations. Many rural older adults have a strong sense of emotional connection and commitment to their locale, which can make relocating particularly stressful. Even if they do decide to leave their rural community, for some current homeowners, finding a buyer for their house if their community is facing a declining population or an economic downturn can be a challenge (Strommen & Sanders, 2018).

Policy Changes Could Help Address Social Isolation

Policy changes can help support rural communities and reduce the risk of older residents becoming isolated. For example, increasing access to high-speed broadband in rural areas could make an important difference in the daily lives of older adults, including enhancing connections with geographically dispersed family, friends, and health-care providers. "Without access to broadband, rural Americans cannot participate in the digital economy or take advantage of the opportunities broadband brings for better education, health care, and civic and social engagement" (FFC, 2020). Looking to the future, advances in artificial intelligence such as driverless cars, smart homes, and robots have the potential to dramatically and profoundly impact the rural landscape and potentially enhance social connections for all rural residents, including older adults. However, limited access to high-speed broadband will likely slow the adoption of these new technologies in rural communities.

As the National Rural Health Association (2020) documents, the cornerstone of many rural communities is the local hospital. When a rural hospital closes, there are severe negative consequences for access to care, the local economy, and the social fabric of the area. Current Medicare reimbursement policies negatively impact rural hospitals.

> Continued cuts to rural providers are creating a hospital closure crisis in rural America, jeopardizing millions of rural patients' access to medical care and devastating the already fragile rural economy. Currently one in three rural hospitals is in financial risk. At the current rate of closure, 25% of all rural hospitals will close within less than a decade.
>
> (NRHA, 2020)

Personal Responsibility to Nurture Social Capital

Rural older adults need to assume some responsibility for maintaining social connectedness in their own private lives. As Lubben (2017) reports, our society has designed entire industries promoting retirement preparation that have focused on building financial capital. However, it is just as important to build the social capital that rural older adults can rely on in their later years of life. The consequence of not attending to cultivating social capital becomes especially apparent in old age in rural communities.

In sum, addressing social isolation as a major threat to the health and well-being of older adults in rural communities will require a multifaceted approach. Rural communities need to be educated regarding the serious consequences of social isolation. Governments and various community organizations need to develop policies and programs to address the problem. Health and social service personnel need to be better trained and have available appropriate practice protocols to identify both those older adults at risk and those who are already socially isolated. Finally, rural older adults need to attend to this important health problem in their own personal lives.

References

AARP Foundation. (2016). *Connect2Affect campaign*. Retrieved from www.aarp.org/about-aarp/press-center/info-12-2016/aarp-foundation-draws-attention-social-isolation-with-launch-connect2affect.html; http://connect2affect.org

Brown, D. L., Glasgow, N., Kulcsar, L. J., Sanders, S., & Thiede, B. C. (2018). The multi-scalar organization of aging-related services in U.S. rural places. *The Journal of Rural Studies*, *68*, 219–229. doi:10.1016/j.jrurstud.2018.09.010

Ciolfi, M. L. (2019). Historical perspectives on research on social isolation, loneliness, and social support. In L. W. Kaye & C. M. Singer (Eds.), *Social isolation of older adults: Strategies to bolster health and well-being*. New York: Springer.

Colibaba, A., & Skinner, M. W. (2019). Rural public libraries as contested spaces of older voluntarism in ageing communities. *Journal of Rural Studies*, *70*, 117–124. doi:10.1016/j.jrurstud.2019.08.007

Cromer, K. J., Wofford, L., & Wyant, D. K. (2019). Barriers to healthcare access facing American Indian and Alaska Natives in rural America. *Journal of Community Health Nursing*, *39*(4), 165–187. doi:10.1080/07370016.2019.1665320

Douthit, N., Kiv, S., Dwolatzky, T., & Biswas, S. (2015). Exposing some important barriers to health care access in the rural USA. *Public Health*, *129*(6), 611–620. doi:10.1016/j.puhe.2015.04.001

Durazo, E. M., Jones, M. R., Wallace, S. P., Van Arsdale, J., Aydin, M., & Stewart, C. (2011, June). *The health status and unique health challenges of rural older adults in California*. Health Policy Brief. UCLA Center for Health Policy Research. Retrieved from https://www.issuelab.org/resources/12947/12947.pdf

Farrell, T. W., Widera, E., Rosenberg, L., Rubin, C. D., Naik, A. D., Braun, U., . . . Shega, J. (2017). AGS position statement: Making medical treatment decisions for unbefriended older adults. *Journal of American Geriatrics Society*, *65*(1), 14–15. doi:10.1111/jgs.14586

Federal Communications Commission (FCC). (2020). Retrieved from https://docs.fcc.gov/public/attachments/DOC-362190A1.pdf

Hawkley, L. C., & Capitanio, J. P. (2015). Perceived social isolation, evolutionary fitness and health outcomes: A lifespan approach. *Philosophical Transactions of the Royal Society B: Biological Sciences*, *370*(1669), 20140114. doi:10.1098/rstb.2014.0114. PMID: 25870400; PMCID: PMC4410380.

Henning-Smith, C., Ecklund, A., Moscovice, I., & Kozhimannil, K. (2018, August). *Gender differences in social isolation and social support among rural residents*. Policy Brief. Minneapolis: University of Minnesota Rural Health Center. doi:10.1097/MLR.0000000000000761

Henning-Smith, C., Moscovice, I., & Kozhimannil, K. (2019, January). Differences in social isolation and its relationship to health by rurality. *Journal of Rural Health*, *5*, 1–10. doi:10.1111/jrh.12344

Holt-Lunstad, J., Smith, T., Baker, M., Haris, T., & Stephenson, D. (2015). Loneliness and social relationships as risk factors for mortality: A meta- analytic review. *Perspectives on Psychological Science*, *10*(2), 227–237. doi:10.1177/1745691614568352

Iowa City Cohousing. (2020). Retrieved from http://iowacitycohousing.org/what-makes-it-unique/index.html

Johnson, J. E. (2002). Why rural elders drive against advice. *Journal of Community Health Nursing*, *19*(4), 237–244. doi:10.1207/S15327655JCHN1904_04

Kaye, L. W. (2017). Older adults, rural living, and the escalating risk of social isolation. *Public Policy & Aging Report*, *27*(4), 139–144. doi:10.1093/ppar/prx029

Lubben, J. (2017). Addressing social isolation as a potent killer! *Public Policy & Aging Report*, *27*(4), 136–138. doi:10.1093/ppar/prx026

Lubben, J., Blozik, E., Gillmann, G., Iliffe, S., von Renteln Kruse, W., Beck, J. C., & Stuck, A. E. (2006). Performance of an abbreviated version of the Lubben Social Network Scale among three European community-dwelling older adult populations. *The Gerontologist*, *46*(4), 503–513. doi:10.1093/geront/46.4.503

Lubben, J. E., Tracy, E., Crewe, S. E., Sabbath, E., Gironda, M., Johnson, C. . . . Brown, S. (2018). Eradicate social isolation. In R. Fong, J. Lubben, & R. P. Barth (Eds.), *Grand challenges for social work and society*. New York and Washington, DC: Oxford University Press.

National Rural Health Association. (2020). Retrieved from www.ruralhealthweb.org/advocate/medicare cuts-hurt-rural

Park, N. S., Roff, L. L., Sun, F., Parker, M. W., Klemmack, D. L., Sawyer, P., & Allman, R. M. (2010). Transportation difficulty of black and white rural older adults. *Journal of Applied Gerontology*, *29*(1), 70–88. doi:10.1177/0733464809335597. PMID: 2P2068835; PMCID: PMC2758564.

Perissinotto, C., Holt-Lunstad, J., Periyakoil, V. S., Covinsky, K. (2019). A practical approach to assessing and mitigating loneliness and isolation in older adults. *Journal of the American Geriatrics Society*, *67*(4), 657–662. doi:10.1111/jgs.15746. Epub 2019 Feb 14. PMID: 30762228.

Scott, G., & Lovell, R. (2015). The rural pastors initiative: Addressing isolation and burnout in rural ministry. *Pastoral Psychology*, *64*, 71–97. doi:10.1007/s11089-013-0591-z

Skemp, L. E., Maas, M. L., & Umbarger-Mackey, M. (2013). Doing it my way. *The Gerontologist*, *54*(4), 693–703. doi:10.1093/geron/gnt052

Skinner, M. W., & Winterton, R. (2018). Interrogating the contested spaces of rural aging: Implications for research, policy and practice. *The Gerontologist*, *58*(1), 15–25. doi:10.1093/geront/gnx094

Strommen, J., & Sanders, G. F. (2018). Perceptions of changing communities among rural elders: Impact on well-being. *Activities, Adaptations & Aging*, *42*(3), 210–224. doi:10.1080/01924788.2017.1398033

TRAIL. (2020). Retrieved from https://trailofjohnsoncounty.org

45
KINSHIP CARE

Sandra J. Bailey

Introduction

As one ages, most individuals look forward to retirement, leisure time, and enjoying family, particularly becoming a grandparent. For some older adults, this image is shattered when they are called upon to parent their grandchildren. According to the U.S. Census, there are approximately 2.5 million grandparents who have the sole responsibility for raising their grandchildren (U.S. Census Bureau, 2017). For the past several decades, the fastest-growing family structure is grandparents raising their grandchildren (Bryson, 2001), increasing from 3% in 1970 to 6% in 2012 (Ellis & Simmons, 2014). Of these caregivers, approximately 25% live in rural areas (Kropf & Robinson, 2004).

Grandparent caregivers are called upon to parent a second time around, for a variety of reasons, and, with the exception of military deployment, most are because of a family crisis. The parents are either unable or unwilling to continue their responsibility to parent their children because of parental death, mental or physical illness, substance abuse issues, incarceration, becoming a parent during teen years, divorce, and financial issues (Bullock, 2004; Letiecq, Bailey, & Kurtz, 2008). These crises are often sudden, thrusting the grandparents into an off-time role of parenting once again. Although the term kinship caregivers covers anyone raising a relative's child, grandparents are frequently called upon to be the caregivers.

Challenges and Adaptations of Rural Grandparent Caregivers

Because of the increase in this family configuration, scholars have begun studying the challenges, successes, and resilience in grandfamilies in urban settings. However, there remains a dearth of information on rural grandparent-headed households. Rural grandparents raising grandchildren are particularly vulnerable to such an unexpected event and are likely not financially prepared to care for them (Allison, 2012). Rural living can be challenging because communities are geographically isolated, generally lack public transportation, and have fewer services (e.g., mental health, specialized medical practices, childcare, support groups, food banks, etc.) readily available for families as compared to urban dwellers (Probst, Moore, Glover, & Samuels, 2004). Geographic barriers and separation often require rural residents to travel many miles to access services and public transportation is commonly lacking (Bauer &

Dolan, 2011). Additionally, populations in rural areas are shrinking and aging more rapidly than urban areas (USDA Economic Research Service, 2017) contributing to fewer resources and services for older kinship caregivers. Issues facing grandparent caregivers are often similar in urban and rural areas but are compounded in less populated areas because of isolation, less support, and lack of services (Robinson, Kropf, & Myers, 2000; Thomas, 2011). Models of support that are found in urban areas may not be effective in rural areas because of the uniqueness of rural living (King et al., 2009).

Demographics of Rural Grandparents Raising Grandchildren

Depending upon the particular rural region of the U.S. under consideration, the demographics of grandparent caregivers can vary. In Georgia, these kinship caregivers are primarily African American with an average age of 67 years (ranging from 50 to 84 years of age), and caring for an average of 2.06 children (King et al., 2009). In Montana, they are primarily white or Native American with an average age of 60 years, generally caring for just under two children (Letiecq et al., 2008). Goodman and Rao (2007) studied Hispanic grandfamilies along the New Mexico border. New Mexico, a largely rural state, ranks sixth in the nation for grandparent-headed families. Although a small sample, these grandfamilies often consisted of more children per family and the families lived in crowded conditions (Goodman & Rao, 2007). There are common themes characterizing all rural grandparent caregivers—they are more likely to be poor (Kreider & Ellis, 2011); have poorer physical and mental health (Minkler & Fuller-Thompson, 1999; Whitely & Fuller-Thomson, 2017); feel isolated (Thomas, 2011); and the event of parenting a second time is unexpected and the new family is in crisis when the children arrive (Bullock, 2004; Letiecq et al., 2008; Kropf & Robinson, 2004). Yet after the crisis, grandparent caregivers can provide a stable home and become resilient as they accept the new family configuration and find needed services (Bailey, Letiecq, Erickson, & Koltz, 2013).

Challenges of Rural Grandparent Caregivers

Economics of Grandparents Raising Grandchildren

Overall, grandparents raising grandchildren have higher rates of poverty than their noncustodial grandparent counterparts (Ellis & Simmons 2014). Grandparent caregivers are more likely to experience poverty than other parents (Kreider & Ellis, 2011) and because many are raising grandchildren outside of the child welfare system, they are eligible for fewer services and governmental assistance than those families in the formal child welfare system (Bailey, Haynes, & Letiecq, 2013). Twenty-one percent of custodial grandparents live below the poverty line in the U.S., and grandmother-only headed households have the highest rate of poverty, yet a large proportion of grandparent caregivers (58%) are in the workforce (U.S. Census, 2014). Some have had to leave paid employment, often grandmothers, to care for grandchildren and others who have retired, typically grandfathers, have had to reenter the workforce to support the new family configuration (Bailey et al., 2009). Bailey, Letiecq, Visconti, and Tucker (2019) found a majority of rural grandparent caregivers in their study had high levels of economic stress, although some degree of economic stress was buffered by utilization of government assistance. Bailey et al. (2013) examined how budgeting for family expenses shifts when grandchildren come to reside with grandparents. Funds may be taken from savings and retirement delayed to support the reconfigured family.

Health and Well-Being of Grandparent Caregivers

Over the past several decades, a plethora of research has been conducted on the health and well-being of grandparents raising grandchildren and the stresses of "off-time" parenting (e.g., Bailey et al., 2019; Bailey, Letiecq, & Porterfield, 2009; Hayslip & Kaminski, 2005; Kelley, Whitley, Sipe, & Yorker, 2000; Letiecq et al., 2008; Waldrop & Weber, 2001). Taking on the responsibility for off-time parenting can take a toll on the mental and physical health of older adults. This challenge is compounded in rural areas where services and transportation options are scarce (Allison, 2012; Bauer & Dolan, 2011).

Off-time parenting impacts the stress levels and mental health of grandparent caregivers. Bailey et al. (2019) found that 48% of rural custodial European and Native American grandparents were experiencing depressive symptoms in the range warranting clinical concern. Isolation occurs, especially for sole grandmothers raising grandchildren (Thomas, 2011). These findings are likewise consistent with previous research findings (Letiecq et al., 2008; Whitley, Fuller-Thomson, & Brennenstuhl, 2015) and may speak to the challenging life events that occur in families when grandparents are called upon to raise their grandchildren. Feelings of isolation can cause ambivalence in grandparents as they struggle to define the boundaries, roles, and expectations of family members (Letiecq et al., 2008).

Physical limitations are common because of the age of grandparents. An early national study of grandparent caregivers found they have more limitations in activities of daily living and reported lower satisfaction with their health (Minkler & Fuller-Thomson, 1999). Physical health issues were reported by rural African American grandmothers and limited financial resources resulted in some grandmothers skipping needed medication and foregoing doctor visits to feed and care for their grandchildren (Clottey, Scott, & Alfonso, 2015). Not surprising, grandparent caregivers often report being tired as energy levels and health have declined with age.

Sources of Support for Successful Adaptation

Although there are challenges for rural grandparent caregivers, there are agencies and organizations that are working to provide services and support. For example, in Montana, the Grandparents Raising Grandchildren Project has a central call center that operates during the week that helps grandparent caregivers find available resources and services. They coordinate a network of 24 local support groups to help grandparent caregivers meet others with similar family situations. Through these local support groups grandparents can share problems, find local sources of support, and develop friendships. The Brookdale Foundation of New York has worked for several decades to support the development of support groups through seed grants distributed across the U.S. (www.brookdalefoundation.org).

When grandparents first take on the role of being the sole providers for their grandchildren, they can feel isolated as their peers are not providing day-to-day care for grandchildren. They may not know anyone else who is in a similar situation. Support groups can be a source of support for the grandparents. Grandparent caregivers in rural areas often lack both the informal and formal supports that are needed as they take on this responsibility (Robinson, Kropf, & Myers, 2000). Some research has begun to address the value of support groups. Strozier (2012) found that grandparent caregivers who participated in support groups experienced greater increases in social support than those who did not attend groups. King and colleagues (2009) found that support groups were one of the most beneficial services provided by a kinship caregiver program as the grandparents appreciated the psychological benefits and contact with others.

In addition to emotional support, networking, and finding resources and services, some members of support groups have moved to take action. In Montana, one local support group worked with a legislator to pass three bills to support grandparent caregivers. Some also plan for educational programs related to kinship caregiving such as how to work with the schools and understanding how to practice trauma-informed care. This transition from crisis to adaptation illustrates that these families can overcome challenges (Bailey et al., 2009).

In 2018, Congress allocated noncompetitive funds to states to develop full kinship navigator programs to assist all kin raising relative children (115th U.S. Congress, 2018). These funds can be used to expand support group networks so that rural grandparent caregivers can receive services. Although there are still the challenges of transportation and limited services, these funds can make a difference in supporting rural grandparents raising grandchildren.

Conclusion

The number of grandparents raising grandchildren continues to increase and is changing the lives of many older adults. Those in rural areas face unique challenges because of isolation, lack of transportation, and limited services. When these families first receive their grandchildren, there is typically a state of chaos (Bailey et al., 2009), yet those who succeed in accessing existing resources and supports can successfully adapt to the new family configuration. Support groups and kinship navigator programs in rural states can help provide critical services for these families, which are crucial for the health and well-being of the grandparents as well as the grandchildren.

References

Allison, V. L. (2012). Econometric analysis of childhood poverty in Georgia. *American Journal of Agricultural Economics*, *94*, 595–599.

Bailey, S. J., Haynes, D., & Letiecq, B. (2013). "How can you retire when you still got a kid in school?" The economics of raising grandchildren in Montana. *Marriage & Family Review*, *49*, 671–693.

Bailey, S. J., Letiecq, B. L., Erickson, M., & Koltz, R. (2013). Resilient grandparent caregivers: Pathways to positive adaptation. In B. Hayslip, Jr. & G. C. Smith (Eds.), *Resilient grandparent caregivers: A strengths-based perspective*. New York: Routledge, Taylor & Francis.

Bailey, S. J., Letiecq, B. L., & Porterfield, F. (2009). Family coping and adaptation among grandparents rearing grandchildren. *The Journal of Intergenerational Relationships*, 7(2), 144–158.

Bailey, S. J., Letiecq, B. L., Visconti, K., & Tucker, N. (2019). Rural native and European American custodial grandparents: Stressors, resources, and resilience. *Journal of Cross Cultural Gerontology*, *34*(2), 131–148.

Bauer, J. W., & Dolan, E. M. (2011). Rural families and work overview. In J. W. Bauer & E. M. Dolan (Eds.), *Rural families and work: Context and problems* (pp. 1–16). New York: Springer.

Bryson, K. (2001, November). *New Census Bureau data on grandparents raising grandchildren*. Paper presented at the 54th annual scientific meeting of the Gerontological Society of America, Chicago.

Bullock, K. (2004). The changing role of grandparents in rural families: The results of an exploratory study in Southeastern North Carolina. *Families in Society: The Journal of Contemporary Social Services*, *85*(1), 45–54.

Clottey, E. N., Scott, A. J., & Alfonso, M. L. (2015). Grandparent caregiving among rural African Americans in a community in the American South: Challenges to health and wellbeing. *Rural and Remote Health*, *15*, 1–11.

Ellis, R. R., & Simmons (2014, October). *Coresident grandparents and their grandchildren: 2012*. US Department of Commerce, Economics and Statistics Administration. Report No. P20–P576. Retrieved from www.census.gov/content/dam/Census/library/publications/2014/demo/p20-576.pdf

Goodman, M. R., & Rao, S. P. (2007). Grandparents raising grandchildren in a US-Mexico border community. *Qualitative Health Research*, *17*(8), 1117–1136.

Hayslip, B., Jr., & Kaminski, P. L. (2005). Grandparents raising their grandchildren: A review of the literature and suggestions for practice. *The Gerontologist, 45*, 262–269.

Kelley, S. J., Whitley, D., Sipe, T. A., & Yorker, B. C. (2000). Psychological distress in grandmother kinship care providers: The role of resources, social support, and physical health. *Child Abuse & Neglect, 24*(3), 311–321.

King, S., Kropf, N. P., Perkins, M., Sessley, L., Burt, C., & Lepore, M. (2009). Kinship are in rural Georgia communities: Responding to the needs and challenges of kinship caregivers. *Journal of Intergenerational Relationships, 7*, 225–242.

Kreider, R. M., & Ellis, R. (2011). *Living arrangements of children: 2009*. Current Population Reports No. P70–P126. Washington, DC: U.S. Census Bureau. Retrieved from www.census.gov/prod/2011pubs/p70-126.pdf

Kropf, N. P., & Robinson, M. M. (2004). Pathways into caregiving for rural custodial grandparents. *Journal of Intergenerational Relationships, 2*(1), 63–77.

Letiecq, B. L., Bailey, S. J., & Dahlen, P. (2008). Intergenerational ambivalence and caregiver coping among grandparents raising grandchildren: Implications for clinical intervention. In B. Hayslip & P. L. Kaminski (Eds.), *Parenting the custodial grandchild* (pp. 3–16). New York: Springer.

Letiecq, B., Bailey, S. J., & Kurtz, M. A. (2008). Depression among rural Native American and European American grandparents raising grandchildren. *Journal of Family Issues, 29*(3), 334–356.

Letiecq, B., Bailey, S. J., & Porterfield, F. (2008). "We have no rights, we get no help": The legal and public policy dilemmas faced by grandparents rearing their grandchildren in informal arrangements. *Journal of Family Issues, 29*(8), 995–1012.

Minkler, M., & Fuller-Thomson, E. (1999). The health of grandparents raising grandchildren: The results of a national study. *American Journal of Public Health, 89*(9), 1384–1389.

Probst, J. C., Moore, C. G., Glover, S. H., & Samuels, M. E. (2004). Person and place: The compounding effects of race/ethnicity and rurality on health. *American Journal of Public Health, 94*(10), 1695–1703.

Robinson, M., Kropf, N., & Myers, L. (2000). Grandparents raising grandchildren in rural communities. *Journal of Mental Health and Aging, 6*(4), 353–365.

Strozier, A. (2012). The effectiveness of support groups in increasing social support for kinship caregivers. *Children and Services Review, 34*, 876–881.

Thomas, E. A. (2011). Cushioning, weathering, place, and community in rural grandmother-mothering. *Issues in Mental Health Nursing, 32*(5), 291–300.

U.S. Census Bureau. (2014). *U.S. Census Bureau, 2014 American Community Survey 1-year estimates*. Retrieved from http://factfinder.census.gov/faces/tableservices/jsf/pages/productview.xhtml?pid=ACS_14_1YR_B10058&prodType=table

U.S. Census Bureau. (2017). *U.S. Census Bureau, 2017 American Community Survey 1-year estimates*. Retrieved from https://factfinder.census.gov/faces/tableservices/jsf/pages/productview.xhtml?pid=ACS_17_1YR_B10002&prodType=table

USDA Economic Research Service. *Rural America at a glance 2017 edition*. Economic Information Bulletin 182. Retrieved from www.ers.usda.gov/webdocs/publications/85740/eib-182.pdf?v=0

Waldrop, D. P., & Weber, J. A. (2001). From grandparent to caregiver: The stress and satisfaction of raising grandchildren. *Families in Society, 82*, 461–472.

Whitely, D. M., & Fuller-Thomson, E. (2017). African-American solo grandparents raising grandchildren: A representative profile of their health status. *Journal of Community Health, 42*, 312–323.

Whitley, D. M., Fuller-Thomson, E., & Brennenstuhl, S. (2015). Health characteristics of solo grandparent caregivers and single parents: A comparative profile using the Behavioral Risk Factor Surveillance Survey. *Current Gerontology and Geriatrics Research*. doi:10.1155/2015/630717

115th U.S. Congress. (2018). *Promoting safe & stable families of 2018, public law no. 115–141 stat 731*. Retrieved from www.govinfo.gov/content/pkg/PLAW-115publ141/html/PLAW-115publ141.htm

46
LATINA/OS

Rogelio Sáenz

Despite common perceptions, Latina/os have always been part of rural America, beginning two centuries ago in southwestern lands that once belonged to Mexico (Saenz, Fox, & García, 2012). For much of the twentieth century, many Latina/o families in South Texas made annual treks throughout the U.S. to work as migrant farmworkers picking a wide variety of crops (Valle, 1994). More recently, beginning in the late 1980s, many Latina/os migrated to new destinations where they were recruited to work largely in meat and poultry processing operations (Marrow, 2011). Latina/os are now the largest minority group in rural America. While little is known about rural Latinos, this is particularly true in the case of Latina/o older adults.

This entry focuses on the rural Latina/o older adult population. In particular, it has two objectives: 1. to provide an overview of the knowledge base regarding Latina/o older adults in rural areas and 2. to carry out an analysis that highlights the population trends of rural Latina/o older adults along with their demographic, socioeconomic, and health characteristics.

The Literature on Rural Latina/o Older Adults

Over the last several decades, there has been a growth of research on Latina/o older adults. From this knowledge base, we know that Latina/o elders tend to have limited socioeconomic resources (Saenz et al., 2012). Yet, Latina/o elders exhibit relatively low mortality and high life expectancy (Saenz & Morales, 2012) compared to their white counterparts. This finding has commonly been referred to as the Latino epidemiological paradox (Markides & Coreil, 1986). Nonetheless, while Latina/o adults live long lives, they do so with more health problems including disabilities, diabetes, and obesity (Garcia, Downer, Crowe, & Markides, 2017). Unfortunately, this body of research has been based almost exclusively on urban areas or large-scale data sets that do not take rural residence into account.

Indeed, there is limited research pertaining specifically to rural Latina/o older adults. The existing literature is based primarily on rural Latina/os in the southwestern part of the U.S., including west Texas (Xu & Rojas-Fernandez, 2003), southwest New Mexico (Averill, 2005), southern Colorado (Hamman et al., 1999; Marshall et al., 1999; Mulgrew et al., 1999), and southern California (Letamendi et al., 2013). An additional segment of the literature focuses on the nation's aging Latina/os (Saenz et al., 2012) in areas where it is difficult to clearly determine if the research site is a designated rural area (Pei, Cong, & Wu, 2019), and large data sets that include rural and urban respondents (Bastida, Brown, & Pagán, 2008; Lee, Parrott, & Ahn, 2014; Salinas, Su, & Snih, 2013).

The scant literature on rural Latina/o older adults has focused primarily on a limited set of topics. These have included diabetes, depression, health-care utilization, health disparities, cognitive functioning, disability, nutrition, prescription medications, religion, and end-of-life planning. There are some primary findings that have come out of this research. For example, aging Latina/os in rural areas in west Texas are more likely than whites to report limitations in ancillary pharmacy services (Xu & Rojas-Fernandez, 2003). In addition, rural aging Latina/os are more likely to experience cognitive functioning limitations (Mulgrew et al., 1999), the prevalence of disabilities (Hamman et al., 1999), and nutritional deficiencies (Marshall et al., 1999) than their white counterparts in two rural Colorado counties. Furthermore, older Latina/os in southern U.S. communities are more likely than whites to live in inadequate housing conditions (Lee et al., 2014). Moreover, Latina/os who live in border counties across the southwest are also more likely to survive to wave five of a longitudinal study, but they are more likely to transition to disability status compared to Latina/os not living in border counties (Salinas et al., 2013). Finally, Averill (2005) has demonstrated the utility of combining critical ethnography and community-based action research to reduce health disparities impacting rural Latina/o older adults in Colorado and southwestern New Mexico.

Data and Methods

Data from the U.S. Census Bureau and the Centers for Disease Control and Prevention are used to develop a profile of the population trends of the rural Latina/o older adults along with the demographic, socioeconomic, and health characteristics of this population. Demographic, socioeconomic, and health data are obtained from the 2013–2017 American Community Survey 5-Year Estimates (Ruggles et al., 2019; U.S. Census Bureau, 2020). Additionally, mortality data are derived from the Centers for Disease Control and Prevention's (2020) WONDER database for deaths occurring in 2013–2017. The data from these sources are based on Latina/os living in nonmetropolitan counties, rather than specifically in rural areas. The use of the traditional rural designation would have significantly limited the breadth of the analysis. Because of the relatively small Latino population in many states, the analysis is based on a five-year period to obtain more accurate estimates than obtained from a single year. The analysis also examines rural non-Hispanic whites and Blacks to lend a comparative perspective to the observed characteristics of rural Latina/o older adults.

The Profile of Rural Latina/o Older Adults

Population Trends

We estimate that there were 245,633 Latina/o elderly living in rural areas in the 2013–2017 period, accounting for 2.9% of the nation's rural population (Table 46.1). The rural Latina/o older adult population increased by 38% between the 2005–2007 and the 2013–2017 periods, outpacing the growth of the Black (10%) and white (9%) older adult populations.

While Latina/o older adults are located in all 47 states that have rural populations, they are concentrated in a few states. Slightly more than half (50.7%) of rural elder Latina/os lived in Texas and New Mexico in 2013–2017. Overall, ten states had more than 4,000 rural Latina/o older adults: Texas (87,228), New Mexico (37,396), Colorado (11,479), Arizona (9,610), California (9,314), Florida (7,207), North Carolina (4,854), Kansas (4,840), Oregon (4,391), and

Table 46.1 Population Trends for Rural Latina/o Elderly and Comparison Groups, 2005–2007 and 2013–2017

Race/Ethnic Group	*2005–2007*	*2013–2017*	*Absolute Change*	*Percent Change*
Latina/o	177,432	245,633	68,201	38.4
White	6,787,348	7,403,799	616,451	9.1
Black	416,817	458,700	41,883	10.0
Total	7,558,032	8,329,811	771,779	10.2

Source: 2007 American Community Survey 3-Year Estimates and 2017 American Community Survey 5-Year Estimates (U.S. Census Bureau, 2020)

Oklahoma (4,182). Latina/o older adults accounted for one-third of all rural older adults in New Mexico in 2013–2017. They also made up a substantial portion of older adults in rural Texas (17%), Arizona (15%), and Colorado (10%).

Demographic Characteristics

There are certain demographic differences by gender among rural Latina/o older adults. First, Latina women outnumber men with 89 males per 100 females, reflecting the higher death rates of men (Table 46.2). Second, aging Latina women are slightly older (median age of 73) than men (72.3). Third, because of men dying at a younger age, women (36.7%) are more likely than men (12.3%) to be widowed. Thus, men (67.6%) are more likely to be married than women (43.1%), but women (30.2%) are more likely than men (19.4%) to be living alone.

Latina/os exhibit greater diversity compared with rural older adults in general. Nearly one-third of Latina/o older adults are foreign-born and approximately one-sixth of all Latina/o older adults are not naturalized citizens (Table 46.2). Latina/o older adults also vary in their language use with half being bilingual (speaking Spanish at home and speaking English well or very well) and one-fourth each speaking either English at home or having limited or no English proficiency.

Socioeconomic Characteristics

Rural Latina/o older adults have limited socioeconomic resources. For example, less than half (49.3%) have a high school diploma or higher compared with 84% of white and 59% of Black older adults (Table 46.2). In addition, households headed by rural Latina/o older adults earn 74 cents for every dollar earned by those headed by white older adults. Overall, rural Latina/o older adults (19.7%) are more than twice as likely to be in poverty compared to their white counterparts (8.8%). While health insurance coverage is nearly universal among aging individuals, nearly 4% of rural Latina/o older adults lack this basic necessity compared with 0.3% of white older adults.

Health Characteristics

Latina/o older adults (45.4%) are more likely to have a disability compared with white older adults (38.1%) (Table 46.2). Yet, despite their low socioeconomic status and high rate of

Table 46.2 Selected Characteristics for Rural Latina/o Elderly and Comparison Groups, 2013–2017

Selected Characteristics	*Rural Latina/os*	*Rural Whites*	*Rural Blacks*
Sex ratio (males per 100 females)[a]	88.9	84.4	70.5
Median age[a]			
Female	73.0	73.8	73.4
Male	72.3	72.8	72.0
Percent current widowed[b]			
Female	36.7	35.6	46.0
Male	12.3	11.8	17.0
Percent currently married[b]			
Female	43.1	48.8	26.8
Male	67.6	72.0	52.4
Percent living alone[b]			
Female	30.2	35.5	38.3
Male	19.4	20.2	29.9
Pct. foreign-born[b]	31.9	1.6	0.8
Pct. not U.S. citizen[b]	15.7	0.4	0.3
Pct. distribution by language category:[b]			
Speak English at home	24.9	97.9	98.7
Bilingual	50.0	2.0	1.1
Limited or no fluency in English	25.1	0.1	0.1
Pct. high school graduate or higher[b]	49.3	83.5	59.3
Median household income of households headed by elderly[a]	$26,706	$36,301	$22,275
Pct. of persons 65 and older in poverty[a]	19.7	8.8	19.0
Pct. of persons 65 and older without health insurance[a]	3.6	0.3	0.7
Pct. of persons 65 and older with one or more disabilities[a]	45.4	38.1	45.7

[a] 2017 American Community Survey 5-Year Estimates (U.S. Census Bureau, 2020).
[b] 2017 American Community Survey 5-Year Estimates (Ruggles et al., 2020).

disability, rural Latina/o older adults die at a lower rate than white older adults. Regardless of age group, Latina/o older women and men have uniformly lower death rates compared with their white counterparts (Figure 46.1). Across the three age groups (65–74, 75–84, and 85 and older), on average, white women and white men have death rates that are 42% and 48% higher than those of Latina women and Latino men, respectively. These findings are consistent with the Latino epidemiological paradox.

Rural Latina/o older adults are particularly likely to die from certain causes. Their leading five causes of death include major cardiovascular diseases, malignant neoplasms, Alzheimer's disease, diabetes mellitus, and chronic lower respiratory diseases. Among these five leading causes of death, Latina/os have higher death rates than whites only for diabetes.

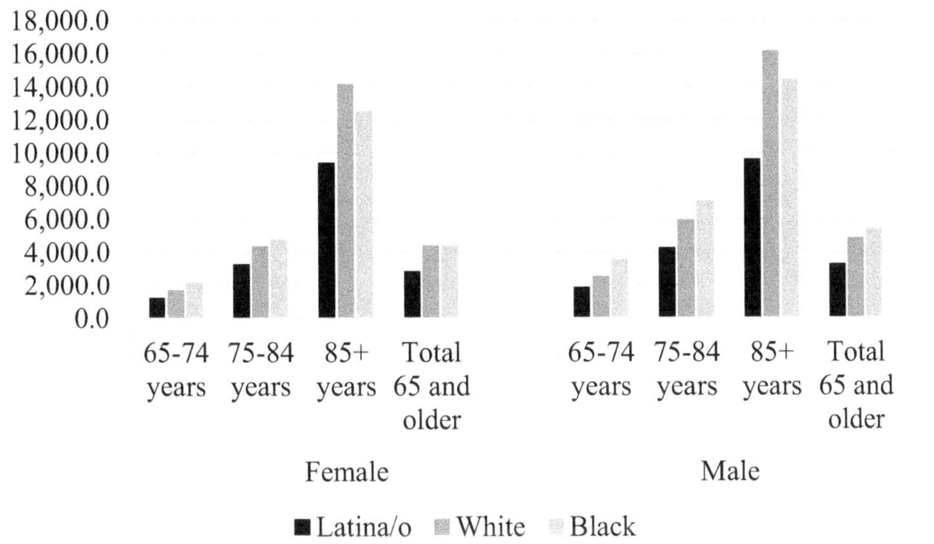

Figure 46.1 Age-Specific Death Rates Per 100,000 Persons for Rural Latina/o Elderly and Comparison Groups by Gender, 2013–2017

Source: About Underlying Causes of Death, 1999–2017 (Centers for Disease Control and Prevention, 2020)

Conclusions

The rural Latina/o older adult population is expanding at a rapid pace compared to other racial groups. The numbers of Latina/o rural older adults will expand substantially in the coming decades not only in traditional areas of the Southwest but also in Latino new destination areas. Latina/o older adults have a variety of challenges stemming from low socioeconomic resources, the lack of health insurance, and a high prevalence of disabilities. Nonetheless, despite the challenges that Latina/os face, they die at a lower rate than do whites, but do so with more health limitations related to diabetes, obesity, and disability (Garcia et al., 2017). Furthermore, it is clear that there is a major need to expand research on rural Latina/o older adults to ensure that they age successfully in their rural communities.

References

Averill, J. B. (2005). Studies of rural elderly individuals: Merging critical ethnography with community-based action research. *Multicultural Aging, 31*(12), 11–18.

Bastida, E., Brown, H. S., & Pagán, J. A. (2008). Persistent disparities in the use of health care along the US-Mexico border: An ecological perspective. *American Journal of Public Health, 98*(11), 1987–1995.

Centers for Disease Control and Prevention. (2020). *CDC WONDER database: About underlying cause of death, 1999–2017*. Retrieved from https://wonder.cdc.gov/ucd-icd10.html

Garcia, M. A., Downer, B., Crowe, M., & Markides, K. S. (2017). Aging and disability among Hispanics in the United States: Current knowledge and future directions. *Innovation in Aging, 1*(2), igx020.

Hamman, R. F., Mulgrew, C. L., Baxter, J., Shetterly, S. M., Swenson, C., & Morgenstern, N. E. (1999). Methods and prevalence of ADL limitations in Hispanic and non-Hispanic white subjects in rural Colorado: The San Luis Valley Health and Aging Study. *Annals of Epidemiology, 9*(4), 225–235.

Lee, S. J., Parrott, K. R., & Ahn, M. (2014). Housing adequacy: A well-being indicator for elderly households in southern U.S. communities. *Family and Consumer Sciences Research Journal, 42*(3), 235–251.

Letamendi, A. M., Ayers, C. R., Ruberg, J. L., Singley, D. B., Wilson, J., Chavira, D., . . . Wetherell, J. L. (2013). Illness conceptualizations among older rural Mexican-Americans with anxiety and depression. *Journal of Cross-Cultural Gerontology, 28*, 421–433.

Markides, K. S., & Coreil, J. (1986). The health of Hispanics in the southwestern United States: An epidemiologic paradox. *Public Health Reports, 101*, 253–265.

Marrow, H. B. (2011). *New destination dreaming: Immigration, race and legal status in the rural American South.* Stanford, CA: Stanford University Press.

Marshall, J. A., Lopez, T. K., Shetterly, S. M., Morgenstern, N. E., Baer, K., Swenson, C., . . . Hamman, R. F. (1999). Indicators of nutritional risk in a rural elderly Hispanic and non-Hispanic white population: San Luis Valley Health and Aging Study. *Journal of the American Dietetic Association, 99*(3), 315–322.

Mulgrew, C. L., Morgenstern, N., Shetterly, S. M., Baxter, J., Barón, A. E., & Hamman, R. F. (1999). Cognitive functioning and impairment among rural elderly Hispanics and non-Hispanic whites as assessed by the Mini-Mental State Examination. *Journal of Gerontology: Psychological Sciences, 54B*(4), P223–P230.

Pei, Y., Cong, Z., & Wu, B. (2019). Risk and resiliency in the relationship between widowhood and depressive symptoms among older Mexican Americans. *Journal of Cross-Cultural Gerontology, 34*, 149–170.

Ruggles, S., Flood, S., Goeken, R., Grover, J., Meyer, E., Pacas, J., & Sobek, M. (2020). *IPUMS USA: Version 10.0* [dataset]. Retrieved from https://usa.ipums.org/usa/

Saenz, R., Fox, A., & García, S. J. (2012). Latino elderly in nonmetropolitan America. In Glasgow, N., & Berry, E. H. (Eds.), *Rural aging in 21st century America* (pp. 115–140). Dordrecht, The Netherlands: Springer.

Saenz, R., & Morales, T. (2012). The Latino paradox. In R. R. Verdugo (Ed.), *The demography of the Hispanic population: Selected essays* (pp. 47–73). Charlotte, NC: Information Age Publishing.

Salinas, J. J., Su, D., & Snih, S. A. (2013). Border health in the shadow of the Hispanic paradox: Issues in the conceptualization of health disparities in older Mexican Americans living in the Southwest. *Journal of Cross-Cultural Gerontology, 28*, 251–266.

U.S. Census Bureau. (2020). *American factfinder: American Community Survey.* Retrieved from https://factfinder.census.gov/faces/nav/jsf/pages/searchresults.xhtml?refresh=t

Valle, I. (1994). *Fields of toil: A migrant family's journey.* Pullman, WA: Washington State University Press.

Xu, K. T., & Rojas-Fernandez, C. H. (2003). Ancillary community pharmacy services provided to older people in a largely rural and ethnically diverse region: A survey of consumers in West Texas. *Journal of Rural Health, 19*(1), 79–86.

47
LEADERSHIP

Linda Silka

Leadership development among rural-dwelling older adults is of great importance. Rural areas need to be able to draw on the depth of experience and resources that older adults can bring to solving long-standing as well as emerging problems. Yet despite the need for rural leaders, the majority of programs on leadership development offer their trainings in urban areas and take for granted that the leadership training and the leadership itself will occur in areas where people can readily come together. People are simply assumed to live in close proximity, and distance and lack of access to transportation (both public and private) are not regarded as posing significant barriers. Models for rural leadership among older adults often need to be different than standard issue generic leadership development programs.

It is important at the same time to recognize that conceptions of leadership are undergoing changes that challenge traditional notions that leadership is about a single leader or a single individual guiding everyone else. Increasingly, it is recognized that effective leadership is about teams of people working together to address challenges and make change (Hart, 2018; Pentland, 2012). The leadership team model makes a difference in how training for leadership is conceived. A single person is no longer deemed the leader, with that "anointed" person being trained to build on those initial assets so that he or she is prepared to lead everyone else. Instead of this single leader model, efforts are increasingly directed at developing leadership training that helps many people lead together. Leadership is increasingly seen as needing to be about collaborative partnership (Bieluch, 2018; MacDonald, Horne, Urioste-Stone, Haskell, & Weiskittel, 2018). Teamwork and collaboration are the new leadership (Hart, 2018; Wolff, 2010). As will be seen, rural elder leadership may be well placed for taking in this form of leadership that is increasingly seen as effective and longer lasting.

Given the importance for leadership models that meet the needs of rural elders, where might we look for models and information? In many states, Cooperative Extension programs continue to serve as an important resource for rural leadership training and leadership development and such programs are attending to new models (Diem & Nikola, 2005). The training often recognizes that to be effective, it must be designed to address the unique challenges faced in rural areas as well as build on the unique strengths that include the roots of rural older adults often being deeper than those of their counterparts in urban areas. Other programs are also emerging. Illustrative examples include *LEAP: Leadership Enhancement for the Active Retired* offered by the Center on Rural Elderly, Kansas City (Schultz & Olson, 1990). And there are now handbooks that can be very helpful. These include *The Community Leadership Handbook: Framing Ideas, Building Relationships, and Mobilizing Resources* (Curphy, Krile, & Lund, 2013)

Much of the emerging rural leadership training also recognizes that the nature of connections among rural people are different than in many urban areas. This understanding comes with strong research support. The scholar Roger Barker very early on completed ground-breaking research on the concept of behavior settings and staffing theory that demonstrated that small settings (e.g., rural areas, communities, and schools) result in people filling multiple roles in ways that are not the case in urban areas. In part, this means that in small settings, people are not siloed into a single role (Schoggen, 1979, 1989). This has important implications for leadership. That research is still remarkably clear in guiding important ways of thinking about rural areas and how to build on the multiple links that exist among people that can strengthen leadership.

In addition, the importance of attending to assets rather than deficits is increasingly being recognized. *Rural Communities: Legacy and Change* (Flora, Flora, & Gasteyer, 2016) is illustrative. The book outlines a capital framework, analyzing many forms of capital—community capital, natural capital, cultural capital, human capital, social capital, political capital, financial capital, and built capital—that must be considered in understanding rural communities and, by extension, leadership opportunities. Older rural residents are often significant sources of many of these kinds of capital.

As much of this summary suggests, within the changing context of leadership, solutions are still being sought with regard to best practices for rural older adult leadership training. There are still significant problems to be solved. One of the challenges of training continues to be that rural people sometimes live so far apart that it is difficult and time consuming to come together for training. To address this challenge, it has been suggested that online training through the internet could be the answer. Here's the challenge. Many rural areas continue to have limited access to the internet. Until the internet is more accessible, this "vehicle" for delivery may not be an option. Moreover, such training often assumes that people have computers and are comfortable with using computers. We know that this differs depending on age. A national representative study by Pew Research Center (Anderson & Perrin, 2017) found that while use by older populations is increasing, it remains substantially lower than in adults of other ages (Fields, 2019) and use by rural older adults is much lower than that of urban older adults (Calvert, Kaye, Leahy, Hexem, & Carlson, 2009). So elder training on leadership using the internet still needs to solve many problems.

In summary, exciting shifts are going on in leadership development that reflect changes in the understanding of leadership and changes in the contexts in which leadership will be enacted. Much is likely to continue to shift as emerging problems in how to grow and use leadership skills become better understood and addressed. At present, those who are looking to develop leadership programs that will work for rural older adults are likely to discover that no single source yet captures all that they need. Building effective programs will call for drawing on and modifying existing approaches to customize their fit to the context in which the rural leadership training will take place.

References

Anderson, M., & Perrin, A. (2017, May 17). *Adoption climbs among older adults*. Washington, DC: Pew Research Center.

Bieluch, K. H. (2018). Leadership as partnership. *Maine Policy Review*, *27*(1), 34–35.

Calvert, J. F., Jr., Kaye, J., Leahy, M., Hexem, K., & Carlson, N. (2009). Technology use by rural and urban oldest old. *Technology and Health Care*, *17*(1), 1–11.

Curphy, G., Krile, J. F., & Lund, D. R. (2013). *The community leadership handbook: Framing ideas, building relationships, and mobilizing resources*. St. Paul, MN: Fieldstone Alliance.

Diem, K. G., & Nikola, M. P. (2005). Evaluating the impact of a community agricultural leadership development program. *Journal of Extension*, *43*(6), Research in Brief.

Fields, J. (2019, May 5). We are leaving older adults out of the digital world. *Techcrunch.com*.

Flora, C. B., Flora, J. L., & Gasteyer, S. P. (2016). *Rural communities: Legacy and change* (5th ed.). Boulder, CO: Westview Press.

Hart, D. D. (2018). Teamwork is the new leadership. *Maine Policy Review*, *27*(1), 30–33.

MacDonald, B. H., Horne, L., Urioste-Stone, S., Haskell, J., & Weiskittell, A. (2018). Collaborative leadership is key to Maine's forest products industry. *Maine Policy Review*, *27*(1), 90–98.

Pentland, A. (2012). The new science of building great teams. *Harvard Business Review*, *90*(4), 60–69.

Schoggen, P. (1989). *Behavior settings: A revision and extension of Roger G. Barker's ecological psychology*. Stanford, CA: Stanford University Press.

Schoggen, P. (1979). Roger G. Barker and behavior settings: A commentary. *Journal of Personality and Social Psychology*, *37*(12), 2158–2160. doi:10.1037/0022-3514.37.12.2158

Schultz, C. M., & Olson, P. (1990). *LEAP: Leadership enhancement for the active retired*. Kansas City, MI: Center for Rural Elderly, University of Missouri Kansas City.

Wolff, T. (2010). *The power of collaborative solutions*. San Francisco, CA: Jossey-Bass.

48
LGBTQ OLDER ADULTS

Sandra S. Butler

Introduction

This entry reviews what is known about the experiences of lesbian, gay, bisexual, transgender, and/or queer (LGBTQ) older adults who reside in rural regions of the U.S. This sexual and gender minority group is very diverse and, while treated together here, the group's components are distinct. The term lesbian refers to women who are physically and/or emotionally attracted to women. Gay, although historically used as a general term for both men and women, more recently has typically referred specifically to men who are physically and/or emotionally attracted to men. The term bisexual describes people who are emotionally attracted to both genders. The term transgender refers to people whose gender identity and/or expression does not align with the sex they were assigned at birth, and queer refers to individuals whose gender and sexual identity are fluid (Fredriksen-Goldsen, 2016).

Recently, the available research on the lives and experiences of LGBTQ older adults has grown substantially. Before the turn of the century, only a scattering of studies were conducted and these were largely focused on gay men and lesbians; but in the past decade, two large, national-sample studies on LGBTQ older adults—one of which is longitudinal and ongoing—have been initiated by a team of researchers at the University of Washington (Fredriksen-Goldsen et al., 2011; Fredriksen-Goldsen & Kim, 2017). Because the population of older LGBTQ adults has been largely hidden because of a history of discrimination, criminalization, and stigma, accessing samples of older adults has been challenging, resulting in samples that often include individuals as young as 45 to 50 years old. Furthermore, there is a dearth of research on LGBTQ individuals living in rural regions, and even less on the experiences of older individuals in the population. Nonetheless, some general themes emerge from this limited research. Before reviewing those studies, it is important to understand the sociocultural context in which today's generation of LGBTQ older adults lived their formative years.

Historical Context

Many of today's LGBTQ older adults were teenagers or young adults prior to the gay liberation movement of the 1970s. They grew up in an environment in which homophobia, transphobia, and risks of self-disclosure were substantial (Butler, 2004). This was a time when being a sexual or gender minority was considered a crime. State sodomy laws were pervasive, only completely overturned in 2003 with the Supreme Court decision *Lawrence v. Texas* (ACLU, 2013). Being LGBTQ at this time also meant being labeled as mentally ill. In the first two editions of the *Diagnostic and Statistical Manual of Mental Disorders* (DSM), published in 1952 and 1968, LGBTQ individuals were classified as child molesters, exhibitionists, voyeurs, and people who committed destructive and anti-social crimes. Homosexuality was not removed from the list of DSM disorders until 1973; "Gender Identity Disorder" was not replaced with "Gender Dysphoria" until 2013 (LGBTQ Task Force, n.d.).

Before looking specifically at the experiences of older LGBTQ individuals living rurally—about which little is known—existing research on the experiences of rural-living for sexual and gender minorities of all ages will be reviewed.

The Rural Experience for LGBTQ Individuals

While rural regions in the U.S. are far from homogeneous, there is evidence that they are generally more conservative than urban areas. Dillon and Savage (2006) reported that the nationally representative General Social Survey found rural Americans to be more likely to attend church and identify as born-again Christians than their urban counterparts. They were also more likely to oppose abortion and same-sex marriage. One of the first articles to look specifically at the "gay experience" in the rural U.S. was titled "The Special Problem of Rural Gay Clients," published in 1980 by Moses and Buchner (cited in D'Augelli & Hart, 1987). They described gay individuals and lifestyles as completely contradictory to rural values of appropriate gender roles, marriage, traditional family living, and religious morality. D'Augelli and Hart (1987) underscored that given the enforced invisibility of sexual minorities in rural areas during the 1980s, little was known about their experiences. Furthermore, they pointed out that non-LGBTQ professionals were not knowledgeable about, nor actively affirming of, their LGBTQ clients in rural areas, and that LGBTQ professionals were cautious about coming out because of fear of loss of jobs and respect.

Since these early descriptions of the LGBTQ experience in rural U.S., a number of small studies have increased our knowledge on the topic. For example, Cody and Welch (1997) examined the life experiences and coping styles of 20 gay men living rurally in northern New England, identifying both positive and negative aspects of nonmetropolitan living. Positive aspects included the proximity to outdoor recreational activities, the beauty of their surroundings, the simplicity of living in a small town, and strong bonds with partners and other gay male friends. Nonetheless, many found rural life isolating. They had few opportunities to meet other gay men and traveled to cities to find gay community. Moreover, they feared losing the friendships they had if they came out (Cody & Welch, 1997). The literature on lesbians in rural environments during this time frequently mentioned the "land bands," which were intentional women's communities created by feminist lesbians between 1965 and 1985 (Bell & Valentine, 1995).

Conducting empirical research on LGBTQ rural populations is particularly difficult as non-metropolitan settings often lack visible gay organizations and communities through which to access samples (Otis, 2008). Oswald and Culton (2003) tackled this challenge and were successful in obtaining a relatively large sample (n=527) through distributing surveys, examining LGBTQ rural life, to organizations and networks they could find in 37 rural counties in Illinois. Findings from that study indicated a fragmented and closeted gay community, with respondents reporting a need to closely manage their disclosure of LGBTQ identity. For a more extensive review of literature on the experience of LGBTQ individuals of all ages living rurally in the

U.S., see Butler (2017). The research regarding rural LGBTQ older adults specifically is sparser still, but a few studies have been conducted and are reviewed next.

LGBTQ Older Adults in Rural Regions

Not surprisingly, the empirical research on LGBTQ older adults in rural regions is also based primarily on small sample studies. For example, two early studies on late middle-aged and older lesbians in New England were qualitative with small samples. Butler and Hope (1999) found study participants to be concerned about health-care access due to poverty and rural residence, but several noted the benefits of sensitive health-care providers, some of whom were lesbians known to study participants personally. Fears related to potential homophobia, should they need long-term care, were also mentioned. Another study of older rural lesbians emphasized the importance of lesbian community to meet social and emotional support needs, which the authors noted might be more difficult to access as study participants grew older and less mobile (Comerford, Henson-Stroud, Sionainn, & Wheeler, 2004).

More recently, Lee and Quam (2013) performed a secondary analysis of LGBTQ baby boomers (most middle aged at the time of the survey; n=1,201) to examine geographic differences among respondents. They found that urban and rural respondents differed with respect to income, levels of "outness," and self-reported LGBTQ identity; rural respondents indicated, on average, lower levels on all three variables. Rural respondents were more concerned with disclosure management, and more guarded with their LGBTQ identity among friends, family, neighbors and co-workers. Also in 2013, a study of Area Agencies on Aging indicated that urban-based agencies were more likely than rural-based agencies to provide LGBTQ outreach and services, to believe addressing LGBTQ issues was important, and to receive requests from self-identified LGBTQ older adults (Knochel, Croghan, Moone, & Quam, 2013). Additional studies focused on LGBTQ older adults in rural areas can be found in Butler (2017).

It is interesting to note that, at the time of this writing, the large-scale national studies of older LGBTQ individuals out of the University of Washington (Fredriksen-Goldsen et al., 2011; Fredriksen-Goldsen & Kim, 2017) have not yet performed any rural-urban comparisons, though respondent zip codes have been gathered (personal communication, Charles Emlet, June 25, 2019). It is likely that this sample is largely urban, given that respondent recruitment took place through large LGBTQ organizations throughout the country and these tend to be located in urban areas.

A few key themes emerge from the limited research on LGBTQ older adults in rural regions. As is true for non-LGBTQ older adults, nonmetropolitan areas present both benefits and challenges to aging. Benefits include the closeness to nature and natural beauty; a slower, simpler pace of life; and, in some cases, opportunities for strong bonds with neighbors, friends, and partners. On the other hand, challenges can include fewer social and health services and transportation options, and lower incomes, which can further compromise access to services and recreational activities. Compounding these disadvantages for LGBTQ older rural residents is the tendency of nonmetropolitan regions to be more conservative and less welcoming to those who do not reflect traditional roles and values. This can lead LGBTQ older adults to carefully manage their disclosure of sexual orientation and gender identity in order to avoid ostracism. One consequence of this is an increased risk of isolation, as LGBTQ communities tend to be smaller and often less visible in rural areas than in cities.

Best Practices

Health and social service practitioners in rural regions of the country may be working in conservative communities that may not always be open to diverse populations. Their older LGBTQ clients may be cautious about disclosure of their sexual orientation and gender identity and may be confronting significant isolation. Best practices for working with LGBTQ older adults in nonmetropolitan regions include:

- Creating LGBTQ-affirmative health and social service settings through printed material, intake forms, and office décor;
- Normalizing LGBTQ identity as a practitioner by being comfortable and open about one's own sexual orientation and gender identity;
- Supporting clients' choices on disclosure;
- Assisting clients to find existing LGBTQ networks and working to create new opportunities for social connections; and
- Actively working against bias and judgment within agencies and the larger community and advocating for civil rights where they don't already exist (Butler, 2017).

Future Directions

The literature reviewed here spans four decades and a time of incredible change for LGBTQ individuals (Zodikoff & Butler, 2015). Three relatively recent Supreme Court decisions reflect this change: *Lawrence v. Texas* in 2003 overturned state sodomy laws; *United States v. Windsor* in 2013 overturned parts of the anti-gay Defense of Marriage Act; and *Obergefell v. Hodges* in 2015 ruled that states cannot ban same-sex marriage.

Another dramatic change, with great potential to ease isolation for all older adults, has been the creation and evolution of the internet. Although some rural areas still lack access to high-speed broadband, this is changing steadily, giving formerly isolated LGBTQ older adults access to online connections and community.

The national organization Services and Advocacy for GLBT Elders (SAGE) has a network of local affiliates around the country. Most of these affiliates are in urban areas, but in 2013, the rural state of Maine established the first statewide affiliate of SAGENet. SAGEMaine has increased knowledge about and visibility of LGBTQ older adults in the state and considerably increased social opportunities for this population (Butler, 2017). Similar initiatives are being carried elsewhere as LGBTQ baby boomers—empowered by a more welcoming legal climate (notwithstanding the backsliding during the Trump administration)—move into their elder years. While challenges continue to exist for LGBTQ older adults living rurally, we are in a time of change that will likely benefit both current and future cohorts of this population.

References

American Civil Liberties Union (ACLU). (2013, June 16). *History of sodomy laws and the strategy that led to today's decision*. Retrieved from www.aclu.org

Bell, D., & Valentine, G. (1995). Queer country: Rural lesbian and gay lives. *Journal of Rural Studies*, *11*(2), 113–122.

Butler, S. S. (2004). Gay, lesbian, bisexual, transgender (LGBT) elders: The challenges and resilience of this marginalized group. *Journal of Human Behavior in the Social Environment*, *9*(4), 25–44. doi:10.1300/j137v09n04_02

Butler, S. S. (2017). LGBT aging in a rural environment. In K. Hash & A. Rogers (Eds.), *Annual review of gerontology and geriatrics* (Vol. 37, pp. 127–142). New York: Springer.

Butler, S. S., & Hope, B. (1999). Health and well-being for late middle-aged and old lesbians in a rural area. *Journal of Gay & Lesbians Social Services, 9*(4), 27–46.

Cody, P. J., & Welch, P. L. (1997). Rural gay men in Northern New England. *Journal of Homosexuality, 33*(1), 51–67.

Comerford, S. A., Henson-Stroud, M. M., Sionainn, C., & Wheeler, D. (2004). Crone songs: Voices of lesbian elders on aging in a rural environment. *Affilia, 19*(4), 418–436.

D'Augelli, A. R., & Hart, M. M. (1987). Gay women, men, and families in rural settings: Toward the development of helping communities. *American Journal of Community Psychology, 15*(1), 79–93.

Dillon, M., & Savage, S. (2006). *Values and religion in rural America: Attitudes toward abortion and same-sex relations.* Carsey Institute Issue Brief No. 1. Retrieved from http://scholars.unh.edu/carsey/12

Fredriksen-Goldsen, K. I. (2016). The future of LGBT+ aging: A blueprint for action in services, policies, and research. *Generations, 40*(2), 6–15.

Fredriksen-Goldsen, K. I., & Kim, H. J. (2017). The science of conducting research with LGBT older adults, an introduction to Aging with Pride: National Health, Aging, and Sexuality/Gender Study (NHAS). *The Gerontologist, 57*(Suppl 1), S1–S14. doi:10.1093/geront/gnw212

Fredriksen-Goldsen, K. I., Kim, H. J., Emlet, C. A., Muraco, A., Erosheva, E.A, Hoy-Ellis, C. P., . . . Petry, H. (2011). *The aging and health report: Disparities and resilience among lesbian, gay, bisexual and transgender older adults.* Seattle: Institute for Multigenerational Health. Retrieved from http://age-pride.org/wordpress/published-articles/

Knochel, K. A., Croghan, C. F., Moone, R. P., & Quam, J. K. (2013). Training, geography, and provision of aging services to lesbian, gay, bisexual and transgender older adults. *Journal of Gerontological Social Work, 55*(5), 426–443.

Lee, M. G., & Quam, J. K. (2013). Comparing supports for LGBT aging in rural versus urban areas. *Journal of Gerontological Social Work, 56*(2), 112–126.

National LGBTQ Task Force. (n.d.). *(In)validating transgender identities: Progress and trouble in the DSM-5.* Retrieved from www.thetaskforce.org/invalidating-transgender-identities-progress-and-trouble-in-the-DSM-5/

Oswald, R. F., & Culton, L. S. (2003). Under the rainbow: Rural gay life and its relevance for family providers. *Family Relations, 52*, 72–79.

Otis, M. D. (2008). Issues in conducting empirical research with lesbian and gay people in rural settings. In W. Meezan & J. I. Marin (Eds.), *Handbook of research with lesbian, gay, bisexual and transgender populations* (pp. 280–299). Florence, KY: Routledge.

Zodikoff, B. D., & Butler, S. S. (2015). Social work with lesbian, gay, bisexual, and transgender older adults. In D. B. Kaplan & B. Berkman (Eds.), *Oxford handbook of social work in health and aging* (2nd ed., pp. 555–564). New York: Oxford Press.

49
LONG-TERM CARE

Carrie Henning-Smith

Introduction

Compared with urban areas, rural areas have older populations, on average, with higher disability rates (Parker et al., 2018; Sage, Ward, Myers, & Ravesloot, 2019; Rural Health Information Hub, 2018). It follows that rural residents have greater needs for long-term care in both home and community-based settings. Long-term care (LTC), sometimes called long-term services and supports (LTSS), is defined as a wide range of services to help individuals with chronic or permanent functional limitations (National Institute on Aging, 2017), including difficulties with activities of daily living (e.g., eating, dressing, bathing) and instrumental activities of daily living (e.g., walking, getting around one's house and around town, managing medications). LTC can take many forms, including care in institutional settings, paid assistance, and care from loved ones.

Unpaid Caregiving

Formal LTC services include institutional care, such as skilled nursing homes, as well as home and community-based services (HCBS), such as help with medical care and chores in one's own home. The majority of all LTC, however, is provided by unpaid family members and friends, often called informal or unpaid caregivers. Every year, tens of millions of people provide unpaid care to loved ones, with an estimated value to society of nearly $500 billion (National Alliance for Caregiving & AARP Public Policy Institute, 2015). Caregiving can put a strain on the caregiver, if they are not given appropriate supports, resulting in poorer health outcomes than their non-caregiver counterparts (Anderson & White, 2017; Hoffman & Wallace, 2017; Ramsay, Reisinger Walker, Ramsay, Compton, & Thompson, 2012; Spillman, Wolff, Freedman, & Kasper, 2014). Rural caregivers may be especially vulnerable to these outcomes, given the greater demand for caregiving in rural areas and the increased barriers to accessing health care and other services (Coburn et al., 2017).

Rural caregivers who juggle their LTC responsibilities with employment outside of the home are much less likely to have supportive services available to them in their workplaces, compared with their urban peers (Henning-Smith & Lahr, 2018b). And supporting caregivers in rural areas requires addressing contextual challenges, such as transportation barriers, an aging population, and geographic and social isolation (Henning-Smith & Lahr, 2018a). That said, there are multiple examples of programs and policies in place to support rural caregivers, including training and education, counseling, respite services, support groups, online trainings, telephone support, and stress management (Lahr & Henning-Smith, 2018). For each of these, consideration of the specific rural environment is necessary when implementing programs designed to be sustainable (Henning-Smith & Blonigan, 2017), and much work is still needed to ensure that rural caregivers receive the support they need to provide good care and remain healthy themselves.

Formal Long-Term Care

In many cases, care from a loved one is either not possible or is not sufficient on its own. In those cases, care in an institutional setting or from paid providers may be necessary. However, while formal LTC services are available in rural areas, rural residents face unique barriers in accessing such care for a variety of reasons, including transportation, workforce shortages, and financial constraints (Coburn et al., 2017; Henning-Smith, Kozhimannil, Casey, & Prasad, 2018; Rural Health Gateway, 2019). Indeed, research finds that there are numerous barriers to LTC for rural residents who need it. For institutional LTC, which may be required on the basis of someone having particularly high acuity and/or on the basis of someone not having a suitable or accessible home situation or available paid or unpaid caregivers, barriers include there not being enough skilled workers to staff local nursing homes, long distances between facilities and patients, difficulty finding a facility that will accept Medicaid (the primary payer of LTC across the country, and especially in rural areas), and a lack of specialized units for particular conditions, such as dementia or complex conditions requiring intensive care (Henning-Smith, Casey, Prasad, & Kozhimannil, 2017; Henning-Smith, Kozhimannil, et al., 2018; Henning-Smith, Kozhimannil, & Prasad, 2017). For rural residents with obesity, dementia, or behavioral health concerns, it can be even more difficult to find appropriate and accessible placement near one's home (Henning-Smith, Casey et al., 2017). Needing to travel long distances to access care can mean that spouses/partners and other loved ones also need to travel farther to visit the patient, which can put a particular strain on rural residents living extended distances from health-care facilities.

In many cases when formal care is needed, HCBS is far preferable to patients compared with institutional LTC, as most people want to remain in their homes and communities as they age and as their health changes, a concept often referred to as "aging-in-place" (Iecovich, 2014). However, there are also barriers to accessing HCBS in rural areas. These barriers include many of the same barriers as those for institutional LTC, such as limited workforce availability and long distances between patients and home care agencies (Coburn et al., 2017). Additionally, housing stock in rural areas tends to be older than in urban areas (Pendall, Goodman, Zhu, & Gold, 2016), which can make it difficult to ensure dwellings are accessible and appropriate for individuals wishing to remain in their homes with functional limitations.

There is evidence that residents of both rural and urban areas go without LTC that they need. In fact, nearly half of older adults (65 and older) in rural and urban areas who need help with toileting report going without help at least some of the time, and nearly one-quarter have unmet needs for help going outside or getting around their home (Henning-Smith, Wu, & Lahr, 2019). Addressing such unmet need in a rural context requires ensuring that there is an adequate workforce, supports in place for unpaid caregivers, and attention to underlying issues like transportation (Coburn et al., 2017; Henning-Smith, Evenson, Corbett, Kozhimannil, & Moscovice, 2018; Henning-Smith, Lahr, & Casey, 2018).

Additionally, the need for LTC is not limited to older adults. Many individuals younger than 65 have functional limitations and long-term disabilities that require LTC. Accessing appropriate and acceptable care for those individuals in rural environments poses its own challenges. Because there are fewer facilities and services overall in rural areas, it is more difficult to find specialized services, especially if individuals need institutional long-term care (Henning-Smith, Kozhimannil et al., 2017). This may lead to younger and middle-aged adults living in nursing homes that were originally intended for older adults; while not necessarily a negative, as opportunities for intergenerational relationships can be incredibly valuable, more care may be needed to ensure that LTC needs of all rural residents are being met.

Future Issues and Implications

The importance of LTC for rural residents is only going to grow as the population ages and as people live longer with many chronic conditions and limitations. Advances in medical care that have allowed people to live—and thrive—well into older age with disabilities, coupled with public health interventions that have allowed more people to remain healthy into later life, when they may develop functional limitations requiring LTC, are all success stories. However, they also create an urgent need to ensure that LTC is available, accessible, affordable, and acceptable to the rural residents who need it. Doing so may mean investing in the health-care workforce for both institutional LTC and HCBS (Coburn et al., 2017) and investing in infrastructure, such as technology and transportation, to make care delivery easier. Additional creative solutions for funding LTC will also be required, as well as supportive services for unpaid caregivers who form the backbone of all LTC across the country, including in rural areas (Henning-Smith, Lahr et al., 2018; National Alliance for Caregiving & AARP Public Policy Institute, 2015).

On a policy level, resources should be devoted to ensuring access to high-quality LTC services and to supporting unpaid caregivers. On an individual level, more work is needed to help people plan for the possibility of needing LTC. On average, individuals underestimate their eventual need for LTC and few people have made concrete plans for such care, should they need it (Henning-Smith & Shippee, 2015). Those plans may include saving for care or investing in long-term care insurance, for individuals with the financial means to do so. It may also mean simply having conversations with loved ones about one's wishes for care so that appropriate plans can be put into place.

Regardless of the specific intervention, it is clear that much more attention needs to be directed to LTC across the country and especially in rural areas, where the need is greater and the challenges to providing timely, high-quality care are more pronounced.

References

Anderson, E. W., & White, K. M. (2017). "It has changed my life": An exploration of caregiver experiences in serious illness. *American Journal of Hospice and Palliative Medicine®*. doi:10.1177/1049909117701895

Coburn, A. F., Lundblad, J. P., Alfero, C., Mackinney, M. A. C., Mcbride, T. D., Mueller, K., . . . Mobley, E. M. (2017). Rural long-term services and supports: A primer. *RUPRI Health Panel*. Retrieved from www.rupri.org/wp-content/uploads/LTSS-RUPRI-Health-Panel-2017.pdf

Henning-Smith, C., & Blonigan, S. (2017). *Rural aging in place toolkit*. Retrieved from www.ruralhealthinfo.org/toolkits/aging

Henning-Smith, C., Casey, M., Prasad, S., & Kozhimannil, K. (2017). *Medical barriers to nursing home care for rural residents*. Minneapolis, MN: The University of Minnesota Rural Health Research Center. Retrieved from https://rhrc.umn.edu/publication/medical-barriers-to-nursing-home-care-for-rural-residents/

Henning-Smith, C., Evenson, A., Corbett, A., Kozhimannil, K., & Moscovice, I. (2018). *Rural transportation: Challenges and opportunities*. Minneapolis, MN: The University of Minnesota Rural Health Research Center. https://rhrc.umn.edu/publication/rural-transportation-challenges-and-opportunities/

Henning-Smith, C., Kozhimannil, K. B., Casey, M. M., & Prasad, S. (2018). Beyond clinical complexity: Nonmedical barriers to nursing home care for rural residents. *Journal of Aging & Social Policy*, *30*(2), 109–126. doi:10.1080/08959420.2018.1430413

Henning-Smith, C., Kozhimannil, K. B., & Prasad, S. (2017). Barriers to nursing home care for nonelderly rural residents. *Journal of Applied Gerontology*. doi:10.1177/0733464817746772

Henning-Smith, C., & Lahr, M. (2018a). *Perspectives on rural caregiving challenges and interventions*. Retrieved from https://rhrc.umn.edu/publication/rural-caregiving-challenges-and-interventions/

Henning-Smith, C., & Lahr, M. (2018b). Rural-urban difference in workplace supports and impacts for employed caregivers. *The Journal of Rural Health*. doi:10.1111/jrh.12309

Henning-Smith, C., Lahr, M., & Casey, M. (2018). A national examination of caregiver use of and preferences for support services: Does rurality matter? *Journal of Aging and Health*. doi:10.1177/0898264318786569

Henning-Smith, C., & Shippee, T. P. (2015). Expectations about future use of long-term services and supports vary by current living arrangement. *Health Affairs (Project Hope)*, *34*(1), 39–47. doi:10.1377/hlthaff.2014.0556

Henning-Smith, C., Wu, Z., & Lahr, M. (2019). *Unmet need for personal care assistance among rural and urban older adults*. Retrieved from https://rhrc.umn.edu/publication/unmet-need-for-personal-care-assistance-among-rural-and-urban-older-adults/

Hoffman, G. J., & Wallace, S. P. (2017). The cost of caring: Economic vulnerability, serious emotional distress, and poor health behaviors among paid and unpaid family and friend caregivers. *Research on Aging*. doi:10.1177/0164027517742430

Iecovich, E. (2014). Aging in place: From theory to practice. *Anthropological Notebooks*, *20*(1), 21–33.

Lahr, M., & Henning-Smith, C. (2018). *Resources for caregiving in rural communities*. University of Minnesota Rural Health Research Center Policy Brief. Retrieved from http://rhrc.umn.edu/wp-content/files_mf/1535129489UMNpolicybriefcaregivingresources.pdf

National Alliance for Caregiving and the AARP Public Policy Institute. (2015). *Caregiving in the U.S.—AARP 2015 report*. Retrieved from https://www.caregiving.org/research/caregivingusa/

National Institute on Aging. (2017). *What is long-term care?* Heatlh Information website. Retrieved October 8, 2019, from www.nia.nih.gov/health/what-long-term-care

Parker, K., Horowitz, J. M., Brown, A., Fry, R., Cohn, D., & Igielnik, R. (2018). *Demographic and economic trends in urban, suburban and rural communities*. Retrieved from www.pewsocialtrends.org/2018/05/22/demographic-and-economic-trends-in-urban-suburban-and-rural-communities/

Pendall, R., Goodman, L., Zhu, J., & Gold, A. (2016). *The future of rural housing*. Retrieved from www.urban.org/research/publication/future-rural-housing

Ramsay, C. E., Reisinger Walker, E., Ramsay, R., Compton, M. T., & Thompson, N. (2012). An exploration of perceptions of possible depression prevention services for caregivers of elderly or chronically ill adults in rural Georgia. *Community Mental Health Journal*, *48*(2), 167–178. https://doi.org/10.1007/s10597-010-9361-x

Rural Health Gateway. (2019). *Long-term care. A collection of federally-funded research projects focused on rural long-term care*. Retrieved from www.ruralhealthresearch.org/topics/long-term-care

Rural Health Information Hub. (2018). *Rural long-term care facilities*. Retrieved from www.ruralhealthinfo.org/topics/long-term-care

Sage, R., Ward, B., Myers, A., & Ravesloot, C. (2019). Transitory and enduring disability among urban and rural people. *The Journal of Rural Health: Official Journal of the American Rural Health Association and the National Rural Health Care Association*, *35*(4), 460–470. doi:10.1111/jrh.12338

Spillman, B., Wolff, J., Freedman, V., & Kasper, J. (2014). *Informal caregiving for older Americans: An analysis of the 2011 national study of caregiving*. doi:10.1093/geronb/gbu004. Retrieved from https://aspe.hhs.gov/report/informal-caregiving-older-americans-analysis-2011-national-study-caregiving

50
MEALS PROGRAMS

L. Carter Florence

Meal Offerings for Older Adults

Meals on Wheels organizations have a notable history beginning in the U.S. in Pennsylvania in the early 1950s and predating the federal supports to deliver nutrition to homebound older adults (Campbell et al., 2015). The concept of people, typically volunteers, delivering food to homebound individuals in need quickly spread throughout the country, resulting in numerous Meals on Wheels programs run with volunteers and supported via donation and small fees from those who were able to afford it. The need to have multiple methods to meet the nutritional needs of older adults has grown into numerous federal supports and the full complement of nutrition programs for older adults delivered through a host of community-based organizations such as Area Agencies on Aging, Community Action Agencies, churches, local government, and independent nonprofit organizations. These organizations exist in both rural and urban settings today.

There are several types of meal offerings made available for older adults. In general, the term senior nutrition program refers to federally supported programming designed to increase access to nutrition for older adults. There are two primary federal agencies with programming that supports the execution of senior nutrition programs—the Department of Health and Human Service's Administration for Community Living and the U.S. Department of Agriculture (USDA). The Department of Health and Human Service's programming, administered through the Administration for Community Living (ACL), focuses on the Older Americans Act (OAA) Nutrition Program. Within the OAA Nutrition Program, there are two main delivery components: 1. Congregate Nutrition Services; and 2. Home-Delivered Nutrition. A third provision under OAA is the Nutrition Services Incentive Program (NSIP). The NSIP exists to encourage serving more OAA-eligible meals by both home-delivered and congregate programs. Grant recipients can choose to receive support through grants and/or directly with the USDA's commodity foods. Within the USDA's administered programming for nutrition, four programs provide additional nutritional benefits to older adults, as well as other priority populations: 1. Supplemental Nutrition Assistance Program (SNAP); 2. Child and Adult Care Food Program (CACFP); 3. Senior Farmers' Market Nutrition Program (SFMNP); and 4. Commodity Supplemental Food Program (CSFP). These federal supports for nutrition bolster many nonprofit and governmental organizations along the continuum of local, grassroots organizations to mail-order, for-profit entities committed to increasing nutrition for older adults in both urban and rural settings. First, we will dive a bit deeper into the nutritional programs administered through ACL and USDA; then we will look at the local community-based organizations and how they approach and innovate to meet the needs of their rural communities.

The OAA-funded programs are designed with three main goals focused on: 1. reducing hunger and food insecurity; 2. promoting socialization for older individuals; and 3. promoting general health and well-being (Colello, 2018). As such, both direct meal programs—congregate and home-delivered—have many components above and beyond the meal itself. Congregate meals are served in a social setting to individuals who travel to a central location, like a senior center or adult day center. Many congregate settings offer services for supporting transportation to and from the congregate site in addition to other health promotion and wellness offerings. As with many other rural initiatives, transportation plays a challenging role in serving rural elders through congregate meals. The 2017 National Survey of OAA Participants found no statistically significant differences in the frequency of use of congregated dining for rural and urban participants, suggesting that congregate dining is accessed similarly in rural and urban areas (Government Accountability Office, 2019).

Home-delivered meals are meals delivered, often by volunteers, to individuals in their residence. Within the OAA provisions, modifications to the delivery can be made in rural areas, meaning some rural-residing older adults may only receive meals one time a week. In this model, meals are delivered frozen and a pre-set number of meals are provided based on funding, client need, and delivery frequency. Many home-delivered meal providers will augment delivery with a daily wellness phone call. The actual supplementary services provided will depend on the local provider for meals. To find a local meal provider, there are two helpful resources, the ACL's Eldercare Locator (www.eldercare.acl.gov) and Meals on Wheels America's Find a Meal (www.mealsonwheelsamerica.org/find-meals).

The USDA's Supplemental Nutrition Assistance Program (SNAP) and the Seniors Farmers' Market Nutrition Program (SFMNP) are designed for low-income older adults to access food through traditional and farmers' market venues, respectively. These are additional options found nationally to combat food insecurity. The Child and Adult Care Food Program supports reimbursement for meals served in adult day care centers. Finally, the Commodity Supplemental Food Program (CSFP) is designed to supplement the diets of low-income older adults.

Who Is Served?

While federal funding through the OAA and USDA may support a portion of older adults (60+) receiving meals, it does not support the full need for nutrition services by older adults. Meals on Wheels programs, which often deliver both home-delivered and congregate meals, report that on average, 39% of their overall funding comes from OAA support (Meals on Wheels America, 2019a). Additionally, OAA has been designed as a public-private partnership and includes provisions for older adults receiving services to pay some amount, if they are able to do so.

To best understand the meal program options available to rural older adults, you must first understand the make-up of older adults in rural communities. This insight lends needed context to the current scope of senior nutrition program options and how they may be accessed by rural-dwelling elders. In 2018, according to the U.S. Department of Agriculture's Economic Research Service's Rural America at a Glance, the majority (85%) of "older-age counties," that is, counties with 20% or more of their population aged 65 and older, are rural (Cromartie, 2018). Rural communities tend to be older for two main reasons. The first of these is that older adults move to rural communities to retire. Secondly, outmigration of younger adults leaves a disproportionately older population remaining in rural communities (Cromartie, 2018). It is necessary to understand how older adults come to live in rural communities when evaluating the options for and utilization of nutrition programs, as well as other support systems. Rural communities with retiree inmigration tend to be closer to large cities as opposed to those counties experiencing persistent outmigration and population loss. These community characteristics may provide insight into the availability and services delivered through nutrition programs.

According to the 2017 Profile of State OAA Programs, 35% of all OAA meal recipients lived in rural areas (Administration on Aging, 2018). A recent study conducted of the Meals on Wheels America membership, which includes both OAA and non-OAA Meals on Wheels providers, shows that 20% of respondents serve mostly or fully rural areas and 62% serve some number of older adults living in rural areas (Meals on Wheels America, 2019b). Meals on Wheels America is the largest national leadership organization dedicated to supporting community-based organizations focused on addressing older adult hunger and isolation. Additionally, a recent Government Accountability Office (GAO) report shows that rural older adults have less access to OAA Title III services (Government Accountability Office, 2019). This is the provision covering home-delivered and congregate meals. This report also documented challenges associated with delivering home-delivered meals in rural areas, including long distances for delivery routes, limited infrastructure (i.e., transportation), and limited broadband access.

Community-Based Innovation in Meal Programs

One of the inherently innovative aspects of nutrition programs is that they are designed for the community they serve. Meal program providers, like Meals on Wheels, are able to leverage this public-private partnership and the flexibility states are allowed to tailor their nutrition services programs to truly meet the changing needs of their community. As a trusted community-based entity, they are able to innovate and adapt to the changing needs of their older adult population. This adaptation and flexibility are seen in rural senior nutrition programs.

Both home-delivered and congregate models of meal delivery are moving to increase the choice in meal offerings, as well as provide culturally appropriate and medically tailored meal offerings. These include considerations such as Hallah and Kosher offerings, pureed and/or meals precut, also known as mechanically soft, and meals formulated for diabetics or other chronic illnesses to name a few. One Area Agency on Aging in rural Maine (Eastern Area Agency on Aging) that has been offering meals for clients with chronic illness for some time was awarded an ACL innovation grant in 2019 to establish and test a technology-enhanced chronic disease self-management program in partnership with the local hospital and a local academic institution. This is just one example of the innovation and flexibility found in rural communities when it comes to accessing nutrition and needed services for older adults.

The significance of nutrition programs like Meals on Wheels, especially in rural communities, is the ability to build trusting relationships and cross the threshold to fully understand the circumstances and challenges facing each individual and how that may change over time. These programs are constantly innovating to meet the growing needs of their communities. One rural example of innovation in meal delivery is found in two very different communities—Southeast Ohio and San Diego County, California, where a technology-enabled client monitoring system was piloted and proof of concept established. In this effort, the local Meals on Wheels programs have been able to test and refine a protocol that has evidence at being an effective system to act as an early-warning system (Morris et al., 2019). Innovation in the delivery system is not the only modification that many Meals on Wheels programs are looking to make. As mentioned earlier, many nutrition programs are also providing innovation in the types of meals delivered.

In some instances, they are exploring Medical Nutrition Therapy and partnerships with healthcare entities to support their offerings. The ability of programs to be flexible and responsive to the needs of the communities they serve is a hallmark of many senior nutrition programs. An important resource for learning more about nutrition programs for older adults and their innovation is the National Resource Center on Nutrition and Aging—nutritionandaging.org.

Key Takeaways

Meal programs in rural communities typically have community-based and federal supports that encourage a responsive and innovative approach to meeting the unique needs within their community. As with many services in rural communities, there is a great and growing need for services, as well as major barriers for delivery of those services. Yet there are tremendous assets in communities that can be leveraged to provide nutritional support to rural elders today and in the future.

References

Administration on Aging. (2018). *2017 profile of older Americans*. Retrieved from https://acl.gov/sites/default/files/Aging%20and%20Disability%20in%20America/2017OlderAmericansProfile.pdf

Campbell, A. D., Godfryd, A., Buys, D. R., & Locher, J. L. (2015). Does participation in home-delivered meals programs improve outcomes for older adults?: Results of a systematic review. *Journal of Nutrition in Gerontology and Geriatrics*, *34*(2), 124–167. doi:10.1080/21551197.2015.1038463

Colello, K. J. (2018). *Older Americans Act: Nutrition services program*. Congressional Research Service. Retrieved from https://fas.org/sgp/crs/misc/IF10633.pdf

Cromartie, J. (2018). *Rural America at a glance: 2018 edition*. U.S. Department of Agriculture. Washington, DC: USDA. doi:10.2139/ssrn.2367409

Government Accountability Office. (2019). *Older Americans Act: HHS could help rural service providers by centralizing information on promising practices*. Washington, DC. Retrieved from www.gao.gov/assets/700/699298.pdf

Meals on Wheels America. (2019a). *How Meals on Wheels is funded*. Retrieved from www.mealsonwheelsamerica.org/docs/default-source/fact-sheets/2019/2019-national/mowa2019factsheets_funding_final.pdf?sfvrsn=c52bb93b_2

Meals on Wheels America. (2019b). *More than a meal comprehensive network study*. Retrieved from https://www.mealsonwheelsamerica.org/docs/default-source/research/comprehensive-network-study-public-summary_may-2020.pdf?sfvrsn=66c6b43b_2

Morris, A. M., Engelberg, J. K., Schmitthenner, B., Dosa, D., Gadbois, E., Shield, R. R., & Thomas, K. S. (2019, June). Leveraging home-delivered meal programs to address unmet needs for at-risk older adults: Preliminary data. *Journal of the American Geriatrics Society*, *67*(9), 1946–1952. doi:10.1111/jgs.16013

51 RURAL MASCULINITIES

Edward H. Thompson, Jr.

Rural living—in the Midwestern northland and Heartland, Appalachia, northern New England, or the Red Rock Country of the Southwest—shares one feature, a thinly populated locale. Whether one thinks of "Rural America" as farmland, ranches, or small geographically isolated communities, it is likely skewed older. Typically, one-fifth of the people in a rural place are over 65, most are still married, own their home, and have lived in the same rural place most of their lives. Rural living is a learned preference. People acquire the *habitus* (preferences, practices) of rural living by embodying the underlying *nomos*. Bourdieu and Wacquant (1992, p. 127) explain:

> [S]ocial reality exists, so to speak, twice, in things and in minds, in fields and in habitus, outside and inside social agents. And when habitus encounters a social world of which it is the product, it is like a "fish in water": It does not feel the weight of the water and it takes the world about itself for granted.

As Wright (1998, p. xi) recognized, many newcomers without the cultural capital of rural life are ill-prepared to live in a tangible rural place; they feel like a "fish out of water." Long-timers have the cultural capital, and they sense threats to their cherished lifestyle, feeling challenged by rural places' lessening distinctiveness and their corporeal aging diminishing wanted self-sufficiency.

Across the U.S., rural places are graying faster than non-rural, and they were already gray. Nearly 85% of the nation's "older age counties" are characterized by their rurality, where at least one-fifth of the county population is age 65 and older (Cromartie, 2017). These counties considerably differ in terms of their aging population—e.g., racial/ethnic homogeneity, rates of poverty—and in terms of the encroachment of city amenities.

Here are two examples. First, Maine and Vermont are the two most rural states in the U.S. (Misra, 2016), with roughly 60% of their populations living in rural places (Smith & Trevelyan, 2019). The nearly exclusive whiteness (roughly 95%) of Maine and Vermont is unlike the remaining rural places in the U.S., which have a much greater mix of races and ethnicities. The marked grayness of Maine and Vermont is part of a national trend that shows an exodus of younger people to cities if not other states where employment and the quality of life are deemed better (Johnson, 2012). Left "aging in place" are older men and women, most who choose to remain in their community. Also increasing rural communities' graying population is some in-migration of newcomers who previously worked and lived in suburban or city places and seek the amenities of a post-retirement "rural lifestyle" (AARP, 2005).

Second, about half of all rural aging men live in the South and Southwest—e.g., the Mississippi and Appalachian valleys, and New Mexico (Smith & Trevelyan, 2019). Misra (2016) estimated that 60% of the graying rural population live east of the Mississippi, and almost half live in the South; here, the health disparities are significantly worse than other parts of the nation and attributable to the cumulative disadvantages of poorer socioeconomics in these rural places, and the men's embodiment of their local culture and ill-health habits (e.g., El-sadek, Zhang, Vargas, Funchess, & Green, 2015).

Appreciating rural places' difference in character also means we must recognize that men differ. The masculinity practices that men adopt as their personal *habitus* reflect their embodied generation, class, ethnicity, and geography. This emphasis on "intersectional" (Crenshaw, 1991) ruralities shaping aging rural men's habitus is unlike most analyses of aging rural men's lives. Scholarship on the relationships between rural living has remained largely ungendered, obscuring the importance of the locally constructed and contested masculinities. Most analyses are predicated on a construction of gender as only a binary (men versus women) and an interpretation of rural men's lives that devalues the so-called feminine over what is understood as masculine, such as ruggedness. This binary helped produce the fabricated "rural masculinity," which was discursively constructed in terms of its counterpart imaginary "urban masculinity" to emphasize the unspoken patriarchal gender relations and notions of self-reliance, hardiness, and restricted emotionality (cf., Levant & Habben, 2003).

Two decades ago Campbell and Bell (2000, p. 539) importantly noted, despite all efforts to portray rurality, there is no such thing as a singular object called "the rural" or "rural masculinity." Their premise matches Connell and Messerschmidt's (2005) concept of "geography of masculinities" and how spaces and places inform dominant/subordinate masculinities. Rural masculinities are locally constructed and contested. The masculinities men embody and perform arise from how race, class, age, generation, and geographies intersect.

Knowing this, there is the problem of lingering imaginaries that misrepresent rural men. Central Appalachian men are imagined as living their lifetime in a homogeneous mountain-dwelling culture (Shapiro, 1978), and aging men are imagined as white patriarchal "rednecks" and "hillbillies" who remain tied to the land in terms of mining and farming (cf., Brandth & Haugen, 2005; Huber, 1995; Morris, 2008). This construction basically depicts Appalachian rural masculinity as clannishness intertwined with whiteness, an economic underclass, deeply conservative religious ideologies, and conservative conceptions of gender. Consider how the 2017 Netflix series *Ozark* similarly portrays the long-term white mountaineers of a fictive Missouri rural community in a culture-clash imagery as being everything urbanites are not: conservative if not backward, white racist, homophobic, and sexist. Stenbacka (2011) would call this "othering the rural."

The facts show that the simplistic tale of "the" Appalachian masculinist culture is flawed as much as mining and farming are infrequent. Generations back but not recently, mountain-top and underground mining once were a primary means for many Appalachian men's economic and masculine capital, even though most men and their families remained in near abject poverty and had much poorer health than places without the industry (Zullig & Hendryx, 2010). Mining now makes up about 1% of total employment throughout Appalachia, behind farming (2.5%) and far behind the newer recreation-based economies (14.5%) that are related to rural places having become weekend and retirement destinations (Appalachian Regional

Commission, 2011; Cromartie, 2017). Netflix's *Ozark* got this aspect of contemporary rural living right, but the Make/Keep America Great campaigns of 2016 and 2020 haven't.

The empirical evidence also is at best equivocal when it comes to the portrayal of rural Appalachian aging (white) men being violence-prone. Whereas regional homicide rates are high in Southern rural areas, there is evidence that the rates are very similar to Western states and reflect a gun culture not a distinctive Southern (or central and southern Appalachian) subculture (Felson & Pare, 2010). In sum, as Carrington and Scott (2008) argued, rural residency is not likely associated with violence any more than non-rural places, because it is neither residency nor an honor culture but the threat to conservative masculinities wherever the men live that can spark violence. Similarly, owing to Northeast and Midwest rural places' whiteness and privileged masculinities, the covenant of independence can be played out among aging white men in terms of suicide (by firearms), a risk that increases significantly when preceded by a major life event such as unemployment or physical health problems (cf., Canetto, 2017; Canham, 2009; Kaplan, Huguet, McFarland, & Mandle, 2012).

A take away from debunking a simplistic view of any rural culture: Researchers, service providers, and policymakers need a much greater sensitivity to nuances of local rural masculinities when it comes to understanding the lives and needs of the men and their aging experiences. Continuing the Appalachian example, old white and black men may equally identify the hills and valleys as home, occasionally visit one another, work together, yet their experiences and discourses about rural living and aging diverge (Catte, 2018; Inscoe, 2001; Smith, 2004). White men's racial privilege and subsequent class privilege shape habitus, including the relations among the men (and between men and women) and racialized rural masculinity practices such as who's visiting is limited to the front porch. Aging black Appalachians have long been made invisible (Catte, 2018), but they are there, distinctly living another Southern Appalachia culture.

No matter where, understanding rural aging men's lives requires deserting the notion of "the" rural masculinity. There might be some similarities across geographies. Yet compared to Vermonters, aging Navaho sheepherders in New Mexico have access to a traditional culture that honors later life and aging masculinities (Lee, 2007; Todacheene, 2015). By contrast, a mostly uncontested way of life is not the case for the aging ranchers living in rural white Montana who now have to navigate population influx, subdivisions, and a deteriorating physical environment that threatens wildlife and place (Wright, 1998).

The rural men O'Lynn (2010) interviewed in his study of caregivers in two northwestern states equally encourage a need to attend to the nuances across rural masculinities. Running through the men's narratives was a near universal unwillingness to ask others for assistance while providing the care work. However, their motives for solo caring differed. One of his examples: men who had moved into the rural communities from urban areas felt they did not have the insider status as "locals," where everybody knows everybody, and these men sensed difficulty in obtaining neighbors' support if desired. Among the "locals," however, it was their long-term geographical isolation and preference of interdependence that distinguished their practices. They knew they had neighbor support should they ask, but their biographies had made self-reliance and ingenuity a prerequisite and preference.

Rural men's negotiation of gender practices as they age is likely to retain much of their earlier preferences and practices—e.g., self-reliance and dependence on wives (cf., Bridges & Pascoe, 2018; Riley, 2016; Thompson & Langendoerfer, 2016). Nevertheless, aging in rural places may be accompanied by noticeable declines in masculine capital and lead to quiet existential suffering. Health issues are common among aging men in rural places; as a group, they have multiple chronic conditions, take a lot of medications, and have high rates of chronic pain.

They have a greater chance of dying a preventable death (Garcia et al., 2017). These men may live long distances to a health-care facility and construct reasons for not seeking health care.

Aging men's narratives will reveal an intersectional life of what it meant to be a rural man worthy of respect. They all share a rural lifestyle, yet their stories expose the differences and inequalities among them. Needed are many qualitative studies to capture the voices and stories of aging rural men's lives, wants and needs, and uniquenesses.

References

AARP. (2005). *Retirement migration in the 2000 census*. Washington, DC: AARP Knowledge Management. Retrieved from http://assets.aarp.org/rgcenter/il /migration_2.pdf

Appalachian Regional Commission. (2011). *Appalachian region industrial report, 2010*. Retrieved from www.arc.gov/images/appregion/jan2011/industryreport-1-13-11.pdf

Bourdieu, P., & Wacquant, L. J. D. (1992). *An invitation to reflexive sociology*. Chicago, IL: University of Chicago Press.

Brandth, B., & Haugen, M. S. (2005). Doing rural masculinity—from logging to outfield tourism. *Journal of Gender Studies*, *14*, 13–22.

Bridges, T., & Pascoe, C. J. (2018). On the elasticity of gender hegemony: Why hybrid masculinities fail to undermine gender and sexual inequality. In J. M. Messerschmidt, P. Y. Martin, M. A. Messner, & R. Connell (Eds.), *Gender reckonings* (pp. 254–274). New York: New York University Press.

Campbell, H., & Bell, M. M. (2000). The question of rural masculinities. *Rural Sociology*, *65*, 532–546.

Canetto, S. S. (2017). Suicide: Why are older men so vulnerable? *Men and Masculinities*, *20*, 49–70.

Canham, S. L. (2009). The interaction of masculinity and control and its impact on the experience of suffering for an older man. *Journal of Aging Studies*, *23*, 90–96.

Carrington, K., & Scott, J. (2008). Masculinity, rurality and violence. *British Journal of Criminology*, *48*, 641–666.

Catte, E. (2018). *What you are getting wrong about Appalachia*. Cleveland, OH: Belt Publishing.

Connell, R. W., & Messerschmidt, J. W. (2005). Hegemonic masculinity: Rethinking the concept. *Gender & Society*, *19*, 829–859.

Crenshaw, K. (1991). Mapping the margins: Intersectionality, identity politics, and violence against women of color. *Stanford Law Review*, *43*, 1241–1299.

Cromartie, J. (2017). *Rural America at a glance*. Washington, DC: USDA ERS. Retrieved from www.ers.usda.gov/publications/pub- details/?pubid=85739

El-sadek, L., Zhang, L., Vargas, R., Funchess, T., & Green, C. (2015). *Mississippi health disparities and inequalities report*. Office of Health Disparity Elimination and the Office of Health Data & Research. Jackson, MS: Mississippi State Department of Health.

Felson, R. B., & Pare, P. P. (2010). Gun cultures or honor cultures? Explaining regional and race differences in weapon carrying. *Social Forces*, *88*, 1357–1378.

Garcia, M. C., Faul, M., Massetti, G., Thomas, C. C., Hong, Y., Bauer, U. E., & Iademarco, M. F. (2017). Reducing potentially excess deaths from the five leading causes of death in the rural United States. *MMWR Surveillance Summaries*, *66*(2), 1. Retrieved from www.cdc.gov/mmwr/volumes/66/ss/pdfs/ss6602.pdf

Huber, P. (1995). A short history of redneck: The fashioning of a southern white masculine identity. *Southern Cultures*, *1*, 145–166.

Inscoe, J. (2001). *Appalachians and race: The mountain South from slavery to segregation*. Lexington: University Press of Kentucky.

Johnson, K. M. (2012). *Rural demographic change in the new century: Slower growth, increased diversity*. Carsey Institute Issue Brief No. 44. Durham and New Hampshire: Carsey Institute, University of New Hampshire. Retrieved from www.carseyinstitute.unh.edu/publications/IB-Johnson-Rural-Demographic-Trends.pdf

Kaplan, M. S., Huguet, N., McFarland, B. H., & Mandle, J. A. (2012). Factors associated with suicide by firearm among US older adult men. *Psychology of Men & Masculinity*, *13*, 65–74.

Lee, L. L. (2007). The future of Navajo nationalism. *Wicazo Sa Review*, *22*(1), 53–68.

Levant, R. F., & Habben, C. (2003). The new psychology of men: Application to rural men. In B. Stamm (Ed.), *Rural behavioral health care: An interdisciplinary guide* (pp. 171–180). Washington, DC: American Psychological Association.

Misra, T. (2016). A complex portrait of rural America. *CityLab*. Retrieved from www.citylab.com/equity/2016/12/a-complex-portrait-of-rural-america/509828/

Morris, E. W. (2008). "Rednecks," "rutters," and rithmetic: Social class, masculinity, and schooling in a rural context. *Gender & Society*, *22*, 728–751.

O'Lynn, C. (2010). Negotiation of constructed gender among rural male caregivers. In C. Winters & H. Lee (Eds.), *Rural nursing: Concepts, theory, and practice* (3rd ed., pp. 193–224). New York: Springer.

Riley, M. (2016). Still being the "good farmer": (Non-)retirement and the preservation of farming identities in older age. *Sociologia Ruralis*, *56*, 96–115.

Shapiro, H. D. (1978). *Appalachia on our mind: The southern mountains and mountaineers in the American consciousness, 1870–1920*. Chapel Hill: University of North Carolina Press.

Smith, A. S., & Trevelyan, E. (2019). *The older population in rural America: 2012–2016*. Washington, DC: U.S. Census Bureau (Presented at the Annual Meeting of the Population Association of America Austin, TX, April 10–13, 2019). Retrieved from www.census.gov/content/dam/Census/newsroom/press-kits/2019/paa/paa-poster-older-population.pdf

Smith, B. E. (2004). De-gradations of whiteness: Appalachia and the complexities of race. *Journal of Appalachian Studies*, *10*(1–2), 38–57.

Stenbacka, S. (2011). Othering the rural: About the construction of rural masculinities and the unspoken urban hegemonic ideal in Swedish media. *Journal of Rural Studies*, *27*, 235–244.

Thompson, E. H., & Langendoerfer, K. B. (2016). Older men's blueprint for "being a man." *Men and Masculinities*, *19*, 119–147.

Todacheene, H. J. (2015). She saves us from monsters: The Navajo creation story and modern tribal justice. *Tribal Law Journal*, *15*, 30–66.

Wright, J. B. (1998). *Montana ghost dance: Essays on land and life*. Austin, TX: University of Texas Press.

Zullig, K. J., & Hendryx, M. (2010). A comparative analysis of health-related quality of life for residents of U.S. counties with and without coal mining. *Public Health Reports*, *125*, 548–555.

52
MENTAL AND BEHAVIORAL HEALTH

Jennifer A. Crittenden

Overview

The impacts of mental health and substance use disorders reverberate throughout rural communities and have significant implications for older adults and their families. Rural areas have shouldered much of the burden of the opioid epidemic, which affects residents across the life span with rural residents having a greater likelihood of experiencing an overdose. While substance use disorder prevalence is similar across rural and urban settings, data suggest that the use of alcohol is higher in rural areas and the impacts of opioid use are more significant in rural regions. Furthermore, close to one in four rural older adults is considered at-risk for depression and suicide compared to their urban counterparts, with older white males being at the highest risk for suicide. Based on 2018 figures, 13.7% of older adults directly report feeling depressed and 22.6% experience worry or anxiety on at least a monthly basis. Rural older adults with depression are less likely to have a regular source of health care and appropriate treatment options (Bocker, Glasser, Nielsen, & Weidenbacher-Hoper, 2012; Ewald, Loganathan, Hasche, & Lochner, 2017; Gale, Janis, Coburn, & Rochford, 2019; Kaiser Family Foundation [KFF], 2020).

Key populations of older adults in rural areas face additional challenges and higher rates of behavioral health (BH) and mental health (MH) issues including veterans and individuals of color for whom health disparities already exist. For rural veterans in particular, those who do access support are more likely to receive pharmaceutical interventions without access to psychotherapy support for their BH and MH needs (Gale et al., 2019).

Isolation and loneliness experienced by rural older adults further increases behavioral health and mental health risk. Prior to COVID-19, 43% of adults 60 and older reported feeling lonely and 24% were considered socially isolated (The National Academies of Sciences, 2020). The recent pandemic has served to only increase the experience of isolation, loneliness, and stress among rural older adults. Approximately one in five adults sheltering in place due to COVID-19 reported that virus-related stress was negatively impacting their mental health. Rural areas are disproportionately affected by COVID-19 because of the high rates of chronic disease and poor health among rural populations. This too translates into more COVID-19 burden for rural residents with over half of adults with fair or poor health reporting that coronavirus stress has negatively impacted their mental health (KFF, 2020).

While rates of MH and BH issues and diagnoses are similar across rural and urban settings, several factors put rural older adults at risk for not receiving the supports they need. First, when compared to urban older adults, rural older adults are less likely to seek out MH services when such help is needed (Hayslip, Maiden, Thomison, & Temple, 2010). This phenomenon has also been noted even when older adults are aware of existing treatment resources and supports (Bocker et al., 2012). In addition, rural areas have ongoing and persistent gaps in mental health and behavioral health service access compared to urban areas. When such services are available, they are likely to require extensive travel, long waits, and translate to briefer visits with specialists. These gaps are further magnified by the lack of transportation and broadband internet for telehealth services (Rural Health Info Hub [RHIH], 2018; Snell-Rood, Feltner, & Schoenberg, 2019).

As many as two-thirds of rural older adults report having been aware of mental health and behavioral health services in their community, yet only a small fraction report using such services (Bocker et al., 2012). What accounts for this difference? In broad terms, MH and BH service access in rural communities can be framed around issues of acceptability and availability of services. For services to be effective for rural older adults, they must be considered acceptable by potential clients. Service acceptability is influenced by factors surrounding trust of the provider, the extent to which services are culturally sensitive and relevant, the perception of privacy, and the provision of services in a non-stigmatizing fashion (RHIH, 2018; Substance Abuse and Mental Health Services Administration, 2016). Availability of services is impacted by the extent to which such services are conveniently located and accessible when needed by older adults and when services are delivered by providers who have adequate training and resources. Interestingly, older adults who are able to successfully connect with services are more likely to have positive views of such assistance and seek it out further in the future (Bocker et al., 2012).

Older adults face multiple barriers in seeking and connecting with MH and BH supports. At the core of this issue is the "boot straps" mentality found in rural areas, which brings a focus on self-reliance and a reluctance to seek help with matters that are otherwise considered private. This mentality coupled with the stigma surrounding the use of mental health services keeps many rural older adults from accessing such services (Brenes, Danhauer, Lyles, Hogan, & Miller, 2015; RHIH, 2018). Reducing the stigma of treatment entails collaboration with primary care, peers, and other stakeholders in rural communities.

Addressing Behavioral Health and Mental Health

Primary Care Integration

The integration of BH and MH services into primary care is a common approach to addressing access and acceptability issues among rural residents. Rural residents demonstrate an inclination to seek BH and MH first at their primary care provider with 54% of MH related office visits occurring in primary care offices as compared to 29% of such visits occurring with a psychiatrist (Cherry, Albert, & McCraig, 2018). Primary care integration can take a variety of forms from shared referrals or contractual agreements between providers, to full integration with BH and MH providers physically situated on-site with primary care (Gale et al., 2019).

Care integration within primary care has been shown to improve patient outcomes such as depressive symptoms and quality of life measures, and integrated care consistently receives high ratings from consumers (Balasubramanian et al., 2017). However, models of integrated care in rural areas are not without challenges. Common barriers noted include the need to overcome workforce and consultative provider shortages as well as provider stigma, provider training gaps, and practice differences between primary care and BH and MH (Gale et al., 2019). Further, such models require that integrative practices be sensitive to local context and culture to effectively serve the diverse patient population found in rural locales (Balasubramanian et al., 2017; Selby-Nelson, Bradley, Schiefer, & Hoover-Thompson, 2018).

As trusted sources of health information and care, the integration of BH and MH into primary care is one method for reducing the stigma associated with receiving BH and MH treatment. Given that specialty providers are not readily available in rural areas, primary care providers should extend their knowledge and training into BH and MH areas as well as geropsychiatric issues. Project Extension for Community Healthcare Outcomes, known as Project ECHO©, is one effective training model that has been used to give rural primary care providers access to specialty mental health training using distance technologies. Project ECHO training has been noted to improve the integration of MH into primary care practice by increasing provider knowledge and confidence in addressing MH issues (Sockalingam et al., 2018).

Technology-Based Approaches

Technological innovations in rural areas have increased access and acceptability of mental health services. As access to broadband and higher-end technologies may be lacking in rural areas, lower tech options such as the use of tele-counseling have been implemented successfully in these settings. Telephone-based psychotherapy has been found to be effective for conditions such as depression and obsessive compulsive disorder (OCD), especially when paired with a medication approach, cognitive behavior therapy (CBT), and carefully monitored by a trained professional (Velasquez, Duncan, & Nelson, 2012).

In addition, as a result of the COVID-19 pandemic, providers are now increasingly using accessible applications for distance visits that can be carried out comfortably from home or the community if technology is readily available. Beyond availability of technology, uptake of home-based telehealth technologies by older adults is influenced by the extent to which older adults perceive the technology to be useful, easy to use, and secure. Older adults are also more likely to use telehealth technologies if recommended by their physician or other trusted health-care provider (Cimperman, Brenčič, Trkman, & Stanonik, 2013). When technology is not available for home-based virtual visits, technology can be integrated into the hospital and primary care settings successfully to connect older patients with remote MH and BH providers such as psychologists and geriatric psychiatrists.

Home and Community-Based Models

The use of community members, peers, and other trusted entities within rural areas serves as the cornerstone for effective early intervention and referral. For example, the community health worker (CHW) approach is a peer-driven health support model that trains community members to take on a variety of health-care roles from health educator, service navigator, to advocate and community organizer. CHWs tend to have lived experience and/or hail from local communities in which they work. Because many CHW efforts are grassroots in nature, CHWs quickly become a trusted source of information and support in rural communities (Infante, Knudson, & Brown, 2011).

The role of the CHW model can be successfully expanded to include a focus on MH and BH. Because CHWs cultivate personal relationships with clients, they are in a position to help identify, refer, and support clients as they obtain BH and MH services. CHWs also support clients between their health-care appointments and prepare them for visits by ensuring that barriers like transportation and insurance are addressed ahead of time. CHWs can also play an important role in supporting self-advocacy and improving medication adherence among their clients (Snell-Rood et al., 2019).

Because of the transportation barriers faced by rural older adults and distance to MH and BH providers, in-home intervention models are a convenient and acceptable modality for engaging older adults in treatment. One such model, the Program to Encourage Active, Rewarding Lives for Seniors (PEARLS), is an evidence-based, in-home intervention for older adults with depression. The PEARLS model is carried out in eight 50-minute sessions over the course of 19 weeks with specially trained care managers. This innovative model has been found to increase quality of life, reduce depressive symptoms, and, for some, bring about remission from depression altogether (Ciechanowski et al., 2004).

The Brief Intervention & Treatment for Elders (BRITE) model offers a community-based approach to screening, identifying, and treating older adults who are at-risk of substance misuse. Under the BRITE model, brief screening and intervention occurs over the course of one to five sessions in-home. For those older adults requiring treatment beyond the brief intervention, treatment sessions can be provided over the course of 16 in-home sessions with follow-up screening completed by phone or in-person as needed. The model has been found to reduce substance misuse risk and depression and suicide risk for participants by identifying and treating older adults who would otherwise not be identified via traditional MH and BH programs. The BRITE model has also been successful in engaging a diverse group of older adults, partly because of its community-based approach as program recruitment is conducted at health fairs, congregate housing sites, and other community locations (Schonfeld et al., 2010).

Summary

Rural older adults face many of the same BH and MH issues as their urban counterparts. However, the unique nature of rural communities creates additional risks such as social isolation and limited provider access. Leveraging assets in the community, such as peer leaders, technology, and primary care, can create opportunities to identify and respond effectively to BH and MH challenges faced by rural older adults.

References

Balasubramanian, B. A., Cohen, D. J., Jetelina, K. K., Dickinson, L. M., Davis, M., Gunn, R., . . . Green, L. A. (2017). Outcomes of integrated behavioral health with primary care. *Journal of the American Board of Family Medicine, 30*(2), 130–139. doi:10.3122/jabfm.2017.02.160234

Bocker, E., Glasser, M., Nielsen, K., & Weidenbacher-Hoper, V. (2012). Rural older adults' mental health: Status and challenges in care delivery. *Rural and Remote Health, 12*. Retrieved from https://pubmed.ncbi.nlm.nih.gov/23145784/

Brenes, G. A., Danhauer, S. C., Lyles, M. F., Hogan, P. E., & Miller, M. E. (2015). Barriers to mental health treatment in rural older adults. *American Journal of Geriatric Psychiatry, 23*(11), 1172–1178. doi:10.1016/j.jagp.2015.06.002

Cherry, D., Albert, M., & McCraig, L. F. (2018). *Mental health-related physician office visits by adults aged 18 and over: United States, 2012–2014*. Retrieved from www.cdc.gov/nchs/products/databriefs/db311.htm

Ciechanowski, P., Wagner, E., Schmaling, K., Schwartz, S., Williams, B., Diehr, P., . . . LoGerfo, J. (2004). Community-integrated home-based depression treatment in older adults: A randomized controlled trial. *Journal of the American Medical Association, 291*(13), 1569–1577. doi:10.1001/jama.291.13.1569

Cimperman, M., Brenčič, M. M., Trkman, P., & Stanonik, M. D. L. (2013). Older adults' perceptions of home telehealth services. *Telemedicine Journal and e-Health, 19*(10), 786–790. doi:10.1089/tmj.2012.0272

Ewald, E., Loganathan, S., Hasche, J., & Lochner, K. (2017). *Access to care among Medicare beneficiaries with and without depression.* Retrieved from www.cms.gov

Gale, J., Janis, J., Coburn, A., & Rochford, H. (2019). *Behavioral health in rural America: Challenges and opportunities.* Retrieved from www.rupri.org

Hayslip, B., Maiden, R. J., Thomison, N. L., & Temple, J. R. (2010). Mental health attitudes among rural and urban older adults. *Clinical Gerontologist, 33*(4), 316–331. doi:10.1080/07317115.2010.503557

Infante, A., Knudson, A., & Brown, A. (2011). *Promising practices for rural community health worker programs.* Retrieved from www.norc.org

Kaiser Family Foundation. (2020). *The implications of COVID-19 for mental health and substance use.* Retrieved from www.kff.org

The National Academies of Sciences. (2020). *The health and medical dimensions of social isolation and loneliness in older adults.* Retrieved from www.nationalacademies.org

Rural Health Information Hub. (2018). *Rural mental health.* Retrieved from www.ruralhealthinfo.org/topics/mental-health

Schonfeld, L., King-Kallimanis, B. L., Duchene, D. M., Etheridge, R. L., Herrera, J. R., Barry, K. L., & Lynn, N. (2010). Screening and brief intervention for substance misuse among older adults: The Florida BRITE project. *American Journal of Public Health, 100*(1), 108–114. doi:10.2105/AJPH.2008.149534

Selby-Nelson, E. M., Bradley, J. M., Schiefer, R. A., & Hoover-Thompson, A. (2018). Primary care integration in rural areas: A community-focused approach. *Families Systems & Health, 36*(4), 528–534. doi:10.1037/fsh0000352

Snell-Rood, C., Feltner, F., & Schoenberg, N. (2019). What role can community health workers play in connecting rural women with depression to the "De facto" mental health care system? *Community Mental Health Journal, 55*(1), 63–73. doi:10.1007/s10597-017-0221-9

Sockalingam, S., Arena, A., Serhal, E., Mohri, L., Alloo, J., & Crawford, A. (2018). Building provincial mental health capacity in primary care: An evaluation of a project ECHO mental health program. *Academic Psychiatry, 42*(4), 451–457. doi:10.1007/s40596-017-0735-z

Substance Abuse and Mental Health Services Administration. (2016). Rural behavioral health: Telehealth challenges and opportunities. *In Brief, 9*(2). Retrieved from https://store.samhsa.gov/

Velasquez, S. E., Duncan, A. B., & Nelson, E. (2012). Technological innovations in rural mental health delivery. In K. B. Smalley, J. Warren, & J. Rainer (Eds.), *Rural mental health: Issues, policies, and best practices* (pp. 149–172). Retrieved from https://ebookcentral.proquest.com

53
MENTAL HEALTH SERVICES

Jean A. Talbot

Mental health (MH) conditions are common among older adults in the U.S. (Institute of Medicine, 2012), and they occur at similar rates among rural and urban residents (McCall-Hosenfeld, Mukherjee, & Lehman, 2014). As the percentage of elders is expected to rise even more rapidly in rural than in urban populations over the next two decades, rural areas may experience a proportionately greater increase in their need for geriatric mental health (GMH) services. This new demand will strain rural MH systems, which already struggle to meet GMH needs.

Rural MH and GMH Provider Shortages

Rural areas face significant shortages of MH specialty providers. Among nonmetropolitan U.S. counties in 2015, 65% lacked psychiatrists, 47% were without psychologists, and 81% had no psychiatric nurse practitioners; moreover, large rural-urban disparities were observed in MH provider supply (Andrilla, Patterson, Garberson, Coulthard, & Larson, 2018). In addition to local MH workforce shortages, rural communities confront nationwide deficits in the supply of GMH experts. Across the country, the number of professionals entering the GMH field is low and decreasing. From 2006 to 2010, fewer than 50% of available geropsychiatric fellowships were filled; from 1996 to 2011, the number of geropsychiatry fellows declined by 50%. In 2010, only 9% of social workers reported that they worked primarily with older adults. Because of the scarcity of GMH specialty providers, other professionals who care for older adults are often called upon to address their patients' GMH issues, but most are not equipped for this role (Institute of Medicine, 2012).

Service Delivery Alternatives to Improve Rural GMH Access and Quality

To address current rural GMH needs and prepare for future challenges, rural stakeholders may wish to explore service delivery models to connect rural elders with GMH specialists in distant locations. The following discussion considers several relevant approaches.

Telemedicine Referral Model

In the now-familiar referral model, an off-site geropsychiatrist or MH clinician becomes the GMH provider for patients at rural health facilities, using telemedicine technologies to offer services such as psychiatric medication management or psychotherapy (Fortney et al., 2019; Rabinowitz et al., 2010). The Fletcher Allen Health Care/University of Vermont Telemedicine Program implemented this strategy, delivering psychiatric care to rural nursing home residents in Vermont and upstate New York via interactive videoconferencing. This initiative facilitated 278 encounters for 106 nursing home residents over six years and was positively evaluated by patients, family members, and nursing home staff (Rabinowitz et al., 2010).

Task-Sharing Models for Rural GMH Service Provision

Although the referral model can sometimes alleviate rural-urban disparities in GMH provider distribution, it does not in itself represent a solution to rural shortages of GMH specialty care. Because GMH specialists are scarce even in urban centers, they may be hard pressed to meet demand in their own areas, and their ability to deliver direct services to remote patient populations is unlikely to match rural levels of need. Thus, rural delivery systems have looked to alternative schemes based on *task-sharing* (Hoeft et al., 2018), in which the GMH specialist role shifts from providing direct patient care to offering training, supervision, and/or consultation to assist nonspecialists in working with elderly patients. By sharing their expertise with rural colleagues who conduct interventions, GMH specialists in distant locations can increase their population impact, enhancing GMH access and quality for older adults in underserved, rural communities.

Building Virtual Communities of Rural GMH Practice

A project of the University of Rochester Medical Center (URMC) provides a noteworthy example of task-sharing to support the delivery of GMH services by rural primary care providers (PCPs) and other generalists. URMC's program was an adaptation of Project ECHO (Extension for Community Healthcare Outcomes), a model developed at the University of New Mexico. ECHO uses group video-conferencing sessions to form virtual communities of practice, in which providers at multiple, underserved sites build clinical skills by obtaining instruction and guidance from specialists at university medical centers, while learning from one another through case discussion. The URMC program, known as ECHO Geriatric Mental Health or ECHO GEMH, connected rural sites across New York State to URMC's interdisciplinary geropsychiatric team, which was composed of a geropsychiatrist, geriatrician, psychologist, psychiatric nurse practitioner, pharmacist, and social worker (Fisher et al., 2017). The program initially served primary care practices and case management sites (Fisher et al., 2017) and later expanded to include long-term care facilities (AHRQ, 2017). The URMC team helped ECHO GEMH participants increase their skills in providing evidence-based treatment to older patients with MH disorders and/or dementia. Participants reported increased confidence in their ability to offer services including psychopharmacology, non-pharmacological interventions, sleep management, and diagnostic evaluations (Fisher et al., 2017).

Telemedicine-Mediated Collaborative Care for Rural Elders

Collaborative care (Fortney et al., 2013; Unutzer et al., 2002) is another form of task-sharing that may be leveraged to increase GMH availability and quality in rural communities. Programs such as IMPACT (Improving Mood-Promoting Access to Collaborative Treatment) have demonstrated the effectiveness of collaborative care for addressing late-life depression in primary care settings (Unutzer et al., 2002). In IMPACT, a psychologist or nurse acting as a depression care manager (DCM) worked with depressed, older primary care patients under the supervision of a PCP and psychiatrist. The DCM provided depression screening, psychoeducation, behavioral activation interventions, support for the PCP's management of antidepressant medication, brief psychotherapy, and symptom monitoring during and after treatment for up to 12 months. IMPACT resulted in greater reductions in depressive symptoms than usual care, while also leading to sustained improvements in quality of life and overall health status (Hunkeler et al., 2006).

For rural primary care practices with no local access to MH specialists and limited resources for care management, telemedicine could facilitate the creation of virtual collaborative care teams, with distant providers performing specialty functions. In one instance of this approach, researchers (Fortney et al., 2013) helped implement a telemedicine-based collaborative depression care program that linked five rural federally qualified health centers with an off-site team consisting of a psychiatrist, psychologist, pharmacist, and nurse DCM. The DCM, whose responsibilities were similar to those of DCMs in IMPACT, conducted interventions by telephone. The off-site specialist team met weekly to discuss cases, supervised the DCM, and made treatment recommendations to PCPs via DCM progress notes. Compared to patients who received primary care-based collaborative care involving on-site nurse DCMs who lacked specialist support, patients treated by telemedicine-based collaborative care teams experienced higher odds of remission, as well as greater improvements in symptoms and quality of life (Fortney et al., 2013). Although this project did not specifically target older adult patients, its successes suggest how telemedicine-mediated task-sharing might be used to extend GMH specialty services to rural elders.

Building a Rural Workforce of GMH Paraprofessionals

A third variation on task-sharing that could enhance rural GMH capacity involves establishing a cadre of local, non-licensed paraprofessionals or behavioral health aides (BHAs) to provide a specifically defined set of direct MH services under the guidance of distant GMH specialists (Hoeft et al., 2018; Kunik et al., 2017). Research suggests that appropriately trained paraprofessionals under supervision can effectively treat MH problems in a range of patient populations (Barnett et al., 2018), including elders (Stanley et al., 2014). Moreover, in addition to filling workforce gaps, BHAs could enhance the cultural appropriateness of rural GMH services; as BHAs are typically recruited from the places where they serve, they are likely to have an insider's understanding of local needs, networks, and norms (Kunik et al., 2017).

The Alaska Tribal Health System's (ATHS) implementation of the BHA model illustrates the potential of this task-sharing strategy for meeting rural GMH needs. The ATHS's BHA program primarily serves Alaska Native people in remote, low-resource areas. The program recruits high school graduates who are employees of Indian Health Service (IHS) and Tribal Health Organizations in villages where services are to be provided (Alaska Center for Rural Health and Health Workforce, 2016). BHAs work in primary care practices and other community-based settings (Alaska Native Tribal Health Consortium, n.d.). The IHS awards BHA certification (Donlon et al., 2018) at four levels; participants complete practica and coursework specific to each level (Alaska Center for Rural Health and Health Workforce, 2016). Services offered at the first two certification levels include psychoeducation, outreach, and referrals. At higher levels of certification, BHAs also provide services such as substance abuse assessments and crisis stabilization, in addition to mentorship of first- and second-level BHAs. All BHAs work under a licensed clinician, who conducts supervision via videoconferencing, telephone, e-mail, and in-person contacts (Alaska Center for Rural Health and Health Workforce, 2016). The state of Alaska allows provider sites to bill Medicaid for BHA services (Donlon et al., 2018). Although the ATHS's BHA program does not focus on elders, rural health systems wishing to adapt this model for rural older adults could include GMH competencies in BHA training and link BHAs to distant supervisors with GMH expertise.

Considerations for Implementing Alternative GMH Service Delivery Models in Rural Contexts

Further research is needed to better understand the factors influencing the effectiveness, cost implications, limitations, feasibility, and sustainability of telemedicine referral and task-sharing models for GMH service provision in rural populations. Nevertheless, existing evidence suggests that strategies along these lines hold promise for improving rural elders' access to quality GMH care. Given that telemedicine is an essential component of these service delivery schemes, their broader dissemination may depend on government agencies' continued efforts to close existing rural-urban gaps in high-speed broadband access (Federal Communications Commission, 2016).

Innovations in workforce preparation, licensing, and reimbursement policies may also be necessary. In the domain of training, professional organizations, schools, and health systems could collaborate on delineating appropriate competencies for paraprofessionals and developing standardized, evidence-based curricula for candidates (Kunik et al., 2017). In addition, to serve as leaders of task-sharing projects, GMH specialists might benefit from training experiences focused on hiring, supervising, and managing paraprofessionals, working with collaborative care teams in rural areas (Kunik et al., 2017), and using telemedicine technologies to perform these functions remotely. In the realm of licensure regulations, state credentialing bodies and professional groups could advance rural task-sharing efforts by working together to establish paraprofessional certification criteria, scopes of practice, and supervision requirements (Kunik et al., 2017). The expansion of interstate licensure reciprocity programs (Center for Connected Health Policy, 2019) could also be helpful in permitting GMH specialists to provide services to rural communities across state lines. Finally, to increase the sustainability of rural GMH service redesign, rural stakeholders could advocate for payers and delivery systems to develop reimbursement schemes covering telemedicine-mediated collaborative care activities (Fortney et al., 2019), GMH specialist consultations to providers (Howe et al., 2019), and paraprofessional services (Kunik et al., 2017).

References

AHRQ. (2017, April). *AHRQ telehealth project helps address mental health needs among rural elderly in New York state*. Retrieved from www.ahrq.gov/news/newsroom/case-studies/201703.html

Alaska Center for Rural Health and Health Workforce. (2016). *Behavioral health aide*. Anchorage, AK: University of Alaska Anchorage.

Alaska Native Tribal Health Consortium. (n.d.). *Behavioral health aide program*. Retrieved August 16, 2019, from https://anthc.org/behavioral-health-aide-program/

Andrilla, C. H. A., Patterson, D. G., Garberson, L. A., Coulthard, C., & Larson, E. H. (2018). Geographic variation in the supply of selected behavioral health providers. *American Journal of Preventive Medicine, 54*(6), S199–S207. doi:10.1016/j.amepre.2018.01.004

Barnett, M. L., Gonzalez, A., Miranda, J., Chavira, D. A., & Lau, A. S. (2018). Mobilizing community health workers to address mental health disparities for underserved populations: A systematic review. *Administration and Policy in Mental Health, 45*(2), 195–211. doi:10.1007/s10488-017-0815-0

Center for Connected Health Policy. (2019). *State telehealth laws & reimbursement policies*. Sacramento, CA: Public Health Institute.

Donlon, R., & Williams, N. (2018). *Case study: How Alaska addresses its health care workforce challenges*. Washington, DC: NASHP.

Federal Communications Commission. (2016). *Broadband progress report: Significant improvements but digital divide persists*. Washington, DC: FCC (FCC News).

Fisher, E., Hasselberg, M., Conwell, Y., Weiss, L., Padron, N. A., Tiernan, E., . . . Pagan, J. A. (2017). Telementoring primary care clinicians to improve geriatric mental health care. *Population Health Management, 20*(5), 342–347. doi:10.1089/pop.2016.0087

Fortney, J. C., Pyne, J. M., Mouden, S. B., Mittal, D., Hudson, T J., Schroeder, G. W., . . . Rost, K. M. (2013). Practice-based versus telemedicine-based collaborative care for depression in rural federally qualified health centers: A pragmatic randomized comparative effectiveness trial. *American Journal of Psychiatry, 170*(4), 414–425. doi:10.1176/appi.ajp.2012.12050696

Fortney, J. C., Veith, R. C., Bauer, A. M., Pfeiffer, P. N., Valenstein, M., Pyne, J. M., . . . Unutzer, J. (2019). Developing telemental health partnerships between state medical schools and federally qualified health centers: Navigating the regulatory landscape and policy recommendations. *Journal of Rural Health, 35*(3), 287–297. doi:10.1111/jrh.12323

Hoeft, T. J., Fortney, J. C., Patel, V., & Unutzer, J. (2018). Task-sharing approaches to improve mental health care in rural and other low-resource settings: A systematic review. *Journal of Rural Health, 34*(1), 48–62. doi:10.1111/jrh.12229

Howe, G., & Hamblin, A. (2019). *Project ECHO: Policy pathways for sustainability*. Trenton, NJ: CHCS.

Hunkeler, E. M., Katon, W., Tang, L., Williams, J. W., Jr., Kroenke, K., Lin, E. H., . . . Unutzer, J. (2006). Long term outcomes from the impact randomised trial for depressed elderly patients in primary care. *British Medical Journal, 332*(7536), 259–263. doi:10.1136/bmj.38683.710255.BE

Institute of Medicine. (2012). *The mental health and substance use workforce for older adults: In whose hands?* Washington, DC: National Academies Press.

Kunik, M. E., Mills, W. L., Amspoker, A. B., Cully, J. A., Kraus-Schuman, C., Stanley, M., & Wilson, N. L. (2017). Expanding the geriatric mental health workforce through utilization of non-licensed providers. *Aging & Mental Health, 21*(9), 954–960. doi:10.1080/13607863.2016.1186150

McCall-Hosenfeld, J. S., Mukherjee, S., & Lehman, E. B. (2014). The prevalence and correlates of lifetime psychiatric disorders and trauma exposures in urban and rural settings: Results from the national comorbidity survey replication (NCS-R). *PloS One, 9*(11), e112416. doi:10.1371/journal.pone.0112416

Rabinowitz, T., Murphy, K. M., Amour, J. L., Ricci, M. A., Caputo, M. P., & Newhouse, P. A. (2010). Benefits of a telepsychiatry consultation service for rural nursing home residents. *Telemedicine Journal and e-Health, 16*(1), 34–40. doi:10.1089/tmj.2009.0088

Stanley, M. A., Wilson, N. L., Amspoker, A. B., Kraus-Schuman, C., Wagener, P. D., Calleo, J. S., . . . Kunik, M. E. (2014). Lay providers can deliver effective cognitive behavior therapy for older adults with generalized anxiety disorder: A randomized trial. *Depression and Anxiety, 31*(5), 391–401. doi:10.1002/da.22239

Unutzer, J., Katon, W., Callahan, C. M., Williams, J. W., Jr., Hunkeler, E., Harpole, L., . . . Langston, C. (2002). Collaborative care management of late-life depression in the primary care setting: A randomized controlled trial. *JAMA: Journal of the American Medical Association, 288*(22), 2836–2845. doi:10.1001/jama.288.22.2836

54
MINORITIES

Cassandra D. Ford, Martha R. Crowther, Keri A. Barron, Mary Ann Kelley, and Jenna Bennett

The distribution and differential experiences of diverse categories of rural elders is evidenced by the diverse backgrounds of the individuals that comprise the broad landscape of this population. As the population continues to age, the communities in which they dwell will be more reflective of the emerging diversity and aging of our nation.

The Presence of Rural Minority Elders

Minority elders are present throughout rural communities in the U.S.; however, there is a greater presence of minority populations in some areas than others. Trends indicate that by 2060, minority elders are projected to comprise approximately 45% of the population of individuals 65 and older (Population Reference Bureau, 2019). The Hispanic population is expanding beyond the Southwest into areas such as the Midwest and Southeast. African Americans are most concentrated in areas of the Southeast (National Rural Health Association, 2013). While the overall population has seen a difference in growth and location trends, a majority of rural elders have remained in their communities over the years or have decided to return to their communities of origin after having worked and lived in different regions of the nation for the majority of their lives.

Reflecting the Diversity of Rural Minority Elders

Special Challenges and Opportunities for Growth

Minority elders face both special challenges as well as opportunities as a result of dwelling in rural communities. The presence of community-dwelling rural minority elders highlights the importance of ensuring that various resources are in place to meet the needs of this group of individuals. A vast number of rural areas are health professional shortage areas, making health-care access a critical need (Douthi, Kiv, Dwolatzky, & Biswas, 2015; Rural Health Information Hub (RHIH), 2019). With the closure of more rural hospitals (McCay et al., 2019), the need for alternative models of health-care delivery is imperative. Health-care services may be provided using telehealth or home monitoring; however, issues related to technology access must be considered. While the number of households with internet access has increased over recent years, an assessment of service availability prior to implementing these services is essential to successful program implementation (U.S. Census Bureau, 2017; RHIH, 2019). Programs to promote social engagement may be limited, underscoring the need for increased awareness regarding social isolation. It is postulated that social isolation and loneliness are a concern for many rural elders (Mullen et al., 2019). Social engagement has many benefits for older adults. Mackenzie and Abdulrazaq (2019) found that an increase in social activities attributed to an increase in social engagement, which contributed to less psychological distress. Boulos, Salameh, and Barberget-Gateau (2017) posited there was a link between social isolation and the nutritional status of older people. Older adults experiencing social isolation or loneliness were at risk for malnutrition. Social engagement also has an impact on the quality of life in older adults, thus having an effect on their physical and mental health (Dalhberg et al., 2015; Neville et al., 2018). Social engagement can be viewed as a difficult task when the limitation of resources and large amounts of land in rural communities are considered. Traveling for work or going to the grocery store can pose as a problem when an individual does not have a car for day-to-day activities. If family or friends are not nearby, then travel can pose an issue to the maintenance of social support (NPR, RWJF, & Harvard School of Public Health, 2019). In addition, transportation to get to health-care services or access other programs may be limited (RHIH, 2019).

As the population continues to age, the question of where to age is of growing importance. In recent years, additional focus has been placed on resources for aging-in-place given large majorities of older adults prefer to remain in their homes. Because of limited resources, other options such as assisted living may or may not be available within the area or close to an individual's residence. Issues such as social support, whether it be from family or friends, financial support, and health-care accessibility must be considered (RHIH, 2019). Caregiving needs, whether from paid or unpaid caregivers, continue to increase as individuals age; yet, there may be limited resources for caregivers or caregiver support (Office of Disease Prevention and Health Promotion, 2019). Caregiver role strain can contribute to the crisis of elder abuse in the US (Jenkins, 2019). Therefore, tools for screening, education, and support for preventive measures must be considered and implemented.

When health-care providers, program administrators, service providers, researchers, or educators are completing an initial assessment and continue working with rural minority elders, it is important to determine the resources that are available and if other mechanisms will need to be put into place. Interventions should be culturally appropriate and culturally sensitive. Ensuring measures are in place to support and sustain quality of life are also factors to consider.

Innovative methods must be utilized to address the unique physical and mental health-care needs of rural elders, particularly related to screenings and diagnosis (Crowther et al., 2018). Health disparities that plague minority populations in relation to conditions such as cardiovascular disease, diabetes, and cancer remain of high concern among minority older adults. Partnerships that are interdisciplinary can provide a greater array of services at various levels (Ford, 2018). Given the dearth of resources in most rural areas, the importance of early screening and detection is crucial for ensuring the prevention and/or treatment of comorbid conditions (Crowther et al., 2018). Once those conditions are diagnosed, an interdisciplinary team must work together to consider the needs of rural minority elders, available resources, and methods for individuals to access them.

Conclusion

As the number and proportion of minority older adults residing in rural (as well as urban) communities continues to expand at an especially rapid pace, it is critical that community resources are in place to accommodate their pressing needs in terms of physical and mental health services and support programs. Any programs targeting rural elders generally, and rural minority elders specifically, will need to account for the unique opportunities working with such populations represent and ensure mechanisms are in place to sustain those efforts.

Additional Readings

Bolin, J. N., Bellamy, G. R., Ferdinand, A. O., Vuong, A. M., Kash, B. A., Schulze, A., & Helduser, J. W. (2015). Rural healthy people 2020: New decade, same challenges. *Journal of Rural Health, 3*, 326–333. doi:10.1111/jrh.12116

Harris, J. (2019). Geriatric trends facing nursing with the growing aging. *Critical Care Nursing Clinics of North America, 31*(2), 211–224. doi:10.1016/j.cnc.2019.02.007

Skoufalos, A., Clarke, J. L., Ellis, D. R., Shepard, V. L., & Rula, E. Y. (2017). Rural aging in America: Proceedings of the 2017 connectivity summit. *Population Health Management, 20* (Suppl 2), S3–S10. doi:10.1089/pop.2017.0177

References

Boulos, C., Salameh, P., & Barberget-Gateau, P. (2017). Social isolation and risk for malnutrition among older people. *Geriatrics & Gerontology International, 17*(2), 286–294. doi:1.111/ggi.12711

U.S. Census Bureau. (2017). *Facts for features: Older Americans month: May 2017*. Retrieved from www.census.gov/newsroom/facts-for-features/2017/cb17-ff08.html

Crowther, M. R., Ford, C. D., Vinson, L. D., Huang, C. H., Wayde, E., & Guin, S. (2018). Assessment of metabolic syndrome risk factors among rural-dwelling older adults requires innovation: Partnerships and a mobile unit can help. *Quality in Ageing and Older Adults, 19*(4), 251–260. doi:10.1108/QAOA-12-2017-0052

Dalhberg, L., Anderson, L., McKee, K. J., & Lennartsson, C. (2015). Predictors of loneliness among older women and men in Sweden: A national longitudinal study. *Aging & Mental Health, 19*(5), 409–417. doi:10.1080/13607863.2014.944091

Douthit, N., Kiv, S., Dwolatzky, T., & Biswas, S. (2015). Exposing some important barriers to health care access in the rural USA. *Public Health, 129*(6), 611–620. doi:10.1016/j.puhe.2015.04.001

Ford, C. D. (2018). Professional associations can nurture interdisciplinary partnerships to better serve rural-dwelling older adults. *Quality in Ageing and Older Adults, 19*(4), 293–303. doi:10.1108/QAOA-07-2018-0030

Jenkins, Y. (2019). Caregivers for the elderly: Clinical issues and intervention. *Women & Therapy, 42*(3–4), 447–468. doi:10.1080/02703149.2019.1622905

Mackenzie, C., & Abdulrazaq, S. (2019). Social engagement mediates the relationship between participation in social activities and psychological distress among older adults. *Aging and Mental Health, 10*, 1–7. doi:10.1080/13607863.2019.1697200

McCay, D. O., Borkowski, N., Hearld, L., Byrd, J., Trimm, J. M., & Duncan, J. (2019). A case study: Organizational and environmental factors associated with Alabama rural hospitals' reported levels of financial distress. *Journal of Health Care Finance, 45*(4).

Mullen, R. A., Tong, S., Sabo, R. T., Liaw, W. R., Marshall, J., Nease, D. E., Jr., . . . Frey, J. J. (2019). Loneliness in primary care patients: A prevalence study. *Annals of Family Medicine, 17*(2), 108–115. doi:10.1370/afm.2358

National Rural Health Association Policy Brief. (2013). *Elder health in rural America*. Retrieved from www.ruralhealthweb.org/getattachment/Advocate/Policy-Documents/ElderHealthinRuralAmericaFeb2013.pdf.aspx?lang=en-US

Neville, S., Adams, J., Napier, S., Shannon, K., & Jackson, D. (2018). "Engaging in my rural community": Perceptions of people aged 85 years and over. *International Journal of Qualitative Studies on Health and Well-Being, 13*(1). doi:10.080.17482631.2018.1503908

NPR, RWJF, & Harvard School of Public Health. (2019). *Life in America*. Retrieved from https://media.npr.org/documents/2019/may/NPR-RWJF-HARVARD_Rural_Poll_Part_2.pdf

Office of Disease Prevention and Health Promotion. (2019). *Older adults*. Retrieved from www.healthypeople.gov/2020/topics-objectives/topic/older-adults
Population Reference Bureau. (2019). *Fact sheet: Aging in the United States*. Retrieved from www.prb.org/aging-unitedstates-fact-sheet/
Rural Health Information Hub. (2019). *Topics*. Retrieved from www.ruralhealthinfo.org/

55
NATIONAL RURAL HEALTH ASSOCIATION

Alan Morgan

The role of the National Rural Health Association (NRHA) in affecting policy change on behalf of older adults in rural communities is considered. Specific examples of NRHA work in the areas of workforce, PACE, telehealth, and the Older Americans Act are presented to illustrate their policy development and advocacy strategies.

More than 25% of older adults reside in rural America. For these individuals, place matters both on a personal and on a policy level (National Rural Health Association, 2020). On the personal level, rural America can represent more than a place of residence, but also a strong sense of self. There can be a connection with place, and with it can also be a powerful sense of community. On the policy level, place or residence can often determine both the adequacy of health resources available to an individual, and the range of general and specialized health-care services that exist within that particular community.

The NRHA is a nonprofit membership organization that promotes policies to ensure the availability of health services for rural older adults through education, research, and advocacy (Committee on the Future of Rural Health Care, 2005). As such, it is both relevant and instructive to examine how the national policy efforts of groups such as the NRHA reflect selected strategies meant to ensure quality health-care services are available for our nation's rural older adults. Offered here is an examination of the ways public policy actors, in particular the NRHA, develops and promotes these aging-related policies of change.

From a historical standpoint, rural communities have served as health-care policy innovation incubators. Small rural communities often present well-defined populations and service areas, which uniquely allow the testing of new health-care approaches. In addition, relatively low competition among rural providers, because of chronic workforce shortages and limited resources, often spur collaboration and creativity among community health-care agencies and organizations (National Rural Health Association, 2019). However, the primary impetus for change in rural settings most certainly is driven by pressures, most notably arising from intense health-care needs, financial pressures, and workforce shortages.

Collaboration across health-care entities in rural communities is reflected in the unique structure of NRHA and in how it develops and promotes policy. The NRHA does not just collaborate with the broad spectrum of rural health-care interests; NRHA is the broad spectrum of rural health-care interests. The association is governed by a board of trustees, who are elected representatives from nine distinct constituency groups and three councils.

These constituency groups include clinical services; research and education; federally qualified health centers (FQHCs); rural health clinics (RHCs); frontier hospitals and health systems; statewide health resources; public health; and students. The councils include the Health Equity Council, the State Association Council, and the State Offices of Rural Health Council.

Elected annually by their respective constituency groups or councils, the board of trustees convenes and collaborates on policy issues. In this way, the NRHA plays the role of network facilitator, bringing together diverse groups. Each of these groups addresses a segment of the rural health community, thus creating a prime venue for collaboration, enabling the association to impact rural health issues in a comprehensive and efficient manner through education, information-sharing, and policy partnerships.

While the NRHA serves as an example of a national external policy agent affecting change, the Federal Office of Rural Health Policy (FORHP) serves as a focal point for rural health policy and grant administration from within the federal government. Located within the U.S. Health Resources and Services Administration (HRSA), FORHP was created in 1987 to advise the secretary of the U.S. Department of Health and Human Services on health-care issues impacting rural communities. In line with the mission of HRSA, FORHP uses its grantmaking ability to build capacity to increase access to care for underserved populations (Health Resources and Services Administration, 2019).

A rural health policy cyclical process has developed over the past 30 years. This process begins with FORHP funding new innovative approaches in rural health delivery through congressionally appropriated federal grants. Lessons learned from these grant activities are shared through professional organizations, such as the NRHA. The NRHA then identifies barriers to both replication and expansion of these policy and programmatic strategies. Policy recommendations are developed by NRHA and shared with policymakers, who, in turn, enact new policy to either address identified barriers or replicate and expand successful initiatives. As barriers and opportunities are identified through this process, the need for additional new approaches are highlighted, and thus, the rural health policy cycle begins anew, with new FORHP grant awards issued as a result.

The strategies that national organizations such as the NRHA employ to affect policy are varied and numerous. However, the overriding goal of all such efforts is to prompt policy change through the provision of data, personal stories of impact, and public engagement. For example, while data may demonstrate that telehealth is effective as a rural behavioral health tool (Langarizadeh, Tabatabaei, Tavakol, Naghipour, & Moghbeli, 2017), it is necessary as well to document the human impact it has on particular rural communities and to demonstrate that there is widespread support for such technology in the health-care sector.

When examining the rural policy development process and its impact on rural elders, it is important to realize that leading causes of death in rural areas are often associated with chronic disease. Not surprisingly, limited access to primary health care for prevention, treatment, and management of chronic conditions and supportive social services is a prevalent barrier for older adults in rural America. Access to primary care services for chronic diseases such as cardiac artery disease, chronic respiratory disease, and type 2 diabetes is critical for enabling older adults to lead both productive and independent lives.

The focus of primary care in a rural context must be on the prevention of illness and on maintenance of health through effective management by using appropriate treatment modalities that older adults find both acceptable and affordable. As such, addressing rural provider shortages, emergency room access, and availability of geriatricians and gerontologists is of paramount importance. Seeking relevant policy changes to address the ongoing and persistent workforce shortages in rural communities have produced successful models and strategies, but access barriers often remain.

In the quest to increase access to care for the nation's aging population, successful health-care accessibility strategies that will have broader positive impacts for rural communities are especially important. This certainly is the case for rural workforce policy and efforts to improve access to rural-based primary care. One example of such a federally supported workforce strategy is the establishment of rural residency programs. As defined by the Rural Training Track Collaborative:

> A rural residency program is an accredited program in health professions education and training in which trainees spend the majority of their time training (more than 50%) in a rural place. A rural program in medical school is an organized and deliberate medical school strategy to produce physicians for rural practice.
>
> (The RTT Collaborative, 2019)

Currently, rural residency programs account for only a small number of first year post-graduate positions presently available in family medicine. However, research shows that roughly half of rural residency track graduates locate in rural areas after graduation. This is more than two times the proportion of family medicine residency graduates who choose to practice in rural settings. Proven success in this approach to addressing rural workforce shortages is the rationale for NRHA's promotion of legislation and regulatory efforts to support and expand this strategy. This particular approach centers around the concept of identifying individuals from rural areas, or with an interest in rural practice, and then training them in rural settings.

Collaboration among national organizations can also drive strategies to address older adult health-care issues. A good example of such a policy collaboration to improve and expand rural health care for older adults can be found in efforts to promote expansion of the rural Program of All-Inclusive Care for the Elderly (PACE) model. PACE is designed to integrate care for frail older adults who are eligible for both Medicaid and Medicare. This population of dual-eligible individuals particularly benefits from integrated care. Some PACE programs are targeted toward all older adults who meet the minimal acuity levels required for nursing home care.

Rural advocates and policymakers have long believed that PACE holds great promise in rural areas. In 2002, the NRHA, the FORHP, and the National PACE Association convened a meeting that brought together PACE experts, policymakers, and rural health-care providers to examine PACE and its applicability for rural communities. An outcome of this national meeting was the development of policy recommendations for change (Fitzgerald, Morgan, & Morris, 2004). While the full realization of the adoption of the PACE model in a rural context remains elusive to this day, the policy concept continues to drive discussion and consideration.

Another ongoing national effort to affect change that directly impacts rural elders is promoting the adoption of telehealth solutions. Telehealth has many potential applications, but for rural-residing older adults, the promise of more home-based care, and, in particular, more readily available behavioral health-care services is particularly promising.

In 2017, NRHA developed an updated national policy paper that recognizes the current state of rural telehealth adoption and provides a good example of the everchanging rural health policy landscape. Despite the promise of telemedicine, it has yet to reach its full potential as a rural health tool/solution from an adoption and utilization standpoint, with further policy adjustments necessary. Reimbursement, licensure, and affordability barriers have long prevented full adoption in rural settings. In fact, only recently is telehealth technology becoming both affordable and accessible, thus enabling a more wide-scale rural adoption.

Regulatory guidance often appears to struggle simply to keep up with the speed at which this technology is evolving. Many of the goals of various health-care reforms in recent years have been to streamline health-care processes and procedures, while reducing the growing cost of health-care delivery in the U.S. Telemedicine has the potential to incorporate technology into the equation for delivering expanded access to a greater number of people at a lower per capita cost.

The NRHA has long advocated for dedicated reimbursement options for telehealth (King, Pigman, Huling, & Hanson, 2018). In 2017, the Centers for Medicare and Medicaid Services (CMS) introduced two new telehealth-relevant CPT codes for Complex CCM—99487 and 99489. While these codes are not specifically telemedicine codes, the provision of these services often includes the use of telemedicine technology. In examining CMS billing data, it becomes apparent that health-care providers are still not yet fully embracing these billing options for telehealth applications. Nonetheless, telehealth offers a practical example of both policy success and policy work that lies ahead to fully realize the potential of the service.

It is important to note that national policy efforts aimed at improving health care for aging rural residents are many and diverse in nature. In 2019, the NRHA was actively engaged in advocating on behalf of the reauthorization of the Older Americans Act (OAA). The OAA provides many critical services for rural older adults and their caregivers including home-delivered and congregate meals; family caregiver support; in-home assistance; preventive health services; job training; protection from abuse; transportation; and other supportive services. The scarcity of transportation options remains a critical barrier for rural older adults needing to travel long distances to access basic health and social services. Transportation, in the context of Emergency Medical Services, are of particular concern for rural older adults (Alonso, Crouch, & Thorell, 2019).

In 2018, the NRHA in collaboration with Tivity Health, the MIT AgeLab, and Jefferson College of Population Health convened and participated in a national summit on rural aging during which a diverse group of stakeholders, including government, faith-based organizations, nonprofits, academia and research groups, the business community, health plans, rural health experts, and aging experts identified priority issues for those living in rural communities. The resulting discussions provided the basis for national policy recommendations related to OAA reauthorization. This collaboration represents an example of diverse national public sector interest groups coalescing on key policy issues of significance to older adults in rural communities.

In each of the preceding policy examples, research, data, and practical impacts on older adults were considered when developing policy. Rural policy development is a collaborative process, involving many actors and varying interests. Of paramount importance to this process is recognizing that access to care not only has a direct impact on health status, but also on the ability for older adults to remain within their communities-of-choice.

References

Alonso, W., Crouch, E., & Thorell, N. (2019). *Telehealth in rural America*. Retrieved from www.ruralhealthweb.org/NRHA/media/Emerg13e_NRHA/Advocacy/Policy%20documents/2019-NRHA-Policy-Paper-Telehealth-in-Rural-America.pdf

Committee on the Future of Rural Health Care. (2005). Quality through collaboration: The future of rural health care. *International Journal of Health Care Quality Assurance*, *18*(4). doi:10.1108/ijhcqa.2005.06218dae.001

Fitzgerald, P., Morgan, A., & Morris, T. (2004). Rural policy development: An NRHA and PACE association collaborative model. *The Journal of Rural Health, 20*(1), 92–96. doi:10.1111/j.1748-0361.2004.tb00013.x

Health Resources and Services Administration. (2019). *About FORHP*. Health Resources and Services Administration website. Retrieved from www.hrsa.gov/rural-health/about-us/index.html

King, N., Pigman, M., Huling, S., & Hanson, B. (2018). *EMS services in rural America: Challenges and opportunities*. Retrieved from www.ruralhealthweb.org/NRHA/media/Emerge_NRHA/Advocacy/Policy%20documents/05-11-18-NRHA-Policy-EMS.pdf

Langarizadeh, M., Tabatabaei, M., Tavakol, K., Naghipour, M., & Moghbeli, F. (2017). Telemental health care, an effective alternative to conventional mental care: A systematic review. *Acta Informatica Medica, 25*(4), 240–246. doi:10.5455/aim.2017.25.240-246

Tasha Brown, Kay Miller Temple, and Josie Rudolphi (2020). National Rural Health Association Policy Paper: Rural America's Senior Citizens: Considerations for Transportation, Healthcare Access, Connectedness, Nutrition and Economics. Retrieved November 16, 2020. Rural American's Seniors https://www.ruralhealthweb.org/NRHA/media/Emerge_NRHA/Advocacy/Policy%20documents/2020-NRHA-Policy-Document-Rural-America%e2%80%99s-Senior-Citizens.pdf

National Rural Health Association. (2019). *About the National Rural Health Association*. Retrieved from www.ruralhealthweb.org/about-nrha

The RTT Collaborative. (2019). Retrieved from https://rttcollaborative.net/rural-programs/

56
NURSING SERVICES

Barbara Ann Graves, Teresa D. Welch, and Foster D. Jones

Introduction

The U.S. Department of Health and Human Services (USDHHS) (2014) identified as a national health priority that all people, including the most vulnerable, should have health that allows a productive life by the year 2020. Fundamental to this priority is the goal of improving access to comprehensive, quality health care services. But access to health care is becoming increasingly complex as growing and diverse populations and rapid health care reform continue to modify the provision of health care services.

Rural dwellers differ from urban dwellers with differences in characteristics, cultures, and economies. While characteristics, such as resilience, self-reliance, and lay care network, often serve rural communities as strengths and assets, other characteristics of rural environments and dwellers may compound existing poor health status (Bushy, 2000; Winters & Lee, 2018). In general, health inequities exist across many social determinants of health (SDOH). Health inequities exist related to age and rural status and are often intensified in the rural environment. Research has shown that rural areas have higher levels of poverty, higher percentages of older adults, and declining populations (Olson, 2018).

Systematic disinvestment in rural areas, often seen in the form of health care service changes and closures, can be expected to adversely affect rural dwellers already known to be older, poorer, sicker, and lacking transportation and insurance. Hospital closures, workforce changes and shortages, compounded by the disinvestment in rural environments have changed both access to and delivery of professional health care services. Additionally, the growing proportion of older adults living in rural areas is expected to further increase and compound current inequities in health outcomes (Bolin, Bellamy, Ferdinand, Kash, & Helduser, 2015a, 2015b; Olson, 2018).

Professional nurses are vital to the provision of health care. They have the knowledge and skills to provide the necessary link to improving access to quality care. Presented here is a brief overview of national trends and developments, current status and availability, and future directions of professional nursing services for the rural-dwelling older adult.

Background

Professional Nursing

As a profession, nurses provide care focused on attaining, maintaining, and recovery of health and quality of life to individuals, families, and communities (American Association of Colleges of Nursing (AACN), 2008). Across the U.S., registered nurses (RNs) are the largest health care profession and form the backbone of the health care industry. Hospitals, free-standing health clinics, nursing homes, health departments, home health services, and hospice services are just some of the areas that maximize the role of professional nurses.

Professional nurses have gained the American public's trust. Based on the most recent Gallup poll, nurses were ranked the most-trusted profession in the U.S. for the twentieth year (Brenan, 2018). They are adaptable and function in a variety of roles, health care specialty areas, cultures, and geographical regions often resulting in demanding work environments. Professional nurses may be baccalaureate or master's prepared. They provide care where needed by functioning in roles both interdependently (with physicians or other health care providers) and independently as advanced practice registered nurses (APRNs). Interestingly, rural communities with professional nurses who reside there have the benefit of a trusted "insider" capable of providing primary care services. Likewise, professional nurses add a resource for leadership capacity. APRNs are RNs who hold at least a master's degree in nursing and have obtained a license to practice using advanced skills in one of the four APRN roles: certified registered nurse anesthetist (CRNA), certified nurse-midwife (CNM), clinical nurse specialist (CNS), or certified nurse practitioner (CNP) (AACN, 2011). It is now common to see APRNs, such as CNPs, fill gaps in health services historically occupied only by physicians. APRNs add a level of invaluable primary and preventive professional health services. This trend is visible in hospitals, private health practices, school-based centers, and most importantly rural health clinics and federally qualified health centers. While some states have recognized independent practice authority for APRNs, many are still limiting scope of practice that often prevents professional nurses from delivering care they are trained to provide.

Trends and Current Status

Rural Nursing Theory

Discussion of professional nursing services for rural older adults must include an acknowledgement that nursing practice differs significantly between rural and urban environments. Rural dwellers and older adults have unique characteristics that present unique challenges to providers. Access to health services, consumption of health care resources, and SDOH are different for older adults living in rural areas. It is important to understand these unique characteristics and challenges for individuals living in rural areas related to the provision of nursing services (Winters & Lee, 2018).

Strong research and conceptual analyses have led to the development of nursing theory to aid understanding of the rural nursing phenomena. Over the last few decades, rural nursing researchers have identified characteristics and concepts of rural populations that are important to nursing practice (Bushy, 2000; Long & Weinert, 1989; Winters & Lee, 2018). The concepts that provide the *rural nursing theory base* are health beliefs, isolation, distance, self-reliance, outsider/insider, old-timer/newcomer, resources, informal networks, lay care network, lack of anonymity, familiarity, and professional isolation (Winters & Lee, 2018).

Deeper consideration of these concepts can provide understanding and direction for future provision of nursing services to older adults living in rural areas and guide future research and theory development.

Access to Health Care

Health care policy changes over the past several decades have drastically impacted access to health services. The rural health environment has felt the impact of these changes in many ways. Significant decreases in health services to the already vulnerable, at-risk underserved rural populations have been compounded by the existing paucity of health resources and has increased health inequities. Of noted importance are the drastic cuts in health services created by the chain of events from the Balanced Budget Act (BBA) of 1997, to the Medicare Prospective Payment System (PPS) of 1983, to the Affordable Care Act (ACA) of 2010. The combination of loss of community health services, health professional shortages, rapidly rising cost, hospital closures, homecare cutbacks, and tighter government payment schedules are just a few changes that have led to greater health inequities for rural populations (Bolin et al., 2015a; Olson, 2018).

Inequities in health status, health outcomes, and health service access based on age, race, ethnicity, socioeconomic status, residential location, location of health services, and other SDOH have been well documented in the literature (Bolin et al., 2015a, 2015b). Rural areas are often designated as health professional shortage areas (HPSAs) indicating health professional shortages. They do not have the attraction for professionals that urban areas can offer, and nurses often prefer to practice in urban communities, rather than rural communities. According to the Workforce Analysis Report (Health Resources & Services Administration (HRSA), 2017), in 2013, only 16% of the nation's RNs worked in rural settings providing health care services to over 20% of the nation's population.

Many issues of supply-and-demand are evident in rural populations. Over the decades, rural health services in general have experienced diseconomies of scale in that long-run average cost increases as output increases (Folland, Goodman, & Stano, 2016). Providing health care becomes too expensive; the providers lose money and close or merge with other services. Because rural areas have a lower population density and rural residents generally have lower levels of income, lack health insurance, and prefer informal care to formal care, the demand for health care is often lower. At the same time, an increase in demand caused by a "sicker" population because of more chronic disease and health status inequities increases the demand for health services.

Health care is a large industry, and supply is affected by variables such as economic incentives, technological change, the size of the health care industry, and most importantly, demand (Folland et al., 2016). Progressive industry does not seek to supply services in an area resistive to change or utilization of services and without the means to pay for services. As rural residents consume fewer health services, less are supplied. These changes in supply and demand in health services perpetuate problems with access to care in rural areas impacting the need for health professionals.

Persistent decline in community hospital occupancy has led to the closure of many rural hospitals. Nationally, between 2010 and 2018, there have been 83 rural hospital closures to add to the already reduced number of community hospitals (O'Donnell, 2014). Community hospital closures have had a profound effect on local communities in terms of changes in utilization of health services and health status. Health service closures in rural areas lead to an increase in distance and travel time. The effect is decreased access to health and preventive services many times provided by professional nurses.

Workforce Shortages

The nursing shortage in the U.S. has been a topic of discussion for decades (HRSA, 2017). This multifactorial issue has many contributing factors. The U.S. health care system is faced with the challenges of an aging population, mandated decreased hospital length of stay, and increased patient acuity. In addition, the demands for increased accessibility and pay-for-performance in a value driven reimbursement structure often leaves professional nursing to bear the weight of patient responsibility (American Nurses Association, 2017a, 2017b). Considering these expectations, the difficulties facing the profession of nursing in maintaining and recruiting experienced nurses to meet critical demands is daunting. According to the U.S. Bureau of Labor Statistics (USBLS, 2016) the average age of a RN working in the U.S. today is 51 years. It is anticipated that more than 500,000 experienced nurses will retire by the year 2022. With a competitive job market and a proliferation of alternative career opportunities for young adults, potential nursing recruits are drawn to other professions with less responsibility and more lucrative compensation (Mester, 2018; Rural Health Information Hub (RHIH), 2018). To avoid a crisis in the nursing workforce within the next decade, the USBLS (2016) is projecting the need for 1.1 million new RNs.

During this national nursing shortage, recruitment and retention of professional nurses in rural areas has been profoundly impacted (RHIH, 2018). The unique characteristics and qualifications for rural nursing practice make recruitment and retention particularly difficult. Although rich with diversity, rural areas often have limited economic resources. Rural regions report limited economic growth, lower median income, and higher rates of poverty than their urban counterparts (Blouin & Podjasek, 2019; RHIH, 2018). Rural nurses must be adept at doing more with less; they are expert generalists with a broad knowledge base and expert clinical judgment, oftentimes balancing competing priorities with little to no support (Mester, 2018; RHIH, 2018; Winters & Lee, 2018). Wages and benefits for rural nurses tend to be less than their urban counterparts, and the lack of educational opportunity and continued education, travel distances and social isolation, the lack of economic opportunity, and heavy workload with no support add another layer of complexity to the recruiting efforts of rural hospitals (USBLS, 2016; Blouin & Podjasek, 2019; Mester, 2018; RHIH, 2018).

Summary of Implications

The USDHHS (2014) has identified the need for improving health care access, reducing adverse health outcomes, and eliminating inequities. While health professional shortages, improvements in scope of practice, and positive reimbursement models are changing the footprint of professional nurses in primary care in rural settings, more is needed. Nurses are uniquely positioned to further impact access to care, health outcomes, and inequities. Many opportunities are created by addressing the noted issues and challenges to professional nursing services for older adults living in rural areas.

When planning and organizing health services for rural dwellers, it is vital to embrace a theoretical framework in the process to provide a better understanding of the unique characteristics, needs, and behaviors of rural dwellers. Consistent application of a theoretical framework provides clarity of purpose and a focused trajectory for health services that would improve efficiency of those services while also maximizing health outcomes. Embracing a theoretical framework when addressing health care issues for rural dwellers would also provide direction for continued research into the nuances of rural life for rural dwellers and the development of evidence-based programs for improving health outcomes among older adults.

To address changing demographics in rural populations, demand on health care resources, and workforce issues, it will be essential to expand current professional nursing scope of practice. This would offer nurses the prospect of increased employment and the opportunity to lead positive change for patients in rural communities. According to the USBLS (2016), 18 of the 30 fastest-growing occupations in the U.S. are in health care. The increased demand for health care services from an aging population and individuals with chronic health conditions will drive much of the anticipated employment growth in the coming decade. APRNs, specifically CNPs, are well positioned to alleviate provider shortages in rural areas if constraints to scope of practice are removed. CNPs currently account for 19% of the primary care workforce and are well prepared to address primary health care needs of rural populations (American Hospital Association, 2019).

References

American Association of Colleges of Nursing. (2008). *The essentials of baccalaureate education for professional nursing practice.* Retrieved from www.aacnnursing.org/portals/42/publications/baccessentials08.pdf

American Association of Colleges of Nursing. (2011). *The essentials of master's education in nursing.* Retrieved from www.tnecampus.org/sites/default/files/docs_and_pdfs/Masters%20Essentials.pdf

American Hospital Association. (2019). *Rural hospitals.* Retrieved September 24, 2019, from www.aha.org/news/insights-and-analysis/2019-03-05-5-strategies-rural-hospitals-are-using-bolster-their

American Nurses Association. (2017a). *Nursing workforce.* Retrieved September 24, 2019, from www.nursingworld.org/practice-policy/workforce/

American Nurses Association. (2017b). *Nursing workforce.* Retrieved September 24, 2019, from https://ana.aristotle.com/SitePages/nursingworkforcedevelopment.aspx

Blouin, A., & Podjasek, K. (2019). The continuing saga of nurse staffing: Historical and emerging challenges. *Journal of Nursing Administration, 49*(4), 221–227. doi:10.1097/NNA.0000000000000741

Bolin, J. N., Bellamy, G., Ferdinand, A. O., Kash, B. A., & Helduser, J. W. (Eds.). (2015a). *Access to quality health services in rural areas—primary care: A literature review in rural healthy people 2020* (Vol. 1). College Station, TX: Texas A&M Health Science Center School of Public Health, Southwest Rural Health Research Center.

Bolin, J. N., Bellamy, G., Ferdinand, A. O., Kash, B. A., & Helduser, J. W. (Eds.). (2015b). *Older adults in rural healthy people 2020* (Vol. 1). College Station, TX: Texas A&M Health Science Center School of Public Health, Southwest Rural Health Research Center.

Brenan, M. (2018). *Nurses again outpace other professions for honesty, ethics.* Retrieved from https://news.gallup.com/poll/245597/nurses-again-outpace-professions-honesty-ethics.aspx

Bushy, A. (2000). Special and at-risk populations. In *Orientation to nursing in the rural community.* Thousand Oaks, CA: Sage Publications.

Folland, S., Goodman, A. C., & Stano, M. (2016). *The economics of health and health care.* New York: Routledge.

Health Resources & Services Administration. (2017). *Rural nursing workforce.* Retrieved September 24, 2019, from www.hrsa.gov

Long, K. A., & Weinert, C. (1989). Rural nursing: Developing the theory base. *Scholarly Inquiry for Nursing Practice: An International Journal, 3,* 113–127.

Mester, J. (2018). Rural nurse recruitment. *Nursing Management, 49*(12). doi:10.1097/01.NUMA.0000544468.98484.b751-53

O'Donnell, J. (2014). Rural hospitals in critical condition. *USA Today.* Retrieved from www.usatoday.com/story/news/nation/2014/11/12/rural-hospital-closings-federal-reimbursementmedicaid-aca/18532471/

Olson, S., & Anderson, K. (2018). *Achieving rural health equity and well-being: Proceedings of a workshop.* Washington, DC: The National Academies Press.

Rural Health Information Hub. (2018). *Recruitment and retention for rural health facilities*. Retrieved September 20, 2019, from www.ruralhealthinfo.org/topics/rural-health-recruitment-retention

U.S. Bureau of Labor Statistics. (2016). *Occupational employment and wages, registered nurses*. Retrieved September 25, 2019, from www.bls.gov/oes/current/oes291141.htm#nat

U.S. Department of Health and Human Services. (2014). *Healthy people 2020: Access to health services*. Retrieved from www.healthypeople.gov/2020/topics-objectives/topic/Access-to-Health-Services

Winters, C. A., & Lee, H. J. (2018). *Rural nursing: Concepts, theory, and practice* (5th ed.). New York: Springer.

57
NUTRITION

Seung Eun Jung and Janice Hermann

Importance of Nutrition

The most recent U.S. Census reported that adults living in rural areas are older than those living in urban areas, with median ages being 51 and 45 years, respectively (U.S. Census Bureau, 2016). Unfortunately, rural older adults have a higher prevalence of chronic health issues such as obesity, cardiovascular disease, and neurodegeneration, which can diminish quality of life (Gamm, Hutchison, Bellamy, & Dabney, 2002; Casey, Thiede Call, & Klingner, 2001; Tai-Seale & Chandler, 2003; Baernholdt, Yan, Hinton, Rose, & Mattos, 2012). Evidence suggests maintaining good nutritional status plays an important role in preventing or delaying chronic health issues (Slawson, Fitzgerland, & Morgan, 2013; Arjuna et al., 2017). Furthermore, malnutrition has been reported to hinder older adults' ability to age-in-place, which is of utmost importance for this population (Getty, Mueller, Amella, & Fraser, 2015).

Common Nutritional Patterns and Practices of Rural Older Adults

Evidence shows rural older adults experience a higher prevalence of poor nutritional status, nutrient deficiencies, and unhealthy body weights (Arcury et al., 2007; Arjuna et al., 2017; Cohen, Greaney, & Sabik, 2018; Ledikwe, Smiciklas-Wright, Mitchell, Miller, & Jensen, 2004). For example, rural older adults' overall diet quality has been reported to be inadequate based on Healthy Eating Index scores. Particularly, consumption of whole grains, fruit, vegetable, and dairy were less than recommended intakes, while discretionary calories exceeded recommended amounts (Vitolins et al., 2007). Furthermore, a higher prevalence of obesity and being overweight has been reported among rural older adults (Gamm et al., 2002). Within this population, rural older adults who consume poor diets in terms of nutrient density are twice as likely to be obese than their counterparts who consume nutritionally appropriate diets (Ledikwe et al., 2004). Additionally, food insecurity among rural older adults is associated with increased rates of obesity for this population (Homenko, Morin, Eimicke, Teresi, & Weinstock, 2010).

Factors Impacting the Nutritional Practices of Rural Older Adults

Because of the geographic isolation of rural areas, the food environment is a major determinant influencing a range of rural older adult dietary behaviors (Arcury, Quandt, Bell, McDonald, &

Vitolins, 1998; Shanks, Haack, Tarabochia, Bates, & Christenson, 2017). In fact, rural older adults face substantial barriers to maintaining optimal nutrition.

Food Deserts

Limited access to affordable healthy foods is a major determinant influencing rural older adults' poor dietary intake. Supermarkets with a variety of healthier foods are more likely to be available in urban areas compared to rural areas (Morland, Wing, Diez Roux, & Poole, 2002). Additionally, limited choices and lower quality food have been reported to be common at rural grocery stores, which further limits access to healthy foods. In fact, rural older adults have reported that poor food quality in rural grocery stores, such as spoiled fruits and vegetables, decreased their desire to consume produce (Shanks et al., 2017).

A previous study indicated that availability of healthy foods in a community is associated with increased fruit and vegetable (F&V) intake (Zenk et al., 2005). High F&V intake is associated with a decreased risk of cardiovascular disease and cancer (Vitolins et al., 2007); however, rural older adults' F&V intake remains lower than the Dietary Guidelines for Americans recommendations (Arcury et al., 2007).

Higher food prices in rural grocery stores compared to urban grocery stores have been commonly reported (Morland et al., 2002; Walker, Keane, & Burke, 2010). These higher prices were explained by rural grocery stores based on lower customer volume, making it difficult to stock a variety of fresh foods; as well as the increased number of convenience stores over grocery stores in rural areas, where healthy foods are often sold at higher prices (Liese, Weis, & Pluto, Smith, & Lawson, 2007). In addition, individuals' proximity to grocery stores negatively affects diet quality and increases the risk of nutrition-related health issues (Larson, Story, & Nelson, 2009).

Studies have indicated accessibility of healthful foods significantly increased rural older adults' F&V and low-fat dairy food intake (Sharkey, 2009; Liese et al., 2007; Sharkey, Horel, & Dean, 2010). Therefore, having fresh, affordable, and nutritious foods available nearby could increase rural older adults' diet quality (Shanks et al., 2017).

Transportation/Accessibility

Lack of public transportation has often been reported by rural older adults as a barrier to consuming a healthful diet (Quandt, Arcury, & Bell, 1998; Bond, Brown, & Wood, 2017). Limited public transportation service is even more problematic for those who rely on family members, friends, and other social supports for transportation to grocery stores (Wright-Morton, Bitto, Oakland, & Sand, 2008). For example, Smith and Morton (1994) reported individuals residing in rural areas travel far greater distances than those who live in urban areas. Rural older adults have also reported they have to drive long distances to purchase groceries because convenience stores were the only food source in their community (Shanks et al., 2017).

A negative relationship between travel distance and diet quality as well as F&V intake among rural residents has been reported (Laraia, Siega-Riz, Kaufman, & Jones, 2004; Rose & Richards, 2004). One possible solution to rural older adult transportation challenges is to develop partnerships between transportation services and nonprofit organizations such as congregate meal sites, food banks, and farmers markets (Bond et al., 2017).

Social Isolation

Rural older adults have also been reported to be at increased risk of poor nutritional status because of social isolation (Ledikwe, Smiciklas-Wright, Mitchell, Miller, & Jensen, 2003).

A study that focused on rural older adults' perception of healthy aging reported maintaining social relationships as one of the most important facets of healthy aging, and respondents referenced their neighbors, friends, and family as influences on their decisions to cook or participate in mealtime (Bacsu et al., 2014). Baernholdt et al. (2012) reported social isolation owing to rural characteristics contributed to poor physical and mental health. A study examining the interrelationship between physical, mental, and nutritional status found poor emotional well-being because of social isolation could contribute to poor nutritional status among rural older adults (Jung et al., 2017); whereas a positive relationship has been reported between social interaction at mealtimes and diet quality (Holmes & Roberts, 2011).

Low Educational Levels

Chen, Cheng, Chuang, and Shao (2014) reported rural older adults tend to have lower incomes, lower education levels, poorer perceived health, and increased risk for malnutrition. Lack of nutrition education in rural areas was also prevalent. The authors suggested limited resources in rural communities as well as educational barriers may be a reason for the absence of nutrition education. Further, rural older adults in this study attributed their health status to chance more than their urban counterparts. It was suggested this may be because of lower education levels in rural areas or circumstances such as food insecurity and poverty that rural older adults feel they have no control over.

Availability of Professional Nutritional Guidance in Rural Communities

Cooperative Extension Service provides informal, research-based education and information to people of all age groups regardless of income, including older adults living in rural communities (U.S. Department of Agriculture, n.d.a). Cooperative Extension Service Specialists and County Educators are located in all 50 states and territories of the nation and strive to improve the lives of others through a variety of education opportunities including programs that help people make informed decisions and lifestyle choices about food and nutrition. Examples of food and nutrition programs offered by Cooperative Extension Service on a community level include healthful eating, nutrition and health promotion, food resource management, food preparation, food safety and food preservation (U.S. Department of Agriculture, n.d.b).

References

Arcury, T. A., Quandt, S. A., Bell, R. A., McDonald, J., & Vitolins, M. Z. (1998). Barriers to nutritional well-being for rural elders: Community experts' perceptions. *The Gerontologist, 38*(4), 490–498. doi:10.1093/geront/38.4.409

Arjuna, T., Soenen, S., Hasnawati, R. A., Lange, K., Chapman, I., & Luscombe-Marsh, N. D. (2017). A cross-sectional study of nutrient intake and health status among older adults in Yogyakarta, Indonesia. *Nutrients, 9*(11), 1–21. doi:10.3390/nu9111240

Aune, D., Giovannucci, E., Boffetta, P., Fadnes, L. T., Keum, N., Norat, T., . . . Tonstad, S. (2017). Fruit and vegetable intake and the risk of cardiovascular disease, total cancer and all-cause mortality—a systematic review and dose-response meta-analysis of prospective studies. *International Journal of Epidemiology, 46*(3), 1029–1056. doi:10.1093/ije/dyw319

Bacsu, J., Jeffery, B., Abonyi, S., Johnson, S., Novik, N., Martz, D., & Oosman, S. (2014). Healthy aging in place: Perceptions of rural older adults. *Educational Gerontology, 40*, 327–337. doi:10.1080/03601277.2013.802191

Baernholdt, M., Yan, G., Hinton, I., Rose, K., & Mattos, M. (2012). Quality of life in rural and urban adults 65 years and older: Findings from the National Health and Nutrition Examination survey. *The Journal of Rural Health*, *28*(4), 339–347. doi:10.1111/j.1748-0361.2011.00403.x

Bond, M., Brown, J. R., & Wood, J. (2017). Adapting to challenge: Examining older adult transportation in rural communities. *Elsevier Case Studies on Transport Policy*, *5*, 707–715. doi:10.1016/j.cstp.2017.07.004

Casey, M. M., Thiede Call, K., & Klingner, J. M. (2001). Are rural residents less likely to obtain recommended preventive healthcare services? *American Journal of Preventive Medicine*, *21*(3), 182–188. doi:10.1016/s0749-3797(01)00349-x

Chen, S. H., Cheng, H. Y., Chuang, Y. H., & Shao, J. H. (2014). Nutritional status and its health-related factors among older adults in rural and urban areas. *Journal of Advanced Nursing*, *71*(1), 42–53. doi:10.1111/jan.12462

Cohen, S. A., Greaney, M. L., & Sabik, N. J. (2018). Assessment of dietary patterns, physical activity and obesity from a national survey: Rural-urban health disparities in older adults. *PLoS One*, *13*(12), 1–15. doi:10.1371/journal.pone.0208268

Gamm, L., Hutchison, L., Bellamy, G., & Dabney, B. J. (2002). Rural healthy people 2010: Identifying rural health priorities and models for practice. *The Journal of Rural Health*, *18*(1), 9–14. doi:10.1111/j.1748-0361.2002.tb00869.x

Getty, M. D., Mueller, E. J., Amella, E. J., & Fraser, A. M. (2015). Differences in medical and life-style risk factors for malnutrition in limited-resource older adults in a rural U.S. state: A descriptive study. *The Journal of Nutrition, Health and Aging*, *20*(2), 121–127. doi:10.1007/s12603-015-0561-5

Holmes, B. A., & Roberts, C. L. (2011). Diet quality and the influence of social and physical factors on food consumption and nutrient intake in materially deprived older people. *European Journal of Clinical Nutrition*, *65*, 638–545. doi:10.1038/ejcn.2010.293

Homenko, D. R., Morin, P. C., Eimicke, J. P., Teresi, J. A., & Weinstock, R. S. (2010). Food insecurity and food choices in rural older adults with diabetes receiving nutrition education via telemedicine. *Journal of Nutrition Education and Behavior*, *42*(6), 404–409. doi:10.1016/j.neb.2009.08.001

Jung, S. E., Bishop, A. J., Kim, M., Hermann, J., King, G., & Lawrence, J. (2017). Nutritional status of rural older adults is linked to physical and emotional health. *Journal of the Academy of Nutrition and Dietetics*, *117*(6), 851–858. doi:10.1016/j.jand.2017.01.013

Laraia, B., Siega-Riz, A., Kaufman, J., & Jones, S. (2004). Proximity of supermarkets is positively associated with diet quality index for pregnancy. *PrevMED*, *39*, 869–875. Retrieved from www.ncbi.nlm.nih.gov/pubmed/15475018

Larson, N. I., Story, M. T., & Nelson, M. C. (2009). Neighborhood environments: Disparities in access to healthy foods in the U.S. *American Journal of Preventive Medicine*, *36*(1), 74–81. doi:10.1016/j.amepre.2008.09.025

Ledikwe, J. H., Smiciklas-Wright, H., Mitchell, D. C., Miller, C. K., & Jensen, G. L. (2004). Dietary patterns of rural older adults are associated with weight and nutrition status. *Journal of the American Geriatric Society*, *52*(4), 589–595. doi:10.1111/j.1532-5415.2004.52167.x

Ledikwe, J. H., Smiciklas-Wright, H., Mitchell, D. C., Miller, C. K., & Jensen, G. L. (2003). Nutritional risk assessment and obesity in rural older adults: A sex difference. *The American Journal of Clinical Nutrition*, 77, 551–558. Retrieved from www.ncbi.nlm.nih.gov/pubmed/12600842

Liese, A., Weis, K. E., Pluto, D., Smith, E., & Lawson, A. (2007). Food store types, availability, and cost of foods in a rural environment. *Journal of the American Dietetic Association*, *107*, 1916–1923. Retrieved from www.ncbi.nlm.nih.gov/pubmed/17964311

Morland, K., Wing, S., Diez Roux, A., & Poole, C. (2002). Neighborhood characteristics associated with the location of food stores and food service places. *American Journal of Preventive Medicine*, *22*(1), 23–29. Retrieved from www.ncbi.nlm.nih.gov/pubmed/11777675

Quandt, S. A., Arcury, T. A., & Bell, R. A. (1998). Self-management of nutritional risk among older adults: A conceptual model and case studies from rural communities. *Journal of Aging Studies*, *12*, 351–68. Retrieved from www.sciencedirect.com/science/article/abs/pii/S089040659890024X

Rose, D., & Richards, R. (2004). Food store access and household fruit and vegetable use among participants in the US food stamp program. *Public Health Nutrition*, 7, 1081–1088. Retrieved from www.ncbi.nlm.nih.gov/pubmed/15548347

Shanks, C. B., Haack, S., Tarabochia, D., Bates, K., & Christenson, L. (2017). Factors influencing food choices among older adults in the rural Western USA. *Journal of Community Health*, *42*, 511–521. doi:10.1007/s10900-016-0283-6

Sharkey, J. R. (2009). Measuring potential access to food stores and food-service places in rural areas in the US. *American Journal of Preventive Medicine, 36*(4), S151–S155. doi:10.1016/j.amepre.2009.01.004

Sharkey, J. R., Horel, S. A., & Dean, W. R. (2010). Neighborhood deprivation, vehicle ownership, and potential spatial access to a variety of fruits and vegetables in a large rural area in Texas. *International Journal of Health Geographics, 9, 26.* Retrieved from www.ij-healthgeographics.com/contents/9/1/26

Slawson, D. L., Fitzgerald, N., & Morgan, K. T. (2013). Position of the Academy of Nutrition and Dietetics: The role of nutrition in health promotion and chronic disease prevention. *Journal of the Academy of Nutrition and Dietetics, 113*(7), 972–979. doi:10.1016/j.jand.2013.05.005

Smith, C., & Morton, L. W. (1994). Rural food deserts: Low-income perspectives on food access in Minnesota and Iowa. *Journal of Nutrition Education and Behavior, 41*, 176–187. Retrieved from www.ncbi.nlm.nih.gov/pubmed/19411051

Tai-Seale, T., & Chandler, C. (2003). Nutrition and overweight concerns in rural areas. In L. Gamm, L. Hutchison, B. Dabney, & A. Dorsey (Eds.), *Rural healthy people 2010: A companion document to healthy people 2010* (Vol. 2, pp. 182–192). College Station, TX: The Texas A&M University System Health Sciences Center, School of Rural Public Health, Southwest Rural Health Research Center.

U.S. Census Bureau. (2016). *New census data show differences between rural and urban populations*. Retrieved from www.census.gov/newsroom/press-releases/2016/cb16-210.html

U.S. Department of Agriculture. (n.d.a). *Extension*. Retrieved from https://nifa.usda.gov/extension

U.S. Department of Agriculture. (n.d.b). *Nutrition programs*. Retrieved from https://nifa.usda.gov/program/nutrition-programs

Vitolins, M. Z., Tooze, J. A., Golden, S. L., Arcury, T. A., Bell, R. A., Davis, C., Devellis, R. F., & Quandt, S. A. (2007). Older adults in the rural South are not meeting healthful eating guidelines. *Journal of the American Dietetic Association, 107*(2), 265–272. doi:10.1016/j.jada.2006.11.009

Walker, R. E., Keane, C. R., & Burke, J. G. (2010). Disparities and access to healthy food in the United States: A review of food deserts literature. *Health Place, 16*(5), 876–884. doi:10.1016/j.healthplace.2010.04.013

Wright-Morton, L., Bitto, E. A., Oakland, M. J., & Sand, M. (2008). Accessing food resources: Rural and urban patterns of giving and getting food. *Agriculture and Human Values, 25*, 107–119. Retrieved from https://link.springer.com/article/10.1007/s10460-007-9095-8

Zenk, S. N., Schulz, A. J., Hollis-Neely, T., Campbell, R. T., Holmes, N., Watkins, G., . . . Odoms-Young, A. (2005). Fruit and vegetable intake in African Americans: Income and store characteristics. *American Journal of Preventive Medicine, 29*, 1–9. Retrieved from www.ncbi.nlm.nih.gov/pubmed/15958245

58
PHILANTHROPY

John N. Feather

Services and programs for older people in rural America are chronically underfunded and understaffed, as are many health and human service programs in general in rural areas. Philanthropy (defined here as grant-giving foundations and corporate charities) can be helpful, but relatively little is directed to serving the needs of older people in rural areas: only 7% of American philanthropy is dedicated to rural issues of any type and less than 2% targets any category of aging (Walsh Center, 2019). How can we make philanthropy more helpful to the one-quarter of the older U.S. population who live in these areas?

Challenges and Opportunities to Philanthropy in Rural Aging

The Rural Philanthropy Analysis Project at Campbell University, with the support of the Robert Wood Johnson Foundation, completed the first comprehensive analysis of rural private funders. They listed some of the challenges facing philanthropy in rural areas (Rural Philanthropic Analysis Project, 2019):

- Rural regions in the United States have as many differences as similarities, and funders often have a difficult time gathering enough knowledge to understand both dimensions.
- The human, financial, and structural assets of rural communities often look quite different than their urban counterparts. Rural leaders may resist unfamiliar but well-intentioned urban models.
- Rural communities may be skeptical of any long-term commitments from private urban-based funders toward rural community improvement initiatives.
- The presence of significant state and federal resources may make it difficult for out-of-area private funders to align their work with common goals.
- The rural nonprofit infrastructure can be sparse, so funders naturally gravitate toward trusted partners that may not be the right kind of leaders for the effort(s).

To provide ways for funders to more effectively collaborate, the project called for a shift in philanthropic practice, including:

- Meaningful ongoing relationships with local, state, and regional funders that are demonstrating success with their rural culture of health work.

- Rural non-health networks that have a state or regional focus and are embracing culture of health concepts.
- Deeper knowledge of individual communities that have created important cross-sector initiatives focused on improving the health of their communities.
- Identification of existing under-the-radar successes from the rural regions of the country and technical and financial support for adaptation to other areas.
- Strategies for adaptation of rural work that recognize differences in geography, culture, and history and that also consider rural Native American communities and other specific populations.
- Understanding of the context of initiatives that fundamentally shift the vitality of rural community life such as electrification and broadband access.
- Support for the development of emerging nontraditional leaders to respond to a rapidly aging leadership population that may lack necessary innovation to support development and growth (Rural Philanthropic Analysis Project, 2019).

Use Aging as a Lens, Not a Focus

For those looking for resources, focusing exclusively on "rural aging" is unlikely to be successful because so few funders support this area, resulting in what is likely to be an extremely limited pool of potential funders. Many times, grant seekers unfortunately hear the response "we don't fund aging" as a blanket response to their inquiries.

A more helpful approach is to use aging as a "lens" or a way of looking at an issue rather than the exclusive focus in and of itself. For example, rather than focusing on support for a program on improving mobility for rural older people alone, grant seekers are advised to find partners who have an interest in improving transportation in general and talking about how directing more attention to the needs of older people improves the transportation options available to the whole community. Making the community better for all includes making the community better for older people, but the emphasis shifts from older people exclusively to residents of all ages in the community. In addition, given the limited resources in rural areas generally, it is unlikely that most communities will be able to develop elderly-only programs.

This approach is particularly important in seeking philanthropic dollars for a number of reasons. All private funders limit their areas of focus because they cannot meet all of the needs of a community. These areas of interest are sometimes determined by the donor of the funds (for example, in the case of family foundations or donor-advised funds at community foundations) or by the areas of interest of the parent corporation (in the case of corporate philanthropy). Given that less than 2% of American philanthropy is directed toward addressing aging-related issues, limiting the search for support to just these organizations is unlikely to be successful.

The most prominent area of current funding in health philanthropy offers a good example of this approach. Social determinants of health (SDOH) cover a broad array of issues but are focused on changing the underlying economic and social conditions that result in some segments of the populations experiencing worse health outcomes than others (Islam, 2019). Rather than focusing solely on conditions that improve individual health (e.g., smoking cessation, diet, exercise), this approach would suggest considering the lack of available healthy foods in certain neighborhoods, the lack of safe and affordable housing, the lack of public transportation that limits access to health care, and other systemic factors that especially create inequalities and more negative outcomes for particular community groups and geographic areas. While it may seem "obvious" that aging is an important consideration in interpreting the impact of SDOH, it is not usually identified as a separate issue. The number of private funders in health is much broader than those who work in the field of aging and understanding the issues that resonate with them will help rural aging programs to strategically position their work in ways that are more likely to be supported.

Philanthropy Is More Than Funding

Those who administer programs for older persons often only approach foundations when they need money. That is a mistake. Foundations play many other roles that can be important in supporting services for older persons (Feather, 2017). One of the most important and frequently practiced roles by foundations in rural settings is acting as a trusted and neutral convener. Foundations provide resources to a community over a long period of time and establish relationships of trust in the process. They can support activities that allow government and social service providers to get to know each other better that will hopefully also help funders better understand the work and the needs of aging service providers.

There is also a special group of stakeholders that is not well understood in philanthropy: the trustees. While it is typical for those seeking funds to try to develop a relationship with foundation staff, it is important to understand that staff are commonly not the final decision-makers on all grants. Trustees in philanthropy vary, but they are usually prominent members of the community rather than experts in a particular field. It is essential that the grant seeker makes it clear how their program answers the key question asked by trustees: how does this make our community better? The assumption is that staff has vetted a proposal carefully, but trustees still have a major decision-making role to play. In addition, trustees, because of their local prominence, are also likely to be closely connected to other leaders in the community. Trustees can serve as a conduit through which to introduce the work of the service provider to a broader range of potential supporters. Thus, it is well worth becoming familiar with the interests and background of a foundation's trustees when seeking funds from that organization.

Examples of Successful Rural Philanthropy Efforts

Campbell University's Rural Philanthropic Analysis Project (2019) has developed a series of four compelling in-depth case studies of foundations that are making a difference in their communities (see the "Resources" section later), including:

- *Northwest Iowa*, focusing on the Community Foundation of Greater Dubuque, which has focused on bringing the region's rural populations and local government and businesses together;
- *Eastern Washington*, focusing on the Empire Health Foundation, which has developed a model closer to a venture capital enterprise than a traditional grantmaking foundation; and,
- *New England*, focusing on the Maine Community Access Foundation and the Endowment for Health (in New Hampshire), which have developed a multistate approach.

One other example, that of the Con Alma Health Foundation of New Mexico, raises a number of particularly interesting issues showing both the complexity and successes of a foundation working integrally in a rural area. Describing the work of rural communities and funders as "small but mighty," the work of the foundation includes:

- Intentionally ensuring that the board, staff, and advisers represent the diversity of the rural areas of the state.

- Investing huge time and energy in developing long-lasting and intense relationships with grantees.
- Working in different ways than normal philanthropy. For example, based on cultural traditions of Native communities, meetings start with a long process of learning about each person in the room (not just organizations) and honoring their contributions. This can be "excruciatingly slow" but is essential for building trust.
- Recognizing that communities know both problems and solutions that best meet their needs. The foundation does not try to impose "evidence-based models" that have usually been developed and tested only in urban areas.
- Understanding the unique history of New Mexico and how it affects issues of racial injustice, often a key issue that prevents communities from coming together. In the state's case, racial trauma often comes from colonialization, first the suppression of Native communities and then the suppression of Hispanics by the dominant Anglo-American culture. Understanding and being able to address these specific issues is key.

The Con Alma Health Foundation is an example of how a deeply committed local funder can have a real and lasting impact on a local community. It is a modest-sized foundation ($14 million in grants over its 20-year history), but it has managed to attract $50 million in additional funding from other foundations (including national funders) through its leadership. It is truly "small but mighty."

Philanthropy for Rural Aging

Philanthropy has always been involved in rural communities and continues to do so, but as rural areas become older, their role needs to dramatically increase. There is no simple or one-sized model as to how this should happen, and indeed, the push to develop a uniform approach will be counterproductive. The most effective philanthropy is deeply engaged over a long period of time in the communities they serve, resulting in the solutions that work best.

References

Feather, J. (2017). *Successful corporate and foundation fundraising for nonprofits.* Retrieved from www.giaging.org/documents/170323_For_Grantseekers_Feather_PPT_Corp_and_Foundation_Funding_with_notes.pdf

Islam, M. (2019). Social determinants of health and related inequalities: Confusion and implications. *Frontiers of Public Health*, 7, 11.

Rural Philanthropic Analysis Project. (2019). *About rural philanthropy.* Retrieved from www.campbell.edu/about/research/rural-philanthropic-analysis/about-rural-philanthropy/

Walsh Center for Rural Health Analysis. (2019). *Building partnership with philanthropies: Emerging strategies for rural communities.* Retrieved from www.norc.org/PDFs/Walsh%20Center/Practice%20Briefs/Rural%20Philanthopy%20Toolkit%20Practice%20Brief_APRIL2019.pdf

Resources

Rural Philanthropic Analysis Project. *About rural philanthropy.* Retrieved from www.campbell.edu/about/research/rural-philanthropic-analysis/about-rural-philanthropy/. Their resource page is the most useful recent analysis of rural philanthropy and can be retrieved from https://blogs.campbell.edu/posts/topics/rural-philanthropic-analysis/.

The Rural Philanthropic Analysis Project has also done a series of in-depth profiles of successful philanthropy in rural areas, including:

- Northeast Iowa (Community Foundation of Greater Dubuque). Retrieved from https://blogs.campbell.edu/rpa-rural-case-study-northeastern-iowa/;
- New Mexico (Con Alma Health Foundation). Retrieved from https://assets.campbell.edu/wp-content/uploads/2019/05/RPA-New-Mexico_LR.pdf;
- Eastern Washington (Empire Health Foundation). Retrieved from https://assets.campbell.edu/wp-content/uploads/2019/07/RPA-Eastern-Washington-LOW.pdf; and
- New England (Maine Health Access Foundation and the Endowment for Health). Retrieved from https://assets.campbell.edu/wp-content/uploads/2019/06/RPA-New-England_LR.pdf.

The Walsh Center for Rural Health Analysis. *Building partnership with philanthropies: Emerging strategies for rural communities*. Retrieved from www.norc.org/PDFs/Walsh%20Center/Practice%20Briefs/Rural%20Philanthopy%20Toolkit%20Practice%20Brief_APRIL2019.pdf. The Walsh Center is part of the University of Chicago.

Rural Health Information Hub. *Rural philanthropy toolkit*. Retrieved from www.ruralhealthinfo.org/toolkits/philanthropy. This seven-module toolkit is based on the Walsh Center report and provided a practical guide to implementing better philanthropy in rural areas. The RHI Hub is supported by the Health Resources and Services Administration, U.S. Department of Health and Human Services.

Feather, John. *Successful corporate and foundation fundraising for nonprofits*. Retrieved from www.giaging.org/documents/170323_For_Grantseekers_Feather_PPT_Corp_and_Foundation_Funding_with_notes.pdf. This is a step-by-step approach to assisting organizations seeking corporate and foundation support, particularly in pointing out the differences from this approach to that typically used for accessing governmental support.

The Daily Yonder. Retrieved from www.dailyyonder.com. The premier daily journalism site for reporting on issues of rural concern like broadband access, health disparities, environmental degradation, and civic engagement. There is also excellent consistent coverage of rural philanthropy.

Giving Compass has a series of rural philanthropy resources that can be retrieved from https://givingcompass.org/?type=news&s=rural. Giving Compass is a philanthropy knowledge hub helping philanthropic-minded individuals and organizations learn, connect, and take action.

59
PHYSICAL ACTIVITY

Erica Robertson and Marilyn R. Gugliucci

Introduction

It is a fact that fewer than 10% of adults (ages 18–64) meet current physical activity recommendations (Tucker, Welk, & Beyler, 2011; Kurti, Logan, Manini, & Dallery, 2015; WHO, 2020), and this percentage is even lower among subsets of the general population, including older adults. Adults living in rural America are less active than urban or suburban adults and twice as likely to report limitations related to activity (Bailey, 2010; Wilson et al., 2009; Kurti et al., 2015).

The term *physical activity*, as referred to here, encompasses the following: fitness, activity, exercise, and recreation unless stated otherwise. According to the World Health Organization, physical activity includes any bodily movement produced by skeletal muscles that requires energy expenditure—including activities undertaken while working, playing, carrying out household chores, traveling, and engaging in recreational pursuits. Physical activities can be categorized into occupational, sports, conditioning, household, or other activities (WHO, 2020).

Rurality and Physical Activity

Older adults who live in rural communities are at a disadvantage as compared with their urban and suburban counterparts in terms of services, resources, activities, and social events—all part of the fabric of the community that supports its residents (Skoufalos, 2017). As a result, rural communities have a higher prevalence of chronic disease, a higher disability rate, a lower prevalence of healthy behaviors (Downey, 2013; Skoufalos, 2017), and a widening gap in life expectancy (Singh & Siahpush, 2014; Skoufalos, 2017) relative to the nation as a whole. A sedentary lifestyle is associated with poorer health, which means increased medical costs because of more practitioner visits and more medications (Greaney, Lees, Blissmer, Riebe, & Clark, 2016).

Within the last decade, the percentage of older adults has grown to 15% of the population in rural areas and 12% in urban areas (Bolin et al., 2015). In Maine, 58% of older adults live in rural communities (Skoufalos, 2017). This demographic shift is occurring as older retirees migrate to rural areas (in part because of reduced cost and preferred living style) and young people move to urban and suburban areas (for reasons of employment and social opportunities). The need for increased health care in rural areas creates additional challenges because of scarcity of available services, trained physicians, and public transportation (Douthit et al., 2015). Improving education on physical activity and providing options for rural-dwelling older adults to engage in physical activity is a step toward addressing health.

Benefits of Physical Activity

Physical activity benefits everyone, and for older adults living in rural areas, there is no discrimination regarding race, ethnic background, sex, functional ability, or age. Older adults with chronic conditions should be involved in physical activity as it can help prevent or control, arthritis, hypertension, diabetes, obesity, heart disease, a number of different cancers, and osteoporosis (U.S. Department of Health and Human Services (USDHHS), 2002; USDHHS, 2018). Physical activity also helps to maintain independent living by improving cognitive and psychological well-being and physical function, including aiding balance and proprioception, mobility, and strength, all of which are attributed to increasing longevity (Gugliucci, Robertson, Wehry, & Weaver, 2019; American College of Sports Medicine, 2018; Chodzko-Zajko, 2014; Chodzko-Zajko, Schwingel, & Park, 2009; Nelson et al., 2007).

To increase levels of physical activity among older adults living in rural areas, it is important to look at why physical activity should be a part of every older adult's life. In a study by Dye et al. (2006), a focus group gathered information on *what motivated* older rural women to be physically active. The most important personal factor was the perceived health benefit or avoidance of a negative outcome if they did not keep moving. Most of the women valued physical activity for the physical and mental outcomes it produced and cited the "use it or lose it" mentality. Disseminating knowledge about the importance and need for moving, in whatever amount one can, could be one of the most beneficial methods of increasing physical activity in older adults who live in rural areas.

Once the perceived health benefit is in place, it is important to address the specific needs and preferences of these older adults in each rural community (Luke & Dzewaltowski, 2000). One of the best ways to build a person's confidence is to suggest participating in any physical or functional fitness activity for a few minutes each day; adding more time while maintaining comfortable exertion and staying within one's ability.

When older adults are physically active, it aids in maintaining their quality of life and more importantly, it can help in maintaining activities and instrumental activities of daily living (ADLs/IADLs), which are key to preserving independence (Gugliucci, Robertson, Wehry, & Weaver, 2019). For many, physical activity is not a fundamental component of daily life and inactivity increases with age. By age 75, about one in three men and one in two women do not engage in physical activity (Resnick & Boltz, 2016; Gugliucci et al., 2019).

In 2018, the U.S. Department of Health and Human Services published the second edition of the *Physical Activity Guidelines for Americans*. It states that for substantial health benefits, adults (general category) should do at least 150 minutes (2 hours and 30 minutes) a week of vigorous-intensity aerobic physical activity (heart rate and breathing rate increase), or an equivalent combination of moderate- and vigorous-intensity aerobic activity (USDHHS, 2018). Preferably, conducting physical activity throughout the week is best, rather than the "weekend warrior syndrome" where vigorous exercise only happens a day or two a week leading to more cases of injury. Including muscle-strengthening activities of moderate or greater intensity involving all major muscle groups two or more days a week provides additional health benefits (ACSM, 2018; USDHHS, 2018).

Since the *Physical Activity Guidelines for Americans* were first published in 2002, research has led to significant updates in physical activity recommendations that were presented in the second edition of the guidelines including:

- All physical activity counts regardless of how long the person does each activity.
- There are immediate health benefits from a single bout of activity; these include reduced anxiety and blood pressure, improved quality of sleep, and improved insulin sensitivity.
- There are more long-term benefits from physical activity, including improved brain health, reduced risk of eight types of cancer (previously two), reduced risk for fall-related injuries in older adults, and reduced risk of excessive weight gain.
- Physical activity helps manage more chronic health conditions; decreasing pain for those with osteoarthritis, reducing disease progression for hypertension and type 2 diabetes, reducing symptoms of anxiety and depression, and improving cognition for those with dementia, multiple sclerosis, ADHD, and Parkinson's disease.

(Adapted from the USDHHS, *Physical Activity Guidelines for Americans*, 2018)

Those in the older adult fitness field recognize that stating all physical activity contributes to health regardless of how long you do it (even for one minute) aids in altering individuals' perception—any movement is *worthwhile*. The updated USDHHS, 2018 guidelines reframe physical activity, offering encouragement to move. For inactive or underactive older adults, doing what they can for as long as they can will be a benefit. For older adults in rural areas, this study supports working on the land, gardening, cleaning the house, walking in the grocery store, walking around the house during TV commercials, and parking further away from an entry door. There are so many ways to include functional fitness into life, regardless of the availability of formal fitness programs.

Programs for Older Adults Living in Rural Areas

Opportunities to participate in organized physical activity may be more prevalent in urban and suburban areas, but successful engagement in functional fitness and physical activity does not require a gym, class, or a paid instructor. The ability to afford participation in a fitness or physical activity program or to find transportation to such a program need not be a barrier, either. Approaches to physical activity that have success in rural areas include home exercise (options presented in Table 59.1); neighbor or buddy system activities (learning from each other and challenging each other to do more); and church and community programs that include participation at recreation centers and health centers. Shopping mall or grocery store walking programs or group exercise programs also are successful in rural areas.

The following online resources from select organizations are designed for older adults or focus on a specific health condition (see Table 59.1). These resources offer a myriad of information and evidenced-based programs to support physical activity for older adults. Any web-based search engine should work and once on the organization home page, search the term "Physical Activity."

Each day, 11,000+ nationally recognized senior centers serve one million adults aged 50+ (National Council on Aging, 2019). Today's senior centers offer fitness programs, job and volunteering information, transportation, and nutritionally well-balanced meals. Senior centers are typically located in urban and suburban areas, but when contacted, they can help connect services and resources to those more rurally located. When a community senior

Table 59.1 Resources on Older Adult Physical Activity

Web-Based Resources
NCOA—National Council on Aging Description: The NCOA is a respected national leader and trusted partner to help people aged 60+ meet the challenges of aging. They partner with nonprofit organizations, government, and business to provide innovative community programs and services, online help, and advocacy. *View*: "Healthy Aging" tab *Search*: Physical Activity
NIA—National Institute on Aging Description: NIA, one of the 27 Institutes and Centers of NIH, leads a broad scientific effort to understand the nature of aging and to extend the healthy, active years of life. NIA is the primary federal agency supporting and conducting Alzheimer's disease research. *Search*: Physical Activity
Go4Life Go4Life offers free, evidence-based resources for older adults in one convenient place for four types of exercise—endurance, strength, balance, and flexibility. *Search:* Encouraging Wellness in Older Patients Information for Practitioners—"Talking with your Older Patient: Exercise and Physical Activity"
AHA—American Heart Association Description: The American Heart Association is a nonprofit organization in the U.S. that fosters appropriate cardiac care in an effort to reduce disability and deaths caused by cardiovascular disease and stroke. *Search:* Physical Activity in Older Americans
ACS—American Cancer Society Description: American Cancer Society *Search:* ACS Guidelines for Nutrition and Physical Activity
Alz.Org®—Alzheimer's Association Description: Alzheimer's Association advances research to end Alzheimer's and dementia while enhancing care for those living with the disease. *Search:* Stay Physically Active *Search:* Exercising the Brain
Health.gov Description: Health.gov is a portal for health-related resources and news from the U.S. government. Information on prevention topics, dietary and physical activity guidelines, and other health resources are provided. *Search:* Physical Activity
University of New England U-ExCEL Balancing Act Program Description: University of New England's Exercise and Conditioning for Easier Living (U-ExCEL) is an auxiliary functional fitness program for older adults. Online training in balance through video and written manuals are free. *Search:* UNECOM U-ExCEL Balancing Act

Note: As Website addresses may change, find "Search" on the home page then type in the term listed under each resource. Gugliucci et al., 2019

Table 59.2 Nationally Accredited Senior Centers

Nationally Accredited Senior Centers
List Form *Website:* NCOA.org/resources/NISC-Accredited-Senior-Centers/
Map Form (Searchable by State or Zip) *Website:* NCOA.org/NCOA-Map/

center is not within commuting distance or commuting is not an option, reaching out to these centers and requesting information or assistance can be beneficial in connecting older adults with available resources (See Table 59.2 for a list of the current Nationally Accredited Senior Centers).

Conclusion

Older adults are a diverse and heterogeneous group regardless of where they live. Rurality is not the determining factor on whether one can be physically active. Older adults exhibit differences in psychosocial factors based on age, race/ethnicity, income, socioeconomic status, location (urban, suburban, or rural), and presence or type of disability. Additionally, internal factors such as motivation, personality, desire, and coping mechanisms will also affect the degree to which persons engage in physical activity or expands their functional fitness (Gugliucci et al., 2019). Anyone willing to try can exercise, whether it be a full body workout or improving grip strength and finger dexterity if wheelchair reliant. The type of activities each person chooses, the decision to be active alone or in groups, and how long the activities are continued are all subject to each person's desires and support system.

References

American College of Sports Medicine. (2018). *ACSM's guidelines for exercise testing and prescription* (D. Riebe, Senior ed., J. K. Ehrman, G. Liguori, & M. Magal, Associate ed., 10th ed.). Philadelphia, PA: Wolters Kluwer.

Bailey, J. M. (2010). *Why health reform can't wait: The benefits of health reform for rural America.* Center for Rural Affairs. Retrieved July 2019, from http://files.cfra.org/pdf/Why-Health-Reform-Cant-Wait.pdf

Bolin, J. N., Bellamy, G. R., Ferdinand, A. O., Vuong, A. M., Kash, B. A., Schulze, A., & Helduser, J. W. (2015). Rural healthy people 2020: New decade, same challenges. *The Journal of Rural Health, 31*(3), 326–333. doi:10.1111/jrh.12116

Dye, C. J., & Wilcox, S. (2006). Beliefs of low-income and rural older women regarding physical activity: You have to want to make your life better. *Women & Health, 43*(1), 115–134. doi:10.1300/J013v43n01_07

Chodzko-Zajko, W. (Ed.). (2014). *ACSM's exercise for older adults.* Baltimore, MD: Lippincott Williams & Wilkins.

Chodzko-Zajko, W., Schwingel, A., & Park, H. E. (2009). Successful aging: The role of physical activity. *American Journal of Lifestyle Medicine, 3*(1), 20–28.

Douthit, N., Kiv, S., Dwolatzky, T., & Biswas, S. (2015). Exposing some important barriers to health care access in the rural USA. *Public Health, 129*(6), 611–620.

Downey, L. H. (2013). Rural populations and health: Determinants, disparities, and solutions [book review]. *Preventing Chronic Disease, 10.* doi:10.5888/pcd10.130097

Greaney, M. L., Lees, F. D., Blissmer, B. J., Riebe, D., & Clark, P. G. (2016). Psychosocial factors associated with physical activity in older adults. *Annual Review of Gerontology & Geriatrics, 36*(1), 273–291.

Gugliucci, M., Robertson, E., Wehry, S., & Weaver, S. (2019). Physical activity for older adults: Supporting social integration. In L. W. Kaye & C. M. Singer (Eds.), *Social isolation in later life: Strategies for bolstering health and well-being*. New York: Springer Publishing Company. doi:10.1891/9780826146991

Kurti, A. N., Logan, H., Manini, T., & Dallery, J. (2015). Physical activity behavior, barriers to activity, and opinions about a smartphone-based physical activity intervention among rural residents. *Telemedicine Journal and e-Health, 21*(1), 16–23. doi:10.1089/tmj.2014.0034

Luke, P. E., & Dzewaltowski, D. A. (2000). Multidimensional scaling and preference mapping: Promising methods for investigating older adults' physical activity perceptions and preferences. *Journal of Aging and Physical Activity, 8*(4), 343–362. doi: 10.1123/japa.8.4.343

National Council on Aging. (2019). *What is a senior center? Facts & benefits most don't know*. Retrieved from www.ncoa.org/national-institute-of-senior-centers/tips-for-senior-centers/what-you-dont-know-about-your-local-senior-center/

Nelson, M. E., Rejeski, W. J., Blair, S. N., Duncan, P. W., Judge, J. O., King, A. C., . . . Castaneda-Sceppa, C. (2007). Physical activity and public health in older adults: Recommendation from the American College of Sports Medicine and the American Heart Association. *Circulation, 116*(9), 1094–1105. doi:10.1161/CIRCULATIONAHA.107.185650

Resnick, B., & Boltz, M. (2016). Incorporating function and physical activity across all settings. *Annual Review of Gerontology & Geriatrics, 36*(1), 293–321. doi:10.1891/0198-8794.36.293

Skoufalos, A., Clarke, J. L., Ellis, D. R., Shepard, V. L., & Rula, E. Y. (2017). Rural aging in America: Proceedings of the 2017 connectivity summit. *Population Health Management, 20*(Suppl 2), Mary Ann Liebert, Inc. doi:10.1089/pop.2017.0177

Singh, G. K., & Siahpush, M. (2014). Widening rural-urban disparities in all-cause mortality and mortality from major causes of death in the USA, 1969–2009. *Journal of Urban Health, 91*(2), 272–292.

Tucker, J. M., Welk, G. J., & Beyler, B. K. (2011). Physical activity in U.S. adults: Compliance with the physical activity guidelines for Americans. *American Journal of Preventive Medicine, 40*(4), 454–461.

USDHHS—U.S. Department of Health and Human Services. (2002). *Physical activity guidelines for Americans* (1st ed.). Washington, DC: U.S. Department of Health and Human Services.

USDHHS—U.S. Department of Health and Human Services. (2018). *Physical activity guidelines for Americans* (2nd ed.). Washington, DC: U.S. Department of Health and Human Services. Retrieved from https://health.gov/our-work/physical-activity/current-guidelines

Wilson, N. W., Couper, I. D., De Vries, E., Reid, S., Fish, T., & Marais, B. J. (2009). A critical review of interventions to redress the inequitable distribution of healthcare professionals to rural and remote areas. *Rural Remote Health, 9*(2), 1060.

World Health Organization. (2020). *Physical activity*. Retrieved from https://www.who.int/health-topics/physical-activity#tab=tab_1

60
POLITICS

Ronald Hustedde

Politics is more than what government and politicians do. It is about the public activities that involve citizens and nonelected leaders and groups to address issues that shape directions for national, state, and local governments. This broader view of politics is shaped by economics, culture, legal, environmental, and social perspectives. It takes place within national, state, and community contexts. It is about influencing public policies and courses of collective action.

Rural American politics have democratic roots that involve five key values. First, deliberation and debate are ways to explore trade-offs about public policy choices before a conclusion is reached. Second, elections are a way to choose government leaders. Third, power is relatively diffused. Fourth, the local unit of government is an instrument for the community to act. Fifth, politics is not limited to voting. For example, politics is often about influence-making by the rural aged and other groups on institutions such as faith-based organizations, nonprofits, and other associations that provide services or a sense of belonging.

The politics of rural aging is diverse and dynamic as the U.S. population ages. It is estimated that 10,000 people reach the age of 65 every day and that this trend will continue through 2030. There are 10.6 million people over the age of 65 who live in rural America. Approximately 17.9% of the U.S. rural (nonmetro) population is 65 years or older compared to 13.7% of the urban (metro) areas. Overall, rural counties make up nearly 85% of the 1,104 "older-age counties"—those with more than 20% of their population age 65 or older. It is estimated that about 80% of rural counties are predominately white while the remainder are Native American, African American, or Hispanic. Five states have rural older age populations that are 65 years of age or older that exceed 50%: Vermont, Maine, Mississippi, West Virginia, and Arkansas. Three states have rural aged populations that are less than 10%: California, Florida, and Hawaii (Smith & Trevelyan, 2018; Rural Health Information Hub, November 1, 2019; U.S. Census Bureau, 2019).

Many rural counties are growing older because they attract retirees who are drawn to their scenic or recreational assets. It is part of their economic development policies. The Economic Research Services classifies one-third of older-age counties as retirement destinations or having recreation-based economies. They include rural counties in the Upper Great Lakes, Ozarks, Texas Hill Country, Appalachians, and the Rocky Mountain West. Most of these counties have seen population growth caused by migration since 2013 (Cromartie, 2018). It should be noted that these retirement destinations are not limited by gated communities or exclusive older adult neighborhoods. Many reside in areas with people of various ages (Glasgow & Brown, 2012).

Other rural counties are growing older because younger adults are moving away for employment, educational, or quality of life reasons. As a consequence, the loss of these young adults and their future children leave behind an older age population. One-third of the nation's rural counties are classified as persistent population-loss counties. They tend to be found in the farming areas of the Northern Great Plains and the Corn Belt (Cromartie, 2018).

These two designations of "retiree destination counties" and "persistent population loss counties" reflect the diversity of the rural aged. The former counties are likely to have access to more resources and national or regional networks than the latter to influence politics. Overall, the rural aged vary by class, wealth, gender, race, ethnic background, sexual orientation, health, and educational status (Lee & Quam, 2013; MacManus, Polk, & Bonanza, 2010; Miller, 2017). These influences are manifested in their politics and the social and economic climate in which they live. As a whole, rural older adults tend to have less income and higher poverty rates than their urban counterparts (Glasgow & Brown, 2012).

National Politics and Rural Aging

The Older Americans Act of 1965 (OAA) is a comprehensive set of programs aimed at improving the lives of older people. It is intended to help Americans stay in their homes. It includes programs such as Meals on Wheels, transportation for doctor's appointments, and other kinds of assistance. The Administration on Aging and state agencies are responsible for administering the program, which includes grants for nutrition, transportation, disease prevention, and other services. While the population of older adults has increased, funding has remained relatively flat since 2010. U.S. Senator Claude Pepper (D-Alabama) was the leading spokesperson from the rural South for issues related to aging, but since his death in 1989, many argue that another prominent advocate for the aged has not emerged. Since the 1980s, there has been a political agenda that prioritizes tax cuts and minimizes or cuts spending on current domestic entitlement and benefit programs such as Social Security and Medicare that are seen by some as unsustainable. President George W. Bush's attempts to privatize Social Security were met with resistance and not enacted (Polivka, 2015; National Council on Aging, 2019).

At the same time, there are prominent national organizations that are advocates for the aged. For example, the National Rural Health Association is a national nonprofit organization with more than 21,000 members. They provide leadership for rural health issues through advocacy, education, communications, and research. For example, in one of their briefs, they argue that Medicare cuts to rural providers are creating a hospital closure crisis in rural America. They claim these cuts are devastating many fragile rural economies. At the current rate of closure, 25% of rural hospitals will close within the next decade. Those closings lead to the departure of physicians, nurses, and other health-care providers and create "medical deserts." These are among the issues being addressed by communities and groups at the national, state, and regional levels (National Rural Health Association, 2019).

There are 17 national organizations that focus on aging issues (Rural Health Information Hub, October 15, 2019). The largest is the American Association of Retired Persons (AARP). They have a membership of more than 30 million people. Coupled with the higher voting rates of older Americans, they are one of the nation's most prominent legislative advocates at the federal and state levels that affect older citizens. They attempt to build bridges between generations and partisan political affiliations.

Some organizations have more focused missions such as the National Resource Center on Native American Aging at the University of North Dakota; it is federally funded with a mission to identify and increase awareness of evolving Native elder health and social issues. They seek to empower Native peoples to develop community-based solutions. Grantmakers in Aging has national conferences and support for addressing aging issues in rural areas. The Connectivity Summit for Rural Aging has taken place since 2017. They bring together leaders and organizations to build a strong foundation for improving the health and well-being of rural older adults. These summits are designed to leverage resources and power from a variety of organizations, agencies, and communities and to build "issue entrepreneurs" who can collaborate for changes at the national, state, and community levels (Skoufalos, Clarke, Ellis, Shepard, & Rula, 2017).

Traditionally, older Americans have been active voters. In the 2018 elections, voter turnout among those 65 and older was 65% for women and 68% for men. At the same time, 38% of women in the 18–29 years age range voted while 33% of men in the same age bracket voted (Misra, 2019). Older people are more likely to see voting as a responsibility and a way to care about a range of issues, not just about aging. For example, they are paying more attention to student debt. It is estimated that 3.4 million people age 60 or older have amassed $67 billion in student loan debt. The average amount owed is about $23,500. The majority of these loans were used to pay for their children or grandchildren's education or for seeking career changes and new skills. Hence, these debt issues are becoming more prevalent as Social Security payments are garnished or older adults are forced to delay retirement (Consumer Financial Protection Bureau, 2017).

Community-Level Interventions

Some Great Plains rural communities have become less sustainable as deaths exceed births and as families and young people move to urban areas. As a consequence, there is decreased revenue from taxes to support health and educational services. There is also less wealth to support grocery stores and social gathering spaces such as restaurants or even faith-based institutions. Some Nebraska communities are attempting to lure former high school graduates back with various incentives. Another strategy for these aging rural communities is to attract multiethnic groups for growth (Glasgow & Brown, 2012).

Other communities are drawing upon the "grey gold" of baby boomers because of recreational and health amenities as a way to augment the tax base and to build volunteerism and stronger communities services. For the most part, boomers have a track record of supporting clean water, healthy government, and purposeful institutions. Communities that neglect to view older adults as assets will have slimmer chances of prospering (Brown & Glasgow, 2008).

Ageism

In spite of their growing numbers, older adults often feel marginalized by the state, culture, and market because of an aging myth that they lack the physical, health, mental, and material resources to be included. The dismissive attitudes by some government and business leaders have provided the fodder for senior groups in rural areas to raise questions and challenges about ageism and the need for greater inclusion through social media. The design of online technology, hardware and software supports, and training workshops can be used to engage and support older adults. Most likely, these kinds of anti-ageism movements will continue to be visible at local, regional, and national levels (Trentham, Sokoloff, Tsang, & Neysmith, 2015).

Intergenerational Conflict or Cooperation

As the aging population of rural communities grows, there is debate that it will lead either to intergenerational conflict or intergenerational cooperation. Some argue that the older generation will consume a higher share of public resources than children, which will lead to intergenerational conflict. Others argue that the potential restructuring of the health-care system and a longer working life of baby boomers, older adult volunteerism, and other connections will lead to intergenerational cooperation. Many organizations such as the AARP are pursuing an intergenerational agenda.

Rural aging issues such as social isolation, housing needs, mental health care, physical health care, and transportation are issues that are shared by younger people in rural areas. Social capital connections among generations are more likely in rural areas because of geographic proximity and shared institutions and networks. Overall, intergenerational cooperation makes sense as part of the politics of rural aging. At the same time, the rural aged are becoming increasingly diverse and are questioning the degree of age-friendliness in rural settings. Health and social care providers are not responding to rural markets, and this is likely to lead to conflict and questions about unresponsive gaps (Skinner & Winterton, 2018; Miller, 2017). Those aging in rural places will have to form alliances with nonprofits and local leaders as part of a resistance to assert their civic rights and responsibilities.

References

Brown, D. L., & Glasgow, N. (2008). *Rural retirement migration*. Dordecht: Springer.

Consumer Financial Protection Bureau. (2017, January). *Snapshot of older consumers and student loan debt*. Washington, DC: U.S. Government.

Cromartie, J. (2018, December 20). *Rural aging occurs in different places for very different reasons*. USDA Economic Research Service in Research and Science. Retrieved from www.usda.gov/media/blog/2018/12/20/rural-aging-occurs-different-places-very-different-reasons

Glasgow, N., & Brown, D. L. (2012). Rural ageing in the United States: Trends and contexts. *Journal of Rural Studies*, *28*(4), 422–431.

Lee, M. G., & Quam, J. K. (2013). Comparing supports for LGBT aging in rural versus urban areas. *Journal of Gerontological Social Work*, *56*(2), 112–126. doi:10.1080/01634372.2012.747580

MacManus, S. A., Polk, A., & Bonanza, D. J. (2010). The politics of aging. In D. Dannefer & C. Phillipson (Eds.), *The SAGE handbook of social gerontology* (pp. 641–652). Thousand Oaks, CA: Sage Publications.

Miller, R. B. (2017). *The rural elderly: Access to mental healthcare*. Retrieved October 16, 2019, from www.aamft.org/iMIS15/AAMFT/Content/Advocacy/Rural_Elderly.aspx

Misra, J. (2019, April 23). *Voter turnout rates among all voting age and major racial and ethnic groups were higher than in 2014*. U.S. Census Bureau. Retrieved October 23, 2019, from www.census.gov/library/stories/2019/04/behind-2018-united-states-midterm-election-turnout.html

National Council on Aging. *Older Americans Act*. Retrieved November 2, 2019, from www.ncoa.org/public-policy-action/older-americans-act/

National Rural Health Association. *Medicare cuts hurt Rural America, advocacy*. Retrieved October 15, 2019, from www.ruralhealthweb.org/advocate/medicare-cuts-hurt-rural

Polivka, L. J. (2015). The legacy of Claude Pepper and the future of aging advocacy. *Generations*, *39*(3), 86–90.

Rural Health Information Hub. *Demographic changes and the aging population*. Retrieved November 1, 2019, from www.ruralhealthinfo.org/toolkits/aging/1/demographics

Rural Health Information Hub. *Rural aging—organizations*. Retrieved October 15, 2019, from www.ruralhealthinfo.org/topics/aging/resources

Skinner, M. W., & Winterton, R. (2018, February). Interrogating the contested spaces of rural aging: Implications for research, policy, and practice. *The Gerontologist*, *58*(1), 15–25. doi:10.1093/geront/gnx094

Skoufalos, A., Clarke, J. L., Ellis, D. R., Shepard, V. L., & Rula, E. Y. (2017). Rural aging in America: Proceedings of the 2017 connectivity summit. *Population Health Management*, 20(Suppl 2), S1–S10. doi:10.1089/pop.2017.0177

Smith, A. S., & Trevelyan, E. (2018). *The older population in rural America: 2012–2016*. ACS-41. Washington, DC: American Community Survey Reports, U.S. Census Bureau.

Trentham, B., Sokoloff, S., Tsang, A., & Neysmith, S. (2015). Social media and senior citizen advocacy: An inclusive tool to resist ageism? *Politics, Groups, and Identities*, *3*(3), 558–571. doi:10.1080/21565503.2015.1050411

U.S. Census Bureau. Retrieved October 23, 2019, from www.census.gov/library/stories/2019/10/older-population-in-rural-america.html

61
POVERTY

Tracey Farrigan[1]

Americans regularly express concern about meeting their basic needs and maintaining a reasonable standard of living as they age (Brenan, 2019; Newport, 2018). This struggle is often measured by the degree to which a person lives above or below the federal poverty level (FPL). The FPL is an absolute measure developed in the 1960s based on a money income threshold for adequate consumption that varies by family size and composition (Census Bureau, 2016). If a family's aggregate income falls below their threshold, all individuals in that family are counted as being poor. The incidence of poverty among the population is then reported as a poverty rate. The most common representation of the relationship between aging and poverty is to compare the poverty rates of three major age groups—children (under 18 years), working age (18 to 64 years) and older adults (65 years or older) (Smeeding & Marchand, 2016). Historically, older adults had the highest poverty rate (Census Bureau, 2019). However, considerable strides have been made in reducing the incidence of poverty for the older population, and for nearly two decades their poverty rate has consistently been the lowest.

While the poverty rate for older adults may be relatively low, it doesn't mean that their economic situation is not deserving of attention. The FPL is a useful measure of income insufficiency, but it fails to convey the precarious financial circumstances often faced by the older population. Many older adults struggle with rising health-care and housing bills and lack of employment opportunities, retirement income, and/or assets that could help absorb those costs (Cawthorne, 2010). For the near poor (those living just above their FPL), one major adverse life event or policy change that is detrimental to their income can land them in poverty (Johnson, Gordon, & Uccello, 2005). The process of aging alone can subject an older individual to and trap them in poverty as their savings diminish, pensions erode, and their dependence on fixed Social Security income deepens. Furthermore, older adults often face insurmountable access issues, such as lack of access to transportation, affordable and nutritious food, health services, civic engagement, and other key public benefits that could help sustain their well-being (Transportation for America, 2011; Ziliak & Gunderson, 2019; Waite & Waite, 2009).

Understanding and addressing these issues will only increase in importance as the nation's 74 million baby boomers continue to age and outlive past generations (Census Bureau, 2018). This is particularly relevant for rural America (Cromartie & Nelson, 2009), where older adults are disproportionately located, representing nearly 20% of the rural population compared to approximately 16% of the total population nationwide. They also make up a larger share of the rural poor than they have in the recent past. Rural communities, like many others across the nation, are challenged with meeting the needs of this population as it ages-in-place (Ormond, Black, Tilly, & Thomas, 2004; Met Life, 2011). However, those challenges are amplified where poverty is widespread and persistent, which is more characteristic of rural areas than elsewhere (Farrigan, 2019).

Historic Trends

The poverty rate for rural older adults is typically higher than the national older adult poverty rate. However, the gap between the two has diminished over time. In 2018,[2] they were only marginally different with the rural rate just above and the national rate just below 10%. Further, historical changes in poverty for rural older adults have largely followed national trends. Those trends have primarily coincided with the implementation and expansion of federal programs aimed at supporting the nation's most vulnerable populations.

It's estimated that after the Great Depression, the poverty rate for older adults was higher than that of other major age groups at around 50% (Altman, 2005). Poverty for most began to decline markedly with the passing of the Social Security Act of 1935, which brought support to older adults and families with children and created the social insurance program (i.e., Social Security). By 1959, the first year that official poverty counts were reported by the Census Bureau, the older adult poverty rate had dropped to 35%. Still, the older adult poverty rate remained higher than the rates for children and those of working age. This changed during the 1960s and 1970s as older adults saw sharp gains in their incomes and subsequent decline in their poverty rate.

The older adult poverty rate decreased by 10 percentage points over the 1960s decade, dropping to 25% by 1970. It fell another 10 percentage points in the early 1970s, reaching 15% by 1975. This was largely attributable to an increase in the level of cash benefits and other changes to the Social Security program in the late 1960s, which drove up median income for older adults and particularly for those with low-income (Engelhardt & Gruber, 2006). Another factor was rising median income among the older employed persons, which increased individual Social Security contributions for those working in qualifying jobs and reduced the likelihood of entering later life in poverty (Reno & Veghte, 2010). In subsequent decades, the older adult poverty rate continued to decline moderately, falling below the working age poverty rate for the first time in the 1990s, and since the early 2000's recession, it has consistently been the lowest of the three major age groups.

Social Security

As with older adults nationwide, today's rural older adults are financially much better off than past generations largely because of Social Security. The rural 65 years and older poverty rate is currently a little more than 10% compared to around 14% for rural working age persons and 20% for rural children. Yet, it's estimated that without Social Security, the poverty rate for older adults would be four to five times higher (Romig, 2010, 2020). That is, nearly half of all rural elders would be living in poverty today, which is similar to the older adult poverty rate in the 1930s.

While Social Security lifts many out of poverty, paradoxically it can contribute to trapping older adults in poverty as they continue to age. Social Security income levels are tied to earnings before retirement. Therefore, low wage earners will receive lower benefits than higher wage earners. The former is also less likely to accumulate assets, substantial pensions, and savings over their working lifetime (Favreault, 2009). Further, they are more likely than higher wage earners to be fully retired when they become eligible to collect Social Security benefits and/or to draw upon those benefits early (Solem et al., 2014). For these reasons, poor aging individuals tend to be Social Security dependent with more than half of their income coming from Social Security. About 57% of all rural older adults and 65% of those 85 years or older fall into that category, meaning that all things remaining equal, they have little to no chance of upward economic mobility.

Economic Insecurity

With limited fixed income, poor older adults are vulnerable to economic insecurity, which means that they do not have the financial ability to absorb economic shocks. Medical care expenses and housing costs are the primary sources of consumption of an aging individual's income, and they are also the most likely to increase significantly with the circumstances of aging (Harrell & Houser, 2011). This puts aging individuals at risk not only of being trapped in poverty, but in deepening poverty as they fall even further below their poverty income threshold. Likewise, near-poor older adults are at risk of falling into poverty. For instance, when accounting for out-of-pocket medical expenses—which are not included in the consumption bundle on which official poverty thresholds are based—the rural older adult poverty rate increases by nearly six percentage points.[3] That's about double the increase experienced by the other major age groups when considering the same expense.

The risk of economic insecurity for older adults as they age is particularly high for women. They face unique obstacles (e.g., lower wages on average than men) in amassing sufficient resources to carry them through retirement and they tend to live longer (Christ & Gronniger, 2018). When many of the support programs were created by the Social Security Amendments of 1965, such as Medicare and Medicaid, the average life expectancy was approximately 67 years for a man and 73 years for a woman. Today, it's about 10 years more for both genders (Central Intelligence Agency, 2019). Longer life expectancies coupled with increasing costs for necessities (particularly health care), as well as divorce/death of a partner, increase the likelihood of aging into poverty for women (Cawthorne, 2008). Currently, the rural poverty rate for women age 65 years or older is 11% and they represent 59% of all poor rural older adults. Those percentages increase to 19% and 67%, respectively, when considering female adults age 85 years or more. In comparison, the poverty rate for rural males aged 65 years or older is 9% and for those 85 years or more it's 14%.

Population Shifts

Many persons living in and moving to rural areas are adults age 65 or older (Cromartie, 2020). While these individuals can bring numerous assets (e.g., tax income and job skills) to rural communities, they also can create unique demands on local governments (Ewing, 2014). A shortcoming of the literature on the impacts of this population, however, is that it often focuses on higher-income older adults who exhibit a tendency to migrate. That migration is frequently captured by rural areas that are classified as either retirement destinations or as having recreation-based economies (Cromartie, 2018). Yet most older adults report that they prefer to age-in-place by staying in their current home and community (Farber, Shinkle, Lynott, Fox-Grage, & Harrell, 2011). Further, estimates based on recent moves indicate that poor older adults are the least likely to relocate long distances if at all. This and other rural population trends (Cromartie & Vilorio, 2019), such as loss of young adults (who have a higher incidence of poverty than do older working age adults), have contributed to the recent increase in the share of aging individuals among the rural poor.

After all-time lows in 2011, the older adult poverty rate has since risen by less than two percentage points to just over 10% and the share of rural poor who are 65 years and older has risen nearly five percentage points to 14%. The latter has rarely ever exceeded the former and never by this much of a margin. Thus, while the poverty rate for rural older adults continues to be relatively low, the age profile of the rural poor has shifted and will likely continue with the aging of the population at-large. This is important to note. For instance, the comparison of poverty rates across age groups alone can hide the growing service needs of the older adult population within rural communities.

Poverty Areas

Just as aging in poverty can create challenges to one's well-being, so too can aging in places where a large share of the population is poor. Many of the issues facing rural older adults are the same ones facing rural America generally, such as provider shortages and limited access to technological advances and broadband (Stenberg, 2013). These challenges are amplified in areas where poverty is prevalent (Farrigan & Parker, 2012). The higher the poverty rate and the longer that it endures in a place, the greater the likelihood that socioeconomic problems become systemic, affecting both the resident poor and nonpoor. For instance, rural areas of enduring poverty often lack access to health care, healthy and affordable food, safe and affordable housing stock, and adequate protective services and transportation systems (Morken & Warner, 2012). Nearly 12% of all rural older adults and 19% of poor rural older adults reside in counties with persistently high poverty rates (20% or higher over three decades) for the total population.

Similarly, poor rural areas may lack sufficient capacity to address the growing needs of an aging population, such as support for housing assistance or other services/investments that directly meet the needs of this segment of the population (Office of Policy Development and Research, HUD, 2013). These challenges can be further compounded where the incidence of older adult poverty is high currently and/or has been persistently high over several decades. Currently, there are 100 counties with high poverty rates (20% or more) for the older population and 90% of them are rural (nonmetro) counties. About half of those counties have had persistently high poverty rates for the older population, 94% of which are rural. They are primarily located in the South and are characterized by low-employment[4] and persistent poverty for the total rural population, while just a few are classified as rural population loss or retirement destination counties (Economic Research Service, 2017). The geographic concentration of poor older adults in rural areas combined with rural older adults being less likely than their urban counterparts to live in nursing homes or other retirement-oriented housing facilities may impact many rural community service decisions (Symens-Smith & Trevelyan, 2019).

Notes

1. The findings and conclusions of this Handbook entry are those of the author, not the U.S. Department of Agriculture and should not be construed to represent any agency determination or policy.
2. 2018 was the most current year of official poverty data at the time of this writing. Unless otherwise stated, all references to current statistics are based on this time frame.
3. Author's estimates using the Census Bureau's Supplemental Poverty Measure, Current Population Survey data, 2016–2018.
4. Less than 65% of county residents ages 25–64 were employed, determined by the American Community Survey 5-year average data 2008–2012.

Recommendations for Further Reading

Administration for Community Living. (2018). *Profile of older Americans*. Retrieved from https://acl.gov/sites/default/files/Aging%20and%20Disability%20in%20America/2018OlderAmericansProfile.pdf
George, L., & Ferraro, K. (2016). *Handbook of aging and the social sciences* (8th ed.). New York: Elsevier.
O'Brien, E., Wu, K., & Baer, D. (2010). *Older Americans in poverty: A snapshot*. Retrieved from https://assets.aarp.org/rgcenter/ppi/econ-sec/2010-03-poverty.pdf
Piggott, J., & Woodland, A. (2016). *Handbook of the economics of population and aging*. Amsterdam: North Holland Publishing.
Rural Sociological Society. (2019). *Persistent poverty in rural America*. New York: Routledge.

References

Altman, N. (2005). *The battle for social security: From FDR's vision to Bush's gamble*. Hoboken: John Wiley and Sons.
Brenan, M. (2019). Americans feel generally positive about their own finances. *Gallup.com*. Retrieved from https://news.gallup.com/poll/249164/americans-feel-generally-positive-own-finances.aspx
Cawthorne, A. (2008). *Elderly poverty: The challenge before us*. Center for American Progress. Retrieved from file:///D:/1%20FY%2019_20/Aging%20and%20Poverty/Aging%20and%20Poverty/Center%20for%20American%20Progress.pdf
Cawthorne, A. (2010). *The not-so-golden years: Confronting elderly poverty and improving seniors' economic security*. Center for American Progress. Retrieved from https://cdn.americanprogress.org/wp-content/uploads/issues/2010/09/pdf/not_so_golden_years.pdf
Census Bureau. (2016). *How the Census Bureau measures poverty*. Retrieved from www.census.gov/topics/income-poverty/poverty/about.html
Census Bureau. (2018). *Older people projected to outnumber children*. Retrieved from www.census.gov/newsroom/press-releases/2018/cb18-41-population-projections.html
Census Bureau. (2019). *Historical poverty tables: People and families*. Retrieved from www.census.gov/data/tables/time-series/demo/income-poverty/historical-poverty-people.html
Central Intelligence Agency. (2019). *The world factbook*. Retrieved from www.cia.gov/library/publications/resources/the-world-factbook/fields/355rank.html
Christ, A., & Gronniger, T. (2018). Older women in poverty. *Justice in aging*. Retrieved from file:///D:/1%20FY%2019_20/Aging%20Poverty/Aging%20and%20Poverty/older%20women%20in%20poverty.pdf
Cromartie, J. (2018). Rural aging occurs in different places for very different reasons. *USDA.gov*. Retrieved from www.usda.gov/media/blog/2018/12/20/rural-aging-occurs-different-places-very-different-reasons
Cromartie, J. (2020). Population and migration. *Ers.usda.gov*. Retrieved from www.ers.usda.gov/topics/rural-economy-population/population-migration.aspx
Cromartie, J., & Nelson, P. (2009). Baby boom migration and its impact on rural America. *Ers.usda.gov*. Retrieved from www.ers.usda.gov/webdocs/publications/46218/9346_err79_1_pdf?v=41056
Cromartie, J., & Vilorio, D. (2019, February). Rural population trends. *Amber Waves*. Retrieved from www.ers.usda.gov/amber-waves/2019/feburary/rural-population-trends/
Economic Research Service. (2017). USDA ERS county typology codes. *Ers.usda.gov*. Retrieved from www.ers.usda.gov/data-products/county-typology-codes
Engelhardt, G., & Gruber, J. (2006). Social Security and the evolution of elderly poverty. In D. Auerbach, D. Card, & J. Quigley (Eds.), *Public policy and the income distribution* (pp. 258–287). New York: Russell Sage Foundation.
Ewing, J. (2014). *Helping seniors age in place*. Health Resources and Sciences Administration. Retrieved from file:///D:/1%20FY%2019_20/Aging%20and%20Poverty/Aging%20and%20Poverty/Helping%20seniors%20age%20in%20place.pdf
Farber, N., Shinkle, D., Lynott, J., Fox-Grage, W., & Harrell, R. (2011). Aging in place: A state survey of livability policies and practices. *AARP.org*. Retrieved from https://assets.aarp.org/rgcenter/ppi/liv-com/aging-in-place-2011-full.pdf
Farrigan, T. (2019). Rural poverty and well-being. *Ers.usda.gov*. Retrieved from www.ers.usda.ogv/topics/rural-economy-population/rural-poverty-well-being.aspx
Farrigan, T., & Parker, T. (2012, May 12). The concentration of poverty is a growing rural problem. *Amber Waves*. Retrieved from www.ers.usda.gov/amber-waves/2012/december/concentration-of-poverty

Favreault, M. (2009). A new minimum benefit for low lifetime earners. *Retirement Policy.org*. Retrieved from www.urban.org/sites/default/files/alfresco/publication-pdfs/411853-A-New-Minimum-Benefit-for-Low-Lifetime-Earners.pdf

Harrell, R., & Houser, A. (2011). State housing profiles: Housing conditions and affordability for the older population. *Assets.aarp.org*. Retrieved from https://assets.aarp.org/rgcenter/ppi/liv-com/AARP_Housing2011_Full.pdf

Johnson, R., Gordon, B., & Uccello, C. (2005). *When the nest egg cracks: Financial consequences of health problems, marital status changes, and Job layoffs at older ages*. The Urban Institute. Retrieved from www.urban.org/UploadedPDF/411265_nest_egg.pdf

Met Life. (2011). *Maturing of America—Communities moving forward for an aging population*. Retrieved from www.aarp.org/content/dam/aarp/livable-communities/old-learn/civic/the-maturing-of-america-communities-moving-forward-for-an-aging-population-2011-aarp.pdf

Morken, L., & Warner, M. (2012). *Planning for the aging population: Rural responses to the challenge*. Retrieved from https://s3.amasonaws.com/mildredwarner.org/attachments/000/000/196/original/de6841e2187c889cdf4a15a7b45512f4

Newport, F. (2018). Update: Americans' concerns about retirement persists. *Gallup.com*. Retrieved from https://news.gallup.com/poll/233861/update-americans-concerns-retirement-persist.aspx

Office of Policy Development and Research, U.S. Department of Housing and Urban Development (HUD). (2013). Aging in place: Facilitating choice. *Huduser.gov*. Retrieved from www.huduser.gov/portal/periodicals/em/fall13/highlight1.html

Ormond, B., Black, K., Tilly, J., & Thomas, S. (2004). *Supportive services programs in naturally occurring retirement communities*. The Urban Institute. Retrieved from https://aspe.hhs.gov/system/files/pdf/73266/NORCssp.pdf

Reno, V., & Veghte, B. (2010). *Economic status of the elderly in the United States*. National Academy of Social Insurance. Retrieved from www.nasi.org/sites/default/files/research/Economic%20Status%20of%20the%20Elderly%20in%20the%20United%20States.pdf

Romig, K. (2010). *Social Security reform: Possible effects on the elderly poor and mitigation options*. Federal Publications. Retrieved from http://digitalcommons.ilr.cornell.edu/key_workplace/506

Romig, K. (2020). *Social Security lifts more Americans above poverty than any other program*. Center on Budget and Policy Priorities. Retrieved from file:///D:/1%20FY%2019_20/Aging%20and%20Poverty/Aging%20and%20Povertry/Romig%202020%20SS%20lifts%20seniors%20out%20of%20poverty.pdf

Smeeding, T., & Marchand, J. (2016). Aging and poverty. In J. Piggott & A. Woodland (Eds.), *Handbook of the economics of population and aging*. Amsterdam: North Holland Publishing.

Solem, P., Syse, A., Furunes, T., Mykletun, R., De Lange, A., Schaufeli, W., & Ilmarinen, J. (2014). To leave or not to leave: Retirement intentions and retirement behaviour. *Ageing and Society*, 1–23.

Stenberg, P. (2013). *Rural broadband at a glance*. USDA Economic Research Service. Retrieved from www.ers.usda.gov/webdocs/publications/42879/37973_eb-23.pdf

Symens-Smith, A., & Trevelyan, E. (2019). The older population in rural America, 2012–2016. *Census.gov*. Retrieved from file:///D:/1%20FY%2019_20/Aging%20and%20Poverty/Aging%20and%20Poverty/older%20population%20in%20rural%20america%20census%20report.pdf

Transportation for America. (2011). *Aging in place, stuck without options: Fixing the mobility crisis threatening the baby boom generation*. Retrieved from http://14America.org/docs/SeniorsMobilityCrisis.pdf

Waite, E., & Waite, L. (2009). Social disconnectedness, perceived isolation, and health among older adults. *Journal of Health Social Behavior*, 31–48.

Ziliak, J., & Gunderson, C. (2019). The state of senior hunger in America 2017. *Feeding America*. Retrieved from www.feedingamerica.org/sites/default/files/2019-06/The%20State%20of%20Senior%20Hunger%20in%202017_F2.pdf

62
PROFESSIONAL ORGANIZATIONS AND ASSOCIATIONS

David C. Wihry

The establishment of trade or professional organizations is a strategy for individuals and organizations to collectively advocate for and serve the needs of their constituent groups. These organizations may be constituted around a specific profession, as is the case with groups such as the Rural Nurse Organization or National Rural Social Work Caucus. They may also be topic-focused, such as the National Association for Rural Mental Health or cross-disciplinary such as the Gerontological Society of America. There are few professional and trade associations devoted specifically to rural aging issues. More commonly, associations are dedicated to either rural or aging issues and have sections, programming, or content focused on rural aging issues specifically. Generally, organizations serve their constituent members through the following services:

- Educational publications—brochures, reports, webinars, and other tools to inform members about issues and best practices;
- Networking—conferences, listservs, message boards, and other venues for networking;
- Research—publishing new research relevant to members through sponsored journals or amplifying research conducted through other entities;
- Policy statements and agendas—positions on legislative and regulatory policy issues affecting constituent members;
- Advocacy—advocacy on policy change, workforce needs, and other priorities of a profession or trade;
- Recognition—recognizing member excellence on issues relevant to a trade or profession; and
- Career development—courses and certificates that help facilitate career development among members.

The following are brief overviews of prominent health and aging-focused professional and trade organizations that also address either or both the aging and rural dimensions and examples of the services they provide to members. The professional and trade organizations highlighted are national in scope. Individual states and regions may have additional organizations or associations that address rural aging needs within these areas. The national groups may also have state affiliates and often list these on their websites.

Professional Associations

AARP—a membership organization with the mission to "empower people to choose how they live as they age" (AARP, 2020). Through its AARP Livable Communities Initiative, AARP has provided educational and planning resources on the topic of rural livability, including hosting a Rural Livability Workshop.

Website: www.aarp.org/

American Association for Geriatric Psychiatry—the AAGP "promotes the mental health and well-being of older people through professional education, public advocacy, and support of career development for clinicians, educators, and researchers in geriatric psychiatry and mental health" (American Association for Geriatric Psychiatry, 2020). The AAGP represents geriatric psychiatrists and other mental health-focused professionals. Services provided to members include a legislative and regulatory agenda, E-Newsletter, Continuing Medical Education, and the peer-reviewed *American Journal of Geriatric Psychiatry*.

Website: www.aagponline.org/

American Geriatrics Society—AGS represents geriatrics health-care professionals. Services provided to members include journals, educational tools for geriatricians, the AGS Annual Scientific Meeting, and the AGS Newsletter. The American Geriatrics Society also provides position statements on issues ranging from Medicare and Medicaid to workforce issues along with policy and regulatory advocacy. The American Geriatrics Society has affiliated programs in some states.

Website: www.americangeriatrics.org/

American Hospital Association—an organization open to both individual members and care providing organizations. It has offered services including a *Rural Advocacy Agenda* and *Rural Report* on health-care challenges and needs in rural areas. The association also maintains a Section for Small or Rural Hospitals that provides services such as newsletters and a Rural Hospital Leadership Team Award.

Website: www.aha.org/

American Psychological Association—APA represents psychology professionals and has the mission "to promote the advancement, communication, and application of psychological science and knowledge to benefit society and improve lives" (American Psychological Association, 2020). APA services to members include networking opportunities, publications, and job search tools. The APA maintains both an Office on Aging and Committee on Rural Health.

Website: www.apa.org/

American Public Health Association—APHA seeks to "improve the health of the public and achieve equity in health status" (American Public Health Association, 2020). It represents public health professionals and works to advocate for public health policies and positions on public health issues. The APHA maintains an Aging & Public Health Section focused on public health needs as they relate to the older adult population.

Website: www.apha.org/

American Society on Aging—ASA represents gerontologists spanning many professions and has the goal "to support the commitment and enhance the knowledge and skills of those who seek to improve the quality of life of older adults and their families" (American Society on Aging, 2020). ASA provides educational resources including blog posts, seminars, and *Aging Today* newsletter. ASA also publishes the journal *Generations* and hosts the annual Aging in America Conference. Educational content includes information specific to rural aging.

Website: www.asaging.org/

The Gerontological Society of America—works to "advance the scientific and scholarly study of aging and promote human welfare by the encouragement of gerontology in all its areas" (The

Gerontological Society of America, 2020). Services provided to members include an Annual Scientific Meeting, electronic newsletter, access to peer-reviewed journals, and numerous other programs. GSA maintains a Rural Aging interest group to elevate rural aging issues and sharing among members on this topic.

Website: www.geron.org/

National Association for Geriatric Education—NAGE's mission is to "represent the collective interests of organizations and groups that provide health professions education in geriatrics and gerontology in the United States" (National Association for Geriatric Education, 2020). Services provided to members include policy advocacy and featuring geriatrics education programs.

Website: https://n-age.org/

National Association for Rural Mental Health—with a vision that "seeks to promote the linkage of the diverse voices of rural mental health" (National Association for Rural Mental Health, 2020), NARMH is focused on raising awareness and addressing mental health and social service needs in rural areas. NARMH publishes the online *Journal of Rural Mental Health* and sponsors the Annual National Association for Rural Mental Health Conference.

Website: www.narmh.org/

National Rural Health Association—NRHA is focused on rural health issues with the stated mission to "provide leadership on rural health issues through advocacy, communications, education and research" (National Rural Health Association, 2020). Services provided include rural health awards, *Rural Horizons Magazine*, Rural Health Policy Institute, and advocacy work. Aging-focused content that has been released by the association includes educational blog content and a policy brief on *Elder Health in Rural America*.

Website: www.ruralhealthweb.org/

Rural Nurse Organization—RNO was "formed for the purpose of recognizing, promoting, and maintaining the unique specialty of rural nursing practice" (Rural Nurse Organization, 2020). The organization is the sponsor of the peer-reviewed publication, *The Online Journal of Rural Nursing and Health Care*, which includes gerontology and geriatrics-focused content. The organization also provides members with access to the *Rural Nurse Connection* newsletter and grant opportunities.

Website: www.rno.org/

National Rural Social Work Caucus—described as an informal organization, the Rural Social Work Caucus works to support the elevation of rural issues within the social work profession. A primary service of the caucus has been the partnership with universities to host a National Institute on Social Work and Human Services in Rural Areas.

Website: https://ruralsocialwork.org/

Trade Associations

National Association of Area Agencies on Aging—n4a is a membership organization for Area Agencies on Aging and Title VI Native American aging programs with the stated mission to "build the capacity of our members so they can help older adults and people with disabilities live with dignity and choices in their homes and communities for as long as possible" (National Association of Area Agencies on Aging, 2020). It engages in policy advocacy related to the needs of its constituent members, providing services such as advocacy alerts, legislative updates, and policy positions. Other services to members include awards, job search, and highlighting best practices. The work of n4a on rural aging has included the publication of an analysis of the structure and services of rural Area Agencies on Aging.

Website: www.n4a.org/

Grantmakers in Aging—a membership organization serving philanthropies, GIA "acts as a relevant and responsive network, resource, and champion, amplifying the voices of older people and issues of aging" (Grantmakers in Aging, 2020). Grantmakers in Aging has instituted programming focused on rural aging, including a *Rural Aging Initiative* to build a network of support for stakeholders working on rural aging issues. The initiative has also resulted in the creation of educational materials for funders on rural-aging topics such as the opioid crisis, mobility and aging, and grantmaking in rural areas.

Website: www.giaging.org/

National Association of Community Health Centers—NACHC represents the network of community-based health centers with the mission to "promote efficient, high quality, comprehensive health care that is accessible, culturally and linguistically competent, community directed, and patient centered for all." Support for health centers includes advocacy, research on the benefit of centers for the American health-care system, and the provision of training, technical assistance, and leadership development opportunities. Services provided by NACHC include a job board, blog, and resource clearinghouse. The association also offers a range of trainings related to topics such as health center governance and financial management.

Website: www.nachc.org/

National Organization of State Offices of Rural Health—NOSORH represents the State Offices of Rural Health and has the mission to "promote the capacity of State Offices of Rural Health and their stakeholders to improve health in rural America through leadership development, advocacy, education and partnerships" (National Organization of State Offices of Rural Health, 2020). Services provided include an Annual Meeting, newsletter, legislative and regulatory position statements, and mentoring program. NOSORH also maintains a quarterly Aging in Rural Learning Group specifically focused on topics related to rural health and aging.

Website: https://nosorh.org/

Leadership Council of Aging Organizations—LCAO "is a coalition of national nonprofit organizations concerned with the well-being of America's older population and committed to representing their interests in the policy-making arena" (Leadership Council of Aging Organizations, 2020). LCAO has identified a legislative agenda in the areas of budget, community services, health, and income security and has published principles on such topics as advanced care and long-term services and supports.

Website: www.lcao.org//

National Association of Rural Health Clinics—NARHC is a trade association for organizations that are part of the Rural Health Clinics Program, the "National Association of Rural Health Clinics promotes rural health clinics as a means of improving and sustaining the availability of quality, cost-effective health care to patients in rural, medically underserved areas" (National Association of Rural Health Clinics, 2020). NARHC's services include educational courses on the Rural Health Clinics Program and a Certified Rural Health Clinic Professional course. The organization also offers a newsletter, discussion forums, and technical assistance webinars.

Website: https://narhc.org/

References

AARP. (2020). *About AARP*. Retrieved from www.aarp.org/about-aarp/?intcmp=AE-HP-FTR-ABOUT

American Association for Geriatric Psychiatry. (2020). *Mission*. Retrieved from www.aagponline.org/index.php?src=gendocs&ref=Mission&category=About%20Us

American Psychological Association. (2020). *About AP*. Retrieved from www.apa.org/about/

American Public Health Association. (2020). *About APHA*. Retrieved from www.apha.org/about-apha

American Society on Aging. (2020). *About ASA*. Retrieved from www.asaging.org/about-asa

The Gerontological Society of America. (2020). *Purposes and mission.* Retrieved from www.geron.org/about-us/purposes-and-mission

Grantmakers in Aging. (2020). *About grantmakers in aging (GIA).* Retrieved from www.giaging.org/about/

Leadership Council of Aging Organizations. (2020). *Our vision.* Retrieved from www.lcao.org/about-lcao/vision/

National Association of Area Agencies on Aging. (2020). *Mission, vision & work.* Retrieved from www.n4a.org/ourmission

National Association for Geriatric Education. (2020). *Mission, goals, and objectives of NAGE.* Retrieved from https://n-age.org/mission-goals-objectives-nage/

National Association for Rural Mental Health. (2020). *About NARMH.* Retrieved from www.narmh.org/index.php/about/

National Association of Rural Health Clinics. (2020). *About us.* Retrieved from www.lcao.org/about-lcao/vision/

National Organization of State Offices of Rural Health. (2020). *About NOSORH.* Retrieved from https://nosorh.org/about-nosorh/

National Rural Health Association. (2020). *About NRHA.* Retrieved from www.ruralhealthweb.org/about-nrha

Rural Nurse Organization. (2020). *Our mission and vision.* Retrieved from www.rno.org/our-mission-and-vision/

63
RELIGION AND SPIRITUALITY

Kristine A. Bundschuh and Michele Dillon

Introduction

Rural Americans in general tend to be more religious than other Americans, and older rural residents tend to be more religious than both their older non-rural and younger rural counterparts (Lyons, 2003). Rural older adults, therefore, have a strong relationship with religion and spirituality based both on their late life stage and their rural location. Such engagement helps older adults develop and maintain community, cope with health challenges and other stressors, and enhance everyday well-being (Arcury, Quandt, McDonald, & Bell, 2000; Yoon & Lee, 2006). Explained here is how and why religion and spirituality provide rural older adults with the tools to manage the aging process. Religion and spirituality are briefly defined, followed by a review of research on the benefits of religion and spirituality in rural older adults' lives. Recent trends in spiritual and religious beliefs, affiliations, and practices among older adults across rural America are presented, and conclusions offered that articulate the challenges to supporting rural older adults' religion and spirituality, as well as recommended readings to further pursue this topic.

Defining Religion and Spirituality

Americans incorporate the sacred into their lives through conventional church-based religion and more individualized spirituality. Though the two constructs are heavily intertwined, Wuthnow (1998) construes religion as dwelling and spirituality as seeking. People practicing religion dwell in a religious institution, communally embracing established beliefs, traditions, practices, and doctrines (Wuthnow, 1998). Spiritual seekers, in contrast, develop their own beliefs and practices through combining religious and mythical elements, including both Western and Eastern spiritual practices. Spirituality is centered on the individual's autonomous search for the sacred, with a focus on self-growth and self-fulfillment (Wuthnow, 1998). Because religion and spirituality are distinct, but related, pathways, they provide different contributions to older adult rural lives.

Religion, Spirituality, and Rural Aging

Religion

In geographically isolated, low-population communities, religion provides older adults with connection and structure. As religion is often practiced in a group setting, it provides external forms of social support and community (Wink & Dillon, 2003). Connecting participants with other local residents is a particular advantage for older adults, who may feel more isolated in a rural setting than those living in more densely populated areas. Along with the social benefits, faith and prayer, whether privately or through communal worship, help older adults cope with declining health (Arcury, Quandt, McDonald, & Bell, 2000). Religious participation is an anchor in the lives of older adults, giving them consistency through rituals and social interactions (Arcury et al., 2000) and is especially salient during a life stage when their personal lives, health, and social communities are undergoing change.

Spirituality

Unlike the social benefits of religion, spirituality provides more intrapersonal support during late adulthood. While spirituality can be sought within a religious setting, many people who practice nonreligious forms of spirituality on a weekly basis benefit from spiritual well-being without regularly attending church (Pew Research Center, 2014). Spirituality is positively related to older adults' well-being through emphasizing personal growth, wisdom in regard to complex personal and societal problems, and participation in artistic and other creative activities (Wink & Dillon, 2003). Rural older adults with stronger engagement in their spirituality have higher levels of social support, psychological well-being, and life satisfaction, and lower levels of depression, compared to non-spiritual rural older adults (Yoon, 2006; Yoon & Lee, 2006). Religion and spirituality provide a framework for processing one's emotions and thoughts when faced with challenges such as increased social isolation, death of a spouse, and ongoing health issues (Yoon, 2006). Spirituality, therefore, provides older adults with mental and social supports to overcome some of the common challenges of aging.

Recently, the role of spirituality has changed among older rural Americans. While older adults have long incorporated the sacred into their lives in formal religious institutions, baby boomers are the first older generation embracing spiritual seeking outside of religion. Born between 1946 and 1964, baby boomers currently span the cusp of middle-age and older adulthood and will soon comprise most of the older population in America. While baby boomers were raised with formal institutionalized religion (mostly within Christianity), they embraced New Age and other more diffuse approaches to spirituality, which expanded with the cultural changes of the 1960s and 1970s (Roof, 1993). This new cohort of older adults have a high sense of spiritual well-being (Pew Research Center, 2014) that characterizes urban and rural baby boomers alike: rural baby boomers are the first generation to identify as more spiritual than religious, compared to previous generations of rural Americans.[1] This suggests that rural baby boomers have developed a toolkit to find nurturance from spirituality in their geographical isolation, being able to reflect on and manage their stresses related to aging without the need for a formal church community.

Rural Older Adults' Religion and Spirituality: Recent Trends

Connecting Religion and Spirituality

Supporting the argument that the distinction between religion and spirituality is more conceptual than empirical, rural older adults equally embrace both terms: 77% identify as moderately or very spiritual, and the exact same proportion consider themselves moderately or very religious. Because most people who identify as religious also consider themselves spiritual, this suggests that among older rural adults, spirituality is partially found within the context of formal religion. The one exception is the West, where 67% of rural older adults say they are religious, but 86% say they are moderately or very spiritual. Since the West is where new forms of spirituality took hold in the 1960s and 1970s (Roof, 1993) and continues to have higher levels of spirituality than religion, it is not surprising that rural older adults in the West are more likely than their rural age peers elsewhere to seek and find the sacred in noninstitutionalized religious contexts.

The Religious and Spiritual Distinctiveness of Elderly Rural Americans

Rural elders are predominantly Protestant (79%) (as is true of rural America in general), followed by Catholic (11%) and nonaffiliated (7%). They are more religious than rural residents under age 65; for example, while 77% of rural older adults consider themselves moderately or very religious, only 61% of other rural residents report a strong connection to religion. Similarly, 42% of rural older adults attend religious services weekly, but only a quarter of younger rural residents do so. Notwithstanding the challenges in accessing religious institutions in rural areas, older rural Americans are somewhat more likely to attend weekly religious services than their non-rural age peers (36%), suggesting, perhaps, that rural older adults are more dependent on religious community for their social support.

Compared to non-rural older adults and younger rural residents, older rural Americans also identify as more spiritual. Seventy-seven percent of rural older adults consider themselves moderately or very spiritual, while only 72% of urban older adults and two-thirds of rural residents younger than 65 say they are moderately or very spiritual.

The fact that older rural Americans are more strongly tied to religion and spirituality than younger cohorts reflects life-course, social, and generational dynamics: older Americans may "need" religion more to help cope with the vicissitudes of aging. At the same time, however, their socialization and experiences of religion and spirituality are historically different to those of younger cohorts—the post-baby boom generations who have come of age in a more secular America. Therefore, the positive role that religion and spirituality play in the lives of older rural Americans today may not necessarily extend to buffering the aging process and challenges that will be encountered by their children and grandchildren.

Regional Distinctions in Religious Beliefs, Affiliations, and Practices

Although the majority of rural older adults are religious, it is important to recognize that their religious affiliations, beliefs, and practices vary by region. This variation is because of broad sociohistorical factors, such that there are far more Protestants in the South and a higher concentration of Catholics in the Northeast, mid-Atlantic, and Midwest (Gallup

News, 2018). Amid large-scale declines in religious affiliation since the late 1990s, the decline in New England is particularly noteworthy, as well as in the West (Gallup News, 2018). These national trends are evident in the profile of aging rural Americans. Rural counties in the South have the highest proportion of older Protestants (86%). The Midwest and Northeast also have a high concentration of Protestants but also claim a modest proportion of Catholics (15% and 17%, respectively). Older adults in the Northeast and West are more likely to be nonreligious than in the South or Midwest, with 15% of Northeastern and 16% of Western rural older adults claiming no religious affiliation. In fact, the West is the only region where the population of nonreligious older adults is tied with the proportion of Catholics (16% for both).

Region also distinguishes religious beliefs and practices. Rural older adults in the South are more likely to report being moderately or very religious (84%), followed by the Midwest (76%), the West (67%), and the Northeast (52%). Whereas nearly half of rural older adults in the South attend weekly services, less than a third in the Northeast or West do so. Some of these differences may be attributed to religious affiliation, but other factors such as local norms and community culture also affect religious engagement.

Challenges to Rural Older Adults' Religion and Spirituality Practices

While religion and spirituality provide supports throughout the aging process, older adults may face challenges to accessing these supports in rural areas. Because of low population in rural communities, the number of sites of worship is lower than in more densely populated regions. In addition to finding the right theological fit within the limited number and range of religious institutions available, older adults must consider the availability of transportation options to the institutions, as public transportation is more limited in rural communities. Finally, they may face barriers in regard to religious institutions' physical accessibility, given that most churches in rural America were built in an era (prior to the enactment of the Americans with Disabilities Act, 1990) when societal consciousness of physical accessibility was relatively dormant. If older adults cannot find, travel to, and be comfortable within a communal space to practice religion, they are not likely to regularly attend religious services.

Older adults' religious attendance has been shown to increase from middle-age to older adulthood (ages 65–75), but then decline in later years (Hayward & Krause, 2013). While not all religious activities require weekly worship, there is a discrepancy between the proportion of rural older adults who identify as religious and those who regularly practice their religion within an affiliated community. Given that religion buffers both isolation and health issues that are prevalent in older adulthood, it is important to consider how to support older adults' continued participation in religion as they age. Future challenges to address include providing accessibility to the physical spaces of religion and connecting older adults with local religious communities if they move into a rural area later in life.

In regard to spirituality, baby boomers are transitioning into becoming older adults, so spirituality practices are on the rise among the population of older adults. This suggests that spirituality practices may become more relevant to the well-being of older adults than traditional religious activities. Therefore, in the future, people concerned with the well-being of older adults may consider supporting more individualized forms of spirituality and creating community-related spaces to practice spirituality, along with traditional religious experiences.

Conclusion

Religion and spirituality play a key role in rural older adults' lives. Spiritual and religious beliefs, affiliations, and practices provide social, emotional, and health-related support during late adulthood (Arcury et al., 2000; Yoon & Lee, 2006). Recent data underscore that rural older adults identify as religious and spiritual more than both non-rural older adults and rural adults who have not yet reached late adulthood. Overall, rural older adults are commonly practicing religion and spirituality, as well as benefiting from their incorporation of the sacred into their lives. Religion and spirituality provide a buffer against the obstacles of both rural living and late adulthood by improving rural older adults' sense of well-being.

Note

1. Unless otherwise cited, trends presented in this entry are from the authors' analyses of the nationally representative General Social Survey (GSS), collected annually from 1998 to 2018. The sample includes 773 adults age 65 and older who live in a rural county, as well as 2,618 rural adults under age 65, and 4,796 older adults who live in non-rural counties. The GSS data file used in this chapter is provided for public access by Smith, Davern, Freese, and Morgan (2018).

Recommendations for Further Reading

Arcury, T. A., Quandt, S. A., McDonald, J., & Bell, R. A. (2000). Faith and health self-management of rural older adults. *Journal of Cross-Cultural Gerontology*, *15*(1), 55–74.

Lyons, L. (2003, March 11). Age, religiosity, and rural America. *Gallup News*. Retrieved from https://news.gallup.com/poll/7960/age-religiosity-rural-america.aspx

Yoon, D. P. (2006). Factors affecting subjective well-being for rural elderly individuals: The importance of spirituality, religiousness, and social support. *Journal of Religion & Spirituality in Social Work: Social Thought*, *25*(2), 59–75.

References

Americans with Disabilities Act. (1990). Pub. L. No. 101–336.

Arcury, T. A., Quandt, S. A., McDonald, J., & Bell, R. A. (2000). Faith and health self-management of rural older adults. *Journal of Cross-Cultural Gerontology*, *15*(1), 55–74.

Gallup News (2018, February 9). The religiously distinct states of America. *Gallup News*. Retrieved from https://news.gallup.com/poll/226844/religiously-segregated-states-america.aspx?g_source=link_newsv9&g_campaign=item_232223&g_medium=copy

Hayward, R. D., & Krause, N. (2013). Patterns of change in religious service attendance across the life course: Evidence from a 34-year longitudinal study. *Social Science Research*, *42*(6), 1480–1489.

Lyons, L. (2003, March 11). Age, religiosity, and rural America. *Gallup News*. Retrieved from https://news.gallup.com/poll/7960/age-religiosity-rural-america.aspx

Pew Research Center. (2014). *Religious landscape study*. Retrieved from www.pewforum.org/religious-landscape-study/

Roof, W. C. (1993). *A generation of seekers: The spiritual journeys of the baby boom generation*. San Francisco, CA: Harper Collins.

Smith, T. W., Davern, M., Freese, J., & Morgan, S. (2018). *General social surveys, 1972–2018 cumulative file*. Chicago, IL: National Opinion Research Center [producer]. Ann Arbor, MI: Inter-university Consortium for Political and Social Research [distributor]. Data accessed from the GSS Data Explorer website. Retrieved from gssdataexplorer.norc.org

Wink, P., & Dillon, M. (2003). Religiousness, spirituality, and psychosocial functioning in late adulthood: Findings from a longitudinal study. *Psychology and Aging*, *18*(4), 916–924.

Wuthnow, R. (1998). *After heaven: Spirituality in America since the 1950s*. Berkeley, CA: University of California Press.

Yoon, D. P. (2006). Factors affecting subjective well-being for rural elderly individuals: The importance of spirituality, religiousness, and social support. *Journal of Religion & Spirituality in Social Work: Social Thought*, *25*(2), 59–75.

Yoon, D. P., & Lee, E. K. O. (2006). The impact of religiousness, spirituality, and social support on psychological well-being among older adults in rural areas. *Journal of Gerontological Social Work*, *48*(3–4), 281–298.

64
RESEARCH ENGAGEMENT

Jennifer A. Crittenden and Carli W. Hutchison

Research in the Rural Context

Despite prevailing myths of rural communities being culturally stagnant, rigid, and outdated, such areas are, in fact, rich with ingenuity, creativity, and tradition, creating limitless opportunities for interested researchers. Because of resource scarcity in rural areas, research in such settings often crosses traditional boundaries of scientific inquiry where researchers may find themselves creating community programming and even addressing culture change as part of their research role. Hand-in-hand with these opportunities are challenges to research engagement. Often such challenges are due to the interplay of individual factors inherent in the aging process itself magnified by the broader environmental context. For example, on an interpersonal level, older adults may be more hesitant to join studies than their younger counterparts. They generally need more time to build trust with researchers, have greater fears about their safety during studies, and may have a limited understanding of research practices and purpose because of infrequent exposure to these activities (Crawford Shearer, Fleury, & Belyea, 2010).

In rural areas, common barriers to recruitment of research subjects include their limited access to transportation, low literacy levels, a wide geographic spread between potential participants, and scarce resources within the community. Compared to their urban counterparts, rural residents tend to have less formal education, poorer health, lower income, are more likely to be uninsured, and suffer from chronic conditions (Miyamoto, Henderson, Young, Ward, & Santillan, 2012). Distance and isolation can make it difficult for participants to travel to research sites, and it can be particularly costly and time-consuming for researchers to reach older adult subjects in rural areas. Internet lag and connectivity issues may further impair research activities and communications with potential older adult study participants. Studies involving rural older adults may also be curtailed in colder regions during the winter season, as older residents may migrate to warmer regions during these months (Fougère et al., 2016; Pribulick, Williams, & Fahs, 2013).

Recruitment Principles and Methods

Recruiting and engaging older adult research participants in rural areas can be challenging, resource-intensive, and require the use of careful planning and strategic partnerships. To build trust among potential research participants, researchers in rural areas may need to partner with well-established and trusted entities, or gatekeepers, in the community that understand the community context and culture. These partnerships can include relationships with a range of organizations, such as Area Agencies on Aging, senior centers, health care practices, and community-based nonprofits. Gatekeeper affiliations of this type not only build goodwill and trust but can create innovative avenues through which research relationships can be brokered with older adults. Given the importance of gatekeepers in rural communities, it is essential to "choose your partners wisely." A successful research gatekeeper demonstrates the following attributes: historical ties to the community, internal commitments to collaboration, knowledge of the community social context, a track record of outreach and engagement within the community, strong relationships with outside entities and institutions, and an inherent level of community trust and respect for its work (Smith, Blake, Olson, & Tessaro, 2002).

Community agencies, as research entry points, face time constraints in supporting research endeavors and may lack relationships with key community members or other organizations. Individual gatekeepers within such organizations need to have a level of trust and understanding of the research process, the availability to assist in making research connections, and the ability to maintain confidentiality (Wu et al., 2010).

While gatekeepers can serve as intermediaries in gaining access to older adult study participants, researchers can directly build trust with potential research subjects through establishing a presence in the community through field work, providing referrals to other trusted organizations as part of the research process, and sharing study information, including findings and recommendations, in engaging and accessible formats (Kammerer, Falk, Herzog, & Fuchs, 2019).

In addition to relationship building, successful older adult rural recruitment entails overcoming persistent barriers within the rural context including lack of transportation, social isolation, and health and functional impairments more often found among rural-dwelling older adults. A variety of research incentives can be used to overcome these barriers including offering monetary incentives for participation; health assessments and screening information to participants for their own personal use; transportation stipends; as well as conducting the research in a congregate setting where older adults can derive the benefits of socialization as part of the research process, and providing the opportunity for personal learning and growth as part of research activities (Kammerer et al., 2019).

Registries

Another solution for increasing recruitment of rural research participants is the use of research registries, databases of individuals interested in volunteering for studies. The following motivations have been noted to drive registry participation: connecting and sharing with other research participants, opportunities for learning, the desire to help others, and cash incentives (Lee et al., 2016). Common concerns regarding registry participation include trust and confidentiality. McSweeney et al. (2018) addressed some of these concerns by employing a user-friendly registry website (Arresearch.org) that showcased testimonial videos from research participants sharing their experiences and discussing the value of research for the community. Their registry website was heavily promoted through the media and proved to be successful in recruiting research volunteers. In the first year, 22,000 site visits were logged resulting in 4,000 registrants by the 18-month mark.

In areas where potential volunteers are scarce, a registry also creates the opportunity for using repeat subjects across multiple studies, conserving research resources. The Center on Aging at the University of Maine recently launched the Maine Older Adult Research Registry providing an avenue for older adults across a rural state to participate in research projects. Recruitment activities for this registry include enrollment at health fairs and community events, and partnerships with existing older adult programs creating opportunities to educate potential members about research and the importance of study participation.

Research Methods

Research methods that address the barriers inherent in carrying out investigations in rural settings center around innovative approaches to partnering with older adults, conducting in-home and community-based research activities, and gathering data in research scarce environments.

Participatory Action Research

The use of participatory action research (PAR) has been shown to be an effective method for creating sustainable efforts that can both engage and empower individuals and communities as both participants and co-researchers. When community members are given agency in the study, they are provided the opportunity to define the research questions, carry out the data collection and analysis, utilize community capacity building, and share and implement their findings as they see fit. PAR can give communities the skills and knowledge needed to create programs and conduct further research on their own as well as create long-lasting partnerships that continue to effect change at the systems level (Blair & Minkler, 2009). When allowed to take control in the study, older adult participants are encouraged to make important decisions in the research design and share their own unique perspectives in the process. Given its focus on sharing power and building trust, this method is particularly well suited for use in rural communities.

In Mey and Van Hoven's (2019) study, six older adults in a rural Norwegian neighborhood were recruited as co-researchers for an age-friendly project aimed at identifying current issues faced by older adults in the area. After the co-researchers were introduced to the age-friendly initiative and received academic research training, they were then given the lead in shaping the research aims, conducting the fieldwork, and making decisions regarding dissemination of the results. The project gave each participant the freedom to focus on the issues they found most pressing based on their data collection and analysis, as well as their ability to choose how issues would be addressed.

Photovoice

Photovoice, which involves study participants taking photos and writing or discussing accompanying captions, is a form of PAR that gives community members control of how their perspectives are documented and shared based on a given research prompt. Photovoice is an accessible methodology for working with low-literacy populations, individuals with disabilities, those for whom English is a second language, low-income individuals, and those who may lack more formal education—all of whom may reside in rural locales (Graziano, 2011; Knowles, Rabinowich, Gaines-Turner, & Chilton, 2015; Shumba & Moodley, 2018). This grassroots approach can enable a deeper look into the lives of those being studied. Photovoice participants are trained by researchers on project frameworks, ethical considerations, and camera use techniques. At the end of the data collection period, individual interviews or focus groups are conducted with study participants to clarify photo significance and meaning, and identify themes and issues among the photos and narratives that are relevant to the research question. Researchers can then make recommendations to the community based on study findings (Novek, Morris-Oswald, &

Menec, 2012; Yankeelov, Faul, D'Ambrosio, Collins, & Gordon, 2015; Rush, Murphy, & Kozak, 2012).

Adapting Survey Methodology

Surveys are a mainstay research approach that can be modified to meet the needs of rural older adults and communities. For rural and suburban communities with distinct neighborhoods or natural gathering points, community-based surveying methods, such as intercept surveying and drop-off/pick-up surveying, provide an opportunity for raising visibility of a research issue and encouraging participation. Personal contact, whether directly with a researcher or an intermediary, can be expected to result in higher survey response rates as compared to traditional paper or electronic surveys. Using drop-off/pick-up surveying, research staff deliver surveys in-person to an individual's home and may also return to pick up the survey or instruct the individual to return the survey by mail. Drop-off/pick-up surveying can also be used in congregate settings, including senior centers, older adult housing communities, and congregate meals sites. While this method is more time consuming and costly than a mailed survey approach, it can: 1. successfully engage older adults who lack transportation; 2. create community understanding and acceptance of the research; and 3. allow research staff to observe, first-hand, the community context and environment (Trentelman, Petersen, Irwin, Ruiz, & Szalay, 2016).

Intercept surveying, like drop-off/pick-up, entails direct face-to-face contact with potential respondents and is often used to study issues of local importance or issues that have place-based significance. For this method, research staff are physically positioned within the community, approach community members about research participation, and conduct a survey or interview in the moment with the individual (Flint et al., 2016). This method can be used at local events where older adults are likely to congregate, including health fairs and at town hall events, such as after local election activities.

In some instances, the use of gatekeepers or intermediaries can complement survey methodologies to increase older adult response rates. This can be particularly beneficial when the research subject matter is sensitive in nature or when the population may be difficult to reach through other methods. For example, Edelman and colleagues (2013) found that partnering with a home-delivered meals program, whose volunteers delivered surveys during their meals visits, led to a higher survey response rate among rural older adults when compared to a traditional paper mailing. The authors attribute this success to the trusting and familiar relationships already established between the older adult and their meals delivery volunteer, making the research process more acceptable to the target audience (Edelman et al., 2013). In similar fashion, Zanjani and Rowles (2012) partnered with local university-based Cooperative Extension agents to assist with mental health research in rural Appalachia. Extension agents are university employees whose role focuses on community education and outreach and whose work entails the building of both trust within the community and relevant resource-knowledge. Their work naturally positions them both within the community but also with established connections outside the community to facilitate the provision of information and referral if needed. Extension agents were found to be instrumental in not only supporting the research but were also successfully situated to implement interventions subsequent to the conclusion of the study.

Summary

Conducting research in rural areas creates rich opportunities for older adults and researchers to explore and inform issues of local importance. A thoughtful selection of partners and methods, including the use of community gatekeepers and participatory approaches, will ensure success in engaging and giving voice to rural older adults.

References

Blair, T., & Minkler, M. (2009). Participatory action research with older adults: Key principles in practice. *The Gerontologist*, *49*(5), 651–662. doi:10.1093/geront/gnp049

Crawford Shearer, N. B., Fleury, J. D., & Belyea, M. (2010). An innovative approach to recruiting homebound older adults. *Research in Gerontological Nursing*, *3*(1), 11–18. doi:10.3928/19404921-20091029-01

Edelman, L. S., Yang, R., Guymon, M., & Olson, L. M. (2013). Survey methods and response rates among rural community dwelling older adults. *Nursing Research*, *62*(4), 286–291. doi:10.1097/NNR.0b013e3182987b32

Flint, C. G., Oldroyd, Z., Wynn, E., Brown, A., Mascher, C., Valle, P. A., Quinton, C., & Unger, B. (2016). Public intercept interviews and surveys for gathering place-based perceptions: Observations from community water research in Utah. *Journal of Rural Social Sciences*, *31*(3), 105.

Fougère, B., Aubertin-Leheudre, M., Vellas, B., Andrieu, S., Demougeot, L., Cluzan, C., & Cesari, M. (2016). Clinical research for older adults in rural areas: The minded study experience. *Age*, *38*(2), 30. doi:10.1007/s11357-016-9892-3

Graziano, K. J. (2011). Working with English language learners: Preservice teachers and photovoice. *International Journal of Multicultural Education*, *13*(1), 1–19. doi:10.18251/ijme.v13i1.354

Jacelon, C. (2007). Older adults' participation in research. *Nurse Researcher*, *14*(4), 64–73. doi:10.7748/nr2007.07.14.4.64.c6044

Kammerer, K., Falk, K., Herzog, A., & Fuchs, J. (2019). How to reach "hard-to-reach" older people for research: The TIBaR model of recruitment. *Survey Methods: Insights from the Field*. Retrieved from https://surveyinsights.org/?p=11822

Knowles, M., Rabinowich, J., Gaines-Turner, T., & Chilton, M. (2015). Witnesses to hunger: Methods for photovoice and participatory action research in public health. *Human Organization*, *74*(3), 255–265. doi:10.17730/0018-7259-74.3.255

Lee, S. B., Zak, A., Iversen, M. D., Polletta, V. L., Shadick, N. A., & Solomon, D. H. (2016). Participation in clinical research registries: A focus group study examining views from patients with arthritis and other chronic illnesses. *Arthritis Care & Research*, *68*(7), 974–980. doi:10.1002/acr.22767

McSweeney, J. C., Boateng, B., James, L., McElfish, P. A., Robinson, D., Hatley, S. E., . . . Indelicato, N. (2018). Developing and launching a research participant registry. *Health Communication*, *34*(10), 1159–1165. doi:10.1080/10410236.2018.1465794

Mey, E., & van Hoven, B. (2019). Managing expectations in participatory research involving older people: What's in it for whom? *International Journal of Social Research Methodology*, *22*(3), 323–334. doi:10.1080.13645579.2018.1563977

Miyamoto, S., Henderson, S., Young, H., Ward, D., & Santillan, V. (2012). Recruiting rural participants for a telehealth intervention on diabetes self-management. *The Journal of Rural Health*, *29*(1), 69–77. doi:10.1111/j.1748-0361.2012.00443

Novek, S., Morris-Oswald, T., & Menec, V. (2012). Using photovoice with older adults: Some methodological strengths and issues. *Ageing and Society*, *32*(3), 451–470. doi:10.1017/so144686x11000377

Pribulick, M., Williams, I. C., & Fahs, P. S. (2013). Strategies to reduce barriers to recruitment and participation. *Online Journal of Rural Nursing Health Care*, *10*(1), 22–33.

Rush, K., Murphy, M. A., & Kozak, J. F. (2012). A photovoice study of older adults' conceptualizations of risk. *Journal of Aging Studies*, *26*(4), 448–458. doi:10.1016/j.aging.2012.06.004

Shumba, T. W., & Moodley, I. (2018). Part 1: A review of using photovoice as a disability research method: Implications for eliciting the experiences of persons with disabilities on the community-based rehabilitation programme in Namibia. *African Journal of Disability*, 7, 418. doi:10.4102/ajod.v7i0.418

Smith, S. L., Blake, K., Olson, C. R., & Tessaro, I. (2002). Community entry in conducting rural focus groups: Process, legitimacy, and lessons learned. *The Journal of Rural Health*, *18*(1), 118–124. doi:10.1111/j.1748-0361.2002.tb00883.x

Trentelman, C. K., Petersen, K. A., Irwin, J., Ruiz, N., & Szalay, C. S. (2016). The case for personal interaction: Drop-off/pick-up methodology for survey research. *Journal of Rural Social Sciences*, *31*(3), 68.

Wu, B., Goedereis, E. A., Crout, R. J., Plassman, B. L., DiNapoli, E. A., McNeil, D. W., . . . Bai, L. B. (2010). Recruitment of rural and cognitively impaired older adults for dental research. *Special Care in Dentistry*, *30*(5), 193–199, 210. doi:10.1111/j.1754-4505.2010.00150

Yankeelov, P. A., Faul, A. C., D'Ambrosio, J. G., Collins, W. L., & Gordon, B. (2015). "Another day in paradise": A photovoice journey of rural older adults living with diabetes. *Journal of Applied Gerontology*, *34*(2), 199–218. doi:10.1177/0733464813493136

Zanjani, F., & Rowles, G. D. (2012). "We don't want to talk about that": Overcoming barriers to rural aging research and interventions on sensitive topics. *Journal of Rural Studies*, *28*(4), 398–405. doi:10.1016/j.jrurstud.2012.03.005

65
RETIREMENT

Helen Dennis

Growth of Rural Retirement Communities

The growth of rural retirement communities has expanded and contracted over the years. During the 1980s, in-migration to rural communities slowed because of the decline of traditional industries of farming and mining. To counter this trend, policies were developed to attract retirees as a means to stimulate economic growth, which received little attention from economic development professionals. Instead, they focused on revitalizing manufacturing and resource-extraction industries (Reeder, 2005). Between 1990 and 1998, rural retirement communities grew rapidly and accounted for a quarter of all rural population growth during that period of time (Anonymous, 2000). The growth rate continued between 2000 and 2007, reaching 3.1% and slowed considerably at the beginning of the financial crisis from 2008 to 2009 to just 1.7% (McLaughlin, 2013). Counties that focused on retirees experienced rapid population growth and increased employment (Reel & Lauder, 2006). They attracted retirees, in part, because of their long history of population growth, experience in appealing to older migrants, their attractive natural amenities, and recreation and tourism industries (Brown, Bolender, Kulcsar, Glasgow, & Sanders, 2011). Despite years of expansion, the anticipated growth of these communities was not a given since only about 5% of retirees were likely to move upon retirement (Anonymous, 2000).

Impact on the Community

Benefits to Rural Communities

Retiree migration is considered an economic development success story (Glasgow & Brown, 2012) often described as "gray gold" (Clark, Lambert, Park, & Wilcox, 2009). For example, the expanded number of health-care facilities, serving significant numbers of older adults, is considered a potential contributor to the economic stability of rural communities, having a positive effect on net in-migration, statistically significant for those 70 years and older (Oehmke, Tsukamoto, & Post, 2007).

In theory, retirees can be an economic benefit to rural communities as consumers of housing, food, entertainment, and health services which, in turn, create jobs and stimulate businesses.

They pay taxes that support services benefiting new retirees as well as older adults aging-in-place and help maintain public services such as hospitals and schools. Retirees bring their assets and capital to the community, benefiting banks that invest their money; they start their own businesses, becoming entrepreneurs using their own finances or enter into joint partnerships with local business people (Reeder, 2005). They raise median family incomes, reduce local unemployment, and add to the economic diversity of the community. Furthermore, retirees enhance volunteerism and support churches, charities, and other civic activities (Reeder, 2005). Surprisingly, retirees have become a labor source for physical jobs once performed by younger workers (Eaton, 2019), which is somewhat contrary to workforce literature regarding physical labor and older adults.

Concerns of Rural Communities

Not all of the impact of retiree migration is positive. Services required for rural retirement migrations can limit the availability of such services to older native residents. With no connection to the public-school system, it is unclear whether retirees would support their public education system or instead support increased taxes on public services that would directly benefit them (Brown, Bolender, Kulcsar, Glasgow, & Sanders, 2011).

The economic impact is woven throughout anticipated changes. An influx of retirees can cause excessive population growth leading to congestion and an increase in housing costs and property taxes, forcing longtime residents to move. Retiree in-migration creates a range of jobs from highly skilled to unskilled, the latter filled by low-income workers who can stress public services such as schools and also decrease taxes. Assuming that inflation erodes retirement income, retirees can become a tax burden as their needs and demands for health services increase. Although diversity is likely valued, different opinions about public policies such as land use, economic development, schools, and taxes can create conflict within the community (Reeder, 2005).

Clearly not all in-migrants to rural communities are self-serving. In one study conducted in a rural Tennessee county, later-life migrants actually were more supportive of funding education than the county's longtime residents. Self-interest, altruism, and knowledge that their taxes would increase served as motivators to support funding for local education (Clark et al., 2009).

In the short term, research suggests that later-life migration to rural communities has a positive impact on local government finance and is referred to as an economic development success. Part of that success is predicated on older in-migrants leaving the community if they experience economic or health problems. If that's the case, their contributions to the community will nearly always exceed the costs of providing them with services (Glasgow & Brown, 2012). However, the overall long-term financial impact of rural in-migration is less clear (Brown et al., 2011), taking into account that most research on retiree attraction strategies focuses on the affluent (Clement, 2004). Uncertainty has evolved into two camps: gray gold for economic development and gray peril as a sign of rural retirees' unwillingness to support local services (Clark et al., 2009).

Profile of Late-Life Migrants to Rural Areas

Late-life migrants to rural areas are better educated, married, and have higher incomes compared to those who are native residents (Brown et al., 2011). They are more aware of available programs and services and in better health (Rogers, 2000). Furthermore, they typically arrive as married couples in their 60s, healthy, with enough income and assets to stimulate real estate and commercial markets. They have professional skills and experiences useful to rural communities often expressed through volunteering (Glasgow & Brown, 2012).

Reasons to Retire and Live in a Rural Community

Reasons to retire in a rural community vary with age. New or recent retirees ages 65 to 69 years typically take advantage of the amenities and move away from locations with high incomes and are attracted to opportunities for education, entertainment, and recreation. Those 70 years and older generally move for health-related reasons and are concerned about the location of health services (Oehmke, Tsukamoto, & Post 2007).

Features That Attract In-Migration

Kathy Greenlee, a fifth-generation Kansan and former Assistant Secretary of Aging at the U.S. Department of Health and Human Services describes her personal view of rural communities, which may be reasons retirees want to relocate there.

> Life in rural America is different. It is quiet. The pace is slower. Personal space is abundant. Ease of movement is an afterthought. You can physically and emotionally spread out. The air is cleaner. You can smell the grass, trees, and freshly cut wheat. You can see the stars and the Milky Way. In the vast middle portion of America, you can see the entire sky from one horizon to another (Greenlee, 2019, p. 7).

Temperate climate, attractive natural resources of mountains and lakes, and championship golf courses are additional attractions (Mclaughlin, 2013), as well as the low cost of living, less noise and air pollution, a slower pace of life, and friendly people (Patterson, 2011).

Retirees from other countries don't necessarily share the same reasons to relocate to a rural community; their definition of amenities is different. Those born in Ristijarvi, Finland, and living elsewhere in the country had a strong desire to return to their remote childhood places. Unlike retiree attractions that are dominant in U.S. communities, such as sunshine, culture and services, these retirees placed a higher value on peaceful, safe unpolluted environments with natural landscapes and low-cost housing (Jauhiainen, 2009).

Marketing Rural Communities for Retirement

Marketers describe the benefits of moving to rural retirement communities emphasizing environments and opportunities for healthy and active aging that also might appeal to all age groups.

Berkeley Springs, West Virginia offers the beauty of nature, small town amenities and is close to Washington and Baltimore. . . . Year-round festivals, live music and theater will keep you busy.

Bozeman, Montana offers a mountain view in a small-town setting . . . that provides outdoor adventure activities, skiing in winter and rafting and zip-lining in the summer.

Concho, Arizona has affordable properties in a small-town setting. . . . with hiking, golfing, hunting and horseback riding within minutes. Day trips to the Grand Canyon . . . are convenient. If you want to escape harsh winters, Concho experiences mild climates for all four seasons (Van De Walle, n.d.).

Need for More Information

The literature describes retirees who move to retirement communities with an emphasis on social services and health care. Information about the attributes of rural retirement communities and the positive and negative impact of retiree migration to rural communities is important, although much of this information is dated and some is speculative. For example, the negative impact often is described in terms of potential rather than actual impact supported by data. Perhaps the largest gap in the research on rural retirement is the study and description of the actual retirement experience for native retirees and those who have migrated. Do in-migrant retirees and native retirees experience retirement in similar or different ways? At what age do they retire? What are their economic, marital, health status, and housing arrangements? Do they live alone? If so, how many and are their needs being met? Are migrant retirees predominantly Caucasian or is there racial diversity? Do retirees continue working past retirement age? How do they spend their time? Do they have encore careers, become entrepreneurs or move on to other employment? What are the service and policy implications?

Since one out of five residents in rural communities is 65 and older, it is timely to learn more about this relatively unknown segment of the population. Rural aging has been referred to as the silent majority (Dudley, 2019). Retirees living in rural America are a significant part of that silent majority.

References

Anonymous. (2000). Aging gracefully? *Forum for Applied Research and Public Policy, 15*(4), 41 [Editorial]. Retrieved from http://search.proquest.com/docview/235137062/

Brown, D. L., Bolender, B. C., Kulcsar, L. J., Glasgow, N., & Sanders, S. (2011). Intercounty variability of net migration at older ages as a path-dependent process. *Rural Sociology, 76*(1), 44–73. doi:10.1111/j.1549-0831.2010.00034.x

Clark, C. D., Lambert, D. M., Park, W. M., & Wilcox, M. D. (2009). Willingness to fund public education in a rural, retirement destination county. *Journal of Research in Rural Education, 24*(6), 1–16. Retrieved from http://libproxy.usc.edu/login?url=https://search-proquest-com.libproxy2.usc.edu/docview/218988954?accountid=14749

Clement, D. (2004, May). Is gray the new gold? *Fedgazette*, 9–12. Retrieved from www.minneapolisfed.org/publications/fedgazette/is-gray-the-new-gold

Dudley, D. (2019, Summer). Keeping the faith in rural America: A longtime denizen speaks about equity and advocacy. *Generations*, 4–5.

Eaton, J. (2019). *The town where retirees can't retire, CITYLAB*. Retrieved from www.citylab.com/life/2019/02/rural-aging-demographics-jobs-places-to-retire/52/.

Frey, W. H. (2019). *How migration of millennials and seniors has shifted since the Great Recession*. Retrieved from www.brookings.edu/research/how-migration-of-millennials-and-seniors-has-shifted-since-the-great-recession/

Glasgow, N., & Brown, D. L. (2012). Rural ageing in the United States: Trends and contexts. *Journal of Rural Studies, 28*(4), 422–431. doi:10.1016/j.jrurstud.2012.01.002

Greenlee, K. (2019, Summer). Why people choose the rural life. *Generations: Journal of the American Society on Aging, 43*(2), 7.

Jauhiainen, J. S. (2009). Will the retiring baby boomers return to rural periphery? *Journal of Rural Studies, 25*(1), 25–34. doi:10.1016/j.jrurstud.2008.05.001

McLaughlin, T. (2013, June 21). Rural retirement can be early and on the cheap. *Reuters*. Retrieved November 16, 2019, from www.reuters.com/article/us-column-rural-retirement-idUSBRE95K0KM20130621

Oehmke, J. F., Tsukamoto, S., & Post, L. A. (2007). Can health care services attract retirees and contribute to the economic sustainability of rural places? *Agricultural and Resource Economics Review, 36*(1), 95–106. Retrieved from http://libproxy.usc.edu/login?url=https://search-proquest-com.libproxy2.usc.edu/docview/214077353?accountid=14749

Patterson, M. (2011, March 17). Rural America as a retirement destination. Washington, DC: U.S. News & World Report.

Rogers, C. C. (2000). The graying of rural America. *Forum for Applied Research and Public Policy, 15*(4), 52–55. Retrieved from http://libproxy.usc.edu/login?url=https://search-proquest-com.libproxy2.usc.edu/docview/235138554?accountid=14749

Reeder, R. (2005). Retiree-attraction policies for rural development. *Economic Research Services, USDA*. Retrieved from https://www.ers.usda.gov/publications/pub-details/?pubid=42156

Reel, S. J., & Lauder, W. (2006). A comparison of rural older adult retiree in-migration in Scotland and the United States: Implications for health care. *Journal of Gerontological Nursing, 32*(10), 12–18. Retrieved from http://libproxy.usc.edu/login?url=https://search-proquest-com.libproxy2.usc.edu/docview/204150312?accountid=14749

Van De Walle, N. (n.d.). *The best rural places to retire*. Retrieved from https://oureverydaylife.com/rural-places-retire-7442268.html

66
RURAL HEALTH CLINICS

Michelle Mills

Rural Health Clinics Established

Federal Policy

The first major federal policy-enabled expansion of rural health services occurred in the late 1970s. The Rural Health Clinic Services Act of 1977 (Public Law 95–210) was enacted to address an inadequate supply of physicians serving Medicare beneficiaries and Medicaid recipients in rural areas and to increase the utilization of nonphysician practitioners such as nurse practitioners (NPs) and physician assistants (PAs) in rural areas (Department of Health and Human Services, 2020). Through the act, PAs and NPs gained much-needed recognition as a valuable part of primary care access in rural communities (National Rural Health Association (2014).

Interest in community health, human rights, democracy and other political trends in the 1960s and '70s also spilled over into the area of rural health, and the first major policy actions to address shortages were carried out. These included, among other things, the establishment of the National Health Service Corps, Hill-Burton construction funding, Medicare, Medicaid, Area Health Education Centers (AHECs), federal and state offices of Rural Health Policy, and the expansion of medical school class sizes, which was assumed to have a "trickle down" effect on the supply of rural doctors. A few schools also established rural-specific medical school and residency tracks, including Jefferson University, the University of Minnesota, and the University of Washington.

Rural health clinics (RHCs) range anywhere from a permanent structure to mobile clinics. Some are provider-based, and others are freestanding. Some are affiliated with a parent entity such as a hospital, and others are not. All federally certified RHCs, however, must, at a minimum, provide outpatient health-care services, emergency care for common life-threatening conditions, and a limited number of in-house lab tests.

RHCs must be staffed by at least one nurse practitioner, physician assistant or certified nurse midwife, who must be on-site to see patients at least 50% of the time. Often the only medical facility in rural communities, RHCs depend on sound business practices, Medicare, Medicaid, private insurance and any available grant funding to keep their doors open. RHCs must be located in a federally designated provider shortage area and are paid an all-inclusive rate of approximately \$84–\$130 per visit furnished by an eligible provider, according to the National Association of Rural Health Clinics (2020).

Today, there are approximately 4,400 RHCs nationwide that provide access to primary care services in rural areas (National Association of Rural Health Clinics, 2020). Currently, legislation exists to help modernize the regulations surrounding RHCs entitled The Rural Health Clinic Modernization Act of 2019. The act seeks to increase the payment to RHCs.

Current Status of RHCs

Resources

The National Organization of State Offices of Rural Health (NOSORH) offers technical assistance, education, and a series of RHC manuals available nationwide and promotes the technical assistance and resources offered through most State Offices of Rural Health (SORH) to RHCs. These resources include guidelines concerning RHC rules/regulations, billing and coding, practice transformation, health information technology, and more (see https://nosorh.org/ for additional detail). The Federal Office of Rural Health Policy (FORHP) and the Health Resources and Services Administration (HRSA) offer online resources through their website (www.hrsa.gov/rural-health/index.html). NARHC, which serves as a national policy voice and has a robust listserv for RHCs, offers resources through their website (https://narhc.org/). The National Rural Health Association (NRHA), a national policy voice and an RHC constituency group, offers education (www.ruralhealthweb.org/). The Rural Health Information Hub (RHIHub) offers a variety of resources, including literature and toolkits (www.ruralhealthinfo.org/). The National Health Service Corps (NHSC) (https://nhsc.hrsa.gov/) offers free education, loan repayment, scholarships, and recruitment services. Finally, the Centers for Medicare and Medicaid Services (CMMS) (www.cms.gov/) has RHC resources.

It's important to note that RHCs do not receive any federal or state funding outside of their services payment reimbursement unless they apply for grants. Likewise, SORHs and other associations that work with RHCs do not receive any funding outside of applied grants to offer technical assistance. The lack of dedicated funding makes the movement toward value-based payment difficult for RHCs that already struggle financially. The financial struggle also makes it difficult for RHCs to expand their much-needed services in rural communities, including those services that will help the aging rural population. Yet in the midst of this seemingly dire situation, there remain innumerable committed individuals who work with and care for the most vulnerable among us.

RHCs provide outpatient primary care services through a collaborative model of health-care delivery that involves physicians, nurse practitioners, and physician assistants. Often the only medical providers in a rural community, RHCs treat patients with Medicare, Medicaid, those with insurance, and those with no insurance.

Rural older adults often face many challenges, including chronic diseases such as cardiac artery disease, chronic respiratory disease, and diabetes. Rural communities have a higher rate of individuals who are either without insurance or are underinsured. They also serve larger proportions of Medicaid and Medicare patients as compared to their urban counterparts. Rural residents generally, and rural older adults in particular, do not have as many choices as urban residents in terms of alternative premiums, issuers, plans, and plan types. Out-of-pocket costs are higher for rural residents and consequently, substantial numbers of individuals don't seek preventive care. As a result, rural Americans are more likely to die from heart disease, cancer, unintentional injury, chronic lower respiratory disease, and stroke than their urban counterparts (Centers for Disease Control & Prevention, 2020).

RHCs are integrating services as they can, either by offering those services onsite or through the use of telemedicine. Unfortunately, the lack of a qualified workforce and outdated rules and regulations are prohibiting RHCs from providing a fully integrated model of care.

Aging in Rural America

RHC Adult Service Offerings

RHCs are focused on the quality of care provided as they depend on patients coming back to keep their clinics in business. Many RHCs nationally are working to increase patient satisfaction, reduce patient wait times, and improve referral coordination. Additionally, RHCs are actively working on ways to solve the transportation issues that exist for their patients in small towns and rural communities. Most rural communities lack public transportation and as the resident population ages, the need to determine ways for older patients to more reliably travel to their RHCs for care becomes increasingly critical.

RHCs are offering management support tools as part of patient and family engagement. Patient and family advisory councils are engaging the public in active partnership with the health-care system to direct care to be focused on patient-centeredness and allow a health-care environment in which patients, families, clinicians, and staff work together as partners to improve quality and safety. These efforts are aligned with CMS value-based care. Patients and families are allies in shared decision-making and in safe medication use, infection control initiatives, observing care processes, reporting complications, and reducing preventable readmissions, all of which lead to improved patient outcomes.

Chronic care management and self-management tools are also offered by RHCs for use by patients to maximize their health and enable them to remain in their homes. These clinical tools give patients a central role in determining their own care at the same time that they foster a sense of self-responsibility for an individual's health and well-being. Providing chronic care management guidelines for patients outside of in-person visits can take place by phone or through secure email. Chronic care management includes care coordination activities that are not typically part of a face-to-face encounter with the patient and can include telephone communication, review of medical records and test results, self-management education and support, and coordination and exchange of health information with other practitioners and health-care professionals. It may also include some face-to-face interaction with the patient or other health-care professionals.

At the same time, RHCs are addressing other patient quality of care challenges, including sharing a patient's health information, such as their electronic health plan, with the patient's other health-care professionals and providers; aging care transitions, including providing referrals and facilitating follow-ups for patients after they are discharged; and coordinating with home and community-based services providers and documenting this activity in the patient's medical record.

Additional key services that are being offered by RHCs to strengthen community-clinical linkages include exercise programs; socialization opportunities, partnerships with local libraries, beauty salons, and recreation centers; conducting community health needs assessments; health fairs; community paramedicine programs; diabetes support groups; healthy cooking classes; 340B drug programs; housing; home health/long-term care; and disability services.

RHCs are also forming close alliances with their local hospitals to better ensure patients receive timely, quality preventive care through transfer communications, follow-up appointments, and medication reconciliation.

Many RHCs have been monitoring diabetes measures and working on processes to improve management and control for their patients. They connect diabetic patients with the clinic's care coordinator who provides education on diabetes management. RHCs also look for opportunities to help some of their most uncontrolled patients with diabetes through adjustments to their treatment plans by setting small goals and developing follow-up plans. Small changes provide patients the confidence to keep making changes and gain control of their diabetes.

Finally, the principles of the patient-centered medical home (PCMH) involves RHCs facilitating a team-based approach within the clinic in complying with a set of standards to organize care around the patient's needs and to coordinate and track care over time. The PCMH is a health-care setting that facilitates partnerships between the patient, provider, and family. Care is coordinated through disease registries, information technology, health information exchange, and other means to ensure patients receive care where and when they need and want it in a culturally and linguistically appropriate manner.

Suggested Resources

American Association of Family Physicians: (www.aafp.org/home.html)

Chronic Care Management and self-management tools: AHRQ (www.ahrq.gov/)

Institute for Healthcare Improvement offers resources on age-friendly health care through their 4Ms, which are four key interventions (What Matters, Medication, Mentation, and Mobility) essential to providing age-friendly care (www.IHI.org/agefriendly)

SAMHSA has a resource entitled Growing Older, Providing Integrated Care for An Aging Population (www.samhsa.gov/search_results?k=Growing+older)

References

Centers for Disease Control and Prevention. (2020, January 7). *Leading causes of death in rural America.* Retrieved from www.cdc.gov/ruralhealth/cause-of-death.html

Department of Health and Human Services. (2020, January 7). *The Rural Health Clinic Services Act of 1977 (Public Law 95–210).* Retrieved from https://en.wikipedia.org/wiki/Rural_health_clinic

National Association of Rural Health Clinics. (2020, January 7). *RHC Modernization Act of 2019.* Retrieved from www.web.narhc.org/narhc/RHC_Modernization_Act_Advocacy.asp

National Rural Health Association. (2014). *Policy brief on rural health clinics, approved by the rural health congress April 2014.* Retrieved from www.ruralhealthweb.org/getattachment/Advocate/Policy-Documents/RHCApril20143-(1).pdf.aspx?lang=en-US

67
RURAL SERVICE NETWORK

Mandana R. Weirich and Kristina M. Hash

Introduction

The rural service network is composed of various formal and informal services, many of which operate with limited funding. Service delivery in these areas relies heavily on informal services to bridge gaps in formal services funded by federal and state programs. The Centers for Disease Control and Prevention (CDC) defines the social determinants of health (SDOH) as the conditions in the place where people live, learn, work, and play that affect a wide range of health risks and outcomes (2018). Addressing the SDOH is the responsibility of those in the aging field and in health care in rural and non-rural communities. Considering the impact of the SDOH, this entry will look at access to health and mental health care, transportation, housing, and advocacy for older adults and their families residing and aging in small towns and rural communities. Services for socialization, recreation, and spiritual connection will also be included as these are important for quality of life for rural elders.

Health and Mental Health Care

The Affordable Care Act (2010) was designed to increase the number of older adults and others having access to health care. Affordable access to care and preventive services greatly improves the quality of life for older adults and better management of chronic disease. While access to insurance is very important, access to doctors, specialists, and case managers is also essential and can prove challenging in rural areas. Managed care organizations in some states have been working on models to bring health care to their patients using a blend of home visits, telehealth technology, and supportive housing models. By targeting populations with chronic and complex conditions, health-care organizations drive down the cost of health care, provide higher quality of services, and improve the health of patients (Centers for Medicare and Medicaid Services, 2019).

Everyone, but especially older adults, benefits when agencies break down "silos of care" and work collaboratively. Collaborations between community hospitals, Area Agencies on Aging, mental health agencies, health departments, and other service providers are a developing trend in the United States. The Support and Services at Home (SASH) model began in Vermont in 2008. SASH was started by the nonprofit housing provider Cathedral Square Corporation to provide a coordinator and a wellness nurse for older residents. As SASH grew to reach over 5,000 residents across the state, their partnerships grew to include community providers interested in improving the lives of older adults. By working together with older adults, gaps in services could be identified and strategies developed to address those gaps. The U.S. Department of Health and Human Services has published four evaluations of the SASH program (https://aspe.hhs.gov/basic-report/support-and-services-home-sash-evaluation-highlights-first-four-years-research-summary). SASH has been replicated in Rhode Island with plans for replication in Minnesota; similar models can be found in states such as West Virginia, Maryland, and Tennessee.

Transportation and Housing

The centralization of services in sparsely populated places and the lack of public transit systems create significant problems of service access for older rural residents (Krout, 2015). Creating an infrastructure of transportation services in rural America will take decades, and in the meantime, innovative solutions are needed to meet the needs of older adults. Services that can be brought to the home, physically or virtually using new technology, are providing solutions to the lack of transportation for many older adults. In addition to programs like SASH, service coordinators and community health workers are highly effective solutions to the transportation problem. Service coordinators are members of the management team in affordable housing communities who help older adults maintain their independence at home by linking residents to services, facilitating health and wellness programs, and providing transportation. According to the American Association of Service Coordinators (AASC), service coordination was started in 1985 and despite its demonstrated effectiveness, stagnant funding has limited its growth. Community health workers (CHWs) are generally members of the community who provide peer support and education. CHWs help individuals manage their chronic disease, provide health education classes, and connect individuals to community supports. CHWs can be found in health-care settings, health departments, or other community settings. Families USA provides detailed information about CHWs and the national trends (https://familiesusa.org/initiatives/community-health-worker-sustainability-collaborative).

Legal Services and Advocacy

Legal and advocacy services are also part of the service network and are critical to meeting the needs of older adults and their families. Adult Protective Services (APS) investigates abuse, neglect, self-neglect, and financial exploitation of vulnerable adults. APS varies from state to state, from the population they serve to how they define abuse. APS does not receive dedicated funding from the federal government and a national reporting system did not exist for decades. In 2015, a pilot project called the National Adult Maltreatment Reporting System (NAMRS) was launched in several states. The system began to collect data from states on the kind of adult maltreatment that was being reported and the result of interventions by APS. Though the program is voluntary for states to participate in at this time, data will be used to find more effective and efficient ways to prevent and respond to adult maltreatment.

Older adults and their families are often in need of legal services and advocacy for such issues as resident rights in skilled nursing facilities, age discrimination, and access to entitlement programs. The Older Americans Act (OAA) funds critical services to help keep older adults living independently. When problems related to the health, safety, welfare, and rights of individuals who live in long-term care (LTC) facilities arise, it is the states' LTC Ombudsman's responsibility to help resolve those problems. LTC facilities include nursing homes, board and care and assisted living facilities, and other residential care communities. The Ombudsman program is mandated under the OAA and is available in all states. Older adults and their families sometimes require legal assistance with accessing programs such as Social Security, Medicaid and Medicare, completing advance directives, help with housing issues, and financial exploitation. To assist individuals with these issues, the OAA funds the Legal Services for the Elderly Program, which includes over 1,000 service providers nationwide. Information about OAA, the Ombudsman Program, and Legal Services for the Elderly Program can all be found on the ACL website.

Socialization, Recreation, and Spiritual Connection

In addition to health and mental health care, transportation and housing, and legal services, rural elders also benefit from access to social, recreational, and spiritual activities and programs. Social isolation in older adults is linked to poorer health, higher health-care costs, and premature death (Weirich & Benson, 2019). To counter social isolation and improve mental and physical health, senior centers provide opportunities for socialization, community education, recreation, nutrition, health screenings, and more. Physical activity and socialization are key components of healthy and successful aging (Kaye & Harvey, 2015). Exercise even in small amounts can improve mobility, reduce pain, and provide a sense of mental well-being. In addition, for rural elders, spirituality and religiousness can increase well-being and quality of life (Yoon & Lee, 2007). Given these health and mental health benefits, formal and (most often) informal services can play a central role in attending to the socialization, recreation, and spiritual needs of rural elders. Churches, senior centers, and groups such as Master Gardeners and Silver Sneakers are a few organizations that can provide such opportunities.

Conclusion

The rural service network is designed to provide needed health-care and other services to persons aging in rural communities. Several state and local initiatives have been implemented to improve access to health promoting and life enhancing services for this population. In the future, collaboration among service providers, improved technology, and further investments will be critical to meeting the needs of our aging society, particularly for those residing in small towns and rural areas.

Further Reading

The Rural Health Information Hub is an online resource supported by the Health Resources and Services Administration (HRSA) of the U.S. Department of Health and Human Services (www.ruralhealthinfo.org/topics).

Families USA, the Voice for Health Care consumers, provides information on four health-care focus areas: coverage, health equity, health-care value, and consumer engagement. They have established the *Community Health Worker Sustainability Collaborative* (https://familiesusa.org/initiatives/community-health-worker-sustainability-collaborative).

To learn more about *Support and Services at Home (SASH)*, please read the following:

Kandilov, A. et al. (2018). The impact of the Vermont Support and Services at Home program on health-care expenditures. *Cityscape*, *20*(2), ePub. Article abstract

Center for Consumer Engagement in Health Innovation brief (August 2018): Care That Works: Support and Services at Home (SASH)

U.S. News Report (August 2018): Aging into a Better Life

The National Adult Protective Services Association provides resources for Adult Protective Services, caregivers, and educators (www.napsa-now.org). The website's APS Resource Center includes research and articles: Putting Research into Practice, Evidence Based Practice Registry, NAPSA APS Abuse Registry Project, Promising Practices, and more.

The Administration on Community Living (ACL) is a part of the U.S. Department of Health and Human Resources. The ACL focuses on advancing independence, integration, and inclusion for people with disabilities and older adults. The ACL website includes resources for practitioners in the aging and disability fields, data, research outcomes, grants, and more (https://acl.gov).

New publication focusing on *social isolation of older adults*. Kaye, L. W. & Singer, C. M. (2019). *Critical topics in an aging society: Social isolation of older adults, strategies to bolster health and well-being*. New York. Springer.

Rural Native elders. There are 567 federally recognized American Indian or Alaska Native tribes and 63 state recognized tribes, and the majority are located in very rural communities. Each community is different in terms of population, traditions, language, landscape, and resources.

To learn more about rural Indian Country:

Goins, R. T., Scarton, L., & Winchester, B. (2019) The first rural community: Indian country. *Generations, the Journal of the American Society on Aging, 43*(2), 76–83.

References

Centers for Disease Control and Prevention. (2018). *Social determinants of health: Know what affects health*. Retrieved from www.cdc.gov/socialdeterminants/index.htm

Centers for Medicare and Medicaid Services. (2019). *Health care professional resources*. Retrieved from www.cms.gov/About-CMS/Agency-Information/OMH/equity-initiatives/ccm/hcpresources.html

Kaye, L. W., & Harvey, S. A. (2015). Providing services to well older adults in rural areas. In K. M. Hash, E. T. Jurkowski, & J. A. Krout (Eds.), *Aging in rural places: Policies, programs, and professional practice* (pp. 138–142). New York: Springer.

Krout, J. A. (2015). Providing services to rural older adults. In K. M. Hash, E. T. Jurkowski, & J. A. Krout (Eds.), *Aging in rural places: Policies, programs, and professional practice* (p. 122). New York: Springer.

The Patient Protection and Affordable Care Act. (2010). 42 U.S.C. § 18001 note.

Weirich, M., & Benson, W. (2019). Rural America: Secure in a local safety net? *Generations, The Journal of the American Society on Aging, 43*(2), 40–45.

Yoon, D. P., & Lee, E. K. O. (2007). The impact of religiousness, spirituality, and social support on psychological well-being among older adults in rural areas. *Journal of Gerontological Social Work, 48*(3–4), 281–298.

68
SENIOR CENTERS

John A. Krout

Introduction

The National Council on the Aging (1991, p. 5) defines senior centers as "community focal points on aging where older adults come together for services and activities that reflect their experiences and skills, respond to their diverse needs and interests, enhance their dignity, support their independence and encourage involvement in and with the community." Over the years, such centers have come to serve as important resources for information on aging and play important roles for older persons, their families, and the community as part of a wide-ranging strategy to meet the needs of older adults (Krout, 1989; Niles-Yokum & Wagner, 2015; Paradasani & Thompson, 2012). Senior centers are of particular importance to rural elders because a lack of resources and lower population sizes and densities limit the development and support of a wider range of rural program options. Centers offer services and activities on-site and link participants with resources offered by other organizations (Krout, 2015; Turner, 2004).

Availability

A well-documented inventory of senior centers nationwide is not available so determining their number is difficult. However, researchers have clearly established that the number of senior centers has grown steadily since their inception in the 1940s spurred by federal, state, and local funding and the interest of older adults in center programming (Krout, 1989; Niles-Yokum & Wagner, 2015). Keller and Sprinkmeyer (2015) put the number of senior centers at 15,000 while the National Council on the Aging puts that number at 11,000 (Paradasani & Thompson, 2012). Few studies have been conducted on rural senior center availability, but at least one indicates that a sizable number of senior centers can be found in rural areas across America. Krout (1989) found that one-half of the 4,000 centers from a 33-state listing were located in nonmetropolitan counties. These data are clearly dated, but the author is not aware of any current national statistics on the number of rural senior centers.

There are a number of reasons to hypothesize a growth in rural senior centers nationwide. First is the general increase in funding for senior centers through the Older Americans Act and the maturation and expansion of the "aging services network." This network, composed of state and local Area Agencies on Aging (AAAs) and community-based service providers that include senior centers, is of particular importance in rural areas (Krout, 2015; Niles-Yokum & Wagner, 2015). Second is the "graying" of rural America because of flat and even declining fertility rates and the out-migration of young adults. As a result, 16.2% of the nonmetropolitan population is 65 and over versus 12.6% in metropolitan areas leading to a growth in the "market" for older adult programs even in the context of general rural population stagnation (Krout & Hash, 2015). Third is the fact that select rural communities, especially those in college towns or with relatively easy access to urban amenities, have seen an in-migration of retirees attracted by lower living costs and other quality of life factors (Krout & Hash, 2015). Finally, the boom in energy production across rural America has brought resources to some rural communities that have been used to support local social services such as senior centers (Krout & Hash, 2015).

Resources

National surveys conducted in the 1970s and 1980s found that rural senior centers have smaller facilities, lower budgets, and fewer volunteer and paid staff than urban centers and this rural disadvantage has likely persisted (Krout, 1989). Sometimes rural centers utilize space in community centers, churches, and fire halls, and centers without dedicated space often serve largely as nutrition sites. The need to co-locate in buildings being used for other purposes (out of necessity) does not necessarily dilute the role of rural centers as area focal points for older adult services and may even assist them in linking with other service providers (Krout, 1989; Kirk & Alessi, 2002). The importance of adequate and affordable transportation to and from senior centers in rural areas cannot be stressed enough. This transportation may be provided by older adults themselves, relatives, friends, or neighbors, or by programs funded by federal, state, and/or local dollars. Regardless, affordable and convenient access to rural senior centers is a key ingredient for success.

One potential way to overcome rural senior center resource deficiencies and transportation challenges is to move to a delivery model that relies less on bricks and mortar and more on "virtual" programming (Keller & Sprinkmeyer, 2015). Here, interaction with peers and information/instruction in a wide variety of areas (e.g., arts, health, financial management, benefits enrollment, etc.) can be done individually or in small groups via online connections. However, a lack of reliable and high-speed internet service and computer ownership, less familiarity/comfort with computers and the internet, and a preference for face-to-face interactions among rural elders may limit the viability of the virtual model. As new cohorts of older adults with more online experience replace older ones in rural communities, this model may be much more acceptable and successful.

Programs and Impact

Depending on their resources, programs found at senior centers typically include meals and nutrition education; health wellness/fitness programs, screening, and promotion; recreation and social activities; education and arts; social services; and information on and referral to other services (Paradasani & Thompson, 2012). Senior centers provide a setting for rural elders to receive services and social support and also to contribute their skills and leadership to these organizations and their communities. Some centers reflect a "social service" model and directly provide programs to economically, socially, and physically vulnerable elders (Krout, 1989). Nutrition (or congregate/in-home meal), social, and recreation programs have been a traditional and core component of rural senior center activity, but many also offer a wide range of programming built on a broader health and wellness model (Krout, 2006; Paradasani & Thompson, 2012).

A study of over 200 rural centers in three midwestern states found that 82% to 97% offered social wellness programs and approximately 80% reported programs for physical wellness programs. Lower levels and much larger variation was found for other wellness dimensions such as emotional, educational, spiritual, and occupational (Russ, 2012). As the number of "old-old" (those over the age of 85) has increased in society and center user populations have "aged-in-place," most senior centers have increasingly offered activities and services for frailer center users and their caregivers (Krout, 1989). Finally, a considerable amount of research has documented many positive benefits from senior center participation. These include improved psychological well-being, social participation and friendships, social support, nutrition, health self-assessment, and many indicators of good health (Paradasani & Thompson, 2012).

The relationships between rural senior centers and other community agencies are extremely important for center programming. Some rural centers are closely connected through planning and funding to AAAs and are designated as official "focal points" and/or have a fairly high degree of interaction with hospitals, home health agencies, legal services, and other components of the community-based care system (Krout, 2015). Senior centers are often a small community's only service and information/referral point for elders, and they serve as a key link to the larger health and human services network. Oftentimes, rural centers rely on and bring outside expertise to participants. Examples of successful rural senior center initiatives include a falls reduction Tai Ji Quan balance program in 36 Oregon centers (Fuzhong, Harmer & Fitzgerald, 2016) and a behavioral lifestyle intervention weight loss program conducted by lay health educators recruited and trained by experts to provide programs to their senior center peers (Krukowski et al., 2013).

Use and Users

Senior centers are well known to older persons, and research has shown that between 15% and 20% of older adults in this country participate in center activities (Krout, 1989). The general lack of availability and accessibility of rural services would suggest lower utilization rates for rural centers. However, research findings on this issue have been equivocal. Some rural community studies have found rates of as high as 25%, while others report rates of less than 10% (Krout, Williams & Owens, 1994). Three decades age, Krout (1989) reported that extant research revealed center participants had low to medium incomes, relatively high levels of social interaction, were female, lived alone, and were in relatively good health. These characteristics have remained fairly consistent over time (Paradasani & Thompson, 2012). Since rural elders are, in general, older, poorer, and more likely to be white than their urban counterparts, one would expect rural center users to reflect those characteristics (Krout & Hash, 2015).

Senior centers and users tend to reflect the demographics, culture, and resources of the community in which they are located. Accordingly, poorer communities will have more economically disadvantaged center populations just as an area with a high proportion of nonwhites will reflect the same participant profile at its centers (Krout, 1989). In addition, survey data suggest that rural centers have experienced a trend toward participants to be "aging-in-place" as indicated by increases in the ages of rural center user populations over time (Krout, 1994; Paradasani & Thompson, 2012). As fewer numbers of "young-old" (65–75 years) utilize centers, their user populations have increasingly consisted of "older-old" adults who have been participants for many years. Rural centers, like most senior centers, are examining their program offerings to better appeal to "baby boomers." In fact, the need to respond to emerging generational differences among older adults is seen as a must by many observers if senior centers, rural or otherwise, are to thrive (Brunt, Strommen, & Stangl, 2019).

Conclusions

Rural senior centers provide a place where older adults go for meals, recreation, socialization, education, and more specialized services. They often provide a link to other aging services in and near their local community. With relatively few resources, many rural senior centers also utilize volunteers regularly. The limited data available on rural senior center participants suggest a need for resources for income support programs (e.g., Supplemental Security Income, food stamps, home heating assistance, tax reduction, and income supplement opportunities). With additional resources, rural centers could better assist participants identify and become involved in these programs through education and referral activities. Health and wellness education and promotion (e.g., nutrition, exercise and stress reduction) as well as a wide variety of regularly scheduled health screening activities (e.g., dental, blood pressure, vision, diet, and diabetes) also appear to be particularly salient for rural senior center populations (Krout, 2015). Unfortunately, many of the program needs noted earlier are often less likely to be met in rural areas because senior centers and the aging services network lack the dollars and health and social service professionals to provide them. Access challenges for center users, including transportation and income, are particularly salient in rural areas. Linkages with other agencies and the adoption of communications technology (e.g., remote broadcasts and videos) can overcome rural senior center resource gaps and accessibility problems, but the lack of any and/or affordable internet service inhibits this strategy.

Rural senior centers face many challenges as the older population grows dramatically in numbers and bifurcates between the "younger old" who are wealthier and healthier and seek stimulating activities outside of congregate settings and the "older old" with multiple chronic health conditions and economic and social challenges. A fundamental challenge for all senior centers including rural ones is to remain relevant as a program provider while America's older population experiences rapid growth, becomes increasingly diverse (in terms of race, ethnicity, sexual orientation, economic status), and has an increasing number of activity options available to them. Rural senior centers have played important roles in the lives of elders for almost 75 years. Their survival and success are a testament to rural ingenuity, staff and volunteer dedication, and strong community support. Maintaining and even expanding these roles today and in the future will require these critical qualities and increased recognition of the need for senior centers by policymakers, funders, and the public.

References

Brunt, A., Strommen, J., & Stangl, C. (2019). Reinventing the traditional senior center in rural areas to attract a new generation of individuals. *Journal of Activities, Adaptation & Aging*. Retrieved July 1, 2019, from https://tandfonline.com/doi/full/10.1080/01924788.2019.1581025

Fuzhong, L., Harmer, P., & Fitzgerald, K. (2016). Implementing an evidence-based fall prevention intervention in community senior centers. *American Journal of Public Health, 106*(11), 2026–2031.

Keller, J., & Sprinkmeyer, F. (2015). Reinventing senior centers virtually. *Parks and Recreation*. Retrieved July 1, 2019, from www.nrpa.org/parks-recreation-magazine/2016/january/reinventing senior centers virtually

Kirk, A. H., & Alessi, H. D. (2002). Rural senior service centers: A study of the impact on quality of life issues. *Activities, Adaptation and Aging, 26*, 51–64.

Krout, J. A. (1989). *Senior centers in America*. New York: Greenwood Press.

Krout, J. A. (1994). Changes in senior center participant characteristics during the 1980s. *Journal of Gerontological Social Work, 22*(1–2), 41–60.

Krout, J. A. (2006). *The aged in rural America*. New York: Greenwood Press.

Krout, J. A. (2015). Providing services to rural older adults. In K. M. Hash, E. T. Jurkowski, & J. A. Krout (Eds.), *Aging in rural places: Policies, programs and professional practice* (pp. 119–134). New York: Springer.

Krout, J. A., & Hash, K. A. (2015). What is rural? Introduction to aging in rural places. In K. M. Hash, E. T. Jurkowski, & J. A. Krout (Eds.), *Aging in rural places: Policies, programs and professional practice* (pp. 3–22). New York: Springer.

Krout, J. A., Williams, M. A., & Owens, O. (1994). Senior centers in rural communities. In J. A. Krout (Ed.), *Providing community-based services to the rural elderly* (pp. 90–110). Thousand Oaks, CA: Sage Publications.

Krukowski, R., Lensing, S., Love, S., Prewitt, T., Adams, B., Cornell, C., . . . West, D. (2013). Training of lay health educators to implement an evidence-based behavioral weight loss intervention in rural senior centers. *The Gerontologist, 53*(2), 162–171.

National Council on the Aging. (1991). *Senior center standards: Guidelines for practice*. Washington, DC: The National Council on the Aging, Inc.

Niles-Yokum, K., & Wagner, D. L. (2015). *The aging networks: A guide to programs and services* (8th ed.). New York: Springer.

Paradasani, M., & Thompson, M. (2012). Senior centers: Innovative and emerging models. *Journal of Applied Gerontology, 31*(11), 52–77.

Russ, R. (2012). Wellness activities of rural older adults in the Great Plains: The online. *Journal of Rural Research & Policy*, 7(1), 1–14.

Turner, K. (2004). Senior citizens centers: What they offer, who participates, and what they gain. *Journal of Gerontological Social Work, 43*(1), 37–47.

69

SOCIAL DETERMINANTS OF HEALTH

Carrie Henning-Smith

Introduction

While access to timely, high-quality medical care is a perennial challenge in rural areas, and while such access matters for the health of rural older adults, what happens outside of the health-care setting is even more important for determining health outcomes and quality of life (County Health Rankings & Roadmaps, 2019; Rural Health Gateway, 2019; Rural Health Information Hub, 2019). This concept is often referred to as the "social determinants of health" (Marmot & Wilkinson, 2005), encompassing a broad array of factors related to where people are born, live, work, and play, and the broad structural, economic, infrastructure, and policy forces that shape one's daily exposures and access to opportunities (World Health Organization, 2008). Taken together, social determinants of health are the most significant contributors to health outcomes and include factors such as socioeconomic status, educational opportunities, employment, housing, transportation, access to food, social support, and environmental/community context (The National Institute for Health Care Management Foundation, 2019).

Social determinants of health are particularly important for older adults, as they have had more time to be exposed to the impacts of such determinants over their lifetimes, leading to accumulated advantage or disadvantage in health (Dannefer, 2003; Marmot, Allen, Bell, Bloomer, & Goldblatt, 2012). Over the course of one's life, social determinants of health shape the available opportunities, resultant health outcomes, and our ability to live independently and age where we choose in older age (Pooler & Srinivasan, 2018). While different definitions of social determinants of health exist, it is generally useful to look at them through the lens of socio-demographic and economic characteristics, community infrastructure and physical environment, and social connectedness. Each of these is discussed in more detail next.

Socio-Demographic and Economic Characteristics

Rural areas tend to reflect lower individual and family incomes, higher unemployment, and older populations than urban areas (Cromartie, 2018; United States Department of Agriculture Economic Research Service, 2017; USDA, 2016). Rural areas also tend to have lower educational attainment levels across all populations, including older adults, in addition to higher rates of uninsurance (Henning-Smith, Prasad, Casey, Kozhimannil, & Moscovice, 2017). The types of jobs available in rural areas are qualitatively different from those in urban areas, too, with more people working in many physically demanding and sometimes dangerous occupations, including agriculture, forestry, mining, and manufacturing (Slack & Jensen, 2008). And jobs in rural areas are less likely than those in urban areas to have benefits to support good health, including employee-sponsored health insurance and paid leave for attending to family caregiving responsibilities (Henning-Smith & Lahr, 2018; Larson & Hill, 2005). These issues may lead to poorer health outcomes over the life course for rural older adults. Further, more adults are remaining in the workforce than ever before, many for economic reasons, but rural older adults are more likely than their urban peers to have trouble finding high-quality, well-paying jobs (Slack & Jensen, 2008).

Rural and urban areas also differ in meaningful ways around racial and ethnic composition. Still, while rural areas tend to have greater percentages of white residents than urban areas, rural areas are becoming more racially and ethnically diverse (Lichter, 2012), and racial and ethnic disparities in health among rural residents are deep and pervasive (Henning-Smith, Hernandez, Ramirez, Hardeman, & Kozhimannil, 2019; James et al., 2017; James & Cossman, 2017). Older adults in rural communities are more likely than younger adults and children to be non-Hispanic white, yet diversity is increasing in all age groups in rural areas across the U.S. And many white, rural-residing older adults are finding themselves with younger community members of different backgrounds than themselves (Lichter, 2012). For the sake of both rural older adults and the communities in which they live, attention is needed to address structural racism and its impacts on health disparities in rural communities (Kozhimannil & Henning-Smith, 2017).

Community Infrastructure and Physical Environment

Almost by definition, rural older adults face different exposures to social determinants of health than their urban counterparts by virtue of the places where they live. Rural areas, while heterogeneous themselves, are qualitatively different from urban environments in terms of their natural and built environments, population density, and access to resources. For example, rural areas tend to have better air quality than urban, but poorer water quality (Fan, Wen, & Wan, 2017; Strosnider, Kennedy, Monti, & Yip, 2017). Rural areas also tend to have fewer spaces in which to safely exercise (e.g., sidewalks, parks, and bike paths) than urban areas (Hansen, Umstattd Meyer, Lenardson, & Hartley, 2015), and access to food, especially for lower-income rural older adults is increasingly challenging in many rural communities (Morton & Blanchard, 2007; Sharkey, Johnson, & Dean, 2010). Meanwhile, climate change is taking a toll on the landscape of rural areas, with important and potentially devastating impacts on many rural livelihoods, such as farming, fishing, and forestry (U.S. Global Change Research Program, 2014).

Rural areas also face distinct challenges related to transportation, including public transportation, safety, and infrastructure (Fan et al., 2017; Henning-Smith, Evenson, Corbett, Kozhimannil, & Moscovice, 2018; Henning-Smith, Evenson, Kozhimannil, & Moscovice, 2017). And rural communities tend to have more limited access to broadband internet and cellular connectivity (Prieger, 2013; Whitacre, Wheeler, & Landgraf, 2017), which can make it difficult for older adults to access resources and connect with others in our increasingly technology-centric society. Together, challenges related to transportation and access to technology can make it more difficult for older adults living in rural areas to access basic necessities, to participate in the civic and social lives of their communities, and to access the health care that they need.

Social Connectedness

For rural older adults to age well in their communities, they also need opportunities to connect with one another and with community resources, services, and amenities. Rural areas face particular challenges and strengths as they relate to supporting older adults as they grow older within their communities, especially related to the social determinants of health (Henning-Smith & Blonigan, 2017; Mattos et al., 2019). In addition to community design and infrastructure, meaningful social interaction is essential for rural older adults' health and quality of life. In fact, loneliness and social isolation have been linked with increased risk of mortality and morbidity (Holt-Lunstad, Smith, Baker, Harris, & Stephenson, 2015), and any focus on social determinants of health should include efforts to promote social connectedness.

There is a growing body of research suggesting that rural residents, and rural older adults in particular, have stronger social ties, larger families, and more social relationships than their urban peers (Henning-Smith et al., 2019; Henning-Smith, Moscovice, & Kozhimannil, 2019). Still, rural older adults are more likely than their urban peers to feel "left out," an important marker of loneliness, and differences exist among rural older adults by gender, with women reporting feeling left out more often than men (Henning-Smith, Ecklund, Moscovice, & Kozhimannil, 2018). It is particularly challenging to address social connectedness in rural areas because of the aforementioned issues around transportation and broadband access, making these multifaceted but crucially important social determinants of health.

Addressing Social Determinants of Health for Rural Older Adults

Any efforts to improve the health and well-being of rural older adults and to address rural-urban and intra-rural disparities in health for older adults need to include a focus on the social determinants of health. Taken together, these constitute the most significant contributor to health outcomes and are instrumental in predicting the ways in which rural older adults go about their daily lives. Because the social determinants of health include so many varied components, efforts to address health by impacting one or more of these components can take many forms, from increasing access to transportation and technological connectivity to building sidewalks and improving access to healthy food.

References

County Health Rankings & Roadmaps. (2019). *What is health?* Retrieved from www.countyhealthrankings.org/what-is-health

Cromartie, J. (2018). *Rural America at a glance, 2018 edition.* U.S. Department of Agriculture Economic Research Service. Retrieved from www.ers.usda.gov/publications/pub-details/?pubid=90555

Dannefer, D. (2003). Cumulative advantage/disadvantage and the life course: Cross-fertilizing age and social science theory. *The Journals of Gerontology Series B: Psychological Sciences and Social Sciences, 58*(6), S327–S337.

Fan, J. X., Wen, M., & Wan, N. (2017). Built environment and active commuting: Rural-urban differences in the U.S. *SSM—Population Health, 3*, 435–441. doi:10.1016/j.ssmph.2017.05.007

Hansen, A. Y., Umstattd Meyer, M. R., Lenardson, J. D., & Hartley, D. (2015). Built environments and active living in rural and remote areas: A review of the literature. *Current Obesity Reports.* doi:10.1007/s13679-015-0180-9

Henning-Smith, C., & Blonigan, S. (2017). *Rural aging in place toolkit.* Retrieved from www.ruralhealthinfo.org/toolkits/aging

Henning-Smith, C., Evenson, A., Kozhimannil, K., & Moscovice, I. (2017). Geographic variation in transportation concerns and adaptations to travel-limiting health conditions in the United States. *Journal of Transport & Health.* doi:10.1016/j.jth.2017.11.146

Henning-Smith, C., Ecklund, A., Lahr, M., Evenson, A., Moscovice, I., & Kozhimannil, K. B. (2019). *Key informant perspectives on rural social isolation*. Retrieved from https://rhrc.umn.edu/publication/key-informant-perspectives-on-rural-social-isolation-and-loneliness/

Henning-Smith, C., Ecklund, A., Moscovice, I., & Kozhimannil, K. (2018). *Gender differences in social isolation and social support among rural residents*. Retrieved from https://rhrc.umn.edu/publication/gender-differences-in-social-isolation-and-social-support-among-rural-residents/

Henning-Smith, C., Evenson, A., Corbett, A., Kozhimannil, K., & Moscovice, I. (2018). *Rural transportation: Challenges and opportunities*. The University of Minnesota Rural Health Research Center. Retrieved from https://rhrc.umn.edu/publication/rural-transportation-challenges-and-opportunities/

Henning-Smith, C., Hernandez, A., Ramirez, M., Hardeman, R., & Kozhimannil, K. (2019). *Dying too soon: County-level disparities in premature death by rurality, race, and ethnicity*. Retrieved from https://rhrc.umn.edu/publication/dying-too-soon-county-level-disparities-in-premature-death-by-rurality-race-and-ethnicity/

Henning-Smith, C., & Lahr, M. (2018). Rural-urban difference in workplace supports and impacts for employed caregivers. *The Journal of Rural Health*. doi:10.1111/jrh.12309

Henning-Smith, C., Moscovice, I., & Kozhimannil, K. (2019). Differences in social isolation and its relationship to health by rurality. *The Journal of Rural Health*. doi:10.1111/jrh.12344

Henning-Smith, C., Prasad, S., Casey, M., Kozhimannil, K., & Moscovice, I. (2017). Rural-urban differences in Medicare quality scores persist after adjusting for sociodemographic and environmental characteristics. *The Journal of Rural Health*. doi:10.1111/jrh.12261

Holt-Lunstad, J., Smith, T. B., Baker, M., Harris, T., & Stephenson, D. (2015). Loneliness and social isolation as risk factors for mortality. *Perspectives on Psychological Science*, *10*(2), 227–237. doi:10.1177/1745691614568352

James, C. V., Moonesinghe, R., Wilson-Frederick, S. M., Hall, J. E., Penman-Aguilar, A., & Bouye, K. (2017). Racial and ethnic health disparities among rural adults—United States, 2012–2015. *MMWR: Surveillance Summaries*, *66*.

James, W., & Cossman, J. S. (2017). Long-term trends in Black and White mortality in the rural United States: Evidence of a race-specific rural mortality penalty. *The Journal of Rural Health: Official Journal of the American Rural Health Association and the National Rural Health Care Association*, *33*(1), 21–31. doi:10.1111/jrh.12181

Kozhimannil, K. B., & Henning-Smith, C. (2017). Racism and health in rural America. *Journal of Health Care for the Poor and Underserved*. Epub ahead of print. Retrieved from https://preprint.press.jhu.edu/preprints/racism-and-health-rural-america

Larson, S. L., & Hill, S. C. (2005). Rural-urban differences in employment-related health insurance. *The Journal of Rural Health: Official Journal of the American Rural Health Association and the National Rural Health Care Association*, *21*(1), 21–30. Retrieved from www.ncbi.nlm.nih.gov/pubmed/15667006

Lichter, D. T. (2012). Immigration and the new racial diversity in rural America. *Rural Sociology*, 77(1), 3–35. doi:10.1111/j.1549-0831.2012.00070.x

Marmot, M., & Wilkinson, R. (2005). *Social determinants of health*. Oxford: Oxford University Press.

Marmot, M., Allen, J., Bell, R., Bloomer, E., & Goldblatt, P. (2012). WHO European review of social determinants of health and the health divide. *The Lancet*, *380*, 1011–1029. doi:10.1016/S0140-6736(12)61228-8

Mattos, M. K., Burke, L. E., Baernholdt, M., Hu, L., Nilsen, M. L., & Lingler, J. H. (2019). Perceived social determinants of health among older, rural-dwelling adults with early-stage cognitive impairment. *Dementia*, *18*(3), 920–935. doi:10.1177/1471301217694250

Morton, L. W., & Blanchard, T. C. (2007). Starved for access: Life in rural America's food deserts. *Rural Realities*, *1*(4).

The National Institute for Health Care Management Foundation. (2019). *NIHCM—addressing social determinants of health can improve community health & reduce costs*. Retrieved from www.nihcm.org/categories/sdoh-2019-infographic

Pooler, J., & Srinivasan, M. (2018). *Social determinants of health and the aging population*. Retrieved from www.impaqint.com/sites/default/files/issue-briefs/Issue Brief_SDOHandAgingPopulation_0.pdf

Prieger, J. E. (2013). The broadband digital divide and the economic benefits of mobile broadband for rural areas. *Telecommunications Policy*, *37*(6), 483–502. doi:10.1016/j.telpol.2012.11.003

Rural Health Gateway. (2019). *Social determinants of health. A collection of federally funded research projects focused on rural social determinants of health*. Retrieved from www.ruralhealthresearch.org/topics/social-determinants-of-health

Rural Health Information Hub. (2019). *Social determinants of health for rural people*. Retrieved from www.ruralhealthinfo.org/topics/social-determinants-of-health

Sharkey, J. R., Johnson, C. M., & Dean, W. R. (2010). Food access and perceptions of the community and household food environment as correlates of fruit and vegetable intake among rural seniors. *BMC Geriatrics, 10*. doi:10.1186/1471-2318-10-32

Slack, T., & Jensen, L. (2008). Employment hardship among older workers: Does residential and gender inequality extend into older age? *Journals of Gerontology—Series B Psychological Sciences and Social Sciences, 63*(1). doi:10.1093/geronb/63.1.S15

Strosnider, H., Kennedy, C., Monti, M., & Yip, F. (2017). Rural and urban differences in air quality, 2008–2012, and community drinking water quality, 2010–2015 — United States. *MMWR: Surveillance Summaries*. doi:10.15585/mmwr.ss6613a1

U.S. Department of Agriculture Economic Research Service. (2016). *USDA ERS—income*. Retrieved from www.ers.usda.gov/topics/rural-economy-population/rural-poverty-well-being/income/

U.S. Department of Agriculture Economic Research Service. (2017). *Rural employment and unemployment*. Retrieved June 19, 2018, from www.ers.usda.gov/topics/rural-economy-population/employment-education/rural-employment-and-unemployment/

U.S. Global Change Research Program. (2014). *Climate change impacts in the United States*. Washington, DC: U.S. Global Change Research Program. doi:10.7930/J0Z31WJ2

Whitacre, B. E., Wheeler, D., & Landgraf, C. (2017). What can the national broadband map tell us about the health care connectivity gap? *The Journal of Rural Health, 33*(3), 284–289. doi:10.1111/jrh.12177

World Health Organization. (2008). *WHO | key concepts*. Retrieved from www.who.int/social_determinants/thecommission/finalreport/key_concepts/en/

70
SOCIAL WORK

Colleen M. Galambos

Introduction

Across the centuries, the rural population in America has declined drastically from a high point of 94% of all Americans living in rural areas in 1800, to 46 million rural Americans or 14% of U.S. residents (Brown, Walters, Jones, & Akinsola, 2017; USDA Economic Research Service, 2016). This shrinking population of rural Americans affects the number of available health and human service professionals, including social workers available to provide health, aging, and social services.

Professional Social Workers: The Numbers

About 106 million Americans live in an area designated as a Health Professional Shortage Area, including mental health. Seventy-six percent live in rural or partially rural locations (Health Resources and Services Administration, 2017). According to Salsberg et al.'s (2017) study, *Profile of the Social Work Workforce*, there is a large disparity across the country in the number of social workers per capita. States classified as rural and frontier have both fewer social workers and fewer baccalaureate and master's programs in social work, making it more difficult for people to obtain professional social work degrees and credentialing. The emergence of online programs in social work have helped somewhat with the access to education issue.

Credentialing

Credentialing issues such as licensure, continue to remain as challenges when there are requirements for face-to-face supervision and in-person continuing education. These requirements remain barriers to social workers living in rural and frontier areas. Not surprisingly, states that are struggling with credentialing issues have a lower number of social workers practicing at the MSW level (Salsberg et al., 2017). In addition, social workers with specialized training in gerontology make up only 5% of social workers in rural areas (Lin, Lin, & Zhang, 2015). Access to post-degree specialization options such as certificate programs in gerontology, continue to remain a barrier to pursuing continuing education programs in gerontology (Monroe, 2015).

Geriatric Workforce Shortages

To add to the lack of social workers in rural areas, the U.S. is experiencing shortages of qualified geriatric health-care providers, including social workers (IOM, 2008; Lin, Lin, & Zhang, 2015; SAMSA, 2019). Given these trends, coupled with the fact that social workers in rural areas are more likely to work with a high percentage of adults over the age of 75 (NASW, Center for Workforce Studies, 2006), rural regions are particularly hard hit by these shortages. In fact, agencies in rural areas are more likely to have trouble filling position vacancies, more likely to outsource social work functions, and more likely to report the hiring of non-social workers than those in metropolitan areas (Brown, Walters, Jones, & Omotola, 2017; NASW, Center for Workforce Studies, 2006).

Only 3% of the social workers in the NASW Workforce Study (2006) practiced in small towns and rural areas. Practice challenges for rural social workers with a gerontology focus include limited access to community resources, medicines, and mental health care (NASW, Center for Workforce Studies, 2006). In a 2017 study, these challenges are reported as concerns across rural social work specializations, with 67% of participants reporting dissatisfaction with community resources, particularly in the areas of medication resources, medical care, and mental health (Talebreza-May, Jensen, & Shay, 2017).

Agency and Practice: The Landscape

Burnout

In addition to recruitment issues, rural social work clinicians are more likely to experience burnout and social workers in smaller communities leave agencies after shorter stays, which creates turnover issues (Brown et al., 2017). Social workers with connections to rural environments, with personal values that align with rural-life culture and those who want to work in rural environments are more likely to have longer tenure at their agencies (Brown et al., 2017).

Burnout and turnover can be mitigated by providing training opportunities, supervisory support, and peer networking opportunities and by creating a culture of positivity that values employee contributions and recognizes day-to-day challenges (Blue, Kutzler, & Macron-Fuller, 2014; Brown et al., 2017; Talebreza-May, Jensen, & Shay, 2017).

Continuing Education

Rural mental health practitioners report in-person workshops as the most frequent method of accessing continuing education and are pleased with the quality of the workshops they have taken (Talebreza-May et al., 2017). However, the major barriers to accessing continuing education events were reported as financial cost, distance to the event, and professional workload conflicts (Talebreza-May et al., 2017). It is important to note that one continuing education area in short supply in rural areas is training to supervise for licensure (Talebreza-May et al., 2017), and the shortage of these training courses may be a factor in the lack of social work supervisors in rural areas.

Supervision

Supervisory support is a strong factor in mitigating burnout and in the retention of rural social workers (Brown et al., 2017). The importance of supportive and regularly scheduled supervision provides an important professional connection in rural areas that helps gerontological social workers receive the guidance they require to perform their job. Open-door policies allow supervisees access to supervisory support as does the use of technology such as video chats, telephone calls, and video conferencing so that workers may access support when the need arises (Blue et al., 2014).

Agency Environment

A variety of publications recognize the importance of positive work environments for promoting the retention of rural social workers. Organizations that engage in ongoing activities that recognize employee contributions and their value are more likely to retain gerontological social workers (Brown et al., 2017). Rural social workers identified the importance of working in environments that are family friendly, flexible, and attuned to personal needs as some of the benefits of working in rural agencies (Brown et al., 2017; Mackie & Lips, 2010).

Networking

Peer networking opportunities is one method to help mitigate isolation and burn out reported by rural gerontological social workers. In one study of the strengths and needs of rural social workers, 98% of participants reported that peer support was important to them. However, 65% rated dissatisfaction with professional networking opportunities in rural areas, and 60% of workers believed that they did not have the same opportunities for peer support as their urban colleagues Talebreza-May et al., 2017). The use of online chat rooms and professional listserv resources such as NASW's All Member Forum (www.socialworkers.org/) and the National Rural Social Work Caucus (www.ruralsocialwork.org/) are resources that rural gerontological social workers can access from a distance.

Roles and Tasks for Geriatric Social Workers

Generalist Practice

The rural landscape for qualified social work professionals relies on generalist practitioners, and this is true for social workers practicing with rural older adults (Pope, Lee, & Loeffler, 2015). Social workers tend to practice as generalists (BSW) and advance generalists (MSW) because of the variety of needs of less populated areas, including complex client and family problems, environmental challenges, and lack of resources (Moore et al., 2016; Waldrop & Kirkendall, 2010).

Roles and Tasks

Rural gerontological social workers are often members of interdisciplinary teams, and the development of strong relationships and boundary setting is critical for effective service provision. The use of collaborative models can enhance service delivery for older adults in rural areas. Examples of these collaborative models include interprofessional teamwork in which members of the team work individually with each other and interprofessional team-based care in which small workgroups are assigned to certain clients (Monroe, 2015).

Rural practicing social workers engage in many roles including counselor, community collaborator, advocate, and educator (Moore et al., 2016). A strength of working in smaller communities is that social workers have opportunities to build community relationships and become leaders who advocate and create services for older adults according to their community needs (Hash, Damron-Rodriguez, & Thurman, 2015).

Workforce studies confirm the depth and breadth of tasks of rurally based gerontological social workers. According to a comprehensive study of licensed social workers that specifically examined social work services for older adults, rural social workers reported they frequently engaged in the following activities with older adults:

1. Communicating with families
2. Accessing community resources
3. Leveraging agency resources
4. Acting as advocates
5. Participating in interdisciplinary activities (NASW, 2006, p. 11).

Finally, gerontological social workers often assume outreach and case management functions. These functions require the rural social worker to be able to work at multiple practice levels with individuals, groups, organizations, and communities (Hash e al., 2015).

Conclusion

In summary, there are many challenges confronted by rural gerontological social workers, including shortages of professionally trained staff. However, these challenges can be mitigated by strong organizational and professional support and access to online resources. Given the many roles and functions assumed by rural gerontological social workers, they have heightened opportunities to become an integral and influential part of small towns and rural communities.

References

Blue, E. T., Kutzler, A. M., & Macron-Fuller, S. (2014). Ethical guidelines for social work supervisors in rural settings. *Contemporary Rural Social Work Journal, 6*(1), Article 2. Retrieved August 8, 2019, from https://digitalcommons.murraystate.edu/crsw/vol6/iss1/2

Brown, A. R., Walters, J., Jones, A., & Omotola, A. (2017). Rural social work: Recruitment, job satisfaction, burnout, and turnover. *Contemporary Rural Social Work Journal, 9*(1), Article 12. Retrieved August 8, 2019, from https://digitalcommons.murraystate.edu/crsw/vol9/iss1/12

Hash, K. M., Damron-Rodriguez, J. A., & Thurman, H. (2015). The role of the human service provider. In K. M. Hash, E. T. Jurkowski, & J. A. Krout (Eds.), *Aging in rural places: Programs, policies, and professional practice* (pp. 235–258). New York: Springer.

Health Resources and Services Administration (HRSA). (2017). *Designated health professional shortage area statistics*. Retrieved August 16, 2019, from https://datawarehouse.hrsa.gov/tools/hdwreports/Reports.aspx

Institute of Medicine. (2008). *Retooling for an aging America: Building the health care workforce committee on the future health care workforce for older Americans*. Washington, DC: The National Academies Press.

Lin, V. W., Lin, J., & Zhang, X. (2015). U.S. social worker workforce report card: Forecasting national shortages. *Social Work, 61*(1), 7–15. doi:10.1093/sw/swv047

Mackie, P. F. E., & Lips, R. A. (2010). Is there really a problem with hiring rural social service staff? An exploratory study among social service supervisors in rural Minnesota. *Families in Society: The Journal of Contemporary Social Services, 91*(4), 433–439. doi:10.1606/1044-3894.4035

Monroe, J. E. (2015). Interdisciplinary teams caring for rural older adults. In K. M. Hash, E. T. Jurkowski, & J. A. Krout (Eds.), *Aging in rural places: Programs, policies, and professional practice* (pp. 189–209). New York: Springer.

Moore, W. R., Pearson, F., Rife, J. C., Poole, K. J., Moore, L. S., & Reaves, A. M. (2016). Reinventing social work education and service delivery in rural areas: An interdisciplinary model for service vulnerable populations. *Contemporary Rural Social Work Journal, 8*(2), Article 5. Retrieved August 8, 2019, from https://digitalcommons.murraystateedu/crsw/vol18/iss2/5

National Association of Social Workers Center for Workforce Studies. (2006). *Assuring the sufficiency of a frontline workforce: A national study of licensed social workers, special report: Social work services for older adults.* Washington, DC: National Association of Social Workers. Retrieved July 18, 2019, from www.socialworkers.org/LinkClick.aspx?fileticket=RIc1kLerL3c%3D&portalid=0

Pope, N. D., Lee, J., & Loeffler, D. N. (2015). Future care planning practices of aging services professionals in rural Appalachia. *Contemporary Rural Social Work Journal*, 7(2), Article 7. Retrieved August 8, 2019, from https://digitalcommons.murraystate.edu/crsw/vol7/iss2/7

Salsberg, E., Quigley, L., Mehfoud, N., Acquaviva, K., Wyche, K., & Sliwa, S. (2017). *Profiles of the social work workforce.* Washington, DC: The George Washington University Health Workforce Institute. Retrieved July 16, 2019, from www.cswe.org/Centers-Initiatives/Initiatives/National-Workforce-Initiative/SW-Workforce-Book-FINAL-11-08-2017.aspx

USDA Economic Research Service. (2016). *State fact sheet: United States summary.* Retrieved August 16, 2019, from https://data.ers.usda.gov/reports.aspx?ID=17854

SAMSA. (2019). *Older adults living with serious mental illness: The state of the behavioral health workforce.* Retrieved August 24, 2019, from https://store.samhsa.gov/system/files/new_older_adults_living_with_serious_mental_illness_final.pdf

Talebreza-May, J. W., Jensen, R., & Shay, N. (2017). An assessment of the strengths and needs of rural social workers in the Northwestern United States. *Contemporary Rural Social Work Journal*, *9*(1), Article 1. Retrieved August 8, 2019, from https://digitalcommons.murraystate.edu/crsw/vol9/iss1/1

Waldrop, D., & Kirkendall, A. M. (2010). Rural–urban differences in end-of-life care: Implications for practice. *Social Work in Health Care*, *49*(3), 263–289. doi:10.1080/00981380903364742

71
STRATEGIC PLANNING

Sally Thomas Buck and Debra A. Laine

Introduction

Strategic planning is critical to successfully move a rural organization toward a vision. It also ensures that needs are prioritized and goals are outlined with specific and appropriate resources in communities. Strategic planning is important for cross-sector organizations with different initiatives to establish common goals for maximizing aging services. A strategic plan established every three years for improvement of aging services allows the coordination of different organizational structures and processes in a community. Without collaborative planning, organizations may fail to link strategic objectives in separate projects with common measures for monitoring progress overtime. Peter Senge views organizations as dynamic systems in a state of continuous adaptation and improvement (Senge, 1990). The ongoing operations of rural organizations, when guided by strategic objectives, constantly adjust to realize the achievements identified by the vision. In other words, strategic planning is effective when it has a destination to aim for, which is the shared vision of the collaborative's achievements and aspirations in rural aging. Moreover, regular strategic planning considers the rapid changes in technology and health care, in terms of both delivery and payment, that may affect strategic objectives.

Trends

The Institute for Healthcare Improvement (IHI) vision for the Triple Aim has fundamentally changed the health-care system and supports the evolution to population health. It focuses on value and quality. Specifically, the approach optimizes health system performance by improving the patient experience of care, including quality and satisfaction; improving the health of populations; and reducing the per capita cost of health care (Institute for Healthcare Improvement, 2004). "The concept of the Triple Aim is now widely used because of the adoption of the Triple Aim as part of the national strategy for U.S. health care" (Whittington, Nolan, Lewis, & Torres, 2015, p. 1). In March 2019, the Department of Health and Human Services (HHS) Secretary Alex M. Azar II announced, "*There is no turning back to an unsustainable system that pays for procedures rather than value. In fact, the only option is to charge forward—for HHS to take bolder action, and for providers and payers to join with us*" (DHHS, 2019). Since then, the Centers for Medicare and Medicaid Services (CMS) have aggressively developed new payment methods that incentivize providers to keep their patient populations healthy while phasing out volume-based, fee-for-service payment models. As of January 2019, there were 518 public accountable care organizations (ACOs) across the United States, with 435 critical access hospitals participating in rural areas (CMS, 2019). These initiatives are focused on serving older adults through Medicare coverage. Through the Centers for Medicare and Medicaid Innovation (CMMI), HHS continues to develop and test innovative health-care payment and delivery models such as ACO and other models that improve quality and drive value within the health-care system (CMS Innovation Center, 2019). These initiatives are transforming health-care delivery by creating incentives for coordinated care, especially Medicare-covered beneficiaries. Successful care coordination requires integration of payment, communication, and care within communities and across organizations providing aging services, including health care, social services, transportation, housing, and public health.

Preparation for Strategic Planning

Before beginning strategic planning, rural-based organizations should ask themselves "Are there other organizations or collaborations that have an interest or focus on aging?" If so, look for other planning efforts in your community that you could join or could enhance your efforts. Some places to look may be:

- Public Health—most states require local public health organizations to do planning. This planning often informs state planning efforts. Contacting the Aging Services Department in your county(s) Public Health department is a start, as they are perfect partners in your planning efforts.
- Area Agency on Aging (AAA)—Older Americans Act funding is administered by AAAs in each state. Some states have one AAA and others have multiple AAAs. Look for a state plan on aging online to see if there are any initiatives that are congruent with your community's needs. Each state is required to submit an annual report to the Administration on Aging and may use local planning efforts to inform the annual report and state plan. The local AAA is an ideal partner in planning.
- Community Health Needs Assessment (CHNA)—every three years, all nonprofit 501(c)(3) hospitals in the U.S. are required by the Internal Revenue Service to complete a CHNA. This is a systematic process involving the community to identify, analyze and prioritize, and address community health needs. CHNAs are becoming a driver of community collaborations and a springboard to launch health improvement initiatives. By contacting your local nonprofit hospital, you can learn where they are in the three-year process and perhaps become part of the planning effort.
- Community Collaborations—spend time thinking about formal and informal collaborations in your community. Develop a list of ones that focus on the aging demographic and approach those to see if there are any efforts toward doing formal planning. Often forgotten, the aging demographic is often a point of focus for faith communities. These potential community collaborators would be ideal partners in your planning efforts.

Strategic Planning Considerations

What Is the Strategic Planning Cycle?

The dynamic and iterative environment of planning, communicating, operationalizing, and adapting describes a strategic planning cycle. Business management writers and thinkers of the

Figure 71.1 Strategic planning cycle

1980s studied organizations to figure out why some succeed while others did not (Kaplan & Norton, 2004). They discovered that successful organizations approached planning holistically. As a result, they devised a planning methodology called the Balanced Scorecard. One of the key aspects of the Balanced Scorecard planning methodology is the strategic planning cycle: Analyze & Plan, Document & Communicate, Execute the Plan, and Monitor & Adapt.

The first step is the Analyze & Plan phase where strategic objectives are identified and agreed upon. Subsequent steps include sharing the strategic objectives with all collaborating partners; identifying the key initiatives that set strategies into motion; executing work plans; monitoring progress quarterly; and adjusting annually (which starts the cycle over again).

Each time through the strategic planning cycle, the collaboration or organization is not at the same place as it was in the previous cycle. If one pictures a Slinky®, it is a circle, but the top of the circle is at two different points. As a collaboration goes through the strategic planning cycle, it learns, grows, makes changes, and leaves the cycle at a new place in terms of experience, capacity, and maturity. Engaging the strategic planning cycle allows the rural collaboration to adapt to the ever-changing environment and stay on course to achieve the shared vision and the desired future of the collaboration.

Who Should Be at the Table?

During this time of rapid change within the health-care landscape and the movement toward population health, it is critical to bring rural stakeholders together from both health-care-based organizations, governmental organizations, and community-based organizations. Just as important to the planning process is to bring representatives from the targeted rural demographic into planning and their potential caregivers.

The list of stakeholders invited to participate in the strategic planning process varies depending on the community's unique characteristics. Carefully consider the stakeholders around aging who can bring information and understanding of the community and who can help strategically consider changes to move from the current reality toward the vision.

Potential Participants in a Given Rural Town, County, or Region

- County public health and aging services
- Faith community representatives
- Area Agencies on Aging
- Community organizations serving older adults
- Local hospitals, clinics, and community health centers
- Behavioral health organizations
- Senior center representatives
- Public schools
- Older adults from the community
- Caregivers/children of older adults
- Local media representatives
- Regional health-care collaborations.

Which Strategic Planning Framework Should We Use?

There are different approaches or frameworks for strategic planning. Each has its strengths and best applications. Each person, or collaboration, may have their preferred approach. The framework selection is based on the preference of the collaboration leadership. In rural communities, the Traditional Strategic Planning framework tends to fit the rural collaborative environment better. Language used here is based on the Traditional Strategic Planning framework as outlined in the Project Strategic Plan Guide and Project Evaluation Plan Guide (Rural Health Innovations, 2019a, 2019b). Details for different planning frameworks (Balanced Scorecard, logic model, and MAPP) can be found in the resources section. It does not matter which framework chosen, just remain consistent throughout your work.

Important Strategic Planning Elements

Vision Development or Check In

When developing an effective strategic plan, commitment to a shared vision is the first critical step. This happens before beginning the Analyze & Plan phase of the strategic planning cycle. A vision identifies the "achievements" of the rural community's aspirations and therefore acts as a beacon for the collaboration.

Environmental Scan and Analysis

This step is undertaken when there is a pause to review significant characteristics of the collaboration's internal and external environment in terms of key barriers and strengths. This is the first step in the Analyze & Plan phase of the strategic planning cycle. It is important within this phase of the strategic planning cycle to take the time to study the rural environment in which your group is functioning. It is here that you can identify the aspects in your community that will assist you in reaching the vision of the group and those issues that are the blocks to achieving the shared vision. Ask "why" at least three times and get as deep as possible in identifying the cause of the blocks, the better the chance that programming can make a difference; this is called a deep root analysis.

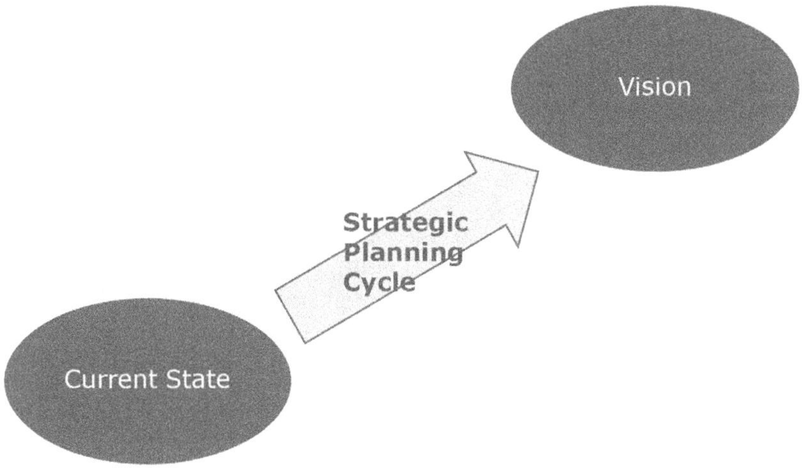

Figure 71.2 Shared vision

Strategic Directions/Objectives

This is a process of identifying the two-to-three-year strategic objectives that will move the rural community collaboration toward its goals. Within the Baldrige Performance Excellence Framework, strategies are the aims or responses that your organization articulates to address major changes or improvement, competitiveness or social issues, and service advantages (NIST, 2019). This is the second step in the Analyze & Plan phase of the strategic planning cycle. A best practice of strategic planning is utilizing the environmental scan and analysis in your community to prepare the planning participants for strategic thinking. A participative process is key to building consensus among stakeholders and identifying meaningful strategic objectives. This is significant for rural collaborations because it furthers relationships and builds trust and understanding amongst partners.

Strategic objectives focus on achieving the group's vision while addressing the identified blocks and taking advantage of the identified strengths. Typically, strategic objectives look out two-to-three years toward the vision. It is helpful for the strategies to be written following the SMART acronym: Specific, Measurable, Attainable, Realistic, and Timely. There are many approaches to identifying and prioritizing strategic objectives.

Alignment

Alignment is the final process in the Analyze & Plan phase of the strategic planning cycle. This key step is checking each of the strategic objectives back to the group's vision. Take time to ask the group, "Does this objective help us accomplish this vision (refer to vision determined at beginning of process)?" There are times when a group lands on good ideas, but these ideas do not help accomplish the vision.

Key Initiatives

Key initiatives refer to significant actions or workgroups needed to develop, implement, support, and move the strategic objectives forward. These are initiatives that take six to 18 months to implement and are key to bringing the objectives to life. This is part of the operationalization phase of the strategic planning cycle. These initiatives are used to develop the work plan for your community. There are several different ways of doing this within the framework that has been adopted.

Measurement

A step that should not be overlooked is to ask, "What does success look like?" for each of the objectives. This step increases the likelihood of realizing success in terms of the group's efforts. Measurement is essential in the Monitor & Adapt phase of the strategic planning cycle. By regularly looking at measures, adjustments can be made in the initiatives if necessary, to ensure success. An added value of measuring your progress is that it will strengthen and sustain the efforts of the group as they see their work moving them closer to realizing their stated vision.

Conclusion

As aging initiatives move forward in your rural community, ideally you will continuously proceed through multiple iterations of the strategic planning cycle. It is important to conduct thorough annual reviews of your community's efforts and outcomes and implement any necessary adjustments. The full planning process is best completed at least every three years with an environmental scan and facilitated discussion to account for changes in funding, policy, demographics, technology, and health issues that impact your community. Always make sure the right stakeholders are included in the process using the vision as the beacon for strategic planning.

Strategic Planning Resources

Brown, K., Campion, D., & Stenger, R. (2001, March). *Strategic planning for rural health networks*. Academy for Health Services Research and Health Policy. Retrieved from www.ruralcenter.org/resource-library/report-strategic-planning-for-rural-health-networks

National Association of County and City Health Officials. (2019). *Mobilizing for action through planning and partnerships (MAPP)*. Retrieved from www.naccho.org/programs/public-health-infrastructure/performance-improvement/community-health-assessment/mapp

The National Rural Health Resource Center. (2019). *Strategic planning; hospital best practices and recommended strategies*. Retrieved from www.ruralcenter.org/srht/rural-hospital-toolkit/strategic-planning

New Frontiers for Funding. (2019). *An introduction to grantmaking in rural aging*. Retrieved from www.giaging.org/documents/170415_GIA_Rural_Aging_Primer_INTERACTIVE.pdf

Rural Health Information Hub (2019). *Strategic planning*. Retrieved from www.ruralhealthinfo.org/toolkits/networks/4/planning/strategic

Rural Health Innovations (2019). *Behind the scenes with strategic planning, part 1 and part 2*. Retrieved from www.ruralcenter.org/rhi/network-ta/development/webinars/behind-the-scenes-with-strategic-planning-part-1www.ruralcenter.org/rhi/network-ta/development/webinars/behind-the-scenes-with-strategic-planning-part-2

University of Wisconsin–Madison Extension. (2019). *Logic models*. Retrieved from https://fyi.extension.wisc.edu/programdevelopment/logic-models/

References

CMS. (2019). *Medicare shared savings program fast facts*. Retrieved from www.cms.gov/Medicare/Medicare-Fee-for-Service-Payment/sharedsavingsprogram/Downloads/ssp-2019-fast-facts.pdf

CMS Innovation Center (CMMI). (2019). *Innovation models*. Retrieved from https://innovation.cms.gov/initiatives/#views=models

Institute for Healthcare Improvement. (2004). *The IHI triple aim initiative*. Retrieved from www.ihi.org/Engage/Initiatives/TripleAim/Pages/default.aspx

Kaplan, R., & Norton, D. (2004) *Strategy maps; converting intangible assets into tangible outcomes*. Cambridge: Harvard Business School Press.

National Institute of Standards and Technology. (2019). *Baldrige performance excellence program*. Retrieved from www.nist.gov/baldrige

Rural Health Innovations. (2019a). *Project strategic plan guide*. Retrieved from www.ruralcenter.org/sites/default/files/Strategic%20Planning%20GUIDE.pdf

Rural Health Innovations. (2019b). *Project evaluation plan guide*. Retrieved from www.ruralcenter.org/sites/default/files/Project%20Evaluation%20Plan%20Guide.pdf

Senge, P. M. (1990). *The fifth discipline: The art and practice of the learning organization*. New York: Doubleday, Currency.

U.S. Department of Health and Human Services. (2019). *Remarks on value-based transformation to the Federation of American Hospitals*. Retrieved from www.hhs.gov/about/leadership/secretary/speeches/2018-speeches/remarks-on-value-based-transformation-to-the-federation-of-american-hospitals.html

Whittington, J. W., Nolan, K., Lewis, N., & Torres, T. (2015). Pursuing the triple aim: The first seven years. *Milbank Quarterly*, *93*(2), 263–300.

72
TECHNOLOGY

Danielle M. Louder

Technology and Older Adults

According to U.S. Census Bureau projections, 22% of Americans will be aged 65 and older by 2050 (U.S. Census Bureau, 2016), and data from the AARP tells us that a vast majority of them (87%) want to age-in-place (Harrell, Lynott, & Guzman, 2014). While a large portion of older adults have become more digitally connected over the past two decades, one-third of those over age 65 report never having used the internet, and half don't have access to broadband at home (Anderson & Perrin, 2017), rather relying on access at public locations, such as libraries, senior centers, coffee shops, etc. Of course, rural residents are less likely than their urban and suburban counterparts to have access to the internet, and coupled with fewer local resources, like public libraries and transportation, the risks for social and health-care isolation are significantly greater.

A 2018 study across multiple rural states found a constellation of factors made it significantly more likely for older adults to use technology, including being married, younger age, fewer depressive symptoms, better self-rated health, and better quality social support (O'Connor, Fuller, & Cortez, 2018). That same study showed that participants who used technology logged just over six hours per week on average, and most (61%) felt it increased their sense of social support (O'Connor et al., 2018). While technology in itself is not the solution to social isolation and successful aging-in-place, it can be a viable tool in promoting independence, as well as helping connect older adults to family and friends, health-care services, and other resources, particularly for those living in rural areas.

While we've seen a 55% increase in the number of older adults using the internet since 2000 (Anderson et al., 2017), a May 2019 Tech Crunch (Fields, 2019) article explains how older adults are being left out of the digital world, with a strong push for investment in accessible devices, connectivity, and technology training to help address the digital divide. That said, some claim that age is not a factor; rather many *choose* not to use technology for a variety of reasons, including lack of interest, concerns with internet security, or simply "unplugging" after retirement.

Technology-Related Trends and Developments

Technology is now a central focus for every industry, and the constant evolution of new devices and applications can be overwhelming to end users of any age, but particularly for those who were born long before computers, smart phones, Wi-Fi, and artificial intelligence became part of daily life. A majority of those aged 65+ report needing some level of assistance with setting up and using new devices (Anderson et al., 2017), and while some technology is developed with older adult needs in mind, or with input from older adult end users, most is not. With the number of older adults steadily on the rise across the U.S., and significant growth in their use of technology, there is an expanding market for solutions geared toward older adults, including, but not limited to, devices, apps, and more. These tools can be particularly valuable for older adults and caregivers in rural areas, as they can help combat social isolation (e.g., video calls, gaming, social media, etc.), provide access to needed services such as health-care and financial management, and bring a world of information to individuals in communities of all sizes.

Many of the projected technology trends for 2020 and beyond are geared more toward industry versus individuals, such as machine learning, robotic process automation, edge computing, and blockchain, and therefore won't be discussed here. That said, experts anticipate further rapid developments in artificial intelligence, virtual reality, the Internet of things (IoT), and cybersecurity, which will continue to make significant impacts on both industry and individuals in the immediate future.

The next section discusses key technology trends and use cases as related to older adults. We will not discuss specific vendors, products, or applications. Rather, it is recommended that organizations and end users carefully research options that are developed for, and/or in collaboration with, older adults. The *National Consortium of Telehealth Resource Centers*, funded through the U.S. Health Resources and Services Administration (HRSA), is an unbiased resource in helping to assess viable technology solutions and collectively covers all 50 states, the Pacific Basin Territories, and the U.S. Virgin Islands.

Artificial Intelligence

With the vast amounts of digital data now available, it is no surprise that artificial intelligence (AI), which leverages those data to make intelligent predictions across a variety of use cases, has continued to explode—think navigation apps, streaming services, smart home devices, personal voice assistants, and much more. These resources can benefit older adults in a number of ways. For instance, built on top of popular smart-speaker technology, personalized voice technology can be used with artificial intelligence to proactively assist older adults and caregivers with managing day-to-day schedules, including medications, appointments, activities, entertainment, and education (e.g., music and audio books), with reminders to support daily routines and help older adults thrive as they age-in-place. Voice technology also has clear benefits for older adults with issues related to mobility, dexterity, and sight, allowing them to maintain independent living—for instance, allowing them to control lights, temperature, and other household functions. AI is also being integrated into wearables commonly used by older adults, such as hearing aids. AI enables the device to interface with smartphones and other computers, and to be "trained" according to individual preferences, which can make the initial adjustment to a new hearing aid a much less frustrating experience than with previous models (Smelser, 2020).

Virtual and Augmented Reality

Virtual and augmented reality have been primarily used for gaming in the past, which has continued to expand rapidly; however, additional use cases are evolving, which have specific relevance for older adults. Either used to immerse a user in a virtual environment (virtual reality—VR) or enhance the existing environment (augmented reality—AR), these technologies are becoming more mainstream, being used for training and education, including high-tech simulations of complex surgeries, entertainment (both within the home and at locations such as libraries), marketing, rehabilitation after an injury, including post stroke, and for post-traumatic stress disorder (PTSD). Some health systems are using VR to stream a virtual rendition of an actual health-care provider into patients' homes, providing guidance similar to what they would receive in the provider's office (Haskins, 2016).

Internet of Things

The Internet of Things (IoT) comprises the broad variety of "things" that are now being designed with Wi-Fi connectivity and that can therefore be connected to the internet, and to each other. As with artificial intelligence, there is an explosion of use cases for IoT within industry, as well as incredible growth for day-to-day use among consumers. With up to 50 billion devices expected to be part of the IoT in 2020, including phones, appliances, cars, medical equipment, wearable sensors, and many others, the ever-expanding ability of devices to "talk" with each other means that IoT can help people of all ages streamline daily activities, lower household expenses (and energy usage), improve health care, help avoid traffic, and much more. In conjunction with artificial intelligence, IoT has the potential to help older adults remain independent longer and stay more connected with the world around them, given the resources needed to access it. Again, these trends hold significant promise for extending capacity of rural residents to age-in-place. However, more needs to be done to create equitable connectivity in rural areas, in order for the resources to be effectively leveraged.

Cybersecurity

Given the rapid expansion of technology and its potential uses across the globe, cybersecurity is also constantly evolving to keep up with emerging threats. As hackers become more adept at identifying ways to work around even the toughest security protocols, technologies must be adapted to strengthen protections. Similarly, industry and consumers, including older adults who are often preyed upon specifically, must be vigilant in choosing reputable products, whether devices, applications, or other technology-related products, and using best practice safeguards, such as implementing password protections and two-factor authentication, checking authenticity of communications before clicking on links, using spam filters, exercising care in sharing information publicly (e.g., social media), using default firewall settings, logging out of apps and websites, and asking for help when in doubt (Protect Seniors Online, n.d.).

Current and Future Challenges

A number of studies have identified common challenges to increased adoption of technology among older adults living in rural areas, with similar findings across the U.S. and globally. These include inadequate internet access, limited digital literacy, a general lack of trust in technology, and technology solutions that are not developed with older adult needs in mind.

Access to Adequate Internet

Much of today's technology relies on a decent internet connection, including resources focused on social interaction, personal health and wellness, financial management, health-care services, and others. Rural areas across the U.S. continue to struggle with adequate internet access, and for older adults with lower household incomes, this challenge is multiplied, as added expenses for internet service providers and cell phone carriers to reach geographically isolated communities are passed on to a much smaller number of consumers. While there are a number of efforts focused on expanding access for both rural and older adult populations, such as those supported by state and federal agencies, they are typically focused on health-care or distance learning initiatives, and individuals are not eligible to apply. That said, thousands of health-care organizations across the U.S. are leveraging Universal Service funds to subsidize internet service fees and enhanced networks in rural areas, thereby improving access for patients and families, through telehealth, patient portals, education, and more. Nonprofit organizations throughout the country, like the Maine Broadband Coalition, are working with local communities, internet service providers, and cell phone carriers to expand access to high quality, affordable internet to better leverage technology in addressing key issues in rural and underserved areas, such as economic development, community health, and aging-in-place. While these programs are certainly making an impact, further investments must be made, combining financial support from public and private, state, federal, and local sources to build an infrastructure that is accessible to older individuals within their homes and/or easily accessible locations within rural areas.

Digital Literacy

There is wide diversity among today's older adults in both internet interest and savvy, with those aged 65 to 69 twice as likely to be online versus those aged 80+ (Anderson et al., 2017). Skill levels range from nonusers, to the highly cultivated, with a number of factors involved, such as time needed to learn, and level of difficulty. The lack of skills and/or confidence to use the internet among older adults, or the "grey" divide, remains a major factor in lower rates of technology adoption, particularly in rural areas. That said, the biggest problem is often confidence versus ability, and providing access to devices and training can bridge the gap. Efforts with older adults have shown the benefits of learning digital skills, including increased social engagement, access to health resources and services, reduced costs associated with travel, and others, but also the importance of understanding digital safety, and how to limit online risk. Older adults who are digitally connected may experience similar issues as younger social media users, including depression, issues with self-image, fear of missing out (FOMO), etc. Alongside technology skills, digital literacy training should cover the potential negative effects of social media and how to avoid them. There are a number of programs and volunteers across the country to assist older adults looking to learn or expand their digital skills. For example, the National Digital Equity Center, which is focused on advancing digital equity and inclusion for all populations, provides digital literacy classes at no cost and includes resources geared specifically toward older adults and aging-in-place. Similarly, programs like Tech Allies in San Francisco provide free devices and in-home training for older adults. Many states and cities are developing digital equity plans to define strategies and approaches to improving access to the internet, promoting digital literacy, and achieving sustainable impacts for residents of all ages.

Trust in Technology (or Lack Thereof)

While it has been noted that adoption rates in technology use among older adults have increased significantly in the past two decades, trust—or lack thereof—remains a core issue for some. Most concerns are related to maintaining privacy of health-care, financial, or other personal data, or a general lack of trust in the technology's ability to provide a particular service, or in the reliability of the information. While it's important that older adults have a healthy sense of cynicism when looking to purchase and use technology that will meet their needs in a safe, effective way, there are opportunities to raise awareness of the significant benefits technology holds in terms of supporting an individual's ability to age-in-place.

Trust is particularly important, from both safety and privacy perspectives, when it comes to use of assistive technology, such as traditional solutions that enable those with motor impairments to use computers, and now intelligent assistive technologies, including service robots, home automation, wearable sensors, IoT solutions, and more (McMurray et al., 2017). While broader than a trust issue, per se, stigma associated with assistive technologies can also be a barrier, although it has become less so as these solutions have become more mainstream and less obtrusive.

Elder Appropriate Solutions

As mentioned earlier, most technology solutions are developed based on the needs and interests of the larger market share, which are younger populations, and are often therefore not appropriate, or relevant for older adults. It's important for technology developers to address factors like age appropriate content and functionality, and other components that are vital for ease of use, such as font styles and colors that are easier for older adults to see, adaptations for vision and/or hearing loss, alternatives to swiping, which can be more difficult for older adults, etc. It's also vital to involve the target audience in development, to ensure that solutions are not designed in isolation from what is important to them and that solutions incorporate routine activities wherever possible. For example, research shows that older adults value face-to-face interaction; therefore efforts like the Allies Program mentioned earlier, which incorporates one-on-one, in-person training on technology for older adults, is more likely to be successful (Proceedings of the 52nd Hawaii International Conference on System Sciences, 2019). Older adults also prefer group efforts and collaboration over competition, so apps designed with that in mind and that incorporate daily activities they are interested in, like swimming and gardening, are more likely to be used long-term.

Generally speaking, older adults have warmed up to technology and see its value through a variety of use cases; however, rural geography can limit that potential for many. Working across sectors to continue to address key challenges, including broadband access and digital literacy, and using opportunities to build solutions that are trustworthy and age appropriate will help ensure that all older adults are able to leverage technology as part of their strategy to age-in-place.

References

Anderson, M., & Perrin, A. (2017, May 17). *Tech adoption climbs among older adults*. Pew Research Center. Retrieved from www.pewresearch.org/internet/2017/05/17/tech-adoption-climbs-among-older-adults/

Fields, J. (2019, May 5). *We are leaving older adults out of the digital world*. Retrieved from https://techcrunch.com/2019/05/05/we-are-leaving-older-adults-out-of-the-digital-world/

Harrell, R., Lynott, J., & Guzman, S. (2014, April). *What is livable? Community preferences of older adults*. AARP Public Policy Institute. Retrieved from www.aarp.org/content/dam/aarp/research/public_policy_institute/liv_com/ 2014/what-is-livable-report-AARP-ppi-liv-com.pdf

Haskins, J. (2016, June 15). *How virtual reality is gaining traction in healthcare*. Retrieved from www.healthline.com/health-news/virtual-reality-gaining-traction-in-healthcare#1

McMurray, J., Strudwick, G., Forchuk, C., Morse, A., Lachance, J., Baskaran, A., . . . Booth, R. (2017, November 2). The importance of trust in the adoption and use of intelligent assistive technology by older adults to support aging in place: Scoping review protocol. *JMIR Research Protocols*, *6*(11), e218. Published online. doi:10.2196/resprot.8772

O'Connor, M., Fuller, H., & Cortez, F. (2018, November 11). Technology use among older adults in rural areas. *Innovation in Aging*, *2*(Suppl 1), 679. Published online. doi:10.1093/geroni/igy023.2528

Proceedings of the 52nd Hawaii International Conference on System Sciences. (2019). *Ensembles of practice: Older adults, technology, and loneliness & social isolation in rural settings*. Retrieved from https://scholarspace.manoa.hawaii.edu/bitstream/10125/59866/0426.pdf

Protect Seniors Online. (n.d.). *10 cybersecurity best practices for older adults*. Retrieved from www.protectseniorsonline.com/resources/cybersecurity-best-practices/

Smelser, D. (2020, February 6). *Hearing aids and artificial intelligence*. Retrieved from www.yourhearinghealth.com/blog/hearing-aids-and-artificial-intelligence/

U.S. Census Bureau. (2016, April 15). *Facts for features: Older Americans month: May 2016*. Retrieved from www.census.gov/newsroom/facts-for-features/2016/cb16-ff08.html

73
TELEHEALTH

Mei Wa Kwong

The Three Telehealth Modalities

Live Video—an interaction that occurs in real time between patient and provider or provider to provider
Store-and-forward—the capture of information that is sent over a secured system and reviewed at a later time by a provider
Remote patient monitoring (RPM)—the constant monitoring of a patient or a patient's condition from a distance.

This chapter was written in 2019, prior to the COVID-19 pandemic. In March 2020, significant steps were taken on the federal and state levels to change, temporarily, telehealth policies to allow the technology to be utilized more fully in response to the pandemic. As of December 2020, some of the temporary policies have been made permanent, though many have not but are still active due to the ongoing public health emergency. If no more permanent changes are enacted, many of the issues outlined in this chapter will still remain. However, as this book is being prepared, it is uncertain what will happen next in the realm of telehealth policy. To get more updated information, please go to the Center for Connected Health Policy, the federally designated national telehealth policy resource center, website cchpca.org.

While older adults have been slower to adopt the use of telehealth to receive their health-care services, attitudes are changing. In a 2019 consumer survey by American Well, a majority of older adults showed a willingness to try telehealth as a means of receiving care (American Well, 2019). The Office for the Advancement of Telehealth (OAT) located in the Federal Office of Rural Health Policy (FORPH) in the Health Resources and Services Administration (HRSA) defines telehealth "as the use of electronic information and telecommunication technologies to support long-distance clinical health care, patient and professional health-related education, public health, and health administration. Technologies include video conferencing, the internet, store-and-forward imaging, streaming media and terrestrial and wireless communications" (Health Resources & Services Administration, 2019).

Telehealth has been around for decades, but it is only recently that adoption of it has accelerated. Part of this reason is that the technology is at a place where it can be used more effectively and cost efficiently, making it more widely available. There is a particular interest in using telehealth to address the health-care needs of rural communities as they struggle with access to needed health-care services.

Older Adults in Rural America and Access

Approximately 25% of over 65-year-old Americans live in rural communities (Skoufalos, Clarke, Ellis, Shepard, & Rula, 2017). These individuals tend to face higher rates of chronic disease and disability, lower life expectancy, and other health challenges that their urban counterparts do not (Skoufalos et al., 2017). In a 2016 survey by the Association of American Medical Colleges, rural communities were seven times as likely as those in urban areas and three times as likely as suburbanites to report they were never able to get the health care they needed (Orlawski & Dill, 2019). This is partly because of a lack of access to health-care providers in rural regions. Rural communities average 39.8 physicians per 100,000 people compared to 53.3 physicians per 100,000 in urban areas (Hing, 2014). If the provider is not in rural communities, the population must go to the provider. However, extended travel for an aging population may not be the best alternative. To address the issue, telehealth is being looked to more often as a solution.

Telehealth Utilization

The concept of using technology to provide care from a distance is not new. Even the use of a telegraph for physicians to communicate with each other is a form of telehealth. However, the rapid advances in technology today allow physicians to be able to communicate more effectively and efficiently not only with each other but directly with patients. The Centers for Disease Control and Prevention (CDC) notes that telehealth could be an effective way to address a multitude of health issues from mental to chronic conditions to acute episodes (Centers for Disease Control and Prevention, 2019). For example, a psychiatrist can conduct a session via live video while the patient is in the comfort of his or her own home allowing those with mobility issues or other conditions that make it difficult for them to travel a means of obtaining services. A wound care specialist can receive a photo of a wound caused by prolonged bed confinement and provide a diagnosis and course of treatment using store-and-forward technology without direct contact with the patient. With the use of RPM, older adults who suffer from multiple chronic conditions such as hypertension and diabetes can have their blood pressure and sugar levels monitored remotely by a health-care professional who can intervene when necessary to avoid a trip to the doctor, or worse, the emergency room. All this can and is being done today via telehealth and is particularly helpful in rural communities with access issues.

Use of telehealth has risen sharply in the last few years. From 2016 to 2017, usage of telehealth grew by 53% nationally but rural growth was only 29% compared to 55% for urban growth (Fair Health, 2019). Telehealth claims with insurance companies saw those in rural areas increase in 2012 to 2017 by 482% compared to 1,289% in urban regions (Fair Health, 2019). The largest group of patients utilizing telehealth in 2017 were pediatric or young adults (Fair Health, 2019). So while telehealth is increasing, it's not growing as rapidly in rural regions and for older adults as it is for younger patients and in urban areas. Some of the reasons for the slow adoption in rural regions are existing policy barriers and connectivity limitations. While the technology has evolved at a rapid pace, the policy that allows for the use of that technology to deliver care has developed more slowly.

Policy Barriers to the Use of Telehealth

Most federal and state telehealth policy is centered on reimbursement. Narrow telehealth reimbursement policies can be the primary factor that discourages providers from offering services through technology. Medicare is the federal insurance program for people 65 years of age or older. In 2019, the Centers for Medicare and Medicaid Services (CMS) estimated there were over 60 million enrollees in Medicare (Center for Medicare and Medicaid Services, 2019). One-fifth of the Medicare population live in rural areas, roughly 12 million people (MEDPAC, 2019).

Medicare telehealth policy has been targeted at rural populations. First introduced in the Balanced Budget Act of 1997 and updated in the Benefits Improvement and Protection Act of 2000 and Medicare Improvements for Patients and Providers Act of 2008, Medicare has been reimbursing for telehealth-delivered services for over two decades in original Medicare, the fee-for-service part of the program. These policies have been crafted to specifically benefit rural areas, but it is also one of the most restrictive policies in the country. Only one modality, live video, is regularly reimbursed under Medicare's telehealth policy (store-and-forward may be used in Alaska and Hawaii demonstration projects). Medicare specifically limits telehealth reimbursement to a small list of eligible providers who may be compensated by the program for services delivered via telehealth. Allied professionals such as audiologists or speech pathologists are not considered eligible. Federally qualified health centers and rural health centers cannot be the provider providing the telehealth service, though they may act as the site where the patient is located during the interaction. Additionally, these eligible providers can only provide a small set of services via telehealth if they wish to be reimbursed by Medicare. Finally, the services must take place in a specifically defined "rural" area that eliminates locations that could be considered rural in other arenas. While telehealth could be used to provide needed services lacking in rural areas, the restrictive policies on who, what, and how those services can be delivered prevent the technology from being used to its fullest capacity.

Legislation would be required to address these limitations in Medicare telehealth policy. While federal telehealth-specific bills targeting these impediments have been introduced over the years, it is only in recent years that there has been legislative movement to address some of these restrictive policies in Medicare. However, these developments have been narrowly focused changes, targeting specific conditions. For example, the 2018 Bipartisan Budget Act expanded where end stage renal disease services and acute stroke treatment could take place, but the existing limitations would still apply to other conditions.

While legislation would be needed to change telehealth Medicare policy, another strategy to expand the use of technology to deliver services in Medicare has begun to emerge. Using its administrative powers, CMS proposed new services to be reimbursed when delivered by telehealth technologies but would not be considered telehealth. Had these services been labeled "telehealth," the statutory limitations that exist would apply and fewer Medicare enrollees would be able to utilize these avenues to receive services. While these services would be provided via telehealth technologies, they would not be called "telehealth."

There are several names CMS has used to label these services: Chronic Care Management, Remote Physiological Monitoring, Transitional Care Management, and Principal Care Management, all of which use some type of RPM technology. There are other services that are called telecommunication-based services, which includes both synchronous and asynchronous virtual check-ins and interprofessional internet consultations. These services all use telehealth technologies, but as they are not labeled "telehealth," the federal statutory restrictions do not apply.

However, not all older adults receive their health-care services through original Medicare. Some may still receive services via Medicaid or Medicare Advantage or private insurers. The telehealth policies for these payers vary and many do cover more services than original Medicare. Under the 2018 Bipartisan Budget Act, Medicare Advantage plans are given greater flexibility to cover telehealth-delivered services to their enrollees. Beginning in 2020, Medicare Advantage plans were not limited by the narrow allowances under federal law in original Medicare and instead are now allowed to cover telehealth-delivered services through any modality and are not limited by location limitations. There are other restrictions such as abiding by state telehealth laws for the patient's location and only certain providers providing these covered services, but Medicare Advantage plans have more flexibility in offering telehealth delivered services to enrollees.

States have been more progressive in dealing with telehealth policy than the federal government. While telehealth policies vary across the states, there are some, particularly in their Medicaid programs, who have adopted policies that treat telehealth similar to services delivered in-person. For example, California Medicaid has allowed the Medicaid provider to decide what modality, live video or store-and-forward, would be appropriate to use to deliver services if certain other conditions are met such as that it is a service that is covered by the program and can be provided via technology (California Department of Health Care Services, 2019).

While most of the policies discussed thus far only cover reimbursement for telehealth services, there are other policy issues to consider when using telehealth such as prescribing, establishing a patient-provider relationship, privacy, and protection of health information. These policy issues are still evolving on the state and federal levels and contribute to providers' hesitancy to offer services via telehealth until clearer policies have emerged. Without clarity and assurance on reimbursement and policy issues, providers continue to be wary of utilizing technology to provide services.

Connectivity Challenges

Broadband connectivity is another issue that impedes the use of telehealth in rural America. Without connectivity, telehealth will not work. In a 2019 study, researchers found that broadband penetration rates decreased as counties became more rural (Landi, 2019). Additionally, counties with inadequate access to primary care physicians generally had poorer broadband penetration rates. Researchers found that broadband penetration rates in rural counties was 62.4% if primary care access was adequate compared to urban counties' 96% rate. This is another reason that telehealth adoption appears to be at a lower rate in rural regions when compared to urban ones.

To address the rural broadband disparities, various federal programs offer subsidies to health-care institutions or groups such as the Federal Communication Commission's Health Care Connect Fund to help with their connectivity needs. The Health Care Connect Fund offers subsidies to help offset the costs of connectivity. While federal programs have offered some relief, the need continues to exist particularly in rural areas. For these communities, until the connection challenges are solved, they will not be able to use telehealth.

Conclusion

Slowly, older adults' attitudes toward telehealth have begun to change and the obstacles for them to utilize it in rural areas are being addressed. However, though telehealth can be used to address health service access issues for aging Americans in rural regions, work is still needed to address the continuing issues both on the operational and policy side that impact the use of telehealth. While telehealth can help address the accessibility barriers and health needs of older adults in these rural communities, challenges still remain.

References

American Well. (2019, June 19). *2019 senior consumer survey finds 52 percent of Americans ages 65+ are open to telehealth*. Retrieved August 29, 2019, from www.americanwell.com/press-release/2019-senior-consumer-survey-finds-52-percent-of-americans-ages-65-are-open-to-telehealth/

California Department of Health Care Services. (2019, August). *Provider manual: Medicine: Telehealth*. Retrieved August 29, 2019, from http://files.medi-cal.ca.gov/pubsdoco/publications/masters-mtp/part2/mednetele_m01o03.doc

Centers for Disease Control and Prevention. *Telehealth in rural communities*. Retrieved August 29, 2019, from www.cdc.gov/chronicdisease/resources/publications/factsheets/telehealth-in-rural-communities.htm

Center for Medicare and Medicaid Services. *CMS fast fact sheets*. Retrieved August 29, 2019, from www.cms.gov/research-statistics-data-and-systems/statistics-trends-and-reports/cms-fast-facts/index.html

Fair Health. (2019, April). *FH healthcare indicators and FH medical price index: A fair health white paper*. Retrieved August 29, 2019, from https://s3.amazonaws.com/media2.fairhealth.org/whitepaper/asset/FH%20Healthcare%20Indicators%20and%20FH%20Medical%20Price%20Index%202019%20-%20A%20FAIR%20Health%20White%20Paper.pdf

Health Resources & Services Administration. (2019). *Telehealth programs*. Retrieved from www.hrsa.gov/rural-health/telehealth/index.html

Hing, E., & Hsiao, C. (2014, May). US department of health and human services: State variability in supply of office-based primary care providers: United States, 2012. *NCHS Data Brief, 151*. Retrieved from https://pubmed.ncbi.nlm.nih.gov/24813076/

Landi, H. (2019, May 21). *FierceHealthcare, "Poor broadband in rural areas limit telemedicine use: A study."* Retrieved August 29, 2019, from www.fiercehealthcare.com/tech/poor-broadband-access-rural-areas-limits-telemedicine-use-study

MEDPAC. (2019, June). *Health care spending and the Medicare program*. Retrieved August 29, 2019, from www.medpac.gov/docs/default-source/data-book/jun19_databook_entirereport_sec.pdf?sfvrsn=0

Orlawski, J., & Dill, M. *American Society of Aging, "Rural America faces shortage of physicians to care for rapidly aging population."* Retrieved August 29, 2019, from www.asaging.org/blog/rural-america-faces-shortage-physicians-care-rapidly-aging-population

Skoufalos, A., Clarke, J. L., Ellis, D. R., Shepard, V. L., & Rula, E. Y. (2017). Rural aging in America: Proceedings of the 2017 connectivity summit. *Population Health Management, 20*(Suppl 2), S1–S10. doi:10.1089/pop.2017.0177

74
THEORY

Leah Kravette

Introduction

As the median age of the U.S. population rises, there is growing public discourse that this demographic shift will have a negative impact, especially in rural areas of the country. Some of these concerns are based in worries about the sustainability of rural economies, but others are based in ableist and ageist notions that if a person can no longer live independently or be involved in the workforce, they are not contributing to society as a whole (Glasgow & Brown, 2012). Alternative perspectives are reviewed by applying selected key theories on aging to rural environments. Activity theory and successful aging demonstrate the positive impacts that older adults have in rural communities. Socioemotional selectivity theory highlights the ways that people value interdependence through fewer and deeper social connections, as their sense of "time left" gets shorter. Cumulative disadvantage theory takes a life-course approach to understand how exposure to structural inequality accumulates over a person's life span, affecting access to resources in older adulthood. These are just a few of many theories on aging, but they provide a sense of the history, scope, and diversity of research in this field.

Activity Theory

Activity theory holds that life satisfaction and well-being are improved when an older person remains engaged in social, civic, or community activities. This theory was popularized by Havighurst and Albrecht's 1953 study "Older People." Havighurst and Albrecht surveyed and interviewed members of a small, midwestern city to establish which individuals were the most happy and well-adjusted, and what impacted levels of well-being. They found that, among such variables as age, health, socioeconomic status, and level of activity, higher levels of activity were the most strongly correlated to higher levels of happiness for the majority of individuals (Havighurst & Albrecht, 1953). Writing in the 1950s, these theorists were primarily concerned about white older men in middle to upper socioeconomic classes who came of age in a work-centered world and did not feel comfortable in the more leisure-centered world they had retired into. Havighurst and Albrecht highlighted the need for this generation to learn how to "play" in ways that were mentally, physically, and intellectually engaging (Havighurst & Albrecht, 1953).

Activity theory also places responsibility for older adults remaining active within the community at large by providing opportunities to be involved in the workforce or civic life.

Through the lens of activity theory, rural communities facing the out-migration of young adults and the in-migration or aging-in-place of older adults can take a positive and proactive view of this demographic shift. Active older adults often bring years of work experience and skills that they are eager to share in their new communities through civic engagement or community service (Glasgow & Brown, 2012). Retirees moving into rural communities can improve the economic life of a small town by stimulating the housing market and shopping at local businesses (Glasgow & Brown, 2012). While a community may face new challenges with an older population, activity theory highlights the benefits to such a shift both for the older adults themselves and for the community-at-large.

Successful Aging

Successful aging is similar to active aging in challenging expectations that older adults pull away from social and public life but differs in its focus on physical and cognitive health and disease prevention. This theory was popularized after Rowe and Kahn published "Human Aging: Usual and Successful" in 1987 and a follow-up publication in 1997 titled "Successful Aging." Successful aging is one of the most popular and well-known theories of aging, and critiques of it have led to important alternative theories. The theory includes three components: "low probability of disease and disease-related disability, high cognitive and physical functional capacity, and active engagement with life" (Rowe & Kahn, 1997, p. 433). Successful aging theorists encourage all adults and society-at-large to consider how lifestyle choices and lifelong health can impact individuals' ability to remain active and healthy into old age. One major critique of this theory is that it ignores structural barriers to health and wellness, placing the impetus on aging individuals to make healthy lifestyle decisions in order to age "successfully." In 2015, Rowe and Kahn addressed these concerns by calling for large-scale societal investments in resources for older adults and a life-course perspective that would value older adults for their unique skills, regardless of their health status (Rowe & Kahn, 2015).

The dual benefits that successful aging theorists promote are particularly relevant to rural communities, which often attract retirees from urban areas and offer many opportunities for social and physical engagement. One researcher studying the health of older adults in rural environments stated that active older adults and rural community's economic and civic sustainability "go hand in hand" creating a positive cycle in which the community develops active roles for its older adults, and older adults become involved with and bolster the community as a whole (Davis, Crothers, Grant, Young, & Smith, 2012). Challenges of rural living can also be addressed through a successful aging lens. For example, transportation is key in older adults' access to social participation, but many rural areas struggle to provide public transportation. If communities commit to valuing older adults by fighting social isolation, they may invest in their public transportation systems, benefiting residents of all ages and supporting older adults to age successfully (Glasgow & Brown, 2012).

Socioemotional Selectivity Theory

Carstensen, Isaacowitz, and Charles's theory of socioemotional selectivity, presented in 1999, takes into account the influence of a consciousness of time as people age. The authors suggest that as individuals age, they become aware of the limited time they have and begin to live in a more present-focused, rather than future-focused, way (Carstensen, Isaacowitz, & Charles,

1999). When individuals are future-focused, they tend to value expanding social and professional networks and intellectual, rational thinking and problem solving. When individuals are present-focused, they tend to spend more time with fewer people with whom they share a strong bond and make decisions based on their emotional state (Carstensen et al., 1999). When there is an increased awareness of the end of life, "short-term goals, such as social connectedness, social support, and emotional regulation assume highest priority . . . focus shifts from the future to the present . . . and emotional experience is characterized by greater complexity" (Carstensen et al., 1999, p. 178).

Socioemotional selectivity theory reframes what is often seen as a process of self-retreat or social isolation into a focus on the development of fewer, deeper, and more complex emotional relationships, which can bring immediate feelings of happiness and comfort. This theory also challenges theories of active and successful aging by centering on the importance of each person's unique emotional experience, rather than on a model of physical "success" and ability. Socioemotional selectivity theory is relevant to aging populations in rural communities because older adults in these communities often report higher levels of happiness than their counterparts in urban environments, even as they generally experience decreased access to health services and higher levels of poverty. For example, one study found that "rurality was seen to be associated with dense social networks although . . . the 'ability to cope with being alone and with isolation was [also] a key feature'" (Milbourne & Doheny, 2012, p. 391). While the older adults in this study had low rates of involvement in community activities, which are future-focused, they highly valued their sense of "place" and the close-knit relationships that they had with key members of their social networks (Milbourne & Doheny, 2012). This study supports socioemotional selectivity's perspective that older adults in rural environments benefit from the richness and depth of their social and emotional relationships by reporting high levels of contentment and inclusion within their communities.

Cumulative Inequality Theory

The cumulative inequality theory of aging challenges the success and activity theories of aging by placing the effects of individual life events on the aging process in the context of structural inequality. Cumulative inequality theory is particularly applicable to rural aging because it attends to the diverse experiences of risk and opportunity that are unique to rural life and which coalesce in older adulthood. The five axioms of this theory bring attention to the ways that social inequality impacts every aspect of human development, from gestation to the circumstances in which people die. This theory calls for an appreciation of older adults as "survivors," who, through navigating risks and opportunities throughout their lifetimes, hold important information about factors that impact older adulthood in an unjust, unequal social structure (Ferraro & Shippee, 2009).

Axioms one and two articulate the role of social systems of inequality in exposing individuals to risks and advantages or opportunities over the course of the lifetime (Ferraro & Shippee, 2009). In one study of older adults in a rural environment, researchers found that "the oldest old (85 years and older) are more likely to have chronic health problems and disabilities, to have relinquished driving, have lower incomes, to be female and live alone, and to exhibit other characteristics suggesting cumulative disadvantage" (Glasgow & Brown, 2012, p. 423). One major contributor to cumulative disadvantage is a history of low-paid work, common in many rural areas (Milbourne & Doheny, 2012). The focus on lifetime exposure to social inequality in axiom one allows researchers to understand the impact of diverse experiences of risk on an individual's aging process.

Axiom two specifies that "disadvantage increases exposure to risk, but advantage increases exposure to opportunity" (Ferraro & Shippee, 2009, p. 335). For example, after World War II, the GI Bill provided financial support for white veterans to buy homes and land, positively impacting their access to financial stability, while African American veterans were excluded from these benefits because of institutionalized racism (McCaskill et al., 2015). Axiom two recognizes that the advantage of white privilege afforded more opportunities to white veterans and their descendants, heightening opportunity for asset accumulation in old age. While there is much research devoted to understanding the challenges faced by rural older adults, studying these trends through a lens of cumulative disadvantage makes evident the longitudinal impact of structural and historical forces on individuals.

Axioms three and four acknowledge the roles of individual agency, availability of resources, and personal narratives in navigating the risks and advantages that people face within an unequal social structure (Ferraro & Shippee, 2009). If internalized, social narratives surrounding experiences of social inequality can have major impacts on individuals' physical and mental health. In one study exploring the heightened rates of suicide among older male farmers, researchers found that values such as "a lifetime working the land, patriarchal family farming and self-sufficiency" (Garnham & Bryant, 2014, p. 232) created internal conflict when combined with the realities of the farming profession, which include high risk of acute and chronic injury and disability. In understanding that increased suicide rates may be tied to farmers' personal identity-based narratives conflicting with the health challenges inherent to agricultural work, a cumulative disadvantage lens may help communities identify creative solutions in providing support for older male farmers.

One can also center the agency of individuals living in rural environments in navigating inequality and building resources. In a 2015 study of an economically disenfranchised rural community, research participants felt high levels of satisfaction with their quality of life because of their connection to the rural environment itself (Milbourne & Doheny, 2012). They also reported feeling a sense of control and agency over their lives because of skills they have developed in response to the structural disadvantages they had been exposed to (Milbourne & Doheny, 2012). Cumulative disadvantage theory would highlight the agency that these participants demonstrate in creating resources and narratives that work to buffer against the negative impacts of structural inequality. Axioms three and four remind us that individuals navigate and name their experiences within structures of inequality in unique ways, which can impact the trajectory of their life course.

In axiom five, cumulative disadvantage scholars call for greater macro-level study of populations across the life span to better understand how the toll of minority stress and lack of access to resources may impact aging in earlier years. In rural communities, older adults already experience limited social and health services compared to their urban or suburban peers (Garnham & Bryant, 2014). Illness and even death in younger or middle-aged adults often happen because of the same structural forces that impact health in older adults, such as lack of access to medical care, high-risk work environments, or institutional discrimination. If populations aged 65 and older are primarily studied, the field is neglecting those who have shorter life spans because of their early exposure to structural inequality.

Conclusion

Rural communities in the U.S. are experiencing a "graying" of their demographics. While this shift may present challenges to communities already dealing with decreased access to resources, it also presents an opportunity for these communities to develop in ways that are more accessible to residents of all ages. The theories presented here provide examples of how research can be used to better understand the diverse implications of this population shift, and how to support the diverse needs of aging rural communities in creative and effective ways.

References

Carstensen, L. L., Isaacowitz, D. M., & Charles, S. T. (1999). Taking time seriously: A theory of socioemotional selectivity. *American Psychologist*, *54*(3), 165–181.

Davis, S., Crothers, N., Grant, J., Young, S., & Smith, K. (2012). Being involved in the country: Productive ageing in different types of rural communities. *Journal of Rural Studies*, *28*(4), 338–346.

Ferraro, K. F., & Shippee, T. P. (2009). Aging and cumulative inequality: How does inequality get under the skin? *The Gerontologist*, *49*(3), 333–343. doi:10.1093/geront/gnp034

Garnham, B., & Bryant, L. (2014). Problematising the suicides of older male farmers: Subjective, social and cultural considerations. *Sociologia Ruralis*, *54*(2), 227–240.

Glasgow, N., & Brown, D. L. (2012). Rural ageing in the United States: Trends and contexts. *Journal of Rural Studies*, *28*(4), 422–431.

Havighurst, R. J., & Albrecht, R. (1953). *Older people*. New York: Longman, Greens, & Co.

McCaskill, G. M., Sawyer, P., Burgio, K. L., Kennedy, R., Williams, C. P., Clay, O. J., . . . Allman, R. M. (2015). The impact of veteran status on life-space mobility among older Black and White men in the deep south. *Ethnicity & Disease*, *25*(3), 255–262. doi:10.18865/ed.25.3.255

Milbourne, P., & Doheny, S. (2012). Older people and poverty in rural Britain: Material hardships, cultural denials and social inclusions. *Journal of Rural Studies*, *28*(4), 389–397.

Rowe, J. W., & Kahn, R. L. (1997). Successful aging. *The Gerontologist*, *37*(4), 433–440.

Rowe, J. W., & Kahn, R. L. (2015). Successful aging 2.0: Conceptual expansions for the 21st century. *The Journals of Gerontology: Series B, Psychological Sciences and Social Sciences*, *70*(4), 593–596.

75
TRANSPORTATION

Robin Phillips and Cara Marcus

Background

Transportation is not just riding in a car or on a bus, train, or bicycle. Transportation is about mobility—a person's ability to get from where they live to the doctor, shopping center, bank, post office, family, or friends, etc. Just as older adults need safe, affordable housing, they need access to food, high-quality medical care, and meaningful activities that help promote happiness.

The nature of older adult housing has changed over the last century. Retirement and over-55 housing and communities are now commonplace. Older buildings are repurposed for new living environments as residents age out of their homes. A rising aging population and age-segregated housing means that more older adults live apart from their families and support systems. Many older people relocate from places they've lived all their lives. Moving later in life can have negative health effects, especially for those subject to involuntary moves. Peterson and Rieck (2017) found that most older adults wish to live in their current homes and "age-in-place" in their own neighborhoods. Retirement communities may not have infrastructure in place for transporting residents to access appointments, shopping, etc. Whether older adults live in their own homes, or retirement or care communities, transportation is the lifeline to independence.

Older adults in rural areas often lack access to transportation available in cities, suburbs, and large towns. Distances between destinations, like hospitals and shopping centers, may be 50 or 100 miles away. The consolidation of consumer goods and social services to distant and urban communities makes accessing health-care services, medications, healthy food, and other necessities more time-consuming and expensive for rural populations. The very geography of some rural areas—jagged terrain, dirt roads, houses high on mountain-tops, flooded creeks, unplowed streets in winter—makes it more difficult for inhabitants to travel.

As people age, they are generally not as able. The change can be gradual. Some older adults are fully mobile (some 90-year-olds run marathons), but walking abilities can run the gamut from fully ambulatory to the use of canes, walkers, or wheelchairs. If people can walk, those living near town centers are generally in considerably less danger of becoming isolated. Isolation can have a negative effect on elder health; a study by Shaw et al. (2017) found that health-care spending was about 23% less for older adults with social connections than those without. But many older people cannot travel unassisted from point A to point B. For our nation's elders,

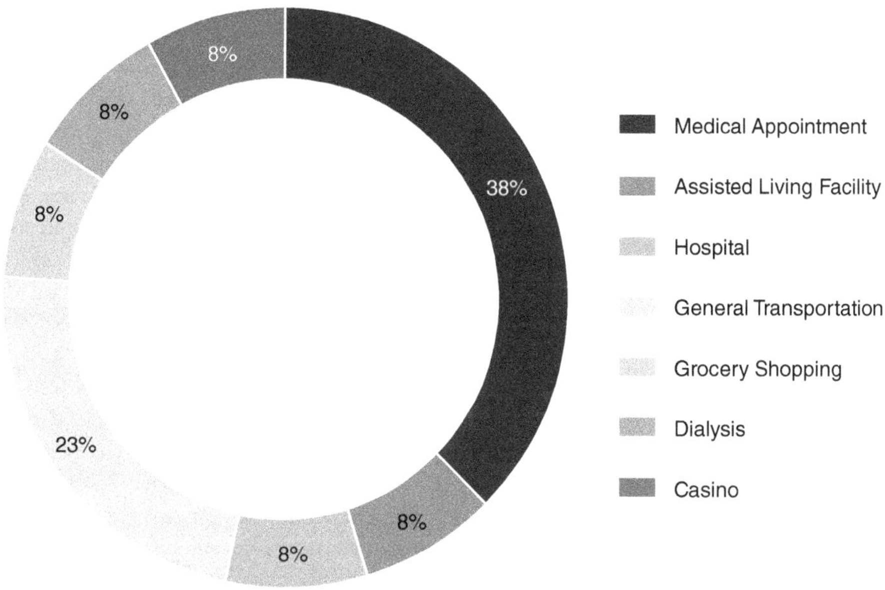

Figure 75.1 Rural older adult destinations

transportation is the key for both meeting their basic needs and maintaining independence and connections.

Rural Older Adult Mobility

Kerschner, Beverly Foundation, Hardin, and Community Transportation Association of America (2006) found that nonemergency medical trips were the most frequent destination for older people. Figure 75.1 shows 2016–2019 data of the breakdown of rural older adults asking the National Rural Transit Assistance Program (RTAP) for assistance locating rides to various destinations (n=31). Particularly for older people, access to medical care is tantamount to wellness, reductions in morbidity, and overall quality of life. According to the American Academy of Primary Physicians (2019), an increase of one primary care doctor per 10,000 people results in a 5.5% decrease in hospital admissions, 10.9% decrease in emergency room visits, and 7.2% decrease in surgeries. Most older citizens have Medicaid health insurance, but many are unaware that this insurance can serve as a conduit to medical transportation.

Older adults need to maintain relationships and positive engagement with their community. Visits to family and friends are so vital to aging individuals in isolated rural areas—maintaining circles of support and improving quality of life. The extent to which isolation and loneliness puts elders at risk has increased as our society spends more time online. Technological advances have influenced rural elders' lives in many positive ways. Smart bracelets can alert a medical team if a person falls and families who may not live near can share pictures on social media. Trips can be booked online rather than requiring that one go to a travel agency. At the same time, people spend less time chatting with neighbors on porches or in neighborhood parks. Furthermore, many people in their 80s and 90s (and even younger) have never used modern technology, and the potential for using a smartphone app to schedule an Uber or Lyft to get to the doctor simply eludes them.

Transportation Challenges

A key issue to be considered is whether someone should be driving a car after a certain age. Research by Kerschner et al. (2006) indicates that people usually live six to 11 years longer than they are able to drive safely, leading to transportation dependency. According to the American Automobile Association (2019), over 200,000 drivers ages 65 and older were injured and over 3,500 were killed in traffic crashes in 2016. AARP, AAA Foundation for Traffic Safety, and many others produce guides discussing when and how to approach someone who should not drive anymore. This is one of the most difficult conversations for families to have, and it becomes even more difficult when someone's parent lives in a rural area where it is hard to get anywhere without a car. Colorado's Older & Wiser Program advises people to start using transit when it is still a choice.

Many rural older adults still want or need to continue working, sometimes into their seventies and beyond. Approximately 30% of retirees return to work, according to data from the Health and Retirement Study (University of Michigan, 2017). Transportation access to the workplace is often more difficult for those in rural areas, but some agencies have found solutions. Estuary Transit District in Connecticut changed many of its routes, schedules, and hours of service to accommodate older riders' work hours. Volunteerism is one solution to transportation-related employment challenges; volunteer transportation programs can help close the gap by transporting older adults who can no longer drive, at the same time that they offer meaningful volunteer opportunities for those who can drive safely. Gonzales et al. (2019) found that older volunteers were at least 1.85 times more likely to report higher self-assessed health than their non-volunteering counterparts. However, volunteer transportation programs may have a difficult time finding qualified volunteers, especially in rural areas.

Taking older people where they need to go is no easy feat. Some riders may not be able to wait outside for long periods of time because of health issues or frailty, and others may develop conditions like dementia, which can cause people to be confused or not even remember where they need to go. Well-trained and compassionate drivers should get to know their older passengers and treat them with high quality customer-focused service and dignity, while providing safe and efficient transportation. Agencies like Envida in Colorado take this a step further by combining transportation with home care and hiring drivers who "do more than drive" by assisting people inside their homes.

The cost of transportation in rural areas is a barrier to many older adults on fixed incomes. For people who need dialysis multiple times a week, paying $10 (agencies have been known to charge as much as $300!) per trip is simply not feasible. Transportation providers have been able to overcome this challenge by finding partners like hospitals and shopping centers that can share costs, and obtaining funding through government, foundations, and businesses, to offer older riders free or reduced-fare rides. For example, the Oklahoma City Foundation awarded a grant to Compassionate Hands in Yukon to operate a free "Care-A-Van" to provide transportation for the area's older citizens.

Many pressing issues affect rural communities today. Disasters are more frequent because of changing environmental patterns and climate change. Older people may need to be transported to temporary shelters or emergency medical care in times of emergency. The growing alcohol and drug epidemic, particularly prescription opioid dependence, is having a profound impact on rural elders. Older victims of drug misuse and abuse will need transportation to medical treatment and educational facilities. Crisis transportation services need to be deliberately planned to ensure the safety of our most vulnerable older Americans.

Creating a Geography of Access

Rural communities must address the transportation needs of older residents to create a full geography of access. They must consider all forms of transportation, including transit, volunteer transportation, ride-sharing, transportation brokerages, feeder routes taking passengers from remote rural regions to transit stations, taxi vouchers, nutrition shuttles, and more. Voucher programs can provide transportation to older adults with limited incomes and include different types of transportation, including transit and taxi service. Area Agencies on Aging (AAAs) often provide free or low-fare transportation to congregate nutrition sites. Most importantly, all transportation plans must include methodologies to ensure that the programmatic infrastructure leads to services that work.

The culture and traditions of aging populations can vary widely in rural areas. U.S. Census Bureau data (2019) confirm over 44 million foreign-born residents and over 3% who belong to more than one race. Even the word "elder" may take on different meanings in different cultures, such as tribal communities. A community is not determined by its population, but rather by its values. Transportation planning should consider the needs of people reflecting all backgrounds and cultures.

A major challenge in any community is being responsive to diverse community requirements in order to create the full spectrum of mobility options. All agencies serving older adults within a particular community are encouraged to engage in joint planning in order to create and implement a shared vision. Community members should not expect the local senior center or AAA to satisfy all older adult transportation needs.

There are many players in rural communities who can collaborate in an effort to ensure that older residents can access the transportation they need, including AAAs, rural planning organizations, community action councils, government councils, and elected officials. Coalition building, where members cooperate for a common purpose to benefit all, has demonstrated success. York County Community Action Corporation in Sanford, Maine, worked collaboratively with a local hospital, community day program, and the Maine Cancer Foundation to develop transportation that made a difference to their rural older residents. AAAs, funded through the Older Americans Act, are designated by states to address the needs of Americans over 60 years of age. AAAs contract with transportation providers to provide transportation and/or directly provide such services. Older veterans may be eligible for transportation through veterans' programs, including Veterans Transportation Services and VA Medical Centers. Although sometimes overlooked, older adults themselves should be included in transportation planning; they often provide the best first-hand insight into what is truly needed.

Innovative older adult transportation models have been instituted by public transit agencies (Hosen, Powell, & Transit Cooperative Research Program, 2011; Transit Cooperative Research Program, KFH Group and A-M-M-A, 2001). Many age friendly communities in small towns and rural communities now include frequent, easily accessible, and low-cost or free transportation to the places these individuals need to go most commonly. Some of the most promising new models are Mobility as a Service (MaaS) and integrative mobility. These models provide outreach and travel training with guidance and information to potential users of the systems. For example, Newton, Massachusetts debuted a microtransit service in 2019 designed for older adults. NewMo enabled individuals to reserve a van that would arrive within 30 minutes, either by calling or via a smartphone app. The ability to call is particularly helpful, as many older adults may prefer not to use an app. The service includes wheelchair accessible vehicles, is low-cost, and takes riders outside town limits for medical appointments. Prairie Hills Transit in Spearfish, South Dakota, began their older adult transportation service with one van. They now cover eight counties and have now taken riders on trips even 75 miles away, including rides for residents living in assisted living centers and nursing homes. The Terrebonne Council on Aging, based in Houma, Louisiana, made more than 32,500 one-way trips in 2018. They have a regular elder transportation program as well as a special shopping service, where older adults can make an appointment up to 30 days in advance for a door-to-door, round-trip, three-hour shopping excursion. Some agencies use out-of-the box thinking to develop truly innovative solutions (Hosen, Powell, & Transit Cooperative Research Program, 2011; Transit Cooperative Research Program, KFH Group and A-M-M-A, 2001). The Colfax, Washington Council on Aging launched a "Postal Bus," which provided both mail service and passenger transportation in the same vehicle, as well as a vehicle pool, where vehicles were shared with smaller social service agencies in their region.

A myriad of federal agencies focus on rural aging-related transportation issues, including National RTAP, National Aging and Disability Transportation Center (NADTC), National Association of Area Agencies on Aging (n4a), the Diverse Elders Coalition, Administration for Community Living (ACL), and National Center for Mobility Management (NCMM). Opportunities are continuously evolving in both coordinated approaches to older adult mobility and social services. Through federal programs like the Federal Transit Administration (FTA) and the Older Americans Act, AAAs are working with health policy, environmental, community action programs, and others to coordinate responses to older adult poverty, isolation, and other critical issues. Funding for older adult transportation is available from many federal programs (including Section 5310—Elderly and Individuals with Disabilities funds), and state and local programs, although most rural agencies seek additional funding to meet the needs and demands of their communities.

Conclusion

In conclusion, aging in rural America poses a myriad of barriers: personal mobility loss, isolation, and an increase in demand for access to health-care services. Communities around the country have risen to the occasion and have pioneered responsive services using a variety of approaches. The future will continue to bring new challenges, but the fundamental resources and systems will continue to respond with innovative services and new technologies to engage and connect rural communities and rural elders.

References

American Academy of Primary Physicians. *Why primary care matters*. Retrieved August 8, 2019, from www.aafp.org/medical-school-residency/choosing-fm/value-scope.html

American Automobile Association. *More than 80 percent of older drivers aren't talking about driving safety*. Retrieved August 8, 2019, from https://newsroom.aaa.com/2018/08/older-drivers-talking-driving-safety/

Gonzales, E., Shen, H. W., Perry, T. E., & Wang, Y. (2019, January). Intersections of home, health, and social engagement in old age: Formal volunteering as a protective factor to health after relocation. *Research on Aging*, *41*(1), 31–53. doi:10.1177/0164027518773125

Hosen, K. I., Powell, S. B., & Transit Cooperative Research Program. (2011). *Innovative rural transit services: A synthesis of transit practice*. Washington, DC: National Academy Press. Retrieved August 8, 2019, from www.trb.org/Publications/Blurbs/166363.aspx

Kerschner, H., Beverly Foundation, Hardin, J., & Community Transportation Association of America. (2006). *Transportation innovations for seniors: A report from rural America*. Pasadena, CA: Beverly Foundation.

Peterson, D., & Rieck, T. (2017). *Aging in place in small urban and rural communities*. Fargo, ND: Small Urban and Rural Transit Center. Retrieved August 7, 2019, from https://www.ugpti.org/resources/reports/downloads/surlc17-006.pdf

Shaw, J. G., Farid, M., Noel-Miller, C., Joseph, N., Houser, A., Asch, S. M., . . . Flowers, L. (2017, January). Social isolation and Medicare spending: Among older adults, objective social isolation increases expenditures while loneliness does not. *Journal of Aging and Health, 29*(7), 1119–1143. doi:10.1177/0898264317703559

Transit Cooperative Research Program, KFH Group, & A-M-M-A. (2001). *Guidebook for change and innovation at rural and small urban transit systems*. Washington, DC: National Academy Press. Retrieved August 8, 2019, from http://onlinepubs.trb.org/onlinepubs/tcrp/tcrp_rpt_70a.pdf

University of Michigan. (2017, January). *The health and retirement study: Aging in the 21st century*. Retrieved August 8, 2019, from http://hrsonline.isr.umich.edu/sitedocs/databook/inc/pdf/HRS-Aging-in-the-21St-Century.pdf

U.S. Census Bureau. *Place of birth for the foreign-born population in the United States*. Retrieved August 8, 2019, from https://factfinder.census.gov/faces/tableservices/jsf/pages/productview.xhtml?src=CF

76
VETERANS

Angeline Bushy

Background

Of the U.S. population (47 million) about 18 million (30%) are veterans, of which nine million are enrolled in the VA/VHA (Veterans Health Administration—Office of Rural Health, n.d., 2016; Veterans Health Administration, 2019). About 18% of the U.S. population reside in a rural or rural remote; veterans comprise 11% of the rural adult population. In 1973, the U.S. Congress legislated implanting an all-volunteer force; and the military draft was eliminated. Since then, soldiers on active duty as well as those in reserve status (Army, Air Force, Navy, Marines, Coast Guard, and National Guard) have been mobilized and deployed to serve in various capacities and global regions. Of the 4.7 million rural and highly rural veterans, more than 2.8 million (58%) are enrolled to obtain health care in the VA/VHA compared to enrolled urban veterans (37%) (Rural Veterans Health Care Atlas, 2015).

Among military recruits, 44% come from rural areas. Those residing in the most sparsely populated zip codes (22%) are more likely to volunteer, an opposite trend from cities. Most enlistees come from southern (40%) and western (24%) states (VA Office of Rural Health, 2016). Upon discharge, a disproportionate number of veterans return to rural communities. While they enjoy the rural lifestyle, many encounter challenges in accessing health care, exacerbated by combat-related injuries and illnesses (NRHA, 2019).

Characteristics of Rural Veterans

The rural and highly rural veteran population is widely dispersed and racially, ethnically, and culturally diverse; and 15% self-identify as a racial or ethnic minority. The majority are Caucasian (91.7%), followed by Hispanic/Latino (6.6%), black/African American (4.9%), American Indian/Alaska Native (1.1%), Asian (.03%), and Native Hawaiian/Other Pacific Islander (0.1%). Most veterans are male (91%) compared to more than half of the nonveteran U.S. population being female. There are an increasing number of female veterans (10%), comprising 7% of all rural veterans. Consistent with national trends, the greatest number of living rural veterans served during the Vietnam area. Each year the number of rural veterans is declining who served in World War II (3.8%), the Korean Conflict (9.3%) and during the Vietnam era (41%). Increasingly, rural veterans served in Middle East Gulf Wars (30%) from 1991 to the present.

Veterans are significantly older than nonveterans. The median age for U.S. veterans is 64 years of age compared to 44 years of age for nonveterans. Rural veterans 65 years of age and over (41%) are older than rural nonveterans (16%). More than half of rural veterans (57%) who are enrolled to receive care through the VA/VHA are over 65 years of age. Compared to the general population in all settings, rural veterans have lower annual family incomes, are less healthy and have more disabilities (Tasseff, Tavernier, Neill, & Watkins, 2019). Of VA/VHA enrolled rural veterans 65 years of age and older, about 75% have medically complex conditions along with chronic comorbidities; and 18% have one or more service-related disabilities.

The older veteran population is often diagnosed with diabetes, obesity, high blood pressure, and heart conditions that require more frequent, ongoing, and costly care. The VA/VHA anticipates the "next" generation of veterans who served in Mideast conflicts are likely to have multiple medical and combat-related conditions that require significant ongoing specialty health care and extensive rehabilitation. Common injuries among Gulf War veterans are associated with improvised explosive devices (IEDs) blast exposure causing mild to extremely severe traumatic brain injuries (TBI), musculoskeletal trauma-related injuries, missing limbs, post-traumatic stress disorder (PTSD), and other behavioral and emotional health problems (VA, n.d., 2019a).

Environmental and occupational hazards can wreak havoc on the body. These conditions tend to exacerbate with age and degenerative processes. With respect to veteran's health-care needs, these will vary depending on the individual's military service history. However, depression, substance abuse, and sleep issues can occur regardless of when or where the veteran served. Moreover, there may be long-term physical and emotional consequences associated with environmental and chemical exposures while serving, such as pesticides, other chemicals, biological warfare agents, prophylactic drugs and vaccines, blasts, noise, radiation, smoke from oil fires and open air burn pits coupled with lack of sleep, fatigue, and carrying excessively heavy equipment.

Rural Social Determinants and Veterans' Health Risks

Social determinants include the conditions in which an individual is born, lives, and works that can impact a veteran's health and well-being. With respect to socioeconomic factors, males (compared to females), have higher incomes, are more likely to be employed, less likely to be single parents, and less likely to live in poverty. With respect to rural veterans, more than half (52%) earn less than $35,000 annually. Likewise, often there are few(er) housing, education, employment, and transportation options available to them in small and more rural communities. Rural older veterans are more likely to be on fixed incomes with fewer financial resources. Compared to their urban counterparts, younger rural veterans may have limited employment opportunities and experience higher unemployment rates. Female veterans have higher unemployment rates compared to their male counterparts and women in general. There is also a higher rate of rural residents who are uninsured or underinsured. Of veterans who are enrolled in the VA/VHA, a significant proportion have another (supplementary) health insurance (e.g., Medicare, Medicaid, and private insurance). Historically, rural residents experience limited access to services across the health-care spectrum; thus, identified as an access disparity in *Rural Healthy People: 2020* (Bolin et al., 2015; HRSA, 2019).

Access to care is also a most significant challenge facing rural veterans. Coupled with rural travel challenges and services at greater distances, there are fewer health-care services and providers in general, and VA/VHA services in particular. Veterans residing in rural and rural remote areas, who rely on the VA/VHA for care, may need to commute a great distance, at times in inclement weather to access services. Along with commuting challenges, a veteran and his or her caregiver(s) may need to take time off from work to travel to and from a VA/VHA facility, coupled with travel-related expenses to access a distant VA/VHA medical appointment.

More specifically, VA/VHA primary care is available within a 30-minute drive for nearly all urban veterans (91%), compared to rural veterans (38%) and highly rural veterans (22%). Fewer than half of highly rural veterans (49%) reside within 60 minutes of VA/VHA primary care services. Average commuting distance for rural veterans is 63 miles to access a VA/VHA provider. Of all VA/VHA enrolled veterans, 25% report that transportation challenges impact their ability to access health care. Among all veterans, 11% do not have a valid driver's license attributable either to a physical or emotional impairment or, in some cases, substance abuse restrictions (i.e., multiple DUIs, etc.). For rural veterans, more than half have only one vehicle in the household (54%) or do not even have a vehicle (5.6%); while 13% must rely on family or friends for transportation.

The Disabled American Veterans (DAV) Van service offers limited transportation services for some rural veterans. The DAV uses volunteer drivers, also veterans (usually retired), to transport local veterans to a VA/VHA facility for appointments. Some rural counties do not have this service. Consequently, in some highly rural areas, two or more counties sometimes collaborate to coordinate DAV transportation services. Depending on driver availability, on a "somewhat" scheduled basis (e.g., weekly, biweekly, bimonthly), the DAV transports area veterans to the nearest VA/VHA facility (DAV, 2019). Yet even when this service is available, only 11% of veterans use a DAV-sponsored transportation service. Various reasons for not using the service are cited by veterans and caregivers; among others, scheduling medical appointments at times other than when the DAV service is available; having to depart from home very early in the morning (sometimes in subzero temperatures); and lengthy commuting time associated with picking up other local veterans en route to the VA/VHA facility. Along with the commute, there often are extensive wait times before departing (until after all riders have been seen by their provider) late in the day for another lengthy commute before being dropped off at one's home. For a veteran who is frail, very old, disabled, or in poor health, such circumstances could exacerbate existing medical conditions and physical disabilities. Despite greater need, rural veterans are less likely than urban veterans to use either the VA/VHA or private sector health-care services. Transportation challenges have been identified as the most significant barrier to obtaining needed care and is the strongest predictor of poor treatment retention among veterans enrolled in the VA/VHA.

Limited Access to Interconnectivity Technology

In many rural regions, communication technology is inaccessible because of limited broadband internet capabilities and sometimes cellular telephone connections. About 30% of rural veterans do not have internet access in the home. (VA, 2019c). Telemedicine/telehealth, along with access to online resources, promotes digital inclusion to support veterans, their families, and caregivers. Digital inclusion can improve access to a continuum of care and could facilitate veterans' participation in their health care.

Mental and Behavioral Health Services

There are insufficient mental and behavioral care providers in most rural areas for both inpatient and outpatient services. Critical rural shortages of this specialty also exist in the VA/VHA. Rural veterans have a higher prevalence of physical and mental comorbidities compared to urban and are 70% less likely to receive adequate and appropriate treatment for traumatic brain injury, PTSD, and behavioral disorders (VA, 2019b).

Misuse of prescription pain medications (i.e., opioids) has increased among veterans of all ages regardless of military history background. The VA/VHA is educating providers, veterans, and caregivers about the risks of opioid dependency and use of alternative pain management interventions (i.e., alternative prescribing practices, and use of complementary therapies such as acupuncture, massage, meditation, and nonaddictive analgesics) (Bernardy & Monatano, 2019).

Homelessness

Point-in-time-estimates ("VA/VHA stand down") suggest, of the adult homeless population, at least 11% are veterans (Statista, 2018). Compared to nonveterans, male veterans are 1.3 times more likely while female veterans are 3.6 times more likely to be homeless. More than half of all homeless veterans have a disability (51%) and a mental illness (49%) (i.e., PTSD, substance abuse). Half of the homeless veterans are 51 years of age or older (50%) compared to the non-veteran population (19%). Older homeless veterans primarily served during the Vietnam era (VA, 2019a).

Females and LGBT Veterans

Females are the fastest-growing veteran population. Females often are uncomfortable in male-dominated therapy settings; thus, their issues and concerns may not be addressed. The VA/VHA is addressing their concerns through Public Law 111–163, Caregivers and Veterans Omnibus Health Services Act. Section 20 (May 2010). Likewise, each VA/VHA facility must have an LGBT Veteran Care Coordinator (VCC) promote best practices to address their concerns (Blosnich et al., 2013; Brown & Jones, 2014; VA, 2018, 2019c).

Congressional Mandates Focusing on Veterans' Health-Care Needs

The VA/VHA health-care system provides care for 5.5 million enrolled veterans. Yet Congress remains concerned that some veterans are not able to access VA/VHA services. The intent of the MISSION Act is to improve access to care for qualifying enrolled veterans with an approved non-VA/VHA "community care providers" (38 C.F.R. §§4.1–4.31) (VA, 2019b).

Finally, most veterans are proud of their service and generally eager to share their story with a health-care provider. In turn, health professionals should become informed about veterans and their military experiences. A veteran's military history could influence the health status of the individual as well as how care is provided.

References

Bernardy, N., & Monatano, M. (2019). Opioid use among individuals with post-traumatic stress disorder. *PTSD Quarterly*, *38*(1). Retrieved from www.ptsd.va.gov/publications/rq_docs/V30N1.pdf

Blosnich, J., Brown, G., Shipherd, J., Kauth, M., Piegari, R., & Bossarte, R. (2013). Prevalence of gender identity disorder and suicide risk among transgender veterans utilizing veterans health administration care. *American Journal of Public Health*, *103*(10), e27–e32. doi:10.2105/ajph.2013.301507

Bolin, J., Bellamy, G., Ferdinand, A., Vuong, A., Kash, B., Schulze, A., & Helduser, W. (2015). Rural healthy people 2020: New decade, same challenges. *The Journal of Rural Health*, *31*(3), 326–333. https://doi.org/10.1111/jrh.12116

Brown, G., & Jones, K. (2014). Racial health disparities in a cohort of 5,135 transgender veterans. *Journal of Racial and Ethnic Health Disparities, 1*(4), 257–266. doi:10.1007/s40615-014-0032-4

Department of Veterans Affairs. (2019). *Profile of veterans: 2017*. Retrieved from www.va.gov/vetdata/docs/SpecialReports/Profile_of_Veterans_2017.pdf

Disabled Veterans Services. DAV. (2019). *Need a ride?* Retrieved from www.dav.org/veterans/i-need-a-ride/

Health Resources and Services Administration (HRSA). (2019). *Health workforce: Health professional shortage areas*. Retrieved from https://bhw.hrsa.gov/shortage-designation/hpsas

National Rural Health Association (NRHA). (2019). *NRHA rural veterans' health initiative: Veterans in rural America*. Retrieved from www.ruralhealthweb.org/programs/rural-veterans-health-initiative

Statista. (2019). *Estimated number of homeless veterans in the United States in 2018, by state*. Retrieved from www.statista.com/statistics/727819/number-of-homeless-veterans-in-the-us-by-state/

Tasseff, T., Tavernier, S., Neill, K., & Watkins, P. (2019). Exploring perceptions of palliative care among rural dwelling veterans. *Online Journal of Nursing and Health Care, 19*(1). Retrieved from https://rnojournal.binghamton.edu/index.php/RNO/article/view/528/450

U.S. Department of Veterans Affairs. (VA, n.d.). *Aging veterans and posttraumatic stress symptoms*. Retrieved from www.ptsd.va.gov/understand/what/aging_veterans.asp

U.S. Department of Veterans Affairs Website. (2018). *Office of Diversity and Inclusion: LGBT*. Retrieved from www.diversity.va.gov/programs/lgbt.aspx

U.S. Department of Veterans Affairs Website. (VA, 2019a). *Homeless veterans: Overview*. Retrieved from www.va.gov/homeless/; https://vva.org/what-we-do/outreach-programs/homeless-veterans/

U.S. Department of Veterans Affairs Website. (VA, 2019b, June 6). *VA MISSION Act: Increasing veterans' access to health care*. Retrieved from https://missionact.va.gov/

U.S. Department of Veterans Affairs Website. (VA, 2019c). *Veterans with lesbian, gay, bisexual and transgender (LGBT) and related identities*. Retrieved from www.patientcare.va.gov/LGBT/index.asp

Veterans Health Administration. (2019, March). *National Center for Veterans Analysis and Statistics*. Retrieved from www.va.gov/vetdata/

Veterans Health Administration—Office of Rural Health. (2016). *Rural veterans' health care atlas: FY 2015*. Retrieved from www.ruralhealth.va.gov/aboutus/ruralvets.asp; www.ruralhealth.va.gov/aboutus/rvhc_atlas_fy2015.asp

Veterans Health Administration—Office of Rural Health. (n.d.). *Caring for rural veterans*. Retrieved from www.ruralhealth.va.gov/docs/ORH_Brochure_2018_v3_1_print_508.pdf

77
VOLUNTARISM

Ke Li and Fengyan Tang

Introduction

Volunteering is one of the most important options for productive engagement among U.S. older adults. According to the 2015 Current Population Survey (CPS), among 62.6 million Americans who had the experience of volunteering during September 2014 to September 2015, 25.1% were adults aged 55 to 64 years, and 23.5% were aged 65 and older (Bureau of Labor Statistics, 2015). Moreover, older adults over the age of 65 reported the highest median annual hours (96) spent on volunteer activities, compared to all other age groups (Bureau of Labor Statistics, 2015).

Volunteering is defined as "any activity in which time is given freely to benefit another person, group, or organization" (Wilson, 2000, p. 215). Some scholars define volunteering somewhat differently by indicating that individuals and their families are not beneficiaries of their volunteer activities (Liu & Besser, 2003). Volunteering has the altruistic nature and leisure concept (Liu, Ching, & Wu, 2017), which indicates that volunteering is free from coercion or moral obligation, and individuals have the free rights to accept or reject the volunteer activities (Stebbins, 2007). The most recent and comprehensive definition of volunteering is "freely chosen and deliberate helping activities that extend over time, are engaged in without expectation of reward or other compensation and often through formal organizations, and that are performed on behalf of causes or individuals who desire assistance" (Snyder & Omoto, 2008, p. 3). The term civic engagement is usually used interchangeably with volunteering in current literature (Martinson & Minkler, 2006). Civic engagement is defined as "the process in which individuals are actively participating in the life of their communities through voting, joining community groups, and volunteering" (Harvard School of Public Health/MetLife Foundation, 2004, p. 3). Even though the concept of civic engagement is overlapping with voluntarism, civic engagement is more focused on formal volunteering at the community level.

Demographic and Contextual Factors of Volunteering

The choice of volunteer activities differs by demographic factors, including age, gender, education, income, and marital status. Women or people with higher education are more likely to engage in volunteer activities (Schwingel, Niti, Tang, & Ng, 2009). Compared with other age groups, volunteers aged 65 and older are more likely to engage in religion-related activities, as 42.7% of them volunteer through religious organizations (Bureau of Labor Statistics, 2015). Male volunteers are more willing to participate in general labor, supplying transportation, and being a coach or referee; by contrast, female volunteers prefer to engage in collecting, preparing and distributing food, and tutoring or teaching students (Bureau of Labor Statistics, 2015). Older men are more likely to perform such volunteer activities as yard work and repair, and older women are more likely to volunteer as cooks or work in religious organizations (Liu & Besser, 2003).

Besides demographic factors, previous studies have demonstrated that there are urban-rural differences in volunteering participation; however, the residential difference between rural and urban communities remains unclear. By examining social participation among Wisconsin older residents, Vogelsang (2016) indicated that rural older adults were less likely to participate in social activities compared with those residing in urban areas, especially in such activities as meeting with friends, attending art and cultural activities, or exercise groups. In contrast, Glasgow and Brown (2012) pointed out that in rural destinations of older migration, older adults actively engaged in social and community activities as leaders and volunteers. Moreover, rural residents are more likely to have intimately social interactions and strong ties to the community (Mair & Thivierge-Rikard, 2010; Keating, 2008). Those higher levels of formal and informal social ties, sense of community, and norms of collective action are significantly related to more community involvement among rural residents (Liu & Besser, 2003).

Effects of Voluntarism on Individuals and Rural Communities

Effects on Individuals

Since retirees are more likely to experience the loss of social roles and former social connections, volunteering and civic engagement provide opportunities for them to make adjustments in later life. Extensive literature has demonstrated that volunteering and civic engagement not only allow older adults to make valuable contributions to society but also improve their physical and psychological well-being as measured by various indicators, including better cognitive functioning and physical functioning, improved self-rated health, higher levels of life satisfaction and sense of self-worth and accomplishment, reduced risk of dementia and decreased cognitive complaints, and reduced depressive symptoms and psychological distress (Choi, Tang, Kim, & Turk, 2016; Morrow-Howell, Hinterlong, Rozario, & Tang, 2003; Schwingel et al., 2009; Tang, 2009; Griep et al., 2017). Especially for older adults who live in rural communities with limited personal and social resources, it seems that they benefit more from volunteering engagement, as such roles may increase the size and vitality of their social network, as well as their perceived power, prestige, access to resources, and emotional gratification (Morrow-Howell et al., 2003). Compared to nonvolunteers, volunteers also benefit from expanded social networks and increased social support from others (Pilkington, Windsor, & Crisp, 2012). Social integration and social influence from peers may promote the exchange of shared norms of healthy behaviors, which further motivate older adults to adopt healthier behaviors to gain beneficial health consequences (Berkman, Glass, Brissette, & Seeman, 2000).

Effects on Rural Communities

Volunteerism has beneficial effects on the development and unity of rural communities. A case study of a volunteer program in rural communities demonstrated that volunteering could maintain communities through promoting close relationships among community members, keeping older adults engaged in social activities, promoting mutual understanding, easing loneliness, and providing accessible assistance to rural older adults (Butler & Eckart, 2007). It is also believed that civic engagement could be an effective way to solve social problems and to empower citizens in rural communities (Butler & Eckart, 2007).

The gap between increased demands for social services and limited resources in rural communities can be filled by volunteering and community activities, such as assistance and companionship provided by older volunteers (Butler & Eckart, 2007). Also, volunteering in rural areas can relieve the pressure of local government agencies when faced with severe budgetary constraints. For example, the Pennsylvania Emergency Management Agency (PEMA) provides a volunteer program named "Citizen Corps," which is ideal for rural communities. In PEMA, volunteers and part-time workers serve as the fire, EMS and emergency management personnel, as well as law enforcement personnel (Pennsylvania Emergency Management Agency, 2019). Moreover, based on the concept of "neighbor helping neighbor," the program calls for rural residents to be active in promoting neighborhood security, to take care of their neighbors when a disaster strikes, and to denote their expertise in medical and public health areas during emergencies (Pennsylvania Emergency Management Agency, 2019).

Challenges of Volunteering in Rural Communities

The Socioecological Model indicates that individuals are affected by contextual factors of their surrounding communities, including interpersonal, institutional, organizational, community level, and structural characteristics (Bengtson & Settersten, 2016; Lu, Xu, & Shelley, 2020). Compared with urban older residents, older adults living in rural communities may face particular contextual challenges. According to the 2005–2009 American Community Survey (ACS), 13.1% of adults aged 65 or older residing in nonmetropolitan areas were below the federal poverty threshold, whereas 9.3% of urban older adults lived in poverty (Glasgow & Brown, 2012). As the poverty rate in rural areas is higher than urban areas, rural older adults may hesitate to get involved in social activities because of the shortage of financial resources and social services (Butler & Eckart, 2007). Moreover, the volunteer opportunities provided for older adults are limited, and older adults may not have sufficient information and access to those limited opportunities, especially in low socioeconomic status (SES) neighborhoods. Community environment and public facilities can also impact volunteering and civic engagement among rural older adults. The extended distance between social service organizations and residential areas and the lack of transportation in rural communities often become the major obstacles to volunteering (Krout, 2001; Butler & Eckart, 2007). Resulting from the shortages of sufficient health care and deficiency of insurance coverage, rural areas are shown to have higher prevalence of mortality and morbidity, which may prevent rural older adults from actively engaging in volunteering (Weinhold & Gurtner, 2014; Anderson, Saman, Lipsky, & Lutfiyya, 2015).

Recommendations for Promoting Volunteering among Rural Older Adults

To promote older adults' volunteering in rural communities, distinct and innovative efforts are needed by considering the characteristics of rural communities and the challenges faced by older rural residents.

Provide Innovative Volunteering Activities to Remove Transportation Obstacles

Unlike urban areas with dense public transportation networks and service centers located in neighborhoods, rural areas have limited transportation for older adults to travel to remote service centers (Kaye & Butler, 2012). To address the issues caused by inconvenient transportation in rural communities, volunteer organizations can design and provide home-based volunteer activities that allow rural older adults to perform volunteering functions within their homes. Optimizing the use of technology in volunteer programs, such as online tutoring and online organizational meetings, has fueled the growth of opportunities available in the older adult's home.

Consciously Identify Needs and Create New Volunteering Opportunities

To make full use of scarce resources in rural communities, volunteer organizations need to conduct careful assessments of available resources and needs for engagement with various activities among rural older adults (Kaye & Butler, 2012). The opportunities for meaningful engagement in voluntarism and civic services should be created and provided for older adults from diverse groups.

Engage Low-Income Older Adults in Volunteering

Financial hardship can be a barrier for low-income older adults to be engaged in volunteering. Compensation and reimbursement can be a useful tool to motivate rural older adults with economic difficulties to participate in volunteer activities (Butler & Eckart, 2007).

Conclusion

Volunteering is a significant public approach to maximizing social integration and increasing health promotion among older adults. Particularly for those residing in rural communities with limited personal and social resources, volunteer engagement may help reduce social isolation, improve social relations, and increase social support. Policy and practice efforts are needed to overcome contextual and institutional barriers to volunteering, expand volunteering opportunities in rural areas, and optimize positive volunteering experience and associated outcomes.

References

Anderson, T. J., Saman, D. M., Lipsky, M. S., & Lutfiyya, M. N. (2015). A cross-sectional study on health differences between rural and non-rural US counties using the county health rankings. *BMC Health Services Research*, *15*(1), 441. doi:10.1186/s12913-015-1053-3

Bengtson, V. L., & Settersten, R., Jr. (Eds.). (2016). *Handbook of theories of aging*. New York: Springer.

Berkman, L. F., Glass, T., Brissette, I., & Seeman, T. E. (2000). From social integration to health: Durkheim in the new millennium. *Social Science & Medicine*, *51*(6), 843–857. doi:10.1016/S0277-9536(00)00065-4

Bureau of Labor Statistics. (2015). *Volunteering in the United States*. Retrieved July 30, 2019, from www.bls.gov/news.release/volun.nr0.htm

Butler, S. S., & Eckart, D. (2007). Civic engagement among older adults in a rural community: A case study of the senior companion program. *Journal of Community Practice*, *15*(3), 77–98. doi:10.1300/J125v15n03_05

Choi, E., Tang, F., Kim, S. G., & Turk, P. (2016). Longitudinal relationships between productive activities and functional health in later years: A multivariate latent growth curve modeling approach. *The International Journal of Aging and Human Development, 83*(4), 418–440. doi:10.1177/0091415016657557

Glasgow, N., & Brown, D. L. (2012). Rural ageing in the United States: Trends and contexts. *Journal of Rural Studies, 28*(4), 422–431. doi:10.1016/j.healthplace.2016.09.010

Griep, Y., Hanson, L. M., Vantilborgh, T., Janssens, L., Jones, S. K., & Hyde, M. (2017). Can volunteering in later life reduce the risk of dementia? A 5-year longitudinal study among volunteering and non-volunteering retired seniors. *PloS One, 12*(3). doi:10.1371/journal.pone.0173885 M

Harvard School of Public Health/MetLife Foundation. (2004). *Reinventing aging: Baby boomers and civic engagement*. Boston: Harvard School of Public Health, Center for Health Communication.

Kaye, L. W., & Butler, S. (2012). *Gerontological social work in small towns and rural communities*. London: Routledge.

Keating, N. C. (Ed.). (2008). *Rural ageing: A good place to grow old?* Bristol: Policy Press.

Krout, J. A. (2001). Community services and housing for rural elders. *The Public Policy and Aging Report, 12*(1), 6–8. doi:10.1093/ppar/12.1.6

Liu, A. Q., & Besser, T. (2003). Social capital and participation in community improvement activities by elderly residents in small towns and rural communities. *Rural Sociology, 68*(3), 343–365. doi:10.1111/j.1549-0831.2003.tb00141.x

Liu, E. S. C., Ching, C. W., & Wu, J. (2017). Who is a volunteer? A cultural and temporal exploration of volunteerism. *Journal of Human Behavior in the Social Environment, 27*(6), 530–545. doi:10.1080/10911359.2017.1295715

Lu, P., Xu, C., & Shelley, M. (2020). A state-of-the-art review of the socio-ecological correlates of volunteerism among older adults. *Ageing & Society*, 1–25. doi:10.1017/S0144686X20000082

Mair, C. A., & Thivierge-Rikard, R. V. (2010). The strength of strong ties for older rural adults: Regional distinctions in the relationship between social interaction and subjective well-being. *The International Journal of Aging and Human Development, 70*(2), 119–143. doi:10.2190/AG.70.2.b

Martinson, M., & Minkler, M. (2006). Civic engagement and older adults: A critical perspective. *The Gerontologist, 46*(3), 318–324. doi:10.1093/geront/46.3.318

Morrow-Howell, N., Hinterlong, J., Rozario, P. A., & Tang, F. (2003). Effects of volunteering on the well-being of older adults. *The Journals of Gerontology Series B: Psychological Sciences and Social Sciences, 58*(3), S137–S145. doi:10.1093/geronb/58.3.S137

Pennsylvania Emergency Management Agency. *Citizen Corps*. Retrieved September 30, 2019, from www.pema.pa.gov/planningandpreparedness/readypa/Pages/Citizenspercent20Corps.aspx

Pilkington, P. D., Windsor, T. D., & Crisp, D. A. (2012). Volunteering and subjective well-being in midlife and older adults: The role of supportive social networks. *Journals of Gerontology Series B: Psychological Sciences and Social Sciences, 67*(2), 249–260. doi:10.1093/geronb/gbr154

Schwingel, A., Niti, M. M., Tang, C., & Ng, T. P. (2009). Continued work employment and volunteerism and mental well-being of older adults: Singapore longitudinal ageing studies. *Age and Ageing, 38*(5), 531–537. doi:10.1093/ageing/afp089

Snyder, M., & Omoto, A. (2008). Volunteerism: Social issues, perspectives and social policy implications. *Social Issues and Policy Review, 2*(1), 1–36.

Stebbins, R. A. (2007). A leisure-based, theoretic typology of volunteers and volunteering. *Leisure Studies Association Newsletter, 78*, 9–12.

Tang, F. (2009). Late-life volunteering and trajectories of physical health. *Journal of Applied Gerontology, 28*(4), 524–533. doi:10.1177/0733464808327454

Vogelsang, E. M. (2016). Older adult social participation and its relationship with health: Rural-urban differences. *Health & Place, 42*, 111–119. doi:10.1016/j.healthplace.2016.09.010

Weinhold, I., & Gurtner, S. (2014). Understanding shortages of sufficient health care in rural areas. *Health Policy, 118*(2), 201–214. doi:10.1016/j.healthpol.2014.07.018

Wilson, J. (2000). Volunteering. *Annual Review of Sociology, 26*(1), 215–240. doi:10.1146/annurev.soc.26.1.215

78
OLDER WOMEN

Jennifer A. Crittenden and Brittney R. Beaulieu

In the context of rural communities, older women can be seen as making significant contributions to social and community life. From informal caregiving to paid employment and formal volunteering, women in rural communities create a safety net for their families and fellow community members. Despite these contributions to community life, rural women face key challenges and issues. While women's issues resonate across rural/urban boundaries, there are special considerations for rural women that impact health, well-being, and quality of life. For example, older men tend to outnumber older women in rural areas, creating risk for invisibility when it comes to women's issues (U.S. Census Bureau, 2019).

Health Disparities

There are significant health differences between urban and rural women with those living in rural areas having a higher likelihood of developing chronic health conditions, overall poor health, and disability (American College of Obstetricians and Gynecologists, 2016). Older women in rural areas experience higher prevalence rates for chronic illnesses and disabilities than those in urban areas. Women in rural areas have a 17% higher chance of getting diabetes, 23% higher chance of being obese, and a 14% higher chance of having depression (National Rural Health Association [NRHA], 2013). These health issues are further compounded by poverty, lack of access to exercise programming, or a safe outdoor environment in which to exercise (NRHA, 2013). The delivery and accessibility of care is more challenging in rural settings as specialists, such as gynecologists, cardiologists, and pulmonologists, can be located hours away in larger hub communities. The experience of disability is common in rural areas with as many as four out of five older rural women reporting a disability (NRHA, 2013). Many older women develop health conditions that require specialists and do not have access to appropriate health insurance to pay for these services (American College of Obstetricians and Gynecologists, 2016).

There are many areas of improvement needed when addressing older women's health in rural areas. Efforts are continuously being made within rural communities to provide transportation to services outside of the immediate vicinity, when older adults are unable to transport themselves. Rural primary care and community-based health care centers are central to identifying and addressing health conditions earlier on in the disease progression. Key screenings for women include those for osteoporosis, falls risk, breast cancer, blood pressure, diabetes, and urinary incontinence (Murukesu, Singh, & Shahar, 2019; NRHA, 2013; U.S. Preventive Services Task Force, n.d.). Early detection of these and other conditions allows for ample time for connecting with more remote specialty care as needed.

Women and Poverty

Poverty has long been a women's issue. The experience of poverty for women is associated with a variety of factors—from access to education and work opportunities to disability and family care responsibilities. Over the course of a woman's life span, poverty has been found to be precipitated by lower overall earnings because of lower pay, part-time workforce participation, and/or caregiving responsibilities. In addition, the loss of a partner through divorce, death, or separation is a common factor that influences a woman's poverty status. For rural older women, widowhood is a significant factor that leads to poverty (Gillen & Kim, 2009).

On a societal and community level, rural poverty, like poverty in urban areas, is firmly rooted in historical sexism and structural racism. In general, rural women are more likely to experience poverty when compared to their urban peers with single women and women within single-earner households being most at risk of poverty (Smith & Pruitt, 2017). Women of color are further impacted by racial inequalities that are prevalent in rural areas, with black/African American rural residents having the highest rate of poverty at nearly 32%, followed by American Indians/Alaska Natives at 31% and Hispanics at 24% (USDA Economic Research Service, 2020). In rural areas, poverty is a significant experience that negatively impacts access to opportunity and the ability to satisfy basic support needs.

Interventions to address poverty among rural older women include financial education that can help women tap into the value of existing assets and understand options for building financial security with fixed income and limited assets (Gillen & Kim, 2009). Several federal programs have been developed that address older adult poverty by providing access to income and employment. The Foster Grandparent and Senior Companion programs, both national volunteer programs, provide the opportunity for supplementing retirement income for older volunteers who wish to give back to their communities. Both programs provide nontaxable stipend income to volunteers in exchange for their service, creating a win-win for rural communities through engaging volunteers and supporting low-income older adults (Morrow-Howell, Backes, O'Neill, & Greenfield, 2018).

Another notable federal program with anti-poverty roots is the Senior Community Service Employment Program (SCSEP), which is designed to provide job training to older adults, building skills for workforce entry or reentry. Program evaluation results indicate that SCSEP successfully engages older women as two-thirds of their clients are female, and women were more likely to exit the program into paid employment at the conclusion of the program compared to their male counterparts. Rural participants were also found to have slightly lower, but similar, rates of employment compared to urban program participants at program exit (Kogan et al., 2012).

Social Isolation

Social isolation occurs for many older women after the death of a spouse, retirement, severe illness, or passing of family and friends. Studies show that communication is important in the healthy aging process (Walkner, Weare, & Tully, 2018). Consistent social connection and social experiences increase dopamine and support the mind's ability to feel happy and motivated

(Berke, 2018). With a lack of natural support, many rural older women face social isolation leading to a variety of negative consequences, including depression, anxiety, and malnutrition (Walkner et al., 2018).

With COVID-19's guidelines of sheltering in place and social distancing, implemented in 2020, older women in rural areas were observed as being unable to see their family members or attend activities at community centers (Bhutani & Cooper, 2020). Many peer centers, senior centers, and community centers were closed because of the pandemic, as community members were told to shelter in place. The closures of these services left many women without the familiar avenues from which to obtain emotional and tangible support required to live a healthy life (Walkner et al., 2018).

Peer centers provide a safe place for individuals to go when they need additional support or to reduce isolation. Many older adults with mental illness attend peer centers to receive structure, support, and to participate in wellness activities (Reinhardt-Wood, Kinter, & Burke, 2018). Peer centers provide activities that give purpose to the individual, while teaching them skills on how to reduce isolation within their home. Peer centers often have crafts and activities targeted toward women, such as paint nights, knitting, coffee groups, and volunteer opportunities. Although many people can communicate via social media, a considerable number of older women in rural areas access a computer at their local library, college, or a family member's home. With the stay at home order put into effect during COVID-19, these computer access points were no longer accessible (Walkner et al., 2018).

Domestic Violence

Social isolation represents a barrier to identifying and addressing a variety of women's issues, including domestic violence, or intimate partner violence (IPV). IPV has long been a key women's issue across the age spectrum, further magnified within a rural setting where social supports and services may be lacking, not fully developed, or accessible. It is estimated that close to 27% of women ages 65 and older experience some form of domestic violence with a lifetime prevalence of domestic violence affecting as many as 55% of women. Nearly a quarter of this abuse occurs within a family or romantic relationship (Brossoie & Roberto, 2015; Pathak, Dhairyawan, & Tariq, 2019). Nine percent of abuse is verbal in nature, and nearly one in five incidences of abuse is perpetrated by a significant other and not a member of the immediate family (Brossoie & Roberto, 2015).

In rural communities, the response to domestic violence can be hampered by a lack of program resources. Privacy is also a barrier to women seeking help in rural communities as it can be challenging to find a provider that does not know the perpetrator or does not have an existing familial connection with the known perpetrator (Brossoie & Roberto, 2015). Many older women fear accepting help, as their partner may find out or it may be difficult to leave the community to ensure safety. In some cases, older women's reports of abuse are ignored because of ageism among providers or an existing relationship between the provider and the perpetrator (Brossoie & Roberto, 2015).

Intimate partner violence is often addressed at emergency shelters after the woman seeks out safety. In rural communities, residents are more likely to know where these shelters are, which makes it difficult for older women to safely obtain support. Further, IPV is driven by a dependence on the perpetrator, which can be reinforced by rural dynamics. For example, without public transportation, an older woman is more likely to rely on their partner for transportation. Older women are also more likely to rely on their partner's retirement income, making it difficult to leave an abusive relationship (Pathak et al., 2019; Zang, 2020). In many cases, the abuser will take control of the victim's Social Security income or household finances so that the victim is financially unable to leave (National Clearinghouse on Abuse in Later Life [NCALL], 2013).

Here, too, rural health-care providers, such as primary care providers, can play a key role in detection and prevention. One simple screen that can be integrated into primary care is to ask whether the older patients feel safe in their home (Brossoie & Roberto, 2015). In addition to medical settings, trusted community members such as mail carriers and hairdressers are being educated on warning signs of IPV (Roberto et al., 2013). These individuals are trained on how to recognize IPV and how to safely refer individuals to needed supports. The hairdresser model specifically teaches hairdressers to identify warning signs of IPV, help their clients to increase their own self-confidence, and help them to identify local IPV resources (McLaren et al., 2010). In addition, faith communities are counted among those trusted entities in rural areas and, like hairdressers and primary care providers, can play a role in identifying and addressing IPV. Faith community leaders are likely to be aware of IPV in their community and, with the proper training, can intervene (Podnieks & Wilson, 2003). Regardless of the trusted source of intervention, women experiencing IPV report that sensitivity toward their safety and personal IPV risk creates a positive outcome (Roberto et al., 2013).

Summary

In summary, rural women face significant health and resource access challenges that, if overcome, can support their well-being and place within community life. Key interventions that support and empower women in rural communities should emphasize health promotion, disease management, the eradication of poverty, and the elimination of domestic violence while placing a special emphasis on social connection and supporting women of color.

References

American College of Obstetricians and Gynecologists. (2016). *Committee opinion*. Retrieved from www.acog.org

Berke, J. D. (2018). What does dopamine mean? *Nature Neuroscience*, *21*(6), 787–793. doi:10.1038/s41593-018-0152-y

Bhutani, S., & Cooper, J. A. (2020). COVID-19 related home confinement in adults: Weight gain risks and opportunities. *Obesity*. doi:10.1002/oby.22904

Brossoie, N., & Roberto, K. A. (2015). Community professionals' response to intimate partner violence against rural older women. *Journal of Elder Abuse & Neglect: Neglect, Abuse, and Violence Against Older Women*, *27*(4–5), 470–488. doi:10.1080/08946566.2015.1095664

Gillen, M., & Kim, H. (2009). Older women and poverty transition: Consequences from widowhood. *Journal of Applied Gerontology*, *28*(3), 320–341.

Kogan, D., Betesh, H., Negoita, M., Salzman, J., Paulen, L., Cuza, H., . . . Cloud, P. (2012). *Evaluation of the Senior Community Service Employment Program (SCSEP): Process and outcomes study*. Princeton, NJ: Mathematica Policy Research.

McLaren, S., Thoms, A., Serin, S., Garad, R., Joyce, A., & McCormick, J. (2010). Hairdressers as a resource in addressing family violence. *Health Promotion Journal of Australia: Official Journal of Australian Association of Health Promotion Professionals*, *21*(3), 236–238. doi:10.1071/HE10236

Morrow-Howell, N., Backes, K., O'Neill, G., & Greenfield, J. C. (2018). Volunteering in later life: Policies and programs to support a resilient aging society. In B. Resnick, L. P. Gwyther, & K. A. Roberto (Eds.), *Resilience in aging: Concepts, research, and outcomes* (2nd ed., pp. 171–189). Cham, Switzerland: Springer.

Murukesu, R. R., Singh, D. K. A., & Shahar, S. (2019). Urinary incontinence among urban and rural community dwelling older women: Prevalence, risk factors and quality of life. *BMC Public Health*, *19*(Suppl 4), 529–611. doi:10.1186/s12889-019-6870-6

National Clearinghouse on Abuse in Later Life (NCALL). (2013). *An overview of abuse in later life*. Retrieved from www.ncdsv.org/images/NCALL_Overview-of-abuse-in-later-life_2013.pdf

National Rural Health Association. (2013). *Rural women's health*. Retrieved from www.ruralhealthweb.org

Pathak, N., Dhairyawan, R., & Tariq, S. (2019). The experience of intimate partner violence among older women: A narrative review. *Maturitas, 121*, 63–75. doi:10.1016/j.maturitas.2018.12.011

Podnieks, E., & Wilson, S. (2003). An exploratory study of responses to elder abuse in faith communities. *Journal of Elder Abuse & Neglect, 15*(3–4), 137–162. doi:10.1300/J084v15n03_09

Reinhardt-Wood, D. L., Kinter, K. T., & Burke, K. (2018). Inception of a peer-run wellness center at a state psychiatric hospital. *Journal of Psychosocial Nursing and Mental Health Services, 56*(12), 31–35. doi:10.3928/02793695-20180612-01

Roberto, K. A., Brossoie, N., McPherson, M. C., Pulsifer, M. B., & Brown, P. N. (2013). Violence against rural older women: Promoting community awareness and action. *Australasian Journal on Ageing, 32*(1), 2–7. doi:10.1111/j.1741-6612.2012.00649.x

Smith, K., & Pruitt, L. (2017). Changing gender roles and rural poverty. In A. Tickamyer, J. Sherman, & J. Warlick (Eds.), *Rural poverty in the United States* (pp. 117–140). New York: Columbia University Press. doi:10.7312/tick17222.11

U.S. Census Bureau. (2019). *In some states, more than half of older residents live in rural areas*. Retrieved from www.census.gov/library/stories/2019/10/older-population-in-rural-america.html

U.S.D.A. Economic Research Service. (2020). *Rural poverty and well-being*. Retrieved from www.ers.usda.gov/topics/rural-economy-population/rural-poverty-well-being/

U.S. Preventive Services Task Force. (n.d.). *U.S. Preventive Services Task Force A & B screening recommendations*. Retrieved from www.uspreventiveservicestaskforce.org

Walkner, T. J., Weare, A. M., & Tully, M. (2018). "You get old. You get invisible": Social isolation and the challenge of communicating with aging women. *Journal of Women & Aging, 30*(5), 399–416. doi:10.1080/08952841.2017.1304785

Zang, E. (2020). Spillover effects of a husband's retirement on a woman's health: Evidence from urban China. *Social Science & Medicine, 245*. doi:10.1016/j.socscimed.2019.112684

79
WORKFORCE

John Dorrer

Overview

Demographic transformation and economic restructuring are having profound impacts on rural America. The loss of jobs and, in many instances, the elimination of entire industries has shattered the destiny and identity of many rural communities. Large numbers of once productive workers with outdated skills are being left behind. The impacts of economic dislocation have contributed to outmigration and population decline. These population losses undermine the maintenance of community infrastructure and institutions. The erosion of social cohesion and decline of living standards are the result. Policymakers are searching for constructive solutions including creative strategies to tap idle rural workers.

Traditional industries such as agriculture, mining, forestry, construction, and manufacturing have been particularly hard hit and slow to recover since the recession of 2008–2009. Men over 50 years of age have suffered the most from job losses in these industries. And while urban America has recovered the jobs lost over the course of the recession, rural America has not. Globalization and technological innovation continue to reshape industry structures and locational choices with adverse impacts on rural America (CED, 2019). Furthermore, the outmigration of younger workers severely limits economic prospects of rural areas over the long term (Porter, 2018).

Retirement decisions are also being upended, including for the aging rural workforce. Increasing life spans and the need for supplements to retirement incomes have stimulated increased labor force participation of older workers (Employee Benefits Research Institute, 2019). For older workers residing in rural communities, however, their abilities to extend working lives and supplement incomes are limited. Declining home equity and other mobility constraints force aging rural workers to remain in place and forego available job opportunities in urban areas.

Struggling workers have lost incomes along with identity and purpose. Many have been forced to turn to income support programs or disability benefits to get by. Deepening pathologies including addiction and mental health problems have afflicted this marginalized aging rural workforce to a higher degree than their urban counterparts. With benefit payments often inadequate to cover living costs, workers end up supplementing benefit payments with part-time employment, if they can find it (Johnson & Gosselin, 2018). Active labor market and well-being policies focused on the aging workforce need immediate attention from policymakers.

Population, Labor Force, and Employment by the Numbers

Long-term demographic changes continue to affect rural America. The share of the U.S. population living in rural counties has dropped and the percentage of those 65 years and older is increasing. Projections indicate that by 2040, the population 65 years and older will number 80.8 million and lead to higher concentrations of an aging population in rural America barring changes to current patterns of migration (Smith & Trevelyan, 2018).

Researchers at the Carsey Institute at the University of New Hampshire identified depopulation of rural areas as a significant factor contributing to rural transformation. Nearly 35% of rural counties are experiencing population loss as a result of outmigration by young adults (Johnson & Lichter, 2019). Such outmigration contributes to lower birth rates and reductions in the prime working age population. These trends impede economic recovery and challenge the viability of some rural regions over the long run.

There are some signs, however, that long-term trends of rural outmigration may be coming to an end. The geographic mobility of Americans is slowing overall. A report from the U.S. Department of Agriculture (2018) indicates that rural (nonmetro) counties added population for the first time this decade. These recent population gains are attributed to increased net migration. Other key positive indicators highlighted include declining rural unemployment, rising incomes, and declining poverty since 2013 (USDA, 2018). Most population gains are occurring in rural regions adjacent to urban centers and/or recreational centers attracting retirees (USDA, 2018).

Employment gains in rural America remain weak. Nonmetro employment represented 16% of employment in metro regions in 2000 and by 2018 had dropped to 13%. Nonmetro regions added jobs over the course of the economic recovery between 2010 and 2018 but at a much lower rate (5.3%) compared to metro regions (17.7%). American Community Survey (ACS) data show that fewer rural older people were employed during 2012–2016 than their urban counterparts (16% and 16.6%, respectively). A higher percentage of rural older people (83.4%)

Table 79.1 Employment Change 2000–2018, Metro and Nonmetro Comparisons

Area	*2000*	*2010*	*Pct. Change 2000–2010*	*2018*	*Pct. Change 2010–2018*
Metro	142,396,424	150,313,128	5.5	176,955,385	17.7
Non Metro	22,974,376	22,588,572	-1.7	23,790,615	5.3

Source: U.S Department of Commerce, Bureau of Economic Analysis, County Business Patterns

Table 79.2 Changes in Key Labor Force Indicators for Workers 65 and Over, 2010 to 2019

Key Indicator	*2010*	*2019*	*Change*
Civilian Labor Force (000s)	6.718	10.663	3.945
Civilian Labor Force Participation Rate	17.4	20.2	2.8
Employed (000s)	6.268	10.347	4.079
Employment-Population Ratio	16.2	19.6	3.4

Source: U.S. Bureau of Labor Statistics, Current Population Survey, Annual Averages

were not in the labor force compared with urban people (82.6%) (Smith & Trevelyan, 2018). States such as Maine, Vermont, Mississippi, and West Virginia are on the leading edge of these trends.

The aging U.S workforce now has a greater share of older workers and their increasing participation has contributed to buttressing U.S. labor force growth (Committee for Economic Development, 2019). Between 2010 and 2019, workers 65 years of age or older have increased their numbers in the labor force by nearly four million. Those 65 years and older reported a labor force participation rate of 20.2%, an increase of 2.8 percentage points during this period. Their employment population ratio (the percentage of the population in that age cohort employed or looking for work) has shown a gain of 3.4 percentage points. A larger presence of older workers in the labor force is creating both challenges and opportunities for employers.

If older workers are to remain engaged in the workplace, however, they will need to acquire new skills, adapt to new technologies and adjust to new workplace cultures. Older rural workers were less likely to have attained education beyond high school and a significantly smaller percentage have completed four-year college degrees (Escobari, Seyal, & Meany, 2019). Trends in the increased labor force participation of older workers are encouraging. Finding good jobs in rural America remains problematic (Partdrige, 2020).

Americans are increasingly unhappy with retirement, suggesting that there could be more older Americans potentially willing to work longer (Shattuck, 2010). The share of newly retired adults who report being dissatisfied with retirement doubled between 1998 and 2014, to 16%. (Johnson & Gosselin, 2018). In another survey of retirees, more than 40% of retirees indicated that they left the workforce earlier than they had planned, citing health problems, a disability, and changes at their company as the most common reasons for earlier-than-expected retirement (EBRI, 2019). The same survey indicates that roughly 80% of workers approaching retirement say they expect to work for pay at some point after they retire, while only 28% of retirees report having worked for pay since retiring. One reason for the increase in older Americans working is their increased longevity and relatively good health at later ages. More than nine out of ten workers ages 55 to 60 report good health (Burtless, 2016).

Health care remains one of the key sectors in the American economy. The availability of rural health-care and home care services, however, is becoming more problematic as hospital consolidation and the lack of physicians is limiting access to health care for an aging population. Furthermore, the health-care and home care workforce in rural America is aging even more rapidly than many other employment sectors. Growing numbers of health-care and social assistance workers are expected to exit the workforce over the next ten years. Their replacements will be hard to find. Maine, for example, is already struggling with this problem (Stein, 2019).

Program and Policy Innovations for an Aging Workforce in Rural America

The curtailment of working lives for many rural workers has exacted both economic and social costs along with personal tragedies. Interventions on behalf of aging rural populations are needed. Such strategies, however, must challenge old assumptions about economic and workforce development. Significant structural and technological changes are redefining the workings of labor markets and the preferences of employers.

The emergence of the digital economy has given rise to new concepts of remote work and the ability to transfer work efforts over the internet. Remote back office operations, outsourcing, call centers, and shared workspaces now provide new possibilities for work in rural regions of the nation. Flexible work arrangements including contingent work and telecommuting offer rural workers more employment opportunities over those physically available in the region.

Labor Market Navigation and Development of New Workforce Skills

The aging rural workforce matured in a labor market environment where employment was stable and unemployment was covered by unemployment insurance benefits (Rogers, 2008). Skill sets and job knowledge typically served workers well over their work lives and on-the-job training was the primary means for mastering new job skills. For many older rural workers, however, their job search methods and career planning skills are rooted in the past. They may not be able to navigate this new, emergent labor market landscape, including choosing the right education and training programs that prepare them for skills in demand (Van Horn, 2015). The right skills remain critical for workers to be able to compete for emerging employment opportunities (Smith & Meaney, 2016). And while education and training opportunities may not be as widely available in rural regions, the increasing availability of low-cost online learning opportunities can overcome such obstacles (Smith & Meaney, 2016).

More proactive efforts must be made to educate workers while they are still employed. Workers will be in a better position to acquire new skills and plan new careers in advance of layoffs and income loss.

Expansion of Employment Programs for an Aging Rural Workforce

More active labor market and economic development policies will be needed to overcome lack of job opportunities, outmoded skills, and general biases that impact older workers.

A more intensive array of counseling and support services customized to the needs of an aging rural workforce should be made available to American workers (Van Horn & Heidkamp, 2019). Adult education programs and America's Job Centers established under the federal Workforce Innovation Opportunity Act (WIOA) can play a key role in improving the labor market literacy and job placement assistance offered to rural workers.

The Senior Community Service Employment Program (SCSEP) is a long-standing community service and work-based job training program for older Americans. Eligibility criteria require that individuals are unemployed, over 55 years of age, and have a family income of no more than 125% of the federal poverty level. The current funding level is $38.5 million. The SCSEP offers an immediate opportunity to expand workforce development programs for this population. In addition to significant funding increases, the SCSEP will require less restrictive eligibility criteria and additional program design features to cover an aging rural workforce that is growing in numbers.

Broadband Is Key to Economic Recovery and Skill Development

Technology is the key to rural workforce development and skill training. Rural regions have not benefited from the necessary connections to broadband. Rural inhabitants are penalized by lack of access to the digital economy, including limits on participating in online education and training. A combination of federal, state, and local investments is needed to bring the full capacity of broadband networks to rural regions. Only when this capacity is fully operational will stranded rural workers be able to compete for employment opportunities that are not place-dependent.

More Emphasis on Rural Economic Development

More active economic development strategies are needed for rural America. The federal Department of the Treasury sponsors the New Markets Tax Credits (NMTC) program. The NMTC encourages private funds to be raised and mandates that 20% of investments be in nonmetro areas. This requirement has led to over $10 billion invested since 2003. The Opportunities Zones Act included in the 2017 U.S. tax reform bill offers up to 100% forgiveness of the capital gains tax for investors willing to invest in distressed census tracts for a stated duration, including underserved rural communities. Incentives to invest, however, should be accompanied by strategies to engage idle rural workers including those over 50. They also need to encourage the relocation of younger workers and their families to rebuild rural populations.

Summary

Worker scarcity and workforce development remain formidable challenges for American business and industry. The quality and availability of human capital remain fundamental drivers of economic growth. An aging rural workforce may be able to find new opportunities to extend their working lives and improve living standards in the context of economic innovation and tight labor markets. Idle workers may once again assume a new purpose. Rescuing aging rural workers, however, will require renewed commitments to invest in economic and skill development, internet technologies, work experience, and internships to effectively connect these workers to current labor markets and concepts of how work is performed. We will need progressive policies that provide incentives and support an aging workforce to extend their working lives and continue to make contributions.

References

Burtless, G. (2016). *Labor force dynamics in the Great Recession and its aftermath: Implications for older workers*. Chestnut Hill, MA: Center for Retirement Research, Boston College.

Committee for Economic Development (CED). (2019, October). *Growing the American workforce: Bolstering participation is critical for U.S. competitiveness and economic strength*. Washington, DC: CED.

Employee Benefits Research Institute (EBRI). (2019, April). *2019 retirement confidence survey: Summary report*. Washington, DC: Employment Benefit Research Institute.

Escobari, M., Seyal, I., & Meany, M. (2019, December). *Realism about reskilling: Upgrading the career prospects of American low wage workers*. Workforce of the Future Initiative. Washington, DC: Brookings Institution.

Johnson, K. M., & Lichter, D. T. (2019, Winter). *Rural depopulation in a rapidly urbanizing America*. National Brief #139. Washington, DC: Carsey School of Public Policy, University of New Hampshire.

Johnson, R. W., & Gosselin, P. (2018, December). *How secure is employment at older ages*. Research Report. Washington, DC: Urban Institute.

Partdrige, M. D. (2020). *Rural America's stagnant economic performance: What's the role of declining dynamism*. Washington, DC: American Enterprise Institute.

Porter, E. (2018, December 14). The hard truths of trying to "save" the rural economy. *New York Times*.

Rogers, W. (2008). The *consequences of recent job growth on older, low income workers*. Retrieved from https://www.researchgate.net/publication/241838568

Shattuck, A. (2010, Summer). *Older Americans working more, retiring less*. Brief 16. Durham, NC: Carsey Institute, Carsey School of Public Policy, University of New Hampshire.

Smith, A. S., & Trevelyan, E. (2018). *The older population in rural America: 2012–2016*. ACS-41, American Community Survey Reports. Washington, DC: U.S. Census Bureau.

Smith, J., & Meaney, M. (2016). *Lifelong learning in 2040*. The Roosevelt Institute. Retrieved from http://rooseveltinstitute.org/wp-content/uploads/2016/08/ Lifelong-Learning-in-2040.pdf

Stein, J. (2019, August 14). This will be catastrophic: Maine families face elder boom, worker shortage in preview of nation's future. *Washington Post*.

U.S. Department of Agriculture, Economic Research Services. (2018, November). *Rural America at glance: 2018 edition*. Washington, DC: Economic Information Bulletin.

Van Horn, C. (2015, June). *Good advice about education and training programs is hard to find*. Washington, DC: AARP Public Policy Institute.

Van Horn, C., & Heidkamp, M. (2019, Fall). Older workers, precarious jobs and unemployment: Challenges and policy recommendations. *Generations: Journal of American Society on Aging, 43*(3).

CONTRIBUTORS

Collette M. Adamsen, PhD
Research Assistant Professor
Center for Rural Health
School of Medicine & Health Sciences
University of North Dakota
Grand Forks, ND

Sandra J. Bailey, PhD
Professor Emeritus
Department of Health & Human Development
Montana State University
Bozeman, MT

Keri A. Barron, PhD, RN
Assistant Professor
Capstone College of Nursing
University of Alabama
Tuscaloosa, AL

Brandy L. Bauer, MFA
Associate Director
Center for Benefits Access
National Council on Aging
Arlington, VA

Brittney R. Beaulieu, BS
MSW Field Intern
Center on Aging
University of Maine
Bangor, ME

Jenna G. Bennett
Undergraduate Student
Capstone College of Nursing
University of Alabama
Tuscaloosa, AL

Mercedes E. Bern-Klug, PhD, MSW
Professor
School of Social Work
University of Iowa
Iowa City, IA

E. Helen Berry, PhD
Professor Emerita
Yun Kim Population Research Laboratory
Utah State University
Logan, UT

Sarabeth L. Biermann, PhD, MSW
Lecturer
College of Social Work
University of Kentucky
Lexington, KY

Traci L. Birch, PhD, AICP
Assistant Professor
School of Architecture
Louisiana State University
Baton Rouge, LA

Robert B. Blancato, MPA
President
Matz, Blancato & Associates
Washington, DC

Erik Blanco, MA
Student
Leonard Davis School of Gerontology
California State University, Los Angeles
Los Angeles, CA

Sally Thomas Buck, MS
Chief Executive Officer
National Rural Health
Resource Center
Duluth, MN

Kristine A. Bundschuh, MA
PhD Student

Department of Sociology
University of New Hampshire
Durham, NH

Angeline Bushy, PhD, RN, FAAN
Professor
College of Nursing
University of Central Florida
Daytona, FL

Sandra S. Butler, PhD, MSW
Professor, Director, & MSW Coordinator
School of Social Work
University of Maine
Orono, ME

Mary Ellen Camire, PhD, CFS
Professor of Food Science and Human Nutrition
School of Food & Agriculture
University of Maine
Orono, ME

Melissa L. Cannon, PhD
Associate Professor
Gerontology: Aging and Older Adulthood
Western Oregon University
Monmouth, OR

Katie E. Cherry, PhD
Emogene Pliner Distinguished Professor of Aging Studies
Life Course and Aging Center & Department of Psychology
Louisiana State University
Baton Rouge, LA

Steven A. Cohen, DrPH, MPH
Assistant Professor
Department of Health Studies
University of Rhode Island
Kingston, RI

Susan M. Collins
Senator & Chairman of the Senate Aging Committee
United States Senate
Washington, DC

Cathy J. Cress, MSW
Consultant for Geriatric Care management

Lifespan Ventures
Santa Cruz, CA

Jennifer A. Crittenden, PhD, MSW
Assistant Professor
School of Social Work
Associate Director
Center on Aging
University of Maine
Orono, ME

Martha R. Crowther, PhD, MPH
Professor
Department of Community Medicine & Population Health
University of Alabama
Tuscaloosa, AL

Helen Dennis, MA
Principal
Helen Dennis & Associates
Specialist on the new retirement
Redondo Beach, CA

Elizabeth DePoy, PhD, MSW
Professor
School of Social Work & Center for Community Inclusion and Disability Studies
University of Maine
Orono, ME

George E. Dickinson, PhD
Professor
Department of Sociology
College of Charleston
Charleston, SC

Michele Dillon, PhD
Dean
College of Liberal Arts
Professor
Department of Sociology
University of New Hampshire
Durham, NH

John Dorrer, M.S.
Labor Economist (Retired)
Topsham, ME

Robert Espinoza, MPA
Vice President of Policy
PHI
Bronx, NY

Tracey L. Farrigan, PhD
Geographer
Economic Research Service
U.S. Department of Agriculture
Washington, DC

John N. Feather, PhD
Chief Executive Officer
Grantmakers in Aging
Arlington, VA

Patricia A. Findley, PhD, MSW
Associate Professor & MSW Director
School of Social Work
Rutgers University, The State University of New Jersey
New Brunswick, NJ

Jessica M. Finlay, PhD
Post Doctoral Research Fellow
Social Environment and Health
Institute for Social Research
University of Michigan
Ann Arbor, MI

Cornelia Butler Flora, PhD
Distinguished Professor Emerita/Research Professor
Sociology
Iowa State University/Kansas State University
Ames, IO

L. Carter Florence, DrPH, MPH
Senior Director, Strategy & Impact
Meals on Wheels America
Arlington, VA

Cassandra D. Ford, PhD, RN
Associate Professor
Capstone College of Nursing
University of Alabama
Tuscaloosa, AL

Leslie Fried, JD
Senior Director

Center for Benefits Access
National Council on Aging
Arlington, VA

Colleen Galambos, PhD, MSW, FGSA
Helen Bader Endowed Chair in Applied Gerontology
Helen Bader School of Social Welfare
University of Wisconsin, Milwaukee
Milwaukee, WI

Roseann Giarrusso, PhD
Professor & Department Chair
Department of Sociology
California State University, Los Angeles
Los Angeles, CA

Stephen F. Gilson, PhD, MSW, BFA
Professor
School of Social Work & Center for Community Inclusion and Disability Studies
University of Maine
Orono, ME

R. Turner Goins, PhD, MS
Professor (Ambassador Jeanette Hyde Distinguished Professor)
Department of Social Work
College of Health and Human Sciences
Western Carolina University
Cullowhee, NC

Barbara A. Graves, PhD, RN
Professor
Capstone College of Nursing
University of Alabama
Tuscaloosa, AL

Mary L. Greaney, PhD, MPH
Associate Professor & Department Chair
Department of Health Studies
College of Health Sciences
University of Rhode Island
Kingston, RI

Kathy J. Greenlee, JD
Chief Executive Officer
Greenlee Global, LLC
Lenexa, KS

Marilyn R. Gugliucci, MA, PhD
Professor and Director

Geriatrics Research & U-ExCEL Older Adult Fitness Program
Division of Geriatrics
Department of Primary Care
University of New England
Biddeford, ME

Meredith C. Hanley, MSW
Director
Community Capacity Building
National Association of Area Agencies on Aging
Washington, DC

Kristina M. Hash, PhD, LICSW
Professor
School of Social Work
Eberly College of Arts and Sciences
West Virginia University
Morgantown, WV

Carrie E. Henning-Smith, PhD, MPH, MSW
Associate Professor
School of Public Health
University of Minnesota
Minneapolis, MN

Janice R. Hermann, PhD, RD/LD
Professor
Department of Nutrition
Oklahoma Cooperative Extension Service
Oklahoma State University
Stillwater, OK

Lyn M. Holley, PhD, FAGHE
Professor
Department of Gerontology
College of Public Affairs & Community Service
University of Nebraska at Omaha
Omaha, NE

Scott A. Horel, MAG
Program Coordinator
Office of Research
Texas A&M School of Public Health
College Station, TX

Judith L. Howe, PhD
Professor

Brookdale Department of Geriatrics and Palliative Medicine,
Icahn School of Medicine at Mount Sinai
Associate Director, Education/Evaluation,
Geriatrics Research Education, and Clinical
Center at James J. Peters VAMC
New York, NY

Patricia Huffman-Oh, PhD, LMSW
Program Manager
Center on Aging
University of Maine
Bangor, ME

Ronald J. Hustedde, PhD
Extension Professor
Department of Community and Leadership Development
University of Kentucky
Lexington, KY

Carli W. Hutchison, MSW
Research Assistant
Center on Aging
University of Maine
Bangor, ME

Foster D. Jones, DNP, CRNP
Executive Director
Capstone Rural Health Clinic
Tuscaloosa, AL

Yvonne C.M. Jonk, PhD
Associate Research Professor
Public Health
Deputy Director
Maine Rural Health Research Center
University of Southern Maine
Portland, ME

Seung Eun Jung, PhD, RD
Assistant Professor
Department of Human Nutrition and
Hospitality Management
University of Alabama
Tuscaloosa, AL

Lenard W. Kaye, DSW, PhD, MSW
Professor
School of Social Work

Director
Center on Aging
University of Maine
Bangor, ME

Ann Kayrish, MBA
Senior Program Manager for Medicare
Center for Benefits Access
National Council on Aging
Arlington, VA

Mary A. Kelley, PhD, MSN, RN
Assistant Professor
Capstone College of Nursing
University of Alabama
Tuscaloosa, AL

Angus S. King, Jr.
Senator
United States Senate
Washington, DC

Leah R. Kravette, MSW, LCSW
Clinician
Adult Community Clinical Services
Center for Human Development
Northampton, MA

John A. Krout, PhD
Professor Emeritus of Gerontology
Gerontology Institute
Ithaca College
Ithaca, NY

Kristie P. Kulinski, MSW
Aging and Disability Program Coordinator
Office of Network Advancement
Administration for Community Living
Washington, DC

Mei Wa Kwong, JD
Executive Director
Center for Connected Health Policy
Sacramento, CA

Debra A. Laine, MEd
Senior Program Specialist
National Rural Health Resource Center
Duluth, MN

Shinduk Lee, DrPH, MSPH
Postdoctoral Research Associate
Center for Population Health and Aging
Texas A&M University
College Station, TX

Carl G. Leukefeld, DSW/PhD, MSW
Professor
Department of Behavioral Science
College of Medicine
University of Kentucky
Lexington, KY

Ke Li, MSW
PhD Student
School of Social Work
University of Pittsburgh
Pittsburgh, PA

Danielle M. Louder, BS
Program Director
Northeast Telehealth Resource Center
Medical Care Development
Augusta, ME

James E. Lubben, MSW, MPH, DSW/PhD
Professor Emeritus
Luskin School of Public Policy
UCLA
Professor Emeritus
School of Social Work
Boston College
Chestnut Hill, MA

Cara Marcus, MSLIS, AHIP
Resource Center Manager
Resource Center
National Rural Transit Assistance Program
Woburn, MA

Sandy R. Markwood, MS
Chief Executive Officer
National Association of Area Agencies on Aging
Washington, DC

Jessica L. Maurer, JD
Executive Director
Maine Council on Aging
Brunswick, ME

Michelle A. Mills, BA
Chief Executive Officer
Colorado Rural Health Center
Aurora, CO

Aimee Moles, PhD, LCSW
Assistant Professor of Research
College of Human Sciences & Education
Louisiana State University
Baton Rouge, LA

Alan E. Morgan, MPA
Chief Executive Officer
Executive Office
National Rural Health Association
Washington, DC

Rebecca C. Morgan, JD
Boston Asset Management Chair in Elder Law
Center for Excellence in Elder Law
Stetson University College of Law
Tampa, FL

Kim Mosby, PhD
Community Engagement Specialist & Postdoc Fellow
Coastal Sustainability Studio
Louisiana State University
Baton Rouge, LA

Joy Moses, JD
Director
Homelessness Research Institute
National Alliance to End Homelessness
Washington, DC

Laura A. Mosqueda, MD
Professor of Family Medicine & Geriatrics Director
National Center on Elder Abuse
University of Southern California
Los Angeles, CA

Sandy Nesin, Esq.
Vice President
Accountable Care Operations and Population Health Strategy
St. Joseph Healthcare
Bangor, ME

Maren Niemeier, MLIS
Information Resources Manager
Rural Health Information Hub
Center for Rural Health
University of North Dakota
Grand Forks, ND

Robin R. Phillips, BA, JD
Executive Director
National Rural Transit Assistance Program
Washington, DC

Andrew C. Pickett, PhD
Assistant Professor
Division of Kinesiology and Sport Management
University of South Dakota
Vermillion, SD

Mindy O. Renfro, PT, DPT, PhD, ECHM
Associate Professor
School of Physical Therapy
Touro University, Nevada
Henderson, NV

Erica S. Robertson, MPH
Fitness Director
U-ExCEL
Geriatrics
University of New England
Biddeford, ME

Rogelio Sáenz, PhD, MS, BSW
Professor
Department of Demography
University of Texas at San Antonio
San Antonio, TX

Kristine Sande, MBA
Program Director
Rural Health Information Hub
Center for Rural Health
University of North Dakota
Grand Forks, ND

Julie R. Schoen, JD
Deputy Director
National Center on Elder Abuse

Keck School of Medicine
University of Southern California
Los Angeles, CA

Chan Shen, PhD
Associate Professor
College of Medicine
Pennsylvania State University
Hershey, PA

Linda Silka, PhD
Professor Emerita
School of Economics
Senior Fellow
Senator George J. Mitchell Center for Sustainability Solutions
University of Maine
Orono, ME

Clifford M. Singer, MD
Medical Director
Geriatric Mental Health and Neuropsychiatry
Northern Light Health Acadia Hospital
Bangor, ME

Matthew Lee Smith, PhD, MPH, CHES
Co-Director and Associate Professor
Center for Population Health and Aging
School of Public Health
Texas A&M University
College Station, TX

Kathleen M. Spencer, MLS, MS
Information Specialist
Rural Health Information Hub
Center for Rural Health
University of North Dakota
Grand Forks, ND

Robyn I. Stone, PhD
Senior Vice President for Research
LeadingAge
Co-Director
LeadingAge LTSS Center @UMass Boston
Washington, DC

Kelley A. Strout, BSN, MSN, PhD
Director and Associate Professor

School of Nursing
University of Maine
Orono, ME

Sharon Strover, PhD
Professor
School of Journalism and Media
Co-Director
Technology & Information Policy Institute
University of Texas at Austin
Austin, TX

Jean A. Talbot, PhD, MPH
Research Associate
Maine Rural Health Research Center
University of Southern Maine
Portland, ME

Fengyan Tang, PhD
Professor
School of Social Work
University of Pittsburgh
Pittsburgh, PA

Edward H. Thompson, Jr., PhD
Professor Emeritus
Sociology and Anthropology
College of the Holy Cross
Worcester, MA

Samuel D. Towne, Jr., PhD, MPH, CPH
Assistant Professor
Department of Health Management and Informatics
Disability, Aging and Technology Faculty Cluster Initiative
University of Central Florida
Orlando, FL

Genevieve M. Waterman, DSW(c), MS, MASM
Associate Director
Digital Economic Security
Center for Benefits Access
National Council on Aging
Arlington, VA

Mandana R. Weirich, MSW
Clinical Instructor
Gerontology Program Coordinator
School of Social Work

Eberly College of Arts and Sciences
West Virginia University
Morgantown, WV

Teresa D. Welch, EdD, MSN, RN, NEA-BC
Assistant Professor
Capstone College of Nursing
University of Alabama
Tuscaloosa, AL

Meredith Whitmire, JD
Vice President
Matz, Blancato & Associates
Washington, DC

R. Constance Wiener, MA, DMD, PhD
Associate Professor
Department of Dental Practice and Rural Health
West Virginia University
Morgantown, WV

David C. Wihry, MPA
Senior Project Manager
Center on Aging
University of Maine
Bangor, ME

William A. Zagorski, MS
CEO
American Senior Care Centers, Inc.
Nashville, TN
Board Chair and Research Committee Chair
National Adult Day Services Association
Fairfax, VA

Erika C. Ziller, PhD
Assistant Professor
Public Health
Director
Maine Rural Health Research Center
University of Southern Maine
Portland, ME

Carl R. Zulauf, PhD, MA, MS, BS
Professor Emeritus
Department of Agricultural, Environmental, and Development Economics
Ohio State University
Columbus, OH

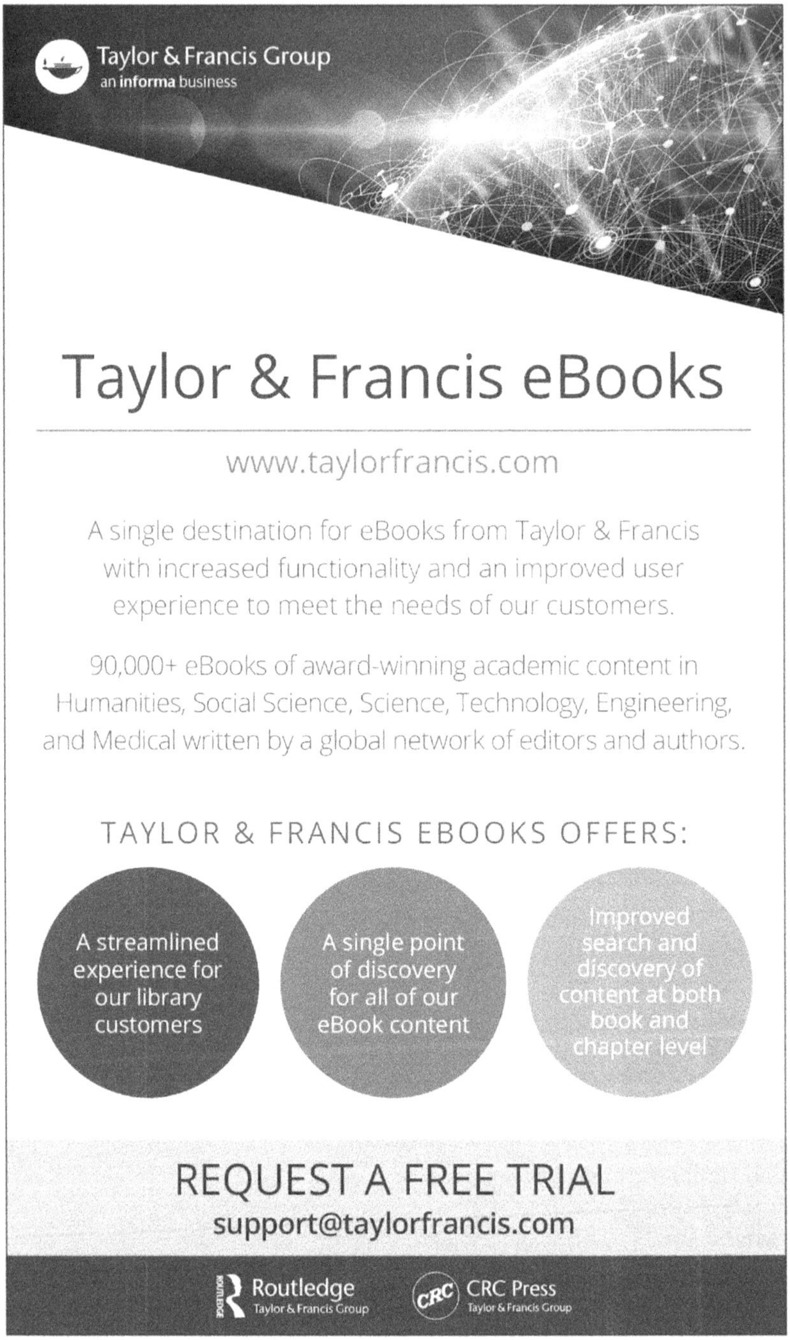

For Product Safety Concerns and Information please contact our EU
representative GPSR@taylorandfrancis.com
Taylor & Francis Verlag GmbH, Kaufingerstraße 24, 80331 München, Germany

www.ingramcontent.com/pod-product-compliance
Lightning Source LLC
LaVergne TN
LVHW080803011026
849160LV00015B/1521